BEECH.

A beautiful forest tree, which from the smallness of its foliage scarcely shews its individuality. Its leading characters are its sharp pointedness at top, and sweeping branches all the way down, elegantly striving to point upwards. Its bark is unlike the generality of other trees, the marks or stripes being mossed, and always horizontally round the trunk, and mostly of a silvery white.

The New Forest Book

An Illustrated
Anthology

Engraved for Rufsels History of England.

WILLIAM II Killed in New Forest Hampshire by Sir Walter Tyrrel.

The New Forest Book
An
Illustrated Anthology

Edited by
JAMES O'DONALD MAYS

NEW FOREST LEAVES
Burley, Ringwood, Hampshire

British Library Cataloguing in Publications Data:
The New Forest Book: An Illustrated Anthology
1. Hampshire. New Forest, history
   I. Mays, James O'Donald
   942.2'75
   ISBN 0 907956-03 3

Set in 10/11 Baskerville by Mathematical Composition Setters, Ltd., Salisbury, Wiltshire

Printed in Great Britain at The Bath Press, Avon

**This book
is dedicated to
MARY**

ACKNOWLEDGEMENTS

The editor is grateful to the following publishers and/or individuals for permission to use the material indicated:

L.J.C. Evans (illustrations and quotations from Heywood Sumner's works); Forestry Commission and John Chapman (passages from *Explore the New Forest*, *Brief Notes*, and other Forestry Commissions booklets and leaflets cited in the contents); Roy Jackman (Domesday Book material); David Stagg ("How the New Forest Has Survived," from *Explore the New Forest*, and extract from *Calendar of New Forest Documents: 1244–1334*); Kathleen Wilson (photographs from C.H. May Collection); Robin Fletcher (illustration, *The Field*) and with Patricia Sibley (extract from *Discovering the New Forest*); Tomothy Sisley and *The Field* ("One Hundred Years of the New Forest Court"); Anthony Pasmore and Pioneer Publications Ltd. (extracts from *Verderers of the New Forest: A History of the New Forest 1877–1977*); Hugh Pasmore ("The Commoners," from *Explore the New Forest*, and passages from "A New Forest Commoner'a Notebook").

Wilfred A. Seaby, Peter Seaby, Philip and Robert Gillmoor (biographical data and other material relating to Allen W. Seaby); A. & C. Black (extracts from Allen W. Seaby's *Skewbald, Sons of Skewbald* and *British Ponies: Running Wild and Ridden*); Harrap Ltd. (extract from Allen W. Seaby's *Purkess the Charcoal Burner*); Catherine McLean (Viscount Bolingbroke); Thomas Nelson and Sons Ltd. (extract from Allen W. Seaby's *The White Buck*); New Forest Association (extract from annual report about Gerald Forward); the late Félicité Hardcastle ("Nature Notes," photographs and other material); Robert Klitz (biographical and other material about Philip Klitz); Dr. Stephanie Tyler and Cambridge University (extracts from doctoral thesis, *The Behaviour and Social Organization of the New Forest Ponies*); Juliette de Bairacli-Levy (material on Augustus John) and with Faber and Faber (extracts from *Wanderers in the New Forest*); Dionis Macnair (material on the Burley Pony Show) and with Eleanor Macnair (extracts from *The Pierrot*).

Susan Picking (extracts from wild-life notes); Eric Ashby (accounts about "Tiger" the fox, and the artificial badger sett, and several illustrations); Eileen Ashby (photography); New Forest Court of Verderers (extracts from the Sutton Collection on Gerald Lascelles); Heather Dorey and other members of the Toomer family (material about "Slut," the sporting pig); Allen Dickson (information on the New Forest fly); Derek Thompson and Hugh Insley (text and illustrations from Forestry Commission leaflet, *Amphibians and Reptiles*); Dr. Colin R. Tubbs (illustrations and excerpts from *The New Forest: A Natural History*); British Tourist Authority (photographs, as credited); Robert Arnold and Simon Keyes of the Hampshire Gallery (extracts from the Gallery's 1977 catalogue on exhibitions of works with a New Forest connection, 1800–1920); Shirley Glick (Sutton Collection).

Brian Stewart and Peter Combes (material on William Shayer); Short Family Collection (photograph of F. Golden Short); Jean Cobb (1875 New Forest Exhibition invitation and related material, essays on conservation of the Forest, and technical assistance); Elizabeth Lewis and Winchester City Museum (material on Heywood Sumner); Iris Worbey (material on Mary Berridge); Belinda Lady Montagu, Hugh Popham and *Esso Magazine* (background to the New Forest Embroidery); Derry Seaton and Mrs. L.K. Errington (material on New Forest Association); Ray Hoare and W.A. Hoare Ltd. (account of the Radnor Stone); Sladmore Gallery and Colin McKelvie (background and illustrations on Geoffrey Dashwood); Basil O'Donnell and Ian Whittington (material on Frank Whittington); Mrs. Eleanor Clarke, Chriss Balcombe and Mike Harlow (background and photographs on Ron Lane).

Isobel Hockey and *International Dolls' House News* (Advertisement of Burleytoys); Jean Westlake (extracts from *Gypsy Caravan: A 100-Year Old Story*; Jude James (background on the Rev. Henry Comyn from *Comyn's New Forest*); E.G.W. Bill, Librarian, Lambeth Palace and Ron Drury (background on the Rev. John K. Craig); Lillian C. Vodrey and the American Shaker Historical Society (the story of Mary Ann Girling); K. Merle Chacksfield (smuggling in the New Forest) and Robert A. Chackfield (vignettes on smuggling); E.E. Cowper and the S.P.C.K. (extracts from *The Moonrakers*) E. Russell Oakley and Century-Hutchinson (excerpt from *The Smugglers of Christchurch*); J.G. Cox and the Southampton City Record Office (extracts from *Castleman's Corkscrew*); Robert R. Wark and The Huntington Library (material on Thomas Rowlandson).

Joan Wilkinson (illustrations and material on Walter Wilkinson); Library of Congress (photographs, Theodore Roosevelt and Dwight D. Eisenhower); *Salisbury Journal* (Sally Taylor's feature on Queen Elizabeth II's visit to the Forest); Arthur T. Lloyd and the Forestry Commission ("Place Names and Personalities" from *Explore the New Forest*); Philip Shanks (background on New Forest Show); Girl Guides Association (extracts from booklet, *Foxlease*); Mrs. Lesley M. Eldred (account of her holiday in the New Forest); Kim Higgins (account of a youth hostel stay in Burley); Anne-Marie Edwards and Arcady Books (extract from *New Forest Walks*); Irene Soper and Arcady Books (recipes from *New Forest Cookery*); Valerie Russell and David and Charles (excerpt from *New Forest Ponies*); Ann Rogers and *Farmers' Weekly* (feature on Fortune Centre); Marylian Watney (account of driving in the Forest); New Forest District Council (extracts from *In and Around the Forest*); Joanna Terry (background on the New Forest Museum and Visitor Centre); Anthony Pasmore and *Industrial Archaeology* ("Surviving Evidence of the New Forest Charcoal Industry"); Anthony Pasmore (extract from *New Forest Commoners*); Mary S. Lovell (material from *A Hunting Pageant*).

The late K. J. Martin (First World War photographs); the estate of Jerrard Tickell (extracts from *Odette*); the Hon. Mrs. E. Pleydell-Bouverie (background on the S.O.E. school at Beaulieu); R.C.B. Ashworth and Patrick Stephens Ltd. (extracts from *Action Stations 5*); National Air and Space Museum, Smithsonian Institution (photography); D.H. Moutray and Macmillan (extracts from *Highways and Byways in Hampshire*); Horace Hutchinson and Methuen & Co., Ltd. (Excerpts from *The New Forest*); The Bodley Head (illustration from *Unknown Hampshire* by Douglas Snowdon); John C. Moore and Chapman & Hall, Ltd. (passages from *The New Forest*); *The Spectator* ("How We Saved the New Forest"); John Murray Publishers Ltd. (extracts from *The New Forest* by Rose de Crespigny and Horace Hutchinson); Susan Gibson (assistance with Heywood Sumner material); Bernard Palmer and *Church Times* (background on the Rev. John K. Craig); estate of A.F. Tschiffely and John Johnson (Author's Agent), Ltd. (material from *Bridle Paths*); Jenny Greene and *Country Life* ("Who Will Save the New Forest?"); Susan Kimpton and Chewton Glen Hotel (photography). Mrs. D.M.A. Irvine (reference material).

The following cultural and educational institutions also provided assistance: The British Library; The Bodleian Library; Special Collections, University of Southampton Library; Hampshire Library Service; Dorset Library Service; Wiltshire Library Service; Hampshire Record Office; Public Record Office; National Maritime Museum; Hampshire County Museum Service; The Tate Gallery ("Colt Hunting" by Lucy Kemp Welch); Richard Green Galleries ("The Bell Inn" by William Shayer); the Mitchell Library, Glasgow; the Museum of Childhood, Edinburgh.

Thanks are due the following for interviews on a variety of New Forest subjects: Chris Charman, Archie Cleveland, Ken Diamond, Maldwin Drummond, Harry Law, Len Mansbridge, Rodney Peckam, Bert Smith, Ray Stickland, the Hon. Mrs. E. Pledell-Bouverie, and Basil O'Donnell.

Of the many who gave unstintingly of their time and advice, thanks are due Hugh Pasmore, Jean Cobb, John Chapman, Anthony Pasmore, David Stagg and Archie Cleveland. On the graphical side, acknowledgement is owed Terry Hood-Cree, John and Maureen Lines, Gerry Beauchamp, and Nicholas Gossip. Kindness and assistance also has come from air Commodore J.H. Greswell, Richard and Elsa Garbett, John Bowker, the Rev. R.H. Lyne, and members of my family. For their patience and advice, gratitude is also due to the typesetters and printers. In an endeavour that has spanned many years and has been interrupted by illness and bereavement, some who ought to be mentioned above have inevitably been omitted. To them, and the legion of helpers who have made possible this anthology, I offer my warmest appreciation.

CONTENTS

ENDPAPERS: Drawings of beech and ash trees were made in the New Forest and are taken from a rare work, *Progressive Lessons Tending to Elucidate the Character of Trees, with the Process of Sketching, and Painting Them in Water Colours* by L. Francia, Member of the Liverpool Academy, Painter in Water Colours to H.R.M. the Dutchess (*sic*) of York, and Secretary to the Associated Painters in Water Colours. Published by T. Clay, No. 18, Ludgate-Hill, London, 1813.

FRONTISPIECE: From Russell's *History of England*.

PREFACE

Assembling this collection of published and unpublished accounts about the New Forest has been both an exhilarating and a frustrating exercise:

—Exhilarating, because of discoveries such as Brusher Mills' technique for catching snakes; what Bramshaw Telegraph Station looked like; the training of Odette as a spy; how the sturdy Diamond farm carts were constructed; the perils of laying the railway line across the Forest; the Commoner's struggle to survive in modern times; the rigorous life of the Agister and the Forest Keeper; Eric Ashby's dogged determination to prove that badgers can live in an artificial sett; Walter Wilkinson's delightful diary and sketches about his peep-show adventures in the Forest—and many others.

—Frustrating because quoting from the mass of material about the Forest has proved impossible. Apart from over 600 books there are hundreds more magazine and newspaper articles and dozens of diaries, journals and letters that deal wholly, or in part, with the Forest. Many of these works, especially in the fields of the natural sciences, forest management, and forest law, are invaluable to a proper understanding of the Forest. Yet the very nature of their subjects has required their content to be written in scholarly rather than everyday language. Few references have been made to these specialized sources; some appear, however, in the bibliography, and others are listed in the Nature Conservancy Council's own excellent bibliography.

This anthology, therefore, deals mainly with those popular aspects of the Forest that have attracted the attention of writers over the past two centuries. Even so, there have been inevitable gaps—especially in accounts detailing the lives of Commoners and Foresters in this century. To compensate for the absence of written records, it was necessary to interview some of the small band of people whose memories go back two generations or more when the character of the New Forest was quite different from what it is today.

A great deal of the content is devoted to the history of the Forest. Without this backward glance it is impossible to appreciate what is left of the Forest today—and how little may survive tomorrow. Today's Forest is but a shrunken core of what it once was. To do justice to the original, larger Forest, it was necessary to include references to some places that lie outside the present boundary. Likewise, it is impossible to overlook such towns as Lymington, Christchurch and Ringwood which though not in the Forest today, have always been closely linked with the Commoners who sold their animals and produce in markets there, and looked upon these places as centres for amusement and sport beyond their own hamlets and villages.

This work differs in two respects from a conventional anthology. As the New Forest is, above all, a visual entity, the format has been adapted to permit maximum use of illustrations. Secondly, the Forest today is one of Britain's major centres of tourism; accordingly, some contemporary information has been included to aid the first-time visitor.

The single, important fact about the New Forest today is that it is under threat of extinction. Commercial pressures are rampant and the powers of the Court of Verderers, the Forest's traditional protectors, may not be sufficient to stem the tide. Without a public response to these threats, this anthology in time will be a mere epitaph to one of the world's last remaining tracts of natural woodland and heath.

It is my fervent hope that reason will prevail and that the Forest will see its ancient "parliament" of Verderers strengthened, so that it will survive as a sanctuary for man, as well as for animal and plant life.

J.O.M.

1
The New Forest:
There's Nothing Quite Like It

Artifacts from the Prehistoric New Forest

Although the New Forest's definitive name and area dates from the reign of William the Conqueror, much can be inferred about its appearance and its inhabitants during prehistoric times. Heywood Sumner, in his *A Guide to the New Forest*, offers his views about the Forest in those days and in the Saxon–Jutish period that followed.

PREHISTORIC

The present-day New Forest provokes question as to the past.

Probably the earliest evidence of man in this district, as in other districts of similar geological formation is supplied by flints that appear to have been hacked with a purpose. *Eolithic*, from Greek *eos*, dawn, and *lithos*, a stone, is the name given to the period of these supposed rude flint implements found in gravel pits on the bluffs which line the Forest side of the Avon valley from Alderbury to Rockford. Specimens may be seen at the Salisbury Museum. Their evidence as human workmanship is still a matter of archaeological discussion and difference of opinion.

Palaeolithic, from Greek *palaios*, old, and *lithos*, a stone.

Well-chipped implements of this period have been found at Wood Green, Fordingbridge, Rockford and along the coast from Chewton Bunny to Milford. Tusks of the mammoth, teeth of the woolly rhinoceros, and antlers of reindeer have been discovered in association with these implements. The old stone men were hunters and probably domesticated the dog.

Neolithic, from Greek *neos*, and *lithos*, a stone, ending in Northern Europe about 2000 B.C.

Flint implements of this period were finely flaked, and were often polished and ground to an edge. Flaked flint knives have been found at Eyeworth, scrapers at Furzehill, and below Picked Post,

and a ground celt (axe-head), has been found on Gorley Hill and is now in the Salisbury Museum. The new stone men domesticated animals, were herdsmen as well as hunters, and made pottery.

Bronze Age, ending in Europe between 1000 and 500 B.C.

During this period bronze was used as well as flint for implements, etc. Bronze celts have been found at Buckland Rings. The barrows in the Forest belong to this period, and their relative frequency, or rarity, indicate the distribution of Bronze Age occupation here. They are most frequent on Beaulieu Heath; there are several on Setley Plain and Sway Common; near Denny and Matley; and near Thorny Hill; they are scattered over the plateau gravel hills of the Northern area. Such barrow excavation as has been recorded indicates a comparatively poor Bronze Age occupation of this District, i.e., neither gold, nor bronze, nor amber objects are recorded in New Forest barrow finds. The pottery of the cinerary urns found is the link of evidence that connects the New Forest barrows with the Bronze Age culture. Without excavation it is impossible to say whether the defensive camps on this District—namely Buckland Rings, Frankenbury, Castle Hill Burley, Castle-place Roe, Malwood Castle, Tatchbury Mount and Dunbury—belong to the Bronze or to the subsequent Iron Age, but from superficial survey we may say that they are pre-Roman. The Bronze Age men

were Agriculturists and Craftsmen as well as herdsmen and hunters.

Iron Age. Between 1000 and 500 B.C. to 43 A.D.

During this period Iron was used in addition to Bronze and flint for implements, etc. The excavations (1911–12) at Hengistbury Head—formerly within the New Forest boundary—shows that this harbour settlement was occupied throughout the Iron Age. Metal-working, spinning and weaving were carried on here; cereals were cultivated, and grain was ground in stone querns; trade connections existed with the continent. This site is classic, inasmuch as here British Iron Age pottery was first identified—though it had been found in 1866, but not identified, in the Highfield pit dwellings, near Salisbury.

Roman Occupation. 43 to 410 A.D.

The Pottery sites around Sloden and Crock Hill were centres of commercial production during this period. "New Forest" ware, (as we call it), was used throughout Roman Britain. This ware was excellent well-turned, ringingly hard pottery; in many instances coated with red-purple glaze. But in gaining hardness it lost certain fine qualities in form and ornament achieved by the Iron Age potters who supplied the settlement at All Cannings Cross, and by the late Celtic potters who supplied the Lake village at Glastonbury. Gain, has generally some loss attendant.

The "streets" named in the Forest perambulations seem to indicate Roman communication with Lepe—which indications are supported by a road surveyor's digging near Butts Ash, cf. "Ancient Earthworks of the New Forest," by the author. At Copy-

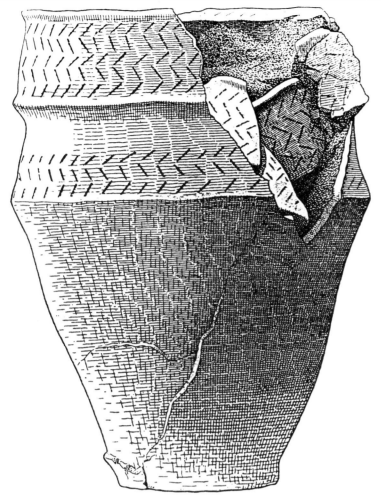

**A CINERARY URN EXCAVATED FROM A BARROW ON
IBSLEY COMMON**
This almost-intact urn is now held by the Salisbury museum.

The New Forest seems to have been populated for many centuries,
albeit sparsely in earlier ages. The Bronze Age barrows (burial
tombs) are to be found in many parts of the Forest, and number
over one hundred.

These barrows never contain objects made of gold, silver or other
valuable substances, an indication that the inhabitants were probably poor farmers and herdsmen. Their sole contents usually are
cinerary urns that held the ashes of early inhabitants. The urns vary
in size and shape, but are simple and often crude in design.

Heywood Sumner, assisted by two others, excavated the Ibsley
urn, illustrated above, during the last week of April, 1921. Other
than a few burnt bones, nothing else was found.

history begin. The Anglo-Saxon
Chronicle gives brief entries that
tell of traditional fighting in this
District between the Britons and
the invading West Saxons from
495 to 519 A.D. and onwards.
The latter date marks the battle
of Charford, or Cerdicsford, near
Downton, and the establishment
of the West Saxon domination
thus far. The Moot earthwork at
Downton—just outside our
Northern limit—is a very fine
example of a Saxon open-air court
of Justice. The numerous place-
names ending in *ton* (homestead),
round Lymington indicate Saxon
or Jutish occupation, and the sea-
farers' camp at Ampress may
belong to this period, a supposi-
tion supported by the adjacent
Norse names of *Rossen* and *Aşkin*
Gutters; while the 'herepaths",
(warpaths) named in the Saxon
boundaries of Ringwood and
Downton, tell us that these ways
were used in Saxon times.

New Forest Pottery Sites

(Sometime before the outbreak
of the second world war—the
exact date is not recorded—the
Girl Guides of Lymington published a slim volume entitled,
*The Guides' Book of the New
Forest*, to help finance their new
club-room. Among the well
known authorities invited to contribute was Heywood Sumner,
the artist-archaeologist. His
short essay, reproduced below
and entitled, *"New Forest Pottery
Sites"*, presents in simple,
straight-forward style, a picture
of what must have been the
Forest's first industry.)

Artifacts...

Continued from previous page
thorn there is a length of Roman
road that appears to lead from the
Roman settlement at Nursling
to--where? After Stony Cross,
traces of this road are wanting.
here are no Roman villa sites in
the Forest, an omission which may

be explained by the prevailing
poverty of the soil here. A villa
was a comfortable country house
belonging to a farm, and no
farmer would choose this soil.

HISTORIC

We now come to periods when
written records of tradition and

Ashley Rails—Amberwood—
Crock Hill—Islands—Thorns—
Sloden, these place-names on the
Northern side of the New Forest
fill the mind's eye of a Forest lover
with visions of the old woods set
amid heathland plains and ridges—of clear amber streams,
flecked with white scum bubbles,

Forest Pottery Sites...

Continued from previous page meandering down little valleys—of great inclosures intersected with wide grass ways—of dark yews and silvery white beams crowning an eminent ridge that ends in a steep bluff, from which extend far views to the West; with all the prospect, far and near, abiding in Forest solitude, save from chance woodman, turf-cutter or sportsman.

This district would have presented a very different prospect 1600 years ago. Then, and here, an Industry was in being. Acrid smell of wood smoke and hum of voices drifted in the air with sounds of wood-cutting from the oak, holly, ash, alder scrub scattered around; a great cattle krall extended along the North-western slopes of Sloden Hill beside the Latchmore brook; led ponies with laden panniers wended their way to Scuts Lane, and the Avon ford—or the Test ford near Nursling; while two miles distant, down Dockens water valley, a cloud of smoke betokened further human activities at Linwood.

All these sights and sounds, and scents were caused by the Romanised New Forest potters having chosen this district as being specially adapted to their craft requirements. Here they found fuel, clay, sand and water, all at hand. Here they constructed their clay kilns, and then when in course of time, the adjoining fuel had been used up, they abandoned such sites, and constructed other kilns where fuel was plentiful. Such usage is suggested by evidence obtained from excavation.

These New Forest Roman kilns were made of clay that (in the process of firing) became terra-cotta. In plan they consisted of a sunken stoke hole leading to a raised circular clay platform about nine feet in diameter, beneath which a flue ran up into a circular combustion chamber in the middle of the platform, about three to four feet in diameter, with a chimney flue, opposite to the stoke-hole flue entry, in order to obtain a good draught.

The combustion chamber was bridged over atop by a vent holed clay *floor*, as regarded from above, *ceiling*, as regarded from below. This was the oven floor of the kiln; on this were piled the pots to be fired; around and over them, wattle work of bee-skep form was fixed, which was covered with earth to retain the heat. When the kiln was fired the heat generated in the combustion chamber passed up into the oven through the floor vent-holes, thus firing the oven charge of pottery, and converting the wattle-work into charcoal; in which condition it, and its earthen covering gradually subsided on to the oven charge, which was then left to cool down. When fit for handling the oven-charge was picked over, the well fired pots were put aside for sale, the mis-fired or mis-shaped pots were cast aside as 'wasters,' and the burnt earth cleared off in preparation for the making of another oven.

The above description accounts for the accumulation of burnt black earth, mingled with charcoal, wasters, and sherds that may be found on all New Forest Pottery sites.

This Industry flourished during the third and fourth centuries, A.D. Excellent hardware was produced, both coarse and fine, of good forms and much variety. During the fourth century the potters shewed their skill in imitating Samian and Rhenish ware forms, decorating them either with white slip or stamped ornament. New Forest pottery has been found on all Roman Sites that have been excavated in this part of Britain, such commercial production and distribution having been made possible by the (then) new means of communication created by Roman roads.

The potters appear to have lived in wattled huts, probably roofed with turves or skins, erected on puddled clay floors, with inside fire-places and outside cooking ovens, which indicate a superior standard of gypsy comfort; but the paucity of relics discovered suggests that they were poor folk.

The Roman evacuation of Britain in the early years of the fifth century put an end to this Industry. It had supplied Romanised requirement and taste, when such demand ceased, pottery production came to a dead halt, the kilns were abandoned, became derelict, and finally forgotten—buried beneath woodland litter, bramble and nettles.

FROM HEYWOOD SUMNER'S *Book of Gorley*

WILLIAM SAILING FOR ENGLAND
This panel is from the Bayeux Tapestry and depicts William's horses as they were landed from France. Some of these same animals may have been brought to the New Forest.

William I Creates the Forest for His Sport

The early history of the New Forest, including its founding by William I, is described in the Forestry Commission's *Brief Notes* from which these passages are taken. Scholars with an interest in the ancient legal aspects of Forest management will find references in the bibliography.

HUNTING PRESERVE

When (about 1079 AD) William I created his "New" Forest in this corner between the Solent and the sea, the land consisted of relatively infertile woodland and furzy waste, sparsely scattered with farms and homesteads.

The act of afforestation in Norman times, and indeed earlier under the Saxon kings, transformed a whole neighbourhood into a royal hunting preserve, placing it under the hated forest law, with all that involved of curtailment of liberty and drastic punishment meted out for any interference with the beasts of the chase or their haunts.

LATER EVENTS

Since the unfortunate peasants who dwelt in the Forest were forbidden to enclose their land lest any fence should interfere with the free run of the deer, their domestic animals were allowed by common right to graze and browse throughout the Forest. This grazing, reinforced by that of the deer themselves, severely diminished the ability of the sparse woodlands to perpetuate themselves. The dearth of new trees became a serious problem during the middle ages, which saw an enormous increase in the consumption of wood, the principal raw material of the time, and enactments were made to enable large areas in the New Forest to be enclosed for establishing woodlands, later to be thrown open when the trees had outgrown the danger to cattle. This process became known as the rolling power of enclosure. The first tree-growing act was passed in 1483 and others followed. The act of 1698 allowed the enclosure of 6000 acres and, as the Crown assumed rolling powers, this meant that the area of woodland would increase beyond that, to the detriment of the Commoners' grazing rights.

There is no record of any sovereign hunting in the Forest after James II. The way was thus clear for the passing of the Deer Removal Act of 1851, under which the deer were ordered to be destroyed, and in return the Crown was authorised to enclose and plant a further 10,000 acres (4047 ha). Under this 1851 Act a unique process began: the registration of all the Rights of Common attached to lands within the area bounded by the coast-Salisbury-Southampton. These rights are exercised on the unenclosed parts of the Forest and

The Domesday Book Chronicles the Forest

(Although the New Forest was sparsely populated at the time the Domesday Book was compiled, it was accorded a folio unto itself.

A representative selection of entries from the Domesday Book about New Forest places has been compiled by Roy Jackman, a Lyndhurst local historian, based on a series of newspaper articles he wrote. Jackman has been prominent in local government activities in the New Forest district for many years, and is also secretary of the Lyndhurst Historical Society. In his spare time he serves as a guide for visitors to the New Forest.)

The Great Survey

1066 is the date most remembered by schoolchildren as the Battle of Hastings—when William the Conqueror defeated King Harold—killed by an arrow in the eye.

William's reign was a troubled one and in 1086 he decided to have a survey of the country and see how it had altered over the preceding 20 years. He therefore divided the country into seven "circuits", Hampshire being in No. 1 circuit, together with Kent, Surrey, Sussex, and Berkshire. The survey took less than twelve months and was eventually collated in "The Book of Winchester", named for Winchester as it was the capital of England in those days. By the 12th century the work became known as "The Domesday Book". As the original manuscript was hand-copied from working papers and verbal observations from the assessors, it must be accepted that there are some

THE DOMESDAY BOOK BEING PRESENTED TO WILLIAM I

inaccuracies in spelling—and possibly, in the data.

Two Pages for Forest

There were some 360 manors in Hampshire and another 101 on the Isle of Wight. The New Forest is unique in that it was allotted a page (two sides) and a small over-run on the bottom of the preceding page. No other part of the 35 shires had such detailed treatment.

The terminology is sometimes strange, though the old English currency of 12 pence to the shilling

and 20 shillings to the pound is used. (This was in use until decimalisation began in February, 1971). A "hide" is frequently mentioned. This was the amount of land needed to support a family, together with their servants. It depended on the fertility of the land, but was about 120 acres. A "virgate" was a quarter of this. Arable land was measured by the number of ploughs needed to cultivate it, and woodland by the number of pigs it could support. The pigs were to eat the acorns

William I...

Continued from previous page

within the perambulation boundary and are today safeguarded by the Court of Verderers who have special statuatory powers to do so. It subsequently proved impossible to remove the deer ... .

The Domesday Book...

Continued from previous page

and beech-mast which could cause illness in other animals. In **MILTON** "the King has woodland in this manor for 20 pigs in his forest valued at 20 shillings."

Mills Were Common

Markets and mills are mentioned in the Domesday Book, although there are only three markets in Domesday Hampshire (none in the new Forest). Mills are more widely mentioned. **MILFORD** had one valued at 30 pence, **FORDINGBRIDGE** two worth 14s 2d, whilst one at **ELLINGHAM** was listed at 7/6, and one at **TOTTON** (the one in the hands of Romsey Abbey) was valued at 10 shillings. **ELING** had two mills worth 25/- as well as a fishery and a salthouse. Sea water was trapped in pans and allowed to evaporate in the sun. The resulting brine was then boiled to leave a deposit of salt. **HORDLE** had six salthouses worth 15 pence, and **DIBDEN** had a salthouse and a fishery.

Honey, like salt, was a valuable commodity. It was used for sweetening, making wax candles and seals for letters and documents, and for making mead to drink. In that part of **ELING** held by the King there was "woodland for 280 pigs and three sesters of honey." A sester probably was a liquid or dry measure, probably about 32 ounces.

The Lord's Role

The people of the villages (and most of England was comprised of small villages) had their position in the community. There was the Lord of the Manor who often had someone on the spot to look after his property. He was the "reeve". Next came the "villein" or villager who held land by service tenure, whereby he had some service to perform for the Lord of the Manor. He had a little more land than a "borderer" or a "freedman"—smallholders with about five acres of land. He paid rent for his cottage and did some service for the Manor, such as ploughing or helping at harvest time. Then there was the "servo" or slave or

bondsman. He possibly lived in communal accommodation and worked for the Lord of the Manor.

The land was owned by the King or one of his noblemen. The survey commissioners went into a lot of detail, as can be seen in the mention of the Manor of Picot. "It was held by Hugh de Port, but William of Chernet (his tenant) claims this land, stating that it belongs to **CHARDFORD** (near **FORDINGBRIDGE**). He adduced his testimony for this from the better—and the older men—of the whole county, and

hundred. Picot brought his opposing testimony from the villagers, the common folk and the reeves, who wish to defend by oath or by a judgment day, that the land holder (Picot), was a freeman who could go with his land wither he would. But William's witnesses refuse to accept any law but King Edward's until it is defined by the King."

"Nova Foresta"

The section of the Domesday Book for the New Forest is headed "IN NOVA FORESTA ET CIRCA"—or "The New Forest and around it." This is the first written record of the area being called the New Forest. Because much of the land was put into the New Forest, its value was either reduced, or put down to nil. Surnames were not used. People were identified by where they came from, or by a personal characteristic, or even by what we would today call a nickname—sometimes not very complimentary. For example, at **TYTHERLEY** near Romsey, the owner's predecessor is referred to as Alwin the Rat.

LYNDHURST was owned by the King and was included in the lands of Amesbury in Wiltshire. It was assessed at two hides and valued at £6 before 1066, but at only 10/- in the Domesday Book. Near **LYNDHURST** is a hamlet of eight houses called **GRIT-**

NAM. At the time of Domesday it was **GRETEHAM** (the "great homestead") owned by a man known as Bolla. It was once valued at 40s, but now at nil. Alum Green is now a small holding with a big house and several cottages; in 1086 it was two hides (240 acres) and once valued at £5, but now at nil, as it is "all in the forest except 12 acres of meadow." This is about its present size.

Brockenhurst Church

There was certainly a church at **BROCKENHURST** for it is specifically mentioned in the Book: "IBI ECCLESIA" (there is a church). **BROCKENHURST** is

---

In that part of Eling held by the King there was woodland for 280 pigs and three sesters of honey

---

the only place in the New Forest to have doubled in value from £2 to £4. It was owned by Aelfric, who had a lot of property in Hampshire and the Isle of Wight. The church mentioned would be the present church of **ST. NICOLAS**. **BROOKLEY**, **HINCHESLEA** and a place called **MAPLEHAM** are also mentioned, although the location of **MAPLEHAM** is unknown.

The Abbey of Romsey held 1 hide in **SWAY** and Earl Roger held two hides, and Edmond 1 hide. Altogether, **SWAY** was assessed at four hides. Hugh Latimer had 1 hide and 1 virgate in **ARNEWOOD**.

The sons of Godric Malf held **MINSTEAD** which was then 3½ hides (420 acres) but is now half a hide (60 acres) as the rest is in the Forest. It was valued at £8, but now at only £1. (These sons may have given the name to **MALWOOD**, which was probably Malf's Wood.)

Earl Roger of Shrewsbury, who had vast holdings in West Sussex, had land extending from **BEAULIEU** to **HIGHCLIFFE**. He had **LYMINGTON** where Fulkwin looked after it for him. It was assessed at one hide (120 acres), and there was one villager, three borderers, and two

Domesday...

Continued from previous page
bondsmen. It had land for two ploughs and was valued at 20 shillings, but now only 15 shillings because some of it is in the Forest. **WALHAMPTON** is mentioned, as is **EFFORD**, which had a mill which "the keeper of the King's House holds." By contrast to Lymington, **HORDLE** was assessed at five hides (600 acres) and there was land for five ploughs. There were six villagers and nine smallholders who had land for four ploughs. There was a mill and six salthouses. It was valued at £8, but now at £5.

Waterside Settlements
"The monks of Winchester had two hides (240 acres) at **FAWLEY**. (This was the old minster at Winchester, founded in 648). There is a small church and four acres of meadow. Hugh of St. Quentin held **LANGLEY** (probably the one at **FAWLEY** although there is another near **TOTTON**) through the Bishop of Bayeux who said he exchanged it for a mill. The half-brother of William the Conqueror (was Odo) who was created Earl of Kent in 1067 and acted as Regent when the King was away. He was later arrested and imprisoned (1082). Odo also had **DIBDEN** which was assessed at five hides, but now only two hides as the other three are in the Forest. There were four villagers 15 smallholders with five ploughs, nine acres of meadow, woodland for six pigs, and a salthouse and a fishery. It was valued at £10, but now at 50 shillings, but it has to pay 100 shillings."

BEAULIEU is not specifically mentioned in the Domesday Book, although **HARTFORD** and **OTTERWOOD** are. There is, however, an area attributed to **THROUGHAM** which is eight hides and two virgates, just over 1,000 acres. The entry continues: "There was land for 17 ploughs (it must have been good, fertile land; this is thought to be around **PARK FARM, BEAULIEU**). Bishop Walkelin of Winchester had two and a half hides, and it was part of the lands of the monas-

tery in Winchester. There was land for four ploughs, but it is now in the Forest. It was valued at £3, but now at nothing.

Hugh of Port holds (in 1086) 1½ hides in Mildeltune (**MILTON**) and William Chernet is his undertenant. (In 1066) Alwin held the manor jointly. There is land for 3 ploughs; on the lord's land is 1 plough and 5 villeins have 2 ploughs. There is 1 serf (slave) and 3½ acres of meadow. In King Edward's time and later (i.e., when Hugh acquired the manor) it was valued at 40 shillings; now 20 shillings. In King Edward's time it was assessed at 1½ hides; now for 1. The woodland of this manor, rated at 20 pigs, the king has in the Forest; value 20 shillings.

Ringwood: Church and Mill
"Before 1066 **RINGWOOD** belonged to Earl Tosti and it was assessed at 28 hides, though part of the area was actually in the Isle of Wight. Then Hugh of Port had it and the area was reduced to 10 hides—about 1,200 acres. When the survey was made in 1086 it was part of the King's lands and assessed at six hides, the other four being in the Forest. There were 56 villagers; 21 smallholders; a church; a mill and 105 acres of meadow. It used to be valued at £24—which included the Isle of Wight property—; later at £16 but now at only £8.10.0.

"The four hides which were in the Forest had 14 villagers and six

smallholders, a mill and woodland for 189 pigs. It was valued at £7.10.0. (This area is thought to be what we now call **BURLEY**).

"**SOPLEY** was held by Edric before 1066 and now by William, son of Stur. It was seven hides—840 acres—; but is now one hide and one virgate—160 acres. It had three villagers and six smallholders: 59 acres of meadow; a mill and enough water for 875 eels. (This is one of the few references to eels.) Later they often formed part of the tithe to the Lord of the Manor by the mill holder. It was valued at 110 shillings."

This will give some idea of the great detail which was collected by the assessors of William the Conqueror. The whole of the kingdom was surveyed in less than 12 months. The book gives a good idea of the country at the time, and many of the place-names can still be seen today.

(NOTE: Other places in and around the New Forest mentioned in the Domesday Book included **BADDESLEY**, **BASHLEY**, **BICKTON**, **BREAMORE**, **BUCKLAND**, **BURGATE**, **COXLEASE** (**FOXLEASE**), **EXBURY**, **EYEWORTH**, **GORLEY**, **MARCHWOOD**, **PILLEY** and **WINKTON**. In addition, three royal manors—**CHRISTCHURCH**, **HOLDENHURST** and **STANSWOOD**, held land in the New Forest.)

The Beauty of New Forest Names

Unless newcomers to the Forest take the trouble to study their maps, they may not realize that virtually every acre bears a name—often, one that goes back for centuries.

Many places are named for people who once lived nearby or in other parts of the Forest, but other sites invoke the magic of the past, some aspect of wildlife, or the splendour of ancient trees.

Consider the appeal, for example of Highland Water Inclosure, Knightswood Inclosure and Hawkhill Inclosure, or of Berry Wood, Gibbet Wood or King's Hat. Likewise, specially planted areas bearing the names of Longbeech, Ravensnest, and Dames' Slough.

And what better names to conjure up those pleasant grazing areas: Sheepwash Green, Wide Lawn, Little Green in Pond, Camel Lawn, Little Eye Green, Plain Green, Greenford, Crabtree Green, Halfpenny Green, and Magpie Green.

(Source: New Forest Management Plan, 1982–91: Forestry Commission)

Doubts about William I Raiding the Forest

That William the Conqueror created the New Forest as his hunting preserve is beyond dispute; that, in the process, he destroyed Forest homes, churches and villages now appears to be without foundation. Nonetheless the belief that William I dealt harshly with Forest places has persisted until recent times, so engrained was it in the teaching of history in British schools.

Rose C. de Crespigny and Horace Hutchinson, in their work, *The New Forest*, published by John Murray in 1895, explain why the allegations against the King are unlikely to be true.

Referring to the reminiscences of our earliest history books, we may recollect that the name of Norman William, the Conqueror, was presented to our horrified views as that of a king who created this vast hunting-ground for his royal leisure at the expense of villages burnt and razed to the ground; of churches treated in a similar barbaric fashion—in fact, of the whole region made desolate and turned into the likeness of a land devastated by war—so that fine covert for boars and wolves might spring up from its ruins.

It was an engaging picture; but even in those nursery days the critical eye of that most realistic age of childhood regarded the ruined villages with suspicion, as an indifferent method of tilling the soil for the growth of covert. At all events, it used to strike us that Norman William must have had a forward-looking and sanguine mind, for, at best, it would be some years before much forest sprang from the ruins; and in those days, if men did not live so quickly as we do, they certainly died more quickly—especially kings; the second William is a ready-to-hand instance. However, there are not wanting other evidences to exonerate the Conqueror from suspicion of an act so contrary to all the artfully conciliatory nature of his general policy.

Domesday Book itself, as well as certain ancient charters, hold record of compensation made, on very modern lines, to owners whose land was put under the forest law: for this, in sober truth, is the meaning of that phrase "afforesting," which has brought so much discredit on the first William. He put this extent of ground —an extent roughly very similar, if slightly larger, so far as our means of judging serve us, to the new Forest of to-day—under "forest law." These laws were severe enough, no doubt, making it a deadly felony to destroy game within the limits to which the forest law applied. Of course there were opponents of the game laws in those days, as there are in these; and, on the whole, the proceeding was, without question, a high-

WILLIAM'S PENNY
William I reigned from 1066 to 1087 and had eight varieties of silver pennies. The one shown is the rarest and shows the king with a sceptre.

handed and "conquerant" one.

But not only is there no trustworthy evidence to show that villages and churches were laid in ruins to form the king's hunting-ground, but there is visible evidence to the contrary, both in the musty writings aforesaid and in the stones and mortar of certain churches—such as those at Brockenhurst and Milford, standing to-day as they stood at the time of the afforesting of the district— churches which certainly ought to have gone the way of ruin, according to the ruination theory of the Conqueror's proceedings.

HUNTING DEER NEAR OLD RUFUS STONE
The original stone was badly mutilated and so was replaced in 1841 by the present Rufus Stone. (Engraving from Mudie's *Hampshire*, 1838.)

"The Red King:" (Death of William Rufus)

Although modern scholars do not accept that William Rufus laid waste to homes and churches in the New Forest, Charles Kingsley nonetheless uses this theme as justification for the "Red King's" fate at the hand of Sir Walter Tyrrel. Kingsley wrote the poem while on holiday in the Forest in 1847.

The Red King

The King was drinking in Malwood Hall,
There came in a monk before them all:
He thrust by squire, he thrust by knight,
Stood over against the dais alright;
And, "The word of the Lord,
    thou cruel Red King,
The word of the Lord to thee I bring.
A grimly sweven I dreamt yestreen;
I saw thee lie under the hollins green,
And through thine heart an arrow keen;
And out of thy body a smoke did rise,
Which smirched the sunshine out of the skies;
So if thou God's anointed be
I rede thee unto thy soul thou see.
For mitre and pall thou hast y-sold,
False knight to Christ, for gain and gold;
And for this thy forest were digged down all,
Steading and hamlet and churches tall;
And Christés poor were ousten forth,
To beg their bread from south to north.
So tarry at home, and fast and pray,
Lest fiends hunt thee in the judgment-day."

The monk he vanished where he stood;
King William sterte up wroth and wood;
Quod he, "Fools' wits will jump together;
The Hampshire ale and the thunder weather
Have turned the brains for us both, I think;
And monks are curst when they fall to drink.
A lothly sweven I dreamt last night,
How there hoved anigh me a griesly knight,
Did smite me down to the pit of hell;
I shrieked and woke, so fast I fell.
There's Tyrrel as sour as I, perdie,
So he of you all shall hunt with me;
A grimly brace for a hart to see."
    The Red King down from Malwood came;
His heart with wine was all a-flame,
His eyne were shotten, red as blood,
He rated and swore, wherever he rode.

They roused a hart, that grimly brace,
A hart of ten, a hart of grease,
Fled over against the king'és place.
The sun is blinded the king'és ee,
A fathom behind his hocks shot he:
"Shoot thou," quod he, "in the fiendés name,
To lose such a quarry were seven years' shame."
And he hove up his hand to mark the game.
Tyrrel he shot full light, God wot;
For whether the saints they swerved the shot,
Or whether by treason, men knowen not,

THE DEATH OF WILLIAM RUFUS, FROM AN OLD PRINT

But under the arm, in a secret part,
The iron fled through the king'és heart.
The turf is squelched where the red King fell;
And the fiends they carried his soul to hell,
Quod "His master's name it hath sped him well."

Tyrrel he smiled full grim that day,
Quod "Shooting of kings is no bairns' play;"
And he smote in the spurs, and fled fast away.
As he pricked along by Fritham plain,
The green tufts flew behind like rain;
The waters were out, and over the sward:
He swam his horse like a stalwart lord:
Men clepen that water Tyrrel's ford.
By Rhinefield and by Osmondsleigh,
Through glade and furze brake fast drove he,
Until he heard the roaring sea;
Quod he, "Those gay waves they call me."
By Mary's grace a seely boat
On Christchurch bar did lie afloat;
He gave the shipmen mark and groat,
To ferry him over to Normandie,
And there he fell to sanctuarie;
God send his soul all bliss to see.

And fend our princes every one,
From foul mishap and trahison;
But kings that harrow Christian men
Shall England never bide again.

Rufus Stone—Famous Forest Landmark

(Heywood Sumner, in his *New Forest Guide*, gives the complete text of the inscription on the Rufus Stone, and adds a comment about a missing word in the inscription.)

The (Rufus) stone has been enclosed by a three-sided cast-iron case bearing the following record in raised letters:

1.

"HERE STOOD THE OAK TREE, ON WHICH AN ARROW, SHOT BY SIR WALTER TYRELL AT A STAG, GLANCED, AND STRUCK KING WILLIAM THE SECOND, SURNAMED RUFUS, ON THE BREAST, OF WHICH STROKE HE INSTANTLY DIED, ON THE 2ND OF AUGUST, 1100.

2.

"KING WILLIAM THE SECOND, SURNAMED RUFUS, BEING SLAIN AS BEFORE RELATED, WAS LAID IN A CART BELONGING TO ONE PURKIS AND DRAWN FROM THENCE TO WINCHESTER AND BURIED IN THE CATHEDRAL CHURCH OF THAT CITY.

3.

"THAT THE SPOT WHERE AN EVENT SO MEMORABLE (SIC) MIGHT NOT HEREAFTER BE FORGOTTEN, THE ENCLOSED STONE WAS SET UP BY JOHN LORD DELAWARE, WHO HAD SEEN THE TREE GROWING IN THIS PLACE.

"THIS STONE HAVING BEEN MUCH MUTILATED, AND THE INSCRIPTIONS ON EACH OF ITS THREE SIDES DEFACED, THIS MORE DURABLE MEMORIAL, WITH THE ORIGINAL INSCRIPTIONS, WAS ERECTED IN THE YEAR 1841, BY WILLIAM STURGES BOURNE, WARDEN."

British Tourist Authority

THE RUFUS STONE NEAR CADNAM

'Happened' is the missing word (see *Remarks on Forest Scenery* by William Gilpin, vol. I., p. 166, Ed. of 1794). Anyone who has had to deal with inscriptions will know that tendency to error lies in wait to confound the inscriber—as here. Even this omission has a variant! (see Gough's Edition of Camden's *Brittania*, vol. I., p. 131—'had happened.'

Precarious Survival of the New Forest

(Ever since its creation the New Forest has been threatened with extinction. Laws have been passed to protect it, but often they have been ineffective or unenforceable. David Stagg has devoted many years to the study of these documents.

A Verderer with a diploma in local history and a background of 32 years archaeological and historical research with the Ordnance Survey, David belongs to several organizations whose aims are to preserve the Forest. His most notable contributions to knowledge of the Forest are the companion volumes, *New Forest Documents: AD 1244- AD 1334* (1979), and *New Forest Documents: the 15th to*

the 17th Centuries (1983). Apart from these two titles, he has produced publications dealing with the Christchurch Court Rolls in the time of Henry VIII, and New Forest woodmen, Commoners, snake-catchers, Agisters, and Verderers.

Reproduced below is "How the Forest Has Survived," from the Forestry Commission's *Explore the New Forest*. In it, Mr. Stagg gives a summary of threats to the Forest from Norman times to the present.)

"The forest law is hereby abrogated". These six words which are contained in the Wild Creatures and Forest Laws Act 1971 mark the formal ending of

forest legislation dating back to at least the twelfth century. The majority of these laws had long become obsolescent, but at one time they were essential for the protection of the forest and the king's deer, and to a lesser extent to define and limit the duties and responsibilities of the inhabitants of the forest.

It is frequently stated that the forest laws were first introduced by King Canute, but this is untrue and the document upon which the claim is based has been proved to be a forgery. The forest laws were made by the Norman kings, the earliest surviving text being that known as the Assize of Woodstock and dated 1184, but this can be shown by documents of the period to be nothing more than a reenactment and possible expansion of the then existing laws, and in fact the very first article refers to the more stringent penalties which had been exacted during the reign of Henry I.

The restrictions, which were intended to protect the game, included the possession of bows and arrows, the keeping of unlawed dogs—that is dogs not lamed so as to prevent them chasing the deer, the setting of traps for deer, and hunting at night. For the preservation of the woods it was an offence to cut timber except under the supervision of a forester, and far more serious was the offence of assarting—the conversion of woodland into arable land, and purprestures—the enclosing of forest land. More information is contained in a document known as "The Customs and Assise of the Forest". This details the customs and laws concerning trespasses to the vert and the venison, the procedure of the Courts, the duty of the inhabitants, and those of the foresters. For instance it gives such detail as the number of sureties in respect of various offences, these being required to ensure the attendance of the offender at the next Forest Court. If a deer was found

The Purkis Family

(From a guidebook, *Topographical Remarks Relative to the Parishes of Ringwood, Ellingham, Ibbesley, Harbridge and Fordingbridge*, published in 1831 by the printers, W. Wheaton of Ringwood:)

The family of Purkis, the charcoal burner, who lent his horse and cart to carry off the body (of Wil-

A wheel of the cart was in their possession till within the last 30 years, and the Lord Lieutenant of the County still pays to this day (1831) an annual fine to the Crown, for suffering the traitor (Tyrrell) to escape by a passage over the River Avon and between the hills into Dorsetshire still known as Tyrrell's Ford.

RUINS OF PURKIS' COTTAGE
This photograph, from the C.H. May Collection, depicts what was left of Purkis' cottage in Canterton Glen about 1901, when it was destroyed by a storm.

WILLIAM RUFUS

liam Rufus), still maintains the same trade upon the selfsame spot (of the killing), and is deemed one of the most ancient in the county.

Precarious Survival...

Continued from previous page
dead it was required than an inquest should be held among the four nearest villages.

The Charter of the Forest AD 1217, the forest's equivalent to Magna Carta, granted some relaxation of the forest laws. It was provided that certain recent extensions of the forests should be disafforested, an amnesty was granted to offenders who has been previously outlawed or exiled, fewer attendances were required at the Forest Courts, certain improvements to private lands within the forest would no longer be regarded as purprestures, rights of common were protected, there were to be safeguards against abuses and extortion by officials of the Crown, and no longer could offences be punished by mutilation or death.

The administration of justice within the forests was done in two stages, first by a local Court which determined whether an offence had been committed but was not empowered to pass sentence, the offenders being referred to the Forest Eyre, or Justice Seat, a Court presided over by the Lord Chief Justice in Eyre and held at irregular intervals around the various forests. The last such Court was held in the New Forest in 1669–70, and although the forest laws remained in force, the New Forest Act of 1698 specifically drawing attention to this point—"the said Forest and every Part thereof shall be subject to and under the Laws of the Forests", the actual enforcement of these laws became virtually impossible.

The 1698 Act was primarily concerned with the establishment of timber Inclosures, but it did give the lesser Courts, held by the Verderers and known as the Court of Swainmote and the Court of Attachment, the power to impose fines for such offences as stealing timber, burning the heath, and destroying the covert. Further powers were given by the New Forest Act 1800 in respect of

unlawful enclosures, purprestures, and encroachments, and an Act of 1819 gave powers over the exercise of common rights, and the right to enquire into the conduct of the under-officers employed in the forest. Throughout this period it was also possible, if less convenient, for more serious offences to be dealt with by the Court of Assize at Winchester.

The greatest threat to the New Forest did not arise from minor encroachments and the destruction of timber, but occurred in 1871 when the Treasury introduced into Parliament a Bill for the Disafforestation of the New Forest. This was a course that had been adopted for other royal forests, but fortunately on this occasion public opinion was aroused and the Bill was withdrawn. Reaction went even further in that a Resolution was passed in the House of Commons that no felling of timber should take place, and no further timber Inclosures be made, pending legislation on the New Forest.

This took the form of the New Forest Act 1877, which is still largely in force and forms the basis of modern day management of the Forest. Under this Act the Crown's powers of Inclosure were greatly limited, and, equally

important, amenity considerations were recognised in that regard was to be given to maintaining the picturesque character of the Forest, with attention being given to its ornamental value. The interpretation and implementation of this Act has from time to time aroused considerable controversy, especially so in the economic conflict between broadleaved trees and the more recently introduced conifers, but an acceptable compromise now appears to have been reached.

Other significant changes over the last 150 years have been more gradual and therefore less perceptible. What was once to all appearances an untouched wilderness has now been fragmented by railways and motor roads. There has been a vast increase in residential development, and around the margins of the Forest have been established an airfield and various industrial complexes. There are now very few areas of the Forest which remain unaffected by the sight or sound of modern technology, and it is this development that represents the present danger. Extreme care must be exercised if the beauty, character and uniqueness of the New Forest is to continue to survive.

Hive Garn Gutter.

FROM HEYWOOD SUMNER'S *Book of Gorley*

The Queen's House in the Past—and Today

(The long and colourful story of the Queen's House is told in a booklet, *The Queen's House, Lyndhurst* published by the Forestry Commission, the text of which is reproduced below.)

Introduction

The Queen's House is the principal building owned by the crown in the New Forest. It is the headquarters of the Forestry Commission's South East England Conservancy and the office of the Deputy Surveyor of the New Forest, and contains the hall where the Verderers of the New Forest hold their ancient courts.

The dominant character of the present structure is that of a mansion of the seventeeth century, but substantial portions of a Tudor building survive within it, as well as earlier relics, and there have been extensive later renovations. It forms nevertheless a remarkable complete unit and has historical significance not only for the New Forest but as an example of architectural development in Hampshire, where it is the only surviving major building of the Charles I period in the county, and displays one of the few examples of seventeenth century brickwork on any scale to be seen here.

The history of the building which has occupied this site is woven of four strands; its origin as the hall or house of the lord of the manor of Lyndhurst, its occupation as a residence and hunting lodge by the sovereign and by tenants of the crown, its accommodation of the courts of justice set up to administer the forest laws and its use as an administrative office.

The Royal Manor of Lyndhurst

The recorded history of Lyndhurst begins in 980, when it was already a royal manor and granted to the Abbey of Amesbury. This "hillock of lime trees" stood at the meeting place of tracks connecting the townships of Southampton, Beaulieu, Lym-

ington, Christchurch, Ringwood, Fordingbridge, Salisbury, Romsey and Winchester, and when the first Norman king, William I, designated the whole area between the river Avon on the west, the Wiltshire Downs to the north, and to the east and south the Test, Southampton Water, the Solent and the sea as his "New" Forest in about 1079 to serve as a safe dwelling place for the beasts of the chase, it followed that the manor of Lyndhurst, the only royal manor in the Forest and lying near its geographical centre, took on an added importance which was to endure down the centuries. By the time of the Domesday survey in 1086 the king had taken the manor back into his own hands and it has remained crown property to this day.

In afforesting the area the Conqueror threw back into the wastes much of the cultivated land belonging to the Forest manors. The only land taxed at Lyndhurst in 1086 was assessed as one virgate, which implies a fairly small holding, but later records show that the manor became a useful agricultural property and may have equalled in size the present enclosed lands around the village.

The enjoyment of these man-

orial lands has over the centuries been granted on various terms to tenants who have included queens of England, noble dukes, landed gentry and forest officials, and many of these have been at the same time Lord Wardens of the Forest and thus responsible for its administration, but the old manor house was always retained for the use of the king himself, and was maintained by the crown and not by the grantee of the manor. In the absence of the king the house was occupied as a residence by one of the Forest officials.

The Royal Residence

The lime-clothed knoll, strategically placed at the junction of the ways and sheltered to the north and west by Lyndhurst hill rising to 300 feet, was an obvious location for the dwelling of the lord of the manor and it is likely that such a building occupied the site in Saxon times, although no evidence of this has been found.

The creation of the royal hunting grounds in the New Forest and the frequent visits by the king and his nobles would have required a more substantial building, greater than the manor itself could support, and other royal revenues, notably those derived from the

Queen's House ...

Continued from previous page
trees of the Forest, were expended to provide accommodation suitable for the number and rank of the visitors. The first documentary evidence that has been identified as relating to this building is in 1297, when an order was issued for "twenty oaks to make laths for the use of the Queen's manor house at Lyndhurst". This was at a time when the first queen of Edward I, Eleanor of Castile, had made Lyndhurst her home in the absences of the king during his wars against the Welsh. The house has been usually referred to as the King's House when a male monarch is on the throne.

In Tudor times the old house was repaired and enlarged, but the main rebuilding of the manor house as a royal abode was carried out between 1634 and 1673. It was begun by Charles I and completed, after the Civil War, by his son Charles II. The original estimate was £1563 12s 6d but it was exceeded and it is said that the Clerk of Works was hanged! The money was raised, in part at least, by the sale of timber from the Forest: a warrant dated 1635 authorised the sale of 250 loads of timber "at the highest profit" for this purpose. Much oak from the Forest was used in the work. The letters patent from Charles I to John Chamberlayne of Lyndhurst call for: "the new building of divers lodgings for our use and service adjoyning to the old house at Lyndhurst in the Newe Forrest as also, a Kitchyn, Pastrie, Larder and other offices, and a stable to contain fortie horse according to the plots and directions given by the Surveyour of our Workes".

The Court of Justice
The size of the stables indicates that the building at this time was to serve as a royal hunting lodge. Charles I hunted from Lyndhurst and in all probability so did Charles II and James II. Thereafter the only sovereign to stay at the house was George III, who came here in 1789 and graciously allowed the local people to watch him at table through the window.

From 1771 to 1850 the tenancy was in the hands of royal dukes. When the Duke of Cambridge, the last Warden of the Forest, died, that office fell into abeyance and it was decided to remove the Deputy Surveyor, the local representative of the Commissioner of Woods, from New Park to the Queen's House; from 1851 to 1915 it was the official residence of the Deputy Surveyors. The living quarters

THE QUEEN'S HOUSE BY ALEXANDER ANSTED
This sketch, taken from C.J. Cornish's *The New Forest and the Isle of Wight,* was made at the turn of the century. Note the signpost indicating the distance of eight miles to Lymington.

were afterwards let privately until 1961.

The vital distinction in the countryside for several centuries from Norman times was between land subject to the forest law and land which lay outside the boundaries of the king's forests. A twelfth century commentator remarks: "The forest has its own laws based not on the common law of the realm but on arbitrary legislation by the king". These savagely restrictive edicts were designed to protect the deer and the coverts where they found their food and shelter in the name of the king's exclusive sport. It was not until the fifteenth century that forests were recognised as a source of timber, the principal raw

material of the time, and the first tree-growing enactments began to reach the statute book, and it was not until the nineteenth century and the passing of the Deer Removal Act affecting the New and Waltham Forests that the ancient character of the forest was changed to one we would recognise today.

The forest laws of the Norman kings required for their enforcement four kinds of courts of justice, the main forest court being that of the Chief Justice in Eyre, who progressed on circuit every three years, and the Courts of Regard, Swainmote and Attachment. Today the only survival, much altered is, the Court of Swainmote and Attachment, generally known as the Verderer's Court.

The Administrative Office
A hall where the forest courts could meet was built within or beside the manor house in 1388, and the present Verderers' Hall is believed to occupy the same site. It was affected by the rebuildings that took place in Tudor and Stuart times. Until the house was altered in 1851 to make it more suitable as the residence of the

Queen's House ...

Continued from previous page

Deputy Surveyor, there were rooms over the hall accessible from the upper floors of the main house; these Tudor rooms were demolished in the rebuilding and an inverted V roof took their place. Additional domestic accommodation was then provided by the building out of two bays on the street side of the main house, but in a style completely at odds with its prevailing character; this extension was removed in 1966. By 1904 additional office space had become necessary for the administration of the Forest and the Deputy Surveyor of the time, the Hon. Gerald Lascelles, had the present offices built over the hall in Tudor style, using early bricks. Although the Forest Eyre was formally abolished in 1817, the last in English history having been held in the New Forest in 1669, the Courts of Swainmote and Attachment continued as a local instrument of regulation, being reconstituted in 1877 and 1949. The Court of Verderers today plays an important role in the administration of the Forest, more particularly being concerned with the enclosed part of the Forest and the health and welfare of the animals that graze there by common right. The Verderers meet in open Court every second month, when the public still has the unique ancient right of presentment to bring matters of Forest concern to the attention of the Verderers and so seek advice and remedy.

The Administrative Office

Originally the management of a royal forest was carried on by an impressive hierarchy of officials, comprising titles and duties of almost Byzantine complexity. The most important was the Lord Warden and in the New Forest this office was generally held by the tenant of the royal manor of Lyndhurst. However the office eventually became a sinecure and the active management of the Forest was devolved upon a Surveyor General of Woods, Forests and Land Revenues of the Crown in 1760.

In 1810 Commissioners of Woods, Forests and Land Revenues were appointed to hold and administer the royal forest property, and the management of the New Forest was thereafter carried out by a Commissioner of Woods in London and a Deputy Surveyor in the Forest, first at New Park and from 1850 at the Queen's House. In 1924 the management of the Forest was transferred to the Forestry Commission, who retained the title of Deputy Surveyor for their official responsible for the New Forest, and who occupied the offices over the Verderers' Hall, letting the main house privately. In 1966/67 however the whole house was adapted to provide office accommodation, but by 1977 major structural weaknesses had begun to manifest themselves and the building was evacuated to enable a thorough survey to be made. This resulted eventually in its complete restoration during 1981 and 1982 to provide modern office accommodation whilst respecting its architectural and historical features, and its importance as a Grade II listed building.

The Queen's House Today

The relics of pre-Tudor work are sparse and enigmatic, but the stone plinths that form the base of the north wall are the lowest courses of the medieval hall. The lowest metre of the Verderers' Hall is undisturbed Tudor brickwork, the sections above having been rebuilt in Victorian times with bricks obtained from buildings of a similar date elsewhere in the area.

The wall south of the central passages on the ground and first floors of the house is Tudor up to eaves height and contains at least two brick mullioned windows, showing that it was an exterior wall before the house was enlarged under the Stuarts.

A Tudor date is also possible for the two "grouped stacks" of chimneys on the north side, both visible from the High Street. The several chimneys do not form a square stack but stand beside each other in a stepped group. The eastern one was linked to the former Tudor upper storeys above the Verderers' Hall; the western may be linked with the Tudor work in the cellars.

The northern half of the house

THE QUEEN'S HOUSE WITH LYNDHURST CHURCH IN THE BACKGROUND
The Queen's House today is the New Forest headquarters of the Forestry Commision, as well as being the seat of the Court of Verderers. It is a Grade II listed building.

Queen's House ...

facing on to the High Street is the result of the rebuilding authorised by Charles I in 1634. The whole of the facade under the four V-shaped dormer windows (that is excluding the front of the Hall and the set-back bay at the west end) dates from this period, but the eastern quarter is no longer original. This Charles I building contains the central corridor; it has no cellars.

Between 1669 and 1674 the house was enlarged for Charles II, the work carried out being the south and west fronts; this increased the principal accommodation by two large and two small rooms on each floor, the new block was equipped with cellars with access from the old house, and a separate roof. The south side has five dormer windows with upright side walls and hipped roofs, unlike those on the north. Its easternmost bay, next to the Verderers' Hall, was built later than the rest, though in the same style, probably during changes in the reign of Queen Anne. The west wall does not end flush with the north wall possibly because during the excavations for the cellars it became apparent that the walls of the pre-existing north side were endangered and the builders decided to leave the critical north west corner of the north side undisturbed by setting back the wall of the new bay by some two feet. The west door and the external flight of steps are modern additions.

The Queen's House carries no heraldic adornments. Since it has never been held by a subject, the only proper arms would be those of the royal house. There do appear however on the rainheads the initials of those monarchs in whose reigns the building was extended or repaired.

They are:

Cast in lead:

A R 1712 and Crown
(Queen Anne)
(on the west end and on the north wall)

G R III 1748 (George III)
(on the south wall of the main building)

E II R 1983
(on the south wall of the Verderers' Hall)

Cast in iron:

V R 1880 (Queen Victoria)
(on the north wall of the main building)

E R 1904 and Crown
(Edward VII)
(on the east end)

The words "Victoria Regina" are also set in tiles over a staircase window on the north side, dating from 1880.

None of these dates forms a reliable guide to the period when

HEAD AGISTER
Brian Ingram standing before the entrance to the Court of Verderers.

any part of the structure was built.

Inside the house the staircase at the west end was installed during the 1982 restoration. The principal staircase, located in the Charles I block, probably belongs to the work carried out in the 1970s; however the only original portions to survive are the treads and risers, the handrail and part of the newels. The staircase in the Verderers' Hall is a copy of this stair constructed in 1904 when the offices were built over it. The rooms on the south side of the house are a fine set of panelled interiors with skirting, dado and cornice. The rooms to the north of the building have simple interiors. The majority of the doors throughout are eight-panelled raised and fielded, and constructed in oak, generally of the late 17th century in date with 18th century ironmongery. The majority of the sash windows are of the early 18th century, in many cases retaining the distinctive crown glass. In the Verderers' Hall the oak panelling is said to have been rescued from the upper rooms during the reconstruction of 1851. The clay tile paving is Victorian. The hall contains a very old prisoners' dock built of oak and hewn to shape with the adze as well as a substantial bench and two oak tables which may be of Tudor date. The last court of the Chief Justice in Eyre was held here in 1669, presided over by Aubrey de Vere, Earl of Oxford, and the hatchment of the royal arms which was then displayed is still preserved, behind the Court Bench. Another relic is related to the ancient Court of Regard. This is an iron stirrup, apparently of Tudor date, and it is said that any dog which could crawl through it was too small to require expedit-ation. Expedition originally meant cutting off a dog's claw so that it could not chase the deer. If the story about the stirrup is true, it is unlikely that the one displayed was so used, since its pattern suggests too late a date of origin. It may however be related to the traditional badge of office of the Forest administration, a stirrup surmounted by a crown.

FRONTISPIECE FROM PERCIVAL LEWIS' *Historical Enquiries* (1811)

Lewis' work, published in 1811, was an early attempt to explain the administration of Britain's forests—including the New Forest. In the frontispiece above, by C. Sheringham, the original Rufus Stone may be seen at the left, ship-building at Buckler's Hard at the water's edge, and the stirrup for "lawing" of dogs on the tree at the right. Present-day enquiries or disputes regarding rights of common are settled by resorting to a definitive atlas, prepared when the New Forest Act of 1949 was enacted. Compiled with a scale of 25.344 inches to the statute mile, it is in use daily by the Clerk to the Verderers when searches are required concerning Forest rights.

The Verderers' Court: Forest Guardian

(In 1977, when the Verderers Court marked the centenary of the enactment of the 1877 New Forest Act, Timothy Sisley wrote the article below for *The Field*. It has been slightly edited to take into account changes over the last decade. Entitled "One Hundred Years of the New Forest Court," it gives a simplified picture of the Court's role as the official guardian of the Forest, and is reprinted here by courtesy of *The Field*.)

In a country and an age in which the past is daily destroyed it is reassuring to be able to record the continuing health of an ancient institution. In Hampshire, the Court of the Verderers of the New Forest this year celebrates its centenary.

In this celebration the Court, which is in effect the governing body of the Forest, commemorates one hundred years of effort to protect the area from threats that have ranged from the encroachment of housing estates to military requisition in both world wars.

Although the modern Court is only a century old it is the natural descendent of institutions which ruled the Forest since before the Norman Conquest. It was resurrected by Parliament in 1877, after a century-and-a-half of peacefully undirected anarchy, in the face of Government attempts to turn the Forest to production of timber for the Royal Navy.

Commissioned Powers

The essential duty of the Verderers' Court has remained the same since then. They are there to preserve the amenities and the character of the area, and as such they have virtually absolute powers within the Forest. It would take Parliament to overrule them.

The New Forest comprises nearly 70,000 acres largely owned, through the Forestry Commission, by the Crown. Of these 20,000 are Forestry Commission woodland Inclosures, over which the Court has no powers. Apart from the

Robin Fletcher

THE COURT BEING OPENED IN A 1977 SESSION
Ray Stickland (left) was the Senior Agister at the time and Sir Dudley Forward (centre) was the Official Verderer.

function of overseeing the general character of the Forest outside these areas, the Court's work is mainly concerned with regulating the livestock put out to pasture by Commoners.

The Commoners are people who hold, by ownership or by rent, land in the Forest to which is attached a Right of Common. This right is largely that of pasturage of horses, ponies or cattle on the Forest, although they have neither entitlement nor access to Forestry Commission Inclosures.

There are ten Verderers, of whom five are elected by the Commoners and four appointed by bodies such as the County Council. The Official Verderer is appointed by The Queen. None of the Verderers need even live in the Forest, although they tend to.

The Verderers sit as the Court once every two months. Their duties and powers fall into two categories, of which the more usual is the hearing of presentments, when a member of the public can call the Court's attention to any matter that he wishes.

The Court has judicial powers, although not that of imprisonment. Anyone who has transgressed against the Verderers' or

the Forestry Commission's bye-laws—the Forest is governed by both—can be fined up to £20.

The work of the Court in looking after the livestock in the Forest is carried out by four paid Agisters, a word reputedly derived from the Norman French for grazing cattle. All horses, ponies and cattle in the Forest are owned by Commoners, who pay a small marking fee to pasture them in the Forest. The deer belong to the Forestry Commission, as representatives of the Crown.

Activities which have been carried out since the eleventh century, are the drifts, when the Agisters and 20 to 30 Commoners, all mounted, divide the Forest and drive the ponies into pounds. The ponies are rounded up to be branded, taken to the Beaulieu Road Pony Sales, (or) are given a health check.

Behind the scenes

However, the life of the Court is not always as gentle and as peaceful as it may seem. A great deal of its work is in preservation behind the scenes. Furious rows have periodically broken out, the last most notable being some years

The Case of the Cows without Tail Marks

Tail-marking (that is, identification) of animals has always been of great importance to the Court of Verderers, who are responsible for the management of animals within the New Forest, and to the Commoners and licensed owners, whose livelihood is affected by rights of grazing.

A particularly contentious case was debated at the Court on 13 January 1908, when the Verderers held that one Commoner had grazed six cows that had not been tail-marked. The hearing was reported almost verbatim in the *New Forest Chronicle* three days later:

Mr. W. G. Bennett, of Tile Barn Farm, Brockenhurst, was summoned for depasturing six cows at Setley Wood, which had not been tail marked, and he pleaded not guilty. The Clerk conducted the prosecution, saying it was instituted in consequence of complaints by other Commoners, who failed to see why they should pay tail-marking fees if others were allowed to go exempt. Further, he said it was not an isolated case on Mr. Bennett's part, and produced the notice which he issued in January of each year, pointing out that neither Commoners or Non-Commoners could cause or allow cattle to be so depastured.

Agister Charles Evemy said he saw the cows in question at Setley Plain on December 4th and 16th, and they were unmarked. The cows were at Setley Wood, which was between Tile Barn Farm and the Vicarage. At first he did not know to whom they belonged, and made enquiries. Finding them grazing again in the wood on December 16th, he went to Mr. Bennett and defendant then said he would pay for them. Upon witness writing out the ticket, and Mr. Bennett finding that he would have to pay again in the following January, he refused to pay, and the case was then reported. Nobody was in attendance with the cows, and witness had received several complaints respecting unmarked cows coming out into the Forest from defendant's farm.

Mr. Bennett said he was in a position to prove that the Agister had marked two of the cows.

Mr. Evemy said he only marked one of defendant's cows last year—a "smoky" looking cow.

Mr. Bennett: Last year you marked four cows, and I am in a position to bring four or five witnesses to prove it. You marked four cows and four steers.

The Agister said he had only marked one cow—the others were heifers and steers.

Agister Albert Evemy having given corroborative evidence, Mr. Bennett asked the Court to allow him to appeal, for he could bring ten witnesses to prove that four of his cows were marked in 1907. He had never intentionally turned out any unmarked cattle into the Forest. His fields were close to Setley Wood, and as sometimes there was no water in the pond opposite his farm they might go down to the pond just beyond the Vicarage to get water. This prosecution he characterised as "only

Oyez! Oyez! Oyez!

The Vederers' Court meets in public session at least five times each year in the Courtroom of the Queen's House at Lyndhurst. The meetings are held at roughly two-monthly intervals, and at the extraordinarily inconvenient time of 10 a.m. on a Monday morning. The meeting is opened by the senior Agister, acting as crier of the Court, with the ancient words inherited from the old Forest Courts:

"Oyez, Oyez, Oyez. All manner of persons who have any presentment to make or matter or thing to do at this Court of Verderers, let them come forward and they shall be heard. God save the Queen."

This opening is spoken from the old oak dock which is still occupied by the accused in Swainmote cases. If there is no judicial business to be transacted, the Court proceeds at once with administrative matters. First of all, now alas almost traditionally, figures of road accidents involving commonable animals and deer are read. Thereafter, decisions of the Court on presentments made at the previous public session are announced. In fact these decisions will have been notified to the persons concerned soon after the previous open Court, and may well have been published in the press.

The Verderers' Court...

Continued from previous page

ago over the Forestry Commission's plans to fell a large amount of hardwood in the Forest. Ministerial intervention was necessary before the Court could claim a victory in the abandonment of the unpopular scheme.

The Court has no power in the Commission's Inclosures, but it can veto almost any other proposals of either the Commission or the County Council if they would tend to destruction of the Forest's character.

It can be reliably assumed that the Verderers' Court is more popular in the Forest now than ever before. It is democratic, capably run and strong, in a good position to meet the challenges of the next hundred years.

The test for the future for the Court is posed by the ever-growing number of visitors and the creeping annexation that their growth brings. The outlook for the Court, and for the Forest itself, will depend on how the Verderers can deal with this problem.

The Five "Rights" of the Forest Commoner

Cows Case...

a trumpery affair," and because of previous disagreements with the Agister. He had offered to pay for his cows last spring, and the Agister had refused to take the money, because he would not also have his dairy cows tail marked. he had paid every year before for 22 years.

In reply to the Clerk, he admitted that he had not stated all these things in a letter he had sent him, respecting this complaint, on December 30th, and added "If everybody paid for their cattle as I do, the Verderers would have a great deal more funds."

At the suggestion of Mr. Tinne, the Court was cleared for the Verderers to consider the matter privately, and the public had nearly half an hour's cold wait in the open ere being admitted.

The Official Verderer said the Court had very carefully considered the case, and he was going to ask Mr. Briscoe Eyre to deliver judgement.

Mr. Eyre said the Court found that Mr. Bennet did have his cows marked year by year, but omitted to do so in 1907; that these cows, which should have been marked had been found straying in the Forest from time to time, possibly between Mr. Bennett's fields, and possibly going down to the pond. If Mr. Bennett knew that, it was an additional reason why he should have had them marked, so as not to violate the by-laws. Under the circumstances, and the cows being sent out without a caretaker, the Court did not see its way to mitigate the fine, and ordered payment of double fees— 18s. and the costs, 11s. (29s. in all).

Mr. Bennett: Can't I appeal?

The Official Verderer: That is for you to decide yourself. The Court has no doubt about the matter, and do not see any reason why you should appeal. That is the decision of the Court after careful consideration.

Mr. Bennett: I wish to give

(Hugh Pasmore, for many years a Verderer but now retired, **explains what a New Forest "Commoner" is, and the rights enjoyed by those who can lay claim to being Commoners. This explanation is reproduced from** *Explore the New Forest* **by permission of the Forestry Commission.)**

A New Forest Commoner is a person who, by virtue of occupying land to which attaches a Right of Common, as registered in 1858, is entitled to certain privileges, all of which originate from the distant past.

The farming Commoner is much influenced by his use of these rights for though he may himself occupy only a few acres, his ability to take advantage of the forest enables him to farm on a comparatively large scale. On the other hand there are many modern Commoners who do not actually farm but have a full time job in the district, for even a garden plot to which attaches the appropriate right entitles the occupier to "farm" the forest.

There are five Rights of Common in the Forest and these are described below:

COMMON OF PASTURE is the most valuable right and enables the Commoner to depasture animals on some 45 000 acres of open forest. This right of grazing is believed to date from the days of William the Conqueror when the New Forest was a hunting preserve and local husbandmen were prohibited from fencing any of their land lest it interfere with the Monarch's sport. It was recognised that this imposed on the

notice I shall have Mr. Evemy up for perjury. I don't know where that will be tried.

The Official Verderer: I think we must go on with the next business.

Mr. Bennett paid the 29s. and made a few other remarks in reference to the action on the part of the Agister.

farmer a very great hardship and he was therefore permitted to allow his beasts to wander over the forest for five summer months (excluding four weeks in June/July—Fench month (20th June to 20 July—when the does normally dropped their fawns). During the winter months (Winter Heyning—22 November to 4 May) when keep was scarce the right was withdrawn so that the deer would not go short.

Over the years extensive changes have taken place and in 1851 an Act of Parliament decreed

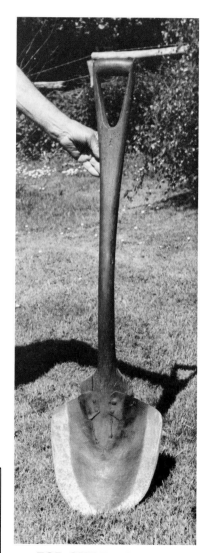

FOR CUTTING TURF
This spade was used by a New Forest Commoner for many years to cut turf. The right of turbary is little used today.

A CONFORMIST CONGREGATION

The Commoners' Rights...

Continued from previous page

that all deer should be destroyed or removed from the forest in return for the Commoners' agreement that 10 000 acres of open land should be fenced and used for timber production. Thus today commonable animals have a legal right to remain on the forest for the whole of the year, though in fact deer have re-established themselves throughout the forest.

It has become a fairly constant pattern that about 5 000 commonable animals run on the forest and in recent times the number of ponies has exceeded the cattle by three to two. Donkeys will be found mainly in the north and west on light or sandy soils but seldom number more than fifty.

The number of Commoners actually using their rights of turning animals on to the forest is in the region of 350 but this is only a fraction of those entitled to do so. In the office of the Clerk to the Verderers are maps prepared by the Forestry Commission showing all the land to which common rights attach and these may be inspected on payment of a nominal fee. Lands bearing rights stretch well outside the forest boundary, even as far away as Bournemouth and Cranborne.

The right to run cattle on the forest is of inestimable value to farmers whose land adjoins the forest, for during wet weather instead of his land being "poa-ched" or cut up by his herd the animals are fed and remain outside, only coming in for milking or veterinary attention. Ponies on the other hand remain permanently on the forest and may well "haunt" (the foresters' name for the district a pony inhabits) an area many miles from its owner's farm, where fortunately for the owner it usually remains within a radius of two or three miles throughout its life.

Though commonable animals (ponies, cattle, pigs and a few sheep) run on the forest as of legal right, they are subject to Byelaws imposed by the Court of Verderers under statutory powers and the owner pays to the Court a grazing fee in respect of each one. Currently (1974) this amounts to £3 per head per annum and is collected by the Agisters for the Court to use to defray the cost of supervising and controlling the animals.

No commonable animal may graze upon the forest unless it is branded with its owner's mark and the Verderers maintain a complete register of these identification brands. Traditionally, ponies are branded on the left or near side in one of three places: on the back where the saddle normally sits, on the shoulder or on the hip. Cattle on the other hand are branded on the right or off side flank. Branding is carried out by clipping the hair as short as possible and then "touching" the hide with a red hot branding iron. Many forest farmers use brand designs which have been handed down through generations of their families. Recently a few animals have been branded with a chemical freeze process which turns the hair permanently white in colour but this is not popular with commoners.

In addition to the forest Right of Pasture there are others less widely used today, though in the past they also were much prized by the commoner.

COMMON OF MAST is the right to turn pigs on to the forest during what is known as the Pannage Season when acorns and beech-mast have fallen and provide excellent feed for pigs, though when green are poisonous to cattle and ponies when taken to excess. Until the New Forest Act of 1964 Pannage dates were fixed from 25 September to 22 November but in those seasons when the acorn fall was late, pigs in search of food invaded local gardens, hence the Act provided for the Forestry Commission after consultation with the Verderers to fix any suitable term of not less than sixty days. The Commoner pays a small fee per animal to the Verderers. On the 3,500 acres of private commons which march with the true forest, local Commoners are not subject to the Pannage

The Forest Beautiful as Gilpin Saw It

Many writers have described the beauty of the New Forest, but few have incorporated the notion of beauty in the titles of their works. The first of those to do so was the Reverend William Gilpin, sometime Vicar of Boldre, whose work was called *Remarks on Forest Scenery and Other Woodland Views*. (1791).

Gilpin's work was divided into "books" as he wrote, but they were not always published separately. Book Three was devoted largely to the New Forest and there are dozens of passages praising its splendour. Some of the sights he saw no longer exist, having long since been overwhelmed by urban development. Other views, happily, do survive, although some of the ancient trees he observed have been cut down, or have decayed. Selected passages follow.

We concluded the last book with a catalogue ... of the principal forests which formerly overspread the island of Britain. None of them at this day possesses its original grandeur. ... (The) New Forest in Hampshire is among the few which have retained any ideas of their ancient consequence; at least it is superior to the rest, on account of the extent of its boundaries, the variety of its contents, and the grandeur of its scenes.

*****

Within equal limits perhaps few parts of England afford a greater variety of beautiful landscape (than the New Forest). Its woody scenes, its extended lawns, and vast sweeps of wild country, unlimited by artificial boundaries, together with its deep views and distant coasts are all in a great degree magnificent. It must still, however, be remembered that its chief characteristic, and what it rests on for distinction, is not sublimity, but sylvan beauty.

*****

Continued from previous page

The Commoners' Rights...

Continued from previous page
dates and their pigs roam throughout the year.

COMMON OF TURBARY entitled the Commoner to cut turf for burning in his dwelling, the rule being that for every turf cut the two adjoining ones must be left, thereby avoiding stripping the area completely. Only one or two Commoners avail themselves of this right today.

COMMON OF FUELWOOD, sometimes referred to as Estovers or Assignment Wood. The Forestry Commission allocates one or more cords of burning wood to certain tenements to which this registered right attaches and as in the case of Turbary the wood has to be burnt in the house. Over the years these rights have diminished in number and today only some eighty commoners enjoy allocations. The Forestry Commission cuts and stacks the wood, usually reasonably close to the Commoner's holding, and assigns the correct cordage to the rightholder who has to collect it.

COMMON OF MARL. This is a right to take Marl from the twenty-three forest pits for spreading on the Commoner's land as a form of manuring. Modern agricultural methods have now rendered this right more or less obsolete.

In 1909 the New Forest Commoners formed an Association known as the New Forest Commoner's Defence Association and today with over 500 members the Association still fulfills its original function of safeguarding the members' rights, whilst at the same time forming a valuable link with the Forestry Commission and the Court of Verderers whereby many difficult forest problems are solved.

PIGS PERFORM USEFUL SERVICE
Ponies can die from eating acorns, especially when green and when consumed in quantity. Thus pigs, when turned out on the open forest during the acorn season, not only satisfy their appetites but help prevent pony deaths. The right to turn out pigs on the forest is called "common of mast."

ETCHING BY JOHN FULLWOOD
The view of a New Forest heath is from C.J.

Cornish's *The New Forest and the Isle of Wight,* published in 1903.

The Forest Beautiful as Gilpin Saw It...

Continued from previous page

Nor was the beauty of the Forest a matter of no concern, even at a time when we might have supposed the pleasures of the chase engrossed men's whole attention. "There are three special causes," says Manwood (author of *Forest Laws,* 1598), "why the Forest Laws have so carefully provided for the preservation of the vert of the Forest. The first is for the sake of cover for the deer; the second is for the sake of the acorns, mast, etc., which feed them; the third is, *propter decorum,* for the comeliness and beauty of the same in a forest. For the very sight and beholding of the goodly green and pleasant woods in a forest, is no less pleasant and delightful in the eyes of a prince, than the view of the wild beasts of chase; and therefore the grace of a forest is to be decked and trimmed up with store of pleasant green coverts." ... I hope I may consider the scenery of the (New) Forest as essential to the very existence of it ... .

... In the Forest vista the trees are casually large or small, growing in clumps, or standing single, crowding upon the foreground, or receding from it, as the wild hand of Nature hath scattered them.

And it is curious to see with what richness of invention, if I may so speak, Nature mixes and intermixes her trees, and shapes them into such a wonderful variety of groups and beautiful forms. Art may admire, and attempt to plant and form combinations and clumps like hers, but whosoever examines the wild combinations of a forest (which is a delightful study to a picturesque eye) and compares them with the attempts of art, has little taste if he do not acknowledge, with astonishment, the superiority of Nature's workmanship.

*****

... the forest vista (gives) a very different air from the artificial one, diversifying the parts of which it is composed so much, that the eye is never fatigued with surveying them, while the whole together presents one vast sublime object. Like a grand gallery of exquisite pictures, it fills the eye with all its greatness, while the objects on each side, continually changing, afford at every step a new entertainment.

*****

... Ober Green ... is chiefly pasturage, patched here and there with heath, and is esteemed one of the best feeding grounds, both for deer and cattle, in the Forest. ... Few counties in England could furnish so many pleasing woodland scenes in so small a compass. He who delights in such scenery will find it in much greater perfection in the wildness of a forest than among the most admired improvements of art. He will find it grander, more varied, and everywhere more replete with those wild, enchanting passages, which the hand of art cannot give.

No Forest Season is Without Great Beauty

"The New Forest is ever beautiful, at every season of the year," says John Wise in his *The New Forest: Its History and Its Scenery.* He adds: "This joyful tyranny of beauty is ever present, at all times and hours, changeful in form, but the same in essence. Year after year, day by day, it appears. ... I believe we may all gain some idea of the glory which each season brings—some glimpses of the heaven of beauty which ever surrounds us—if we will seek for them patiently and reverently. ... They are attainable only upon this one condition—that we go to Nature with a docile, loving spirit, without which nothing can be learnt."

The extracts that follow reinforce John Wise's point that the New Forest is beautiful in all seasons. In which season is the Forest at the peak of its glory? That, Wise suggests, rests in the mind of the beholder.

SPRING

(From *The New Forest: Its Traditions, Inhabitants and Customs*, by Rose de Crespigny and Horace Hutchinson, John Murray, 1895)

In springtide the budding leaves of beech and oak tree form a veil of most delicate lace-work, green and translucent, so that the sun-rays passing through it are tinged with the warmth of the same delicate green, and all colours and outlines are made soft beneath it. Through the chequered meshes of this veil the sunbeams steal and fleck the ground with alternate light and shade. The thorns are decked in a bridal garment of snowy blossom, sweeping away like the trains and flounces of a woodland nymph draped for Pan's great wedding feast. The tangle is putting forth green or red-brown buds, and below, again, is the softest carpet of moss or sward laid on the most mysterious passages which lead in and out and down vast avenues of the stalks of the bracken fern.

The bracken itself is uncurling on the top of those delicate stems, opening its tender young eyelids on the beautiful world. So it goes on, a forest—a new forest—of delicate stems and uncurling heads—on, on, as far as the eye can reach, until one expects to see the fairies and pixies (whom one *knows* to be there) peeping around the stems, or coming, in glad troupes, down the green passages. In spring the Forest is a fairy-land.

SUMMER

(From "Summer in the Forest," by W. H. Hudson in *Longman's Magazine*, January, 1900)

At the end of the third week in June we know without the almanac that spring is over: nowhere in England perhaps is one more sensible of the change to full summer than in that warmest corner of Hampshire within the angle of land formed by the Solent and Southampton Water.

The cuckoo calls less and less frequently, and the nightingale has ceased singing. The passionate season is plainly over for the birds; their fountain of music is running dry. Voices are harsher and colour deeper than in May and early June. One of the commonest sounds in all the open woods and along the lanes is the curious musical note of the young blackbird. It is like the chuckle of the adult, but sharper, and is the hunger call of the young bird as he sits concealed in a bush or on the ground among the corn or weeds; when he has been left unfed for a long time he emits this shrill note at intervals of ten to fifteen seconds. It may be heard distinctly two or three hundred yards away. The cornfields and waste weedy grounds are everywhere splashed with the intense scarlet of poppies. Summer has no rain in all her wide hot heavens to give to her green thirsty fields, and has sprinkled them with the red fiery moisture from her own veins.

The young bracken has sprung up as if by miracle to a height of four to five feet. It spreads all around me, an unbroken sea of brilliant green, out of which rise the tall red columns of the pines supporting the dark woodland roof. One could not very well sit down among this waist-deep

SPRING ON THE LYNDHURST ROAD, A SKETCH BY ALLEN SEABY
Although a well known artist, Seaby also wrote four children's books set in the New Forest.

The Forest Seasons...

Continued from previous page
bracken, and it was a weariness to wade in it. I found it more agreeable to pass through it and down into the oak wood on the farther side, where I could pick my way through the undergrowth of holly, thorn, and bramble, and find open spaces to sit and stand in.

Here, more than in the open, it is felt during the last ten days of June that spring is over, that it is full summer. Birds songs are few and not loud; the wren, wood wren, and willow wren being almost the only singers. A family party of jays, the young birds not long out of the nest, screamed at me for a few moments, then became silent. Then I disturbed a pair of green woodpeckers—these, too, with young out of their breeding-hole, but unable to fly; and the parent birds, half crazed with anxiety, flitted round me from tree to tree, and clung to the bark with wings spread and crest raised, their loud laugh changing to a piercing cry of anger that pained the sense.

All the passion and music had gone out of the bird and into the insect world; the oak wood was full of a loud continuous hum like that of a distant threshing machine; one unbroken deep sound composed of ten thousand thousand small fine individual sounds, but diffused and flowing like water over the surface under the bushy tangle.

AUTUMN
(From *The New Forest* by Mrs. Willingham Rawnsley, A. & C. Black, 1904)

A path winds through short grass that is golden yellow in the sunshine. On one side is a belt of wood, on the other open moorland, sloping upwards and crowned with beech-trees, whose now leafless branches melt into soft billowy masses of red-purple shadow in the middle distance, flecked here and there with touches of russet-orange colour, where some leaves yet linger, and glow with richest red as the sunlight touches them. Beyond them is a strip of far-distant moor, in colour a pure deep blue.

The path leads on into the shade of a grove of oaks, the green of whose foliage is scarcely touched by the hand of autumn, whose subtle presence they have, so far, boldly defied; only his breath upon them is shown by a deeper, richer olive shade over the mass of foliage, against which the rugged stems stand out in pale rosy lights and gray shades.

The belt of the wood on the left is almost bare of leaves, but the bracken, red-russet and brown, nestles lovingly around the feet of every tree-stem and twists in and out of the gray-lichened wood-paling that bounds it.

The heather blossom on the moorside has long been dead, but it still keeps a warm crimson hue, shaded at the roots into brown madder, at the foot of its tangled tufts. ... The ... birch, to the left, is a young tree, and its one slender, erect stem shines silvery-white in the sunlight, as it tapers gradually upwards; a rounded mass of golden-yellow foliage hides the topmost twigs, while the lower branches are bare and plainly visible, of a warm, red-madder colour, against the background of olive-gray oaks and their deep shadows.

The light of sunshine upon this golden-rich mass of colour is indescribably delightful to the eye, and forms the brilliant keynote to the whole picture, contrasted as it is against the blue-purple distance, the cerulean shade of the lower sky, or the pure cobalt blue above.

WINTER
(From "In the New Forest" by Charles W. Wood in *Argosy* magazine, February, 1881)
One night, darkness fell upon a green world ... The next morning ... everyone was amazed to find the world white. Through the night the silent and unseasonable visitor had fallen thick and fast, and was falling still.

It seemed no time for prolonging one's sojourn in the New Forest. I felt inclined to pack up

CASCADES OF SNOW AND ICE AMONG THE BEECH AND HOLLY TREES
This wintry scene was made in the ancient and ornamental woods near Burley.

The Forest: Mother Nature at Her Best

The beauty and charm of the New Forest has rarely been so well described as by J.A. Owen in *Forest, Field and Fell* in 1895.

A writer for *Blackwell's* magazine and author of *On Surrey Hills, Annals of A Fishing Village* and *Forest Tithes*, Owen knew the Forest when it was peopled by Commoners. The extracts here include his praise of the New Forest, as well as some of the customs and superstitions he encountered when visiting its inhabitants.

The New Forest has a peculiar charm of its own, one that consists not so much in the grandeur of individual trees, but in the masses of wood, the long solemn aisles of trees, the groups of sombre yews contrasted with neighbouring whitethorn, the sylvan glades, purple-clad hills, and long stretches of heather and gorse. And here one finds oneself in company with Dame Nature in her best and most unspoiled aspects. All is still so little changed, if, indeed, changed at all, since the times when the wolf and the wild boar ranged here.

Through their winding courses the same streams flow as of old, licking out deep pools by the gnarled roots of oak and beech, washing over shallows of rolled and rounded pebbles; the lily and iris there still gladdening the eye, milkwort waving blue heads, wood-sorrel lifting its delicately veined cups, and wood-anemones hanging their fair heads, as they have done for centuries. You might travel far and wide and not find such another combination of all that is lovely and also grand in scenery.

Hares' brains are supposed still to be a useful tonic for children that have come into the world before their time. Children afflicted with fits are still passed through cloven openings in ash-trees. A certain lichen again is used in a lotion for strengthening weak eyes; whilst the fat of the hedgehog is used to lubricate stiff joints. Bread baked on Good Friday, the forest folks believe, will keep good for seven years, and it will also cure certain complaints.

There is an amusing proverb in use here about upstarts: "A dog is made fat in two meals." A curious idea is prevalent in the forest about the death's-head moth; they believe firmly that this insect was never seen until after the execution of Charles the First.

There is scarcely a village or hamlet in the New Forest but has its pixy field or mead, or its pixy's cave. That mischievous spirit, which is known under the name of "Laurence", still obtains possession of those whom "the gods wish to ruin." "Laurence has got on him," they say of one who is lazy. A tricksy fairy, the forest folk believe to this day, tempts their rough native ponies to stray. Also, they say that he lives in bogs, into which he entices the unwary. "Colt-pixies" such as he are termed; only the first-born may consider themselves to be free from his spell. The caterpillar is known, as in the days of the first translation of the Bible into English, as the "palmer-worm." A woodlander talks of feeling lear-like when he is hungry, using a corruption of the word "learnes," old English for emptiness, which reminds one of the German "leer."

The names of the forest villages are almost unchanged, and the natives of these are many of them descendants of Cerdic, who fought at Burley about the year 495 A.D. In that notable battle five bat-

The Forest Seasons...

Continued from previous page

and depart. The old postman—the most popular of all public characters—when he arrived with the letters, said the snow was so thick upon the trees that branches were breaking in all directions with the report of small guns. But presently the snow ceased, the leaden sky rolled away, the sun came out with all the brightness it wears on such occasions.

Improving the opportunity, I started for a long ride in company with my good host, without whose guidance I should quickly have gone astray in the mazes and thickets we proposed to explore. I was again mounted upon the little Pride of the Forest, and as he tossed his head, and snapped at the stirrups and reared in the exuberance of his youthful spirits, it was evident that he meant to have his own share of fun and enjoyment out of the afternoon.

We were bound for Mark Ash, almost the finest part of the New Forest: though where all is so beautiful comparison seems invidious. It would be difficult to describe the wild grandeur of the wood after we entered within the bounds of Boldrewood and Mark Ash. ... High above our heads, meeting like the Gothic arches of a Cathedral, wide branches spread and blended together. Often we stood enclosed as by walls, in these natural temples, the trees standing out from each other in long and lovely aisles for a great distance, the sky but not the daylight completely shut out. Every branch was lined with snow; everything was white and dazzling; the barer branches ran in white veins, and clung and clasped each other like things of life. A white fretwork was above and around us.

Branches, some of them as large as small trees, lay prone upon the earth, borne down by the weight of the snow, and obstructing our path. Even as we stood, wondering silently at all this strange beauty, branches cracked and fell to the earth—as the old postman had said—with the report of small guns.

The Forest: Mother Nature at Her Best...

Continued from previous page

talions were slain between sunrise and sunset. And these people use old English words such as are now never heard elsewhere.

There is an indescribable charm about this varied scenery of wood and moor, which perhaps gives more pleasure than any other that I know. The eye delights itself in gazing on the large massive oaks, the tall, shapely beech stems, covered with lichen; the sea of waving bracken or the flowing cotton-grass. Gentle undulations covered with heather are here broken by plains of greenest turf, over which is borne on the breeze the distant neighing of forest cattle, or the sound of the hurried flight of the wood-dove. And we sit and watch the shadows lengthen, and the haze of evening creep on, while the sun sinks ... after flooding all things with a golden light that fills us with vague, mysterious presentiments of some coming morning of promise.

Rockford Common

FROM HEYWOOD SUMNER'S *Book of Gorley*

2
People of the Forest

The Tames of Bolderwood: Father and Son

Henry Tame is one of few people to have lived in three centuries; he was born in 1796 and died in 1901. He was 103 years and six months old when he passed on.

Henry had a son, also named Henry, who was an equally well known New Forest character. The elder Tame was a gardener, Methodist preacher, and in his spare time occupied himself by visiting the sick and distributing religious tracts. Henry Tame the younger was a great story-teller. Two writers give accounts of the Tames in their books: Heywood Sumner in his *Book of Gorley*, and Miss Sarah Robinson in her autobiography, *My Story*. Sumner also has a portrait sketch of the father while Miss Robinson includes a photograph made (probably by herself) in Henry's last year.

Sumner's account of the two Tames follows:

My first visit to the Tames Farm at Boldrewood was in the year 1882. Old Tame had been Mr. Duckworth's gardener at Beechwood, and at the time I write of had retired, and was living with his son and daughter-in-law, still able, however, to do regular garden work, and occupying a tiny room and a large four-post bed. He was then an old man of 84, shrewd, wise in his garden craft, ready in speech, and a staunch Dissenter. He lived on into this century, and died at the age of 103.

In the years 1897 and 1899 I had long talks with the old man. He spent time every day in writing texts on slips of paper, which he wrapped carefully round smooth stones, and gave to the keeper's children to be dropped on the road as they went to Minstead or Emery Down. Some one, he said, would pick up the little parcels, would open them and read the papers, and just as David overcame Goliath with a sling and five smooth stones, so his stones, winged with texts, would surely find their billet.

Old Tame had been a Wesleyan preacher, so his talk was naturally reminiscent of his Chapel experience, and the following is a record, taken down at the time, of some of our conversations when the old man was over 100 years of age.

"My eyesight's garn, can't see'ee, but I've been reading the Bible." "Does B. read to you?" "No" (with a grave chuckle), "the Lard reads to me. He called me away from where the men was a-mowing, when I was 21, beside a girt dog's tomb, and then I knelt down behind that stone, and prayed to the Lard. But I kep secret: so I fell away agen, and live in sin for ten years. I was sitting in the church at Bramshaw, in the old sinful ways, and I was a-looking at the parson and a-thinking, I shan't get much good out of 'ee, when the Lard call me the second time, His vaice comed out o' the wall, 'This is no place for 'ee.' So I know'd I was called for His service, and I comed out o' church, and never been in one since. Yes; I took up with the Wesleyans, and I preached, and so they all took and hated me. In the world'ee shall have tribulation, and I knew my enemies would try to over-throw me. They kep on saying things to my master agen me. One day I was a-praying agen my enemies, by the hot-water pipes in the greenhouse, and the Lard heard me, and He took me up from behind, so I knew that I was in the hand of the Lard; and when I come out, my master he comed to me and says, 'Tame, I'm a-going away for a bit; here's £5 for 'ee to pay the wages, and for to keep 'ee going while I'm away. And so my enemies was all confounded, and so they always have a-been." Then he went on multiplying stories of his enemies, showing how tiresome and wicked they had been, and how continually they had been confounded. When I had an opportunity, I tried to change the subject by saying that I was staying at Bournemouth, and had ridden over on my bicycle, at which he sharply rapped out, "Another of the works of the Devil," and fresh fuel was added to his fiery anathemas on the wiles of the wicked. So my plan failed.

Old Tame died in 1901, and his strong character and great age have made him memorable in this countryside. He was a point of interest in the Forest—like one of the most ancient trees—and stories are "minded" of the old man's sayings and doings. When he was 100, he was dissatisfied with some boots that were made for him at Lyndhurst—they were too thin—so he went to complain. The bootmaker retaliated: "They're thick enough for any walking you'll want," to which old Tame replied: "Well, I've begun my second 100 a good sight stronger that I did my first."

His son, Henry Tame, is a valued and constant friend, and his vigorous talk always has that

Old Tame

The Tames, Father and Son ...

HENRY TAME AT 103
This photograph was made in 1901, the year Henry died. Sarah Robinson in *My Story* states that Henry Tame was "converted" at the age of 21; throughout his life he called on ailing friends and neighbours and, when there was time, wrote out religious tracts. "He prayed over his *messenger-stones* (to which the tracts were attached) continually," wrote Miss Robinson, "and believed that *some* would prove a blessing to the finders."

Continued from previous page
rare quality of hitting the mark. He is a first-rate story-teller, and his stories are humorous and to the point. Thus, I was talking to him about a field here that is called "Paradise." "That minds me," he said, "of a lawsuit about a piece of land that was washed out by a flood. The lawyers, they kept on a-talking about how the land lay afore the flood, and one of 'em calls his witness: 'What's your name?' – 'Adam.' 'Where do 'ee live?' – 'In Paradise.' 'How long have 'ee lived there?' – 'Afore the Flood.'"

Here are some more of Henry Tame's stories given without their setting, but they were always called forth by the turn of the conversation.

"One of the Crown tenants, he got behind with his rent, but kept on coming to the audit dinner just the same. Well, the Crown, they talk it over, and then they said as how he owed 'em a lot of money, and mustn't do it agen, and so they'd let 'en off, but, till he paid his rent reglar he mustn't come to the audit dinner. So he said, 'Thank 'ee.' But he told me that he'd rather owe the money, and have the dinner."

"One of Lord Mount Temple's tenants was asked to join in a general request for reduction of rents on the estate, and he said he quite agreed with 'em, but didn't see how he could ask for a reduction, as he hadn't paid any for some years."

"Peter Warren, of Tharney Down, son of the smuggler, kept cattle, and made his living by selling his heifers to butchers at Bourne. One day they tell 'en that one of his heifers was took bad, and he had to run home like billy-o to cut his throat, and save his life."

"That minds me of the man who always put his chair particler at dinner, and used to eat his-self up to the table—then he know'd that he'd finished. But one day they bested 'en, for they shifted his chair, and bimeby he found that he didden't get no nearer—tho' he kept on eating—so he never know'd when he'd finished."

Bad Husbands, Beware of Skimmington

(A century ago it was common practice in the New Forest for neighbours to take matters into their own hands when a husband was known to mistreat his wife. This custom was commonly known as "Skimmington" and was described by de Crespigny and Hutchinson in *The New Forest* (1895) from which the extract below is taken.)

The foresters still keep up the good old custom of "Skimmington," or "rough-music," played with pots, pans, kettles, tea-trays and all kinds of music outside the house of a man who is supposed to ill-treat, or behave ill to his wife.

The serenade is an expression of social opinion, more forcible than harmonious, which no doubt serves a good moral purpose. A villain is seldom so hardened a villain as to be indifferent to the publicity thus given to his villainy.

The Art of Encroachment

(For centuries it was possible for families to "squat" in the New Forest long enough to build a fireplace, a crude hut, and to annex a small piece of surrounding land. In his *The New Forest and the Isle of Wight*, C.J. Cornish describes how the encroacher set about staking his claim. The practice continued up to the end of the 18th century.)

It is said that in the old days of encroachments, custom ruled, that if a house were once built, *roofed*, and a fire lit within, it was not in the power of the Crown to pull it down. Occupation, and not architecture was the object of the squatters, and the game of house-building in the forest was soon played with a skill born of long practice, which baffled the spasmodic fits of energy on the part of the authorities. It reached such a stage of perfection that the art of building, roofing, putting in a chimney, and lighting a fire within the space of a single winter's night was at last attained; and the curl of smoke rising defiantly in the gray of a December morning was the signal that the squatter had triumphed, and that henceforth he was irremovable.

Some of these little cabins are still used, though more commodious dwellings have been added to them. Others stand, or are tumbling down, in the gardens of later buildings. Fifty years of settled and prosperous occupation have not given them the complacency of the humdrum cottage.

Brusher Mills—the Best Known Forester

Royalty and nobility have been associated with the New Forest virtually since its creation, yet no name is better known than that of Harry (or Henry) "Brusher" Mills.

Brusher was born in 1840 and for the first half of his life was little known outside his circle of family and friends in the New Forest. Then he learned how to capture snakes alive, including poisonous ones, and by 1884 had turned this delicate technique into a paying business. He found that Lord Londesborough in Lyndhurst and the Zoological Gardens in London were prepared to pay for live reptiles in almost any quantity.

By 1889 Brusher could say he had captured two thousand vipers. It had been only five years since he had seriously turned his attention to the newly-developed occupation. The local press had earlier written up his exploits, but it was probably a Fellow of the Royal Astronomical Society, Major General A.W. Drayson, who first brought Brusher to the attention of the nation. Drayson wrote about Mills in a national sporting journal and also in the widely read *Boy's Own Paper*. In the excerpts below, Drayson tells how he accompanied Brusher on an expedition in the New Forest and recorded a precise, snake-by-snake account of what happened.

Soon Mills' name was known the country over and as visitors flocked to the New Forest in increasing numbers, many sought out the colourful snake-catcher. Brusher accommodated his admirers by showing off snakes in a container and on occasion, would even release them in front of startled on-lookers and then demonstrate how easily they could be recaptured. Several post-card publishers sent photographers to the New Forest to make pictures of Brusher in action, and by the turn of the century post-cards of him could be bought in shops throughout southern England.

Just how Brusher came by his nickname is a matter of conjecture. Some people hold that it was conferred because he brushed the ice clean for skaters on Foxlease Lake; others say he performed an equally important cleaning job of the pitch for the Lyndhurst cricket club. For the greater part of his snake-catching days Mills lived in a crude forest hut, not unlike those once frequented by the charcoal burners. He died in mid-summer, 1905 and was buried at Brockenhurst churchyard where his distinctive headstone may be seen. He kept no record of the number of reptiles he caught, but the total is estimated at between 30,000 and 35,000.

There is nothing very remarkable about English snakes or adders, yet, when it is known that in a certain district in England nearly two thousand adders have been killed by one man during a period of six years, it follows that not only must the reptiles have been numerous there, but the man must be expert and have some knowledge of their habits in order to have achieved such success.

For many years I have been a periodical visitor to the New Forest in Hampshire, generally in the early summer and autumn. My eye has been fairly trained for snakes, having resided some years in India in a district where poisonous snakes were numerous, and during my various visits to the New Forest I have killed about twenty vipers, and have seen, perhaps, forty snakes. While staying there, I heard that there was a man in the forest who in six years had killed upwards of 1900 vipers, but I had grave doubts of the accuracy of the statement. Recent experience, however, induces me to believe that the statement is true, and the man himself, who had no object in deceiving, has confirmed it.

During the latter end of May last, I was walking to the west of the Brockenhurst Wood, and saw a man clothed in a long velveteen coat, which I recognised as having once belonged to the Duke of Beaufort's hunt. The man was about 5ft. 3in. in height, but the coat had evidently been made for a man at least 6ft. high. A stout pair of leather gaiters above thick boots protected the lower part of his legs, and the pockets of his coat contained small tin canisters. Seeing that the man was searching among the bushes, I asked him what he was doing, when he informed me that he was looking for snakes and vipers. In reply to my inquiry as to the use he made of these, he said that for the vipers he received one shilling per head, and that he sent the snakes to the Zoological Gardens. These were probably for the Elaps, and other snake-eating reptiles.

The man told me his name was Mills, but was popularly known in the New Forest as the "Brusher," or Brusher Mills. From off his back he took a bag containing six or seven snakes, and, on opening the lid of his tin boxes, he showed me four adders—two small, and of a light red colour, and two larger and dark brown. He asserted that the red vipers never grew any larger than those he showed me, but were equally as venomous as the larger brown species. The implements he employed to catch the vipers were a stick about four feet long, with a forked end, and a pair of very long scissors, the ends

The Art of Encroachment...

Continued from previous page

They never quite lose the hasty, half-defiant look which is their birthmark, though their present owners enjoy a degree of security, independence, and general good-will, which their honourable and industrious lives fully justify.

BRUSHER MILLS RESTING ON A LOG WITH HIS CATCH OF SNAKES
The most important item in his snake-catching equipment was a pair of long-handled tongs. They are seen here dangling from his chest. Other safeguards to minimize bites were his knee-high boots. On the ground is his pole, used for probing the undergrowth. This photograph of Brusher has appeared in numerous books about the New Forest. (The original print from which this plate was made once graced the public rooms of the Fox and Hounds in Lyndhurst, and is now held in a private collection.)

TONGS IN ONE HAND, SNAKE IN THE OTHER
An artist's impression of Brusher Mills by Lancelot Speed in C.J. Cornish's *The New Forest and the Isle of Wight*.

Brusher Mills

Continued from previous page

of which were flat, and consequently blunt. The viper when seen was pressed down by the forked stick, and then grasped just below the head by the blunt scissors. To hold a small snake in this manner was easy and safe, as the reptile could not move its head, and could not consequently bite; in fact, when thus pinched by the scissors, its mouth could be opened, and a close inspection made of its fangs.

Several important questions at once suggested themselves to be asked of the "Brusher", first, what was the greatest length of any English snake that he had caught? 6ft. 4in. was the answer, and two upwards of 5ft. 2in. Now, as the longest English snake I had ever seen was only 4ft. 2in., these measures struck me as being most unusual; but I was assured that no mistake had been made. To my next question, whether he had ever seen a viper swallow its young, he replied that on two occasions only he had done so, but on these two occasions he assured me there was no mistake about it. Having walked some miles with the Brusher without seeing a snake or viper. I made an engagement

with him to come to my lodgings on the following morning in order to devote the day to snake and viper catching. We started at about 10 a.m., the sun shining at intervals, and but little wind blowing, a condition of weather very suitable to finding snakes or vipers basking outside of their secure retreats.

Ascending the hill to the south of Emergy Down, I followed Brusher, who walked rapidly, and did not appear to search the ground with any great care. His eyes, however, were well trained, for suddenly, pointing under a small bush, he called my attention to a viper, distant about five paces, and coiled up among some dead leaves. We remained motionless, whilst two companions, who were some paces behind us, came up, and, after some time, also perceived the viper. The reptile now began to move, and Mills, with a rush, placed one foot on its neck, and, extracting his long scissors from the buttonholes of his coat, nipped the viper's neck with these, and held it up for our inspection. This viper was nearly two feet long and about three inches in circumference. Being desirous of showing the poison fangs, Mills held the viper by the neck with his finger and thumb, and, opening its mouth, pressed a lucifer match against the fangs, and caused some poison to be emitted. This poison was of a green colour, and had a sort of oily look about it. The fangs were about one-tenth of an inch long. This creature was deposited in one of the tin boxes, and we continued our walk.

During about an hour nothing was seen, but Mills then pointed to a small bushy clump, about five feet in diameter, and stated that he had seen a viper run into it. Taking off his coat he commenced scraping at this bush, tearing it and the leaves, so as to clear the ground. The first object exposed was a lizard, then a slowworm, and finally the adder. Pressing my stick on this creature, I held it firmly to the ground, and Mills, with his scissors, caught it by the neck. "That's a viper," said Mills,

The British Tourist Authority

DETAIL FROM BRUSHER'S GRAVESTONE IN THE BROCKENHURST CHURCHYARD

Brusher Mills...
Continued from previous page

as he held up the wriggling reptile, which was about eighteen inches long and of a brick-dust red colour; "he will never get any bigger, but he is just as venomous as the large adders." "Then you think there are two kinds of these reptiles," I inquired. "Oh yes, two quite different kinds; this is a viper, the other was an adder. They are of different shapes, and this one you see is thinner." This information is, I believe, not in accordance with the accepted theories of naturalists, but a man who during six years has caught thousands of these reptiles, and who is evidently well acquainted with their habits, is entitled to have his say. On continuing our walk towards Boldre Wood, Mills suddenly jumped forward, and very nearly caught a snake just as it was disappearing among some bushes. This snake was 4ft. 2in. long, and thicker than usual—a result not due to its having lately fed. A walk through Knightwood inclosure, where we had a good view of a fallow doe, completed our day's journey.

On further inquiry from Mills, I found he placed great faith in the curative properties of adder's fat. He had in his pocket a small bottle containing scarcely a quarter of a pint; this he valued at thirty shillings, and asserted that it would cure deafness, and also was an antidote to the bite of a viper. On asking for evidence on this latter case, he told me that he had once been bitten on the finger by an adder; he instantly ran his knife into his finger, placed his thumb on the large vein in his arm inside the elbow, and allowed the blood to spurt out of his finger. When the bleeding ceased, he poured adder's fat in the wound, and in half an hour all pain had ceased, and he felt no ill-effects from the bite. This result was to him a proof of the efficacy of adder's fat. I am disposed to believe that the bleeding prevented the damage, and, though adder's fat may have specific charms, this case gives no proof thereof. Considering the number of adders that there must be in the New Forest, it is curious how few people or animals are bitten by them. The reason is that all snakes do their best to escape, and rarely if ever bite, unless obliged to do so in what they consider self-defence.

The life led by such a man as

Two Gibbins Stories about "Brusher"

The two anecdotes below concerning Brusher Mills are related by H.E.J. Gibbins in his book, *Gipsies of the New Forest and Other Tales*.

Of late years (Brusher) made much more money, and with far less labour, by catching trippers in Lyndhurst street, and exhibiting to them his paraphernalia. When several young people had descended from a brake or "Tally Ho," he would unobserved drop a live snake from his pocket. Then followed a stampede of the fair sex, a scramble, and a hue and cry. The reptile was soon recaptured, and, enclosed in a tin or bottle, was safely returned to his pocket. Then, taking off his hat, he would go round with it to the visitors, who tipped him liberally.

. . . .

A rather comical incident took place at his funeral. He fell dead in the yard of an inn after having eaten his supper one Saturday evening, July 1st, 1905. The inquest was held on the following Monday, and the funeral fixed for Tuesday, at four o'clock at Brockenhurst. But a relative and some friends who were about to follow made up their minds in the morning that they would prefer to have the funeral at three o'clock instead of at four, and accordingly despatched a small boy with a message to that effect to the Vicar, who, rather amazed at such a message at that time, went out to see what the boy meant. When asked what it was he wanted, the little boy said:

"Please sir, Brusher Mills wants to be buried at three o'clock."

The Vicar replied:

"Well, my boy, I suppose you have not brought me any letter from Brusher Miller?"

"No, sir."

"Well, then, the funeral must take place at four o'clock as arranged. I cannot take any messages from him today."

Gerald Lascelles: Greatest of the Surveyors

The top administrative position of the Forestry Commission for the New Forest is Deputy Surveyor. This position has been held by many able men, but none has filled the job so well—and for such a long period—as Gerald William Lascelles. Born in 1849 and educated at Eton and Cambridge, his first awareness of the New Forest came in 1875 when he married Constance Augusta Mary Fitzclarence, the only child of J.B. Phillipson of Bramshaw House, Lyndhurst.

Five years later, when only 30, he was appointed Deputy Surveyor of the New Forest by Lord Beaconsfield. He remained in this position for 35 years, proving himself a competent administrator and and a keen follower of out-door pursuits. Almost the only critic of Lascelles' policies was the conservationist, Auberon Herbert, who maintained that the Deputy Surveyor ordered the planting of many trees that "don't belong to the Forest" and that he sought to fell some plantations of ancient oaks for profit. Lascelles was a prolific writer. His works include a volume on falcony and another on shooting. For many years he was the manager of the Old Hawking Club, but was saddened to see less and less public interest in falconry. His autobiography, *Thirty-Five Years in the New Forest* (1915), was favourably reviewed by almost every major newspaper and journal in the land. He died on 11 February, 1928, at the age of 78.

The extracts below, chosen at random from his autobiography, illustrate Lascelles' genius for administration, his appreciation of history, and his love for the New Forest.

When I came to the Forest there were but four responsible keepers left. As their colleagues had died or retired, under keepers were appointed in their places. These men were under no supervision but that of the Deputy Surveyor, and, as they were as a rule merely promoted labourers, they were not the class of man to be allowed to act independently. No definite orders had ever been given to them, and they seemed to think that so long as they looked after the preservation of foxes and pheasants, and kept a mild check on poaching, generally all the rest might be allowed to slide.

Rabbits were supposed to be kept down by the keepers in the plantations, but they never accounted for them when killed, and everything in the shape of rare birds that they could get hold of they regarded as perquisites. With some trouble I discovered the

Why Waste Alcohol When Water Will Do

(A.F. Tschiffely was a 20th century William Cobbett who liked riding his horse for sheer adventure. He kept copious notes about the people he met and the places he visited and subsequently turned these into books. In his *Bridle Paths* (William Heinemann, 1936), he relates an incident in the life of a famous New Forest snake-catcher.

Brusher Mills...

Continued from previous page

Mills is certainly free and independent. He is practically his own master; he goes out or stays at home, as he likes, and if he catch one viper and one snake a day, earns an average labourer's wages. Having been born in the Forest, and lived there all his life, he knows every portion of it, and frequently acts as a guide to visitors, showing them the finest trees, and also some of the most beautiful portions of the Forest.

Although Tschiffely does not name him, the snake-catcher almost certainly was Brusher Miller.)

The New Forest has always been a place where extraordinary characters are to be met.

Among these used to be a dirty, ragged and unkempt man who ... was a snake-catcher.

An elderly gentleman who was a keen collector of snakes—an ophiologist, as he called himself —used to pay this snake-catcher good prices for specimens with rare or peculiar markings on their skins.

Now, as it happened, the bearded terror of New Forest snakes had one great weakness, namely, a craving for alcohol. Invariably, his hard-earned money went straight into the coffers of distillers and brewers —often highly respected and benevolent gentlemen who are

indirectly responsible for not uncommon occurrences when people see snakes and other reptiles which in reality are not there.

However, there was nothing like that about our old snake-catcher, whose eyes never deceived him when he was out in the forest on business.

One day, as with his forked stick he poked about in a heap of leaves, his crafty eyes fell on a grass-snake which had most extraordinary white markings all along its wriggling body. Before the unfortunate reptile had time to slither to safety, or even to hiss, it was safely inside the bag the man always carried for this purpose.

With a smile of anticipation the old snake-catcher followed tortuous paths through his green domain until he arrived at the house of the rich ophiologist, who surely would pay a good price for the unique specimen of snake in the bag.

Gerald Lascelles...

Continued from previous page

Southampton bird-stuffer who was in the habit of regularly paying them 3s. 6d. per head for all king-fishers he could get. Everything in the shape of a bird of prey was, of course, looked upon as vermin, killed, and if possible sold. Had it not been for this laxity, the honey buzzard might have continued to be a far more regular breeder in the Forest than I have found it to be.

The four remaining head keepers, though they had far higher pay and better houses than the under keepers, had in charge only one of the thirteen "walks", or keepers' beats, in the Forest. They had no authority over the under keepers, who each had a similar "walk" which he considered his own, free of supervision.

Everything was in a state of chaos, and I set to work to clear out what was verily an Augean Stable. First of all, I had to persuade the Treasury to give me one other head keeper at a somewhat lower salary than the four existing ones. Each of these, and they were all excellent men, continued at their existing wage, but their places were each cut down to the limit I had decided on, as they fell vacant, and new men were appointed at what was quite an ample wage.

I divided the Forest into five districts, containing so many "walks" each, and placed each of my five men in charge of one, with twelve under keepers among them. Each man had so many under keepers under his authority, and these men had no defined districts, to the boundaries of which they confined their energies as before, but had to attend to whatever duties were set them in any part of the district of the head keeper wherever he chose to send them. He was entirely responsible for their good work, and was supported heartily if he had any well founded complaint to make against any of his subordinates.

Full instructions for all the keepers were carefully drawn out;

GERALD LASCELLES

each man had his printed and signed copy, and realised that a deliberate breach of those instructions meant instant dismissal. In compiling this list of rules and orders, I had in view the object of preserving all the fauna of the Forest of every kind—not merely, as gamekeepers are apt to think, game birds and ground game only. I had to make my men understand that I desired the same care taken of the nest of a buzzard or a fern owl as of a pheasant.

Special rules were made as to particular care being taken of the rarer birds likely to occur, and orders were given that every instance of a strange visitor was to be reported to the Deputy Surveyor at once. And there was to be no killing of any birds save a few scheduled ones. All bird's-nesting was to be rigidly prevented. Of course these were rather novel ideas to some of the men, but, after a change or two had been made among them, they all settled down well to their work, and in some cases became keen and intelligent observers of wild life.

In what is locally called "the April month," viz. from about 15th March to the end of April, when hunting people from all parts of England flocked to the New Forest to finish up in that delightful climate and scenery the ordinary hunting season, I found that quarters in the old Royal hunting box that I occupied were keenly in request, and my spare bedrooms were continuously booked as one party succeeded another. And more than that, the inns and lodgings of the village were overflowing at that season,

Why Waste Alcohol When Water Will Do...

Continued from previous page

A deal was immediately made, whereupon the old gentleman —who was an invalid—asked the great hunter to be kind enough to go to the study and place the singular snake into a jar filled with alcohol which he would find on the desk.

Thanking the buyer for his kindness, the snake-catcher went to do as he was requested. Some time later, when the daughter of the house happened to go into the study, she was startled to see a bearded, dirty tramp stretched out on the divan, snoring melodiously.

Assisted by the strong arm of the gardener, the chauffeur carried the sleeper into a shed, from where, after having slept a sleep of the just, he made his way to his favourite "pub."

Although everybody in the house wondered what had made the snake-catcher so sleepy, the mystery was only solved when—some days later—the source of a most offensive smell was discovered.

Instead of alcohol, the jar which contained the coiled-up, and very much decomposed specimen of a strangely marked grass-snake, was found to be filled with plain water.

Unforgettable Character: Gerald Forward

GERALD FORWARD IN HIS 70s

(Gerald Forward (1898–1980) probably is the only person ever to have been both an Agister and a Verderer in the New Forest. There are few people in the long history of the Forest who were as knowledgeable as he about it, and even fewer who could speak up in its defense so effectively and with such vigour. Three years before Gerald died, a fellow Verderer— Hugh Pasmore, paid tribute to him in the annual report of the New Forest Commoners. That account follows.)

New Forest Commoners are frequently what is known as "Characters", and many of a byegone age have become almost legendary. Not all were quiet gentle people in the past, and the same is true to-day. Gerald Forward would certainly never be called quiet or gentle. Dynamic and forthright would be nearer the mark, and his uncompromising and stubborn attitude typifies the type of Commoner who in past generations fought for and preserved for us the New Forest as it is to-day. Though he will argue fiercely and tenaciously it is seldom he is wrong in facts and his knowledge of forest life and forest lore is encyclopaedic.

His plea that because he lacked an expensive education and therefore cannot compete with more active brains is ludicrous indeed, for there can be few who, when they know their subject, can be so devastating and convincing as Gerald. That he has made bad friends through his unrelenting attitude, he is the first to agree, but the fault lies not on his side, for whatever the disagreement he never fails to buy his adversary a pint when next they meet in a pub. This then, is the man who is certainly unique in that he has been both Agister and Verderer of the New Forest. One can but wonder what transpires in the Verderers' Court in Committee, for nothing is more certain than that Gerald Forward is no 'Yes' man, and it would indeed be interesting to listen in on one of those occasions when he does not see eye to eye with his fellow Verderers.

War Service

Gerald was actually born in Dorset, but came with his parents to live at Burley in the New Forest before he was a year old. By the time he started school at the age of five he was a proficient rider, and

Lascelles...

Continued from previous page and contained many a good sportsman who was paying a brief visit to see the spring hunting. These, of course, of either sex, had to be gathered in to join our party, and I think I have seen as many cheery, informal dinner parties one after the other during the April month, as the old house can ever have sheltered in its earlier days, far back as they go.

The (last renovators of the Queen's House—1851) could not leave well alone. They decided that panelling of any kind was unsuited to a drawing or principal living room. Therefore they covered over with rough planking the walls of the drawing-room but luckily left the panelling behind it, not very much injured. Over this

planking was stretched canvas, whereon was pasted a wall-paper of quite remarkable hideousness.

A very handsome carved wooden mantelpiece, typical of the date of the building had been in this room. It was removed, and a plain white marble slab, with two uprights, placed in its stead. Luckily the canvas stretched over the walls was very rotten, and under my investigations it gave way sufficiently to give an idea of what might be underneath. I quickly examined into this, and, to my joy, found the panelling intact. Better still, I had recently discovered in a loft over a stable, a carved mantelpiece for which I could not account. On bringing this to light, the outline on the paint of the panels showed that it

was the original mantelpiece that fitted into its old place perfectly in the drawing-room of the house as it formerly was.

I soon besought the Office of Woods to carry out the restoration of this room to its original form. What they would not do, I myself supplemented, and the result was a very pretty old room exactly in keeping with the rest of the house.

One of the stipulations I made in the builder's contract was, that no brick should be used in an addition to the old building that was not certified to be at least two hundred years old. When the contractor ran out, I provided him with the remainder from the walls of the old derelict garden at Boldrewood, abandoned for many years, but of considerable age.

GERALD FORWARD (CENTRE) WITH FRIENDS AT THE ROYAL OAK IN FRITHAM

Forest Character: Gerald Forward

Continued from previous page
during his school years he spent much of his time with Charles Evemy, the Agister, and Tom Holloway, a colt owner of some substance, breaking ponies and colt hunting all over the Forest. Thus from his earliest days his life was bound up with horses and never has he been separated from them since. In September 1915, at the age of 17 (putting his age forward to the prescribed minimum of 18) he joined the Royal Field Artillery as a Regular, signing on for 7 years. Three months later he was in France and from thence he moved to Italy. Back in France in March 1918, he went on to Germany and then returned to England. As a Regular, demobilisation was not for him, and early in 1919 he was off to Palestine.

Here, judging by a faded photograph, Gerald briefly forsook horses, for he is depicted as a good looking young sergeant in tropical

kit, riding, of all things—a camel! Finally in November 1922 he returned to England and the New Forest as a civilian, and here he has remained every since. For two years whilst living at Burley he worked for the Forestry Commission and recalls that he helped to build the gravel road through Oakley Inclosure. The work did not appeal to him and in 1924 when Jesse Taylor retired as Agister, Gerald, with others, applied for the job. He was appointed and took up work with Frank Shutler and Hubert Forward, his brother, who were the other Agisters of the day. When Shutler retired, Gerald and Hubert carried on alone until about 1943 when they were joined by Johnny Bradford and Ted Saunders.

After 25 years as Agister, Gerald Forward left the service of the Verderers in 1949, having as great or perhaps greater knowledge of the New Forest than any other man alive. Fortunately as it turned out, that knowledge was not shelved, and when he was elected Verderer in 1959 he pro-

ceeded to turn his lifetime of experience to the benefit of the Forest and all who live in it. One must not forget also that he is a leading figure in all the established Forest Associations, being on the Councils of most of them, and that he was one of those called upon for advice when both the 1949 and 1964 New Forest Acts were being drafted.

Well-earned Coin
At one time Gerald was one of the big pony owners in the Forest, all springing from the purchase at the age of 12 of a colt from Rosie Young of Burley. Reflecting on his colt hunting days he remarked that the first colt he ever caught belonged to this same Rosie Young. She offered him half a sovereign if he could catch a foal whose mother had died, and Gerald collected one or two other boys and found the colt at Ferny Knap. They chased the pony on foot, finally getting to terms with him in a gravel pit at Clumbers where Gerald collared it. That half sovereign was never spent and is

Félicité Hardcastle: Forest Naturalist

The New Forest was fortunate when Félicité Hardcastle's widowed mother chose it as the place to live out her remaining years. Mrs. Hardcastle's life had been disrupted when her husband, a lecturer to the Oxford Extension Delegacy, died before he could assume duties as Director of the Armagh Observatory.

She came to the village of Burley and it was here that her daughter, Félicité, grew up and compiled a remarkable record of service to her local community and the New Forest. For nearly three decades she was Cubmaster; for this service to young people she was awarded the Scouting Medal of Merit. She was also a parish councillor, school governor and archaeologist. She was awarded the British Empire Medal in 1987.

It was not by chance that she was interested in the natural sciences. Her great-grandfather was the noted astronomer, Sir William Herschel, and on her mother's side, her grandfather was Sir Edward Clive Bayley, for many years a statesman and archaeologist in India. She had no need to travel afar to observe nature's laboratory; there was more than enough to record in her own immaculate garden, her beloved Long Pond nearby, and the adjacent Forest.

Her monthly "Nature Notes," started before World War II and resumed thereafter, continued until the end of 1986, and was the most popular feature of the village magazine. Anyone who had seen or found a mysterious insect, bird, or antiquarian object, knew that Miss Hardcastle could identify it and supply history or background in the next issue.

As lecturer Miss Hardcastle introduced thousands of young people, some handicapped and some from deprived urban areas, to the wonders of the New Forest. This she did at the national youth centre at Avon Tyrrell where her illustrated talks on the Forest were seized upon by the youthful visitors. Her *Records of Burley* originally appeared in 1951, and was reprinted in a greatly expanded version in 1987. It is outstanding for its detailed documentation of local people, homes, and customs, and contains hundreds of photographs. She died in early 1988.

The extracts that follow are from Miss Hardcastle's "Nature Notes," selected randomly over recent years, and grouped according to the calendar year.

Gerald Forward ...

Continued from previous page

to-day a treasured possession in his household.

Again looking back he remembers earning one shilling each from Harry Young and Johnny Forman of Burley by walking seven miles from Burley to the Pony Fair on Swan Green in 1912, when the men led the mares on halters and Gerald had to make sure that the loose foals did not stray from the cavalcade. Asked about the price of ponies in the old days he said that at the first of

Ensors sales at Beaulieu Road two of his foals sold for 10/- the pair, bought by Frank Biddlecomb!

Gerald married in 1926, having met his wife, Alice, in Ipswich in his Army days. As he puts it, he courted her for two months in Ipswich, and then for two and half years by post! Now after 40 years they are quietly and happily living out their days in Fritham, but still unceasingly working for the Forest they both love so well.

(Editor's note: Gerald died in 1980.)

JANUARY

In the days when men were closer to nature they recognised animal traits, virtues and vices, in their neighbours and certain phrases and adjectives became common usage. Run like a scared Rabbit, blind as a Mole, sly as a Fox (and) batty (or) bats in the belfrey. The birds seem to be used less frequently, but we do have chatter like a Magpie, cocky as a Sparrow, and "as the Crow flies." There are, of course, complimentary terms: strong as a Horse, patient as an Ox, quiet as a Mouse, gentle as a Lamb, Dog-like devotion, wise as an Owl, swift as an Eagle, and so on. People in the Middle Ages may have spoken ungrammatical English, but they certainly enriched our language by their observations. Read Shakespeare! ... The bitter east wind persisted until 7th January when snow again covered us, yet more deeply. ... Our Winter birds have at last arrived. Mrs. Belstead reported Siskins back on her bird table in Copse Road.

FEBRUARY

It is interesting to study the "pecking order" at the bird table. It certainly does not go by size. On the whole I find the Great Tit is the boss, but the Nuthatch often takes over. Next come the Blue Tits, then the Robin. The Blackbird, for all his size, puts up no fight, and is certainly seen off by the Nuthatch. The Thrush is so timid he will come only when none of the others are there. Of course, in times of real hunger there is a general amnesty and all feed together. ... The Hazel's "lamb-tails" have been out since January; now come the Birch and the Alder. But all catkins don't hang down. Bog Myrtle and about 16 species of willow all grow *up* the stem. Oak and Beech and Ash cluster together like tassels.

MARCH

Easter Day being much earlier than last year, Palm Sunday falls

Hardcastle...

Continued from previous page
on the last day of this month. The name, of course, derives from the Biblical story of the triumphal entry into Jerusalem by Jesus when crowds strewed branches of palms on the road before Him. Not many trees are in leaf in March or even early April, and all are not suitable for processional purposes. The Hawthorn is one of the earliest, but it is far too prickly to hold or wave and certainly not to be recommended for an Ass to walk on. Willow has for many years been used in England and so has acquired the name of Palm. ... According to our ideas nature can move incredibly fast or tediously slow. Consider the speed at which light travels, or the centuries it takes to form a stalagmite. This train of thought started on 4th March after the first frost-free night for about two months, when I found three Stylosa Irises already in flower. I wish I could have sat there and watched them actually growing. It couldn't have taken them more than two hours! ... The Curlew was back on Long Pond in mid-March and despite snow and hail storms, our normal residents are getting on with nest building as usual.

APRIL

When I was a child I was told by my aunt, "You mustn't kill Earwigs because they are kind to their young." I wasn't particularly fond of that Aunt, so I took no notice and continued to squash Earwigs whenever I met them. However, "with years that bring the philosophic mind," I learnt she was right. The female lays up to 80 eggs in the Autumn, guards and licks them continually to prevent mold forming till the young hatch in the Spring. They feed on carrion, leaves, roots, and, alas, the blooms of many garden plants —especially Dahlias. ... The Slow-worm is neither slow nor a worm; it is a legless lizard. It is perfectly harmless and a good gardener, eating slugs and snails. It suffers from man's stupidity which

FÉLICITÉ HARDCASTLE
Her "Nature Notes" sparkle with local colour.

urges him to kill anything that looks like a "viper." Like other lizards they have a protective device. If they are caught by the tail, it breaks off and the Slow-worm departs and you are left with the tail end only. Nature has equipped all lizards with this escape mechanism and they can grow a new tail in about three months. ... The first foal was reported on 18th April, but I didn't see the first swallow until 28th April, though I believe there were earlier sightings.

MAY

What a blessing it is not to have constant heavy traffic, jet planes or even express trains thundering past our windows at night. Listening to *silence* is very rewarding. "The things that go bump in the night" are always interesting and not always easy to identify. There are footsteps, scufflings, squeaks, chirps, grunts, shrieks, besides the recognisable barks, mews and hoots of dogs, cats and owls. Ponies and cattle move about at night more than one realizes, and so do deer. Hedgehogs make quite a lot of noise scuffling among the leaves under bushes and often keep up a constant chirping sound. The pattering of tiny feet and little squeaks mean mice, perhaps on the roof or the window sill, but grunts and heavier movement probably come from a

badger searching for grubs and slugs. The shrieks often mean the end of a successful rabbit hunt by a stoat, weasel or fox. Luckily, they cease abruptly. Foxes are very active when they have a litter of cubs to feed, but often that blood-curdling scream is just the call of the vixen and will be answered by the dog fox's four short barks. The "roding" of Woodcock can be heard at dusk and dawn, and I have several times heard the cuckoo start up about 3 a.m. From Long Pond I can hear the quacking of Mallard and the whistle of Wigeon and from far out on the moor the shurring of the Nightjar. Sadly the Nightingale is scarce and I have never heard it from my cottage.

JUNE

There are plenty of wasps about now, and one in particular persists in flying in at my bedroom window every half hour. (Why can't they find their way out as well as in?) I got tired of chasing her off, and finally caught her in a jar and took her to the far end of the garden. She was back again within the hour; I am quite sure it was the same one. There is a great temptation to kill these insects, but they do help to reduce the Aphid pests which will afflict us this summer. ... It was a great relief to see so many Tadpoles in Long Pond this year. Frogs and Toads are becoming an endangered species in many places. Here in the Forest we are lucky and still have numerous ponds. In the old days every village had its pond, but along came the Health Authority and said: "Horrid, smelly water, dangerous to health and children; fill it up and make a car park," so the frogs lost their ancestral spawning places. ... Mrs. Tanner brought me a Lime Moth. It was sitting on the bonnet of their car and was cleverly manoeuvred into a large plastic bag. Its rather sleepy condition and its still crumpled wings indicate it had only just hatched from its Chrysalis state. When fully expanded they are very large, handsome moths, cinnamon

LONG POND, BETWEEN BURLEY AND BRANSGORE
This pond, located only a few minutes from her cottage allowed
Félicité Hardcastle to feature it in many of her "Nature Notes."

years. Certain species do come in periodic waves and no one quite knows why. Climate and wind direction play a great part, as many of our butterflies and moths come over from the continent. Even with the most favourable conditions, it is a marvel how such frail wings can cross the Channel where there are no "service stations" or "lay-bys" to supply resting places. ... During the beginning of August when the Perseid meteors were due, the night sky was consistently hazy and the moon was full. I saw only one, but it was exceptionally fine. It started by leaving a long orange trail, and then the head exploded in a brilliant white and green flash. ... Mr. Trafford brought me two half-grown Elephant Hawk moth caterpillars found in Garden Road. One was dark brown, the other a bright green. Both have the characteristic "eye" marks near the head and a black horn at the rear. They feed on Bedstraw and Willowherb.

Félicité Hardcastle

Continued from previous page
brown in colour with darker markings which vary in shape.

JULY
Recently I was shown a very curious flower found by Mrs. Knapton. It was a Foxglove with a single enormous flower at the tip of its stem, more like a Campanula than a normal Foxglove. This is typical of a malformation called "fassiation" which occurs in a number of different species. Foxgloves seem particularly prone to it. Often it takes the form of an enlarged flower, but sometimes of a double stem. I have an example of this at present in my garden: two beautiful white flower heads on a single double-thickened stalk, formed like Siamese twins. These forms also occur in Delphiniums and certain lilies. For many years I kept a branch of Winter Jasmine two fingers in thickness, which had curved round to form a perfect Shepherd's crook. Apparently

this aberration is caused by the enlargement of a single cell at the growing tip to the exclusion of the other normal ones. ... Nearly all Forest flowers are now "protected." Besides the Spotted Orchids we have the Early Purple Orchid, the Fragrant, Butterfly, Marsh, Beem Lady's Tresses and the little green Bog Orchids. All these can be found in the parish of Burley though some are very local. Perhaps the tiny green Bog Orchid is the most difficult to find as it really does grow in very wet bogs surrounded with Sphagnum moss, but for beauty I give my vote to the slender, white-scented Butterfly while the rosy-pink Fragrant takes the prize with its delicious Vanilla perfume.

AUGUST
At the beginning of this month there was a veritable "explosion" of butterflies, Brimstones and Peacocks being the most numerous, with Meadow Browns and Gatekeepers running them close. Several people reported Clouded Yellows and I myself was thrilled to see one again after many blank

SEPTEMBER
Our magnificent September "Harvest Moon" is a deep orange-red and reminds me of the many different colours people have attributed to her. There is the mythical BLUE moon, the WHITE moon that beams at the end of the "Long, Long Trail," the PALE moon by whose light Scott advised people to visit Fair Melrose, the SILVER moon, the RED harvest moon, the BRIGHT moon, the YELLOW moon, and the "Long Glories" of Tennyson's WINTER. Sentimental poets have always loved the moon because it rhymes with June, tune, croon, and swoon. The apparent variation in size and colour is due both to its elevation and the atmosphere through which we see it; yet all the time it is really covered only in greyish dust. ... My garden is swarming with tiny frogs. It is difficult to avoid treading on them and I am afraid the mower has taken its toll. I fear many of mine will be eaten by the family of grass snakes who

The Smiths—A Family of Forest Keepers

Bert Smith comes from a family of New Forest workers going back three generations. His father and his brother Gilbert were Keepers, and his grandfather was a long-time employee of the Forestry Commission.

Holly Hatch Cottage where Bert was born in January, 1905, when his father was Keeper, still serves as the residence of a New Forest Keeper—although, in Bert's eyes—it lost much of its charm when its original brickwork was rendered. Having spent the first 20 years of his life at Holly Hatch Cottage, he was back again for 15 years (1935–1950) as Keeper. When he became Head Keeper of the New Forest, he was moved to Bolderwood where he remained for another 20 years. His total service with the Forestry Commission was just over half a century. In the interview below, Bert describes the Forest of his youth and compares the state of the Forest then with its present condition.

Despite its many changes, the New Forest is still close to Bert's heart. "To live in the Forest," he says, "is to live more naturally."

"Junior" but when father died, the Junior was dropped. There were five children in the family, all but one being born at Holly Hatch Cottage when father was Keeper.

It was a cold day in January, 1905 when I was born—the 24th. Snow lay thick upon the ground and the poor midwife who came out from Ringwood had a terrible time getting to the cottage, my parents later told me. In those days the track was rough and unimproved.

School in Fritham

Our nearest school was Fritham. It was three and a half miles each way and I started going there when I was five. We had mixed classes, boys and girls. People had big families in those days. There were 11 in one family, and they were all going to Fritham school when I was. When the children reached the age of 10 they were supposed to continue school at Bramshaw, but that was

Félicité Hardcastle

Continued from previous page

will find them tasty morsels, but I hope at least some will survive— they deal so efficiently with the slugs.

OCTOBER

Major Millar had a surprise when he went to put on his leather gardening glove and found the thumb was completely blocked. What he extracted was a beautifully made tube of leaves, the half-inch circular and square pieces looking as if they had been cut out with scissors. Actually, there were two little trumpet-shaped constructions which fitted into each other, sealed at both ends with a circular cut leaf. This was the work of the Leaf-Cutting Bee, a small, solitary insect, which choose holes in walls, trees, banks and even keyholes, in which to build its nest for the single egg. Rose leaves are its favourite material. Each "tube" is about two inches long with a filling of pollen and honey surrounding the egg. The thumb of the glove was an ideal site and the construction was completed in the two days since the glove was last worn. ...

My father was a Keeper for 49 years and I was Keeper for just over 50 years, so between us we put in almost exactly 100 years of "keeping" for the New Forest.

His name was the same as mine, Benjamin Bertie. When I was quite young people called me

NOVEMBER

I always reckon the first week in November to be the best time to see the autumn colouring. This year it started earlier, certainly among the garden trees and shrubs. My Sumachs were like bonfires and the Azaleas varied from deep maroon to vivid scarlet. The Beeches and Horse Chestnuts were turning to pure gold by mid-October. ... The winter migrants have arrived. A Redwing was seen in the first week of this month. There are plenty of berries to welcome them, but give me a "green Christmas!" ... Complaints are coming in about Herons taking goldfish from lily ponds. Mr. Holdsworth says the bird actually stands on the net covering and catches the fish through it. ... I see we are promised a "mini Ice Age." I am so glad I shall not be here to see—and feel, it!

DECEMBER

I am hoping my Glastonbury Thorn will have at least a few flowers on it. Last year the buds all got frosted, but its flowering is often known to wait till Twelfth Night (January 5th) which was the old date of Christmas before the calendar was changed in 1752. That is the day good country folk should "wassail" their apple trees, toasting them in cider and singing. "Stand fast, root; bear well, top; pray God send us a good heavy crop." ... Mrs. Watney put her letters on the bench by the door for the postman to collect. He didn't call that day and when she went to take them in, she found unmistakable signs of mice and two of the letters had corners eaten off. In each case it was the corner with the stamp that was missing. Does the Post Office gum have some irresistable attraction?

> *"I always reckon the first week in November to be the best time to see the autumn colouring."*

NATURE'S WALKING STICK

When walking in the Forest, Bert Smith likes to pick up fallen sticks and fashion them into something of use. Here he is holding a walking stick made from a piece of holly whose root made a perfect handle.

The Smiths: A Family of Keepers ...

Continued from previous page

another three miles and it was too much to walk. So I stayed on at Fritham until I was 12, although— being an infant's school—there wasn't much to do.

When I left school at 12 the first world war was going on and the Forestry Commission had to maintain the tracks throughout the Forest because a great deal was going on in the area at the time. My first job was helping to keep up the timber tracks. I had no other formal schooling except for

Forestry Commission training when I was 19, but the Forest itself was my real school.

Mother was Mentor

As a young lad I got to know a great deal about the Forest from my parents, especially my mother. Father taught me as well, but he had his work to do and was away a great deal. Mother was very patient with us and at every opportunity taught us about Forest wildlife.

We had wild animals all around us, but nothing like the number of injured ones we see today from passing cars. We might come across the odd animal that was lame—maybe a disjointed leg. We'd get the vet out and afterwards look after it for a time. Besides the deer—always plentiful, we had the birds, squirrels, badgers, and foxes.

Mother taught my brother Gilbert and me how to enjoy badger watching, one of her favourite pastimes. Mother would make us take turns, but would not allow us to watch together. I remember one night when I wanted to go with mother and Gilbert, she refused. "No," she said, "when it comes to badger watching, one's ideal, two's plenty, and three's too many." It's been my life experience that her words of wisdom still hold true for badger watching.

You see, the more people there are, the more noise there is. Mother explained that every movement you made had to be very slow, because it might make a bird fly away. All birds have warning notes. The animals—the deer, fox, and badgers—read all these notes and can tell exactly what's going on.

A Pet Badger

We used to keep a badger at one time. His mother got killed on the road. That was back in the 1930s, when the cars started becoming more common. There were three young badgers in a place called the Old Park. I managed to pick up one of them because they were gradually dying, as the mother was gone. So we fetched it back and my wife reared it. She called it Geoffrey. It used to follow her everywhere.

We had it until it was fully grown. We used to let it out at night and it would wander about and come back into the house the next day. It would curl up and get in under the couch—a place where it was dark. One spring after it got to be of a certain age, it just walked off, went down into a big badger set and introduced himself to some more. It came back occa-

The Smiths: A Family of Keepers ...

Continued from previous page

sionally, but gradually it weaned itself off from us. We felt happy about that. It was a male. It paired up with a female and forgot about us—naturally.

The New Forest was split into two areas then with a Head Keeper for each. At first I had the southern part of the Forest; later I had the northern part, so I have had all of the Forest to look after at one time or another. As a result, I know it like the back of my hand.

Forest Versus Towns

To live in the Forest one is living more naturally. You are living with all the wild life. You *must* be interested in wildlife. A town never appealed to me. If I go into a town, I know what I want when I go there. I get it and I'm out and gone again. I like my wildlife; I've enjoyed it all my life.

Of the four types of deer in the New Forest the fallow is my favourite, because they're so friendly. I started a deer sanctuary at Bolderwood in 1963 when we had a very bad winter. The deer were dying all around us, so I went out and cut ivy off the trees. The deer found it. Every morning I had more and more deer waiting for me. I had over a hundred outside waiting for me to cut some ivy for them. This is how I started the deer sanctuary.

They even called for me. They made noises for me to come outside. I wouldn't have believed it before it happened, but it's true. I had a few that used to come when we had bad weather who would go into the shed. I opened up the door and they went inside and lay down. I would go in there with them, but they wouldn't take any notice of me at all. They were very friendly, but I never handled them. They can be dangerous. Sometimes I would stand outside and call out and a hundred or more deer would just gallop and form circles around me. I used to feed all kinds of things. Potatoes mostly. As a real tit-bit, there's nothing to beat mint sweets. You

couldn't feed them many, naturally, but they were crazy for mints. I always had some in my pockets and I'd be walking along and they would be putting their noses into my pocket.

The Forest has changed a great deal since I was young, and I'm afraid—not for the better. In the years just before 1970 we were really clearing out the hardwoods. It was pitiful to see it. I've said to a lot of people a good many times I wish I could have had a film made of the New Forest like I first knew it. If I showed it to you today, you wouldn't recognize it. There are areas of woodland that were solid hardwoods that are now three parts conifers. There's not the same wildlife in the Forest, or bird life, butterfly life or insect life. Conifers don't produce insects and such, like the oak. The oak is the best producer for insects. There are 200 types of insects, and lots of birdlife.

I did a trapping survey once to see what wildlife—voles, and that type of thing—there was in the conifers. We put out traps, and were supposed to record what we caught and then release them. We sat there and watched and caught nothing. In the hardwoods, you'll catch something practically every night—a vole, mouse, woodland mouse—all types of things. The best place was along woodland streams where the hardwoods grew. It was very interesting—I rather enjoyed doing that. The only thing in favour of conifers is for crows to nest in, or roost in. The trouble about that is the crow is a pest—vermin, really. The worst vermin are the magpie and the crow. The more magpies and crows you have, the less other forms of wildlife you will have.

The magpie is the worst bird that there is. They take the eggs, they take the young. What used to get me was when an animal was in distress in a bog, mired down, the first thing a magpie does when he comes upon an animal in a bog that can't escape is to peck its eyes

out. They are terrors, alright. We always had plenty of other birds when we were allowed to destroy the magpie. In the olden days at Holly Hatch we could lie in bed at night and hear nightingales all around us, but you can't hear a nightingale anywhere now. They're all gone. Where have they gone? Magpies. Many people don't realize this, but it is so.

Birds Taken

Other birds that have disappeared? The skylarks have gone now because they are a ground-nesting bird. They are very vulnerable to magpies and crows. You can see an old crow sitting on the moors somewhere—or even a magpie—just watching every bird going to and from its nest. "There's breakfast, there's my tea, supper or what have you." He's straight in and gone with them. There are less and less magpies in the Forest now because there is less birdlife—less food— for them. They are terrors—they don't miss.

But the New Forest hasn't always been just trees and plants and wild life. Before the Second World War we had the Schultze Gunpowder Factory at Fritham. It was a German-owned firm in those days. There were quite a lot of people living in Fritham then, and many more came from nearby places to work in the factory.

There are still some of the old places left where the gunpowder was stored. Once there must have been about 30 buildings on the site; now there are only two or three. There were several serious accidents at the gunpowder factory. The track from Fritham to Holly Hatch passed close to the gunpowder factory, situated in the valley to the right. One day, when we children were returning home after school, there was a tremendous bang in the valley. We couldn't see the factory for the trees, but just at the moment we looked a huge amount of debris was suspended in the sky. Instantly it fell and we all knew there had an explosion with several casualties.

The Smiths: A Family of Keepers ...

Continued from previous page

I was about 17 when I learned to shoot. Father wouldn't let me use a gun before then. He would take me out vermin-shooting with him and allow me to take a gun, but no cartridges. We were mainly after magpies, crows and jays. I learned to mimic some of the birds and at times this has come in handy.

Birds, too, can mimic, and I think the starling is the cleverest of all. They mimic almost any other bird and even some animals. They are very greedy but can't help it. I like them. I wouldn't injure them in any way, for they do a lot of good. I like to hear the cuckoo when it first arrives, but I have never heard one after about June 16th.

I can mimic a pheasant and have caught poachers by doing so. It can be a bit dangerous, but before the poachers aimed in my direction I would stand up. You never did see such a fright in your life!

Deer poaching has gone on for a long time, but it seems to be getting worse. In my time the Keepers were sworn in as special constables with the same powers as police. They would radio us and then we would work together. The system was effective.

The modern poachers are very cruel. They come out with their headlights on and shoot to kill the deer, but sometimes they only wound them. Of course the deer scramble off. I can't tell you the number of wounded deer I have come across and have had to put down.

The Orphaned Fawn

Once in Frying Pan's Bottom I was with another Keeper and saw something. "Look," I said, "There's a dead deer down there." We saw this white stomach sticking up. We went down and found a dead doe. She had a little fawn, just barely alive, and we could see a path where it had been walking around and around his

dead Mum trying to feed. He had been there for I don't know how many days. I think I would have done something to that fellow if I had caught him. That really hurt.

It was too late to save the little one; he was by now unconscious. The most peaceful way was to put him down.

Some of the deer I have come across had their eyes blasted out by the poachers—terribly cruel.

Last Boar Killed

Sometimes wildlife has to be killed for good reasons. My grandfather Charlie Bessant, was the last person to kill a wild boar in the New Forest. That was in 1907. The boar was at Wood Fidley in the southern part of the Forest. He had been making a nuisance of himself and Gerald Lascelles, the then Deputy Surveyor, instructed Grandfather to kill him, which he did.

I often wonder what happened to the boar's feet because Lascelles had them made into inkwells. The last one I saw was at the Queen's

"THE ROOM WHERE I WAS BORN"

Holly Hatch Cottage was built during 1808–1809 and has been home for many happy Forest families. Bert Smith was born there in 1905 when his father was Keeper. Pointing to the room where he was born, Bert recalls he was later told that a deep snow had fallen on the January day he was born, and that the Ringwood midwife who came to attend his mother found it difficult going over the rough Forest track.

The Smiths: A Family of Keepers ...

Continued from previous page
House in Lyndhurst. Lascelles was the best Deputy Surveyor I ever knew. He was interested in all wild life. The New Forest isn't a true Forest without its wild life—you *must* have it.

War-time in the Forest
The New Forest was a busy place during the Second World War. There were big airfields at Stoney Cross, Holmesley and Beaulieu and large army camps scattered all over the place. The Canadians were at Bolderwood and there's a memorial cross there now at the spot where they used to have their religious services. You can still find the concrete patches where some of the war-time gun-sites were.

Not far from Holly Hatch is Broomy Lodge which was a very hush-hush place during the war. I and the other Keepers were sworn to secrecy about all that was going on in the Forest, but we knew that secret navigational research was going on at Broomy. The Germans must have thought something unusual was taking place there, too, for they dropped bombs all around the place. Holly Hatch is only half a mile away and we caught some of the bombs. Once the windows were blown out of the cottage. Our chicken house was blown to bits, and a lot of the garden was destroyed. I remember how the blast blew all the roses off their stems.

We had about 30 bombs within half a mile of Holly Hatch, probably intended for Broomy Lodge. Broomy was in the middle of nowhere, yet the Germans persisted in trying to hit it. I wonder if someone had given their location away. Once we had "Daisy Cutters" at Holly Hatch, blast bombs that would devastate everything in a small area. We had two horses in a nearby field and I fully expected to find them dead, but they were alright. Incendiary bombs were common and we could expect them to drop almost any night when it rained.

Plant Life Disappearing
The modern Forest is also affecting plant life. Take the wild columbine, for example. There are only about three places in the Forest where it has survived. They used to be quite common. There was once a big patch near Holly Hatch where I was born, but the oaks were cut down. They planted conifers in their place and that killed them. That's what happens.

The same goes for the "fly" orchid. I know where the few surviving plants are, but I don't disclose it to anyone. People would go and dig them up, and they soon would disappear.

Many of our rare birds are becoming even rarer. Take the Dartford Warbler. There are not many of them left in the Forest. The right habitat for them is there, but it's not looked after. The Dartford likes a tight, hard cover—not great, long lanky gorse. They don't let the Warbler's natural habitat stay there now.

Cover Important
When we had the Forest cover under our (Forestry Commission) control, we used to keep it down. It could be burned, every nine or ten years. Not burn the lot, but only so much and it would come up thick again, and all the birds would transfer across to it. Now the Nature Conservancy has stopped it all and we have very little bird life out there.

We used to have plenty of Dartford, hobby hawks and honey buzzards. They are now all gone. The

---

Gilbert Smith's Book
Bert Smith's brother Gilbert was the subject of a limp-cover book published in 1986. Entitled *Gilbert Smith: Man of the New Forest*, the 82-page volume contains both black and white and colour illustrations and is available from Paul Cave Publications, 74 Bedford Place, Southampton, Hants.

---

oak woods were the favourite spot for the honey buzzards to nest in, but many of them have been cut down.

When you go into an oak woods all the trees are individual—no two oaks are the same. Conifers all look alike, and are depressing. We are lucky in having some old oaks still—and some wonderful beeches. The trouble is, nothing is being done about replacing those that fall or have been cut down. Oak is in demand, so an entire area is not cut any more—only one here and there, what we call "knocking."

The Coming of Cars
The beginning of the end for the New Forest has been the motor car. When people came to the Forest and walked or used horses, it was unspoiled. In the last 30 to 40 years the car has taken over. Traffic is enormous, tracks are worn, animals are killed. I don't know why people have to tear through the Forest.

With the coming of cars camping has greatly increased. When I last lived at Holly Hatch I issued only about a dozen camping permits in a year. That was before the last war. Most visitors walked, carrying packs on their backs.

When cars became common, people went right down into the woods as far as they could go. They'd stop there, camp or have picnics, and leave their litter behind. Some would light fires in the claws of a big oak or beech. Where that fire was lit, a couple of years later, decay would set in.

I would say to those people: "You come back and look at that tree in three or four years' time and you'll see that you started that tree on its last days by lighting that fire there." It was then an offense to light a fire in the Forest, but to light it there—to me—was a double offense. "Oh, we lit it there," they'd say, "because it was safer." But, of course, the safest thing was not to light it at all.

Today, thankfully, the large camp sites accommodate the campers and the Forest does not suffer so much from them.

Len Mansbridge: A Commoner's Life Today

Len Mansbridge comes from a long line of New Forest Commoners. His father, grandfather and great-grandfather were all Commoners, and possibly there were generations of Forest Commoners in the family before them.

Today, however, he is one of very few commoners to earn total living from the land. Mansbridge likes to recall how his ancestors relished "the good life," but he fears the time may be fast approaching when hard-working, self-sufficient Commoners will be no more.

I was born in 1917 at Longdown, just about a mile from where I live today. When I was a lad, all the people around us were Commoners, and had been for generations.

They'd run a few cows on the Forest. The cows would go out in the morning and come home at night. They were milked then and sometimes be turned out again at night. Within a radius of about two to three miles from where I was born there were about a dozen little holdings, each one supporting a family. All of them are gone now. This is true of the Forest generally, but I have first-hand knowledge of this immediate area which I've known all my life. In some cases the original farmhouses have been renovated or enlarged, or both, and now command great prices, but the old small-holdings themselves are gone, I'm afraid, forever.

Hard-working people
Commoners didn't give hard work a second thought in the old days. Take my grandparents, for instance. My grandfather had five sons, two of whom worked at home. Everyone pitched in. They milked the cows, made the butter. Grandmother used to drive the pony and cart into Southampton twice, sometimes three times, a week. She had a steady round of customers who were only too pleased to buy her fresh butter, cream and eggs. She did this most of her working life—until she was eighty. It wasn't until my grandfather died that the youngest son took over, and they bought a little van—but they still continued making the rounds in South-

ampton.

Life was conducted by strict plans. Grandmother would load up the cart at about eight in the morning, everything having been made ready the night before. Off she would go and she would come back home about four o'clock. She made the butter in the old-fashioned wooden moulds; the moulds had different designs—all attractive. I can still remember

when they used to skim the milk. They would put it out in pans and skim it by hand. Later the mechanical separators came along. The buttermilk we called "separated milk." Grandmother used to bottle it up and sell it, too, in Southampton. It brought a lower price than whole milk. My grandparents also had a few pigs and chickens—the chickens were always free range. They usually kept a couple of hives of bees—not for commercial use, but just to provide honey for the family.

Vegetables, Too
Grandfather also had his little market garden—we called it "Granfer's Field"—where he grew all kinds of vegetables: carrots, turnips—pretty well every-

DONKEYS HELP TO MAKE ENDS MEET
The growing popularity of "Donkey Derbys" has led Len Mansbridge to breed donkeys as a sideline. They thrive on the Forest and Len feels their value as a tourist attraction has not been fully appreciated. Donkeys have been a tradition in the Mansbridge family since Len was 13 years old.

Mansbridge: the Commoner's Life

Continued from previous page

thing. He also grew apples, and would take them into Southampton and sell them. He never made cider—both he and my grandmother were teetotalers. I never knew them to take a drink. What grandfather liked when he relaxed was smoking a cigar.

They were regular chapelgoers. Grandmother ran the local chapel, the Wesleyan one at Longdown. It was burned down not too many years ago. On the other side of the road from the chapel was the school. When the school closed, the chapel moved into the school building. But that, too, is now finished.

School Days

I went to this little school in Longdown for a few years. That was my very first school. There were two teachers: one the headmistress, and a younger one. There were about 25 to 30 of us, most years—all local children. But there were half as many again of gypsy children. A gypsy compound was located at Longdown at that time. Until I was in my teens the gypsies used to camp in various places around Longdown. At different times of the year they would go off fruit-picking. Then the compound was made and they had to all live in it.

I got along fine with the gypsies. One of the old ones worked for me here on the farm. He could go out in the Forest and see a plover flying round and he would just watch him. And then he would walk straight to his nest. Another thing he used to do, when the salmon came up the Beaulieu River to spawn, was to lie down on his stomach and he would tickle the salmon and catch them.

No Eggs Lost

Where the gypsies used to camp —in the days before the compounds—was just outside my grandfather's farm. They were just on the edge of the Forest. I remember one old boy, Matty Jeff, who had only a little tent—a "ben-

der"—and his legs and feet would be outside. It was just somewhere he could get his body in. He used to do all his cooking there. Well, grandmother's hens used to escape and go all over the compound. They would make their nests there. Then a gypsy would come to grandmother and say, "Mrs. Mansbridge, you come with me—I've found a nest of eggs." They would take her there and she'd get them.

My wife and I have three children, all married. My only son works with me on the farm, has his own animals. He and his young family actually live away from the farm. My holding has 42 acres. I used to rent it, but eventually I bought it. It's nearly all grassland, with just a little woodland. Actually it was about 30 years ago that I ploughed all the grassland— some of it probably for the first time in living memory. In the woodlands there are oak, birch, beech, some conifers. At one time the woodland was pure forest, I would think, because there are oak trees there that have more or less come to the end of their day. These last few years we have had several to be blown over by the wind. Whether I would be advised to sell off these old trees now and replant, I just don't know.

I have the same situation with beeches. Over the last five years or so I must have lost 30 big beeches. They just died off, and you can see some of their trunks standing today. My own opinion is that they must have a disease, similar to the Dutch Elm disease. What makes me think this is that when I was in Belgium judging New Forest ponies, I stayed on a small estate similar to mine, and I got talking to the Baron who owned it and he said what they do on the Continent when they notice this disease in a beech, is to inject the tree with a hormone, and that stops it.

Emphasis on Beef

I always had beef cattle. It's mainly Galloway cattle that I have now. I suppose I have about 135

cows and quite a number of heifers —nearly up to the 200 mark, all told. I sell most of the bull calves around about six to eight months old. The heifers, we keep them.

Actually I operate something like the ranch style. The Galloways live on the Forest the year round. In the wintertime they browse on gorse, birch trees, whatever. I take them a little hay—not every day—but when its needed. The cows are all around this immediate area. Nowadays we have to test them, usually in the second or third month of the year, and also they have to be marked by the Agisters. So we do the lot together—the testing and the marking. The Agisters do the tail marks, put the tags in, and we worm them,—all on the same day.

I may wean off something like 40 calves which we then brand, mark and turn out on the Forest. This year, I turned some out in February. They went into another part of the Forest, because if I put them out here with the cows, they'd go back and suck the cows. When they are away on the open Forest, they get used to grazing and away they go. When they go out, they'll be from nine to 14 months old. They stay out the first summer, the next winter, and the next summer. In the second summer I bring some in and put them to the bulls for replacement. Those that get in calf, do, and those that don't run again out on Forest and I sell them as beef animals. These Galloway cattle don't become big animals, but the heifers—after they get to, say, two and half years old—they get fat on the Forest.

Keeping Cattle Mobile

The cattle that are turned away from home—last year, I suppose there were from 40 to 50—they would average out eating about a bale of hay apiece. It was good hay, mind, but that's all they needed in the winter. But they'd clear it up and then go on grazing. If I'd given them a lot of hay, they'd just eat that and stay in one place the whole time.

If they are on the move, they'll

Mansbridge: the Commoner's Life

Continued from previous page

keep themselves warm and fit. Those cattle that are out there look as well as, if not better than a lot of those that are inside.

I sell my cattle mainly through the Salisbury and Shaftesbury markets, and occasionally the Ringwood market. The main farm income is from cattle. My wife keeps the chickens—I do have a couple of sows and a few sheep. If we want one in the freezer, we just go out and take one. Ponies are a different story. Today they are a liability. It wasn't always so.

At one time I exported a lot of ponies. I used to drive up to Great Yarmouth with a load of ponies and put them on the boat and then drive back. It was a terrible bind —you just had to keep going. Those shipped out of Great Yarmouth went to Holland. Those that went to Sweden I took myself. A fellow from Sweden came here one day and I showed him some of my ponies. He kept coming back and I eventually took them over myself. The ponies went not only to Sweden, but to Germany, France, and Belgium. Really, ponies were my life. The export ponies were mainly for riding, although in Sweden they used to break some for driving. I've got photographs showing how they are used with sleighs. The person I sold the first lot of ponies to from Sweden, he wanted them to live on the mountains. That was in Skara. The best thing about the Forest ponies is their temperament.

Continental Exports

The exporting of New Forest ponies to the Continent went on for some time, I'd say the peak was from about 1955 to 1975. I also took a lot of ponies to France. After I took some over, I got to be known over there and afterwards people came over to see me—and occasionally they do now. In the course of one year, I sold one chap 600 ponies, going backwards and forwards. They were mostly for riding schools. I found that in most countries on the Continent they didn't have a small pony for the children, and the riding schools wanted something for children. I am sure this is where most of the ponies from England ended up. In Sweden, the people thought a great deal of their Forest ponies.

The Forest pony got good marks all round—they were sure-footed, they could ride in the mountains, and they had good temperaments. They're breeding their own over there now. We sent out their foundation stock; now they're breeding their own, they have their own stud books. When I was over there judging the Forest ponies, they would have been the descendants of the original stock.

Donkeys for "Derbys"

I have a number of donkeys on the Forest as well. They actually pay me more than the ponies. I supply the donkeys for some of the "Donkey Derbys." It started up some years ago when I took some to the Southampton Speedway for their Donkey Derby. I suppose I have something like 20 now. How do the Derbys work? Well, I take the donkeys to the Derby and the organizers get the kiddies out from the crowd to ride them. The donkeys are quite safe to ride, although sometimes children do fall off. But usually there's no harm done.

All the same, I have to take out insurance on them. At the end of the Derby, I pick up the donkeys and take them home again, and turn them out on the Forest. In the course of a year the donkeys might take part in four, five or six Derbys. Also, there are a number which are taken away for fêtes— church fêtes, that kind of thing. I had two churches that had donkies for a number of years on Palm Sunday. On these occasions, I don't charge. So the donkeys earn their keep. I've had it in mind for several years to ask the Verderers if the donkeys could run free in the Forest because they are such a tourist attraction—which they definitely are—and I think the owners ought to have something back from that.

A REMINDER OF THE HORSE-AND-CART DAYS
Len Mansbridge stands inside the frame of an old Diamond cattle truck made at the firm's Lymington works.

Mansbridge: the Commoner's Life

Continued from previous page

Moss, Leaf-mould, and Fern

We used to sell moss and leaf-mould to Toogoods, the well-known Southampton seedsmen and nurserymen. They would wrap it around plants because it held the moisture in. Nowadays it is often used in hanging baskets.

When I was collecting moss, I got to know where it was all over the Forest. Sometimes I would get a telephone call from Toogoods saying, "We've got to have 20 bags today." We'd have to move fast, and sometimes my wife would drop everything at home and help.

Everyone used to cut fern in the olden days. You bought your fern ticket from the local keeper for a shilling a load. The fern was for bedding down animals, and all the small-holders had their special patches of fern in the forest. We respected each other's territory; you knew there was a tree there and that was as far as you could cut. Fern isn't used much today because straw is so cheap and it is always baled. I believe there is still one person near Godshill who cuts and bales fern, but its use has pretty well died out.

Fern and Grazing

There's something else about bracken. A lot of people might laugh at this, but you only have to stay and watch, and you will see it's true. In the winter when the bracken is dead, you'll see Forest ponies going there, raking it away, and finding good grass underneath. Now, when the bracken used to be cut there would always be a lot of grass underneath, and you'd see the animals coming back and grazing. That is how we've lost a lot of grazing land on the Forest today—there is so much fern, left to spread, that it's destroying the grazing.

The Changing Forest

The New Forest has changed in many ways and what the future holds I'm just not able to say. Today there is so much pressure on the Forest—and from so many sides.

There's little doubt but that a lot of Commoners have been driven out of the Forest because of the attraction of industry—the Esso oil refinery and other nearby businesses. Some of the old, original Commoners' sons and grandsons work at at Esso, getting quite a good wage. They may have a couple of ponies still—just as a hobby—but that's all. That's quite different from years ago when Commoners kept animals for a living. They had a few cows, and the ponies helped. We used to reckon the ponies paid the rent. Today people come and buy a pony or two without realizing they've got to keep an eye on them the whole time. It's like when you get "red water" in the Forest, caused by ticks. If you don't catch and treat the infected animal in time, she'll die.

Motor Traffic

Another thing that is killing the Forest is motor traffic. I mean, how far are we from London now? They measure it in minutes instead of miles.

The proposed Lyndhurst by-pass is a sore point with me. If you've got a wife and a little family and you enjoy watching cricket in the Forest, what better place than at Lyndhurst? Now they want to put the by-pass there and the cricket ground will be cut off. If they put in a bridge or underpass, what will happen to the ponies, donkeys and cattle that used to roam freely over the area? They'll not use it at all for a while —that's their nature—but when they do, they'll not go back. They'll have just a few tit-bits there, no more, and they'll slowly starve. Today they can go right back on the Forest into the gorse. But if there's a bridge or underpass, it'll be too much trouble for them.

Uncontrolled Growth

It's my opinion that it won't be too many years before the New Forest is overgrown. I was up in the Fritham area recently and was surprised to see how much holly trees and brambles are encroaching on the Forest. You don't realize it until you actually walk through the area and study it. Then you say: "I walked through easily the last time I was here; now you can't get through at all."

There are certain parts of the Forest that can't be burned now. They won't let us burn the gorse in some areas now, even if it is higher than a man. It's no good for anything. The Forest animals help to keep the undergrowth under control. The ponies used to browse freely on the holly and whatever, in the winter. Likewise, holly was cut extensively at Christmas. At Lyndhurst Road station you could see truckloads and truckloads of holly going to London for the Christmas season. In those days the holly was controlled by grazing and cutting, but not today.

I hope my son will carry on after me. He has more ponies than I do. But I have to admit it won't be easy for him in these changing times.

Life of the Forester

(Philip Klitz, in his *Sketches of Life, Character and Scenery in the New Forest,* describes the forester's life in the middle of the last century.)

Contrast the life of the "lean and smutch'd artisan" with the life of the forester, and what a change is visible!

From the rising of the sun to its going down, his hours for the most part pass under "the open firmament of heaven." Here may be found the daring dear stealer, fleet of foot, cunning in strategy. ... What a variety is there in the forester's avocations! Through turf-cutting, furze-cutting, broom-vending, wood-cutting, bark-peeling, carting, potato-growing, the thrifty forester attains his *ne plus ultra.*

Maldwin Drummond: 25 Years A Verderer

Maldwin Drummond's family originally came from Scotland, but for over 200 years there have been Drummonds in the New Forest and a number have been Verderers. One was George III's banker, another was an eminent soldier, and another was Vicar of Fawley.

The original family seat was at Cadland, which Maldwin remembers from childhood. That house was demolished shortly after the end of the second world war and the site is now occupied by the Esso oil refinery. The present seat, Cadland House, was built as a fishing lodge in the 1780s and later was expanded. Legend has it that, when a fire started in 1786 during the lunch hour, the family calmly moved the dining room table onto the lawn and continued their repast—consuming a fine haunch of venison and some good wine to dispel the gloom. There was another fire in 1916 and, in 1935, the house was rebuilt for the last time.

Maldwin, in common with thousands of other British children, spent part of the war in the United States. On return he continued his education at Eton and the Royal Agricultural College in Cirencester. His time is now divided between over-seeing the Cadland estate and a variety of civic interests— the most important of which is his service as a New Forest Verderer. He was first elected to the Court of Verderers in 1961 and is now the longest serving member of the Court.

In the interview below he looks back over his time as Verderer and reflects on events which, in his view, have shaped the destiny of the Forest. He regards the conflicting interests in the Forest as a "plus" so long as no one group attempts to stifle another. "These competing interests," he maintains, "are the lifelines of the Forest. Our strength is in diversity. But if one interest overwhelms another that could lead to disaster, and in no time the Forest would be covered with bricks and mortar."

During my time as Verderer there were probably two events that were to greatly affect the future of the New Forest. The first actually started before my time, but its reverberations continue. That was the decision to make the A31 a principal route to the west and now connected with the M27 to the Forest. Sir John Mills, then a Verderer, took the view that the main road leading to the south-west should come to the north of the Forest. If that had taken place, some of the problems faced by the Forest today wouldn't be so great. The A-31, inevitably I suppose, in time, will be a motorway. It's virtually one now. I used to call it a "motorway by stealth." This road has put the pressure on the Forest from the early 1960s to the present day.

The most momentous thing in my time was clearly the fencing and gridding. Ponies used to go almost up to Salisbury and Totton, creeping up the lanes—all over the place. We had to have pounds at that time. This unrestricted movement of ponies caused a lot of animals to be killed because people never knew where they would come upon them. though fencing and gridding the Forest was impossible.

I was on the New Forest District Council at the time and when the subject was discussed the Councillors used to shake their heads and say, "But what of the expense?" and "It's just not possible." Anyway, the fencing and gridding did take place in 1964. It probably was one of the most significant events in the history of the Forest.

Humour in Court

A presentment can be made to the Court of Verderers on almost any subject although, of course, most are directly concerned with the New Forest. I remember an interesting one, some years ago, when ponies frequently interrupted picnics. On this occasion a good lady got up and asked the Verderers if fire-brooms could not be supplied all over the Forest for picnickers to beat off the ponies when they disturbed their picnics. Then there was a gentleman (perhaps that's a misnomer), a few years back who got into a disagreement with the Official Verderer and to emphasize his point brought to the Court a goat with a label around its neck saying it was the "Official Verderer."

What work in the Forest has given me the most pleasure? Well, there are a number of things. I enjoyed my time as President of the New Forest Association, but I suppose the New Forest Museum has been a real passion of mine for a very long time. You see, I think there are two basic problems facing the New Forest. One has to do with local government, and I was able to see this while serving on the District Council and the County Council. That problem, simply put, is that local government doesn't really understand the Forest. I don't think they would pretend to. The other problem is that the Foresters and Commoners don't always understand local government.

Bringing People Together

This mutual misunderstanding goes much deeper than is at first apparent. For example, people in the villages of the Forest—Burley, Brockenhurst, and so on—tend to be somewhere in between. Some residents are actively "Forest" while others are actively "village". There are, of course, some who are actively "Forest and village". It is my hope that the New Forest Museum will bring people together. They will be able to see that there is a "culture" within the Forest, that they have a common heritage whether they live in a

Drummond...

Continued from previous page

village or the back-of-beyond, or even on the outskirts of the Forest. I think the museum will knit people together by a proper understanding of the history and uniqueness of the place in which they live.

People who live away from the Forest sometimes think the Forest people are already closely knitted. In fact, people living in Beaulieu, for example, probably know very few residents of Burley, or of Minstead, and so on.

There is a school of thought that says museums are dusty places with glass cases covered in cobwebs. To get around this stereotype and also because the building will house a visitors' centre, we had decided to call it the "New Forest Centre." This was based largely on responses from a survey we conducted in the Forest. We asked people what they thought the building should be called, and the one that came out on top was "The New Forest Museum and Visitors Centre."

Themes of the Forest

It won't be a dust-and-cobwebs museum. Instead, it will take particular themes and work right through them. There won't be that number of artifacts, but those that are selected, important artifacts where will have a real story to tell.

When you enter into the Museum you will find "Geology" —the setting of the Forest—and then you will come to "History" where, for example, you will learn about the killing of William Rufus. Then you'll get to the Commoners, the Foresters, and so on. It will all be related to the New Forest Embroidery.

The Museum is totally independent. It will have an advisory board and an education officer who organizes programmes inside and outside the museum for everyone. What we want to do is to use the Museum as the starting place—but with the whole of the New Forest serving as the exhibit.

Visitors, therefore, will be directed here, there and everywhere. The idea is to get people to see the Forest as a *whole* rather than to tour the Museum and think they know all about it.

Sadness over By-Pass

One of the saddest episodes in my time as Verderer has been the long-running conflict with the Hampshire County Council over the Lyndhurst by-pass. It is unfortunate that the County Council has come in for a lot of bad publicity over this issue. Probably the county's conservation policy is the most forward-looking in Britain. That, ironically, is why we in the

MALDWIN DRUMMOND

Forest were taken unawares by the Council's initiative over the by-pass. We though the County Council would look after the interests of the Forest at all times, but we were mistaken. Here was another case of misunderstanding, or under-estimating the Forest's interests. I think the main complaint in the Forest is the worry that there may be oil underneath and the department of Energy or even the oil companies themselves will now try and override the Verderers following the precedent of the Hampshire County Council.

Competing Interests

The Forest has a number of conflicts running through it, many of which clash one with the other. There is the Commoning interest, the Forestry Commission's need to grow timber, the natural history interest, the interest of the visitor, and there is the interest of the local resident. Now all of these conflict.

It would be a disaster if any of those interests overcame completely the others. This indeed has happened in places outside the Forest.

I believe the Verderers have a job to see that these interests are balanced. That, it seems to me, is the task of the Court of Verderers in a nutshell. As long as we can do that, the future of the Forest should be assured. But if, for example, all the visitors went away—which some people might say is a good thing—if this happened, it would be very bad for the economic health of the Forest. On the other hand, if the number of visitors becomes too great we've got enormous problems.

All these interests have their "plus points." Growing broadleafed timber does. The visitors do, for if they come to love the Forest they will help to preserve it when threats arise.

I feel very strongly that by understanding the "lifelines" of the Forest we can help it to survive in the future. We have to look at history to identify these thin "red lines" that have held the Forest together since before the time of William the Conqueror. Once one of those red lines—whether it be Commoning, silviculture, or whatever—is cut by an opposing interest, we will lose that strength which we know from history, has allowed the Forest to survive.

For example, the grazing habits of the Commoners have over the years done so much to enhance the beauty of the Forest. If these Commoners' rights were interrupted, irreparable damage would result and the Forest would become devalued. Before we would realize it, the Forest would be built over with bricks and mortar.

Ponies and Cattle Essential

It is not an over-statement to say the continuing right of commoning—and its good health—preserve the Forest from exploitation and over-development. The ponies and cattle are to the Forest what the apes are said to be to Gibraltar.

If they go, we are lost.

Ray Stickland: the Agister's Arduous Tasks

> Ray Stickland was born in 1922 at Alderholt on the fringes of the New Forest. After brief sojourns in Redlynch and Wood-mancote, he came with his parents to Linwood when he was 15, and has remained there since.
>
> He was a popular Agister for 37 years, never turning down a request to help an ailing animal in any kind of weather or any hour of the night. He retired only on his doctor's advice after developing hypertension. In the interview below, he tells of his first duties as Agister and describes some of the more memorable incidents he dealt with. Not the least of obstacles put in his way was piping hot parsnip wine on a winter's day.

I loved riding horses and I used to go out with the Commoners when they had to catch their ponies. I didn't have any ponies at the time. So I got more and more used to the Forest and I liked it. When the next Agister's job came up, Mr. Forward—who was then Agister—rang me up and said 'Why don't you put in for the job?' I fortunately got it. That was November, 1947.

Agister for 37 years

Unfortunately I had what is known as hypertension. I felt alright, but I happened to have a blackout one day and the doctor, seeing my age was then 63, thought I ought to think about retiring—especially because I was working on my own so much. I was miles from anywhere when I had the blackout and had to pull myself together when I came round. I didn't want to retire but I had to. I had been an Agister for 37 years when I had to give it up.

Riding a horse is still required of an Agister today for he has to get to parts of the Forest where you cannot get to with a vehicle. He has to look at the animals. It's a little easier nowadays, for the Agister carries a bleeper. So he can call in from any house to the police and know where there's a problem. They know if they've got to get straight home or not.

My first day on the job I rode in a point-to-point race. It made me realize that when you became an Agister you were on a 24-hour a day job. Next day I met another agister—from the Brockenhurst area—and his job was to show me

around and tell me what I had to do. I was a bit surprised at him because he took me off, got his field glasses out and had a look round at the ponies. He seemed to know whom they belonged to, and that was that.

A Pub "Education"

The next stop was at a pub. I thought to myself, "Everything I do has to go in a diary and as I don't frequent pubs very often; what shall I do?" Well, we were there for an hour and a half and we saw several Commoners coming in and out. We got to chatting with one who had his son with him, and when we got back to where I had left the car at Picket Post it was half past two. My fellow Agister said, 'Now, you'd better go home now.' I thought to myself—knowing I had to keep the diary—what I should write, so I put down "Inspected ponies with Agister X in that area" and that was it for the day.

"Over the Broomstick"

When it came time to mark the animals, I had to follow the old marking book to know where to go. There were so many small Commoners in those days—not any longer, for the Forest has changed quite a lot since. Then you'd go where there would be just one person with a couple of cows, or one cow and two little

heifers out, and he'd wean a calf, or something like that. I remember going out to Godshill and I asked for a certain Commoner, where he lived. I found a young lad and he said, "Oh, that's our Dad." He gave me one name for his father and another for his mother, and I couldn't understand that until I learned from another Commoner that his parents never got married, but they only jumped over the broomstick. Anyway, I managed to find my way around the Forest without any problem, but it's so changed now. Even in the village I live in there's only about two or three people that turn out animals whereas there used to be a dozen or more.

The trouble now is that when the old people die out, their homes are so valuable they are bought up by people from away. Most of them are not interested in having animals. Of course, we have had a few people who don't even live in the Forest, but have large herds of animals. One man used to have about 500 head of cattle—he had a farm near here. They were Galloway-type cattle. He used to keep a good many here, but he also had farms in Sussex and Lockerly. I've had to go to Sussex to mark 300 cattle in a single day on my own. I've branded each one, ear-marked it, tail-marked it —done the three things, with five blokes helping me pushing them through, and clipping them out. They clipped the hair away so that I could get at it with the brand, and we had about five brands going at the same time—the same brand. We started at half-past seven in the morning and I finished at four o'clock. The next day we loaded them on the train and took them off at Ford-ingbridge, came home that night and drove them back up the

> *"The trouble now is that when the old people die out, their homes are so valuable that they are bought up by people from away."*

STICKLAND AND ONE OF HIS RETIREMENT PRESENTS
When he retired in 1984 after 37 years as Agister, Ray Stickland
received several mementoes from friends and admirers. He is shown
here holding one of the gifts—a painting of himself, in Agister's
uniform, executed by Tiptoe artist, Rosemary Sarah Welch.

Ray Stickland: Tasks of An Agister ...

Continued from previous page
Forest. That was before the
Fordingbridge line was taken up.

If a pony changes ownership, a
new brand has to be applied. It's
an offense to brand on top of an
old brand—so you have to find
another place. There's generally
room for another brand if you look
carefully.

The knack of Ear-Tabbing
For cattle, we change the ear-tab
every year. It's plastic—a different
colour. We cut out the old one and
put the new one in its place. We
thought it was going to be very
difficult when we had to use the
same hole—which we were told we
had to do. If you didn't, the Verderers said, you have an animal
which had gone out for several

years, looking like a pepper-pot!
After a bit of practice you'd be
surprised how easy it is. You just
get hold of the ear and your
finger'd go there to where the hole
was—it was only a tiny hole —and
you could snip in the tag quite
happily. To get the old one out,
we'd use a pair of special secateurs
like wire-cutters. Something like
electricians' wire-cutters. This
changing of ear-tags is still done

every year, and that animal is
recorded in the book. You put
down the owner, his herd number,
the number of the animal -- which
is shown on the tag, and you put
the Commoner's number
alongside of it. So you have the
check in case anybody rings up
and says he has found an animal,
you ask them to give you the
number and you just look in the
book, and you can tell to whom it
belongs.

Four Calls in One Night
In all my time as Agister, 1958
was my worst year. That year I
had 180 accidents to animals—
just in the northern part of the
Forest. That is, north of the A31
(running from Cadnam to
Ringwood). At that time the main
roads were not fenced. The most I
have been called out was four
times in the same night.
Fortunately I am one of those
people who can fall asleep easily
and after 10 minutes, I feel as
bright as ever, and can then go on
again.

I have had the police pull up at
my house at 3 o'clock in the morning, tap at the door and say,
"Come on, we want you quick,"
and they would take me out to
Picket Post or someplace like that,
and bring me back. They'd come
in and have a cup of tea. We had
to work with the police constantly
and I got on well with them. They
treated me well. They have to get
their job cleared up, we have to do
the same. You go there and find
an animal with a broken leg, and
you know what you've got to do.
You see one that's been hit by a
car and is standing up.

The Crucial Decisions
You've got to give it the benefit
of the doubt. Then, you get up

> *"The most I have been called out was four
> times in the same night. Fortunately I am one
> of those people who can fall asleep easily and
> after 10 minutes, I feel as bright as ever, and
> can then go on again."*

Ray Stickland: Tasks of An Agister ...

Continued from previous page

again the next morning—it doesn't matter what time the accident was—you get up at first light and pop out and see that animal. If he's hit where *you* can't see—like in the stomach where he bleeds inwardly, and you can't tell, the vet may not be able to tell you. If that happened, the animal would be dead by morning. If he's alright by morning, normally he would get over it. If there were instances where we had doubt and the animals belonged to Commoners we know well, you have to use your own initiative—then you might call in the vet.

I had only one Commoner tell me off for shooting an animal. I said to him, "Well, you didn't see it laying in the middle of the main road." He still said, "You shouldn't have shot it without letting me see it." I told him: "Well, we couldn't let it stay there, and it couldn't get up." He apologized to me afterwards when it was pointed out to him that the animal had a broken back—that is, after it had been taken to the slaughter-house. I made it my business to find out what the injury was. If you were used to running your hand over the middle of the animal's back, you can get a pretty good idea if the back's broken.

An Agister has authority to destroy an animal if he feels it should be done, and the Verderers will stand by him. Nine times out of ten the Agister has to make a decision on the spot and if the animal has to be destroyed, there's nothing to do but go to the owner afterwards and tell him.

Key Role for the Wife

The Agister's wife is the main one who answers the phone. Really, one's wife is a great help all the time.

The Forest keepers deal with the deer accidents, but if the police can't find the keeper they ring an Agister. We never refuse to go when this happens.

We also have had cattle rustlers in the Forest. Going back some years, up at Fritham, they hung a loop up between two trees. This animal, a big one, got caught in it, and was chopped with an ordinary axe. His head was split open. Happily, they did catch somebody for that. But I went one night to an accident and shot a real fat animal north of Godshill—it must have been eight or nine months old—just before Christmas. It had a broken front leg—broken right off. It was a Galloway-type and I knew exactly whose it was, so I knew I didn't have to bother before destroying it. I happened to be in Godshill that morning with the chap who had the job of picking up the animal, and he turned to me and said, "What happened to that animal? Have a look at it."

The Vanished Haunches

I did, and somebody who knew how to use a knife had run the knife around and taken both haunches out—without skinning it—and just left it with the tail coming straight down. They took the best of the meat out of it, and just left it as it was. I expect they had a good Christmas dinner out of that. That was the only experience I ever had where an animal that had been left overnight was tampered with. There was one other time when an animal was found dead under suspicious circumstances and the police were called in and I had to go out. Looking round, looking for clues, my eyes were sharp enough to pick up an empty 22 bullet shell. They had the clue then that the animal had indeed been shot. But I don't think anything more was found.

Cars Kill Most Animals

Most animals that die or get killed are victims of car accidents —perhaps eight or nine out of ten. Old age takes a few—sometimes you come across them. Sometimes young three-year olds were at risk because of condition, but the Agisters are tight on them now. We like to get the owner to take them in.

Occasionally in the spring of the year when we have in the bogs what is called "spurty grass"— then the grass shoots are greener— the animals get in too far and can't get out. There's no standard way of getting a pony out of a bog, you take on each case as you find it. Sometimes you have to call the Fire Brigade for help. They roll the animals over on a sheet, one side or the other—whichever way they can get at them. You pull them along on the sheet afterwards to firm ground. It can be dangerous for the rescuers as well, for soon you start sinking and you feel the ground all like a jelly.

The pony normally won't go into a bog, but will stay on a footpath. But when they see this sort of grass that grows a bit greener, especially in dry time, that can be a danger. Sometimes we get people who don't know the Forest—people on riding horses— they get stuck in bogs. Normally a Forest pony doesn't get into bogs unless he's slips off the side coming up the pathway beside the bog. Perhaps he's been knocked over by another animal and pushed in there when they were playing.

A Difficult Winter

Speaking of especially difficult cases, I remember the winter of 1962. I had two calls: first to go to Hyde common—I was told there was a pony bleeding to death. I couldn't go out with a car because we were snowed in, so just put an extra coat on and a rug on my horse because he was clipped out.

> *"He apologized to me afterwards when it was pointed out to him that the animal had a broken back—that is, after it had been taken to the slaughter-house."*

> *"She heated up some home-made parsnip wine in a saucepan to keep me warm, but actually it made me a little bit woozy. She gave me a tumblerful, but there was a little drop left in the pan. 'Drink that drop,' she said, 'you don't want to waste it.' And I did."*

Ray Stickland: Tasks of An Agister ...

Continued from previous page

That was a good pony, one I had had for years. There was about a foot of snow. I rode on to Hyde and all it was, was a pony that had pricked its nose in the gorse and a spot or two of blood came from where he had pricked his nose. Of course, blood on snow looked a lot more that it really was.

Then, I went on from there to Woodgreen—which is quite a journey from here—and found a mare that had a snare, badger wire, on her hind leg. I arrived at this small farm and they knew where the pony was, and we walked her in. We got some hot water because it was so cold the wire would stick to your fingers. Finally I got the wire off and I tied her to my own horse and rode on with her then back to its owner at Telegraph Hill and put her in his field and she got over it alright. Then I had to make my way back home. It was dark when I got home and my wife was a bit worried for I had been gone since half past eight in the morning. But I was alright. I never caught cold or anything.

Peril of Parsnip Wine

I'll tell you why. The owner's sister was the reason I didn't have any ill effects. She heated up some home-made parsnip wine in a saucepan to keep me warm, but actually it made me a little bit woozy. She gave me a small tumblerful, but there was a little drop left in the pan. "Drink that drop," she said, "You don't want to waste it." And I did. When I got back to Amberwood I said to myself: "I'll never make it," but the horse took me home, and that was that. That's the nearest I have ever been to not knowing what I

was doing.

I suppose the most exciting thing that happened to me in my life was when I was presented to the Queen when she visited the New Forest in 1979.

The biggest change in the Forest in my lifetime has been the disappearance of smallholders. When a place is put up for sale, a small man is not able to come in and buy it. Many of them are only weekend cottages. I might have been able to keep my son in the Forest, but the planning people wouldn't let me build a bungalow for him—so that was the end of that.

Agister's Hard Life

The time may come when it will be difficult to find enough Agisters. There are quite a number who are interested, but when they find out about the particulars—being on call 24 hours a day and so on—they have second thoughts. But when I put up, I was one of 15, and they were mostly Forest people.

Regarding the motorways and all the people who visit the Forest, I think the Forestry Commission has done a good job of controlling them. People have to use the campsites now whereas in the old days they could go anywhere. It was common then to find a car right in the middle of the Forest, stuck, and needing to be pulled out. This rarely happens now, thanks to the barrier ditches, dragons' teeth and the like. I don't think it's right to deny people the

Forest Superstitions

(John Wise, writing in *The New Forest: Its History and Scenery*, recalls some of the superstitions and proverbs of a century ago.)
Plenty ... of old love superstitions remain—about ash boughs with an even number of leaves, and "four-leaved" clover, concerning which runs a Forest rhyme:
  "Even ash and four-leaved clover,
    You are sure your love to see
    Before the day is over."
Again, "A poor, dry thing, let it go" (a sort of poacher's euphemism); "The grapes are sour" is said of the Forest hares when the dogs cannot catch them, and so (is) applied to things which are coveted but out reach. "As bad as Jeffreys" ... preserves the memory of one who, instead of being the judge, should have been the hangman. Again, too, "Eat your own side, speckle-back" is a common Forest expression, and is used in reference to greedy people. It is said to have taken its origin from a girl who shared her breakfast with a snake, and thus reproved her favourite when he took too much.

Passing, however, from particulars to generals. let me add for the last: "There is but one good mother-in-law, and she is dead." I have never heard it elsewhere in England ... .

chance to enjoy this beautiful part of the world.

Death under the Conifers

Another thing that has changed is the trees. I'd like to see the oaks come back again. As soon as these conifers get up, the ground is killed underneath them. There's no greenery.

Under hardwood trees you always get greenery, but where you have these dense conifer plantations in the Forest there's just no life going on at all.

> *"The time may come when it will be difficult to find enough Agisters."*

Gems from a Forest Commoner's Notebook

(Hugh Pasmore was born in Southampton in 1908, but came to the New Forest when he was 25 and has remained there since.

From 1969 to 1980 he was a member of the Court of Verderers, having been the appointee of the Ministry of Agriculture.

It was while serving as Verderer that he wrote a monthly column, "A New Forest Commoner's Notebook," that appeared in half a dozen weekly newspapers in and around the New Forest. These columns were eagerly awaited not only for any official news emanating from the Court, but also for nature notes and events—some dramatic, some happy, and some sad—reported to him by New Forest Agisters and other contacts in the Forest.

His son Anthony is now a New Forest Verderer and is the author of the highly regarded history, *Verderers of the New Forest* (1977). As one observer said, "What Hugh and Anthony don't know about the Forest ain't worth knowin'."

Hugh lives in retirement with his wife, Margaret, at Fritham where they are only a short distance from many well-known Forest beauty spots and landmarks. In his spare moments he edits the monthly magazine, *Forest Views*, for seven nearby villages and hamlets. Up to now he has resisted editing a collection of his "Commoner's Notebook" columns, but has kindly given permission for inclusion here of a few extracts.)

HUGH PASMORE AND "DRIFTER"
Acquired when six months old, "Drifter" is now almost 29 years old.

An Able Agister
(December, 1971)

It goes without saying that a NF agister is a versatile and resourceful man for he is daily faced with fresh problems for which there are no precedents. Even so there are occasions when he excels himself, and such an occasion was just before Christmas when two agisters, "Georgie" Cook and Brian Ingram, were called to Brockenhurst. Here they were confronted with a mare impaled on a piked iron fence some four feet high. Nine of the iron palings were imbedded in the pony between the foreleg and abdomen to a depth of about two inches and it was clear she had attempted to jump the railings with tragic results.

Ordinary mortals faced with such a predicament would probably have put a bullet in the mare's brain without further ado, but the agisters had noticed a drainage tractor with lifting bucket working a few hundred yards away, and the operator willingly rushed to the stricken animal. A rope round the mare was attached to the bucket which then lifted the animal straight up clear of the railings and deposited her on the ground on the side. A local vet was quickly on the spot and having done what he could pronounced the animal had a 50-50 chance. Normally such incidents result in days of nursing only to be followed by the death of the patient, but the owner tells me that this little mare never looked back. Swellings abounded but heavy doses of anti-biotics kept infection at bay and now, after three weeks, it would be almost impossible to tell the pony had been in trouble.

Nesting Birds
(July, 1981)

Just when I thought that my trials and tribulations caused by birds nesting in sites which interfered with my daily routine were over, a pair of spotted flycatchers entered the lists. At our front door is a hanging flower basket with geraniums and other flowers. Obviously the flycatchers approved the colour scheme and set up home amidst the flower stems. The evening before the nest was discovered my wife gave the basket a thorough watering, without, apparently, infererring with the household arrangements and

From A Commoner's Notebook ...

Continued from previous page

the following day came the first of four eggs.

All would have been well if the bird had been amenable to our comings and goings, but as soon as one approached within 10 yards off she went to the nearest apple tree. In view of the number of times our front door is used it was clear that there was no hope of hatching young flycatchers if mother spent more time off the nest than on. So once more our daily life was disrupted—the postman left letters in a cardboard box at the front gate, and a notice balanced on a garden chair directed all callers to the back door. Even the painters who were doing up the house deferred work near the front door until last. The hen started sitting as soon as the fourth egg arrived, and for fourteen days serenely watched the chaos she was causing. Then arrived four grotesque little creatures with apparently insatiable appetites. For a further 13 days the nestlings grew rapidly, swelling over the edge of the nest until suddenly all had disappeared. For a further four days the parents fed them in the garden and now they appear to be fending for themselves, happy to stay in the vicinity. My bird book sounds an ominous note 'The spotted flycatcher is a creature of habit, returning year after year to a favourite nest site.' Heaven preserve us from this annual nightmare.

Threepenny Piece
(September, 1967)

Anecdotes of the past are always of interest and there seems no end to the variety of happenings in the Forest in bygone years.

Bob Andrews of Ringwood, who follows his father's footsteps in being a leading Commoner, told me a story of his youth when a would-be mis-appropriation of a Forest pony was frustrated in an unusual way. In his very early days, he and his brother were being driven along the Bolderwood road when his father spotted one of his mares with a foal near the Portuguese Fireplace. Not having his iron in the trap, he could not brand the foal in the usual way, but he told the boys to catch the foal which was not very wild. He then took one of the old-fashioned small three-penny pieces, noted the date, and making a tiny slit in the skin under the mane, slipped it in.

The pony carried no brand and at the end of a couple of years it had disappeared from the Forest, but Harold Andrews never forgot a colt, and one day he spotted it in a Lyndhurst field, bearing another Commoner's brand. At once he tackled the Commoner and a fierce altercation ensued. However, the evidence was unassailable, and when the coin had been located, the new "owner" had to give way, and with a vague muttering of having been mistaken, he handed back the colt to its true owner.

Cuckoo Thwarted
(July, 1978)

It is twenty years since last I had a cuckoo reared in my garden. On that occasion a pair of chaffinches worked themselves almost to death coping with the fledgling's enormous appetite. This year once again I have been involved with this, in some respects, not very likeable bird. Firstly, I discovered a cuckoo's egg in a hedgesparrow's nest and after consideration we decided that if we sacrificed the dunnock's nestlings the cuckoo would soon be off to Africa, whilst if we removed the cuckoo's egg the hedgesparrows would be with us throughout the winter. So the cuckoo's egg now adorns my mantelpiece. Alas it was in vain, the young hatched only to be devoured by a marauding magpie. Shortly after, a Cadnam farmer, Tom Penny, phoned to say he had a fledgling cuckoo in a hedgerow nest. He and his son James had been trimming a field hedge by hand and had discovered the young cuckoo overspilling from a robin's nest. Typical of countrymen they had carefully left six feet of hedge to preserve the nest. The youngster resented instrusion and swore violently at us, showing the brilliant orange interior of his mouth.

Rutting Season
(November, 1976)

During the first week in November we were riding quietly through Eyeworth Wood into Island Thorns Enclosure when we disturbed three or four fallow does, and almost at the same time heard in the distance a crashing as though a pony was trapped in a fallen tree, and was breaking branches in an endeavour to free itself.

At once we rode towards the sound, and on getting closer, the penny suddenly dropped. The crashing was the sound of antlers coming into violent contact. Sure enough, about 100 yards away through the undergrowth we could see two bucks circling each other and attacking with heads down. Unfortunately we viewed the con-

FOILED BY A SILVER THREE-PENNY BIT
The ingenious use of a hastily-inserted coin, when branding was not possible, allowed the rightful owner to reclaim his pony.

From A Forest Commoner's Notebook...

test for only a minute or two, for one decided he had had enough, and set off with the other in hot pursuit. The sodden ground was churned up in a circle of about forty feet and the fight, though short, had obviously been fierce.

(October, 1976)

New Forest ponies are renowned for being quiet and reliable for riding. However I have found they possess very definite wills of their own, and on occasion they will dig in their heels and indicate they wish to do what they want and not what the Owner wants.

Continued from previous page

Normally this merely means a battle from which the rider should always emerge victorious. However a certain pony in the Cadnam area, known as Macgregor, when exhibiting this trait caused his young lady rider considerable embarrassment.

On a fine sunny morning she was enjoying the beauty of Cadnam Common when on rounding a clump of gorse bushes she came upon two couples in the nude enjoying a sunbathe. Now Macgregor thought this was well worth investigating, and stopped dead in his tracks. His rider fever-

ishly kicked, tugged and implored him to move on but Macgregor had his own ideas and despite the ever increasing embarrassment he was causing refused to go forward; however he did elect to go backwards which would have been all right had not one of the couples been directly in his path. This was too much and, throwing dignity to the winds, his rider leapt off and tugged and hauled Macgregor by the rein until she gained the comparative safety of the far side of the bushes. Macgregor was not her favourite animal for the next week or two.

GIRLS AT THE BURLEY PONY SHOW
Sketch by the artist-author Allen W. Seaby; the drawing was executed between the two world wars when the show was in its heyday.

3
Creatures of the Forest

A Plucky Student Studies Pony Behaviour

From 1965 to 1968 a Cambridge University student, Stephanie Tyler, spent thousands of hours observing the behaviour of the New Forest pony.

The result of her study was a doctoral thesis, *The Behaviour and Social Organization of the New Forest Ponies*, completed in 1969. It also appeared in the *Animal Behaviour Monograph Series* (Vol. 5, Part 2, 1972).

Later Dr. Tyler spent six months in the United Arab Emirates, four years in Ethiopia (where she, her husband and two small children were ambushed by Marxist guerillas and held for eight months in captivity), and a further year in Tanzania. In recent years she has worked in the more peaceful surroundings of the Wye valley for the Royal Society for the Preservation of Birds.

A selection of excerpts and photographs from Dr. Tyler's doctoral thesis is given below. These are introduced by a passage from Hugh Pasmore's "A New Forest Commoner's Notebook," a regular feature of newspapers in the Forest area when Mr. Pasmore was a Verderer. Published in February, 1969, it relates how Stephanie Tyler arrived with little knowledge of Forest ponies, but doggedly set about observing and recording their habits.

Four thousand hours of patient observation of NF ponies! What a stupendous effort this must have been. Dawn to dusk in all weathers and at all times of the year, and in many cases throughout the night as well. Yet this is precisely the achievement of Stephanie Tyler of Girton College, Cambridge, whose thesis I have just had the intense pleasure of reading.

Most of us whose connections with commonable animals have taken us into the forest during the past three years have come upon her quietly watching, noting and following ponies in one of her three chosen localities. (Backly Plain in the north, Longwater and Holland's Wood in the centre). Now at the end of these long years her knowledge and deductions have been recorded in what must be the most comprehensive thesis on the subject, and one which has been submitted for a Ph.D.

When she first arrived in the forest she confessed she had no idea how to go about the task or what she might hope to glean and this makes her work all the more praiseworthy. Even the most ardent critic would be forced to admit that the book contains a mass of carefully authenticated information which upsets many previously held theories, and I have no doubt that it will be a standard book of reference for many years to come.

PONY THESIS

Leadership

When ponies left the open daytime grazing areas in the evenings for the valleys and woods in the early mornings and when they moved to the "shades" or drinking places, they sometimes moved as much as a mile without grazing. These movements were more integrated and were initiated by any member of a group, even by an immature animal. This animal began to walk purposefully away from the rest of its group, whereupon the other ponies usually soon began to walk after it. Occasionally one or more ponies did not see their group companions move away but they usually looked up after several minutes and then trotted or galloped after them ... .

Usually a group of ponies walked in single file. ... Young foals, however, did often walk alongside their mothers. The order of the file in a group of ponies was not always constant but some patterns did emerge. When the ponies were walking some distance, the pony leading initially, if a young animal, soon stopped until a more dominant animal had overtaken it. In small family groups, the mother invariably led with her offspring following behind her in their order of age. Foals were alongside or immediately behind their mothers, followed by yearlings and then two to three-year-old or older offspring.

Foodplants

Although the ponies were normally grazers, browsing was important during the winter and early spring. Gorse, *Ulex europaeus*, was of great importance both as shelter during strong wind and rain, and as a food plant at such times... . Plants of the dwarf gorse, *Ulex minor*, were also selected by the ponies when they were grazing over the heaths and they often pawed with their fore-feet at the gorse plants before browsing them. This was presumably to crush and soften some of the spines... .

Heather plants, *Calluna vulgaris* and *Erica*, seemed to be of relatively little importance in the ponies' diet, despite the large areas covered by these species ... . Leaves and shoots of brambles, *Rubus*, were browsed between autumn and spring, when ponies also took both leaves and leafless shoots of oak, *Quercus* and beech,

Pony Behaviour...

Continued from previous page

Fagus sylvatica... Leaves of holly, *Ilex aquifolium*, together with gorse provided almost the only food when snow was on the ground. Most leaves were removed to a height of about eight feet up to which ponies could stretch their heads.

Acorns had a great effect on the movement of some of the ponies, completely disrupting their normal daily pattern. They remained under oak trees for much of the day in October grubbing for fallen acorns instead of moving out onto the open woodland clearing. It is known that individuals can become "addicted" to acorns and that the ingestion of large numbers of prematurely fallen green acorns can cause poisoning and death (Garner 1967)...

Bracken, *Pteridium aquilinum*, was the only other plant that was recorded as being eaten in any quantity. During the summer day when ponies were grazing out on the open grasslands, they sometimes moved into clumps of bracken which they browsed for short periods of up to half an hour. They then returned to the grass... .

Behaviour of the Newborn Foal

First day foals showed a strong tendency to follow any large moving object; they frequently followed siblings or mares other than their mothers; several followed the observer and one even trotted alongside a van which was driven slowly past it. By their second day, foals did not show this response to other ponies or objects and they only followed their own mothers, walking behind or alongside them or trotting or galloping by their sides when the mares moved quickly. One foal, born in woodland, showed a marked attraction to a particular tree on its first day. It remained close by the tree, even when its mother moved up to five yards away, and it nibbled the tree,

STEPHANIE TYLER, PATIENT OBSERVER OF PONIES

walked around it and to and from it.

However, a successful mother-foal relationship was formed, although some Forest Commoners observed that the attachment to a fixed object, such as a tree, can occasionally upset the relationship. A foal will sometimes completely ignore its mother and try to suck from the tree; the mare will eventually desert it ...

A mare's behaviour on her foal's first day was therefore directed to keeping her foal near her and away from all other ponies, until it was able to recognize her. Foals usually seemed able to recognize their mothers by their second day by smell, and

their mothers then approached them infrequently compared with on their first day.

Young Foals

(Young foals) lay for 70 to 80% of their total resting time up to the age of two months ... . Although in cold winds and rain, foals tended to stand rather than lie down when resting, many other factors determined whether they stood or lay. They usually stood when they were on rough or hummocky ground and when the vegetation was long or dense as in the valleys; they also usually stood when their mothers were grazing on the heaths where they moved

Student Observes Pony Behaviour...

on several paces between each mouthful due to the sparse distribution of *molinia* and gorse.

When young foals were lying down, their mothers—if not resting by them—grazed repeatedly away from them and back towards them, or in circles around them. The distance a mare moved from her foal on its first day was very small, rarely more than five yards, but the distance increased with (the foal's) age. ... When a young foal was standing resting, it usually stood immediately behind its mother, and almost each time she moved, it approached her ... .

Mutual Grooming

(Mutual Grooming) is an important part of social contact between ponies. It occurred when two animals stood facing each other, and nibbled at the neck, mane, fore legs and withers of their partners, mostly parts of the body that would not be reached easily during (self) grooming. ... Occasionally a third animal joined in, but such occurrences were rare and brief. If a foal or other young pony approached its mother when she was already mutually grooming, it sometimes started to nibble and groom her at the same time.

Mother Licking Head

Mares began to lick their foals a few minutes after their birth and then licked almost continuously for up to half an hour. After this, licking was less frequent, but occurred intermittently and for short periods throughout the foal's first day. It was concentrated around the head and tail region of the foal, especially when the foal was sucking. ... After a mare had licked her foal, she discriminated between it and other foals; the latter were threatened whenever they approached the mare whereas she touched her own foal, nuzzled it, and allowed it to suck.

MOTHER LICKING FOAL

STANDING RESTING

MUTAL GROOMING

Some Examples of Pony Behaviour
As Observed by Stephanie Tyler

"Adult ponies were ... dominant over the cattle and tended to obtain the best sites in the shade."

"Acorns had a great effect on the movement of some of the ponies, completely disrupting their normal daily pattern. ... It is known that (some ponies) can become 'addicted' to acorns and that the ingestion of large numbers of prematurely fallen green acorns can cause poisoning and death."

"One foal, born in woodland, showed a marked attraction to a particular tree on its first day. It remained close by the tree, even when its mother moved up to five yards away, and it nibbled the tree, walked round it, and to and from it."

"Jackdaws and magpies were observed perching on the ponies and actually plucking hair in the spring."

Relations with Other Creatures

Donkeys. Very few donkeys are depastured on the Forest but a pair was present for a year on one study area. The two donkeys moved about together and usually grazed separately from any pony groups. Only one interaction was seen between donkeys and ponies; a ten month pony filly kicked out at the two donkeys when they were grooming near her.

Cattle. Before 1914 few cows were turned out on the Forest but since the last war, their numbers have increased to over four thousand, well-exceeding the pony population. There is direct competition for food between the cattle and the ponies but most of the cattle, both dairy cows and beef animals, are generally taken onto the small-holdings and farms for the winter and supplied with food.

Ponies and cattle used the same grazing areas in summer daytime and shaded together under the same trees or on the same hill. Adult ponies were, however, dominant over the cattle and tended to obtain the best sites in the shades. Foals were often threatened and chased by cows but some play was observed between foals and calves.

Deer. Of the four species of deer present in the Forest, the fallow deer, *Damadama*, was the only species that occurred in large numbers on the two study areas. Competition for food with the ponies probably did occur as especially in the early mornings and evenings of winter and spring, deer, ponies and cattle could often be seen grazing together. The deer, however, had access to the Forestry Commission enclosures, which ponies and cattle had not. One interaction was observed between a pony and a fallow deer when a yearling filly threatened a doe that moved too close to her. ...

Birds. Many birds, particularly starlings and corvids, collected hair from the ponies for nest material when the ponies were

Student Observes
Pony Behaviour...

Continued from previous page

Colt-Biting

Mutual grooming bouts between colts and fillies were common, but the colts usually became rough. They gripped their partners' necks, bit at their heads, fore and hind legs, reared up and even mounted them. The fillies then tried to leave, first often laying back their ears and biting or kicking out at the colts.

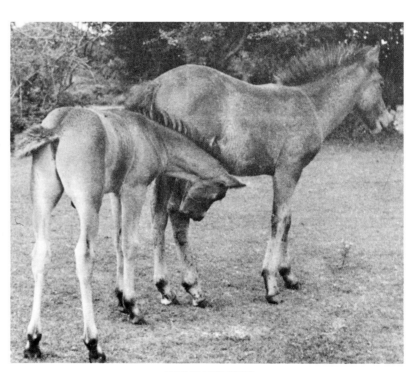

COLT BITING

Horses and Donkeys

(In his book of equestrian rambles, *Bridle Paths* (William Heinemann, 1936), A.F. Tschifely relates how his mare displayed a fierce dislike of donkeys.)

Coming out into an open space I saw a number of forest ponies grazing among high bracken. Disturbed in their peace they looked up, while a stag, followed by timid does, with graceful speed sought refuge in the forest.

Suddenly Violet began to snort with fear; and presently I noticed three donkeys behind a bush near us.

I then remembered having been told that the mare was afraid of nothing and that she never shied, except on seeing—a donkey.

She made such a fuss that I let her have her head, whereupon she galloped away as if we had been face to face with some dangerous beast of prey.

After a while she stopped and —from a safe distance—looked back at the three donkeys who watched us with typical, sleepy asinine interest.

Then, for some time, I amused myself by letting Violet do as she liked, allowing her to trot up and down, prop, snort and fuss until she grew tired of showing off.

As I continued my journey of exploration, I wondered why donkeys were Violet's pet aversion and only fear, but after thinking it over, I came to the conclusion that this must be a lady's secret I would never solve.

The Herbal Mare

(According to Juliette de Bairacli-Levy, as recounted in *Wanderers in the New Forest* (Faber, 1958), the New Forest pony is an instinctive herbalist.)

The forest pony—as are most native ponies—is an instinctive herbalist, and also knows the virtues of the various springs of water: I have been much impressed by the herbal knowledge that they reveal, especially the mares, and they know the medicinal plants and their seasons for the taking of them. The mares show much desire for the tiny flowering shoots of the white and blue milkwort which is abundant in the forest areas where artificial petrol-burning of the moorland has not been carried out. This small plant increases milk production.

They will take all the watercress within reach; and they have a passion for the forest wild onion which grows in abundance during the spring months and which, some old foresters say, was spread over the forest and its environs, especially the Fordingbridge area, by the Gypsies, who greatly value it as a tonic and medicine for their ponies and their dogs and also as blood tonic for themselves.

Burley Pony Show Remembered

(For three quarters of a century the Burley Pony Show was a prime attraction of the New Forest, and visitors converged on the village from near and far.

Dionis Macnair, a New Forest Verderer who was associated with the show during its latter years, traces the history of the event and recalls the colour and excitement it brought to participants and spectators alike.)

The Burley and District New Forest Pony Breeding and Cattle Society's first show was held in Manor Park on August Bank

Student Observes Pony Behaviour...

Continued from previous page moulting in the spring. Jackdaws and magpies were observed perching on the ponies and actually plucking hair in the spring; at other times of the year they pecked around the mane and were probably feeding on ticks and lice. Little attention was paid by ponies towards these birds although very young foals showed some interest in their movements and mares sometimes seemed irritated by magpies on their backs. At first they kept turning their heads and biting at the birds but each time the magpies moved back out of reach until eventually the mares ignored them.

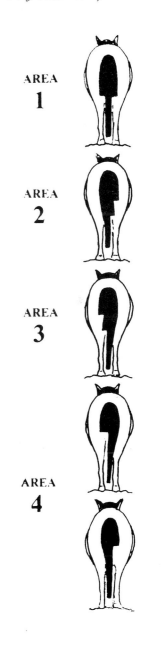

TAIL MARKS

The New Forest is divided into four districts and at present one Agister supervises the depastured animals in each district. The tail of each animal is cut out as shown in the sketches below, to indicate that its owner resides in, or adjacent to the district indicated. (From *The New Forest Pony Stud Book*.)

AREA 1

AREA 2

AREA 3

AREA 4

Tate Gallery, London

Burley Pony Show Remembered...

Continued from previous page
Holiday, 1906.

The Pony Show was Burley's "Great Day." It began with the arrival of Commoners with their mares and youngstock tied behind their carts, or round the necks of riding ponies. Foals were never haltered and it was not unknown for a foal, wanted for judging, to be found in the beer tent.

Cattle and pigs that had run on the Forest were also judged, but were very unmanageable. There were donkey races, too, but these came to an end after someone cheated by actually training a donkey to run. There were classes for ponies in Forest trucks—the small farm waggons that were driven standing up, as in a milk float. Bets were placed on those who could remain upright longest after spending an hour in the beer tent.

Ladies in enormous hats competed in the harness class. There were also classes for "Children's Hunters" and for "ponies suitable to carry a man to his work." The potato race was a popular feature, usually followed by the climax: races for Forest ponies around the

"COLT HUNTING IN THE NEW FOREST"
Lucy Kemp-Welch was only 27 when she completed the above painting of colt hunting in the Forest. She had wanted to undertake it two years earlier, but her tutor, Professor Herkomer, persuaded her to wait until she had passed into the "life class" at art school. Recalling the event in the year of her death, she said: "It was sound advice." Kemp (1869–1958) was born in Bournemouth. Her sister was Edith Kemp-Welch, the landscape and portrait painter. Lucy started exhibiting at the Royal Academy in 1895. She learned to sketch ponies at a Bournemouth veterinary hospital and in the New Forest itself. "Colt hunting" was shown at the Royal Academy in 1897 after which it was acquired for the Chantry Collection. It has appeared in many books and journals as a striking example of equestrian art.

perimeter of the park and ending in front of the Manor.

The flower show had a large marquee and was well attended. The Burley Band, pride of the village, added to the festivities which ended with dancing in the

main ring.

Alas, times changed and the show went into gradual decline. In 1981 it was moved to the permanent show-ground site at New Park, Brockenhurst, where it has remained since.

When Forest Deer Fight to the Death

(Rival bucks can fight one another viciously during the rutting season, with the sound of the clashing antlers echoing through the Forest. Gerald Lascelles, in *Thirty-Five Years in the New Forest*, describes a particularly furious battle that took place in 1905.)

Like other deer, the New Forest bucks, fight desperately in the rutting season—not unfrequently even to the death. A curious case occurred about 1905, when two bucks were found still warm, but both dead, in the bottom of a drain, with their horns so firmly locked together, that it was almost impossible to disengage them. The

Growing up amongst the Deer of the Forest

21 Fallow Deer
(16 April 1976, aged 13)

Today I went to Mill Lawn at 4.45 a.m. In Mrs. X's field a herd of 21 fallow deer were grazing. It was a dull, full moon. I heard the common snipes and the tawny owls calling and hooting. ... I (then) went to the glade (in the inclosure) and saw a fine roe buck with antlers in velvet. He ran a little way and stopped and stared, then gave a loud and throating alarm call, and ran away, continuing to 'boah' loudly for a long time.

"Rustoff" Arrives
(31 July 1977)

At 6.15 a.m. at the cross-paths in the inclosure I saw a tiny, fluffy roe buck whom I didn't instantly recognize as the buck I now call 'Rustoff' (the one with the black antlers). But I soon noticed his unobservant ways as he fed in the ditch beside the path. Soon, though, he saw me. ... If it had been any other roe, he would have disappeared years ago, but being Rustoff, he pretended not to mind, and put his head down to eat. Suddenly, up shot his head. No, Rustoff, I hadn't moved! His head returned to the bracken, then up it

In almost every part of the New Forest children have the opportunity to observe wild animals first-hand. Even if deer, foxes and badgers do not actually "invade" the family garden, they are never far away.

Susan Picking, who grew up in Burley, started keeping notes and making sketches and photographs of deer when she was 13 (1976). During the following ten years her observations continued, permitting her to confirm many patterns of deer behaviour. Susan obtained an honours degree in biology from the University College of North Wales and for several years was co-leader of Arctic wilderness explorations, adventures that allowed her to study the elk and reindeer of northern Scandinavia. She has owned a New Forest pony for 12 years, has won several awards for wildlife photography, and enjoys writing fiction for children. She also does oil and watercolour painting, and makes animal models in clay. She is competent with .22 and .303 rifles at indoor and outdoor ranges.

shot again. He repeated the performance endlessly, determined to catch me out. ... But as I was still as stone, he gave it up and began to eat ivy from a conifer. He appeared to be waiting for someone as if it were a meeting place. I sensed this, but was silly enough not to look carefully around for his friend, whoever it might be. When he rounded the bend in the path, I rose to follow him. Then I saw her—his doe, of course. She saw me, but I don't think she recognized me. She took a step or two towards Rustoff, and then turned

and cantered away slowly along the path, followed by the little black-antlered fellow.

An Enormous Red Deer
25 August 1977)

At 6.25 a.m. I was amazed to see an eNORmous red deer standing stoutly on the path ahead, with its head in a yew tree. I quite expected it to be a great stag with massive antlers, but when it turned its head I saw it was a hind—probably the same one that I had seen earlier. I put a tree

When Deer Fight

Continued from previous page
heads of both had to be cut off and removed together, before the bodies could be got out of the drain.

It would appear as if one buck had turned to fly, and his pursuer had locked the horns together by an attack from behind, falling on to the defeated deer into the drain, and turning right over, locked as he was by his horns, had broken his neck. His super-incumbent weight probably suffocated the under-most deer quickly. But had this not happened, they must surely have perished miserably from starvation. The heads, locked together as they were found, now hang in the Verderers' Hall at the King's House.

SUSAN, AS A TEENAGER, WITH HER PONY "PIP"

RECORD BOOK

In this notebook Susan kept a diary of her observations.

Growing up...

Continued from previous page

between herself and me, and proceeded to advance, only to find that she had disappeared in the way that they do. Therefore, as I approached the spot, I was incautious. I examined where she had been feeding and took another step forward. Suddenly I saw her! There, not a stone's throw away from me—the other side of the flooded river—she stood busily eating a bush with her behind towards me. I sank down, astonished, for she was so huge and near. She must have swum across the river. The camera was already loaded. I raised it. She turned, saw me, took a step, and then "click", The picture was taken at less than 60 feet. She bounded away startled.

Buck Wallowing
(1 October 1977)

At 6.25 a.m. as I was walking beside the inclosure through the woods toward the open area, I saw a fallow doe just outside the woods. As I approached, another doe shot past me, uttering "Boh!" loudly, and the first doe joined her.

I then noticed a small animal nearer to me than the does, who were now feeding round some

A TRIO OF FALLOW DOES
This sketch was drawn from real life observation.

gorse bushes. I then saw that it wasn't a small animal, but only part of an animal! It was a fallow buck wallowing. He repeatedly licked his back and scraped his (moderate) antlers in the mud. He did this for a long time before emerging and scraping his head on a forefoot, and scraping his back with impatient movements. I must describe this wallow, which I examined later on. It is about six to ten feet across—a rough circle—and three feet deep in the middle, coming up to only a foot or so at the sides. The floor was of very muddy peat, scored with slots, scrape marks, and generally well churned up.

The buck looked at the six does, and then advanced slowly in my direction. He saw me and I took a photograph. He was alerted, but kept putting his head down to eat before bouncing off.

FROM NEW FOREST TO WORLD EXPLORER
Susan Picking has continued her wildlife studies, begun at the age of 13 in the Forest, in other parts of the world. The reindeer and elk of Scandinavia fell under her gaze when she was co-leader of Artic wilderness expeditions.

Growing up...

Continued from previous page

5½ Inches of Snow
(17 February 1978)

I was delighted to be able to deer-watch this morning in 5½ inches (14 cm) of crisp snow. Although snowy, the air wasn't as cold as I expected. I hung the thermometer in a tree for five minutes and it changed from 50 degrees to 25 degrees. ... At 7.20 a.m. I saw a fallow deer in the woods. I quickly identified it as a fallow deer, a 1977 fawn, making her way in the woodland border towards the inclosure. She was going uphill and was startled when another doe, an older one, joined her. I squatted down beside a tree and was delighted when the doe-fawn came my way. She walked straight towards me with her head half up, but didn't see me. She apparently didn't even hear the mechanical click of the camera, and after a short time, wandered behind some thick scrub.

A Clear Morning
21 April 1980

It was a clear morning and the birds began to sing at 5 a.m. At 5.30 I saw about five fallow deer on the end of the lawn. At 5.50 I saw three fallow does by the inclosure. Having surveyed me from a distance, they entered the inclosure at 6.07. The May is in flower and the silver birch leaves are coming out. The beech is about to leaf and the chestnut is already out. There was a red morning sky. We have had over two weeks of hot, cloudless weather.

Discovering A Rutting Scrape

(One of the most recent guides to the Forest is *Discovering the New Forest* by Patricia Sibley and Robin Fletcher (Robert Hale, 1986). With nine maps and 54 photographs, the authors take the reader into every corner of the Forest while exploring wildlife, people and buildings. The passage below, reproduced by their permission, describes how they sud-

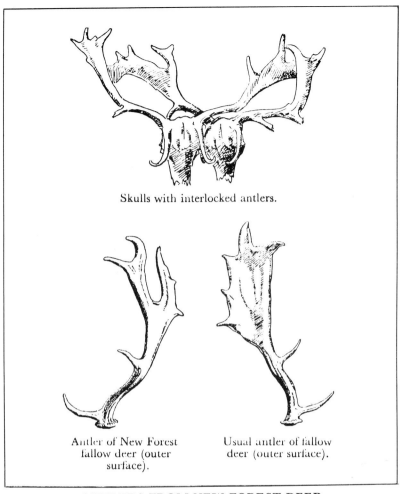

Skulls with interlocked antlers.

Antler of New Forest fallow deer (outer surface).

Usual antler of fallow deer (outer surface).

ANTLERS FROM NEW FOREST DEER
This sketch is taken from *The White Buck*, a children's classic written by Allen W. Seaby.

denly came upon a "rutting scrape" of the fallow deer.)

On a still, misty day the wood was truly amber, bracken fading to pale browns, oak and beech leaves, yellow and tawny, dropping slowly through the damp air, patterning the forest floor with colour – except in one place where it was black – we had found a rutting scrape.

... thousands of visitors to the forest leave again without sight of a single deer. The sanctuary at Bolderwood is your best chance, otherwise remember they move out of cover at twilight. Like birds, fallow do not worry much about a stationary car and will trot unconcernedly past, so it makes a good hide. Most of the year they are very quiet animals, a doe gently whickering to its fawn perhaps; the most startling sound made by a doe is its bark, so deep and sudden it resembles a shot going off. This means she is anxious, or suspicious—an eerie sound at dusk.

Only once a year does the buck become vocal: this is in October when the mating season begins; then he starts 'groaning', a strange guttral moaning sound almost like belching which we had heard night after night in the woods during the last few weeks—on a still night it will carry half a mile or more. At this time the buck returns to his rutting place, or stand, of the previous year. This one in Amberwood is some sixty feet across under a grove of Scots pine, the ground churned into a morass of black, trampled mud, the trunks flayed where bucks had threshed with their antlers, marking out their rutting territory and leaving the scent from glands below the eye.

The World's Only Half-Deer, Half-Horse?

REMARKABLE HYBRID, FROM THE NEW FOREST. DRAWN FROM LIFE, BY GEORGE LANDSEER.

This remarkable filly (seven months old) was found a short time since in the New Forest and is evidently of a mixed breed between the horse & the deer. Her mother a pony mare, was observed to associate with some red deer stags in the New Forest for some months and at last this foal was seen by her side. The nose shows a proximity both to the stag & horse, her forehead is round like that of the deer; legs slender & distinctly double, colour brown, lighter under the belly, & tail like a deer.

This extraordinary animal is the property of T.G. Attwater Esq. of Attwater at the village of Bodenham 5 miles from Salisbury. Dr. Fowler of that city has inspected the Hybrid & is quite satisfied of the correctness of the preceding statement & Col. Buckley (a keeper of the New Forest) is of a similar opinion. Dec. 9th 1848

(In 1848 a firm of print-makers in Salisbury issued the above sketch showing a hybrid deer-horse found in the New Forest.

Research has failed to turn up mention of other such hybrids either before or after the 1848 specimen became known. As deer and horses have long lived side by side in the New Forest, it would be interesting to know what conditions made possible the conception of the hybrid and why more such specimens have not been reported.

The drawing was made by George Landseer, and the exact text beneath the print (slightly blurred in the reproduction above) is as follows:)

This remarkable filly (seven months old) was found a short time since the New Forest and is evidently of a mixed breed between the horse & the deer. Her mother (a pony mare) was observed to associate with some red deer stags in the New Forest for some months, and at last this foal was seen by her side. The nose shows a proximity both to the stag & horse, her forehead is round like that of the deer; legs slender & distinctly double; colour brown, lighter under the belly, & tail like a deer.

This extraordinary animal is the property of T. G. Attwater Esq. of Attwater at the village of Bodenham, 5 miles from Salisbury. Dr. Fowler of that city has inspected the Hybrid & is quite satisfied at the correctness of the proceeding statement & Col. Buckley (a Keeper of the New Forest) is of the similar opinion.

A Victorian Lament for A Poacher's Victim

Deer poaching always has existed in the New Forest and it continues there today. Apart from constituting a crime, the practice often leaves a wounded animal to die a slow, painful death.

Philip Klitz, who was born at Lymington and continued the great musical traditions of his family, so loved the New Forest that all his life he collected true stories, legends and poems about it. Five years before his death at the age of 49, his *Sketches of Life, Character and Scenery in The New Forest* was published.

This work includes "The Wounded Stag" a poem that tells of the death of a handsome stag in Rhinefield Walk at the hands of a ruthless poacher. Klitz does not say who wrote the poem, but given his own musical talents, he may well have been its composer.

THE WOUNDED STAG.

It was a lonely winter's eve;
    The moon's pale beaming light
Shone brightly forth, so soft, so clear,
So calmly through the atmosphere,
That all on earth, both far and near,
    Look'd pure and silv'ry bright!

The twinkling stars came peeping out,
    And willing seem'd to try
Who'd shine the brightest, fairest, best,
The while all earth lay hush'd in rest,
Yet, ever and anon, to test
    A cloud came sailing by.

The bracing coolness of the air,
    So crisp, so pearly grey,
Play'd o'er the surface of the brook,
Which, ever as a leap it took,
Would gently stop, as if to look
    At what had check'd its way.

The forest trees of leaves bereft,
    Stood forth in outline bold,
Their branches tipp'd, as oft of yore,
In glitt'ring rims of frosted hoar;
The furze in folds was mantled o'er
    By snow so chill and cold.

That gentle slope which summer time
    Had deck'd with bright green fern,
Was cover'd o'er by bitter frost,
And all its lovely freshness lost,
As to and fro, in storms 'twas tost,
    By winter, cold and stern.

'Twas such a night in Rhinefield Walk;
    The keeper was at rest,
When all at once he thought he heard
A sound—it was not voice, or word—
Perchance the plaint of some lone bird,
    By lawless fowler prest.

But see! who lurks in yonder glen,
    And noiseless steals along?
I fear thou'rt bent on aught but good;
Too well they calling's understood;
Nay, leave the stag to range the wood,
    He will not want it long!

Thou wilt not, surely, kill and steal,
    And break the laws of God;
Nay, leave him to the cold, cold bed,
Whereon he rests his branching head;
O, do not send him with the dead,
    By artifice and fraud.

He'll beat thee, man, if, face to face,
    Unarm'd, thou wilt appear;
Let nature's weapons prove the truth—
Thou could'st not, though thou'rt yet a youth,
Withstand the onslaught, fierce, uncouth,
    Of a brave forest deer.

Shame, shame! on man, who thus betrays
    Both cruelty and fear;
Who skulks behind a hedge to kill,
By dint of art or cunning skill,
A creature form'd by God's own will,
    A coward is, that's clear.

I glory in the lawful sport,
    That's given to man in chase;
But in that sport give space and breadth—
A single chance of life or death—
And not at once deprive of breath,
    But win by strength or pace.

Why e'en the bird which high on wing
    Hangs floating in the air,
The sportsman true would scorn to take,
Whether in field, by bush, or brake,
On marsh, or mount, or on the lake,
    Unless the game is fair.

Hark! hark! now, through the brittle air
    The echo of that gun,
Around it flies—now back again,
But not a sound will e'er remain
To drown the moan of dying pain
    So treacherously won.

Continued on next page

A Victorian Lament for A Poacher's Victim

Continued from previous page

But all thy skill, thou poaching elf,
    Will bring no gain to thee;
For see! what's this comes limping near,
Moaning loud with pain and fear?
By heav'n! 'tis the wounded deer—
    Now from the foe he's free!

And whither would'st thou wend thy way,
    Thou injured harmless thing?
Ah! to the keeper's lodge—I see,
For he has e'er been kind to thee:
When roaming in the forest free,
    Thy fodder he would bring.

Last night he fed thee at the gate
    That leads down to the farm,
The while thou lick'dst his hand with glee,
And he in turn caressing thee:
He little though this sight to see!
    His favorite come to harm.

And thou would'st call him from his rest,
    By butting at the door;
He hears thee now,—quick from his bed
He lifts his weary, dreaming head;
But now all sleep has from him fled,
    And he has grief in store.

Here, wife and Mary! Edward, George!
    Come, see the wounded deer;
Some poaching rogue has shot poor Jack,
And see, he's broke the poor thing's back!—
Ned, go and find a stout warm sack,
    And quickly bring it here.

Fetch cloths, we'll staunch the bleeding wound,
    There's life left in him still!
Ah! good kind keeper, 'tis in vain,
For nought but death can ease the pain,
A few short minutes yet remain,
    And he's beyond thy skill!

The children all with tearful eye,
    The keeper and his wife,
Crowd round the dying stag, whose eye
Expressive rests on those close by,
Who vainly hope, yet kindly try
    To save the poor thing's life.

And see, now from his dying face
    The trickling tear-drops fall;
The poor dumb creature cannot tell,
Who wounded him, or why he fell,
But seems to speak a last farewell,
    To keeper, wife, and all.

Look! keeper, look! once more to raise
    His drooping head he tried;
One ling'ring look, that seem'd to say
"Kind master, can't you let me stay?
O, why should I be sent away?"
    And then the poor stag died.

How New Forest Deer Survived the Removal Act of 1851

(The 1851 Deer Removal Act sought to get rid of all deer in the New Forest on the grounds that they caused unacceptable damage to private property. Also, young trees in the Forest were then, as now, vulnerable to deer. As Gerald Lascelles recounts in *Thirty-Five Years in the New Forest*, even the severest of measures did not succeed in exterminating the animals.)
At the period of the Deer Removal Act, when the deer became a burning question, it was stated that the number had been cut down, from about 3000 to 4000 in recent years, to the number of 2000. Even then, there was considerable anxiety in various

quarters to get rid of them—and this was arranged to be done.

According to the Act, the deer were to be wholly removed from the Forest within two years. No effort was spared to bring this about. At first the great bulk of them were simply shot down. But as they became scarcer and wilder, all sorts of means had to be adopted. Nets were used, and the deer were driven into them, set at the well-known tracks and paths through the woods; hounds were freely employed to drive the deer into the nets and up to guns posted in likely places. Finally, hunting pure and simple had to be resorted to, and a deer when found was run down by the bloodhounds each keeper used to assist him in his duties. At the end of the two years, the Act had been carried out as far as was possible in a wild densely wooded country like the New Forest.

But it was impossible to carry

out the provisions of the Act down to the very last deer, or to know for certain whether or not a few of the fugitives were left in various parts of the thick coverts up and down the Forest. Probably a few did survive. But it was overlooked by those who drafted the Act that in many parts of the Forest it is bounded by thick woods, the property of private landowners. The hotter the pursuit in the Forest grew, the more the deer sought refuge in these woods. In some they were killed just as they were in the Forest. But in others they met with more hospitable treatment, and as the Deer Removal Act grew to be more disliked, the deer that remained were viewed with more kindly eyes.

People forgot the damage they had done, and thought with regret of the palmy days of the Forest, with its herds of deer constituting one of its most attractive features.

The True Story of "Tiger," A Gentle Fox

Best known for his wildlife films of the New Forest and his coloured photographs and post-cards of Forest scenes and animals, Eric Ashby and his wife, Eileen, have also managed to nurture several fox cubs that were orphaned for one reason or another.

In the copyrighted account below, Eric tells the story of Tiger who arrived at the family cottage when only five days old. He relates how the cub was raised and grew up with other rescued foxes only to meet an untimely end.

The voice on the phone was asking: "What does a baby fox cub look like?"

It seemed the tiny mite was found in a disused pig-sty used as a store for hay and straw, and Rosalind, thinking it was a kitten, had left it for 24 hours expecting the mother would return and take it away. But sadly the newly born cub was cold, still and apparently dead, with pieces of straw in its tiny mouth which it had been trying to eat. After being picked up in warm hands—much to her delight—it gave a little squeak, and so began the chore of encouraging it to feed at two-hourly intervals.

I was shown the helpless but now active little cub when about five days old, a dark brown little mite squirming along with legs splayed out, squeaking as it moved like a clockwork toy.

At three months old, when the owners of Tiger (as he was named) went away for a holiday, we were delighted to look after him for a few days in our living room. He was surprisingly clean, using newspaper in the corners of the room, welcoming us in the mornings with tail wagging, excited cries followed by puddles of delight. We found him more intelligent than a puppy of the same age and a great time consumer during the day.

On the owner's return from their holiday, they asked if we could find a home for Tiger as they considered it was not fair to keep him, as both Rosalind and her husband were at work during the day, often followed by meetings in the evenings. But we could find no one willing to take on the responsibility of keeping a wild animal with all the work involved and no likelihood of taking a holiday. So we decided to build a large outside grass pen where he could be kept safe until the hunting season ended.

Risks to Bottle-Fed Foxes

Normally it is not possible or fair to set free bottle-fed foxes as they become too attached to human company and would soon be killed, but Tiger had a particularly nervous disposition and feared strangers, so we thought he would have as good a chance as any wild fox having been kept safe during the most vulnerable period. It is said that the average life of a wild-reared fox cub is only 18 months, because of the problem of finding sufficient food and an empty territory, not to mention the many human hands against him.

He had been named Tiger, we were told, because he growled when any attempt was made to take a bone from him.

It took at least a month to get all the materials together and to build the outside pen—meanwhile indoors plaster was being torn from the walls and lino scratched from the floor by growing claws. Actually, a fox is not suitable as an indoor pet!

Gentle and Intelligent

We were learning a lot from this experience—the gentle and intelligent nature showed in play when he would mouth our hands and never bite, though one had to be careful to avoid his needle-sharp teeth which would draw blood on soft human hands. We found the stories of dog foxes smelling strongly quite unfounded, his fur was more pleasant than a domestic dog's, though of course adult dog foxes do have strong scent glands which they use to mark their territory.

We did not want Tiger to be imprinted on humans but to know his own kind, so in July we gave him two cub companions obtained from the R.S.P.C.A. for him to play and live with.

Soon after the three cubs were safely installed, we had a letter from a young Isle of Wight couple who wanted a home for an 18-month old vixen named Sheba. She was rescued as a tiny cub after almost drowning in a stream and reared on a bottle. We found her to be a very tame fox, loving human company, but unfortunately was very scared of the three cubs—not having remembered her own kind. Fortunately Sheba was diurnal whereas the cubs were mainly nocturnal. However, she was continually being disturbed by the lively cubs even when trying to sleep. To solve the problem we added another run adjoining the first with a connecting pophole which

ERIC ASHBY WITH "SHEBA"

The True Story of Tiger...

Continued from previous page
was closed at night to allow the new vixen a good night's rest.

Sheba loved visitors and we invited as many people as possible to see and stroke her, and to enjoy the fox greeting of touching noses. The exception was when the Chairman of the New Forest Hunt Club backed away when she approached with tail wagging—perhaps his experience of foxes was limited to hunt digs when he could be bitten when pulling foxed out by their tails. Another hunt supporter—an elderly man—asked to see Sheba but he could not be persuaded to enter even the pen!

We were now keeping four rescued foxes, all having quite different characters. One thing they did have in common—an inbred fear of the hunt. The barking and other noises from the Alsatian kennels 150 yards away did not worry our tame foxes, nor did the dogs disturb the wild foxes and deer often seen around the kennels. Traffic sounds nearby seldom disturbed them either. But the sound of distant fox or buck hounds would cause them to run around the pen in fear, sometimes climbing the wire fence in their anxiety. No amount of comfort from us would pacify their fear. Such is the inbred alarm instilled by generations of foxhunters.

Delicate Rearing
Our foxes had comfortable poultry houses with covered boxes inside filled with dry grass, but often even during hard frost or dry snow they would prefer to be curled up on the frozen ground. During this time my wife, Eileen, could still stroke Tiger, now well grown with heavy winter coat, but would not allow me to touch him, probably because he was reared by a woman.

Sheba could never be set free; she was far too tame and would never survive in the New Forest where foxes are much persecuted. However, Tiger, and the two R.S.P.C.A. foxes had an ingrained fear of strangers and would therefore have a reasonable chance of survival in the wild after the difficult winter period.

Tiger seemed to be very fond of Sheba and wanted to play with her but at every advance Sheba would run away and hide in her house. She came into season for three days during February, 1986, as is usual with vixens and became very unsettled. For the first time she wanted to escape from the pen, but would still have nothing to do with Tiger. Then came a great surprise and delight to us, when a fortnight later in March she started playing with him and having a wonderful time.

After dark on the first of May we closed the pophole joining Sheba's run with her companions, and opened the door for them to go free, the intention being to leave the door open for some weeks—placing back-up food in the run each night. We caught glimpses of the other two for a day or so but Tiger completely disappeared and this made us very worried.

Tiger Comes Home
However, two days after his release we were most excited to see Tiger at the back door in the early morning. He was very shy but became more confident as the days went by, so much so that I, who could never stroke him in the pen, could now do so. Once he had made sure who it was, he would come running up wagging his tail, obviously very pleased to be talked to.

In due course he would follow me "helping" in the garden, furiously digging where I had been working, often right up against the garden tool! He enjoyed playing ball, jumping clean over the four-foot garden hedge after it or chasing it on the lawn like a dog. On his own he would sometimes walk unsteadily on top of the close cut hedge. He was a fun-loving animal with a great sense of humour. When I lay down on the lawn he would come up and gently rub his face on each side of my head or jump on my back to ruffle my hair.

One would have thought that an animal kept penned up and then given its freedom would not voluntarily be confined again but Tiger was keen to return to play with Sheba every evening. What games they played! Hectic chasing, first one then the other, rolling over and over in excitement, with quiet cries of delight. When Tiger had enough he would be waiting at the door to be let out, and away he would go.

Tiger and the Deer
In the evening Tiger loved to play with our cat who would be on the field waiting for him. He would also play with the fallow deer when they came near the cottage, bouncing up to a buck, whereupon the buck would chase Tiger and so it would go on until he was tired of the game. Another time, he would just be curiously sniffing the deer, as on one evening when an old buck was lying down chewing the cud, Tiger came up and lifted the buck's tail by the middle and dropped it as if he wondered where it had been. We had wonderful times watching and being with Tiger.

Although Tiger had not been inside our cottage for six months, one night at 11.30 p.m. I opened the back door to find him outside. He shyly came into the kitchen, then on into the living room and up the stairs to lie down on a mat on the landing, just as he used to do as a cub! I stepped over him and went to bed. At 4 .a.m. I found him still asleep and thought it best to let him out.

We often saw him on the road outside and marvelled at his traffic sense. The fast traffic did concern us but our big worry was the coming cub-hunting season which was to start in early August in the Forest.

Then one morning in September I saw him on the lawn at 7 a.m. but at 7.20 heard hounds in full cry less than a mile away. We never saw him again. Later I was told a dog fox had been killed by a car. He must have been very

"Us Won't Be Drov," Motto of Foresters and Their Hog

The "Coat of Arms" of the New Foresters is said to be:
"Three hogs *regardant*, with motto, "Us wunt be drov."
An old rhyme runs:
"Grintie, grintie, grunt; Us be arl tew blunt,
Naw use Hampshire hogs but to show the way to bogs."

Although the days have gone by when large herds of swine fed in the forest and 'swineherd' was a distinct vocation, when great trees stood in their thousands over many parts now bare —yet the pigs form quite a feature of Forest scenery; the wise old sows that roam do not get *bogged*; no creatures are more knowing or more humorous. But treat them with respect and be careful not to get between them and their progeny! (From *My Story*, by Sarah Robinson)

ILLUMINATED LETTER
My Story, **Sarah Robinson's autobiography, contains several charming accounts about New Forest pigs.**

In the Time of Wild Hogs

(A century and a half ago the New Forest was the home of large numbers of wild hogs. Strictly speaking, they were not wild boars, but descendants of domesticated hogs who—through years of living wild, had developed many of the traits of the Continental boars. The Forest wild hog was described by an anonymous writer in the 14 September issue of *The Penny Magazine,* reproduced here from the Sutton Collection held by the Court of Verderers.)

The domesticated breed left to run wild in the forest for so many generations as to have, in some degree at least, has reverted to the original type. As in the wild boar, the volume and strength of the New Forest hog are concentrated upon the anterior part of the animal, the shoulders being thick and the neck massive, as compared with those of what are esteemed the most valuable domesticated breeds. The wild hog of the New Forest has certainly not the same volume of body as the indolent tenant of a sty or a farmyard, but there is a vigour and fleetness to which the other has no pretensions; and one who forms an opinion upon this species of animal from what is seen in domestication, is greatly in error as to its real characters.

It is a heavy and lumbering animal; and instead of being able to gallop along, which is the natural swift motion of all the Pachydermata, to which order the horse and hog belong, simple walking with the alternate foot seems a painful operation. The appearance of the forest hog, when left to find his own food in the forest, is very different from this. In the hinder parts he is light and slender, while he is strengthened in front, has an elevated crest on the neck and shoulders, with a thick mane of bristles which he can erect at pleasure.

His colour, also, approaches to

The Story of Tiger...

Continued from previous page
distressed and so concerned that he did not notice the danger on the road.

Poor Tiger. We do miss him. And so does Sheba. For four days she went right off her food. She has changed to a nocturnal fox and is rarely seen in daylight, no longer welcoming visitors with tail wagging and excited cries.

During the Autumn and Winter Sheba would rarely come out of her home to welcome visitors. The happy light had gone from her eyes. The coming Spring saw a slight improvement when she sometimes enjoyed the warm sunshine.

We had been so fascinated keeping these beautiful creatures that the original grass pen made for Tiger had been increased to four runs to provided fresh and interesting playgrounds.

To try and get Sheba interested in life I was making a further much larger adjoining pen when we introduced Sheba to Vicky, a rescued vixen born in May, 1986. We had cured her of mange and rickets soon after we had her at a few weeks old, and now we were overjoyed seeing them play together, but Sheba still continued to be mainly nocturnal.

Arrival of Cubs
Later we were given two young cubs, Jack and Jill, who had been unearthed by a bulldozer. For a few days they lived in our box-room and then were taken out to one of the grass runs for a short while each day. While they were enjoying the fresh air I noticed Sheba running up and down the fence line carrying a piece of rabbit and calling quietly to the cubs. What a delightful picture it made when we let her join them. Sheba turning over on to her back with the cubs piling on top of her.

The old contented light had come back into Sheba's eyes.
(© Copyright by Eric Ashby, Badger Cottage, Linwood, Ringwood, Hants.)

"Slut," the Famous Sporting Pig Whose Fame Knew No Bounds

Toward the end of the 18th century two brothers, **Richard** and **Edward Toomer**—both New Forest Keepers, developed the hobby of breaking in pointers and setters. One day a sow chanced to pass by and after she responded well to a morsel of oatcake, the two brothers decided to train the animal as a sporting pig.

The story of "Slut's" training and subsequent achievements came to the attention of the nation when her exploits were documented in *Rural Sports*, a delightful compendium of sporting adventures that first appeared in 1801. The compiler of *Rural Sports* was William Barker Daniel (1753-?1833), a Cambridge graduate who took holy orders but appears never to have been beneficed. Instead he spent most of his life indulging in sports of many kinds. Little is known of Daniel himself, but his two-volume work was the first serious effort of an author to record contemporary British field sports in detail and with illustrations. So successful was *Rural Sports* that it was revised and reissued in three volumes in 1812, with a supplementary tome the following year.

Daniel also documents the shooting exploits of **Richard Toomer** who once engaged in a marksmanship contest with a **Mr. Mist.** The competition took place at **Moyle's Court** where Toomer was *blindfolded* and brought down first, one rook, then another, from a nearby tree.

The engraving of "Slut" from Daniel's work is reproduced here along with extracts about the pig. A painting of "Slut" adorned the wall of Brockenhurst's Olde Tea House from 1930 to 1952 where it was seen by thousands of visitors to the Forest. The tea house was owned by Mr. and Mrs. C.H. Toomer and when the business was sold, the painting passed out of the family.

(A supplementary account of "Slut's" accomplishments appeared in Sarah Robinson's *My Book*, from which a brief excerpt also appears here.)

Daniel's Account of "Slut" from Rural Sports

Of this most extraordinary animal will here be stated a short history, to the veracity of which there are hundreds of living witnesses:

Slut was bred in, and was of that sort which maintain themselves in the New Forest without regular feeding, except when they have young, and then but for a few weeks, and was given when about three months old, to be a breeding sow, by Mr. Thomas, to Mr. Richard Toomer, both at that time Keepers in the Forest.

From having no young, she was not fed, or taken very little notice of, until about 18 months old, when seldom observed near the lodge, but chanced to be seen one day when Mr. Edward Toomer was there. The brothers were concerned together in breaking pointers and setters, some of their own breeding, and others which were sent to be broke by different gentlemen. Of the latter, although they would stand and back, many were so indifferent that they would neither hunt nor express any satisfaction when birds were killed and put before them.

The slackness in these dogs first suggested the idea, that by the same method any other animal might be made to stand, and so as well as one of those huntless and inactive pointers. At this instant the sow passed by, and was remarked as being extremely handsome. Richard Toomer threw her a piece or two of oatmeal roll, for which she appeared grateful, and approached very near.

From that time they were determined to make a sporting pig of her. The first step was to give her a name, and that of "Slut," (given in consequence of soiling herself in a bog) she acknowledged in the course of the day, and never afterwards forgot.

A Fortnight's Training

Within a fortnight she would find

Wild Hogs...

Continued from previous page
that of the wild boar as still found in the continental forests, being generally dark brindled, and sometimes entirely black. His ears, too, are short, firm, and erect; and when he is excited, there is a fiery glance or glare in his eye. His spirit is also true to these indications; for a single dog, untrained to the sport, must be staunch indeed before he will venture to go in upon the wild hog of the New Forest.

These hogs are social animals, and generally seen in small herds, led on by one patriarchal male. In their peregrinations of the forest they do little mischief, and appear to fear as little; for if a dog makes his appearance, the natural instinct of the animals is aroused, and the most powerful of the herd advance to the front and stand in hostile attitude; and when they are thus excited by the presence of what they feel to be their natural enemy, they are not quite safe even for human beings. In their native glades, or in the depth of the beechen forests, they are animals of no inconsiderable beauty, their forms being light and elegant, and their bristles having almost a metallic lustre, which shows very brightly in the straggling sunbeams among the trees.

THE ORIGINAL ENGRAVING OF "SLUT" FROM DANIEL'S *Rural Sports*

"Slut," the Sporting Pig…

Continued from previous page

and point partridges or rabbits, and her training was much forwarded by the abundance of both which were near the lodge. She daily improved, and in a few weeks would retrieve birds that had run, as well as the best pointer. Nay, her nose was superior to any pointer they ever possessed, and no two men in England had better.

They hunted her principally on the moors and heaths. Slut has stood partridges, black-game, pheasants, snipes and rabbits in the same day, but was never known to point a hare. She was seldom taken by choice more than a mile or two from the lodge, but has frequently joined them when out with their pointers, and continued with them several hours.

She has sometimes stood a jack-snipe when all the pointers had passed by it. She would back the

dogs when they pointed, but the dogs refused to back her until spoke to, their dogs being all trained to make a general halt when the word was given whether any dog pointed or not, so that she has been frequently standing in the midst of a field of pointers.

Jealous Dogs

In consequence of the dogs not liking to hunt when she was with them (for they dropped their sterns and shewed symptoms of jealously), she did not very often accompany them, except for the novelty, or when she accidentally joined them in the Forest.

Her pace was mostly a trot, was seldom known to gallop, except when called to go out shooting. She would then come home off the Forest at full stretch (for she was never shut up, but to prevent her being out of sound of the call or

whistle, when a party of gentlemen had appointed to see her out the next day, and which call she obeyed as readily as a dog) and be as much elevated as a dog upon being shewn the gun.

She always expressed great pleasure when game, either dead or alive, was placed before her. She has frequently stood a single partridge at forty yards distance, her nose in a direct line to the bird.

Sarah Robinson's Postscript

(In her autobiography, *My Book*, Sarah Robinson repeats much of Daniel's account above, and adds the following contemporary information:) The Toomers lived several miles apart, at Rhinefield and at Broomy Lodge.

Slut frequently went by herself from one lodge to another in the hope of being taken out for shoot-

ANOTHER PAINTING OF "SLUT"
This representation of "Slut" hung on a wall of Brockenhurst's Olde Tea House for many years.

Sporting Pig...

Continued from previous page

ing. When five years old she was sold for ten guineas to Sir Henry Mildmay of Dogersfield Park (from whose grand-daughter I heard most of these particulars).

Slut pointed as well as ever for some years, and was then sold to Colonel Sikes. Her portrait and history appeared in Daniel's *Rural Sports*. Eventually she became fat and slothful, ending her career as bacon.

A Forest Legend

(The Sutton Collection of Gerald Lascelles' papers, scrapbooks and illustrations, includes a New Forest "legend" about a badger-baiter who came to see the error of his ways. The account originally appeared in an unidentified sporting journal.)

Once upon a time there was a great hunter put over the Forest, he had many hawks, hounds, and horses, and he hunted almost all the year round. But there came a very hot dry summer when he could not hunt, and he knew not what to do. Then it entered his mind he would have some badger-baiting, and he would draw the

earth near the village, where he had seen some badgers very busy all the spring, thinking no one would disturb them there. Accordingly he set on his dogs to draw the badgers. Now the badger is an inoffensive animal, but has long claws, a strong jaw, and powerful teeth; and these badgers would not bolt, but stuck to their earth, and so bit and fought that the hunter and his dogs could not prevail against them.

There was then a great uproar in the place by reason of the badger-baiting; the villagers liked the badgers, and the villagers were moreover disturbed in the quiet possession of their burial ground, which was near to the badgers' earth. So there was a great cry raised, and complaint was made to the Governor of the land of the hunter's doings. And the Governor was angry with the hunter because he was cruel to the badgers and vexed the villagers, not letting them and their wives and their little ones be buried in peace; and he bade the hunter to leave the badgers alone, and to disturb the villagers' burial ground no more.

When the hunter read the Governor's letter, he was sore troubled in his mind, and he knew

that in the Forest there was no man on his side. . . . . . . Little by little his eyes were opened to the wrong he had done; he sought the priest of the place, confessed, and gave alms to the poor. Moreover he made an offering of a curiously-wrought silver chalice to the chapel of the burial ground; and the villagers were no more disturbed in the possession of their burial ground.

Thence-forward the hunter had a kind word for all his neighbours, rich and poor alike. The trees that he planted grew, there was great plenty of game and venison, and the hunting in the Forest was better than ever. Amen.—Note.— We are informed that the badgers' earth mentioned in the above legend was only four miles from Brockenhurst.

Lawing of Dogs

(To prevent large dogs from injuring Forest deer, an unusual "test" was once performed. In his autobiography, *Thirty-Five Years in the New Forest*, Gerald Lascelles relates how the test was applied.)

One of the cruellest enactments was that concerning the "expedit-ation" or "lawing" of dogs. But even this was not quite so bad as it sounds. By the laws of the Forest, a dweller within its verges might keep a small dog "for the protec-tion of his house and chattels." But he might keep no hound or dog of such size that it might chase a deer or fawn with any prospect of success.

Such a dog, then by strict law had to be "expeditated," or to have his three front toes cut off with an axe, so as to debar him for ever from running fast enough to chase anything—let alone a deer.

And the test was whether he would pass through a certain large stirrup which hung in the Ver-derers' Hall at the King's House at Lyndhurst, where the Forest courts were held. If the dog would pass through the stirrup he was a little dog, only fit to guard house and chattels, and free of all risks; if he would not pass, he was liable to the penalty.

Peregrines atop Lyndhurst Church

(The New Forest has never been renowned for the sport of falconry, but during Gerald Lascelles' time as Deputy Surveyor (1880–1914) Lyndhurst residents had the rare opportunity of seeing some of the finest hawks ever to be trained for hunting. In the autobiographical extract below, Lascelles tells of his love of falconry and how he brought the Hawking Club's birds to Lyndhurst.)

Although the New Forest is a country so unsuitable for hawking that, except on a very few occasions I was unable to follow the sport there, yet my life at the King's House, and in fact wherever I have been, was so bound up with the training of hawks and with falconry, that it would be impossible to omit mention thereof in any sketch of my pursuits during my New Forest life.

I do not know when I first took to falconry. I cannot remember the time when I was not devoted to that pursuit. Although quite ignorant of its practice, I devoured all books I could get upon the subject, and in my Eton days endeavoured to put in force what I learned from reading them upon any unhappy kestrel I could get hold of.

In the autumn of 1871 the question of reviving the Hawking club was mooted, and then and there letters were written off proposing to start the club again. All the old members gave support, and I was requisitioned to act as Manager and Hon. Secretary, a position I have held ever since. It now (1914) covers forty-four years.

We began well in 1872, with a remarkably good lot of hawks, such a lot as the Dutchmen, who catch them on their "passage" or migration do not get hold of every year. When a few years after, I took up my appointment in the New Forest, I moved the hawks to the south with me.

Accordingly, the headquarters of the Old Hawking Club were transferred to Lyndhurst, and,

though the hawks were not flown there, the mews where they dwelt was an object of interest to a great many of my neighbours, and other travellers, from Mr. Gladstone to Kaiser Wilhelm, both of whom paid visits thereto, as did many other distinguished personage.

The most attractive sight afforded by the hawks to the people of Lyndhurst came during July and August, when the young peregrines, to the number of eight or nine, were flying "at hack," —that is to say, in perfect freedom, all round the village, using, as a rule, the pinnacles and tower of the church as their chief resting place. As they began to get stronger on the wing, their evolutions, as they chased one another

LASCELLES WITH A PEREGRINE IN THE GROUNDS OF QUEEN'S HOUSE
This photograph was used as the frontispiece of Lascelle's autobiography, *My Thirty-Five Years in the New Forest.*

HERONS AT VINNEY RIDGE, A BYGONE SIGHT
Nature lovers once marvelled at this well known herony which, in
1861, was home to 50 pairs. Of them John Wise wrote: "In the
morning and evening and, in fact, all through the day, one incessant
clamour was going on, and under the trees lay great eels which had
fallen from their nests."

Peregrines at Lyndhurst...

Continued from previous page
around the spire and all over the
village, were very beautiful to
watch.

I have seen six or seven chevy-
ing one another all over the village, and perhaps half a hundred
visitors and inhabitants standing
in the street watching the aerial
show. So long as these young
hawks come regularly to their
food, morning and evening, they
are just as secure as fowls let out to
feed. But ere long symptoms are
shown that they have, one at a
time, learned•to procure food for

themselves. Steps are then at once
taken to secure them, and the
happy period of liberty, which
rarely extends to more than three
weeks, is at an end.

During my life at Lyndhurst, a
great many first-class hawks—
hawks such as perhaps have had
no superiors—passed through the
mews at the King's House. Of the
young hawks that used the spire so
persistently in their youth were
many very superior game hawks,
coming most of them year by year
from certain eyries in the precipit-
ous cliffs of north-west Donegal.
Whether it was the intensely wild
and stormy surroundings of their
birthplace, or whether it was a
peculiar strain of dark-coloured

Ups and Downs of Forest Birds

(Over 70% of all species of
native British birds may be
found in the New Forest,
according to Rose de Crespigny
and Horace Hutchinson in their
book, *The New Forest*. In the
extract below, the authors discuss some of the rarer species.)

Observations on Forest Birds

Of three hundred and fifty four
species of birds commonly recognised as natives of Great Britain,
we believe we are right in saying
that as many as two hundred and
fifty are, or were, to be found in
the New Forest. The march of
civilisation does not always mean
a decrease in bird life. It means
rather that certain kinds, especially the wilder kinds, and above all
the birds of prey, diminish, but
their decrease is commonly
accompanied by a proportionate
increase in the number of those
smaller birds whom they were
wont to harry.

It is probable enough that
events have followed this course in
the Forest. We know, for instance
that the kite, the honey and
common buzzards, the marsh and
hen harriers were common birds
in the Forest a while ago. Now we
may say that they are virtually
extinct, and the small birds have
no doubt increased accordingly in
boldness and numbers.

Some years ago lapwings were
numerous on Brook Common.
Now they are rarely there, though
they still haunt the wilder plains.
It is a pity they should diminish,
so graceful as they are in their
motley plumage and tumbling
flight. Moreover, they are a good
friend to the farmer.

The hen harriers... have nearly
gone. A few years ago we used
peregrines that haunted those pre-
cipitous cliffs, I cannot tell; but
year by year hawks of the highest
class were sent us from those
eyries to mature round Lyndhurst
spire.

"Butterfly Baronet" Sights Rare Robin

(The late Viscount Bolingbroke (1896–1974) lived at South Gorley and Crow Hill for the last 28 years of his life. As a naturalist he contributed notes to county archaeology and natural history publications, and for several years wrote weekly columns for the *Ringwood and Fordingbridge Journal.*

He was an authority on butterflies and moths and his private collection is at the National Museum of Wales; other specimens are with the Natural History Museum in London.

Viscount Bolingbroke kept diaries of his explorations in the New Forest area and, among them, is the excerpt below recorded on Christmas Day, 1949, while passing through Burley Street.)**

While passing a cottage near the bus stop at the beginning of Burley Street, I noticed a remarkably coloured robin fly up from the grass verge.

After watching it at various angles, I got to within six yards of it for a full ten minutes. First on the ground, then on the top twig of a holly bush, and finally on the arm of the seat near the bus stop.

Its plumes appear to be thus: all the usual olive-brown of the upper parts is replaced by fawn right right up to the crown. Breast, the usual red, which made a striking contrast with the fawn.

The visible tail features: white, although I couldn't see if the white reached the base of the tail. Primaries and secondaries: white but the wings fawn like the rest.

It apparently is just as tame and unconcerned as any other robin. Because it was Christmas Day, I did not make any local enquiries concerning it, but will call at the cottage next to the bus stop at the first opportunity.

A very interesting bird and quite gripping to come upon.

New Forest Insect Life

(Rose de Crespigny and Horace Hutchinson, co-authors of the highly regarded 1895 work, *The New Forest*, point out in the passage below that no other area of Britain is so blessed with entomological treasure as the New Forest. Sadly, changes in forest management practices have reduced the number of species in recent years.)

THE New Forest is a district perhaps more precious to the entomologist than any other in Great Britain. The variety of insect life that finds its home and its food in the abounding and various flora is legion. Several species of *lepidoptera, coleoptera,* and *hymenoptera* —butterflies, beetles, and flies— are found in the Forest that have not been found elsewhere, and few of the varieties better known to English entomology are wanting.

It is singular enough that of all the British butterflies only one species has never been taken in the Forest—namely, the Camberwell Beauty. It is, of course, a very rare species; but it has been taken in the county of Hampshire, and it seems remarkable that having come so close it should not have wandered to the Forest. That it should have done so, of recent years, at least, and have escaped notice, is scarcely conceived.

Probably a satisfactory explana-

*Ups and Downs
of Forest Birds...*

Continued from previous page occasionally to see them hovering, but for the last year or two we hear nothing of them.

Owls abound. There are four varieties in the New Forest, and of these the tawny owl appears the commonest. Now and then, as you go through the woods, you may surprise from its roost a ghost-like white screech owl, which will flit uneasily before you in the blinding glare of the sun.

The hoot of an owl "carries" astonishingly far on a quiet night, and often you may hear three or four calling to one another, as if in conversation.

*Birds to be Seen
on Ober Water*

(From the Forestry Commission's leaflet, *Ober* Water Walk. Stonechat illustration by Hugh Insley.)

At the car park chaffinches are the most common, but robins and several species of tits can be seen. Woodpeckers are more often heard than seen. The yaffle of the green woodpecker is a characteristic forest sound. Dead trees are retained where possible by the Forestry Commission and provide nests for woodpeckers. Stonechats may be seen on the gorse bushes near to the car parks where they loudly scold anyone entering their territory.

tion for the absence of the Camberwell Beauty from the list of the Forest butterflies may be found in the virtual absence of the willow— on which the caterpillars of this species feed—from the list of the Forest trees.

Possibly the greatest "find" ever made in the Forest was the *Niobe* fritillary, taken in 1869 by a Mr. Gerrard, of Lyndhurst. There is considerable variety in different specimens of the commoner species of fritillary; and at a cursory glance Mr. Gerrard ascribed his prize to one of these commoner kinds. A more thorough inspection proved it without doubt to be the *Niobe,* which, up to that time, had not been taken in England.

New Forest Insect Life...

Continued from previous page

Common Fritillaries

Fritillaries of the commoner sort are among the most numerous of the butterfly kind in the Forest, and among the most beautiful—beautiful as they sail on level wings of sheeny bronze, and yet more beautiful when they settle and show, with erected wings, the pale greens and yellows of the underparts. Wood Arguses flit across the sunlit glades and patches, and out on the open heath are the Blues of every variety moving and settling, like living gems of turquoise. Hair-streaks and Skippers dart to and fro with their startling suddenness of flight. Peacocks, Painted Ladies, and Tortoise-shells are ubiquitous with their brave hues.

Linked to Honeysuckle

The White Admirals, so plentiful here, but so local, may be seen flitting down all the Forest glades with their own peculiar grace of movement, settling on the leaves of the oak trees, then off again for another flight. But though the mature insect appears to affect the oak of preference, the caterpillar feeds on the honeysuckle whose luxuriance may well account for the abundance of the butterfly in the Forest. Nowhere else in England is this butterfly to be found in anything like the same numbers, and nowhere else is the profusion of honeysuckle so remarkable.

Far less common here than the White Admiral, the Purple Emperor is yet more numerous in the New Forest than in any other locality. It is an oak-loving butterfly, loving especially to sail over the topmost branches of the oak trees, whence it can laugh down in imperial scorn on the green nets of the collectors below.

The Clouded Yellow

Certain seasons seem peculiarly favourable—though the reason is not, humanly speaking, obvious—to certain species of butterflies,

---

NEW FOREST FLY
This is the notorious insect whose motion is detested more than its bite by horses and other animals. The fly, *Hippobosca equina*, is found in other areas of Britain where it has no special name. It abounds, however, in the New Forest and for at least a century and a half has found its way into Forest literature.

The Notorious New Forest Fly

(Many writers have put pen to paper to describe the New Forest Fly, but few have succeeded so well in portraying this pest as William Gilpin and Sir Thomas Dick Lauder, who edited Gilpin's classic *Remarks on Forest Scenery*. Their accounts first appeared over 150 years ago, but the behaviour of this insect is as notorious today as when first described, despite ecological changes and the advent of chemical repellants.

The New Forest fly (*Hippobosca equina*) is thus described by Gilpin:)

(A) species of fly (that) should not be passed over ... is one of the great nuisances of the forest. In form it is not unlike the common black fly, and about its size, but its colour is different. It is a bright-coloured, brown insect, well cased, strong, and very retentive of life. It has a sidelong, crawling motion like a crab. The horse is its favourite quarry, though it attacks the cow and other animals.

You may sometimes see hundreds of these insects nestling under the tail and belly of such horses as are patient of them, as the New Forest horse commonly is by long sufferance. But to such horses as are unaccustomed to these teasing insects, they are a grievous torment, though it is doubtful whether they are blood suckers, or subsist only on such juices as exude through the skin. In this latter case they offend the horse only by tickling him, for which operation their legs are well adapted, appearing, in a microscope, armed with sharp talons, like pothooks.

(To Gilpin's account, Sir Thomas Dick Lauder adds:)

... No one who has not had experience of the misery (the fly) creates when crawling with its wriggling and sideling motion over the back, can form any idea of it. And then it clasps so close with its flat body and bowed legs, that one may undress and dress a dozen times before it can be detected; and when detected, it is very difficult to kill it, for it lies quite flat, and appears to have no substance, and when any attempt is made to crush it, the moment the pressure is removed, away it runs wriggling as if nothing had happened to it.

The New Forest horse, or any horse which has been for some

The Clouded Yellow is one that is singularly capricious in its appearances.

There is a common tradition that they appear in their legions every seventh year, but we have it on excellent authority that this is a fable. Many have been the theories advanced by way of explanation, some deeming that the eggs lie dormant, and hatch out only under the specially favourable conditions, others that the butterflies are blown over from the continent, like a cloud of locusts. None of the explanations are satisfactory, but the fact of the capricious appearances of the creatures remain.

Not the least of the New Forest's attributes as a natural woodland, interspersed with expanses of heathland, is it's habitat for every species of British reptiles, save one (the wall lizard).

One cannot spend a summer's day in the Forest without coming across several types of reptiles or amphibians. If there is not time for an extended walk, the naturalist can go to the Holidays Hill reptiliary and see *all* the Forest reptiles and amphibians.

To aid naturalists and interested visitors the Forestry Commission has issued an attractive leaflet, *Amphibians and Reptiles*. Written by Derek Thompson and profusely illustrated, it describes the species, their habits, and tells in which kind of Forest terrain they are likely to be found. The leaflet is available at the reptiliary; its text is given below.

Reptiles and Amphibians Abound in the Forest

Holidays Hill Reptiliary

Location

Holidays Hill is situated two miles west of Lyndhurst on the A35 Bournemouth road. From Lyndhurst turn right at the sign indicating Holidays Hill camp site, through the campsite and the reptiliary is by the keeper's cottage at the north end of the site.

All the reptiles and amphibians of the New Forest may be seen at the reptiliary.

The reptiliary has a dual function. One of helping you learn about and appreciate reptiles and amphibians, and a second function of breeding reptiles for release, particularly sand lizards and smooth snakes.

New Forest Fly...

Continued from previous page

years naturalized to the New Forest, appears to be little annoyed by it; but it is a very dangerous thing to go there with riding or machine-horses which have never experienced this plague, for we have seen such animals driven actually frantic, and rendered quite unmanageable by the assaults of myriads of these vexatious creatures.

Protection of reptiles and amphibians

All wild animals and plants in the new Forest are protected and it is a byelaw offence to collect, pick, remove or in any way harm the Forest flora and fauna.

In addition certain rare creatures and plants, including the sand lizard and smooth snake, are protected by the 'Conservation of Wild Creatures and Wild Plants Act 1975'. This Act makes it an offence to take, possess or offer for sale, these rare creatures.

Please observe and enjoy, but do not interfere with the New Forest wildlife.

Amphibians and reptiles

All the British reptiles occur in the New Forest with the exception of the introduced wall lizard. Of the amphibians all three species of newt, the common frog and toad as well as one exotic frog, the European tree frog can be found. The rare natterjack toad was recorded once or twice in the past, but is not now thought to exist as a Forest species.

The Forest has become increasingly important as a haven for reptiles and amphibians, largely because of heathland destruction elsewhere. Even in the Forest, overburning of heathland and selfish collecting of reptiles for sale as pets, had reduced sand lizards to the point of extinction.

Although reptiles are identified with heath and waste areas, within the group each species has its own habitat requirements. Thus smooth snake colonies are associated with sunny heathland valleys with damp ground in the bottom, and a good lizard and small mammal population. Sand lizards are restricted to dry sandy heathland with exposed patches of sand

HOLIDAYS HILL REPTILIARY

Reptiles and Amphibians in the Forest...

which the females require to deposit their eggs. Grass snakes tend to stay in the Forest bogs and wet valley bottoms, while adders, common lizards and slow worms are more generally distributed, and can even be found in gardens.

There are over fifty ponds in the Forest, including several deliberately constructed by the Forestry Commission for conservation purposes. These together with the numerous bogs and streams provide a large choice of habitat for the amphibians—frogs, toads and newts.

Adder

The adder or viper (*Vipera berus*) which is the only venomous snake occurring in Britain is the most common snake in the New Forest. It is easily recognised by a diamond shaped dark zig-zag pattern down its back. However, several colour varieties occur in the Forest including a red variety in which all the normally dark brown or black scales are various shades of earthy red; and there is also a completely black melanistic form. The latter type has often been responsible for bites because people have thought that as no zig-zag pattern shows on the back, that they could not be adders and have picked them up.

The adder gives birth to live young usually in August. The mating period is in April and early May some weeks after the adults have emerged from hibernation. It is commonly thought that the "dance of the adders" is the courtship display of male and female adders. In fact this display is usually between two males competing for the same female and one of the participants usually retreats leaving the female to the other. Males grow to about 46 cms in length and females to 60 cms.

Adders are well known for their habit of basking in the sun. However, on the hottest days they often retreat to water, and like the smooth snake they will drink water in hot weather. They feed on insects, slugs, frogs, toads, liz-

Continued from previous page
ards, small mammals, as well as the eggs and young of small birds. They usually strike and kill larger prey with their venom before eating it; but smaller creatures are devoured whole, without being struck first.

Adders will not bite unless they are molested, and we ask that you leave those interesting creatures well alone. It is a byelaw offence to interfere with or catch any wild creature in the Forest.

A person who is bitten by an adder should be taken to Poole or Southampton General Hospital as quickly as possible. Fatal bites are rare in this country, but the effects of the bite are often much more serious in young children than in adults, mainly because the potency of the venom is in inverse proportion to the size of the creature bitten.

Grass snake

The grass snake (*Natrix natrix*) which can be immediately identified by its cream or yellow collar is by far the largest British snake. One of the largest grass snake ever recorded in England was one of 172 cm (5 ft 8 ins) found in the New Forest in 1947, but normally they seldom exceed 120 cm (4 ft).

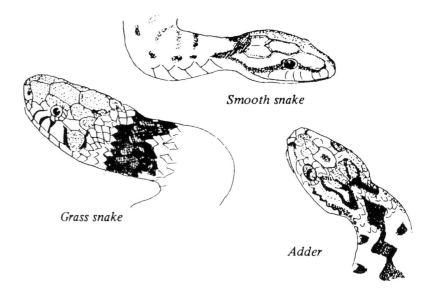

Smooth snake

Grass snake

Adder

Grass snakes inhabit mainly wet areas such as valley bottoms and bogs, and can often be seen lying in water on very hot days. They are olive green in colour with dark spots on the side and back, and white and black scales on the belly. As mentioned, they have a distinctive yellow collar.

After mating in May, the females lay their eggs in June and July. The snakes choose sites with warm moist decomposing vegetation in which to lay, the heat incubates the eggs, often compost or manure heaps are used. Sometimes several females will lay in a single compost heap if it is particularly suitable so that when the young hatch in August and September a "plague" of baby grass snakes all 7 to 8 cms long can occur.

Grass snakes are of course quite harmless; however, if they are picked up they hiss strongly and exude a foul smelling liquid from their anus, the smell of which is difficult to wash off.

Grass snakes feed on frogs, toads, newts, tadpoles and any small creature which they come across, even taking fish.

Like all reptiles and amphibians, grass snakes hibernate and are among the first to

Reptiles and Amphibians...

seek refugee in the Autumn not venturing out again until April the following year.

Smooth snake

The smooth snake (*Coronella austriaca*) which is rare and locally distributed, is so named because its scales are extremely smooth and polished, unlike the adder and grass snake which have strongly keeled (ridged) scales.

It was not discovered as a British species until 1859 when one caught near Bournemouth was sent to the British Museum for identification. One caught near Ringwood six years earlier was preserved by its collector but not reported until after publication of the Bournemouth record.

Its stronghold around Bournemouth has long since been built over, but the snake although rare is still found in small colonies in Hampshire, Dorset and Surrey.

The smooth snake is quite harmless but is unfortunately sometimes killed in ignorance by people mistaking it for the adder. Unlike the adder which has a red eye with vertical slit pupil, that of the smooth snake is yellow with a round pupil. It is a slender grey down the whole length of the back.

Its favourite haunts are dry, sandy hillsides overgrown with heather and gorse, sloping down to a marshy valley. The snake sometimes kills large prey such as lizards and small mammals by throwing two or three coils around the prey animal in its mouth. However unlike its tropical cousins (20 ins) it is in fact the smallest of our three snakes.

Unlike the adder the smooth snake gives birth to its young in individual egg sacs which are ruptured as the young snakes are born.

Sand lizard

The sand lizard (*Lacerta agilis*) like the smooth snake is a rare species in danger of extinction in Britain. Although protected by the byelaws it has declined to the point of extinction in the New Forest. Although illegal collecting of these animals for sale as pets has been partly responsible, over-burning of the Forest heathlands has also taken its toll.

Mature male sand lizards can be distinguished from the females by their bright green flanks and underparts. This green is especially vivid during the breeding season.

The sand lizard eats much the same food as its smaller relation the common lizard, taking beetles, grasshoppers, flies and moths.

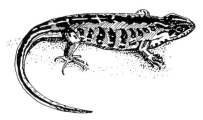

SAND LIZARD

Large prey is shaken vigorously to stun it before being eaten. It grows to about 20 cms in length.

Mating takes place in May and June, and there is considerable competition amongst males for the females. Once a male has paired with a mate he usually accompanies her closely keeping all other males away.

The eggs are laid in June or July in loose sand, where they are incubated by the heat of the sun, and hatch some seven to twelve weeks later. Before myxamatosis was prevalent, suitable loose sand was often provided by rabbits scraping and digging their burrows. Now in order to save the species this often has to be provided by conservationists turning over turves to expose loose sand, so that the females may lay their eggs.

Sand lizards are social creatures often living in small colonies on suitable areas, a practice which unfortunately makes it more vulnerable to unscrupulous collectors.

Common lizard

The common lizard (*Lacerta vivipara*) is the only British reptile found in Ireland. it is distributed throughout Britain and is common in the New Forest.

It is smaller than the sand lizard, reaching only 16 cm in length compared with the sand lizards 20 cms. In colour they are grey brown with darker markings on the head and body, and the males have a bright orange underbelly.

As with the sand lizard they feed off small insects and spiders and are extremely fast in pursuit of their prey.

Mating takes place in April—May and the gestation period is about three months. As its name implies the viviparous lizard produces living young the only member of the genus (family) to do so. Four to eight young are born, and at birth they are black in colour, and measure only 2 cms in length.

Lizards swim well, and will often dive into water to escape danger, they have been known to spend some minutes under the surface hiding from an enemy.

Unlike the snakes which have no external ears, the lizards have relatively large ear openings, which can easily be seen. There are other distinctions between snakes and lizards, such as their moveable eyelids, and a short flat tongue. None of the snakes have these characteristics.

All members of the lizard family are able to shed and regrow their tails. This process is known as autotomy and is a protective mechanism so that if seized by a predator the animal is able to escape, leaving its enemy holding only the tail.

Slow worm

The slow-worm or blind worm (*Anguis fragilis*) as it is sometimes called is certainly not blind, but can be rather slow and deliberate especially when stalking prey. This legless lizard is often found in gardens and cultivated areas where it consumes large quantities of slugs, its principal food. It grows to about 40 cms long.

The colour of slow-worms varies between individuals, and

Reptiles and Amphibians...
Continued from previous page

they can be brown, bronze or greyish. Usually males are greyish and the females brown or bronze with a dark stripe running down their backs. There is also a blue spotted variety. The cause of the blue spots is not known, these are not present at birth, but are usually obtained in the third or fourth year of life.

Mating occurs during late April or May, and there is often rivalry between males for a particular female, some old males bearing permanent scars on their bodies.

Slow worms live longer than other lizards, and records show that some have lived for thirty years. One male lived in Copenhagen Zoological Museum for fifty-four years.

Young are born live, the litter size varying between six and twelve. When born they are a most beautiful pale gold, but as growth proceeds they take on a more sombre hue.

Common frog

Frogs are extremely variable in colour, no two specimens being exactly alike. The skin which is smooth gives the impression of being permanently moist and is yellow, brown and green with darker spots.

Four species of frog occur in Britain although only the common frog (*Rana temporana*) is native. The edible, marsh and European tree frogs have all been introduced at various times. The edible frog was liberated during the 1830's in Norfolk and Cambridgeshire and since that time in the southern counties also. The marsh frog was introduced into Romney Marsh in 1935 where it still survives.

The common frog is widely distributed throughout Britain and Ireland.

Breeding starts in March and April, many frogs gathering at a single pond. Unlike the toad the frog's spawn is laid in large round masses each containing up to 4000 eggs.

Once the breeding season is over the frog spends much of its

COMMON FROG

time on land, though mainly in damp places where it feeds on worms, slugs and insects. Most frogs hibernate in or near water, often many together in one place. Many other animals depend on frogs for food, from grass snakes which eat the tadpoles as well as the adults, to large birds such as herons, and mammals such as the otter.

European tree frog

Many attempts have been made to introduce the European tree frog (*Hyla arborea*) not many of which have been successful. Most successful colonies have succumbed during severe winters, although two colonies on ponds in the New Forest still survive.

A small active frog, leaf green in colour and with large pads on its feet and toes to enable it to cling to branches, the tree frog is extremely noisy. From early spring until mid-summer it spends its time in ponds, but from mid-summer until autumn, when it hibernates, it spends its time in bushes and trees near the breeding pond. On warm still evenings its rapid "burring" call echoes through the Forest air.

Common toad

Toads (*Bufo bufo*) can be distinguished from frogs by their warty textured skin and ambling rather than hopping gait.

They are frequently found in gardens where they are most active during the evening and early night, often wandering some distance in search of slugs, worms

and insects which they feed on. Sometimes they have a favourite daytime resting place, to which they constantly return.

During the latter part of March and beginning of April, toads migrate to their breeding ponds, where they gather in huge numbers. The males cling to the backs of the spawning females, and release their spermatozoa into the water to fertilize the spawn as it is laid. As it meets the water toad and frog spawn swells enormously as the albumen surrounding the egg absorbs water. Usually toads prefer to spawn in deeper water than frogs so that while frogs will spawn at the pond margin, the toads will spawn out in the centre. Rather than laying large masses of spawn as does the

COMMON TOAD

frog, toad spawn is laid in the form of a long bootlace.

Water is essential for amphibians to breed in, and the infilling of even the most insignificant village pond can contribute to the destruction of these interesting creatures.

Newts

Smooth Newt (*Triturus vulgaris*)
Palmate Newt (*Triturus helveticus*)
Crested Newt (*Triturus cristatus*)
All three species of newts are found in the ponds of the New Forest. Two of these, the smooth and the palmate newt are closely related and difficult to distinguish from one another. Both are pale brown or green with dark spots on their smooth skin. The males of both species develop black spotted orange bellies and crests along their back and tail in the breeding season. The palmate newt however, has very slight palmation (webbing) between the toes on its hind feet, and in the breeding season the males have a thin filament extending for one millimetre beyond the rather blunt

Reptiles and Amphibians in the Forest

Continued from previous page tipped tail.

The crested newt or warty newt is dark grey or black in colour and as its name implies has a warty skin, and the males develop a fine serrated crest along the back and tail in the breeding season.

On the underbelly they have a bright orange colour dispersed by black markings.

Like all amphibians newts depend on water in which to breed. After mating the females do not simply disperse their spawn into the water as do frogs and toads but carefully and secretively lay individual eggs. Sometimes they fold two water plant leaves together and lay the egg between, the egg coating sticking the leaves together until it hatches.

After the breeding season newts leave the water and hibernate under logs and stones on land.

They have the unusual ability to regenerate parts of their bodies, especially limbs or tails which become damaged or lost, and form perfect replacements, this is known as autotomy.

Newts are voracious feeders and the crested newt will feed on the

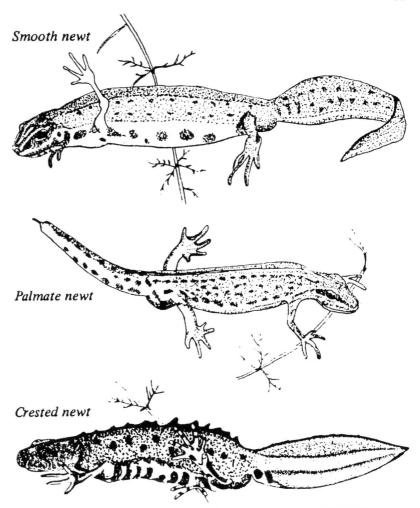

Smooth newt

Palmate newt

Crested newt

NEW FOREST NEWTS DRAWN BY HUGH INSLEY

tadpoles of the other two species of newt. They hunt by both sight and smell, and are very quick at seizing any prey which comes within reach. Worms, slugs, snails and insects form their main diet on land, while when in water they feed on aquatic larvae and crustacea.

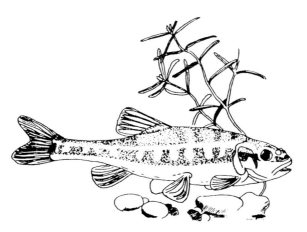

MINNOW, BY HIGH INSLEY
Drawing taken from the Forestry Commission's leaflet, *Ober Water Walk* (1984).

4
Things That Grow

Mystery of the Forest's "Groaning Tree"

In the middle of the 18th century the New Forest village of South Baddesley attracted visitors from all over the nation because of its mysterious "groaning tree."

F. E. Stevens, author of *The New Forest Beautiful*, was one of many writers who described the tree in later years. "A noise was frequently heard which seemed to come from the neighbourhood of the tree," he explained. "Everybody living near it heard it, but the commonly accepted explanation—accepted only because there was no better available—was that the noise was the bellowing of stags in the Forest ... . But in time it was recognized that the groaning noise came from an elm tree of no great age and apparently in sound condition."

"People came to see it," Stevens continues, "there were even royal visitors—and the scientists debated fiercely about it. Many held that friction at the roots caused it; some said there was water in the tree, but neither seemed to fit all the available evidence. The tree became a great attraction and even had the dignity of having a guide-book written about it."

A copy of that guide-book, published in London in 1742 by a member of the Royal Society identified only by his initials, is held by the University of Southampton Library's Cope Collection. Its title page and a wood-engraving of its frontispiece are reproduced here. Below are selected passages from the guide-book, and F. E. Stevens' comment on the death of the tree.

THE
Hampſhire Wonder;
OR THE
GROANING TREE.
BEING
A full and true Account of the GROAN-
ING TREE, in the New-Foreſt, near
Limington in *Hampſhire*.
WHICH
Has been heard for ſome Time paſt by Thou-
ſands of People, who come from all Parts
to hear this amazing and portentous Noiſe.

By P. Q. M. D. F. R. S.

LONDON:
Printed for *W. Smith*, near Temple-Bar.
M,DCC,XLII.

TITLE PAGE OF PAMPHLET
The pamphlet, which at four pence was not cheap in 1742, was published in London and earned the South Baddesley elm national attention.

The Hampshire Wonder: or The Groaning Tree

At about two miles distant from Limington in a solitary part of the New Forest, stands this famous tree, which has been heard to groan like a human creature in the agonies of death, for several hours together. What is most surprising in it, is that the tree is not old and decay'd or hollow, but a thriving young tree in the full vigour of youth.

So that it is looked upon by the virtuosi as the most surprising thing in its kind that has happened in England, or perhaps in Europe, for above these hundred years, since Queen Elizabeth's days.

Now tho' this groaning tree in the New Forest has not yet been observed by the most curious literati to have the least tendency towards walking, yet as by its groaning it appears to be undoubtedly dissatisfied with its present situation ... there are some who pretend to affirm that it is very reasonable to conclude that in all probability this New Forest tree will ... in a short time begin its travels and are under some apprehension that a new-built chapel in that neighbourhood will be in imminent danger, in case it should make its progress southwards, of being overthrown, even as the chapel was overthrown in the days of that good Queen ... .

We will for the present confine our account to the amazing groans which are now every day heard to proceed from its trunk, and these indeed are so terrible and shocking to human nature, that few who hear them have power to stir from the place till proper cordials have been administered to revive their sinking spirits and confounded imaginations.

They resemble in some manner the groans of a dying person, but withal so hollow and stupendiously deep, that they seem to proceed from the inmost centre of the earth at least, and are so terrifying to the ear of human mortals, that it astonishes the very clergy themselves who have been to listen to it. Tho' some learned divines (as there are many in the neighbourhood) have been requested to come and pray by the tree, yet none has hitherto done it, whether it be that they want faith enough to believe that there is a poor confined spirit in the tree, or that if there were, they think their faith is not strong enough to remove the tree and release it.

Now, besides this common groaning, there are many people of credit and reputation in their way, who aver that it has been heard to speak, or rather to groan articulately. Some even of my own aquaintance have positively declared it to me that they themselves have had it from people in

Why Trees Were Pollarded

(Gerald Lascelles in his autobiography, *Thirty-Five Years in the New Forest*, describes the practice of "pollarding" as it was carried out in some of the old woods of the Forest.)

A ... point (that) will strike any observer of trees as he wanders through these ancient groves ... is that almost every beech—and some oaks—are pollarded. And it is perhaps to this treatment that they owe their great size and their age, exceeding the average life of the beech. But why was this pollarding done? And under what circumstances?

The reason is to be found in the method of cultivation practiced in the early days of these encoppicements, viz., to farm them out upon lease to various tenants under very strict conditions. The crop realised was mainly the underwood, and used no doubt for fuel and charcoal. It was not permitted to fell timber trees, nor to cut down trees such as oak and beech which might ultimately become timber. But a sort of cultivation by pollarding on underwood lines of young trees seems to have been permitted.

Ridley Wood ... is one of the most beautiful woods in the whole Forest. It consists almost entirely of pollarded beeches, with wide spreading heads of numerous different stems, some of them very large dimensions, forming, both individually and as a whole, woodland scenes of very great beauty. It has amply repaid the care that was bestowed upon it in its early days. ... The effect, quite apart from scientific forestry, is certainly most beautiful. The great spreading trees, covering, no doubt, five times the space they ought to occupy, ... to the ordinary lover of beautiful forest scenery, ... are very dear.

All this pollarding of trees was finally extinguished by the Act of William III in 1698. By that Act it was made a punishable offence for

WOOD-ENGRAVING OF THE GROANING TREE
One unaccountable fact was that the groaning elm was the same age as several adjacent elms, but had grown to a considerably larger size.

Mystery of the Forest's "Groaning Tree"...

Continued from previous page
the neighbourhood, who say it has been heard to utter: "O walp! walp! It is thou who makest not only me but the whole nation to groan."

(The author of the booklet then explores possible causes of the groaning, using some factual and philosophical arguments. F. E. Stevens, writing about the tree

nearly 200 years later, gives the end of the story of the South Baddesley phenomenon: "The explanation was never discovered. A hole was bored in the trunk after which it ceased to groan, and that whetted scientific curiosity more than ever. The tree was uprooted and the closest investigation made, but the cause of the groaning was never found.")

POLLARDED BEECH PHOTOGRAPHED BY LASCELLES

Why Trees Were Pollarded...

Continued from previous page
any keeper to top or lop any timber tree ... . We can therefore safely assume that all the old pollards forming the woods so greatly appreciated by the public are not less than 200 to 300 years old. Probably the latter date is more nearly the correct one.

Some Forest Trees that Have Been Named

Over the centuries hundreds of New Forest trees have been given names. Many such have long ago decayed and are all but forgotten. The most famous of existing trees is undoubtedly the mighty Knightswood Oak near Lyndhurst. The names of some trees are localized—known only to the inhabitants of the immediate area. A tree need not be named because of its size, shape or association with some historical event; it may have been the trysting place of grandfather and grandmother, or a quiet spot for meditation by one heavily laden with worldly troubles.

F. E. Stevens lists a few of the better-known Forest trees with names, (*The New Forest Beautiful* Methuen, 1925). Some sadly no longer exist.

... At Minstead are two very famous oaks known as "Adam" and "Eve". There is (also) the Scissors Beech at Bank, ... so called because the branches intersect so curiously. Then at Vinney Ridge ... is the great Eagle Tree, with a girth of nineteen feet, one of the very giants of the Forest. Quite close, too, is that very oddly named wood, Birchen Hat, which won its name because of the resemblance of the tree-tops to hats.

Other individual trees or groups of them which are notable are St. Peter's Oak, outside Lyndhurst in the Lymington direction, a great oak near Burley, said to have been planted when William III was king, and the beech known as "Pretty Beech" at Furzy Lawn.

One of the most remarkable of the trees that ever grew in the Forest was that described in the Bath Society's papers, which was quoted by Gilpin and serves to show how dependent the Navy was in the day of the wooden walls on the well-grown Forest oaks. This tree, cut down in 1758, had branches nearly forty feet each way.

"Its head was all knees and crooks, aptly suited to naval purposes; its bole or shaft was short, not exceeding twenty feet in length, but it was full six feet in diameter at the top and perfectly sound. It was felled in an unusual manner for the preservation of its crooks, which were cut off one by one, whilst the tree was standing, and lowered by tackles to prevent them breaking."

In order to save a particularly large and valuable bough a bed of faggots—some hundreds were used—was made to catch it as it fell. Even so, half the bough was so heavy as to crush a timber carriage to pieces, and a special carriage had to be sent from Portsmouth to convey it to the dockyard. The record quoted shows that this tree was bought in the first instance for £40. The next purchaser gave £100 for it and he made a hundred per cent profit out of his purchase. "The breadth of the tree across, near the ground, was twelve feet, and it had three hundred rings of annual growth."

Burley way, in the western Forest, the moor country, are the "Twelve Apostles"—the Foresters of old time had the most arresting way of fitting effective names to the conspicuous objects of their countryside—mighty oaks which are beginning to fail, and have to be stayed—those which remain—by iron bands.

The same knack of neat naming has given character and a place in Forest tradition to "The Naked Man". It is but a bit of a tree, blasted long years ago, near Wilverley, on the road from Brockenhurst to Burley, but its bare arm points mutely to heaven, and in its desolation and impotence, upon the lonely heath one sees a certain fitness.

Why, I wonder, should a stump win a name at all? It doesn't happen in the other Forests. Perhaps it is because the Foresters are

ST. PETER'S OAK
This handsome specimen was located between Lyndhurst and Brockenhurst, and was remarked upon by F. E. Stevens (*The New Forest Beautiful*) as late as 1925.

New Forest Trees that Have Names...
Continued from previous page

able in their minds to give an individuality to the trees which are their friends. It isn't easy to "get the idea across", but every Forester feels that way about those trees which stand out in especial lordliness from among their fellows. They *are* friends.

There are several others which need to be mentioned, and none more famous than the Cadenham Oak at Cadnam, right on the other side of the Forest, near the road from Southampton, which is supposed to bud either on Christmas Eve, or on old Christmas Day. The story varies, or more probably the date varies. Wise thought it not unlikely that a few buds did sometimes show themselves about that time, having regard to its situation, and it has been hinted by much less grave authorities, that the meagre suggestion of bud which has been seen has either been placed there by artificial means or that auto-suggestion and strong beer have helped.

Gilpin took a lot of trouble to investigate the matter. "I engaged one Michael Lawrence," he said, "to send me some of the leaves as soon as they should appear. The man, who had not

the least doubt about the matter, kept his word and sent me several twigs, on the morning of the fifth of January, 1782, a few hours after they had been gathered. The leaves were fairly expanded and about an inch in length. From some of the buds two leaves had unsheathed themselves, but in general only one. ... I sent some

of the leaves to one of the ablest botanists we have, Mr. Lightfoot, author of the 'Flora Scotica', and was in hopes of hearing something satisfactory on the subject. But he is one of those philosophers who is not ashamed of ignorance where attempts at knowledge are mere conjecture. He assured me that neither could he account for it in any way, nor did he know of any other instance of premature vegetation, except the Glastonbury Thorn."

In the "Salisbury Journal" of January 10, 1786, it was stated that a lady—

"attentively curious in everything relative to art or nature, made a journey to Cadenham on Monday, the third instant, purposely to enquire on the spot about the production of this famous tree. On her arrival near it, the usual guide was ready to attend her, but on his being desired to climb the oak and to search whether there were then any leaves on it, he said it would be to no purpose, but that if she would come on the Wednesday following (Christmas Day) she might certainly see thousands. However, he was prevailed on to ascend, and on the first branch which he gathered appeared several fair new leaves, fresh sprouted from the buds and nearly

THE "TWELVE APOSTLES"—AS SKETCHED 150 YEARS AGO
This plantation, on private land, was well known when the Dukes of Bolton "reigned" at nearby Burley Lodge in the 18th century. Already in a state of decay 150 years ago, the once mighty oaks are falling one by one.

How Old Are the Trees of the New Forest?

(Although the soil of the New Forest is not conducive to producing trees of great age, many Forest trees nonetheless date from the English Civil War period and a few are slightly older.

Dr. Colin R. Tubbs of the Nature Conservancy Council, in his 1986 work—*The New Forest: A Natural History*—classifies the ages of Forest trees into A, B and C categories, with the A group being the oldest and C the youngest. The following extract from his book indicates that the largest oak and beech trees in the Forest have girths of seven metres (about 23 feet). The girths of the oldest hollies are only half that of the ancient oak and beech, and probably go back only to Queen Anne's reign (1702–14).)

Most woods consist of two or more distinct generations of trees, the age of which has been established by counting the annual growth rings of fallen or felled trees. The oldest (A) comprises mainly oak, beech and holly of large girth which are either pollarded or have large spreading crowns suggestive of growth in relatively open conditions. A-generation yew also occurs locally and probably, the occasional mas-

Colin Tubbs

AN ANCIENT BEECH IN BRATLEY WOOD
This tree, a pollard type, is among the oldest (A-generation) to be found in the New Forest.

Trees with Names…

Continued from previous page
an inch and a half in length. It may be imagined that the guide was more amazed at this premature production than the lady; for so strong was his belief in the truth of the whole tradition that he would have pledged his life that not a leaf was to have been discovered on any part of the tree before the usual hour."

"In some years," went on the chronicler of this occasion, "there is no doubt but that this oak may show its first leaves on Christmas morning as probably as on a few days before, and perhaps this was the case in the last year, when a

gentleman of this neighbourhood, a nice and critical observer, strictly examined the branches not only on the Christmas morn, but also on the day prior to it. On the first day not a leaf was to be found, but on the following every branch had its complement, though they were then but just shooting from the buds, none of them being more than a quarter inch long. The latter part of the story may easily be credited that no leaves

are to be seen on it after Christmas Day, as large parties yearly assemble about the oak on that morning, and regularly strip every appearance of a leaf from it."

Then there are the very famous yews of Sloden, none of which have ever been named, and a mighty specimen at Brockenhurst, eighteen feet in girth. There, too, is a mighty oak, now dead, which measured twenty-five feet round the bole.

How Old Are the Trees of the Forest?...

Continued from previous page
sive crab tree is from the same period. Some coppice stools of alder are also probably very old. The A-generation can be separated into an older sub-generation of mainly open-grown, commonly pollarded trees; and a younger unpollarded sub-generation which arose in gaps among the older trees or in places from which they had been removed. In the oldest sub-generation, which includes many senile and decaying trees, oaks are scarcer than beech, but they are less so in the younger sub-generation. Holly, both pollarded and unmutilated, occurs in both.

The largest surviving oaks, all pollards, are 5–7 m in girth at breast height. Nicolas Flower, in 1983, listed thirty-nine such trees, and I can add at least three more, but there are many times that number of old pollarded oaks 4–5 m in girth, and some maidens, which I believe are of similar age. Only four oaks are known which exceed 7.0 m girth: the largest is 7.4 m, which is not large for old oak trees on richer soils and reflects the low growth rate achieved in the Forest. The oldest oaks dated by counts of annual growth rings (mostly from fallen trees subsequently sawn at the butt) date from 1640–50, but these were comparatively vigorous maidens free of rot, which postdated the older, usually more degenerate trees. The latter I thus deduce to be of late 16th- or early 17th-century origin. The oldest and largest trees are massive, but few survive intact. Most have lost limbs and are dying back, confirming that not much more than about 400 years is the maximum life of an oak in the poor New Forest soils.

The earlier sub-generation of beech are of smaller girth and presumably younger than the oldest oaks. Flower listed ten beeches over 6.2 m in girth, the largest of which was 7.4 m (Queen Bower SU$_2$288043). Beeches, mainly pollards, of 4–6 m girth, however, are still abundant and there are numerous pollards of 2.8–4.0 m which clearly grew up with the larger trees and are thus similar in age. The difficulty in obtaining growth ring counts from most old beeches is that they are usually rotten in the centre, but the oldest sound beech counted was 347 in 1963, thus dating from 1616. A further nineteen trees proved to date from 1616–60.

The oldest holly was 254 years old in 1963 and thus dates to about 1709. Many counts were of stems dating from 1709–65. However, the oldest hollies are clearly coppice stems arising from stools of much greater age and commonly 3–4.5 m in girth, whereas the largest stems are 2–2.5 m girth. It would seem that stools coppiced in the 17th century regenerated and were pollarded in the 18th century. I strongly suspect that the oldest holly stools and root systems, like the oldest alder stools, are of 16th-century age or earlier, for the plant seems nearly indestructible in its capacity to regenerate from rootstock after felling and fire.

The younger, non-pollarded element of the A-generation mainly comprises beeches and oaks 2.5–4.0 m in girth. The range in girths among trees which clearly arose simultaneously has proved considerable, depending on local soil variation and the vagaries of competition within the stands. However, the form and cohesiveness of the later A-generation stands make them a distinctive element in the woods.

The B-generation is much younger and arose at woodland margins and in places where it can be conjectured the older A-generation trees had died or been felled after the establishment of the later part of the A-generation. Most B-generation oak and beech are in the girth range 1–2 m but there are many exceptions and some overlap with the A-generation. The B-generation is biased in species-composition towards those locally dominant in the A-generation, but birch is frequent (though often now moribund), ash occurs on richer soils, notably in valley bottoms, and yew, Scots pine, crab, rowan, whitebeam, willow and hawthorn are widespread. Hawthorn and blackthorn scrub, mostly now disintegrating with age and stock damage—the interior of thorn thickets are much used by ponies and cattle for shelter—colonized alluvial valley floors.

The C-generation is younger still, and is similarly species-variable. It represents the further colonization of gaps, glades and clearings and expansion of woodland margins, mainly by birch and oak. The paucity of species in the A-generation compared with those which arose subsequently is mainly explained by its age, which exceeds the life span of most species available for colonization except oak, beech, holly and yew.

The "Langley Oak," Felled by Order of A Bishop

(Occasionally New Forest oaks reached a circumference of more than 30 feet. One such, known as the Langley Oak, is described in *A Few Topographical Remarks Relative to the Parishes of Ringwood, Ellingham, Ibbesley, Harbridge and Fordingbridge*, published by Wheatons of Ringwood in 1831).
The trees of the Forest seldom rise into lofty stems, but are twisted into the most fantastic forms—a peculiarity supposed to arise from the gravelly nature of the soil.

The Langley Oak, felled in 1758 by order of the Bishop of Salisbury, presented 300 rings of annual growth, while the trunk measured 36 feet in circumference.

ALL THAT REMAINS OF THE NAKED MAN TODAY
The origin of the name of this "tree" is lost, but the likely truth is that generations ago—when it was first shorn of its branches, it resembled a naked man. The legend that it was used by excisemen for hanging smugglers en route from the coast to the depths of the Forest, is not borne out by records. Today, when viewed at the angle shown above, the Naked Man more nearly resembles a gaunt horse. It is best reached from the Wilverley Plain car park.

TWIN OAKS
This pair of entwined oaks once stood near Cadnam and was a much photographed sight of the area. It is not uncommon for trees, either of the same or of different species, to grow together in this manner in the New Forest.

"THE BOUNCING TREE"—A LOCALIZED NAME
Several generations of children in the Bisterne Close district of Burley have swung on the amazingly long branch of this great pollarded beech, 19 feet in circumference.

TYRREL'S OAK
The arrow shot by Sir Walter Tyrrel is supposed to have glanced off this oak before killing William II. The Rufus Stone now marks the spot.

The Aged and Majestic "Knightswood Oak"

British Tourist Authority

ONE OF THE BEST KNOWN SIGHTS IN BRITAIN: THE KNIGHTSWOOD OAK

Located approximately two miles south of Lyndhurst, just off the A35, this ancient oak exemplifies the pollarding once practiced on trees of the New Forest. It is probably about 600 years old and has a girth of 21 feet. The tree is still growing; in 1862 the oak's girth, as measured by John Wise, was 17 feet, four inches. Despite its great height and the loss of its neighbours, it survived the devastating storm of October, 1987.

Some of the Less Appreciated Trees

> The New Forest has long been noted for its stately oaks and beeches, but it also boasts a variety of "lesser" trees. Some abound throughout the area while others—such as the yew—are confined to only a few districts.
>
> Rose de Crespigny and Horace Hutchinson wrote about some of the smaller trees in their 1895 work, *The New Forest*, from which the passage below has been excerpted.

Before the enclosure was made at Sloden there was a magnificent show of fine old yew trees. A goodly number still remain at the upper end of the enclosure—a remnant that testifies very amply to what their glory must have been in their prime. Some are splendid specimens, and if you stand underneath and look up at the delicate red berries, with the light shining through them, against the intensely dark green of the foliage, you may believe yourself in a wonderful fairyland surrounded by a host of little fairy lanterns.

In the old days the forester can have been at no lack of good yew timber for his bow, for specimens of these splendid trees are to be seen everywhere throughout the Forest. It was specially the boast of the English yeoman that none but he could bend his bow. The phrase has reference to the peculiar English style of archery in which the bow was not *drawn*, as the French drew it, by drawing the bowstring towards the archer, but, *bent* by pushing the bow, with straightening left arm, away from the body.

The Forest is rich, too, in another tree of peculiar but very opposite beauty—the birch, whose graceful feathery foliage and silver stem gleaming whitely throws into such fine contrast the more solid glories of the stouter trees. They grow in especial profusion in the neighbourhood of Lyndhurst and Brockenhurst.

The Scottish fir, of which we have spoken before, is so numerous now, and blends its fine colour and outlines so harmoniously with the hues and contours of the indigenous trees, that it is difficult to believe that previous to 1776 there

was not in the whole area of the Forest a single conifer.

The firs were first planted by way of an experiment in Ocknell

Gorley Firs

(FROM HEYWOOD SUMNER'S *Book of Gorley*)

Clump, and have multiplied and replenished the earth ... amazingly. The Douglas fir has also been introduced and thrives well.

Larch has been planted here and there, chiefly as a protection to seedlings of other species, but experience seems to show that the larch does not make much headway in southern England. The ash and mountain ash are to be seen occasionally, but are not common.

Of the lowlier growths, the blackthorn or wild plum is perhaps the commonest and certainly the most impressive. Its bloom, preceding its foliage, comes forth, under the cherishing of the most cruel winds of spring, in clumps of feathery whiteness thrown out against the purple-black—sloe-

black—wood.

And the sloes themselves, the fruit of the blackthorn, abound in the autumn, and are plucked by the people to the tune of five shillings a bushel, wholesale, to be made into sloe-gin, an excellent liqueur.

This blackthorn and its beauty are not without its thorn, both actual and metaphorical – the "blackthorn winter," as the forester calls it, comes "sure as death and taxes" after a snap of biting wind, often with snow upon its wings, in spite of the kindliest promise of some warm spring days.

The "merry" tree, as it is called, the small cherry tree (French *mérise* and *mérisier*) grows abundantly. Once an annual fair was held for the sale of its fruit. A part of Bramshaw village is locally known as the Merry Orchard.

The wealth of ivy is a beautiful feature of the Forest. It climbs the trees and then comes hanging in long trails that sway with the breeze. It forms a kindly covering for old and naked trunks, embracing them and clothing them with the beauties of its own cool foliage, ever green.

In spring the hawthorn is luxuriant, and at every turn one sees the sheets of its snow-white blossom. The spindle-berry bush with its gorgeous fruit—gorgeous but poisonous as the nightshade—appears here and there, and now and again we come upon a crabapple.

The hollies ... are a large and most pleasant feature of the New Forest. All the year round their rich dark foliage gleams among the tenderer greens of summer or more sombre winter hues, and at the latter season they are decked with such a wealth of scarlet berries as one can scarcely credit who has only known the holly berry as a Christmas decoration. The holly grows to so great a size as to place it outside the list of undergrowths—it takes its place among the Forest trees.

The Richness of New Forest Flora

(Whether among the ancient woodlands or on the open heathlands, the New Forest abounds in wild flowers and other plants. A sampling is contained in de Crespigny and Hutchinson's *The New Forest* (1895), from which the extracts below are taken.)

The Forest is rich in marsh flowers and most of those productions of flora which are lovers of soft boggy soils.

Foxgloves are fond of growing in the banks of the streams and here and there among the trees, and the tangle is a mixture of blackberry and dog roses. The bramble, however, is not very luxuriant: it is not a good blackberrying country.

But the "predominant partner," so to speak of it, is the honeysuckle. It grows in wonderful and wonderfully beautiful profusion. It is predominant in the tangle, but, not satisfied with that, it winds its stealthy way through the midst of the densest hollies, climbs the stems of the barest and unfriendliest trees, and finally justifies its intrusions by thrusting forth, here, there, and everywhere, when least expected, a glorious head and spray of most luscious, beautiful and golden blossom, throwing into all the air around its own sweet intoxicating scent. The stems of the honeysuckle grow to quite a stalwart size, and one of the present writers had a strand of three stems of honeysuckle, intertwined by their natural growth, that had not a less united thickness than an ordinary man's arm.

Of heather there is a great abundance. Though it scarcely grows to the height or bushiness of some of the Scottish heather, still less to that of some of the great clumps of the Irish bogs, it can nowhere in the world be excelled in the brilliant splendour of its bloom.

There are three distinct kinds of heather in the Forest—the early "bell," the larger kind of the common heather, and the smaller flowered "ling," which blooms latest and most profusely. All of them are found in that white variety which is supposed to bring so much good luck to the finder. It is disputed which kind of white heather is the most potent in this regard; but in all probability they are much on an equality.

From year to year there is a good deal of difference in the beauty and splendour of the heather bloom; and it is to be noted that the years which produce the finest crop of purple heather are also the years in which the white heather is most abundant. It appears, therefore, that the white colour can be in no way regarded as a morbid condition of the other, on the analogy of the albino variety of rabbits, ferrets, and so on.

That curious plant, the carnivorous "sun-dew," is very common, and there are some places where wild lilies of the valley are abundant.

Ferns grow finely in the Forest shade. The royal fern, *Osmunda regalis*, still seen in marshy places. The lady fern and the sweet-scented fern are common. The hart's tongue occurs, but more rarely, and the poly-pody is fairly plentiful, generally choosing for its home the mossy clefts and forks of the old oaks. Of mosses themselves the Forest produces at least one variety peculiar to the locality.

Toadstools and fungi of every sort, size and colour abound. There are big brown and yellow ones, scarlet and white ones, and tiny little fellows scarlet all over. In some years mushrooms are fairly plentiful, and in the local opinion no mushrooms are equal in flavour to those that grow in the Forest.

Fern Cutting

(When the New Forest was heavily peopled with Commoners, fern cutting was a big event of the autumn. In *Sons of Skewbald*, Allen Seaby describes the cutting, the carts that carried away the fern, and what it was used for.)

Autumn is, perhaps, the most beautiful season in the Forest. True the furze is at its dullest (except the dwarf sorts), although even in October a few golden stars can be seen twinkling among the green. Country folk have a saying that Britain will never be conquered while the furze is out, and certainly blossoms may be found at any time of year. In autumn the heather, too, has replaced its purple by umber, but the fern makes up for any absence of bloom. After the first frosts it begins to turn—yellow, orange, then sienna. From Wilverley Cross the plains or uplands for miles look all one hue—purplish-brown—that of the dead fern.

At this time the ponies find the open Forest, usually quiet except for the hunts and the rounds of the riding schools, strangely noisy. The farmers and other folk possessing stables or cow-byres are out. They cut down the fern with scythes and collect it as bedding for their beasts. Some bring their farm carts and pile up the fern as high as a wain of hay.

One and all receptacles have four stout poles, slanting upwards out of the car corners to sustain the load, which is packed by a worker on top as great forkfuls are passed up to him. Fern cutting is perhaps more picturesque and certainly richer in colour than the meadow haymaking.

Sally's aunt wanted supplies of fern as bedding for her cows and pony. Her "fern ticket" told her where it was to be cut; she had paid her three-and-sixpence per load to the authorities. ... The fern was dry enough to cart directly it was cut—unlike some years when the heaps had to be spread out and dried time after time. ... Several days were spent at work around the Naked Man, where the fern grew thick and tall.

Moyles Court Oak.

MOYLE'S COURT OAK HALF A CENTURY AGO
Heywood Sumner sketched this view of the famous oak in the early 1930s when it appeared as the frontispiece of his *Local Papers*. At that time he found the tree to have a girth of 20 feet, 4 inches, measured at a point four inches above the ground. Despite many storms and modern intrusions (the rustic track has long since been replaced by tarmac) the ancient oak still survives.

Heywood Sumner on the Death of An Old Tree
(From *Local Papers*, "Trees and Anno Domini")
One cannot gaze on a fine old tree without reverence—the reverence due to achievement, to age, to a span of life so infinitely greater than that of any other living thing.

It is this dim sense of personality in achievement—of a presence inspiring reverence—that imparts pity and resentment at the spectacle of such a tree being felled. We behold the violent end of a woodland Being whose age may accord with a decade of centuries. This is the last act; when wedges have been driven to ease the final saw-cuts ... until the tree-top quivers, slants, begins slowly to heel over, and gradually—then abruptly the whole living landmark pitcfhes downwards, with rending crack from the butt-hold, followed by a thump of impact as branches, limbs, and trunk crash together to the ground.

We have been present at an execution and feel ashamed to have been onlookers.

Once There Was A Noble Beech in Eyeworth...

(Major General A. W. Drayson, a fellow of the Royal Astronomical Society, did much to bring the New Forest to the attention of the nation a century ago.

In the 1 August 1871 issue of *Good Words for the Young*, Major General Drayson describes the King's Beech in Eyeworth Wood. This majestic specimen has long since fallen, like many of its contemporaries.)

Those who admire magnificent timber should pay a visit to the New Forest.

The largest beech with which we are acquainted in the New Forest is in Eyeworth Wood; it is locally known as the King Beech, and certainly is a grand tree. The trunk of the tree at the lowest part is fourteen feet two inches in circumference.

At about thirty feet from the ground the stem is about fourteen feet in circumference. The topmost twigs are ninety-eight feet from the ground, and the branches extend eighty feet from side to side.

Here is a sketch of the King Beech, the size of which can be judged by comparison with the man near it.

5
Arts and Crafts

The New Forest: A Magnet for the Artist

With its contrasting scenery and teeming animal life, the New Forest has long been popular with the artist. In May, 1973, the Hampshire Gallery in Bournemouth organized an exhibition of works by artists who either lived in or near to the Forest, or who painted subjects there during 1800–1920. The gallery's catalogue of that exhibition, compiled by Robert Arnold and Simon Keyes, has now become a valued work for anyone interested in art of the New Forest.

Hampshire Gallery has kindly given permission to include here some of the catalogue's contents: the introduction below; the story of the New Forest Exhibition of 1875, and biographical notes on the Reverend William Gilpin; J.T. Young; William Shayer, Snr.'s three sons—William Joseph, Henry Thring and Charles; Albert Durer Lucas; John Emms; Sidney Pike; Arthur Batt; Arthur H. Davis; Frederick Golden Short; Hugh Wilkinson; and Creswell Hartley Desmond.

Painters of the New Forest: 1800 to 1920

Through the centuries, although changes have taken place, the Forest and moorland has kept a character of its own, retaining something of that wild unspoilt look, where man can be nearer to nature and animals still play a part in the way of life. Residing in such an area must affect one's attitudes and pattern of living always attracting those who's interests are best satisfied by such an environment.

Many artists have painted in the New Forest, among them some of the leading painters of the English School but we are interested in those who were born or lived for a period of time in the Forest or the surrounding centres of population and were influenced by the environs of the area.

Various painters were active, particularly in the larger towns around the Forest in the first part of the nineteenth century. Tobias Young of Southampton was often drawn to the Forest for his subjects. William Gilpin became vicar of Boldre in 1777 and although he had acquired his reputation as a water-colourist and writer on art prior to this, he continued to pursue his artistic activities to some extent. William Shayer was painting at Southampton from the early eighteen twenties and later his sons followed the same profession. They continued to paint in the area until the late seventies, the Forest and its folk featuring in many of their works. At Chilworth, for fifty years from 1850 onwards, A.D. Lucas was quietly painting his fine still-lifes, mostly wild flowers. Two animal painters, John Emms and Arthur Batt had established themselves in the Forest before 1870 when it would appear that there was enough money and sufficient interest in animal painting to support them. Both lived and worked successfully into the twentieth century. Arthur Davis and Sidney Pike, living to the West of the Forest, frequently found themselves drawn to the woods and moorlands for their subjects. Frederick Golden Short was, by the turn of the century, well established at Lyndhurst as a landscape painter, whilst those semi-professional artists Hugh Wilkinson and Creswell Hartley Desmond kept art alive in the Forest past the first quarter of this century. Throughout this time, from eighteen hundred onwards, there were other artists, mostly amateur, working in the area but these have drifted into oblivion.

Many of the people mentioned who were contemporary with one another would have been friends joining each other in artistic activities. The Southampton Art Society after its foundation in 1885 was the meeting place for many of them, all those painters alive in the Forest from that date onwards showed their work in the annual exhibition at one time or another.

The changing patterns of life in this century and the confused position that the artist found himself in, appear to have created conditions not suitable for the pursuit of painting as it had been known in the eighteen hundreds and early nineteen hundreds. With the twenties came the end of an era, the passing of Golden Short in 1936, Hartley Desmond and Hugh Wilkinson at a later date, saw the severence of the links with the Victorian period. Art in the New Forest could never be the same again.

Reverend William Gilpin

Little need be written here about the Rev. William Gilpin as there exist several books on the subject. His appointment to Boldre as vicar brought him to the Forest and he was, we think, the first known artist to reside in and paint scenes of the New Forest.

He was born at Scaleby Castle near Carlisle in 1724, his father John Bernard Gilpin being an amateur artist and his brother Sawry Gilpin becoming an outstanding professional painter specializing in animal subjects.

William Gilpin had considerable influence on the art of the day

"FOREST SWINE"—A SKETCH BY THE REVEREND WILLIAM GILPIN

William Gilpin…

Continued from previous page
through his books and essays on
the picturesque in landscape. He

GILPIN'S TOMB (*Remarks on Forest Scenery***)**

was also the author of biographical
works, Lectures on the Catechism
of the Church of England and
various other religious subjects.
Headmaster of Cheam school

from 1752 until 1777, he was
appointed vicar of Boldre in 1778,
retaining the office until his death.
During twenty six years in the
New Forest his interest in art continued and he wrote and illustrated two volumes, published in
1791, titles "Remarks on the
Forest Scenery".

The Rev. William Gilpin found
time to give lessons and advice,
mostly on his favourite theory of
the Picturesque, to those amateur
artists who visited the vicarage.
Painting in watercolour was at
that time a popular past-time
among the gentry.

In the last years of his life Gilpin
prepared a number of drawings to
be sold at Christies, the proceeds
to provide an endowment for a
school for poor children at Boldre.
The sale took place in 1802 and
1804 raising a considerable sum.

Few of his drawings are in circulation and Forest scenes are
rare.

The Rev. William Gilpin passed
away in 1804 aged 80.

J. T. Young

Little is known about the artist J.T. Young. It has been suggested that two artists existed, probably brothers, J.T. Young and Tobias Young, but recent research in Southampton leaves little doubt that there was in fact one artist with signatures on his works varying, perhaps at different periods. The subject matters for his paintings also varied, as well as painting landscapes, there exist some historical paintings by his hand.

Mildenhall near Marlborough is thought to be his birthplace but when he was born is not known. In the year 1803 the Southampton Chronical gives his address as Hanover Buildings, Southampton.

The first recorded exhibited painting by his hand appeared in the Royal Academy in 1811 and was a Mill scene on the Thames. In 1817, the date of his next Academy Picture, the subject is "View in the New Forest" between Lyndhurst and Lymington and his address is given as 1, Hanover Buildings, Southampton. In 1822 his third and last Academy picture, a landscape, was sent from a London address.

There is no doubt that he resided for a number of years in Southampton, the area in and around that city and the New Forest being the favourite subjects for his brush.

Painting mostly landscapes of a cabinet size, he does not forget the smallest details of foliage, particularly in the foreground. Usually the inclusion of figures and animals painted with an individual charm add to the interest. When signed the signature is often difficult to locate, sometimes forming part of the foliage.

The works of J.T. Young are not numerous. The city of Southampton possess a history picture "The Judgement of Solomon", the Victoria and Albert Museum have five watercolours, all landscapes.

J.T. Young died at Southampton in 1824.

Arthur H. Davis

A native of Southampton, Arthur H. Davis was born in 1847. Educated at Southampton he showed early inclinations towards art which resulted in him attending the South Kensington Art School in London.

It is not known when he came to reside in Bournemouth. In 1872 when 25 years old he exhibited a painting in the Royal Academy from a London address. On his death in 1895 his obituary in the Bournemouth Guardian mentions that he was a Bournemouth resident for some twenty years.

Primarily interested in landscape painting, many of his pictures depict scenes around Christchurch in the New Forest and along the Solent. He made several paintings trips to Devon. His pictures have considerable charm, showing a good choice of subject and are usually topographically correct. Using a full brush he handles paint cleverly and confidently with a fine touch for details. His colour sense is strong with a dominance of heavy green.

A constant exhibitor at local exhibitions, including the Southampton Art Society, he occasionally sent pictures to Suffolk Street and other London Galleries.

The Regent Street New Forest Exhibition of 1875 contained several scenes by his hand.

A generous and impetuous person with much enthusiasm about matters in which he was interested, his early death was a great loss to local art circles. He left a wife and three young children.

Hugh Wilkinson

Hugh Wilkinson was born at Ealing, London in 1850. Little is known of the first part of his life, we know he qualified as a barrister and for a time practiced law. Always wishing to devote his full time to painting, this was not practical until he inherited an annuity in about 1878. His love of the New Forest, frequently visited on holidays, decided him to take up residence at Brockenhurst and spend his time painting the wonderful scenery of the area. His work met with considerable success as his ability to depict landscapes and trees was recognized. Exhibiting from 1870 he had forty two pictures in the Royal Academy and a large number in other London exhibitions. The National Gallery of Australia purchased an oil of a forest tree for their collection. Russell-Cotes Museum, Bournemouth has a winter scene in the New Forest purchased from the artist in 1926.

Hugh Wilkinson, whose art was self taught, had an individual style especially in the application of paint. There is some similarity between his work and that of F. Golden Short but Wilkinson is stronger in handling and colour. Particularly appreciated in his own time were his paintings of trees, a contemporary press report describing him as "The finest painter of trees."

His income supplemented by the sale of his pictures enabled him to assist several artists less fortunate who fell upon hard times, some coming to stay at a house in Brockenhurst purchased by Hugh Wilkinson for this purpose. Vernede a London landscape painter and Frank Brooks the portrait painter were among those who stayed for a time.

For nearly seventy years Hugh Wilkinson painted his Forest scenes, enjoying his chosen profession. He died in his ninety ninth year in 1948.

Arthur Batt

The early life of Arthur Batt has not been revealed through research and we know only that he was born in 1846 in Whitchurch.

Where he received his artistic training and when he first began to paint is not known. Our first reference to him occurs in 1884 when a picture entitled "The Highway Board" was exhibited by him in the Royal Academy, his address given as Hall Lodge, Lyndhurst; further paintings

"FARMYARD FRIENDS," AN OIL ON PANEL BY ARTHUR BATT

Arthur Batt...

Continued from previous page
shown in 1885 and 1887 at the Academy were sent from this address. Shortly after, Arthur Batt moved to "The Briars", Brockenhurst just a few miles away. In the early nineties he had a house built with a garden studio in Avenue Road, Brockenhurst, and here he lived until his death in 1911.

A member of the Southampton Art Society, the titles of his pictures appear in the catalogues of their annual exhibitions from 1885 until 1910 usually showing four each year.

Remembered as a small dark man, Batt was interested in music and was a member of the local chapel. He raised a family of eight children, educating them himself in preference to their attending the local school. One daughter, Edith, painted local forest scenes very similar to those of her friend F. Golden Short from whom she received lessons. She exhibited frequently in the Southampton Art Society.

Without doubt it is as a painter of animals that Arthur Batt is best

remembered. Donkeys held a special attraction and many of his compositions include this animal. His pictures have a quality and charm reflecting the forest and its animals with truth and an understanding of the environment. His subject pictures are often amusing in the story they have to tell. Animal portraiture was an important part of his oeuvre and among his clients, for whom he painted horses and hounds, was Lord Rothschild of Tring.

Lessons in painting and drawing also helped his income and it is interesting to note that Lucy Kemp Welch, who later became an outstanding animal painter, received her first instruction from him.

Of the twenty eight pictures that Arthur Batt exhibited in London, the Academy exhibit of 1885 titled "The Culprit" attracted the most attention and he was invited to send it to the Adelaide Exhibition, where it was awarded "Gold Medal of the Year".

Now that animal paintings are again popular and the qualities of

Victorian painters appreciated, works by Arthur Batt find a ready sale, not just locally but also in the London Art Market.

John Emms

Born at Blowfied, Norfolk in 1841, little is known to us of John Emms' early life.

His interest in art took him to London and it is possible that he assisted Mr. Frederic Leighton, later Lord Leighton, in his studio for a time. We understand that it was as Leighton's assistant that Emms came to the New Forest to help in the execution of the fresco "The Ten Virgins" in Lyndhurst church. Leighton travelled from London to Lyndhurst at the weekends during the summers of 1864–1866.

It was from 16, Earls Court Gardens, London that Emms sent his first picture to the Royal Academy in 1866 titled "The Birds Nest". At this time birds and incidents involving birds were his favourite painting subject (perhaps the owl in the Lyndhurst

**HASSELL'S "VIEW ON THE NEW FOREST" REVEALS THE WILDNESS
OF TWO CENTURIES AGO**

John Emms...

Continued from previous page

fresco is the work of John Emms) and further pictures at the Academy in 1867 and 1868 were titled "The Fate of the Village Jackdaw" and "Pigeons".

His visits to Lyndhurst would have introduced him to a wonderful area of country where animals and wild life abounded and there existed gentry and those of means who could be likely customers for his paintings.

1872 finds him back in the Forest residing at Lyndhurst. His ability to paint animals soon found him clients, he was a success with his brush and socially. An accomplished horseman, his activities in the hunting field would not only be enjoyable but doubtless helped in finding subjects and customers for his work. Short trips to other parts of the country, probably most by invitation, brought him work painting horse, hound, dog portraits and subject pictures.

In 1880 Emms married Miss Fanny Primmer the daughter of a local head gamekeeper and after the wedding decided to work from a London studio, not returning until 1888 when they built a house and studio at Lyndhurst. Emms remained in Lyndhurst, apart from further short stays in other parts of the country and trips both to Scotland and Ireland, until his death in 1912 aged 71.

An artist of great ability his early pictures were carefully painted and show the use of glazing but later he developed a direct and rapid style using a limited palette. Emms executed a large number of paintings. At his best he is able to portray animals especially hounds and dogs with that vital alive look that seems to reveal their character and personality. His hunting scenes are among his best works, always lively, they show his knowledge of the subject acquired by experience in the hunting field.

John Hassell

(John Hassell, whose date of birth is unknown, died in 1825. He first came to the attention of the art world when he exhibited a "View of Stonehenge on Salisbury Plain" at the Royal Academy in 1789.

Thereafter his fame grew and he wrote or illustrated many works, some of them encompassing specific regions of the British Isles. He was a water-colour painter, engraver and drawing master.

His best known topographical books are *A Tour of the Isle of Wight* (1790), *Views of Noblemen's and Gentlemen's Seats* (1804), *Tour of the Grand Junction Canal* (1819) and *Rides and Walks Round London* (1820).

It seems likely that Hassell visited the New Forest in connection with his visit to the Isle of Wight in 1790.)

A successful painter until later in life when illness prevented him from working, he was a man of

John Emms...

Continued from previous page

genial disposition and strong personality, with a reputation as a humourist. On his death he was survived by three daughters and a son.

A member of the Southampton Art Society he showed a number of his paintings at their annual exhibitions. Between 1864 and 1884 Emms exhibited twenty paintings at the Royal Academy and nearly seventy more at various London Exhibitions. The London Exhibition of 1875 on the beauties of the New Forest included three of his pictures.

There is a picture in the National Gallery of Scotland of a wire haired terrier by Emms, Southampton Art Gallery have a number of his works and there is one in the Russell-Cotes Art Gallery, Bournemouth.

Albert Durer Lucas

Albert Durer Lucas was born at Salisbury in 1828, his father Richard Cockle Lucas the professional sculptor was something of an eccentric. In the 1850's the family moved to Chilworth where Albert's father designed and built an unusual house which he called Chilworth Tower; made of much timber beaming and brick it proved not to be weatherproof and some years later a new abode "Tower of the Winds" was constructed nearby.

Having early in life developed artistic tendencies Albert was able to assist his father in various branches of art and later, when he took to painting, he still occasionally found time to carve and model.

Chilworth Tower, being very large, afforded Albert with enough room not only for a studio but also a picture gallery where he was able to display his works. It is without doubt that his metier was the painting of small finely finished still-life and flower oils and these have great merit and charm. His work appears to owe very little to any other artists influence and indeed there is about it a feeling that his approach is slightly naive.

It is said that Lucas was of a modest and retiring disposition, this is reflected in his approach to painting, never attempting to work on a large scale and being limited in his painting accomplishments. His rare figure subjects are very carefully painted but have little merit in the drawing or conception, this also applies to his attempts at landscapes. The subjects for his pictures are usually the wild flowers and heathers that grow in the area, arranged in a small vase or on a ledge. He would often choose that the picture should have a message to convey and small objects sometimes adorn the ledge, such as a wedding ring or gold sovereign, the appropriate caption completing the picture. The inclusion of moths, butterflies and insects minutely painted occur in many of his works. A neat small printed signature A.D. Lucas is sometimes accompanied by a large signature on the back of the canvas or board.

A frequent exhibitor in London he showed thirty seven pictures in various exhibitions in the Metropolis between the years 1859–1878. In 1880 one of his paintings was selected for an international exhibition in Melbourne, Australia, where it was awarded a gold medal.

A member of the Southampton Art Society, he exhibited in 1887, 1889 and again in 1906.

Lucas married and had one son who died while still a boy. He resided the last thirty three years of his life at 50, Padwell Road, Southampton, where he died in 1919 aged 90 years.

Southampton Art Gallery has several of his paintings.

Creswell Hartley Desmond

Reaching into the past has failed to reveal details of the early life of the artist. Born at Lambeth in 1877 we know that as a young man he spent some of his time in Paris, his interest in art bringing him into contact with noted painters who had studios in the French capital.

In 1890 Creswell Hartley Desmond moved to Spout House, Boldre, here he lived with his mother and sister Phoebe, an artist, sculptor and wood carver in her own right.

Art was Creswell's main occupation and obsession, although it did not have to support him financially. A painter of ability, he was able to portray figures and animals equally well. The Forest and its life presented him with ideas and subjects which he successfully transferred to canvas. Those pictures sent to the Royal Academy through the early part of this century were often received with enthusiasm by both public and press.

Dogs frequently figured in his paintings and he would, on occasions, turn to historic subjects, for example "The Red King" portraying the death of Rufus or "The Witch" shown in 1910 and reproduced in the Royal Academy Illustrated Catalogue of that year.

He could paint carefully but often employed a looser technique especially on his larger canvases. Creswell was also a good portrait painter and his ability to carve and model were other artistic achievements. Several bronzes were exhibited.

About the time of the first world war, Creswell became increasingly interested in wild animals, particularly members of the cat family. The following years saw him producing paintings of leopards, tigers etc., visiting London and other zoos to sketch. These are often effective but owe nothing to the area in which he lived.

Ill health robbed him of enthusiasm for painting and later years produced very little in the way of pictures.

After his death in 1953 his sister arranged an exhibition of his works at Spout House which was well received.

The Leighton Fresco in Lyndhurst Church

Leighton's Frescoe

(While visiting his Lyndhurst friend, Captain Hamilton Aide, in 1862, the artist Frederick Leighton painted a fresco for the parish church.

Entitled "The Wise and the Foolish Virgins," it included Lyndhurst girls who at first hesitated—not wishing to be known as foolish virgins.

The description of Leighton's work is taken from C.P. Phillips' *New Forest Guide*. Despite some initial anxiety about the fresco's ability to resist the damp British climate, it endured for a century before it was cleaned and retouched.)

British Tourish Authority

LORD LEIGHTON'S FRESCO IN LYNDHURST CHURCH

The subject of Mr. Leighton's picture is the Parable of the Wise and Foolish Virgins, consummately wrought out by means of fifteen figures of life size, with several attendants, the space covered being about twenty-four feet long by eight feet high, and occupying the whole of the wall space beneath the eastern window of the church.

From the central arch, around which the vine bears clusters of its luscious fruit, issues the Saviour as the Bridegroom—a figure of noble form and beneficent countenance, bearing in his hand a lily, emblem of spotlessness, and attended by a joyous company of angels filling the air with melody from the instruments they carry. Turning towards the right the Bridegroom welcomes one of the five Wise Virgins, who has pressed forward from amid her companions with her burning lamp.

Near her an angel of mercy supports the outstretched arm, and encourages the approach, with her lamp, of a damsel whose intensely nervous countenance and flaxen hair bespeak her youth and timidity. A magnificent figure occupying a prominent position in the group and bearing her lamp above her head probably typifies life and activity. A group of doves near a playing fountain and a fruit-laden orange-grove, standing out against the deep blue of the midnight sky, with, at the extremity of the picture, "Vigila" personifying Watchfulness, tending a burning lamp, complete the major group of the composition.

On the other side of the central figure are the Foolish Virgins, shut out from the Bridegroom by an angel with outstretched arms, full of forbidding power. Their lamps are gone out through neglect, and whilst intense despair is depicted on the countenances

---

Painters of the New Forest...
Continued from previous page

Sidney Pike

This landscape painter, lived for more than ten years in the Christchurch area.

Born in 1846 it was not until 1889 that he moved to the South Coast. He was familiar with the Forest area before this date as we find he had several paintings in the Bournemouth Fine Art Society Exhibition of 1886 and one of them was a New Forest view.

Exhibiting from a Taplow address in the Royal Academy from 1885 until 1889, he continued to show pictures in London for the next ten years from Christchurch and later Pokesdown, Bournemouth. By 1899 he had moved to London, exhibiting from 69 Elizabeth Street, Belgravia. His last Academy picture appeared in 1901. Six years later his death is recorded as taking place in Chelsea.

In all, forty paintings were exhibited by him in the Metropolis. His pictures appeared regularly in the Southampton Art Society's annual exhibitions.

A prolific painter, he mostly chose for his subjects, forest scenery, the country lanes around Bournemouth and Christchurch and river views on the Avon and Stour. Effects of light at the beginning and end of the day often add colour and atmosphere to his pictures.

William Shayer and His Love of the Forest

William Shayer, Snr., was born in Southampton and lived there most of his life. His work was nationally respected and had he chosen to reside in London, it is likely his fame and standing would be even greater. Three of his sons were artists: William Joseph, Henry Thring, and Charles.

William Shayer's love of the New Forest is reflected by the large number of subjects he painted there, among them gypsy encampments, rural inns, and domestic scenes. His biography below was written by Brian Stewart for the Southampton Art Gallery's 1987 exhibition catalogue of William Shayer, Snr.'s works.

William Shayer 1787–1879

William Shayer's evocative landscape paintings admirably present an image and spirit of rural life in Southern England. The landscape he most made his own was the New Forest: the woodland glades, gypsy camps, their characters and animals all are portrayed with perception, sympathy, and humour.

Little is known about William's early life. He began earning his living in Southampton as a painter of rush bottom chairs and later moved to Guildford to work as a coach painter. From Guildford he moved to Chichester to continue his work for a master coach builder by the name of George Parsons.

In September of 1810 William Shayer married Parsons' niece Sarah Lewis Earle, the daughter of Robert Earle who ran '*The*

Courtesy Peter Combes
WILLIAM SHAYER, SNR.

Anchor Inn' in Chichester. The marriage appears to have been somewhat hasty for it was only seven months later that his son William Joseph was born.

Shayer's career as an artist was

helped considerably by the patronage of Michael Hoy, a popular and wealthy Southampton merchant, who owned extensive estates at Midanbury, Thornhill and the Isle of Wight. According to *The Hampshire Town and County Herald*, Hoy "with the munificence of a true patron of art employed Mr. Shayer until his rooms were almost covered with his works and thus gave this native artist the means and the heart to prosecute his toilsome way".

The artist's way became more 'toilsome' on the 29th June 1823, when his first wife, Sarah, died leaving five children. This must have been a particularly hard time for Shayer, for he was by no means an established artist, and to earn a living as a landscape painter and bring up a large family without the support of a mother cannot have been an easy task. *The Hampshire Town and County Herald*, in a later review of Shayer's work exhibited in 1827 wrote "His touch is firm and free, and light, his feeling for chiaroscuro good, and his distribution of lights generally happy.

He remarried sometime before 1825 when his son Henry Thring Shayer was born, the new wife and mother being Elizabeth Wallter, daughter of William Waller, landlord of '*The Duke's Head*', Putney. Shayer's living from this point appears to have gradually become more secure, his fortunes helped by the opening of the Society of British Artists—a gallery sympathetic to hanging the work of landscape painters. Shayer eventually achieved the remarkable total of 426 exhibited paintings in the major London galleries; 338 at the Society of British Artists, 6 at the Royal Academy and 82 at the British Institution.

Shayer was also helped by the opening in 1827 of *The Hampshire Picture Gallery* in the High Street of Southampton. The proprietor of the gallery was Henry Buchan, a significant figure in the history of Southampton who did much to

---

Leighton's Frescoe...
Continued from previous page

of four of them, a veiled figure nearest the Saviour, by her utter prostration and emaciated hands, testifies with eloquent suggestion her realization of the words of the sentinel angel immediately above here, "Too late! too late! ye cannot enter now."

The owl, emblem of sloth, the rent wall, and the broken tree are suggestive accessories to this portion of the composition, which, in its colouring and the guilt and terror characterizing the whole of the actors in the scene, forms a

contrast full of dramatic power with the well-nigh supernatural radiance and beauty of the figures in the corresponding portion of the fresco. At the extremity of this side "Ora," standing under a Gothic porch, corresponding to one at the opposite end, a figure full of grief, personifies Prayer, an angel above seemingly recording the sympathy thus expressed.

Of the design and execution of this splendid work little can be said in exaggeration, so intensely dramatic and impressive is it.

The Remarkable Shayer Family of Artists

(Three of William Shayer's sons, one by his first wife and two by his second, also were artists. None, however, attained the level of his father. New Forest scenes continued as a popular theme, especially with oil paintings executed jointly by Henry and Charles.)

The Other Shayers

William Joseph Shayer

William Joseph Shayer son of William Shayer was born at Chichester and baptized on 10th May 1811. He moved with his family to Southampton sometime before 1820.

Following in his father's footsteps he set out to be a professional painter, receiving tuition from his father, he was able to help William Snr., and later reached a standard that enabled him to paint on his own behalf. Attracted to animal painting, he developed a style reminiscent, but somehow more precise than his father's, lacking his decorative appeal and overall perfection.

William Joseph Shayer married Susannah, daughter of Joseph Slater, Architect of the theatre in Southampton and soon after decided to seek his fortune in London where he appeared to meet with some success, painting animal subjects, horse portraits and sporting pictures. He signs his works W.J. Shayer, those signed W. Shayer Jnr., are probably early works before his move to London.

In 1841 he exhibited an oil of greyhounds in the British Institute and in 1858 and 1885 sporting oils were shown in the Royal Academy.

There is no evidence that he ever again lived away from **Continued on next page**

A 1832 PAINTING BY WILLIAM SHAYER, SNR.
Shayer was fond of rural subjects. Although the locale of the above scene is not identified, it may be the New Forest.

William Shayer...

Continued from previous page encourage the arts in the area.

Shayer moved next door to Buchan's Gallery in the autumn of 1828 taking residence at 158 High Street (the Gallery was at number 159). He stayed in the High Street until about 1832–33 when he moved to number 10 Hanover Buildings. In 1842 he was registered as living at Nursling, but by 1843 he moved to Bladon Lodge in Shirley, where he remained until his death 36 years later. Shayer reputedly chose to live in Shirley because of the beautiful skies that are typically to be seen in that locality.

Sir Walter Gilbey in his *Animal Painters* states "Shayer's talent was recognised by his brother painters, some of whom, among them Sidney Cooper, urged him to come to London and take his place in the art world which they assured him was his. These invitations Shayer resolutely declined, he was content with his life, could sell his works as fast as he painted them, and preferred to go his own way."

Shayer's love of the countryside of the South Coast, which prevented his move to London, is clearly evident in his paintings. His reluctance to leave Hampshire for London may have enhanced the quality of his work, but it was certainly detrimental to his career, for his fame would have been far more widespread if he had not cut himself off from the publicity that London would have provided.

On the 9th March 1866 Shayer's second wife Elizabeth died. At this time the artist was beginning to suffer from a number of ailments, particularly gout, and sometime after 1871 he lost his sight. It says much for Shayer's strength of character that at a most advanced age he suffered for five long years from the acute pains of renal cholic, the result of stones in the kidney. Eventually his kidney became infected and he passed into a coma, which lasted for three days until finally on the 21st December 1879, at the age of 92½ years, he died. He was buried in the churchyard of St. James' Church, Shirley, where his grave can be seen today.

Shayer Family...

Continued from previous page
London for any length of time, but those oils signed W. and H. Shayer point to collaboration with his young half-brother Henry and were probably painted at Southampton.

W.J. Shayer died at Twickenham, Middlesex in 1892.

Henry Thring Shayer

Henry Thring Shayer, son of William Shayer by his second wife Elizabeth, was born in 1825 at Southampton.

Little is known of his life. He took to painting and for many years until his father's death resided with him at Shirley. Paintings signed Henry Shayer do not appear to exist, it is very possible that he helped his father, particularly with backgrounds of his paintings. There are quite a number of oils, mostly Forest views and ploughing scenes with figures, signed H. & C. Shayer and these are a result of his collaboration with his brother Charles. It can be assumed that Charles would paint the figures whilst Henry painted the landscape. These paintings are attractive in colour, style, and subject, with well painted figures and accessories in neat landscapes. There is a tendency for the greens to be rather towards the emerald compared with William Snr. There also exist oils similar to those signed H. & C. Shayer but signed W. & H. Shayer, indicating co-operation with perhaps Shayer Snr., but more likely W.J. Shayer could have been involved.

On his father's death Henry moved to Wandsworth with his brother where he died in 1894 aged 70.

Charles Shayer

Charles Shayer was born in 1826, son of William Shayer by his second marriage, painting became his profession, not marrying and living with his father in the family residence until moving to London after the death of his father in

Courtesy Short Family Collection

FREDERICK GOLDEN SHORT IN HIS LYNDHURST STUDIO

F. Golden Short— Forest Born and Bred

(He was) born in Lyndhurst in 1863. Both his father and mother were prominent local residents. J.G. Short was the local chemist and with his wife shared a great interest in photography, often exhibiting photographs of the Forest. Frederick received his education locally and then, showing an inclination towards art, was sent to Southampton Art School, which was founded in 1855.

His father was greatly interested in the New Forest and was often involved in illustrating, with his photo slides of local scenery, entertainments and lectures given in the vicinity, including Southampton and Bournemouth. The lantern slides, coloured by his son F. Golden Short, were much appreciated; later Frederick showed these slides himself at local functions to the accompaniment of poems, songs and piano music.

Loath to leave the Forest Area for long, Golden Short did visit London and the North of England during the late 80's and made several visits to Devon and Cornwall on painting trips. Sketches by him of views in the Mediterranean area exist, inferring a short trip abroad.

Living most of the time in Lyndhurst, knowing and loving the Forest in all its moods and seasons, Golden Short portrays the local scenery with a truth and understanding that has not been achieved by any other artist. His colour is fine and accurate and his handling of paint good. Those views away from the Forest and his occasional marine subjects are not perhaps as convincing.

1879.

Influenced greatly by the work of Shayer senior, he painted figures and cattle in landscape settings and the occasional sporting subject, he is responsible for many of those Shayer family paintings, which do not quite make the grade of William senior. Signing his pictures Charles Shayer his recognition has suffered a great deal from the unscrupulous, who have removed or altered his signature, hoping to pass off the work as that of his father. Those pictures signed H. & C. Shayer are a result of his collaboration with his brother Henry.

Charles Sayer exhibited one painting in Suffolk Street, London, in 1879. It can be assumed that most of his pictures were sold direct to interested dealers.

He died at Wandsworth aged 88 in 1914.

F. GOLDEN SHORT'S LYNDHURST COMMON AND CRICKET PITCH

Frederick Golden Short...

Continued from previous page

A member of the Southampton Art Society, he was on the committee and a constant exhibitor for many years, his works often attracting particular attention. He occasionally sent paintings to the Royal Academy and other London Exhibitions.

Frederick Golden Short gave lessons in painting and as an accomplished musician also instructed on the cello. For many years he was organist at the local Baptist Church. The original drawings illustrating "Autumn Leaves", a much acclaimed publication on the New Forest, were by this artist and were reproduced in the London Illustrated News of December 1881.

Golden Short died at Lyndhurst on July 29th 1936 having lived his life in the heart of the Forest and of those artists mentioned perhaps he is the one that reflects the glories of this area best. During his lifetime he saw the struggle to preserve the Forest meet with partial success and it is pleasant to think that perhaps his pictures have helped people to appreciate the most beautiful forest in England.

Southampton Art Gallery has several of his paintings.

BEECHES IN ALUM GREEN.   TWO SENTINEL TREES IN MARK ASH.

TWO VIGNETTES FROM *Autumnal Leaves* **BY SHORT**

A NEW FOREST SCENE BY F. GOLDEN SHORT

The New Forest Exhibition of 1875

> In 1875 the New Forest was threatened with extinction. The Deer Removal Act was already in force and the 1851 Enclosure Act allowed more open areas of the Forest to be enclosed for commercial production of timber.
>
> To draw national attention to the possibility that the New Forest was on the point of being wiped off the map, leading artists arranged a national exhibition of their works in London. National dailies and journals devoted space to the campaign to save the Forest. The result of this effort—largely sparked by the New Forest Exhibition of 1875—was the passage in 1877 of the New Forest Act, a measure which to this day incorporates safeguards for the preservation of the Forest.
>
> The background to the Exhibition is taken from the Hampshire Gallery's 1973 New Forest exhibition catalogue; the poem from *Punch* and quotations from other national periodicals are from the 1875 Exhibition catalogue.

Art Saves the Forest

Art has played its part in helping to preserve the New Forest, making people more aware of its beauty. This is best illustrated by the way local people organized an exhibition of paintings of the New Forest shown at Gallery 294, Regent Street, in order to bring to the attention of those in the Metropolis the beauties of the New Forest and to promote its preservation and use as a recreational area.

This exhibition in 1875 was part of a campaign in protest at the Deer Removal Act and The Enclosure Act of 1851, which allowed the enclosure of certain areas for the growth of timber which would, if allowed to continue, destroy the Forest with its open spaces and Commoners Grazing rights, eventually leading to the planting of timber in all suitable areas. After prolonged protest, Parliament passed "The New Forest Act" of 1877 which recognized the commoner's case, abolishing the ill defined and disputed "rolling power" of the Crown that had allowed extensive afforestation and re-establishing the ancient Court of Verderers to represent the commoners and protect their rights.

The exhibition lasted three months and was a great success. Artists such as Alfred Vickers, Alfred Parsons, Copley Fielding, W.L. Willie, Fred Hines and T.L. Rowbotham were represented by Forest views. Included in this exhibition were two local names, A.H. Davies with four paintings and John Emms with three. John Short, whose son (F. Golden Short) was later to become the Forest Artist, exhibited photographic views.

From *The Times* (April 21)

THE OLD NEW FOREST.—We hear rumours of a projected exhibition of works of landscape art illustrative of the scenery of the New Forest, to be opened in May next, under the auspices of the New Forest Defence Association. This scheme, which originates with a few public-spirited gentlemen, is set on foot with a view to making more widely known the varied and peculiar beauty of this delightful district, which, invaluable alike to all lovers of thoroughly English scenery and English art, is threatened with utter destruction by enclosure, by fir planting, and by the indiscriminate sale of old historic timber.

From the *Daily News*

FORESTS AND ENGLISH ART.—"A Landscape Painter" write to the *Daily News*:—"Having read in several papers that the New Forest, Hampshire, is in danger of being enclosed—for the benefit of a few and the loss of many—I must be forgiven for putting my pen to paper to deprecate, in the strongest terms, such an act. I am a landscape painter, and feel that its destruction would be the greatest loss to artists.

Standing as it does in its primitive state, it presents opportunities for the study of nature in perhaps her grandest and most picturesque forms. The elegance and stateliness of its trees—beech, birch, and oak—the lovely undergrowth, infinite in variety of line and tint, and the sombre, I had almost said the solemn tone which characterises it, makes this forest singularly improving and instructive to the artist. Nor should the opportunities it affords to sportsmen—the hunting, shooting, and fishing—be forgotten; nor the grand field it offers for study of entomology and ornithology. Really, if all our forests are to be done away with, what will become of dear old England? I beg to enclose my card, and if you can spare space for these few lines they may help to keep our New Forest as it is, with its many attractions, a thing of beauty and (I trust) of joy for ever. I have studied for forty years in most of the forests of England, including Dean and Sherwood Forests, and I have no hesitation in saying that these forests are as nothing in point of beauty to the New Forest."

From the *Standard*

THE NEW FOREST.
SIR,—The letter which you published some time ago in your valuable journal announcing an intended exhibition of works of art illustrating the scenery of the New Forest has been read by me with the liveliest satisfaction. There is no doubt whatever that this forest has a poetical original beauty which is without a rival not only in these islands but also on the Continent, and the artist may well be pardoned if on this subject he has perhaps a stronger feeling than even the politician and sanitarian. A selfish feeling in the first instance, it is true, for if a short-sighted and unstatesmanlike policy was to decide against the

THE INVITATION FOR THE 1875 NEW FOREST EXHIBITION
Never before, or since, has Britain been so united in trying to save the New Forest as in 1875 when a New Forest art exhibition was mounted during the summer in London. The official invitation depicted an ancient tree being cut down at the very moment an artist was painting it. The secretary, G.E. Briscoe Eyre, a Verderer, was perhaps the ablest defender the New Forest ever had.

The Committee request the honour of a visit from.................... and Friends to the

New Forest Exhibition

held at their Gallery; 294 Regent Street (nearly opposite the Polytechnic) during May, June, and July 1875

G. Morrison Esqr. Treasurer
G.E. Briscoe Eyre Esqr. Hon. Sect

Art Saves the Forest...

Continued from previous page
preservation of the forest, the artist would be the first loser, being deprived of one of the very few places in Great Britain and anywhere else, that are suitable for the study of forest beauty. But I am quite sure that in this question the whole nation will heartily side with the artist.

The Englishman, who always is the first to visit and to appreciate any spot abroad that may be famous for its romantic beauty, is sure not to allow this last specimen of virgin woodland in his own country to be swallowed up by a prosaic Commission for Woods and Forests. It is a well-known fact that not a few English artists of note considered the New Forest as their favourite resort for study and recreation, and also from abroad a number of painters of forest land-scapes are attracted every year by its unique scenery. I cannot better conclude my letter than by quoting the following sentence from the letter of a brother artist which I have just received; writing from a well-known spot in the Bavarian high forests, he says—"There are no trees to be found here like those in the New Forest."—Apologising for taking so much of your valuable space, I am, Sir, yours sincerely,

A FOREIGN ARTIST.

Strong Tradition of Art in the Forest

Although well known artists have long regarded the New Forest as a cornucopia for their works, foresters themselves—whether living in villages or on small-holdings—also have had an appreciation for art.

It was not uncommon to find in the humblest cottage a representation of a favourite sylvan scene, forest animals or plant life. The work may not have been of the highest quality, but it served to show that the forester possessed an inherent love of the beauty about him.

In the forest villages art societies have flourished for well over a century. Lyndhurst, the "capital" of the New Forest, probably has the area's longest continuous record of local exhibitions. The town, moreover, has nurtured artists who have gone on to make their names on the national and

New Forest
ART EXHIBITION

THE NEW FOREST HALL,
LYNDHURST.

FIFTH YEAR.

WILLIAM GERRARD, *Manager and Hon. Sec.*

SOUTHAMPTON:
PRINTED AND PUBLISHED BY H. KING, HANTS ADVERTISER CO., LIMITED.
MDCCCXCII.

Poem Printed by *PUNCH*, 27 March 1875

THE NEW FOREST.

"LORD HENRY JOHN MONTAGU-DOUGLAS-SCOTT on Tuesday evening, March 17, obtained a Select Committee to inquire into the enclosure of the New Forest."

PUNCH thanks you, scion of the bold BUCCLEUCH,
  Now, when you need of elbow-room is sorest,
For bearding the utilitarian crew
    Who'd cut up the New Forest.

O the long leagues of heath and sunny furze!
  O the great oak-trees, haunted by the squirrel!
The glades, delight of daily picnicers,
    Where RUFUS died by TYRELL!

There is no pleasant corner of those woods
  But breeds its legends plenteous as its throstles,
Which sing in summer hours sweet interludes,
    Amid the "Twelve Apostles."*

Who has not eaten rashers at the "Crown",
  And gone to Church by Faith's or Fine Art's urgin's,
To see the fresco, pride of Lyndhurst town,
    LEIGHTON'S ten lovely virgins?

Are there five wise ones anywhere about?—
  Will there be five wise men on this Committee,
Who'll make the Forest safe beyond a doubt?
    If not, the more's the pity.

'Tis not good wheat you grow on forest land,
  But health and joy, in wild walk, coppice briery,
And broad heath, on whose sky-line, grey and grand,
    Cuts stately Christchurch Priory.

If such delight be good for human brains,
  Why from the catalogue of pleasures strike it?
Let's leave to England, while the chance remains,
    One scene of *As You Like It*.

*Twelve oaks (of which about four or five now stand) which must have been old trees when WILLIAM RUFUS was killed.
  LEIGHTON'S fine altar-piece of the *Parable of the Virgins* is alone worth a trip to the Forest.

Strong Tradition of Art in the Forest...

Continued from previous page

international scene.

In 1892, for the fifth year in succession, a New Forest Art Exhibition was held in the town. Staged at the New Forest Hall, it was organised by William Gerrard. The catalogue, considered so prestigious as to be held by the British Library, contains 20 pages and lists 390 works. Forest scenes predominated, among them Beaulieu Mill, woodland views, Tyrrell's Ford, a view of Brook, a keeper's cottage, sunsets, seasonal scenes, and groups of old foresters. Sidney Pike displayed several paintings; Rose de Crespigny and Emily Short also exhibited. Prices ranged from one guinea to £42.

Persons Engaged in Literary or Professional Work

(In 1875, when Britain could point with pride to its vast number of literary giants and leaders in the sciences and arts, 128 of these eminent people signed a petition to save the New Forest from destruction and to preserve its ancient "parliament," the Court of Verderers. They declared:)

"(We) believe that (the) New Forest is in variety and beauty, unique as an open space," the petitioners, wrote. "To destroy such a district would, in the opinion of your Petitioners, be an act which no equivalent obtained in money or other material wealth, could render otherwise than one of reckless waste. No other tract has quite the same characteristics as the New Forest, and its destruction would be a permanent loss to the means of enjoyment and recreation of Her Majesty's subjects."

(Of the 128 men and women who signed the New Forest petition in 1875, 81 (or almost two-thirds) later were included in the Dictionary of National Biography. Among them were:

Robert Browning, T. Carlyle, John Ruskin, Jean Ingelow, Coventry Patmore, William Allingham, Julia Margaret Cameron, E.J. Stone, Herbert Spencer, J. Llewellyn Davies, Richard Quain, Warren De la Rue, Richard Garnett, Russell Martineau, W.M. Rossetti, Christiana G. Rossetti, A.C. Swinburne, Jos. D. Hooker, Dora Greenwell, James Bryce, A.P. Stanley, Moncure D. Conway, Margaret Gillies, Anna Swanwick, Elise C. Otté, Austin Dobson, Henry Morley, Annie Keary, Arthur J. Munby, Percy Gardner, A.S. Murray, Richard D. Blackmore, Richd. Owen, S.C. Hall, Anna Maria Hall, Edmund W. Gosse, M.A. Mackarness, Sidney Colvin, W.H. Corfield, Frederick Pollock, Charles A. Fyffe, and C. Kegan Paul.

Courtesy Winchester City Museums

**HEYWOOD SUMNER AT HIS HOME, CUCKOO HILL,
ABOUT 1928**

Heywood Sumner:
Artist and Archaeologist

(The brief biography of Heywood Sumner below is taken from the foreword of a catalogue for an exhibition of his work shown at Winchester, Cheltenham and Portsmouth in 1986; it was written by Elizabeth Lewis, curator of Winchester City Museums.)

Among the artists of the Arts and Crafts Movement *George Heywood Maunoir Sumner* (1853–1940) deserves to be better known.

Sumner was born in Alresford, Hampshire, into a family of Anglican clergy. He studied at Oxford and Lincoln's Inn, London, in company with his childhood friend W.A.S. Benson who later became a successful metalwork designer and whose sister, Agnes Benson, Sumner married in 1883.

His first publication *The Itchen Valley*, a collection of etchings, appeared in 1881 and he continued to publish illustrated books throughout his life. In each one the design of cover, illustrations, text and ornament were carefully integrated. A strong graphic line characterises all Heywood Sumner's mature work, whether it be a picture in a children's book, a cartoon for a sgraffito mural, a floral wallpaper pattern or even the drawn survey of an earthwork.

Starting by decorating the houses of his relatives, Sumner experimented with the current revival of the Italian art of sgraffito, a technique of incising designs in coloured plaster. Direct, bold and colourful, Sumner's narrative designs and ornamental patterns covered the walls of 11 Victorian churches and chapels in the British Isles; characteristically he also turned his hand to stained glass, mosaic, painted gesso and inlaid alabaster. Perhaps the most notable, and today the most complete, scheme is in the great church of All Saints at Ennismore Gardens in London (executed 1897–1903) where sgraffito, stained glass and tesserae all contribute to the rich interior. By contrast, Sumner brings the Welsh landscape indoors in his delightful murals in the little church at Llanfair Kilgeddin, between Abergavenny and Usk (1888). Two rare surviving pieces of furniture are also known, designed with his brother-in-law W.A.S. Benson, exquisitely incised and inlaid with coloured wax stopping.

By the 1890s Sumner was living in Kensington and in great demand as a designer, producing wallpapers for Jeffrey and Co, textiles for Alexander Morton and Co and 'improving' prints for schools and missions for The Fitzroy Picture Society. Works in all media were selected for international exhibitions from 1893–1914, at Antwerp, Brussels, Turin, St Louis, Ghent and Paris. Sumner was a founder-member of the London-based Arts & Crafts Exhibition Society and active in the Art Workers' Guild where he would sometimes entertain his fellow members, C.R. Ashbee, Walter Crane and W.R. Lethaby, with renderings of Hampshire folk songs. They called him 'The Shepherd'.

Yet in 1904 he put his busy career and his colleagues in London behind him and returned to Hampshire, moving his family into the new house he had

NEW FOREST VIEWS
Queen's Bower (above) and Bushy Bratley (left), as sketched by Heywood Sumner in the "Artists' Edition" of Wise's *The New Forest* (1883).

Heywood Sumner...

Continued from previous page designed and built at Cuckoo Hill, South Gorley, in the New Forest. Here he was able to devote himself to country interests. Many of his most lyrical water-colours date from this time, but he had also started systematically to record the natural and manmade landscape that surrounded him. *The Book of Gorley* was begun as a personal journal of his way of life, and includes anecdotes and illustrations of the people and history of the New Forest. It was published in 1910 by the Chiswick Press. There followed meticulous field studies of the ancient monuments in the region, encouraged by Sumner's archaeologist friends O.G.S. Crawford and J.P. Williams Freeman, both regular visitors to Cuckoo Hill. Exploratory walks with his five children and very long bicycle rides in

Trust Established for Artists and Craftsmen

With each passing decade Heywood Sumner grows in stature as artist and archaeologist, but most of all as one of the great authorities on the New Forest.

His *Book of Gorley* and *A Guide to the New Forest* are "musts" for anyone hoping to form a collection of New Forest references. Successful exhibitions of his art have been held at the Red House Museum in Christchurch and at Winchester, Cheltenham and Portsmouth.

A particularly happy event occurred in 1987 when the earliest version of his *Book of Gorley* was published in a full-colour, original manuscript edition by J.M. Dent. This was made possible by the generosity of L.J.C. Evans, great-nephew of Sumner, and other members of the Evans and Heywood families, in allowing use of original manuscript material.

A Heywood Sumner trust, devoted to charitable purposes in the field of arts, crafts, archaeology and church decoration, is to be established with royalties from sales of Dent's edition of the *Book of Gorley*. Readers wishing to find out more about this trust should contact L.J.C. Evans at Little Acre, Alderpark Meadow, Long Marston, Tring, Herts HP23 4RB.

Heywood Sumner...

Continued from previous page
search of ancient earthworks were daily activities for Sumner.

Heywood Sumner had turned to the excavation of archaeological sites at the age of 58, and did most of the digging single-handedly; he recorded and published some 13 different sites in about 20 years. He died in seclusion soon after the outbreak of war, in 1940, aged 87.

The Press

"THE PRESS" FROM *The Book of Gorley*
Sumner gives a detailed account of cider-making in *The Book of Gorley*, adding his own opinion that the "best cider is pure apple-juice, fermented, without any addition, and kept in a cask or drought." (Below) A scene from *The Book of Gorley*.

Greenford Bottom & Pinnick
H.S.

"BURLEY NEW COTTAGE," A WOOD-ENGRAVING BY MARY BERRIDGE

Courtesy Iris Worbey

MARY BERRIDGE IN THE NEW FOREST

Wood-cut Artist, Mary Berridge

The manpower shortage during the first world war brought the artist, Mary Berridge, to the New Forest as a member of the Women's Land Army. Her wood-cuts of the Forest were few and are rare today.

Originally from Redhill, Miss Berridge moved to Folkestone in 1914 and remained there until her death in 1963. Some of her woodcuts were reproduced in *The Studio* in 1917 and 1920. She exhibited a wood engraving of Salthouse, Norfolk, at the Royal Academy in 1933, and during 1933–1935 also exhibited at the Royal Scottish Academy and the Society of Women Artists.

Her use of the graphic line technique is reminiscent of the style of Heywood Sumner.

A COTTAGE NEAR HUBBARD'S HOME ON WOODGREEN COMMON

E. Hesketh Hubbard founded The Print Society, an international organisation of print makers and collectors, and looked after the society's affairs from his home on Woodgreen Common, on the edge of the New Forest. He wrote several definitive works on prints, including *On Collecting and Storing Etchings*, and also was a member of the Institute of Oil Painters. His most productive period was the decade immediately following the first World War.

Allen Seaby, Popular Author and Artist

Allen William Seaby (1887–1953) was born in London, but spent most of his life in Reading where he studied art and later become Professor of Art at Reading University.

He combined his twin interests, nature and art, to produce several works that became classics of their time. His *Birds of the Air* (Black, 1931) and *British Ponies: Running Wild and Ridden* (Black, 1936) were widely acclaimed. The latter work includes 32 pages on New Forest ponies with 26 pen-and-ink or pencil drawings. Another, earlier reference was *The British Bird Book* (T.C. & E.C. Jack, London and Edinburgh, 4 vols., 1911–13). From 1921 to 1931 he also produced four standard references for students of art.

His last published works (he was then 85) were illustrations for two Ladybird books in Brian Vesey-Fitzgerald's *British Birds and Their Nests* and *A Second Book of British Birds* (William Hepworth, 1954).

For many years Allen Seaby brought his family to the New Forest for summer holidays. Here he learned first-hand about the New Forest pony which was to feature in several of his children's books. The most popular, *Skewbald: the New Forest Pony* (Black, 1923), was followed by a sequel, *Sons of Skewbald* (Black, 1937). Two other works had New Forest settings: *The White Buck* (Nelson, 1939) and *Purkess, the Charcoal Burner* (Harrap, 1946). In the extract below from *British Ponies: Running Wild and Ridden*, Seaby describes the "catching-in" of a pony.

"Catching in" A Pony

It was during a camping holiday in the New Forest that I first became interested in stud-bred ponies, that is, those born and bred in a free state. Here, they were all around me. At dawn, I might be awakened by the sound of their munching close by my sleeping place. My open tent door faced the east, and early one morning, as the level rays of the rising sun fell on my face, I opened my eyes to see a little way off a mare and her foal, haloed in rosy light.

The ponies came so close and seemed so tame, that I believed them to be as domesticated as the cows turned out into the Forest from the little farm from whence we got our milk, although I could admire the way they harmonized with the landscape, whereas the cows looked, to my mind, somewhat out of place. But when the farmer rode one evening on the moor with his young daughter to "catch in" a pony, my eyes opened.

These creatures placidly brows-

ALLEN W. SEABY

ing on a stretch of open land before me suddenly turned into wild animals. The "hunters", mounted on ponies as rough looking as those they pursued, wanted to "cut out" a three-year old from the herd, and drive him off the Forest into the farmyard. The ponies, realizing the situation, raced away, mares calling to their foals, manes and tails waving, hoofs thudding—all the peacefulness of the scene suddenly dis-

sipated by sound and movement. The fleeing ponies rapidly diminished in size to mere specks and disappeared.

They must have been turned, for almost immediately they galloped back, the riders at their heels, shouting, waving, and wheeling their mounts, when a breakaway threatened. The ridden ponies entered with zest into the spirit of the chase. They anticipated the course taken by the hunted ponies and, when the ground admitted, went straight for their objective. More than once a rider had to flatten against his or her pony's neck to avoid being scraped off by an overhanging branch.

It was a beautiful evening; the sun still guilded the near hilltops; the stretch below, in cool shade, gave plenty of space for the hunt to move in. ... I now looked on the Forest ponies with more understanding eyes. Creatures which had to be hunted like this could hardly be described as tame, even if classed as domesticated.

Childhood Days in the Forest

(Wilfred, son of Allen Seaby and the first director of Belfast's Ulster Museum (1962–1971), recalls how the Seaby family came to know and love the New Forest.)

It was C.I. Evans—for many years Headmaster of Leighton Park School, Reading, who introduced my father to the New Forest Ponies.

This is likely to have been about the time of the First World War, for it was in 1918 that he took the family camping in the New Forest for the summer holidays. The first camp proved disastrous for it rained from the time we pitched our tent at a farm near Beaulieu Road station until we woke up the next morning.

This was the first experience

Childhood Days
in the Forest...

Continued from previous page
that mother had had of camping,
and with the nervous worry of it
all and fearing we should all go
down with pneumonia, she had
one of her sick headaches, and
begged father to pack up and
move to a boarding house. This
we did and spent the rest of the
holiday at Lymington. We tried
again, however, in the lovely
summer of 1919 at the same site in
the Forest and father was able to
cycle around and sketch the ponies
and scenery for his first pony story,
Skewbald, which was published by
Black in 1923.

Father eventually decided the
family should have a more permanent holiday base in the New
Forest, so in 1928 he bought a
small triangle of land adjoining St.
John's Road at Wootton, and
there built a wooden hut which
could be used at various times of
the year for holidays. He and my
mother would go there with various members of the family, some
sleeping in the main hut and
others in an annex hut or in tents.
Many are the walks we have taken
together on the commons, along
the streams, and through the
inclosures—father with his sketch
book often stopping to draw
groups of ponies or a particular
feature in the Forest itself. We also
attended some of the pony shows,
such as that at Burley; here father
was in his element and would ask a
girl on her mount to pose for him
while he did a quick sketch.

A DIGNIFIED AGISTER, CHARLES EVEMY
The artist and author, Allen W. Seaby, sketched this impression
of the Agister on one of the many visits the Seaby family made to
the New Forest. Evemy's service extended from the 1880s to the
age of the motor car.

**LYNDHURST-BROCKENHURST
ROAD**   (From *Autumnal Leaves*, 1881)

The Story of A Remarkable Embroidery

(Belinda Lady Montagu, who designed and executed the New Forest 900th Anniversary Embroidery in 1979, is a tireless advocate and teacher of the craft of embroidery.

After fine arts training at London's Byam Shaw School of Art and the Central School of Arts and Crafts, she took the City and Guilds certificates in embroidery at the Southampton College of Art. Her subsequent experience included teaching embroidery on a world cruise of the Queen Elizabeth II; producing presentation cushions for the Queen, HRH the Prince of Wales and the Queen Mother; and ecclesiastical embroidery for Salisbury Cathedral and St. Luke's Garrison Church at Soest, Normandy (a frontal to commemorate the 1944 landing by the 3rd Division).

In 1986 Batford's published her book, *Group Work in Embroidery.* She has been to Bali twice to assist women and girls in developing a local cottage embroidery industry. In 1986 she completed a feasibility study of the project and in 1988 returned to establish an embroidery studio and train a manager and 20 girls in canvas-work techniques.

"History Embroidered," reproduced below, appeared in the Summer, 1980 issue of *Esso Magazine.* In it Hugh Popham tells how the original idea grew into reality with eighty volunteer embroiderers contributing to the project under Lady Montagu's guidance.)

LADY MONTAGU WORKING ON THE EMBROIDERY

THE NEW FOREST'S nine centuries of recorded history have a tapestried quality, as if within its boundaries time itself had been slowed down. Kings and courtiers gallop through the coverts, and the stags scatter; one disreputable king dies in mysterious' circumstances; another, hardly less disreputable, makes a royal visitation, bearing gifts; a well-loved queen plants a commemorative oak. Except by the harsh laws of their ancient privilege, the comings and goings of these grandees barely touch the frieze of common folk who, against the backcloth of the woodland, eke out their narrow lives and fight for their own ancient common rights, of pannage, turbary, fuelwood and marl. The towns and cities of this corner of Hampshire lie beyond the forest's edge, the so-called perambulation, villages are few and scattered; the characteristic dwelling is a cottage backing on the wilderness through which creep and run and fly and slide the forest's smaller inhabitants, hedgehog and adder, badger and fox, smooth snake and toad, innumerable birds, and butterflies as bright as they are rare. Like all idylls, since this one, too, is only the frame of human lives, the forest has its darker aspect.

The great oaks are felled for ships of war; the soil, much of it, is poor; and the penalties for infringing the forest law, the king's law, are death or mutilation. The forest has its martyrs, as it had its mysteries, its wise women, its verderers and agisters. And, like its laws and customs, even the vocabulary of the forest has a living ancientness, handed down from the older England, before the coming of the motor car and the caravan and the continental frame tent. Along its southern frontier lies the sea, to which, from

A PANEL FROM THE EMBROIDERY
In the centre is the Rufus Stone, while at the right is Mary Dore, a celebrated witch who lived at Beaulieu in the 18th century. Beside her is a cat, symbolic of Mary's alleged power to turn herself into a cat at will.

New Forest Embroidery...

Continued from previous page
Buckler's Hard, the *Agamemnon* (64 guns), the *Swiftsure* (74 guns) and the *Euryalus* (36 guns) sailed to fight the French; from which came, via Barton Cliff or Hengistbury Head, the smugglers with their silks and taffetas, their brandy-kegs and spices; from which come today the swarms of pleasure craft. In a little less than a thousand years, the New Forest has come full circle, from being the playground of the Court to being the playground of the multitude.

To Maldwin Drummond, sailor, landowner, environmentalist, elected Verderer and President of the New Forest Association, the 900th anniversary of the forest's establishment as a royal hunting preservee seemed worthy of something more durable than, say, a fireworks display, a television documentary (though it got that too), or a feast; and thinking about this odd, anachronistic corner of England, he came to the conclusion that, indeed, a tapestry might be the answer. The Association agreed, and a sub-committee was formed to see it done.

By chance there lives in the forest an artist, Belinda Montagu, trained and skilled in the arts of embroidery, and she was commissioned to design the tapestry and, with outside help, transform her design into reality. The forest has, also, its historians, its naturalists and foresters, with their accurate first-hand knowledge; and, along its eastern border, a number of major companies—Esso among them—who were prepared to contribute to the cost. They are, after all, the modern inheritors of the forest's former trades, charcoal-burning, pottery, shipbuilding.

For the artist, the commission was a challenging one, for the finished work had, ideally, to resolve a number of conflicting demands. it must be contemporary in style, and yet be true to the legendary element of the forest's history; it must be both represen-tational—for the trees and flowers, the birds and insects, would have to satisfy the critical eyes of foresters and botanists, ornithologists and entomologists, not to mention her technical adviser on such subjects, the naturalist Colin Tubbs—and, at the same time for an artistic unity that would be greater than the sum of its parts. It was to be quite large—25 feet long by just over 2 feet deep—and there was a great deal to be included in it. Belinda had never tackled anything so complicated before, and the trickiest questions of scale, of historical accuracy, of placing and of colour, had to be satisfactorily answered. For, finally, in order to fulfil its purpose, which was essentially celebratory, public, theatrical, it had to bold enough to strike the beholder's eye at a distance before drawing it in to the detail. Above all, it must be fun.

First came a series of rough sketches; then a cartoon, full-size, on which she could juggle the various themes and motifs of the design. She took as the armature, as it were, the forest trees, a screen of oak and beech and pine to run the whole length of the picture, and the changing seasons, starting with high summer on the left and working through the year to summer again on the extreme right. Marching with them—but not always precisely where they should be: that is the artist's licence—are the historical events and places; the death of William Rufus; the presentation to the Cistercian monks of a model of Beaulieu Abbey by King John; the coming of the railways, and so forth, to the planting of the oak sapling by Queen Elizabeth II. These fulfil the design's obligations to what might be termed 'hard history', the facts and dates of the textbooks. But there are other figures too: Gerald Lascelles, the 19th century's great Deputy Surveyor, Brusher Mills, the last of the snake-catchers; and Mary Dore, the witch, with her grimalkin. Here is Perkin Warbeck, who sought sanctuary in the abbey, in his golden cloak; and Lewis Carroll's Alice (Hargreaves, née Liddell), who is

> *"An article in the local paper mentioned that volunteers were needed to help with the work, and the response was remarkable. It was if half the population of the Forest consisted of embroiderers in search of an artist."*

Forest Embroidery...

Continued from previous page
buried in Lyndhurst Churchyard. Most various and delightful of all, in and out of the undergrowth that borders the foreground, go the forest's lesser denizens, the deer and the ponies, the rabbits and hedgehogs; and among the branches of the trees the birds, not forgetting such special inhabitants of the forest as the Dartford warbler and the honey buzzard. Even, faintly on the horizon, may be discerned Fawley's private forest of chimneys, and, more faintly still, the pylons which carry electricity from Calshot power station.

Once the design was completed, there remained the question of turning it into its proper form, an 'embroidered wall-hanging'. Although it is loosely referred to as a 'tapestry', technically this is not one. In a tapestry the design is woven into the cloth: this, on the other hand, is what embroiderers call 'canvas work', in which the picture is created by stitching on a canvas backing. Only in this case Belinda has used collage as well, so it is truly a mélange of two slightly different techniques. Call it 'embroidered'; that decorative word suits it admirably.

But no one embroiderer, however nimble-fingered, could hope to produce such a major work in the time; and how it was achieved is a story on its own. An article in the local paper on the subject mentioned that volunteers were needed to help with the work, and

the response was remarkable: it was as if half the population of the forest consisted of embroiderers in search of an artist. Belinda was inundated with offers of help from people, none of whom were to be paid, and of whose skill she had no knowledge. The latter was a risk that had to be accepted.

And it worked. It worked, indeed, on two separate levels, for it not only produced the finished work of art on time, but generated an interest and enthusiasm locally which no *fait accompli*, however magnificent, could have done. In the final count, eighty-five people, two of them men, had a share in it, and displayed for the most part, exemplary skill.

The design was ready, the outworkers were eager. The main task now was to allocate to each of them some part of the picture, draw it on canvas, provide the appropriate materials—to make up, in short, dozens and dozens of individual 'kits'—post them off, and wait, heart in mouth, for the results. Belinda herself undertook all the figures, and the tremendous labour of sewing all the finished fragments together into a triptych of three seamless, unified panels. Her workroom became a cross between a studio, a rag merchant's den and sweatshop.

Gradually, like a gigantic jigsaw puzzle, the picture began to grow, in all its gaiety and vigour. The first panel of the three—an added complication was that it had to be designed thus, to fit between the windows in the Verderers' Hall—was completed in April; all three were ready for the unveiling in

December. Present at the ceremony were all the members of the scattered team which had worked on it, able to see for the first time how their own contributions fitted into the whole. There was one irony. During the preceding months the Verderers' Hall had been found to be on the verge of collapse, and had had to be closed for major repairs; so, for the time being, the tapestry is on display in the local council chamber at Lyndhurst, and has been on show at the community centre and various country shows in the forest.

> **The New Forest Embroidery is now permanently sited at the New Forest Museum and Visitor Centre in Lyndhurst.**

Everywhere it has aroused intense enthusiasm, which is gratifying to those involved, but not at all surprising. After the initial impact of the whole design from a distance, the colour and vitality of it, a closer inspection reveals the myriad details. "People spend twenty minutes or half-an-hour studying it", Belinda says in some awe.

Such close and pleasurable scrutiny from all manner of different people attests the work's success. It has a sort of magic. And truly it celebrates in a unique and delightful way, the ancient magic of the forest.

One endearing touch is worth a final mention. The work is unsigned; but the observant may notice, towards the extreme right of the right-hand panel, a rider on a grey horse with two whippet hounds at heel. They depict Belinda herself on the horse on which, for many seasons, she used to hunt, and the two dogs, one black, one white, which she still has.

(A booklet reproducing the whole of the New Forest Embroidery with accompanying explanation, is available from The Secretary, New Forest Association, Rockford End, Ringwood, Hants BH24 3ND, at a nominal charge, plus postage.)

> *"It has a kind of magic. And truly it celebrates in a unique and delightful way, the ancient magic of the Forest."*

Memorial at Bolderwood Honours Forestry Commission Chairman

The Making of the Radnor Stone

"Since William the Conqueror first claimed the area for the Crown, the Forest's picturesque glades and extensive heaths have been regarded as a national rather than as a regional possession," wrote William Pleydell-Bouverie, the 7th Earl of Radnor in 1960.

Lord Radnor at that time was Chairman of the Forestry Commission; four years later he was appointed Official Verderer of the New Forest. Ill health forced his resignation in 1966.

To honour the memory of Lord Radnor the Forestry Commission decided to erect a memorial at Bolderwood. The task of obtaining a suitable stone, designing and executing it, was given to Raymond Hoare and his family firm, W.A. Hoare, Ltd., of Bournemouth.

Ray was educated at Bournemouth Grammar School and the town's College of Art, where he studied lettering and carving. He first planned a career with the Indian Army, but Partition in 1947 ended that dream. He therefore joined the family business where he has since been concerned with design and production. Over the years he has executed countless memorials, coats of arms and plaques. One commission that gave him particular pleasure was designing two de Rothschild family memorials in the private burial ground at Exbury, and another to the memory of Lionel de Rothschild. In recent years there have been commissions to honour heroes of the Falklands War and the "Cockleshell Heroes" at the Royal Marines establishment at Hamworthy.

In the account below Ray describes the difficulty of finding a stone suited to the New Forest environment, and how the Radnor Stone design was developed.

Forest Subjects

Although the original idea was for a simple, repetitive motif of leaves or flowers down the sides, it became clear that Lady Radnor had a preference for specific Forest subjects to be incorporated in the carvings. Much research went into this, resulting in quite accurate representations of Forest flora and fauna based on a Forestry Commission publication. I believe there are 31 species portrayed. The stone was erected in 1970. The work took about six months

RAY HOARE
Planning the Radnor Stone involved consideration of the damp Forest climate.

Choosing the Design

After the Forestry Commission commissioned the work, I presented designs to them for selection by the Dowager Countess of Radnor. She chose a sketch of a simple rectangular stone with foliage carving on the sides. The Commission then put me in direct contact with her. With her very considerable help, the final design emerged.

I selected Westmorland Green Slate because there is really no local indigenous material which would be suitable amongst the Douglas firs of Bolderwood. Purbeck stone, which I often use, would soon be covered in algae and suffer from dripping moisture

and lack of light.

Carving Problems

The front and back were natural siren surfaces which presented a problem for the letter-cutter who was obliged to look for the shape of the letter and the bottom of the "v" cut. Provided the chisel is left at the correct angle, it does not matter that the width at the top of the "v" varies.

In keeping with the verticality of the design, the letters were greatly compressed and rather freely drawn to give a rhythmic pattern over the whole of the face, except for the Radnor coat of arms—all of which was incised, "v" cut, in a smooth sunken panel at the top right.

to complete, including the several design stages, obtaining the stone, and completing the drawings.

I sometimes wonder if my work on the Radnor Stone influenced me to move from Bournemouth to the edge of the Forest some three years after the memorial was erected. I walk the Forest frequently and love it dearly. In semi-retirement (whilst remaining the firm's chief designer) I hope to spend even more time getting to know it more intimately.

THE RADNOR STONE AT BOLDERWOOD
Carved in Westmorland Green Slate, the stone is able to withstand all kinds of weather. It is only a short distance from the Bolderwood car park.

FROM SIDE PANELS
(Above and right)
Familiar Forest flora and fauna specimens adorn the sides of the stone.

It was Lady Radnor's wish that a considerable range of Forest subjects should be incorporated into the design of the stone.

A New Forest Sculptor: Geoffrey Dashwood

When you consider the delightful cluster of sporting artefacts, pictures, sculptures and other collectibles with which the sportsman delights in filling his study or gunroom, we tend to forget that there is a long, rich and fascinating tradition of sporting art in Britain and France.

The British contribution has come principally in the form of paintings, with the masterpieces of artists such as Stubbs, Thorburn, Lodge, Rickman and Harrison pre-eminent. Few continental artists have managed to achieve quite the same consistent excellence on canvas and paper.

Europe remains the home of the mainstream tradition of sporting and wildlife sculpture, however, the best known of which are the celebrated *animalier*-type bronze sculptures from the workshops and foundries of France, Belgium and Germany, depicting sporting and equestrian scenes.

There is something very special about a really inspired sculpture of a favourite animal or bird, sensitively sculpted and finely cast in bronze, a metal which lends itself especially well to creating a rich and evocative texture, colour and patination.

All the best sporting art stems from a special artistic talent allied to a deep and close affinity with the creatures, their ways and the world of traditional country sports.

Geoffrey Dashwood is one such. A sportsman, an expert field naturalist and an eminent sculptor of British wildlife and game species, he lives in a cottage on the north-west fringe of Hampshire's New Forest.

There, in a bright, naturally-lit upstairs studio, he sculpts the birds and animals he has seen around him and which he has lived among, sketched, painted and sculpted since boyhood, when at the age of 15 he won a place at the Southampton College of Art.

Geoffrey Dashwood's artistic training and studies have always

Bryan Alexander

DASHWOOD IN HIS GODSHILL STUDIO

National and international recognition has come early for Geoffrey Dashwood, a Godshill sculptor who models in clay or wax, and casts mainly in bronze. Born in 1947, he won a place of merit to study fine art at the Southampton College of Art at the age of 15.

For five years he was an assistant keeper in the New Forest, but when his works of art—undertaken on a freelance basis—attracted the attention of experts, he abandoned "keepering."

Dashwood exhibits annually at the Society of Wild Life Artists and the Royal Society of Miniaturists, and his works are also on view at London's Tryon, Sladmore and Malcolm Inness galleries, as well as in the fine arts departments of Harrods, Garrard, and Asprey. His mallard drake bronze won the 1986 Henry-Brett Award for the best wildlife sculpture at the Society of Wildlife Artists' exhibition. Sculptures by Dashwood have been exhibited in France, Germany and the United States, as well as at many public galleries in the United Kingdom.

Colin McKelvie, writing in the Summer, 1987 issue of *Shooting Life*, assesses Dashwood's work.

gone hand in hand with his practical enthusiasm for the study of wildlife and his active participation in country sports.

He became a member of the New Forest wildlife staff, with a particular interest in deer, which he has studied, photographed and stalked in the Forest for many years.

Among his recent limited edition bronzes are fine studies of a fallow buck at the gallop, a delicate roebuck pausing to scent the air and a dramatic, life-size sculpture of the head of a six-pointer

buck.

Having become a freelance artist specialising in wildlife work, Geoffrey undertook a variety of illustration and design commissions for the Forestry Commission. Hampshire County Council, The Nature Conservancy Council and The Game Conservancy.

In 1982, however, he was drawn towards a specialisation in sculpture, which he now prefers to painting and drawing.

Painstaking modelling in clay and wax is a prelude to the skilful casting in bronze of each

MALLARD DRAKE

Sladmore Gallery

Dashwood...

Continued from previous page
individual sculpture, for which Geoffrey uses the services of a small and dedicated family firm that produces castings to the most exacting standards.

A member of the Society of Wildlife Artists and an associate of the Royal Society of Miniaturists, Geoffrey exhibits regularly with the leading London galleries, including *animalier* bronzes, as well as working on special commission for the fine art departments of Asprey's, Garrard's and Harrods.

Provincial galleries in England and Scotland have also exhibited his work, and his bronzes were on display in France in 1985 and in Germany last year.

As the sportsman and the naturalist grow more skilled and knowledgeable, so the sculptor also develops his work in new directions, modifying his approach as he experiments with new styles and techniques.

For Geoffrey Dashwood this has meant a gradual move away from the smaller *animalier*-style bronzes, with their sober, traditional tones of burnished bronzes and predominantly russet tints, towards a series of life-sized sculptures of gamebirds and water-fowl.

While still cast in bronze, these large and dramatic pieces reveal a new and bolder play of subtle, natural colours and a special patination which is an unusual and exciting departure from the more familiar and conventional style.

Geoffrey's work finds its way into several prestige London galleries. It is on permanent display at the Sladmore Gallery in Bruton Place, where they gave him his first one-man exhibition in November, 1987.

Individual commissions from enthusiasts and collectors made up a large proportion of his work too, and he has sculpted special pieces for collectors in Europe, the Middle East, Australia and the U.S.A.

At the age of 40, Geoffrey Dashwood is one of a handful of Britain's young wildlife artists, who, though successful and well-established, are still experimenting with new techniques and exploring fresh areas of their craft.

The eagerness of discriminating collectors in Britain and abroad to acquire his work and commission new, exclusive items is testimony to his success.

GEOFFREY DASHWOOD WITH COCK PHEASANT

(Bryan Alexander)

EXAMPLES OF GEOFFREY DASHWOOD'S WORK
(Counter-clockwise)
(Top right) English (grey) partridge
(Top left) Cock pheasant
(Left) Kingfisher
(Bottom left) Woodcock
(Bottom right) Roe buck
(*Photographs: The Sladmore Gallery*)

Frank Whittington, the Gentle Toy-Maker

Frank Whittington (1876–1973), whose New Forest Toys Brockenhurst factory brought him world acclaim for more than two decades, was an artist in the broadest sense of the word.

While his woodcarvings gained favour with the Royal Family and were admired on both sides of the Atlantic, Whittington was gifted in other fields. He was fond of playing the cello and loved sport—especially tennis. He was Secretary of the New Forest Lawn Tennis Club (1920–1924) and a keen player well into his 70s. A devout Christian, he attended St. Saviour's Church, Brockenhurst, where he also was a church-warden.

These interests sometimes were merged into a work of art as, for example, when he once carved a trio, "The Musicians," showing Bertram Lewis, violin; Samuel Clifford, cello; and Edie Marr, piano, playing their instruments. Earlier Whittington had quietly sketched the group as they performed in a subscription concert at the Balmer Lawn Hotel before the Second World War. The woodcarving is now held by the Russell-Cotes Museum in Bournemouth. When Frank Whittington went to play the cello with friends, he strapped the instrument to a home-made frame on his bicycle, donned his trousers with clips, and pedalled away.

He was best known, however, for his toy woodcarvings. After working in a munitions factory during the First World War he came to Brockenhurst and began making toys on a small scale in his home. The public responded immediately and in 1922 he was obliged to set up a small factory which eventually employed about 16 men and women. In the account which follows Basil O'Donnell—who worked many years for Frank Whittington—tells how the toys were made and of the fame they achieved.

My father was partly responsible for Frank Whittington coming to Brockenhurst. Originally from Reigate, Mr. Whittington worked at a factory near Redbridge (Southampton) making ammunition boxes during the first world war. There he got to talking with my father, who was also working in the factory, and he must have liked the sound of Brockenhurst, for he came there after the war.

Both Mr. and Mrs. Whittington were artists. Mrs. Whittington went by her professional name, Marjorie Hood, and she did both paintings and commercial art. Some of the advertising artwork that once decorated our railway carriages was done by her. Mr. Whittington's artistic gift lay mostly with sculpturing in wood.

Once he made a horse for the famous actress, Elizabeth Bergner. It must have cost hundreds of pounds, for a huge amount of time and material went into it. I'll never forget the day it left the old goods yard at Brockenhurst station. It was heavily wrapped in corrugated card-board and brown paper, but even then it still looked very much like a real horse—about the size of a foal.

Dogs Were Popular

When people heard about Mr. Whittington's work, they would come to him and ask for carvings of their dogs. It was no good their bringing the dogs to the studio, so he had to work from photographs.

I suppose I was about 16 when I first started working at the toy factory. That would have been about 1925. At first my job was to get up early in the morning and fill the coal scuttles and clean the shoes. Considering all the wood and sawdust lying around, we were lucky that we never had a fire. But then Mr. Whittington wouldn't allow smoking on the premises. If anyone had to have a smoke, they went outside.

Later on I worked on almost all the equipment in the factory and became a kind of mass-producing woodcarver. That was because the toys were made in sections: the head, body and tail in one piece, and the legs stuck on the sides. All the toys were made to scale, and so were valuable for educational purposes.

Mr. Whittington always took a new man in hand and went right

GIRLS PAINTING TOYS AT WHITTINGTON'S BROCKENHURST FACTORY
Allen Seaby, artist and author of several New Forest books, visited Frank Whittington's workshop in the 1920s and sketched this view of girls putting the final touch to animal woodcarvings.

Whittington ...

Continued from previous page
through the whole procedure with him—even showing him how to grind his chisel and how much edge to leave on. Once the new man was instructed, he was left to work on his own.

In the Workshop

Although Mr. Whittington made a modest start with the toy-making business, he soon had to provide more space and take on more help. At our peak I suppose we must have had about 13 men and boys turning out the rough toys and three girls painting them.

In the workshop we used deal wood (pine or fir) imported from North America by Howard's, a Southampton timber firm. We bought long, pre-cut boards and from one board we could make hundreds of toys. Deal wood is soft and easy to cut. The most important piece of equipment was a big jig-saw capable of cutting five to six inches of wood. First we would stamp out the animals—section by section— from patterns made of linoleum. Some of those old linoleum patterns, by the way, are still around Brockenhurst.

The jig-saw was powered by an old Petter engine kept in the engine house just outside the workshop. It was made in Yeovil and was very reliable. Just occasionally it "struggled" a bit under the workload and we would have to have a mechanic out, but in the main it was easy to operate and dependable.

Step-by-Step

Once the individual pieces of an animal were cut out on the jig-saw, they were planed smooth. We had to take great care in squaring off the insides of the legs so they could be glued properly. With a horse, for example, the head and the tail could be one piece, with the legs added. Horses could come in all sorts of positions—sitting, lying down, kneeling. With a fox, he could be standing or running.

We used only one kind of glue, a special one for wood that came

WHITTINGTON AT WORK ON HIS "MENAGERIE"
Besides New Forest animals, Whittington's factory produced Noah's Arks complete with a wide range of animals and birds. His frequent visits to the London Zoo and the Natural History Museum enabled Whittington to turn out carvings of authentic appearance and proportions. At one time his Brockenhurst factory made over 60 breeds of dogs.

from Scotland. It came in great big chunks. The old burner was going all the time with the glue pot on it. This glue was fast-setting, although as a rule we would let the toys stand overnight.

The girls did the painting. If we were doing an animal—say an elephant—in grey, they would dip the entire animal in a big dish of grey paint, and do the touching up afterwards on the eyes, the tusks, and so on. The zebra was tricky to paint. After putting it into the paint bath for the background colour, the girls had to add all the stripes by hand, one at the time. Sometimes Mr. Whittington used to go and help the girls, for he was the artist. He was so fast he could

turn out toys about three to the girls' one.

Queen Mary's Patronage

Once we expanded into the additional shed and took on more people our production rate went up. In the end we were selling to Harrods, Selfridges, and other big London shops. But it was the British Industries Fairs that gave Mr. Whittington his biggest boost. These fairs were held regularly before the second world war and were great opportunities for small industries to show off their wares. Mr. Whittington decided to exhibit one of Noah's Arks with all the animals in it.

Whittington ...

Continued from previous page

Outside the door of the Ark was a little thread of fine wire—virtually invisible—with a dove on it. The Prince of Wales was at this particular fair with his mother, Queen Mary. Much to the Queen's annoyance, the Prince kept breaking away from the royal party. At last, she went to find him and there he was, gazing at the Noah's Ark. She ordered two dozen of the Arks on the spot, and of course, that made us. This got into all the papers—the *Evening Standard*, the *Evening News* and others.

After that we had almost more visitors to Brockenhurst than we could cope with. Sometimes we had a job to work, so many people were crowding round. Orders poured in from everywhere. There were far more visitors to Brockenhurst in those days than now. We had Europeans, Americans, Chinese, Japanese and others. Many arrived in England on the great ocean liners at Southampton and within minutes they would be on their way to the New Forest and our Brockenhurst factory by coach. No admission fees were charged, for the visitors almost always bought toys.

NEW FOREST ANIMALS BY WHITTINGTON

Other Woodcarvings

We did other carvings besides animals. For example, there were nice little milk-maids with their pails. We had to use a special little lathe to turn out the pails. Afterwards we would glue them on top of the maids' heads. We also did old stage-coaches. The had real wheels which we would get from Armfields in Ringwood. They were cast there and came ready to be added to the coaches. The coaches also had tiny little chains—all done to scale. Most people would buy a team of horses to go with the stage-coaches.

My pay as a wood-carver, after deductions, was £3.5.10 for a 40-hour week. That was a fair wage, considering how cheap the toys were—sixpence or a shilling each in most cases. Of course the toys would have cost much more if they had not been mass-produced and assembled. But we did make some carvings from a single piece of wood. Mr. Whittington kept a book listing all the specially ordered pieces he made and there were lots of well known people in it.

He made nativity sets for several churches in the area. One was for St. Saviour's here in Brockenhurst; it still comes out every Christmas. He also made replicas of the old timber carts— just like the real thing, except on a small scale. Outside the workshop he had a showcase with examples of the carvings we made. When all these things were being made, Plumleys the Carriers would come almost everyday to the shop and take away a load of toys for Brockenhurst station from which they would be shipped to London and other places.

World War II

With the outbreak of the second world war the North American deal became impossible to get.

WOOD-CARVINGS CAPTURE A BYGONE ERA
The romantic period of the stage coach is represented in this tableau created by Frank Whittington. It shows a West Country coach with its team of horses drawn up in front of the George Hotel, a noted Axminster hostelry. Whittington made the entire "living picture", including the hotel facade and the villagers gathering to meet the coach. This was a departure from his usual work, which consisted mainly of animals.

Making Farm Carts from New Forest Trees

For almost a century New Forest Commoners in the eastern half of the Forest came to equate the name of Diamond with the finest in farm carts and waggons.

The original business was founded by Jacob Diamond in Lymington in 1856. He was succeeded in the late 1800s by his son, Joseph O. Diamond, who in turn, was followed by his son, Charles Joseph Diamond. The fourth (and last) generation of the family to make horse-drawn vehicles was Kenneth H. Diamond; he took over the business in 1933 and continued until his retirement in 1976.

In the interview below, Ken Diamond recalls how the family firm catered to the needs of the New Forest Commoner and others requiring horse-drawn vehicles.

A DIAMOND NAME-PLATE
From a cattle cart used by the Mansbridge family near Ashurst.

In the period leading up to the 1914-1918 war we had perhaps our peak period of producing carts and waggons. The firm then employed six men: a coachsmith, shoeing smith, two wheelwrights and two coach painters. These six not only made new vehicles, but carried out a great deal of repair work on many types of older horse-drawn vehicles.

Our range of vehicles might seem surprising to some, given our small size. Father made a glass-sided horse-drawn hearse in the mid-1920s. It was used extensively during that period and was drawn by a pair of black horses driven by my elder brother, Eric. The firm also made, at this time, a horse-drawn refuse collection vehicle for the then Lymington Borough Council. It bore on its sides the lettering: "Burn your refuse and save your rates." Many of the horse-drawn delivery vehicles used by shopkeepers in Lymington and nearby villages were made and maintained by Diamonds. These included bakers, butchers, draymen, and oil and hardware merchants. We also repaired and painted to G.P.O. specifications the old handcarts used by the Lymington Post Office.

Meticulous Hand Work

It is amazing how much work was done by hand and how crude were the working conditions. For example, my grandfather used to assist the sawyers when trees were cut into planks, by hand, over a sawpit. The smiths made their own spanners, chisels and other cutting tools from worn-out files. All the iron-work was filed to bright hue by the smith before the painter put on the first of many coats of paint. Likewise, when fine lining was required, the coach painter—Charlie Jenvey, had to be a highly skilled operator to do this by hand. Over his many years with the firm, Charlie must have painted many miles of fine lining with his special brushes. I still have his brushes and mahogany case. Some of Charlie's lettering was done in gold leaf.

There were as many as a dozen iron tyres being heated at the same time, a process that was necessary so that the tyres would expand and drop over the wooden wheels. The smith's shop was composed of three forges, three anvils, two

Whittington ...

Continued from previous page

Mr. Whittington gave us a week's notice and closed down. Soon I was off to the war. When it was over and I was de-mobbed, I learned Mr. Whittington was staying at the Watersplash Hotel and almost totally blind. I used to drop by and take him out for a walk three or four times a week.

Eventually he went to live with his son Ian in Tunbridge Wells. He was 97 when he died in 1973. He was a wonderful man and his toys brought happiness to thousands of people.

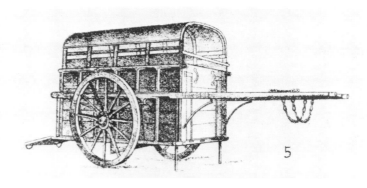

DRAWING OF CATTLE TRUCK USED IN THE FOREST
The Diamond family used handbooks of drawings, from which this one of a cattle truck is taken, to prepare specifications for the horse-drawn vehicles they made. So precise were their standards that the blacksmith would be given the diameter of an iron tyre *before* its wooden wheel was made.

Making Carts...

Continued from previous page
hand-drilling machines, a tyre-bending machine, and an "upsetting" machine to reduce the diameter of the iron tyres. There was also an apparatus to press in the "clincher" rubber tyres fitted, in latter times, to the wheels of carriages and other horse-drawn vehicles. There were also two "platforms" for tyring wooden wheels.

Six Weeks for a Waggon
Adjacent was a large vehicle body-building shop capable of accommodating several waggons and a number of smaller carts. These wagons, including the wheels, took about six weeks to make. The smith, incidentally, was given the diameter of the iron tyres *before* the wheels were made, so demanding was the standard of the shop.

One exciting aspect of our work was the arrival of huge, heavy vehicles used by circus and fairground people. They turned up whenever they were in the area for essential repairs and attracted much attention because of their accompanying steam-traction engines.

Very little of the work in making horse-drawn vehicles was placed outside the firm. Timber, of course, we bought, and we had to take great care to see that it was properly aged.

Despite the labour-intensive nature of the business—much of it highly skilled, the need for us to make many of the tools used, and no heating and only candle-light much of the time, the firm produced a steady flow of horse-drawn vehicles for over a century. Powered machinery did not come along until my time when we installed a heavy-duty bandsaw and a planing machine driven by a reliable three horse-power Petter stationary oil engine.

It was the coming of motor vehicles that killed off the horse-drawn carts, waggons and commercial vehicles. This development, however, was partly offset by making bodies and cabs for

HORSE-DRAWN VEHICLES AT THE OLD CROWN INN LYMINGTON
This picture, made about 1909, shows an array of vehicles drawn up in front of the old Crown (now the Toll House) Inn. The waggon on the right has "Diamond & Son, Cart and Waggon Builders," painted on its tailboard. These vehicles would have been used for general haulage; the covered waggons were employed to transport corn and other commodities from nearby farms. The Crown, conveniently located near the junction of the Sway and Brockenhurst roads, allowed thirsty drivers to partake of liquid refreshment.

the first commercial lorries and delivery vehicles.

Making the Wheels
In the making of waggons and carts the biggest time consumer was wheels. It takes a long time to make wheels from raw materials. First you have the "stock" (or hub), made from pieces of round elm. These were available in various lengths and sizes and were kept in stacks to air-dry until needed. After choosing a rounded piece for a stock, it was placed in a hand-operated lathe to be fashioned into the required shape. The stock was then hand-morticed so as to take 10, 12, 14 or 16 spokes, and then it was fitted with "stock bands" at each end by the smith. These were shrunk onto the wood while hot.

The spokes, which had been hand-shaped, were then fitted very carefully into the stock and

hammered into place. Great care had to be taken to see that each spoke was driven in "true" or else the rim of the tyre would not be "true." The outer ends of the spokes were then formed into round "tongues" and the "felloes" (rim sections) bored and fitted, with one felloe accommodating two spokes.

The felloes were bored and dowelled at each end and then secured by a wedge driven into each spoke end. Eventually the tyre was heated and placed on the wheel, which was screwed down tight to the steel "platform." The tyre was cooled by cold water to avoid burning the felloes.

A Cart For £25
Everything had to fit accurately. I suppose, from start to finish, the making of wheels took nearly half the entire time to make the waggon or cart. Orders were pro-

Making Farm Carts...

Continued from previous page

cessed in strict rotation; nobody was allowed to jump the queue. A two-wheel cart would not have cost more than £25 in the 1920s. Even by 1946, when I made the last of our heavy-duty tipping farm carts—that was equipped with new Dunlop pneumatic tyres and steam-bent axle shafts, the price was only £50. Wages and materials, of course, were cheap and in proportion to the selling prices. The men, by the way, were always paid in gold sovereigns.

We used several kinds of wood in making our carts and waggons. The framework would be of ash, including the front crosspiece (known as the "nose piece"). the rear one (known as the "shuttle-length"), and the main bed. Also in ash were the fore and hind undercarriages. The floor was of elm boards, the spokes of oak, and the felloes for the lighter vehicles were made of ash. Of all the woods used, the spokes in oak were the most durable. They outlasted everything else. The original source of most of our wood was the New Forest. We used no imported timber in our vehicles.

Hot Weather Problem

There were few real problems in making carts and waggons, but there was one practice we frowned on. If a farmer, during severely hot weather, found the iron tyres on his cart had expanded and become loose, he would simply drive to the nearest stream and remain there until the metal cooled down and tightened. We strongly discouraged this, for the practice allowed water to get into the various joints of the wheel and thereby shorten its working life. The correct procedure— admittedly more time consuming—was to take the tyres off with a cold chisel or sledge hammer, reduce the diameter, and then rejoin the tyre and refit it to the wheel. This

JOSEPH AND CHARLES DIAMOND AND STAFF CIRCA 1909
The workshops were in Lower Buckland Road, Lymington. Between them the group above could produce a wide variety of horse-drawn vehicles. Each person had a speciality: blacksmith, coach-smith, wheelwright, coach-painter or whatever. The cart shown at the right was known as "a pair of Forest trucks". These vehicles were used extensively in hauling timber from the New Forest. Two other timber specialist vehicles employed in the New Forest were the timber carriage and the timber "nib."

KEN DIAMOND HOLDING BRASS CAPS

Tom Charman and His Unusual Carvings

Tom Charman of Godshill was what may be called a folk character of his time. From the mid-1920s until 1933 he exhibited his unusual wood-carvings at the annual Artists and Craftsmen's Exhibition in London. People came year after year to his stand, but not just to see his carvings.

"He had a stall with his name above it—TOM CHARMAN, CURIO CARVER," his son Chris recalls. "He was a very good raconteur and people used to flock to hear his stories—and he also sold quite a few carvings. Still, it was a meagre living, even when he had to support only my mother and himself.

"That was before I was born. They lived simply. You might say they were among the first of the so-called 'self-sufficiency' people. It's fashionable now, but they were doing it in the 1920s. For example, they had goats, ponies and other creatures. I was brought up on goat's milk. I can't say I ever cared for it much.

"Father never received much publicity about his stall at the London exhibition because he lived in the 'pre-media' period. My mother always tried to get father to make more practical carvings—toasting forks, paperweights, and so on. But he preferred carvings for art's sake. My mother was the practical parent, my father the dreamer. By the time I was born my parents had started making pottery. After that my father had less time for wood-carving. He kept it up whenever he could snatch a few minutes, but no longer as a commercial venture. He died in his late seventies."

What was it like to visit Tom Charman and see his collection of fascinating carvings? Juliette de Bairacli Levy was privileged to stay with the Charmans in the 1950s when she was working on her book, *Wanderers in the New Forest* (Faber and Faber, 1958). In the accompanying extract, she describes how she examined the strange, but charming carvings by the light of a log fire one evening.

Of Many Forest Things

Among the things to keep that I was putting away from my cottage, were two carved wooden figures given to me by the Charmans, one of the head of a forest pony—the wild-eyed and maned savage pony of former days; the other a forest spirit, monstrous but compelling. Both figures were the work of Tom Charman, husband of my friend Margaret and father of the much-liked Christopher and Danae.

Tom Charman had been a wood-carver of genius. He would roam the forest, taking the natural pieces of wood which he found on the trees and bushes or mostly discarded on the ground, and which suggested to him the forms of birds and beasts, or human and near-human creatures. Gorse boughs and gorse and heather roots, holly and birch, seemed to be the woods that he used most often and most successfully. Nothing could be more typical of the New Forest.

Original Character Saved

The pieces of tree or shrub that Tom Charman brought back from his days in the heart of the forest would then be planed, carved and polished by the wood-artist, the original character of the wood which had caused its selection never being lost.

The Charmans have a big wooden chest filled with the artist's best work. I passed one interesting evening in their cottage examining the fine and original forest carvings, as they were brought out of

Making Farm Carts...

Continued from previous page
process we called "cutting and shutting."

People cared less about comfort and were more prepared to endure hardship in those days. One day my father was asked to make a new body and cab on a Model T Ford chassis for a farmer. In setting forth his order, the farmer told my father: "I don't need a roof on the cab. I want to enjoy the fresh air. Just a seat and doors will do."

CHRIS CHARMAN WITH ONE OF HIS FATHER'S CARVINGS

Godshill: A Pottery Using New Forest Clay

Founded by Tom and Margaret Charman in 1920, Godshill Pottery has remained in the family. It continues today under the watchful Christopher, his wife Kate, and sister Danae.

Tom started by making wood-carvings but found it difficult to make a living. He and Margaret then began to make pottery, using New Forest clay dug up outside their home.

Since the clay was unrefined the potter was continually forced to pick out flints and patch up the scarred surface as the pot was shaped. In the early days, also, pots were fired at very low temperatures—about 980 degrees Centigrade—leaving them in a very brittle state.

Today's products from Godshill Pottery are made quite differently. Some New Forest clay is still used, but Devon clay is added. A complicated refinement process results in a pot far superior to the crude one turned out by the pottery's founders. In the interview here, Chris Charman describes the various processes; he also relates the "ups and downs" of the crafts business.

I still dig up clay outside the door here. There is a gravel "cap" here about three feet deep, after which you come to clay.

I skim off the gravel in an area of about 10 square yards at the time, and then put down corrugated iron sheets around the hole. On these sheets I throw up the clay as I dig it, making a big bank. We can use the first three "spits" (a spit is about a spade's length) of clay. This is alluvial or top clay—the best for using in pottery. If you dug deeper, you'd get a lot of green sand with the clay. That's no good because the clay would become less and less plastic.

New Forest Clay

We supplement this local clay with clay brought in from near Newton Abbot in Devon. The proportion is about half and half.

The Devon clay is called "ball" clay. It has a quality halfway between fine china clay and earthenware clay. It is white and very plastic because of the fine particle size. It is cleaned and dried after being dug up in Devon, and comes in bags like cement. So you are not paying for water when buying several tons of ball clay.

The New Forest clay is first put into a baker's dough mixer. Water is added a little at the time until the mixture is like a thin soup. Then I pour the liquid through a sieve, a fairly course 20-mesh one, that will catch all the root hairs, flints, and so on, which are in the local clay.

After this the mixture goes into settling baths where it remains until all the water rises to the

Tom Charman ...

Continued from previous page

the chest. Forest pony, snake and toad, they came, Gypsy, and tree spirits; there was wood turned into door-knockers and book-holders, toasting forks and bellows-tops, walking-stick and umbrella heads, and many other objects.

As I was shown the contents of the chest, we all sat around a log fire, and every one of the strange wooden figures as they came into the firelight, was made more lovely, being touched with the flickering crimson and the gold.

A SIXTY-YEAR OLD FOREST INDUSTRY
Godshill Pottery, located two miles east of Fordingbridge on the B3078 road, is a favourite halt for New Forest visitors.

Godshill Pottery...

Continued from previous page

surface. Excess water is then siphoned off, leaving a thick sludge. This sludge is then returned to the dough mixer and the Devon clay is added. The two clays are mixed together for a time and then removed and put into air-tight bins. This mixture is better if it can be kept at least a month before using; the bacterial activity induced by aging makes the molecular structure more adhesive, and therefore more plastic.

The Production

Clay is weighed out into lumps —different weights for different articles. The pots are then hand-thrown on a potter's wheel, and afterwards put aside to dry naturally. At the "leather-hard" stage handles can be added, the base of the pots turned and the "slip" decoration applied. "Slip" is clay coloured with oxide, one on top of the other and pulled while still wet, with the tip of the brush. It's similar to feathered icing. This is the heart of the operation. Then, when the pots are bone dry they go into the kiln and are fired over a period of 18 hours at a temperature of 960 degrees Centigrade. The pots come out "biscuited"— that is, hard, but still porous. We then dip them in the glazes and place them back in the kiln. They are then re-fired to 1160 degrees Centigrade at which temperature the glaze fluxes and becomes a gloss, giving the pot its final finish.

Our work here is a team effort. It has evolved that we make certain shapes and certain items. We make them, decorate them and then combine on the chore of glazing.

We all do the artistic work, using the same materials and colours. Inevitably, we influence each other; yet there's a cohesive pattern to the pottery. Unless you work in the place, you wouldn't be able to tell which person made what. So the tradition builds up.

We look closely at the shape of each of our wares. One can tell if a shape is degenerating and might

say, for example: "That pot should have more of a belly on it— it's too straight—you have to tighten up that shape a bit."

As for the public, domestic decorated pottery is very much in demand—from coffee mugs to jugs, vases, casseroles and so on. Almost everything sells well. I used to think mugs sold better than anything else, but now everything goes.

Practical Use Important

We have about 45 different lines. The customer goes more for the practical than the artistic. We get customers who like the design and say, "I couldn't possibly use this." I reply: "Well, it's made to be used."

For our oven-ware we add a material known as "grog" to the clay. Grog is fire-clay, reground to

the consistency of sand. You add that to the clay and it opens it up. When the pot is then glaze-fired, the composition of the wall of the pot is not so tight and fused. It is therefore able to withstand thermal shock better.

Most of our business is "passing sales"—that is, it comes from people passing by our premises. I don't like doing commissions and try to avoid them if I can. Likewise, we never send anything by post, unless it is a very small object, like an ashtray. Otherwise, they would all get smashed.

No Advertising

We used to have an advertisement in the Rural Industries Bureau booklet of countryside shops, but we don't anymore.

You can keep life ticking over by being a potter but you will never get particularly rich in this country unless you are one of the elite, "one-off" potters. The domestic conception of pottery is good

SIMPLE, CLASSIC DESIGNS PREVAIL

Most of the pottery's output is geared to everyday home use. Here Kate Charman holds a bowl decorated in an attractive but conservative style.

DECORATIVE OBJECTS TAKE LONGER TO MAKE

Besides oven-ware and other functional kitchen items, Godshill Pottery also produces some decorative objects. Danae Charman displays a tray of such items, among them animals frequently seen in the Forest.

Faggotting: An Ancient Craft

(The New Forest, with its bounty of fallen branches, fostered the craft of faggotting in bygone days. H.E. Livens, in his village history (*Nomansland*, 1910), relates how families joined together to provide a few extra shillings in income.)

Faggotting was an industry, in which all hands, down to the youngest, could help. In fact, apart from the carting, the work was mainly done by the women and children, and given a large family and due application, a profitable business might be carried on. A cart-load of small wood, consisting of as much as could be piled up on two wheels, cost only a shilling, and served to make some 4,000 bundles.

The children were employed in breaking the sticks into short lengths with their hands and placing them in the proper quantity in a hole in the ground between four upright pegs, ready to be pressed down and tied under the tying-board. This would be done by the mother, or one of the older boys. Every bundle had afterwards to have its ends trimmed with the hatchet.

The usual price for faggots was a shilling a hundred; occasionally one-and-twopence could be got.

Godshill Pottery...

Continued from previous page

in one sense, for people will make room for an object if it is useful. On the other hand, if it does have a use, its monetary value is low in comparison to a strictly art object. So you are "had" both ways. One just has to make a living by sheer repetition.

A lot of crafts are debased nowadays because the actual use to which they can be put is gone. Plastic has virtually replaced the old village potter. There used to be a pitcher and a nice bowl for washing one's hands and face in the morning. Today there's the tap and basin.

It's the debasement of pottery that I find most distressing at some of the craft fairs. The genuine craftsman, for example, will do marquetry or inlay work—beautifully crafted. They are lovely because they are legitimate. But when you see a very nice *terra cotta*

pot covered in sea-shells stuck all around it, that's really debasement.

JOSIAH KING, NOMANSLAND FAGGOTTER

Ron Lane's Wood-carving Philosophy

"I Love Wood and Will Never Dictate to It"

Ron Lane was born on the edge of the New Forest in the village of Dibden Purlieu in 1921. The magic of the Forest cast a spell on him early in life and he had no hesitation in giving up a secure position with the nearby Esso refinery for a new career in sculpturing in wood.

"There was the terrific draw of ... the New Forest where all my ideas are born," he said at the peak of his artistic output. "... each and every day I could walk before breakfast with a mind freed of everyday worries, free to accept and absorb the beauty that is to be found when one is in tune with nature."

Ron's sensitive wood-carvings met with instantaneous acclaim. He exhibited and lectured throughout Britain and frequently appeared on radio and television. Pathé News did a feature about him in its "Look at Life" series. His handiwork sold all over the world and he was invited to Canada to lecture and exhibit. Fine examples of Ron's work may be found throughout Britain. The parish church of Blackfield owns a pair of candlesticks, carved in Honduran mahogany, in the form of a young man and a young woman kneeling and offering light. The Lyndhurst parish church possesses a Madonna (in English walnut) in its Lady Chapel.

Sadly, Ron died in 1976 at the early age of 51. His shocked friends and admirers quickly established a memorial fund to award annual prizes for the best wood-carvings by an adult, and by a young person, in the New Forest area. For a decade after Ron died his widow—now Mrs. Eleanor Clarke—has presented prizes for the area's best sculpture in wood.

The passages below, taken from some of Ron's lectures and interviews, reveal his love of nature and how he applied it to wood-carving.

I believe that modern man is missing the ability to use his hands. The craftsman of old is rapidly disappearing and (is) becoming a specialist.

Today's craftsman seldom sees the finished article and cannot be permitted to reach the high standard which he so longs for.

*****

It was in the village of Dibden Purlieu on the very edge of the New Forest that I was born in 1921, a very different place then. ... As with all families there is bound to be one dim wit; it was me. The only way in which I was possibly stronger than the others was in the gift of a vivid imagination, and even this got me into trouble more than once.

Even then I found I could tell my highly exaggerated stories to the trees and know there would

not be any comeback. They just listened!

The Trees, My Friends
It was these trees and the wildlife that surrounds them that really captured my imagination; we

seemed to belong together, each absorbing the life and movement of the other. So, often I watched the rippling movement of the stoat or weasel, and then found it repeated in the limb of a tree. Or the stump-like shape of the tawny owl huddled to the trunk of an old oak, its feathers blending with the bark, again mirrored in an old log—the knots perfectly taking the place of the blinking eyes.

Although I was not aware of it at the time, these things were making a lasting impression on my mind (and) setting the seal on my life for the future.

*****

... for ten years I enjoyed (my work at Esso) working on illustrations for training purposes (but) I was missing the feel of a good cutting edge slicing through timber and obeying my command. So in the evenings, on a portable bench that fitted neatly into the kitchen sink, I started carving animals and shapes again —an advance on my childhood whittling.

The years had changed my style: more mature pieces started taking shape and I felt for the first time I was really creating something of importance. People were impressed and a demand for my carvings was beginning. ... My

FOX CARVING BY RON LANE

RON LANE
The well-known Waterside wood-carver died just as he was winning international recognition.

Ron Lane...

Continued from previous page
carvings started to sell but, as with most artists, the price to begin with hardly paid for the timber.

Original Shape and Grain
I was working in my own style, largely from scrap timber found in the garden and the Forest, using the original shape or grain pattern to lead me in the design. The grain (helped) in suggesting powerful muscles, or the lightness of a bird on the wing, or the liquid lines of a swimming otter. No stain ... used, no drawing first—just let the wood lead and control.

I started evening and afternoon classes ... which helped the purse a little, and (worked) all the hours that God gave. A small one-man exhibition followed and art shops were soon asking for my work. A display at the New Forest Show really started things rolling. Then a brief television show on my work helped to make my name to be more widely known. More television followed and requests started rolling in for my illustrated talk, "Wildlife and Wood."

Then came a chance to exhibit with the Society of Wildlife Artists in London. I did not expect to get any of my six pieces exhibited, but joy, oh joy, all were shown, and I was now on the map—being made a member at my first exhibition.

Visitors were now coming from all over the globe to my tiny studio and gallery. They included old craftsmen, naturalists, television personalities, and many famous names—and those who just loved wood.

His Philosophy
I am often asked why my work is ... different. This is difficult to answer, but I firmly believe that it is because I love wood and will never dictate to it. It must lead *me* and dictate the movement and mood—each small piece (being) a piece in its own right. Try to dominate nature and the results will be disastrous.

My eyes study these simple pieces (of wood) until the natural markings show me the wild creatures that lie within. (The wood must) not be turned into a replica of some animal or bird, but (rather it should suggest) the atmosphere of the wild creature that I learned to know through years of watching.

I have learned, too, the discipline of the craftsman and his love for his tools. Only with this love can good work be done.

Copyright Chris Balcombe

ANDREW PHILLIPS, YOUNG WOODCARVER
Mrs. Eleanor Clarke (right), widow of Ron Lane, is shown presenting Andrew with a set of fine wood-carving tools after he won the 1987 competition among young craftsmen.

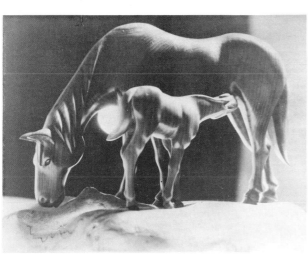

Mike Harlow

MARE WITH FOAL

Children Loved the Pre-war "Action" Toys

Wooden toys that "exploded," or collapsed, or had moving parts were a specialty of a New Forest firm, Burleytoys, that flourished in the decade leading up to the Second World War. In the interview below Rodney Peckham, who worked at the toy factory from the age of 16, tells how the toys caught the public imagination. Burleytoys are now much sought after by toy collectors.

I started working at Burleytoys about 1932 when I was 16. The business was a joint venture between two men, Colonel Mumby and C. T. Eaton. The business started up in the small workshop at the rear of Colonel Mumby's garage.

The first toy we produced was what we called a "Buster" fort. This was an "explosive" fort made of wooden pieces. It's mode of operation was simple: there was a chair-spring in a small box, held down by a lever which, in turn, protruded at the back and was covered by a tower. A little gun, using an elastic band and firing wooden shells, allowed the child to hit the fort. This blow pushed the peg out, releasing the spring, and all the pieces blew apart. When knocked down, these pieces fitted nicely into a small box.

"Buster" Fort Patented

All the toys were Mr. Eaton's inventions. His "Buster" fort was an original concept which he patented. About 1934 the "factory" was moved from Colonel Mumby's garage to a building of its own.

From the outset Mr. Eaton strove for quality above profit, as he had no need of money. The factory, built specifically for toy-making, had four workshops and an office in front shaped like an ark. There were only four of us working on toys when we moved from the garage, but business so prospered that we at one time employed about 30 people—half of them girls. The girls did the finishing off—rubbing down between the coats of paint, and the packing.

Eventually we produced a considerably range of toys. We developed a larger "Buster" fort which was two-tiered. From this we expanded the idea into a "tumbler" fort, one which fell down instead of blowing up when hit. This was made of plywood panels hinged at the corners.

Ships and Dolls' Houses

We also made a battleship game which consisted of a battleship and a submarine. They used the same "explosive" device employed in the forts, all harmless where children were concerned. The battleship and the submarine fired at each other and the first to get hit, "blew up."

One line we made that didn't blow up was dolls' houses. They did, however, fold up into pieces and could be packed away neatly in a small box. We had two basic types of dolls' houses: one thatched and the other, Tudor. The thatched model was a simple, single storey house. The thatch was simulated by using a coating of Scotch glue which, while still wet, was covered with sawdust. Afterwards, we spray-painted it from different angles. The Tudor model followed the conventional black-and-white architecture.

The "Buster" fort sold for 10 shillings, a good price for pre-war days. Dolls' houses cost more. Our main outlet in London was Gamages; they took them by the gross—everyone we could make. A tremendous number were exported to America. The American toy trade came to know about our Burleytoys when they visited the British Industries Fair which used to be held at Olympia annually.

Great Ocean Liners

Passenger liners plied the oceans in those days and we had great success with models of some of the more famous ones. There was a basic model of the *Queen Mary*, and also one of the *Queen Elizabeth*, the *Empress of Canada*, and many others. They sold for 3/11.

Although not exact replicas,

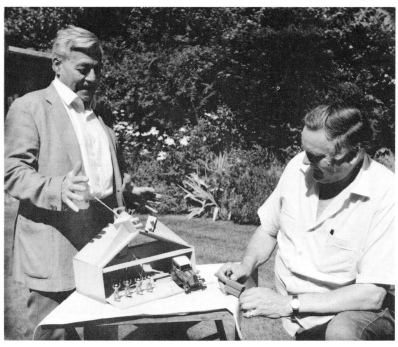

A "RAID" ON A TEXAS SALOON
Rodney Peckham (left) jumps as saloon starts to collapse after Harry Law fires small pellet at roof. Customers stand with raised hands as "getaway" car leaves. Peckham made the "action" toy; Law received it as his seventh birthday gift.

A selection from the fascinating

Burleytoys

Range of "Action" Toys

"BUSTER" FORT No. 1   **10/-**
(Patent No. 413,006)
Blows up when hit by a direct shot

THE "BURLEY" GUN   2/11

Send for complete lists to

PERCY GOODWIN LTD.

27 Paper St. and 31 Whitecross St.
London, E.C.1
Sole Concessionaires

or to the manufacturers :—

EATON & MUNBY LTD.

BURLEY, Nr. RINGWOOD, Hants.

FOLDING DOLLS' HOUSES

The Doll's Cottage   -   -   -   -   -   -   12/6
Two-room Bungalow   -   -   -   -   -   25/-

BRITISH LINERS   -   -   3/11

Reproductions of famous British liners beautifully finished,
true to colour, guaranteed to float. A very attractive
line which displays well

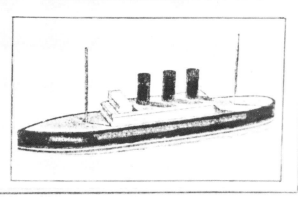

All these Burleytoys are now collectors' items. This advertisement appeared in the *Games and Toys Trade Directory and Diary* for 1935 and is reproduced by courtesy of *International Dolls' House News* (P.O. Box 79, Southampton).

Children Loved the Pre-war "Action" Toys

Continued from page 146

these liners—constructed of cedar, had decks, bridges and funnels. By special order, we did make ships to exact specifications. Once I made one of the *Queen Mary* after obtaining the specifications from the Cunard Line; another time I made an exact model of the *H.M.S. Hood*.

Each ship was about 14 to 15 inches long and had to float. Mr. Eaton would come along and pick out one model from each batch we made, and test it in water. If it didn't float without listing, he would throw the whole batch out. That happened only once, as I recall.

We also made sets of tug boats and barges. The sets were made of blocks of cedar, about 10 inches long, the inside of which was carved out. This inside piece was then fashioned into a tug boat, and the piece carved from the tug was made into a dinghy. Thus, from the original block, resembling a barge, there were these two additional boats—each nesting in the next larger size.

Fish, too

We also made fish that were as near to the actual shape as modern machinery would permit. They operated on the "otter principle," i.e., with a string attached about a third of the way back of its head, it would "swim" naturally when pulled. We made no effort to reproduce precisely a salmon or a trout, or whatever; the toys were simply "fish." These, too, were made of cedar.

We developed an experimental elephant that actually "walked," but never put it into production. In later years we made sets of trains and something we called "Biff Bats." These latter were something like table tennis bats with three holes punched out, each hole bearing a number. Attached to the bat by means of an elastic string was a soft ball. The object of the game was to toss up the ball and make it land in the hole with the highest number; that way, you would defeat your opponent. Operating on the same principle was a game called "Crown It," consisting of a hollowed-out cup with the ball attached.

Best Sellers

Although the British liners, forts and dolls' houses were our best sellers, another popular item was the "Texas Saloon." Using the "Buster" fort device inside, the saloon—when hit, allowed the door to open up suddenly, from which emerged at high speed a little car with "gangsters" inside. The little cars were about the only thing we didn't make ourselves; they were imported from Germany for $4\frac{1}{2}$d each.

Burleytoys was both nationally and internationally known, and featured in the toy trade journals. The red cedar we used came from Canada and if we hadn't stopped because of the war, we would have been obliged to close in any case as the supply would have been cut off. We used cedar because it was both light, and floated easily.

Agents' commissions bit heavily into the profits of the toy-making and eventually the factory switched to making bee-hives, again using cedar which was weather-resistant and did not need treating. The Ministry of Agriculture's experimental station gave Burley Hives top marks, and soon this line became both popular and profitable. The war, however, put an end to this line, and the factory had to close.

A WINNER AT THE 1939 NEW FOREST AGRICULTURAL SHOW
Only a few weeks before the outbreak of the second World War, this exhibit of Burley Hives won the Award of Merit at the New Forest show.

6
The Holy and the Unholy
Minstead Church As It Was Being Built

Although no detailed record exists of the building of Minstead church, Allen Seaby, in *Purkess the Charcoal Burner* (George C. Harrap, 1946) offers a fictionalized account of how the work may have been undertaken.

Minstead was having a holiday, holy day, to be precise. All work in the fields was stopped. The women had put on what finery they possessed and pleaded with their menfolk to smarten themselves up. Soon all were at their doors, watching parties of visitors as they passed. These were mostly gentry or even nobility, but that was nothing out of the way for Minstead, used to seeing royalty itself coming to hunt in the forest.

To-day was no time of festivity or secular show. Who was this riding in her litter, her household knights escorting her on either side, a procession of priests and officials following? It was the Abbess of Romsey, and the villagers bent reverently as she passed. A little later and another procession came by and knees bent still more, for here rode he who was to take the chief part in the day's proceedings, no less a personage than the Bishop of Winchester, with an imposing train of followers. The Bishop was to dedicate the new church at Minstead.

Solemn Procession
After the cortège had passed the villagers followed humbly. They made their way through rows of littermen and grooms with horses waiting outside the sacred precincts, and almost blocking the road. Soon the churchyard was crowded. There was hardly an inch of spare room. Only a few would be admitted to the final rites within the church, but all could watch the procession being formed of gorgeously arrayed ecclesiastics, preceded by acolytes swinging censers, and a full-voiced choir. They marched solemnly round the new edifice standing on

its knoll. The well-wrought stones showed up in the sun, for this building was quite other than the mud-walled church of earlier days.

Old Aldred had got his way at last. Although he had long retired from office, yet he had lived to know that Minstead was to be provided with the desire of his heart—for which he had worked and prayed—a stone church. Stone from the Purbeck quarries had been broken out with wooden wedges, wetted so that their expansion forced open the cleavage lines in the rock. The blocks of stone were roughly dressed and put aboard ship. The vessels sailed up Southampton Water and landed their heavy cargoes at Eling. Thence the stone had been dragged on noisy sleds drawn by

oxen to Minstead—an awkward journey. More than once a sled sank into a soft part of the road and had to be pulled out with the aid of teams, unhitched from other sleds, and brought to the spot. However, the loads reached their destination, nearly the worst part of the journey being that last steep bit of hill before the site was reached, now cleared of the old church.

After the site of the old church had been cleared the plan of the new one was marked out with wooden pegs. Then the trenches for the foundations were dug, and the bottoms rammed with 'punners' to consolidate the ground. Now all was ready for the building to begin. When the foundations had been laid in the trenches and levelled the walls of wrought stone began to rise quickly. Soon it was necessary to erect scaffolding to enable the upper part of the church, including the chancel

British Tourist Authority

MINSTEAD CHURCH AS IT APPEARS TODAY
The church is one of the oldest in the New Forest, going back at least to 1279 when the list of rectors begins—but some parts of the building are decidedly of earlier age.

Minstead Church...

Continued from previous page
arch, to be built.

Aldred nearly lived on the site while building was proceeding. Although he could not see the rising walls, for his eyes had gradually covered over with a film, yet he could feel them. He patted the stones as they were set up until the masons, not unkindly, edged him out of their way and made him a comfortable seat in the sun, promising to let him know when the chancel arch was finished. Presently the arch on its temporary framework of timber was ready for the keystone to be set, and a mason fetched in the priest so that he could be present when this operation was about to be performed. He heard (he thanked heaven that his hearing was still fairly good) the keystone gently tapped into place with a wooden mallet.

The Roof Completed

Then the carpenters could start work on the roof, and soon they put up a little flag, which was a signal that the timber work, including the ridge-pole was ready for the tilers. These put on the tiles, which were thin slabs of stone fastened to the laths by wooden pegs driven into holes punched in the tiles. Aldred shed tears of joy when the master-builder told him that the roof was finished and the church now ready for its fitments and furnishings.

There was one disappointment; the church had no tower, but a bell-tower would have been of no use, for bells in those days were only to be found in great churches. Neither Brockenhurst nor Boldre had towers as yet, so Minstead folk had no need to feel ashamed of their church. As for timber, a New Forest church was not likely to go short. Long before they were required some good trees were felled. The trunks were stripped of their branches, dragged to the timber-yard, and, after being barked and lying there for a

British Tourist Authority

UNUSUAL TRIPLE-DECKER PULPIT AT MINSTEAD

season, were sawn into sizes suitable for beams, rafters, and planks. All these were stacked cross-wise, so that the air could circulate freely between them to continue the process of seasoning. When well seasoned the master-builder had them taken to the site and showed the carpenters what he required, great cross-beams for the roof and middle-sized ones for rafters. The measurements were marked on the wood, so that there should be no mistake.

When the sawing was completed the adzes were brought into play. These were nasty-looking tools, the blade set, not as with the axe, but like a hoe. They required expert handling, for the strokes were made towards the legs of the workers, but, knowing their job,

they stood astride the beams and so escaped injury. With the adzes they removed all trace of the saw. It was important to work carefully; too deep a cut and the whole surface had to be gone over again. The timbers having been mortised, tenoned, and notched, holes were bored for the dowels, or wooden pins, which were to hold the framing together. Unlike iron bolts, wooden fastenings did not stain the timber.

Now the church stood finished, including its strong door. Was it absolutely finished, within and without? Well, one thing was missing, which the folk noticed and discussed among themselves. There was no great iron ring bolted to the door, a ring to which

Judge Jeffreys Condemns A Gracious Lady

Lady Alice (or Alicia) Lisle has been described by biographers as "a victim of judicial murder."

Daughter and heiress of Sir White Beckenshaw of Moyles Court, she was born about 1614. At 16 she became the second wife of John Lisle, a man who later was to play a leading role in the dethronement of Charles I. Subsequently he was rewarded with high office by Oliver Cromwell.

Although Lady Alicia was assumed to be largely sympathetic with her husband's anti-royalist views, she herself—on hearing of Charles I's execution—said she "had shed more tears for Charles I than any woman then living did." During the Monmouth Rebellion she gave shelter to two men fleeing for their lives. Betrayed by a villager, she was subsequently arrested and tried by Judge Jeffreys at Winchester.

Her trial, sentence and execution are described in the following passage from F.E. Stevens' *The New Forest Beautiful* (Methuen, 1925). A fresco entitled, "Alice Lisle Concealing the Fugitives," may be seen in the Palace of Westminster.

Poachers Sheltered

(In his *Calendar of New Forest Documents: 1244–1334*, David Stagg cites the case of a vicar of Boldre who knowingly harboured poachers.)

It is presented and proved by the said Verderers and by John the son of Thomas, steward of the said (New) forest, that Thomas Passavoinet the servant of Richard Blaunchard, the Vicar of Boldre (sic), and Simon le Fletchere of Wereborne, on the day of St. Thomas the Apostle in the 5th year of king Edward (21 December 1276) killed a doe and carried it to the house of Richard the Vicar of Boldre, who harboured them, knowing of the offense.

About the middle of the following night he sent Thomas with the venison on his horse to Salisbury, and the foresters took Thomas with the venison and took him to the prison at Lyndhurst. The following morning, in accordance with the assize of the forest, the steward searched the house of the Vicar at Boldre and found the entrails and offals of the beat, and the Vicar and Simon were taken and retained in prison until delivered by writ and by bail.

The story of Lady Alicia Lisle, of Moyles Court, which lies, by the way, just on the margin of the Forest, is one of the epics of sacrifice. It is the most poignant of all the tragedies and the broken lives which Judge Jeffreys left behind him when he raged back and forth throughout southern and western England, slaking his insensate hate in the Bloody Assize.

The Lady Alicia lived on the fringe of the hates and terror which were the unhappy influences of the Monmouth rebellion, but she was a woman, pitiful before all else, and when the two fugitives from Sedgmoor fight, drifting like chaff before the winnowing of the King's men, came to Moyles Court, knowing, perhaps, the big heart of the châtelaine, the door was opened to them. The Lady Alicia saw only their plight; regarded their hunger as of greater moment than their mistaken adherence to a lost cause, and gave them the succour of the priest's hole.

But their enemies were more closely upon their heels than either they or the pitiful Lady Alicia knew. Their presence within the house was suspected if not actually known. They may, indeed, have been tracked; it is not an impossibility, remembering the terror and the betrayals which were the fruit of terror, that they were headed that way, and permitted first to make their plea for sanctuary.

At all events there was a search, and Hicks and Nelthorpe were revealed. Treachery was in all likelihood the explanation, for priest's holes and hiding-places in houses like Moyles Court gen-

Minstead Church...

Continued from previous page
a fugitive, whether innocent or not, might cling and claim sanctuary – that is, if he could reach the door before his accusers seized him. However, there was a good-sized ring to the latch, and that must suffice.

MOYLES COURT: TODAY A PRIVATE SCHOOL

THE TOMB OF LADY LISLE AT ELLINGHAM CHURCH
After Lady Lisle was beheaded at Winchester, her body was turned over to friends who brought it to Ellingham. The grave is situated to the right of the church entrance.

Judge Jeffreys Condemns A Gracious Lady...

Continued from previous page
erally managed to retain their secrets until danger was overpast. The Lady Alicia, treated with a measure of contumely which scorches us with shame, knowing as we do what human kind is capable of in the stress of war, was hailed before the Black Judge.

Jeffreys constituted himself counsel for the prosecution as well as Judge. He bullied the jury until they felt that they, too, were on trial for their lives, and that a verdict favourable to the accused would very conceivably place them in peril. To the meanest intelligence the act of the accused was one of pure charity; had the fugitives been King's men she would most likely have acted in the same way.

But with the scales of justice thus weighted with venom, hardness of heart and something infinitely worse than uncharitableness, it was not surprising that Lady Alicia was unable to prove that her act, which she admitted, was one of pity. It was one of those cases in which the result was a foregone conclusion.

The awful savagery of her sentence, to be burned alive, following the final indignity of being drawn upon a hurdle to the place of execution, was lightened in part, and death, a merciful thing, came to her in the Market Place at Winchester by the axe. She was buried at Ellingham in a stone tomb near the door in 1685.

William Gilpin's School at Boldre

(W. Frank Perkins, in his 1927 local history **Boldre,** *describes the Rev. William Gilpin's famous school.)*

(Gilpin) founded and endowed a school designed for the education of 20 boys and 20 girls; the children of day labourers of the parish who were clothed and educated, the boys being taught "reading, writing, and the first four rules of arithmetic;" and the

A SCHOOL ENDOWED FOR THE POOR

girls to "read, knit, or spin, sew or mend their own clothes." There were separate classrooms for boys and girls. The room for boys was 25 × 14 ft. with a covered roof. Adjoining was a "commodious little mansion" for the master... in which the girls were taught. The master was paid a salary of £24 per annum and the mistress £12. The school was opened on 1st July 1791.

THE MOST CONSIDERATE VICAR EVER?

There was a time when every vicar knew each family in his parish, including the names and ages of all the children, father's occupation, and the attributes and faults of father and mother.

Knowing this information was one thing, but putting it in writing was another. The vicar who did this best was probably Henry Comyn, who came to Boldre as curate in 1812 and who, in 1817, compiled 22 notebooks about the people in his parish. He did this, almost certainly, for his successor, the Reverend Charles Shrubb, who at first attempted to update the mass of information Mr. Comyn had left him. Eventually, he was obliged to abandon the effort, either because it was too time-consuming or because he was not so interested in the members of his "flock."

At the time Comyn produced his notebooks Boldre and Brockenhurst were a combined parish comprising a sprawling area of the New Forest. As such, the notebooks are a valuable record of social conditions in early 19th century England. After much painstaking research and annotations, Jude James—the local historian, produced *Comyn's New Forest* in 1982.

The work embraces over 600 entries naming more than 3,000 inhabitants of the Boldre/Brockenhurst area, and is an invaluable source of information about family structure, genealogy, occupations, living conditions and other elements of social history.

Getting Lost on the Way to Church

(Charles W. Wood, writing in *Argosy* magazine in February, 1881, tells how he got lost looking for Minstead Church and, instead, became on the receiving end of some home-spun philosophy.)

...Sunday morning I started with the intention of going to Minstead Church but, missing the road, never saw Minstead Church that day.

Turning presently a little to the left instead of to the right, I entered a long road skirted on either side by the forest. Far down at the end might be seen something that looked like the commencement of a village; surely, a church was not far off.

At length I came upon an open space, a few cottages, an inn or two, a pond and a small green. But the last stroke of eleven had ceased to vibrate on the air, no church bell could now be heard and, what was more, no church was visible.

Knocking at the nearest inn door, being Sunday and church time it was barred and bolted, it was opened by a pleasant looking woman who stared in some amazement at the enquiry as to whether this could possibly be the village of Minstead.

"Minstead, sir!" cried the woman. "And you come from Stoney Cross! Law bless me! Why, you've come miles out of your way. You ought to have turned right instead of coming down the hill. Well you have had a walk. Though it's an uncommon fine day, to be sure. And I always do say that if you must lose your way, better do it on a fine day than a wet one."

Here the good woman paused for breath and, making the most of the opportunity to get a word in edgeways, I inquired for a church.

"Church!" returned the dame. "Oh, we've a church, sure enough. But you'll be awful late, sir. Anyhow, they'll let you in and, if you miss the prayers, why you'll be in time for the preaching. You might say the prayers to yourself, like, as you go along the road."

Another pause, and I looked about for the said church, but looked in vain. The woman saw my perplexity and again came to the rescue.

"Oh, if you're peering for the church, you'll peer long enough before you find it, leastaways unless you're blessed with a crooked vision that can see around the corner. You bear to the left, here, and keep straight along the road, and by and by you'll come to the church at the top of the hill. It's a good mile from here."

"Your churches about the New Forest are for the most part at the top of a hill," I observed.

"Yes, sir," she answered, laughing. "I have heard that remark before and I believe it is true. Well, it's uphill getting along in life and I suppose they thought they'd give us a little of it in getting to heaven."

John Howard Lived in the New Forest

(The noted penal reformer, John Howard, lived at Brockenhurst for three years. John Bullar, in his 1801 guide, *A Companion in A Tour Around Southampton*, describes this brief period in the life of Howard.)

A little out of the road (from Brockenhurst), on the left, adjoining the church, we see Brockenhurst House. It has a very grand forest view, in the highest style of picturesque beauty.

Watcombe House, situated in the same park, claims our notice on account of the worthy character who once inhabited it: no less a person than the late very benevolent Mr. (John) Howard. He settled here soon after his second marriage in 1759.

During his three years' residence at Brockenhurst, his bounty and amiable disposition so endeared him to his poor neighbours, that he is still remembered with grateful veneration.

Shortly after quitting this village, he entered upon those plans of extensive (penal reform) benevolence which have ranked him high among the names Britain is proud to own.

New Forest Vicar, Convicted on Morals Charge, Wins Appeal after His Brother Leads National Campaign to Clear Name

John Kershaw Craig, the first Vicar of Burley, was the central figure in one of the most bizzare cases in modern British ecclesiastical history.

Born in 1801, he was the youngest son of the noted water-colour artist and miniature painter, William Marshall Craig. The elder Craig was much favoured by the Royal Family; among his patrons were Queen Charlotte and the Duke and Duchess of York.

John Kershaw obtained his B.A. from Magdalen Hall, Oxford, in 1828 and eleven years later was named the first Vicar of Burley. On 9 November 1843 he signed an audit of the accounts relating to construction of the new church (St. John the Baptist). The cost of erecting the church and a small residence for the minister had been estimated at £2,000. Subscriptions and donations, in fact, came to £2,046. The largest contribution, £200, came from John Lefevre. Another £105 was subscribed in the name of the late king, William IV. The Rt. Hon. Sturges Bourne gave £100.

The only other substantial donor was George Rooke Farnall (£100), originally a Bristol solicitor, but now resident at Burley Manor. Farnall and Mr. Craig were shortly to be set on a course of confrontation that was to involve nearly every household in the village and receive the attention of both local and national newspapers.

Burley was then inhabited almost entirely by villagers whose roots went back for generations. The gentry hardly existed and Mr. Craig, who was an evangelical, considered village folk as his "flock." He and George Rooke Farnall seldom saw eye-to-eye, and at one time Farnall is reported to have put his fist in Mr. Craig's face. Eventually Farnall developed various charges of incompetence and immorality against Mr. Craig and on 17 January, 1845, the Bishop of Winchester notified the Vicar that a Commission of Inquiry would be held. The inquiry, held at Ibsley, saw dozens of Burley residents making affidavits against Mr. Craig.

Later the Vicar was brought before the Court of Arches where he was acquitted of five charges ranging from adultery to visiting the bedrooms of his female servants. He was found guilty of the sixth charge: kissing or attempting to kiss one Ann Smith, and tickling one Jane Shelley. For this offense he was sentenced to suspension from his benefice for two years, ordered to pay £250 exceeding his emoluments for a further three years, and to pay the costs (estimated at not less than £1,000).

Mr. Craig's elder brother, Edward, also a clergyman, set about trying to vindicate the family name. The only way an appeal could be mounted against a verdict by the Court of Arches was to apply to the court of the Judicial Committee of the Privy Council. This Edward did by privately publishing an 80-page pamphlet, "Statement of the Case of the Office of the Judge Promoted by Farnall against the Rev. J.K. Craig in the Arches Court of Canterbury with Remarks on the Proceedings and Judgment." The pamphlet, published by the law booksellers, William Benning & Co., in Fleet Street, London, revealed many faults in the trial, not the least of which were contradictory evidence and amazing incompetence by the judge, Sir H.J. Fust.

Edward Craig's zeal carried the day and in February and March, 1849, the appeal was heard. Before the court could conclude its hearings members were confounded when George Rooke Farnall brought forth new charges of adultery against Mr. Craig. The court rightly held that whereas Mr. Craig had not been found guilty of adultery in the original case before the Court of Arches, these new charges could not be entertained in their (appeal) court.

Charges and counter-charges were made by the opposing counsels, with the credibility of witnesses' statements much in doubt. At last, the court ruled that the original decision should be reversed.

Mr. Craig lived out his days in Burley, dying three weeks short of his 88th birthday. He was buried in Burley churchyard and his 46 years is the longest period served by a vicar of Burley. The *Ringwood Illustrated Almanack* praised his many fine qualities and called him a man of "great and gentle nature."

His brother Edward, who successfully organized the appeal, survived the Privy Council appeal by only a year.

The passages that follow include excerpts from Edward Craig's pamphlet, extracts from the press, and items from the obituary of the Vicar.

From Edward Craig's Pamphlet

(Edward's pamphlet not only helped to raise funds, but focussed national attention on what he considered to be injustices in the original Court of Arches trial.)

I am the elder brother of the Rev. John Kershaw Craig, older by 12 years. I superintended his education, and sent him to College. I avow my unqualified belief in my brother's innocence (my conviction that he is an injured and oppressed man). ... In the conduct

New Forest Vicar...

of his defence before the Court of Arches I took no part, that was in other hands; but I watched the proceedings in the cause, and I heard the judgment—I sat by its cradle—I followed the hearse.

From that sentence an Appeal is in due course. It can at last be accomplished only at an expense, which is in itself a barrier, almost unsurmountable. It cannot be estimated at less, I believe, than from £1,200 to £1,500.

Enough has become known through the channel of the daily press to excite an unusual degree of interest, if not of astonishment and alarm, which must await the final issue. ... The object of the statement contained in (this pamphlet) is to place before the public the true character of the proceeding and judgment.

In the month of May, 1839, the Rev. John Kershaw Craig (who is of 47 years, and has a wife and four children) was presented by the Lord Bishop of Winchester to the Incumbency of the District Church of Burley, situate in a rude part of the new Forest near Ringwood, in Hampshire, which previous to the year 1838, had been under the sole care of Dissenters.

Enter Mr. Farnall

The prosecutor in this (Court of Arches) case, Mr. George Rooke Farnall, was formerly in business as an attorney in the city of Bristol. At the commencement of Mr. Craig's incumbency, he was (by virtue of his marriage) a person of acquired importance in Burley parish, where he is still (1848) resident.

Resolutions (were) passed and signed at a meeting of churchwardens, overseers, and 47 of the principal farmers, yeomen, and other inhabitants of Burley parish, 17th Feb. 1842, which shew unequivocally the then state of the district, of which Mr. Farnall is the person to give account:

"That this meeting much regret that attacks of the coarsest kind

are continually made from time to time upon the public character of their Minister, both anonymously and by name, and they also much disapprove of a continual writing of every imaginary evil to the Diocesan. They earnestly wish that his Lordship (the Bishop of Winchester) would at once put a stop to this, and confer with the churchwardens: otherwise they fear the peace of the district will be continually disturbed."

In the small (Burley) church of (the) district (... in the year 1831, 415 persons, now perhaps 600, a

MR. CRAIG'S HOME AT PICKET POST
So well known was the name of Mr. Craig's home (Dilamgerbendi Insula) that it was so noted on Ordnance Survey maps of 1869. Sir John Mills of Bisterne is credited with solving the meaning of the name. The first word is believed to be a Romany version for "home;" the second, Latin for "island." Taken together, they meant the home from which the Isle of Wight could be seen.

great part of whom are labouring poor) there are 98 seat renters, 216 regular attendants at church, and 143 others whose attendance is more or less frequent. Neither the letting of the seats nor the number of the congregation has been at all diminished by the prosecution, proceedings or judgment.

Origins of Clash

The origin and history (Farnall's) quarrel with Mr. Craig appear (in the trial) but incidentally and can now be only so ascertained, inasmuch as the offered proof of both was deemed by the Judge to be

inadmissable, as irrevelant or immaterial to the issue. That it was of early date is certain, from the fact established on the cross-examination of one of (Mr. Farnall's) own witnesses, that on an occasion in the year 1840, he put his fist in Mr. Craig's face; on which occasion he also threatened to knock him down.

It is no trifling matter for any clergyman to bear up against the *great* man of such a parish as Burley, when personal enmity is backed by the professional experience of an attorney (a reference to

Mr. Farnall's profession). I read in the judgment of Sir H.J. Fust (at the Court of Arches trial) that if there be animosity in Farnall towards Mr. Craig, "there appears to be a pretty fair share of it on the 'part of Mr. Craig towards Mr. Farnall,' as if there were no difference between unjust attack, and just, if it be indignant, defence. Mr. Craig is to be held responsible for all that is amiss, and he has credit for nothing that is good.

The Charges

It (was) charged against him (in

New Forest Vicar...

the Court of Arches) *generally*, that he was in the habit of going in an undressed state at night into the bed of his female servants after they had retired to bed, and therein remaining with them frequently for several hours, and with being then guilty of "adultery, fornication or incontinence."

In further and following articles, Mr. Craig is charged with indecent conduct towards a young female, then in his service, in Verely Wood, in the month of May, 1844. Then with an act of adultery alleged to have been committed with the same young person in Ridley Wood on the 3rd of June in the same year. Then with a visit to the bedroom of his three female servants, on a night happening in the month of December, 1844. Then, with an act of adultery, fornication or incontinence with one or two female servants, in the same bed with the other also. Then, with a habit of unbecoming and indecent familiarities with the same females.

And lastly, with a familiarity ... which I must quote at length, because it is the *one* and *only* charge which has been held by Sir H.J. Fust to be proved against him:

"That on a Sunday, shortly before Christmas, 1844, two or three young girls who were your (Mr. Craig's) parishioners—and among them one Ann Smith—went to drink tea in the kitchen at your house; and that after tea your wife played to them in the drawing room upon the organ, and with you sang or chanted part of the service of the Church. And that the said girls having had their supper in the said kitchen, you after the supper, being in the said kitchen, pulled back the chair whereon the said Ann Smith was sitting, and putting your hands round her, kissed or attempted to kiss her. That on the said occasion, you with one of your hands, tickled the aforesaid Jane Shelley, saying you did so to see if she was jealous."

The Sentence

For (this last charge) Mr. Craig was sentenced by that right honourable person (Sir H.J. Fust) to suspension from his benefice (*ab officio et a beneficio*) for the space of two years; ordered to pay the sum of £250 for three further years; and left to pay the whole amount of the costs incurred by him in his successful defence against the other charges, which cannot be so little as £1,000.

(Edward Craig then uses 40 pages of his pamphlet to refute evidence and to cast doubts upon the competence of the judge, Sir H.J. Fust. An example relates to the charge of adultery against Mr. Craig occurring in Verely Wood in May, 1844. The *only* witness for this charge was Farnall's servant, a man named White. Mr. Craig had at one time occupied Verely Farm, where the alleged act occurred, but had given it up in 1842. Edward Craig resumes his rebuttal:)

It turns out that by no possibility could (this alleged act) have occurred subsequently to the year 1842, and it was therefore out of date. The observations of Sir H.J. Fust upon this point are to this effect:

"How it came to find its way into the Articles that this was 1844 does not seem exactly explained, but that it was intended as a fraudulent representation, that it was done for the purpose of creating prejudice to Mr. Craig, does not appear to me to be at all a necessary consequence."

New Charges Made by George Farnall

(Both *The Times* and the *Hampshire Advertiser* described how, on 13 February 1849, the court of the Judicial Committee of the Privy Council considered altogether new charges against Mr. Craig at the time the court was considering the appeal by the Vicar against his conviction on a single charge of kissing and petting. The new charges, also preferred by Mr. Farnall, related to adultery and were based largely on the statement of one Moses Sims. The account from the *Hampshire Advertiser* follows:)

An affidavit by one Moses Sims, a servant in the home of Mr. Craig from January, 1845, to May, 1848, was produced. Sims said during the whole of that time one Charlotte Sims was also in the employ of Mr. Craig, and that in April, 1847, Mr. Craig frequently spoke to him (Moses) about the pregnancy of Charlotte Sims, "the fact being manifest at that time by her appearance," and told him (Moses) she was going to Jersey with her father and that Mr. Craig promised to accompany them. Further, that on or about 21 May, Mr. Craig left home, Charlotte Sims having taken her departure the previous day.

Visit to Jersey

Upon the appellant's return after a lapse of about a week, Mr. Craig, informed him (Moses) that he and Charlotte had been to Jersey.

After an absence of 15 weeks or thereabouts, Charlotte Sims returned to the house of Mr. Craig, she then being much reduced in size and having been, as is believed, delivered of a child during her absence. Moses Sims said he had seen Mr. Craig conduct himself with indecent familiarity towards Charlotte Sims, and her sister, Jemima, who was also a servant in the home.

He had, one evening in the month of February, 1848, observing a light in the dining room of Mr. Craig's house, looked in at one of the windows and had there seen Mr. Craig and Charlotte Sims in the act of immoral intercourse on the floor. On another occasion, in the same month, going into the same room, he found Charlotte Sims rising from the floor, on which were the cushions from the carriage, and Mr. Craig standing near her arranging his dress.

Moses Sims also claimed that

New Forest Vicar...

Charlotte Sims was delivered of a child on Monday, 26 November, in Mr. Craig's house, and this fact was confirmed by an affidavit of Mr. Stephen Westcott, surgeon of Southampton, to the effect that he had attended her during her confinement.

(In the hearing) there were allegations that witnesses had been tampered with by plying them with refreshments at the local public house (the Queen's Head). John Lewis, landlord, confirmed this.

Other Affidavits

Affidavits were produced alleging Mr. Craig had taken "indecent or unbecoming familiarity" with five girls (Amelia Archer, Charlotte Sims, Jemima Sims, Jane Shelley and Ann Smith).

Mr. Craig denied all these allegations.

Praise for Mr. Craig

(Burley originally was a part of the parish of Ringwood, and it was in the columns of *The Ringwood Illustrated Almanack for 1889* that a long obituary of Mr. Craig appeared. Excerpts from this tribute follow.)

Many pilgrims on their way to Bolderwood must have had their attention arrested by a house standing on a commanding eminence on Picket Plain, and bearing the high-sounding name of "Dilamger-bendi Insula," which means, that it possesses a beautiful view of the Isle of Wight. In this house for the past half-century has dwelt the Rev. John Kershaw Craig, Vicar of Burley, who has gone to his final rest.

As he was a man of striking individuality of character and powerful mind, who stood out from his fellow man with whom his lot was cast—even as his house on the plain stood prominently above the dwelling abodes in the valleys around, I have thought his

BURLEY CHURCH TODAY
Here the Rev. John Kershaw Craig began his ministry in 1839. He died 50 years later.

memory deserved something better than that it should lapse into oblivion without a notice.

An Evangelical

In his theological views Mr. Craig belonged to the old Evangelical School, and in his manhood had been an enthusiastic adherent of the party. Yet he did not share in its bigotry and narrow-mindedness, but he was broad and tolerant in his views. Like many others of the old school of the Clergy, he was a great classical scholar and was proficient in the dead languages, including Hebrew, and also was acquainted with modern ones.

Among other ventures, Mr. craig once started a local Magazine, called *The Hawk*, but as all light and frivolous reading was strictly tabooed, it lasted only for a year. He was also an accomplished chess player, and of anything that

tended to mental and moral culture, he was a warm advocate.

He was a great patron of cricket and, in the village matches, generally presented the highest scorer on either side with half a crown. He also loved to organize Old-fashioned fetes for the diversion of the parishioners, and even revived the Maypole. He sometimes gave a general invitation to the gipsies who rove the Forest, and hospitably entertained them.

Mr. Craig had little faith in doctors, but rather believed in fresh air and right living. The great age he attained showed this little eccentricity was not altogether absurd. Many stories are told of him which show he had a quaint and original vein in his nature. He conducted Religious Worship with a simplicity that was displeasing to those who like an ornate and elaborate ritual.

He was of very courteous and

A Nation Torn by the Plight of the Shakers

In the long history of the New Forest and its religious institutions nothing has so attracted public interest as the ousting of the Hordle "Shakers" from their premises in Vaggs Lane near New Milton.

In 1873 a remarkable woman, Mary Ann Girling, established her religious group in New Forest Lodge (now a private nursing home) and for a while the community prospered. Mary Ann possessed almost hypnotic powers over her flock, but she was no good at managing the commune's financial affairs. Deeply in dept by 1878, the Shakers were evicted from New Forest Lodge ten days before Christmas. A national outcry followed and most of the national press carried the story. A leading weekly, *The Graphic*, dispatched an artist to capture in sketches the plight of Mary Ann and her followers and accorded the Shakers front-page treatment in its next issue.

The story below of the Hordle Shakers is reproduced with permission of America's Shaker Historical Society and its author, Lillian C. Vodrey.

The Hampshire property in the New Forest to which Mother Girling fled (in 1873) with her twelve loyal disciples in order to pursue the life of peaceful meditation (they were not permitted in London) was contributed by one of the very few well-to-do Shaker converts. It consisted of a house called New Forest Lodge and the thirty-one acres on which it was situated in Vagg's Lane in Hordle. Stables were also included. The lodge became the dwelling house, and one of the stables served as the chapel. This property was purchased by a Miss Julia Wood, who was generous enough also to buy the livestock and the farm implements the little group needed to work the land. In return, they were to pay the interest on a £1,000 mortgage on the property.

So great was Mary Ann Girling's oratorical and hypnotic power that within three years of establishing herself in New Forest, the number of her devotees grew from her original flock of twelve to a membership of 140. By 1875, 60 women, 45 children and 35 men, mainly of the laboring class, had given up their local homes for this Victorian utopia, putting their meagre assets into the common pool.

Centre of Attention

We are told that the commune continued bravely for fourteen years. Their extraordinary behavior, for they were the *Shaking* Quakers just like the earlier Manchester group, brought crowds flocking Sunday after Sunday from as far away as Salisbury, Bournemouth, and Southampton to gape at their strange gyrations or to pity their privations. By this time they had become national news. Vagg's Lane was packed with vehicles of all sorts from donkey carts to large brakes drawn by three or four horses which brought the curious sightseers from as far away as twenty miles to see and hear the Shakers.

The conduct of the community was the same as that established by the American Shakers. Each member was required to surrender all his worldly goods to the society; and the members of the commune lived on this capital, which was augmented from time to time by the contributions made by outsiders at the Sunday religious services open to the public.

Hard Times Come

At first this large Shaker family lived fairly comfortably, though frugally. But soon the capital was used up, and the contributions from outside dwindled. For Mother Girling, while she was a firm and kind and loving leader of her flock, evidently had none of the business acumen characteristic

New Forest Vicar...

Continued from previous page

gentlemanly bearing, but at the same time possessed a very firm disposition. When his principles were at stake, his was not the nature to be dictated to by the squire of the village or anyone else.

The Funeral

He was buried in Burley Churchyard on Friday, September 20th, 1889, and a friend and myself, who greatly esteemed the old Clergyman, resolved to pay our tribute to his departed worth by being present at the ceremony. With this intention we made our way to Burley and were glad to see that a large number of his old parishioners had gathered in the Churchyard to witness the last scene in their old pastor's career.

Slowly and solemnly the minister, an old friend of the deceased, read the burial service, while around the grave were clustered the homely villagers in reverential attitude. Pride and wealth were not represented, but I think it was a far better tribute to the labours of the departed in his sacred calling, that his mourners were chiefly the poor and lowly.

The Churchyard is prettily situated on an eminence, surrounded by stately trees, and the natural beauty of the place lent a soothing sadness to the scene. The place and the occasion were such as to have inspired an artistic or poetic mind to a great work.

We lingered a brief space and glanced at the graves and the epitaphs. Then, with thoughts somewhat sadder and less restless than usual, slowly sauntered homeward over a lovely stretch of the Forest, recounting as we went, anecdotes of the dead man who, to us, had seemed of a great and gentle nature.—*A.H.K.*

THE GRAPHIC

AN ILLUSTRATED WEEKLY NEWSPAPER

VOL. XI.—No. 267
Regd at General Post Office as a Newspaper

SATURDAY, JANUARY 9, 1875

WITH EXTRA
SUPPLEMENT

PRICE SIXPENCE
Or by Post Sixpence Halfpenny

1. New Forest Lodge, the Recent Home of the Shakers, Hordle, Hants—2. Interior of the Chapel: The Prophetess addressing the Community—3. The Dance—4. Barn at Batchley Farm, the Shakers' Present Abode—5. Mrs. Girling, the Prophetess—6. Exterior of the Chapel—7. Scene on the High Road upon the Night of the Eviction—8. Off for a Walk—9. The Shakers' New Hall, built of Unburnt Brick, and now Falling in Pieces.

THE SHAKER SETTLEMENT IN THE NEW FOREST

The Plight of the Shakers...

of her American counterparts. It is true that she believed that, like them, her community should be self-supporting. She saw to it that the members did their share of the work of maintaining themselves and their property. But she would not allow them to accept any pay for the outside work they did. When local farmers needed her able-bodied men to help with the haymaking and other agricultural endeavors, she gladly let them go to their assistance. But they were not allowed to accept any payment. She did permit those farmers who wanted to, to make small contributions to the general fund, but that was all. So preoccupied were Mother Girling and her group of English Shakers with their dream of a life to come (their millenium) that they lost all sense of the real and practical side of their present life.

Mother Girling kept no accounts. All the money she received from the sale of the personal property of her followers and from the Sunday service contributions from outsiders went into one fund. As long as it lasted, she was able to go to the Lymington shops nearby, for the cloth for garments and leather for shoes, all of which these New Forest Shakers made just for themselves with no surplus to be sold in the public market place. For the first year or two, they were able to meet the rates and taxes and interest on the £1,000 mortgage on the land and the lodge provided them by Miss Julia Wood. However, this was true only for the first year or two. After that, there were no more members to turn over all their worldly goods to the society; and the contributions from the outsiders who attended the Sunday services, dwindled to practically nothing. Mrs. Girling was unable to pay the interest on the mortgage. The mortgage was foreclosed. The sheriff's deputy ordered them out of New Forest Lodge.

No Documents
Never was Mother Girling's lack

> **"The household goods were placed upon the high road with two or three pianos and harmoniums, 77 beds and bedding, farm produce., etc., supposed to be worth about £1,000"**

of business responsibility more evident than at the time of this crisis. It was soon apparent that Miss Julia Wood never took the legal steps necessary to convey the property to Mrs. Girling, nor did Mother Girling ever demand a document to substantiate the transaction between her and Miss Wood. Nor would she take any steps to defend her claim to the property. She had firm scruples against going to law. This reluctance on her part made her an easy prey most of her life to her predatory enemies. So she and her flock of 140 men, women and children were ejected from New Forest Lodge on December 13, 1874.

A newspaper, the *Hampshire Independent*, published a graphic account of the cruel eviction of Mother Girling and her New Forest Shakers which took place on December 15, 1874. It reads as follows: "The mortgagee gave notice to foreclose, and the sheriff's officer ejected them. The household goods were placed upon the high road with two or three pianos and harmoniums, 77 beds and bedding, farm produce, etc., supposed to be worth about £1,000. Then the inmates, numbering upwards of 140, including 40 children were ejected, Mrs. Girling, the 'Mother' being the first to be moved. ... The others grouped themselves around her and commenced singing, appearing to regard their hard lot as only a portion of the persecution which

those who are the Lord's must expect to undergo in this world. Hundreds of visitors were on the spot to see the ejectment. There was a fierce east wind blowing with heavy rain and sleet and snow. The keen icy blast penetrated the thin dresses of the women and little ones. The furniture was soaked and spoiled. Hay, straw, and beans were strewn about the road; and the scene was one of terrible privation and desolation.

A Piteous Sight
"After some hours of misery, the children were removed to a neighboring cottage. A woman who was ill at the time was taken by her husband to a place of shelter. The Rev. E. Clissold offered the others the protection of a barn, but they declined it. They said they would not leave their 'dear Mother,' and through all the terrible night they remained in the rain and snow, the sound of their hymns and prayers mingling with that of the storm; and the morning found them half-perished with the bitter cold but defiant of all consequences and sturdily refusing to leave the spot, saying they were in the Lord's hands and He would do with them as seemed Him best. Bread and cheese and milk were kindly bestowed on them; otherwise, they had scarcely anything to eat. In the evening, a heavy snowstorm came on, and there was every prospect of another terrible night, but about 9 o'clock they were per-

> **"through all the terrible night they remained in the rain and snow, the sounds of their hymns and prayers mingling with that of the storm"**

Plight of Shakers...

Continued from previous page
suaded by Sergeant Timkin, partly with the threat of removal to the Workhouse, to accept the shelter of a barn about half a mile distant."

From Hand to Mouth

They remained in this barn for about three weeks, but the place was not large enough for them all to sit down at one time. Then they received the offer of another larger barn. Some four or five weeks later, they moved to a field in Vagg's Lane which Mother Girling leased, but on the expiration of the lease, they were again turned adrift and lived for several weeks on the roadside. Later, Mrs. Girling succeeded in renting two acres in neighbouring Tiptoe, where they erected huts and tents, including one large wooden building which they used as a place of worship. Here they remained, a gradually dwindling family, until Mother Girling's death in 1886, at which time the community family broke up and scattered. But there was no word of complaint against their persecutors, only expressions of grief for the break-up of their community life, as that was what their ejectment from New Forest amounted to. Mother Girling never really recovered from the exposure and hardship she suffered that awful night in December, 1874, nor from the mental anguish caused her by the sufferings of her helpless flock of women and children.

Death by Cancer

There were, prior to Mother Girling's demise, eleven deaths among the members of the community. Hers was the twelfth. When any member of the group died, he or she was buried with the usual rites of the established church in Hordle parish churchyard in a single line of graves. A tree of the macro-carpus type, an evergreen, possibly a yew, for a road nearby is named Yew Lane, was planted at the head of each grave. The twelfth grave at the extreme end of the line is that of

Mary Ann Girling: Leader of the Shakers

MARY ANN GIRLING

An East Anglian, Mary Ann Girling came from a humble background, but possessed amazing qualities. The brief biography below is taken from an American work, *Modern Spiritual History*, published in 1879.

Mary Ann Girling—maiden name, Cloughton—was the eldest of seven children. Her father was a farm labourer in a small village near Lowestoft, Suffolk, and according to his social position

Mother Girling, who died of cancer on September 15, 1886, after many months of painful suffering. At the head of her grave, the customary yew tree is very small compared with the others. The tree planted at the time of burial died, and so did a second and a third, and for years there was nothing to mark her grave. Then an old admirer of her life work planted a fourth tree. This one is still living, though (in 1979) it was making a very poor growth.

With the death of Mother Girling, the New Forest Shaker community died, too. Certainly, their eccentricities and strange opinions and behavior did not justify the harsh treatment they received.

was a man of good repute. She was born about 1830 and so uneducated and illiterate that when arrived at womanhood she could scarcely read or write. She was, in her youth, impetuous, strong-willed, and passionate, somewhat tall, and in figure well made. At the age of 20 she married George Girling, a sailor, by whom she had ten children, eight of whom died in infancy, and two, a son and daughter, still survive. During her husband's absence on the sea, she helped to support her household by millinery and dressmaking. It was not until after several years of her marriage that she evinced any disposition for religious thought or conviction, and this was brought about by the death of her last child.

... *and Her Rules*

Mary Ann Girling's rules were strict and each follower was expected to follow them to the letter:

Rule 1st.—That all who were admitted must have received the spirit of the same faith, and give evidence of it in purity and holiness of life.

2nd.—That upon entering, each must give up all that they possessed in money, goods, clothing, or valuables to Mrs. Girling, who was to dispose of the same for the benefit of the whole family, according as she was directed by God so to do.

3rd.—That no parent shall in any way interfere with the management or education of their children, nor yet correct them or otherwise, as all government is to be left to Mrs. Girling; and the teachers are to submit to her decrees in all things.

4th.—That no brother or sister be allowed to go out of the grounds, on their own pleasure, without permission.

5th.—That no private corres-

"The Soldiers' Friend" Loved the Forest

Although Sarah Robinson died at the turn of the century, her life remains a prime example of how one person can profoundly influence the lives of many.

Born in 1834 in Sussex, her family moved several times during her childhood. At 20 she was told by a surgeon that she would never enjoy a normal, healthy life and that, above all, she should not marry. Undeterred by this prognosis, she resolved to follow the precept that "the unmarried woman careth for the things of the Lord."

When her family moved near to Aldershot, she rented a temporary "soldier's home" and set about teaching soldiers how to read. In 1864 she sent 650 letters of inspiration to servicemen around the globe; by 1872 the figure had risen to 2,200—plus 625 parcels. During this time she visited soldiers in camps all over the south, lecturing and distributing copies of the Bible and *Pilgrim's Progress*. These visits totalled nearly 200, and some lasted as long as a week. Sarah, moreover, did not hesitate to visit public houses where soldiers gathered. She was soon aware of the poor living accommodations for the men, and eventually her crusade led to the provision of better quarters.

Sarah is best remembered for founding the Soldiers' Institute at Portsmouth, a large building that catered to many needs of the servicemen. She poured her life savings into it, and raised thousands of pounds from others. Military authorities supported her efforts, and on one occasion the Prince of Wales visited the Institute in the company of the Duke of Cambridge.

A visit to soldiers on maneuvers in Dartmoor was particularly destructive to Sarah's health, and thereafter she was unable to walk. Her ability to travel decreased and when she did go about, she was obliged to do so lying down. Now confined to a wheel chair, she erected a modest cottage in Bisterne Close, Burley, where she lived out the rest of her days. Ever ingenious, she had erected raised flower beds which she could admire and tend from her wheelchair. She looked upon her move to the New Forest, despite her infirmity and age, as a new chapter in her life. She met many Forest "characters" and learned about others. Extracts from two of her books, *The Soldier's Friend* and *My Book*, give the flavour of life in the New Forest a century ago.

narrow stairs, tiny windows, and general stuffiness of these doll's houses; in *our* Hut we had five good-sized airy rooms, a wide light passage from end to end and, no stairs.

Sublime Solitude

Within a year, roses and creepers had covered the ugly walls, while the door at the end opened directly on to the greensward of the Forest, between two old hollies. Big trees around us, with an undergrowth of holly and bracken. No one within half-a-mile, except a dear old Christian couple in the cottage at the other end of the field, who supplied us with dairy produce and veg-

SARAH ROBINSON

Mary Ann Girling ... and Her Rules

Continued from previous page
pondence be kept up with the friends or kindred of the Family, and that all correspondence to and fro be submitted to Mrs. Girling, whose decision is final.

6th.—That all gifts, of whatever kind, made to the members, must be given up to Mrs. Girling, so that they might be for the benefit of all without partiality.

7th—That all letters received by the members be handed to Mrs. Girling for perusal, and all monies or remittances be taken by her for

We went to Burley, met Woodman Sims, and came to terms about building in the north-west corner of his field, Bisterne Close. My good friend our builder from Portsmouth was almost ready to weep at being required to put up the long, low Hut I had planned, "just like a cowhouse," when, for the same money, I could have "a sweetly pretty little cottage." Too well I knew the cramped rooms,

the mutual benefit.

8th—That no undue intimacy of whatever kind must exist between brother and sister, and their daily life is to be such as becomes the Children of God.

etables. One could sit out among the trees in any direction without seeing a creature other than the forest ponies and cattle; rabbits, and birds everywhere, while the notes of jays, woodpigeons, and green woodpecker or "yaffle," showed how real was the solitude.

Northward of the Hut is a comparatively open space, honeycombed with rabbit-holes, and carpeted with heather and bracken; this slopes down to extensive bogland, dotted with furze bushes; and dangerous in some parts where the cotton-grass hangs out warning plumes; sometimes ponies or cattle get bogged and may even lose their lives here.

The Soldier's Friend...

Continued from previous page

Classes for All

After a while I opened a Men's Bible Class on Sunday afternoons in our kitchen, to which the foresters came from long distances; then there was a request that women should be admitted; so we built a kind of *annexe* to seat about sixty, and threw it open to all for various meetings, including one for children, whom I did not admit with the grown-ups. One could only wonder where all the people came from, or how they came to know of the "Hut." This went on for years, till quite a distinct track became trodden down through the trees to our door.

The young men about here seem too solid and too comfortable, either for soldiering or emigration. But one dear old woman, who walked some miles to see the "Hut," told me she had three grandsons soldiers—"they all know the Lord, and one of them can pray *beautiful*." Several women had sailor sons; one had lost hers in the *Victoria*; he had only been married a few weeks, as he and his sweetheart had deferred their marriage *eight* years that he might support his mother: the young widow, with the mother and sister all attended our meetings, Christians.

I cannot claim to be *old* in Burley estimation, for I soon

SKETCH FROM SARAH'S AUTOBIOGRAPHY

found the people here considered seventy the prime of life. One woman to whom I spoke of the happiness of being prepared for death, said, "But I'm not going to die yet, I'm only eighty-four!" A man whom I asked "What do *you* call old?" replied, "Well I should say when a man is past ninety he is getting on in years." Farmer Tame of Boldrewood died at a hundred and four, and there are several strong old persons around here long past eighty. The Old Age Pension has been a great boon in many families, though the old folks seemed to manage somehow

before that. One old man of eighty-eight applying for parish relief for the first time, remarked it was only for himself; his old woman could still earn her living. People had not expected us to stay here in the winter, and told us the snow was sometimes four or five feet deep in our corner and no one would be able to get at us: that at times the cottagers were short of food and necessaries from the roads being blocked. Ringwood, our nearest town, was some miles distant. One man seemed greatly concerned, and wondered what we would do without any doctor near.

I told him what another had said in a similar place, "*We mostly dies natural deaths*." All the same, we made preparations in the way of stoves, shutters, curtains, great store of fuel and foods; and so did very well though the winter proved a severe one with much snow. The silence seemed profound when no wind stirred, and the forest looked like a fairy dream, the great white motionless trees with blue sky above and blue shadows beneath them; and still more weird in moonlight; with a feeling of being buried away in this profound solitude. Our meetings were perforce suspended.

"THE HUT" WHERE SARAH LIVED

TWELVE GOLDEN RULES,

WHICH LEAD TO HAPPINESS IN THIS WORLD,
AND IN THE NEXT.

I.

THE *ready Penny* always gets the beſt Bargain. He who buys upon Truſt, muſt not complain if he be cheated. The Shop-keeper ſuſpects the Cuſtomer *who buys on Truſt*, and thinks he means never to pay; and therefore he takes good Care to be beforehand and charge accordingly.

II.

THE beſt Pennyworth is to be had where moſt fit together, in the open Market; and Bargains are often cheaper in the latter End of the Day. When honeſt Men have done their Work, it is better for them to *go to Market, than to the Ale-houſe.*

III.

WHEN Times are hard, why ſhould we make them harder? Is it not enough to be taxed once by Government, without being taxed twice by Folly, thrice by Drunkenneſs, four Times by Lazineſs, and ſo on? A good Man, even in hard Times, will do twice as well as a bad Man, in the beſt of Times. Let us all then riſe up *againſt ourſelves*, who thus impoſe the higheſt Taxes upon us, and we ſhall ſoon find that Times will mend. *Let us do our beſt*, and we ſhall find it to be a true Saying, that " God will help thoſe who help them- " ſelves."

IV.

TIME IS OUR ESTATE. It includes our Property. If we waſte it, or loſe it, we can *never, never*, purchaſe it back. We ought therefore neither to allow an idle Hour, nor to throw away an idle Penny. While we employ our Time and our Property (however ſmall that Property may be) to the beſt Advantage, we ſhall find that a Liveli-hood *may be made in any Situation of Life;* and that the poor Man who once wanted Aſſiſtance him-ſelf, may become able to aſſiſt others.

V.

INDUSTRY makes a Purſe, and FRUGA-LITY finds Strings for it; neither the Purſe, nor the Strings will coſt any Thing. He who has it, ſhould only open it as Frugality directs, and he will be ſure to find a uſeful Penny at the Bot-tom. *The Servants of Induſtry* are known by their Livery; it is always *whole* and *whol-ſome.* Look at the *ragged Slaves of Idleneſs*, and judge which is the beſt Maſter, INDUSTRY or IDLE-NESS.

VI.

MARRIAGE IS HONOURABLE; and the married State, when entered into with Affection and Prudence, is of all Conditions of Life the *moſt happy.* But to bring a Wife Home to ſtarve, ſhows neither Prudence nor Affection. Let young People therefore treaſure up *all the Surplus of their youth-ful Earnings*, and they may marry with Confidence, and live in Comfort.

VII.

DRUNKENNESS is one of the moſt beaſtly of all Vices. It is alſo one of the moſt miſchievous. The Drunkard loſes his Friends and his Buſineſs: he ruins himſelf and his Family. He will never be happy at Home; and he who is not happy at Home, will never be happy any where.

VIII.

THE Labourer's Wife has not often Meat to dreſs; but when ſhe has, if ſhe *roaſt* or *broil* it, ſhe waſtes Half of it in the Fire; if ſhe boil it, ſhe loſes a Third of it in the Water; but when ſhe ſtews it gently, thickening the Liquor with a little Meal, ground Rice, Potatoes, Peas, or other Vegetables, making it ſavoury with fried Onions, Herbs, and Seaſoning, ſhe gets the Good of the Whole. Let her keep the Veſſel covered: the beſt Part goes off in Steam.

IX.

HONESTY, we are told, is the beſt Policy. The honeſt Man therefore will generally get the moſt Buſineſs; while the Knave is generally de-tected, and is always deſpiſed. Honeſty, connected with Induſtry, may be ſaid to make a poor Man's Fortune. He who will do his Maſter's Work fairly will always have the Preference.

X.

ALL Wickedneſs, though it begin *in Pleaſure*, will end in *Miſchief*. Remember therefore, when you ſin, you are ſwallowing the Devil's *Bait*, and you may depend upon it, you will feel the *Hook* next.

XI.

THERE is ONE SIN, however, to which we are tempted by no Advantage; and that is *Swear-ing.* When you ſwear, therefore, remember you are ſerving the Devil without Wages.

XII.

IF to theſe Rules we add RELIGION; which leads us not only to avoid Wickedneſs, but, through Faith in Chriſt, to lead holy Lives, we want Nothing elſe to make us comfortable in this World, and everlaſtingly happy in the next.

T. BAKER, PRINTER; HIGH-STREET, SOUTHAMPTON.

EARLY 19TH CENTURY HANDBILL CIRCULATED IN FOREST AREA
Since newspapers were expensive, anyone with a cause to promote printed and distributed handbills on the streets, at stage coach stops and public places. This one, printed in Southampton, is held by the University of Southampton's Cope Collection.

(Above) Forest bluebells and (below) pigs at pannage

(Photographs by Eric Ashby)

"The Bell Inn," (Bramshaw), by William Shayer, Sr.   (Richard Green Galleries)

The death of Rufus: panel from New Forest Embroidery   (Belinda Lady Montagu)

The Ornamental Drive in spring (above) and (below) in autumn

(Photographs by Eric Ashby)

This rare "bird's eye" view of the New Forest is held in the Special Collections of the University of Southampton Library. No date is assigned, but the National Maritime Museum ascribes it to the early 1920s.

Small-holders then populated the Forest, most being self-sufficient in food. This was the era that Heywood Sumner knew and loved, and which is reflected in so much of his art.

The old Southampton-Dorchester railway

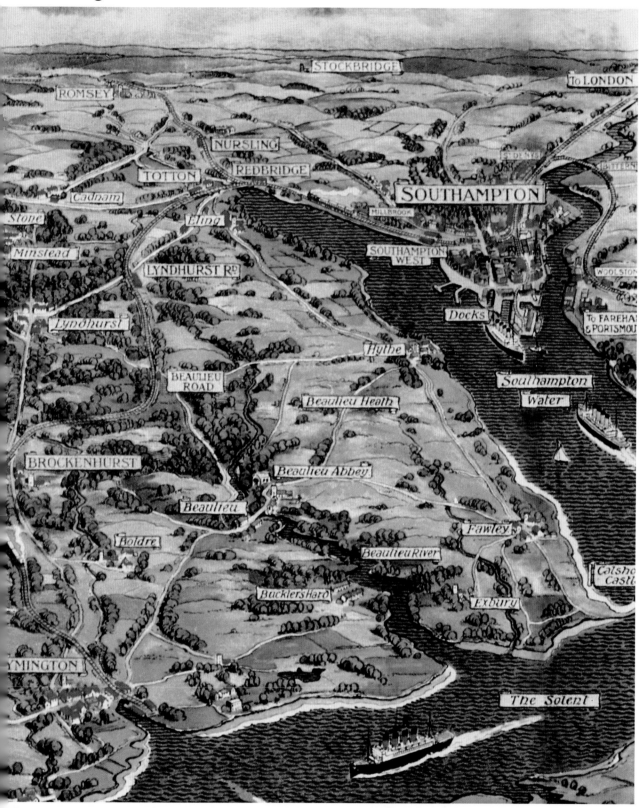

line was in operation, and the "map" probably came from one of its carriages. Southampton was the world's premier passenger port with virtually all of the great liners of the period calling there. Standing on the foreshore of the Forest, the on-looker marvelled at such well known giants as the *Leviathan, Mauretania, Berengaria, Olympic, Acquitania, Majestic, Empress of Canada*, and *Arundel Castle*.

Commercial and residential development on the Forest fringes was negligible.

The New Forest from Rockford Common

(Photographs by Eric Ashby)

Ancient beech trees at Undersley, near Burley

Odette (Mrs. G. Hallowes)

(Photograph by John Gill)

"Brusher" Mills

(From an old post-card)

"The Chace," Heywood Sumner's New Forest tapestry

(Hampshire Museum Service)

The rare wild gladiolus   *(Photographs by Eric Ashby)*   **Female tawny owl at nest hole**

Fallow buck in summer coat

7
Tales That Have Been Told
How the Keeper's Daughter Lost Her Lover

Charles Kingsley (1819–1875) was the son of the Rev. Charles Kingsley, originally of Battramsley House in the New Forest. Young Charles followed in his father's footsteps and was himself ordained in 1842. Plagued by ill health, he took time off from his duties as rector at Eversley in northern Hampshire for a holiday in the New Forest in the summer of 1847. During this time he composed the poignant ballad reproduced below, and another work with a New Forest setting, "The Red King." The ballad may be sung to a number of tunes, including "Barbara Allen."

A NEW FOREST BALLAD

Oh she tripped over Ocknell plain,
  And down by Bradley Water;
And the fairest maid on the forest side
  Was Jane, the keeper's daughter.

She went and went through the broad grey lawns
  As down the red sun sank,
And chill as the scent of a new-made grave
  The mist smelt cold and dank.

"A token, a token!" that fair maid cried,
  "A token that bodes me sorrow;
For they that smell the grave by night
  Will see the corpse to-morrow.

"My own true love in Burley Walk
  Does hunt to-night, I fear;
And if he meet my father stern,
  His game may cost him dear.

"Ah, here's a curse on hare and grouse,
  A curse on hart and hind;
And a health to the squire in all England,
  Leaves never a head behind."

Her true love shot a mighty hart
  Among the standing rye,
When on him leapt that keeper old
  From the fern where he did lie.

The forest laws were sharp and stern,
  The forest blood was keen;
They lashed together for life and death
  Beneath the hollies green.

The metal good and the walnut wood
  Did soon in flinders flee;
They tost the orts to south and north,
  And grappled knee to knee.

They wrestled up, they wrestled down,
  They wrestled still and sore;
Beneath their feet the myrtle sweet
  Was stamped to mud and gore.

Ah, cold pale moon, thou cruel pale moon,
  That starest with never a frown
On all the grim and the ghastly things
  That are wrought in thorpe and town:

And yet, cold pale moon, thou cruel pale moon,
  That night hadst never the grace,
To lighten two dying Christian men
  To see one another's face.

They wrestled up, they wrestled down,
  They wrestled sore and still
The fiend who blinds the eyes of men
  That night he had his will.

Like stags full spent, among the bent
  They dropped a while to rest;
When the young man drove his saying knife
  Deep in the old man's breast.

Continued on next page

JANE'S TRUE LOVE WAS KILLED IN BURLEY WALK, SHOWN HERE

Conan Doyle: "Steel True, Blade Straight"

(Thousands of Sherlock Holmes admirers flock annually to Baker Street in London, but few realize that Holmes' creator, Sir Arthur Conan Doyle (1859–1930), is buried in the churchyard of the New Forest village, Minstead. Doyle was born in Edinburgh and took his M.D. from Edinburgh University in 1885. His medical knowledge was to feature in many of the Sherlock Holmes adventures. For eight years he practiced at Southsea. In 1890 he wrote the historical novel, *The White Company*, which opens at the Cistercian monastery in Beaulieu. The excerpts below demonstrate Doyle's powerful writing as the incorrigible John of Hordle refuses to follow the straight and narrow path laid down by his religious superiors.)

The Incorrigible John of Hordle

(The brothers filed into the Abbey, following two of their number leading a young novice—remarkable for his huge stature and the defiant expression on his face.)

HOW THE BLACK SHEEP CAME FORTH FROM THE FOLD

The great bell of Beaulieu was ringing. Far away through the forest might be heard its musical clangour and swell. Peat-cutters on Blackdown and fishers upon the Exe (Beaulieu River) heard the distant throbbing rising and falling upon the sultry summer air. It was a common sound in those parts—as common as the

British Tourist Authority

CONAN DOYLE'S GRAVE IN ITS PEACEFUL FOREST SETTING

chatter of the jays and the booming of the bittern. Yet the fishers and the peasants raised their heads and looked questions at each other, for the Angelus had already gone and Vespers was still far off. Why should the great bell of Beaulieu toll when the shadows were neither short nor long?

All round the Abbey the monks were trooping in. Under the long green-paved avenues of gnarled oaks and of lichened beeches the white-robed brothers gathered to the sound. From the vineyard and the vine-press, from the bouvary or ox-farm, from the marl-pits and salterns, even from the distant ironworks of Sowley and the outlying grange of St. Leonard's, they had all turned their steps homeward.

It had been no sudden call. A swift messenger had the night

How the Keeper's Daughter Lost Her Lover...

Continued from previous page

The old man drove his gunstock down
  Upon the young man's head;
And side by side, by the water brown,
  Those yeomen twain lay dead.

They dug three graves in Lyndhurst yard;
  They dug them side by side;
Two yeomen lie there, and a maiden fair,
  A widow and never a bride.

The Incorrigible John of Hordle

Continued from previous page
before sped round to the outlying dependencies of the Abbey, and had left the summons for every monk to be back in the cloisters by the third hour after noontide. So urgent a message had not been issued within the memory of old lay-brother Athanasius, who had cleaned the Abbey knocker since the year after the Battle of Bannockburn.

With a bow to the Abbot, which had in it perhaps more pleasantry than reverence, the novice strode across to the carved prie-dieu which had been set apart for him, and stood silent and erect with his hand upon the gold bell which was used in the private orisons of the Abbot's own household. His dark eyes glanced rapidly over the assembly, and finally settled with a grim and menacing twinkle upon the face of his accuser.

The chamberlain rose, and having slowly unrolled the parchment-scroll, proceeded to read it out in a thick and pompous voice, while a subdued rustle and movement among the brothers bespoke the interest with which they followed the proceedings.

'Charges brought upon the second Thursday after the feast of the Assumption, in the year of our Lord thirteen hundred and sixty-six, against brother John, formerly known as Hordle John, or John of Hordle, but now a novice in the holy monastic order of the Cistercians. ... 'The charges against the said brother John are the following, namely, to wit:

'First, that on the above-mentioned feast of the Assumption, small beer having been served to the novices in the proportion of one quart to each four, the said brother John did drain the pot at one draught to the detriment of brother Paul, brother Porphyry, and brother Ambrose, who could scarce eat their own meat of salted stock-fish, on account of their exceeding dryness.'

At this solemn indictment the

British Tourist Authority
CLOISTERS AT BEAULIEU ABBEY

novice raised his hand and twitched his lip, while even the placid senior brothers glanced across at each other and coughed to cover their amusement. The Abbot alone sat grey and immutable, with a drawn face and a brooding eye.

'Item, that having been told by the master of the novices that he should restrict his food for two days to a single three-pound loaf of bran and beans, for the greater honouring and glorifying of St. Monica, mother of the holy Augustine, he was heard by brother Ambrose and others to say that he wished twenty thousand devils would fly away with the said Monica, mother of the holy Augustine, or any other saint who became between a man and his meat. Item, that upon brother Ambrose reproving him for this blasphemous wish, he did hold the said brother face downwards over the piscatorium or fish-pond for a space during which the said brother was able to repeat a Pater and four Aves for the better fortifying of his soul against impending death.'

There was a buzz and murmur among the white-frocked brethren at this grave charge; but the Abbot held up his long quivering hand. 'What then?' said he.

'Item, that between Nones and Vespers on the feast of James the Less the said brother John was observed upon the Brockenhurst road, near the spot which is known as Hatchett's Pond, in converse with a person of the other sex, being a maiden of the name of Mary Sowley, the daughter of the King's verderer. Item, that after sundry japes and jokes the said brother John did lift up the said Mary Sowley and did take, carry, and convey her across a stream, to the infinite relish of the devil and the exceeding detriment of his own soul, which scandalous and wilful falling away was witnessed by three members of our order.'

'What hast thou to say, brother John, upon these weighty things which are urged against thee?'

'Little enough, good father, little enough,' said the novice, speaking English with a broad West Saxon drawl. The brothers, who were English to a man,

The Incorrigible John of Hordle . . .

Continued from previous page
pricked up their ears at the sound of the homely and yet unfamiliar speech; but the Abbot flushed red with anger, and struck his hand upon the oaken arm of his chair.

'For the matter of the ale,' continued brother John, 'I had come in hot from the fields and had scarce got the taste of the thing before mine eye lit upon the bottom of the pot. It may be, too, that I spoke somewhat shortly concerning the bran and the beans, the same being poor provender and unfitted for a man of my inches. It is true also that I did lay my hands upon this jack-fool of a brother Ambrose, though, as you can see, I did him little scathe. As regards the maid, too, it is true that I did heft her over the stream, she having on her hosen and shoon, whilst I had but my wooden sandals, which could take no hurt from the water. I should have thought shame upon my manhood, as well as my monkhood, if I had held back my hand from her.' He glanced around as he spoke, with the half-amused look which he had worn during the whole proceedings.

'There is no need to go further,' said the Abbot. 'He has confessed to all. It only remains for me to portion out the punishment which is due to his evil conduct.'

He rose, and the two long lines of brothers followed his example, looking sideways with scared faces at the angry prelate.

'John of Hordle,' he thundered, 'you have shown yourself during the two months of your novitiate to be a recreant monk, and one who is unworthy to wear the white garb which is the outer symbol of the spotless spirit. That dress shall therefore be stripped from thee, and thou shalt be cast into the outer world without benefit of clerkship, and without lot or part in the graces and blessings of those who dwell under the care of the blessed Benedict. Thou shalt come back neither to Beaulieu nor to any of the granges of Beaulieu, and thy name shall be struck off the scrolls of the order.'

'So much for thy spiritual punishment,' he cried. 'But it is to the grosser feelings that we must turn in such natures as thine, and as thou art no longer under the shield of holy church there is the less difficulty. Ho there! lay-brothers—Francis, Naomi, Joseph—seize him and bind his arms! Drag him forth, and let the foresters and the porters scourge him from the precincts!'

As these three brothers advanced towards him to carry out the Abbot's direction, the smile faded from the novice's face, and he glanced right and left with his fierce brown eyes, like a bull at a baiting. Then with a sudden deep-chested shout, he tore up the heavy oaken prie-dieu and poised it to strike, taking two steps backward the while, that none might take him at a vantage.

THE GATE HOUSE, BEAULIEU
(Sketch by Alexander Ansted from C.J. Cornish's *The New Forest and the Isle of Wight*.)

The Favourite: *Children of the New Forest*

Captain Frederick Marryat (1792–1848) was a distinguished naval officer who received British and French awards for his gallantry and contributions to scientific navigation. In 1830, at the age of 38, he left the navy to pursue a career of writing. For most of the next two decades he turned out books at a rapid rate, sometimes producing two popular titles in the same year. He was plagued by ill health dating from fevers suffered in tropical areas, and for the last eight years of his life concentrated on children's books. Some of these became classics and one of the most popular was *The Children of the New Forest* (1847). It went into many printings under several publishers. The two extracts reproduced here are taken from the Dent's "classics" edition and set the stage for the story, as well as revealing the kindness and philosophy of old Jacob Armitage, the children's mentor and protector.

THE BURNING OF ARNWOOD, THE NEW FOREST HOME OF COLONEL BEVERLEY
(Taken from an edition published by H. Hurst in the second half of the last century)

The Incorrigible John of Hordle...

Continued from previous page

'By the black rood of Waltham!' he roared, 'if any knave among you lays a finger-end upon the edge of my gown, I will crush his skull like a filbert!' With his thick knotted arms, his thundering voice, and his bristle of red hair, there was something so repellent in the man that the three brothers flew back at the very glare of him; and the two rows of white monks strained away from him like poplars in a tempest.

The novice was a strategist as well as a man of action. Springing forward, he hurled his unwieldy weapon at brother Ambrose, and, as desk and monk clattered on to the floor together, he sprang through the open door and down the winding stair. Sleepy old brother Athanasius, at the porter's cell, had a fleeting vision of twinkling feet and flying skirts; but before he had time to rub his eyes the recreant had passed the lodge, and was speeding as fast as his sandals could patter along the Lyndhurst road.

The circumstances which I am about to relate to my juvenile readers took place in the year 1647. By referring to the history of England of that date they will find that King Charles I, against whom the Commons of England had rebelled, after a civil war of nearly five years, had been defeated, and was confined as a prisoner at Hampton Court. The Cavaliers, or the party who fought for King Charles, had all been dispersed, and the Parliamentary army under the command of Cromwell were beginning to control the Commons.

It was in the month of November in this year that King Charles, accompanied by Sir John Berkely, Ashburnham, and Legg, made his escape from Hampton Court, and rode as fast as the horses could carry them towards that part of Hampshire which led to the New Forest. The king expected that his friends had provided a vessel in which he might escape to France; but in this he was disappointed. There was no vessel ready, and after riding for some time along the shore he resolved to go to Titchfield, a seat belonging to the Earl of Southampton. After a long consultation with those who attended him, he yielded to their advice, which was, to trust to Colonel Hammond, who was governor of the Isle of Wight for the Parliament, but who was supposed to be friendly to the king. Whatever might be the feelings of commiseration of Colonel Hammond towards a king so unfortunately situated, he was firm in his duties towards his employers, and the consequence was that King Charles found himself again a prisoner in Carisbrook Castle.

But we must now leave the king, and retrace history to the commencement of the Civil War. A short distance from the town of Lymington, which is not far from Titchfield, where the king took shelter, but on the other side of the Southampton Water, and south of the New Forest, to which it adjoins, was a property called

JACOB DISCOVERS TROOPS
These illustrations were made for the George Routledge edition.

HUMPHREY'S SUCCESS
Self-sufficiency was to be the key to the children's survival.

PATIENCE IN TEARS
Her agony over Edward was short-lived, for they were soon to be married.

The Favourite: Children of the New Forest. . .

Continued from previous page
Arnwood, which belonged to a Cavalier of the name of Beverley. It was at that time a property of considerable value, being very extensive, and the park ornamented with valuable timber; for it abutted on the New Forest, and might have been supposed to have been a continuation of it. This Colonel Beverley, as we must call him, for he rose to that rank in the king's army, was a valued friend and companion of Prince Rupert's, and commanded several troops of cavalry. He was ever at his side in the brilliant charges made by this gallant prince, and at last fell in his arms at the battle of Naseby. Colonel Beverley had married into the family of the Villiers, and the issue of his marriage was two sons and two daughters; but his zeal and sense of duty had induced him, at the commencement of war, to leave his wife and family at Arnwood, and he was fated never to meet them again. ...
(Colonel Beverley's four children escaped from Arnwood which the Roundheads had set to the torch and, after many adventures, found shelter with the old forester, Jacob Armitage.)

Time passed; the month of November came on without anything to disturb the daily employments of the family in the forest: when one evening Jacob, who had returned from hunting with Edward (the first time they had been out since the season commenced), told Alice that she must

A CLOSE CALL
Humphrey greets the suspicious officer, but Edward saves the day.

do all she could to give them a good dinner the next day, as it was to be a feast.

'Why so, Jacob?'

'If you cannot guess, I won't tell you till the time comes,' replied Jacob.

'Well then, Humphrey must help us,' replied Alice, 'and we will do what we can. I will try, now that we have some meat, to make a grand dinner.'

Alice made all the preparations, and had for dinner the next day a piece of baked venison, a venison stew, a pair of roast chickens, and an apple pie—which, for them, was a very grand dinner indeed. And it was very well dressed; for Jacob had taught her to cook, and by degrees she improved upon Jacob's instructions. Humphrey was quite as clever at it as she was; and little Edith was very useful, as she plucked the fowls, and watched the things while they were cooking.

'And now I'll tell you,' said Jacob, after saying grace, 'why I asked you for a feast this day. It is because exactly on this day twelve-month I brought you all to the cottage. Now you know.'

'I did not know it certainly, but I dare say you are right,' replied

A Civil War Story by the Vicar of Sopley

> **The Rev. J.F. Vallings was Vicar of Sopley for 40 years and at his death in 1929 had reached the age of 76. An Oxford graduate, he was both a student of theology and the English Civil War. He wrote several books on theology and one fictional work on the Civil War, *The Severing Sword*, an excerpt from which is quoted below. Mr. Vallings makes use of actual Civil War incidents in other parts of Hampshire, while setting his story in the New Forest. He captures the Forest dialect and reveals how cunning Forest characters thwart the plans of the invaders. Appropriately, a vicar plays a prominent role.**

The wayfarers felt too tired to go on much further, and, feeling safe from pursuit for the present, they buried themselves in the heart of an enclosure, whence some startled deer trotted away. Here was a saw-pit and a woodman's rough shelter. With logs or faggots for pillows, they were soon far into dreamland.

As they slept, a peasant passed by seeking for some stray cattle with his mark V upon them. Seeing the sleepers, he stept softly up, his dog sniffing round the unconscious forms. The man peered into their faces, and recognised both the sleepers.

"As sure as I be Tom Vatcher to Burley that be Parson Willis and young Master Compton. What be un a doing thicce pleace? It be a queer carner un be got into, I allow. How easily us might cut their throats and make off wi' their money. But us ud be terr'ble sorry to hurt nor a hair of their heads. Parson was that kind to my old mother down to Avon when she was took of the browntitus, and the young Master was allus so free like, it did un good to a poor man to meet un with his cheerful face. He be a downright straight un. Shall us wake un?"

Tom scratched his head; but the dog had also recognised an old sporting friend in Marmaduke, and by profusely licking his face, and by jerky little happy barks, roused him for a few moments, only to fall asleep again in that delicious indifference which contemplates getting up as worse than death by torture.

Tom proceeded to crack his whip. This time the clergyman awoke, and instantly rousing his companion, pointed to the newcomer. Recognition and friendly greetings followed.

Tom guided them by a short cut towards Boldre Wood and the friendly charcoal-burner's hut, and promised if he came across any pursuers he would take care to direct them out of harm's way.

Herein he was as good as his word, for about an hour afterwards, when the fiery Corporal and the few Avon troopers he could inspire with his vengeful ardour came trotting past Holmesley enclosure bound for Lyndhurst, he gravely informed them he had sighted a couple of runaways making southward, doubtless for Lymington or Beaulieu, where a boat might be secured. Further he so gained their confidence that they, rigidly following his minute directions, were soon floundering in some choice bogs, whence at last they emerged in piteous plight of man and beast, too exhausted to continue the chase.

It was about noon when the two Royalists reached the charcoal-burner's hut. This was a rough erection of turf clods and heaps of brushwood and furze. Inside, a heap of straw, some dry ferns, a wallet and flask, a wooden platter and cup, and a rough blanket or two, appeared to be all the furniture which dignified the domicile.

They entered in, and resumed their interrupted slumbers, being much too fatigued to be nice about the accommodation.

The master of the house himself soon entered. His hands were very black, so was his face; his eyes and

---

Children of the New Forest...

Continued from previous page
Edward.

'And now children, tell me,' said Jacob, 'has not this year passed very quickly and very happily—quite as quickly and quite as happily as if you had been staying at Arnwood?'

'Yes, more so,' replied Humphrey, 'for then very often I did not know what to do to amuse myself, and since I have been here the days have always been too short.'

'I agree with Humphrey,' said Edward.

'And I am sure I do,' replied Alice; 'I'm always busy, and always happy, and I'm never scolded about dirtying my clothes or tearing them, as I used to be.'

'And what does little Edith say?'

'I like to help Alice, and I like to play with the kitten,' replied Edith.

'Well, my children,' said Jacob, 'depend upon it, you are the most happy when your days pass quickest, and that is only the case when you have plenty to do. Here you are in peace and safety; and may it please God that you may continue so! We want very few things in this world—that is, we really want very few things, although we wish and sigh for many. You have health and spirits, which are the greatest blessings in life. Who would believe, to look at you all, that you were the same children that I brought away from Arnwood? You were then very different from what you are now. You are strong and healthy, rosy and brown, instead of being fair and delicate. Look at your sisters, Edward, do you think that any of your former friends—do you think that Martha, who had the care of them, would know them?'

Edward smiled and said: 'Certainly not; especially in their present dresses.'

From Forest Observer to World Authority

(Ethel Stevens was only nine years old when her father became Vicar of Burley in 1889. She became keenly interested in the gypsies, their customs and speech, and this interest continued after she left the village. In 1915 Mills and Boon published *Allward*, her story of New Forest gypsy life as seen through the eyes of young Mary Allward.

This early interest in customs and life of a different society grew and, later as Lady Drower, Ethel became a leading authority on a Near Eastern sect, the Mandaeans. She accompanied her husband, Sir Edwin Drower, to Iraq when he was appointed the territory's Judicial Advisor in 1921. For the next 25 years she was able to visit and observe the Mandaeans.

Lady Drower received many awards, including honorary degrees from the Universities of Oxford and Uppsala. She died in 1972 at the age of 92.)

(In the passage below from *Allward*, a gypsy woman explains why she delays "dookerin" until the next day.)

Photographs courtesy Félicité Hardcastle

THE VICAR'S DAUGHTER WHO ROSE TO FAME
Ethel Stevens (left) as a young lady and (right) as Lady Drower. Her childhood interest in the gypsies of the New Forest led her to study another group, the Mandaeans, in the Near East when her husband was appointed judicial advisor there.

We were camped up by Minstead Mill, and there was two ladies stayin' up at the Compton Arms. When my mother called in at the gennleman's with her basket one day the two ladies wuz there, looking at his picters. He always had a pleasant word for her, and the two ladies they asked her to dooker them.

She says, "Not today, my pretty ladies, the stars isn't right for it, but I'll come and dooker you tomorrow up by Stoneycross."

She said that artful, look, because if a lady or gennleman puts their hand in their pocket sudden, without expectin' it, it's

---

Civil War Story
by Sopley Vicar . . .

Continued from previous page
hair were all as black. He seemed to be himself a forest of hair. He had a broad, squat figure.

He bent over the sleepers with a look of amazement. Then, as he recognised them, an amused gleam came into his eye, changed into a grave and tender expression as he spoke aloud to himself—the way, sometimes, of a very lonely man.

"It be Parson Willis. These be a queer zart o' times. The Lard be wi' un howsomedever. Many a time have he and young Compton been rummaging about thicce pleace. And he brought a runagate to think o' his sins and know his Saviour. Anythinks Dickon can do for them Dickon'll do."

SOPLEY CHURCH IN THE REV. J. F. VALLINGS' TIME
This sketch by Douglas Snowdon is taken from *Unknown Hampshire* published by The Bodley Head.

Passages from Three of Allen Seaby's Books

A generation of young people came to know the New Forest and its wild life through Allen W. Seaby's trilogy: *Skewbald* (1923) and *Sons of Skewbald* (1937), both published by A. & C. Black, and *The White Buck* (1939), published by Thomas Nelson.

Representative passages from the three books are reproduced here. "The Family of Foxes" is taken from *Skewbald*, "At the Pony Sale" is from *Sons of Skewbald*, and "A Terrified Fawn" is from *The White Buck*.

"The Family of Foxes"

Instinct and his mother taught Skewbald to notice all that was going on, to keep his eyes "skinned."

When they were in the woods, the harsh notes of the jays made him start, and from his mother's movements, he learned that some-one was about. Once in spring, browsing on the young shoots of a hawthorn-bush, he almost nosed against two dormice fresh from their long rest, sleek and tawny bright, among the green tufts. ...

Sometimes a fox trotted by, or sat up and looked at him impudently, and, as it happened, he got tolerably familiar with a family of foxes. The lair was in a bank between the roots of an old oak. Skewbald's mother, as she went by, snuffed the air, and, indeed, the smell, whether of fox or high viands, was perceptible even to human nostrils. So Skew-bald snuffed too, and whenever he passed the hole, the odour remin-ded him of what dwelt there.

One fine evening, as he idled at a little distance, he perceived movement outside the hole. It was not rabbits, so he went closer, and saw the little fox cubs, lithe and furry. One lay on its back gnawing at a moorhen's wing, two were engaged in a tussle, and one curled into a ball with his tail over his nose, pretending to be asleep; but when the vixen came up, and after looking around, sat down calmly amidst her family, the mis-chievous cub got up, came behind her and worried her tail, until she turned, and seized him in her jaws, so that the yelped.

At the Pony Sale

On the way the mare gave no trouble but trudged on, Sally at her side, the two foals ambling along together, making little chases after one another or staying to nibble at a tussock. It was a beautiful morning to uplift the heart, sad as the girl felt at the idea of parting from her young friends. The morning mist was dissipating rapidly from the lowel levels; the sky was cloudless; long shadows stretched from the hollies and bushes, from the ponies and Sally herself. She knew of short cuts, went through enclosures, down hills by forest paths, heather fringed, and across moors where mossy bogs lay on either side of the track. Once they crossed a Forest bridge, the skewbalds preferring to splash through the shallow water rippling over its pebbly bed. ...

The scene was a busy one when Sally arrived on the sale ground. A number of ponies were there tied to the rails of a fence, and folk had begun to congregate at the ring roped around, with the auc-tioneer's box in a commanding position. ... Sally tied up the mare at a vacant space and looked around. She knew she had to notify the auctioneer's clerk and find out when her turn would come to enter the ring with her ponies. As she stood, hesitating to leave the two colts to their own devices among this throng of people, not to say dogs, she noticed two men passing along the line of waiting ponies. One, a tall, stout red-faced man, was smartly dressed. He wore a well-cut tweed suit, in his hat-band was a slip of jay's blue patterned wing, and he sported a heavy gold chain. His companion was an undersized, wizened man whose collar, leggings and boots told he had something to do with

From *Observer to Authority*...

Continued from previous page

sixpence instead of a shilling. But if they knows you're comin' a-purpose to see them, they has to give you a bit extry so as not to look mean. And these was rich, look. Besides, my mother wuz afraid they might smell the drop of drink she'd had that day.

So she says, "If I tells you true, you'll not fergit to treat the poor gypsy woman handsome, will you, my pretties?"

(Ethel Stevens' powers of description come through in the extract below detailing Mary's trek from Thorney Hill to Burley.)

(Mary) walked rapidly along the high road (at Thorney Hill) towards Burley, meeting many of the villages in their Sunday clothes who looked askance at the unkempt gypsy girl.

She soon left the last house behind her and, turning off onto the heather, stood looking over the wild heath that lay between her and Burley, bosomed in distant trees. The long pond in the valley gleamed and mirrored the great cumuli, heavy with unfallen rain.

The clearness which spoke of rain near at hand brought Burley Beacon nearer by two miles. The heather, still wet from the morn-ing's heavy showers, was dark green-brown at her feet, becoming purple on the further slopes. The brown bracken was plum-coloured in the distance. The colours were rich and vivid.

Near her there was the steady sound of cropping—a pony, its shaggy hide red as fire in the transitory sunlight, was busily feeding. A peaty bracken and heather-sweet smell rose to her out of the valley, as it were, the very soul of the heath and bog.

Passages from Seaby's Books. . .

horses; he was plainly horsey in type.

The two paused along side the mare and her colts, both of whom at the moment had their heads under her, one on either side.

"Twins!" exclaimed the big man, and more quietly to his companion: "Well, Jim' we shan't be likely to find anything today more suitable?"

A Terrified Fawn

In the grassy rides of the enclosures an occasional pony may be seen. He had donned his winter suit, say of deep bay, which glows sombrely, while the hair of mane and back reflects the blue light of the northern sky. In such conditions, if you had seen the white fawn (and at this season and through the winter the deer do not always hide during the day) in a shady glade, he would have appeared an icy blue, save where

the afternoon sun penetrated and dropped a spot of pure gold on his back. He had cut his teeth by now, and was no longer dependent on his mother. He had learned to partake of what she herself ate, all but the bramble and holly leaves, too prickly for his yet tender lips.

That first frost of autumn, which changed so much the appearance of leaf and frond, caused movement to take place among the deer population. The fallow bucks, who had harboured by themselves for three-quarters of the year in the outlying enclosures, made their way to the central wooded area, home of the does and their fawns.

The white fawn was terrified when he saw the strange-looking intruders. They were like his mother in shape and with the same familiar scent, yet they had on their heads what looked like dead

branches. How fierce the bucks looked and how their antlers clashed together as they challenged one another! The fawn shrank against his mother's side, although he was soon pushed away from her.

The bucks ran round the does seeking to attach to themselves a herd. These circular tours soon brought a buck into collision with another male. With heads down they charged. Their antlers crashed and the rivals did their best in what was little more than a shoving match. Seldom did they harm one another save for an accidental bruise. On rare occasions, however, antlers may become so interlocked that the combatants are unable to separate, and if not found in time, both die a miserable death. In the Verderers' Hall at Lyndhurst hang the antlers of two bucks wedged together in this way. The unfortunate creatures could not free themselves and were found dead, their bodies still warm.

British Tourist Authority

GRAVE OF THE GIRL WHO WAS "ALICE"
This grave in Lyndhurst churchyard is that of Mrs. Reginald Hargreaves who was the "Alice" in Lewis Carroll's *Alice in Wonderland*.

8
The Forest at War

Buckler's Hard: Steeped in Naval History

(For two centuries Buckler's Hard has played an important role in Britain's naval history. From 1745 to 1822 more than 50 vessels were built there for the British Navy, among them some for Lord Nelson's fleet. During the 1914-18 war motor launches were built there. In the second world war wooden mine-sweepers, built elsewhere, were fitted out there. Nearby some of the floating docks and artificial ("Mulberry") harbour units were constructed, and when naval craft assembled all over Britain's south coast for the invasion of Normandy, the Beaulieu River was one of the rendez-vous areas.

Today it is easy for the visitor to appreciate Buckler's Hard's contribution. A maritime museum has models of the famous "hards," and the old "Master Builder's House" has been expanded into a hotel and restaurant, while retaining the original maritime flavour.

John, Second Lord Montagu of Beaulieu, in his 1909 work, *Buckler's Hard and Its Ships*, tells about the site's early history, three famous ships of Nelson's fleet built there, and reflects on the lasting quality of "brave Englishmen" whose vessels were constructed there.)

Early History
The early history of Buckler's Hard is shrouded in the mists of time, but it is probable that it was a fishing and agricultural village from very early times. On the Beaulieu River there are only six places along its nine miles of estuary where the gravel soil stretches right down to low-water mark, and Buckler's Hard is the principal of these. Therefore when John, second Duke of Montagu, was looking out for a place at which to create and encourage local industry—to wit, shipbuilding—it was natural that he should

British Tourist Authority

TRANQUILITY BELIES BUCKLER'S HARD'S BUSY PAST
Two centuries ago some of Britain's most famous naval vessels were built here. The two world wars again saw Buckler's Hard making valuable naval contributions. Today a small maritime museum documents the site's past glories. The visitor may also enjoy riverside nature walks or a cruise on the Beaulieu River.

have chosen Buckler's hard. The name of Buckler's Hard, or, as it was originally spelt, Buckle's Hard, is probably derived from a local family, the Buckles, who lived there for generations; and as for the term "hard", it is used along the South Coast to describe a landing-place in the case of rivers or estuaries where the banks in other spots are specially soft.

Extensive quay frontages were offered at a yearly rental of 6s. 8d. apiece, on a ninety-nine years' lease; three loads of timber were given gratis for every house erected, and the cheapness of water-carriage from Buckler's Hard was strongly insisted upon.

At many adjacent points on the coast shipbuilding had long been going on—at Southampton, Lymington, and elsewhere. The Duke wished to attract a firm to settle at Buckler's Hard, and went to some pains to induce a builder to come.

Enter Henry Adams
The firm of Wyatt and Co. appears to have been attracted

to Beaulieu by the advantages offered by the Duke, and in September, 1743, they commenced operations. The result was that in 1745 they launched the *Surprise*, 24 guns; in the following year the *Scorpion*, 18 guns; and in 1749 the *Woolwich*, 44 guns. It is expressly stated, in a business abstract compiled for the firm of Adams and Co. in 1801, that "Henry Adams was overseer to building the above three ships." This is the first mention of this veteran shipbuilder, who, born in 1713, was only thirty years of age when he undertook the responsible task of superintending the building of the *Surprise*. For sixty-two long years he was destined to build and design ships of war.

The *Salisbury and Winchester Journal* of July 11, 1789, when the *Illustrious*, 74 guns, had been launched on the Beaulieu River on the previous Tuesday stated: "This makes the twenty-first of the line that Mr. Adams has built at Buckler's Hard, besides which he has built as many more at other places."

Buckler's Hard...

Continued from previous page
Nelson's Ships

The (same newspaper) of 10 April, 1781, contained an account of the launch of the *Agamemnon*, which I give here: "There was launched at Buckler's Hard the *Agamemnon*, a fine 64-gun ship, built by Mr. Adams, of that place. " Her gun-deck was 160 feet in length, her keel measuring 132 feet, with a burden of 1,384 tons.

She rapidly became a famous ship, and in February, 1783, Horatio, Lord Nelson, was appointed as her Captain, and in the following October she kept up a gallant running fight with four French frigates and a brig corvette.

She was in every affair of importance in the Mediterranean, and whilst in command of her Nelson lost his right eye, at the siege of Calvi. The *Agamemnon* played a noble part at Copenhagen, and bore her full share in Sir Robert Calder's action off Capte Finisterre. The battle-thunder of Trafalgar raged around her, and in the following year she was with Sir John Duckworth off St. Domingo, when five sail of the line struck, amidst ringing English cheers. Nelson's *Agamemnon*, after a glorious career, was finally wrecked in Maldonaldo Bay, in the River Plate, in May, 1809.

The *Euryalus*, 36, was built at Buckler's Hard, and launched on June 6, 1803. Need one say more of her than that she, with the *Agamemnon* and the *Swiftsure*, were the three Buckler's Hard ships which fought at Trafalgar, and that to the *Euryalus* was assigned the honourable task of watching the allied fleets of France and Spain in Cadiz Harbour; that she signalled their coming out to Nelson's fleet in the offing, and that after the battle she right gallantly took the *Royal Sovereign* in tow.

The *Swiftsure*, 74, was launched in 1804, when a large number of spectators assembled to witness the launch, the day being very fine. Next year she was at Traf-

1803 CALL FOR MEN

Mid-way during the Napoleonic Wars, the Rev. Henry Drummond, Vicar of Fawley took the initiative in organizing volunteers from Fawley, Beaulieu, and Dibden. This is the hand-bill circulated among the public.

At a MEETING of the principal Inhabitants of FAWLEY, BEAULIEU, and DIBDEN, held at the NEW INN, at FAWLEY, on the 8th Day of August, 1803, the following RESOLUTIONS were agreed to:

RESOLVED,

I. That it is expedient, as well for the Relief of the aforesaid Parishes, as for the Advantage of the Service, that the People be invited to come forward as Volunteers, so that the Call for Service from the several Classes, under the Acts of Parliament of the 43d of the King, may be obviated.

II. That Volunteers be accepted in greater Numbers than absolutely required by the Act, or by the Secretary of State's Communication to the Lord Lieutenant of the County.

III. That a Subscription be opened for assisting the Government Allowance for Clothes and Accoutrements, so that they may be made as near as possible to the Regulation for the Army, but, on no Account, of a superior Quality.

IV. That the Subscriptions be put into a General Stock Purse, for the Benefit of the aforesaid Parishes.

V. That the Uniform of the Volunteers as nearly resemble those of the Regular Regiments as possible.

VI. That the Men willing to come forward as Volunteers, be requested to assemble at Eight o'Clock on Sunday Morning the 14th Instant, at Ash Down; and that such Clauses of the Defence Act, as relate to their Situation, be read to them, and explained; as also the Resolutions of this Meeting.

VII. That a Book be prepared, in which the Names of the Volunteers shall be entered, as soon as requisite Explanations shall have been made to them.

VIII. That Admiral PARRY's obliging Offer to act as Treasurer be accepted.

IX. That the Thanks of this Meeting be voted to the Chairman, the Rev. HENRY DRUMMOND, for his very polite Attention and able Assistance this Day.

X. That this Meeting now adjourn to Tuesday the 16th Instant, at Twelve o'Clock; then to meet at the New Inn, Fawley.

XI. And that a General Meeting of the Parishes of Fawley, Beaulieu, and Dibden, be held at Hill Top Gate, on Sunday the 21st Instant, at Nine o'Clock in the Morning.

HENRY ROGER DRUMMOND, Chairman.

T. Baker & Son, Printers; Southampton.

Stiff Rules for Yeoman Cavalry

(In 1830 Andrew Robert Drummond of Cadland was appointed Captain of the "Cadland Troop of Yeomanry Cavalry" by the Duke of Wellington. A year later the troop was fully organized. It's *Rules and Regulations*, adopted "democratically" at various troop assemblies, reveal the heavy pecuniary threat under which the volunteers lived. Nonetheless, belonging to a local military unit had great appeal, and the unit flourished under its proper name, the "New Forest East Troop.")

RULES, &c.

I.

Every Officer not attending Parade shall be fined £1 10s. Not

algar, and on November 26, 1813, her boats captured off Corsica the French privateer schooner *Charlemagne*, 8 guns and 93 men.

Old Spirit Lives on

Where the caulking-hammer resounded is now a peaceful meadow, and wild-fowl and herons haunt the once busy banks. The oak gave way to metal. Shall the dominion of the seas be overshadowed by the dominion of the air?

Thus Time brings its changes, and the sails and wooden walls give place to steel armour and steam-turbines. But the spirit of the brave Englishmen who fought by flood and ebb, by shore and on open sea, remains.

The 1895 Manoeuvres: 13,000 in the Forest

FIELD STATE, MANOEUVRES, AUGUST 31, 1895.

General His Royal Highness the DUKE OF CONNAUGHT, K.G., K.C.B., Commanding. Aides-de-Camp—Captains Lord Bingham; E. W. Blunt; M. McNeill. Assistant Adjutant-Generals—Colonels T. Kelly-Kenny, C.B. (Chief Staff Officer); H. S. G. Miles. Deputy Assistant Adjutant-Generals—Lieutenant-Colonel Hon. F. W. Stopford; Majors J. Wolfe Murray; H. E. Belfield; Lieutenant-Colonel C. W. H. Douglas (Acting). Commanding Royal Artillery—Lieutenant-Colonel Wallace. Commanding Royal Engineer—Colonel Sir A. W. Mackworth, Bart.

Corps as Brigaded.	On Parade	Casualties. Sick.	On Duty.	Total.	Total at Manoeuvre Ground	Horses. On Parade	Not on Parade	Total.	Guns.	Names of Commanding Officers
Major-General H. M. Bengough, C.B.										
5TH BRIGADE (DETACHED TROOPS)										
½ Squadron 3rd Hussars	55		15	15	70	55	9	64		Captain Patton-Bethune.
16th Field Battery, Royal Artillery	64	2	62	64	128	58	27	85	6	Major Keir.
2nd Bedfordshire Regiment	465	5	26	31	496	9		9		Lieut.-Colonel Young.
2nd Cheshire Regiment	463	2	29	31	494	7	2	9	2*	Lieut.-Colonel Hare.
2nd Worcestershire Regiment	456	5	26	31	487	7	2	9		Lieut.-Colonel Egerton.
1st Royal Scots Fusiliers	430	5	58	63	493	4	3	7		Lieut.-Colonel Spurgin.
1ST INFANTRY DIVISION. Major-General Sir W. F. Butler, K.C.B.										
Lieutenant-Colonel C. M. H. Downing.										
Squadron 3rd Hussars	113		24	24	137	113	14	127		Major Wogan-Browne.
3rd Field Battery, Royal Artillery	66	1	53	54	120	62	14	76	6	Major Dunlop.
13th " "	66	1	51	52	118	62	19	81	6	Major Lambart.
77th " "	49		49	49	98	50	7	57	4	Major Bland.
Royal Engineers	150		47	47	197	45	11	56		Major Maxwell.
1ST BRIGADE. Colonel L. J. Oliphant.										
2nd Grenadier Guards	510	14	12	26	536	14		14		Colonel Ricardo.
2nd Scots Guards	531	17	18	35	566	8		8	2*	Colonel Fludyer.
1st Northumberland Fusiliers	454	21	26	47	501	7	2	9		Lieut.-Colonel Cherry.
1st Coldstream Guards	544	5	22	27	571	6	4	10		Colonel Graves-Sawle.
2ND BRIGADE. Lieutenant-Colonel Stopford Sackville.										
2nd Leicestershire Regiment	467	4	23	27	494	6	5	11		Lieut.-Colonel Gregg.
2nd Middlesex Regiment	667	12	30	42	709	6	4	10		Lieut.-Col. Hughes-Hallett
1st Argyll & Sutherland Highlanders	460	5	21	26	486	3	5	8		Lieut.-Colonel Hannay.
4th Rifle Brigade	454	5	24	29	483	5	4	9	2*	Major Kenyon-Slaney.
Medical Staff Corps	57		51	51	108	75		75		Surgn.-Lieut.-Colonel Miller
2ND INFANTRY DIVISION. Major-General Sir C. Warren, G.C.M.G.										
Lieutenant-Colonel Yorke.										
Squadron 3rd Hussars	109	3	20	23	132	109	11	120		Captain Oswald.
57th Field Battery, Royal Artillery	65	5	53	58	123	59	18	77	6	Major Galton.
58th " "	46	2	50	52	98	52	17	69	4	Major Baldock.
69th " "	66	1	56	57	123	63	14	77	6	Major McKenzie Grieve.
Royal Engineers	100	2	35	37	137	40	9	49		Captain Jeffreys.
3RD BRIGADE. Major-General C. F. Clery, C.B.										
2nd Norfolk Regiment	507	3	37	40	547	4	5	9		Lieut.-Colonel Shepherd.
1st Border Regiment	577	4	24	28	605	6	3	9	2*	Lieut.-Colonel Hinde.
1st Seaforth Highlanders	444	13	40	53	497	8	2	10		Colonel Murray.
2nd East Lancashire Regiment	599	21	37	58	657	4	5	9		Lieut.-Colonel Evans.
4TH BRIGADE. Major-General W. E. Montgomery.										
2nd South Wales Borderers	462	3	12	15	477	5		5		Lieut.-Colonel Browne, V.C
1st Connaught Rangers	560	11	13	24	584	5	3	8		Lieut.-Colonel Brook.
1st Royal Dublin Fusiliers	472	15	12	27	499	3		3		Lieut.-Colonel Riddell.
2nd Shropshire Light Infantry	544	4	13	17	561	3		3		Lieut.-Colonel Murray.
Medical Staff Corps	79		30	30	109	15		15		Surgn.-Major Macnamara.
Military Police	38				38	23		23		
NOT ON PARADE	. .	2	590	592	592		456	456		
Total	11189	193	1689	1882	13071	1001	675	1676	46	

PRINTED AT HEAD-QUARTERS, BROOMY PLAIN, NEW FOREST. * Machine Guns. ARTHUR, GENERAL, Commanding Manoeuvre Force.

The Duke of Connaught led the "invasion" of the New Forest. Manoeuvres caused severe disruption to the life of the Commoners. So numerous and complicated were claims against the military that the ensuing compensation procedures proved a model for future years. (For a detailed account of the effect of the the 1895 manoeuvres in the Forest, see Anthony Pasmore's *Verderers of the New Forest*.)

Stiff Rules . . .

Continued from previous page

attending Inspection £2 0s.

II.

Every Non-commissioned Officer not attending Parade shall be fined 15s.—Inspection £1.

III.

Every Private not attending Parade shall be fined 5s., and days of Inspection 10s.

IV.

SICK CERTIFICATE

No excuse sufficient, except certificate of Sickness, which must be made through the Sergeant of the Squad to the Commanding Officer. Agreed unanimously.

V.

Fines to be collected by Sergeant of Squad, and applied at the end of each year as majority of Troop think best. Agreed unanimously.

VI.

Any man seen wearing his uniform when not on duty, (except with the permission of his Commanding Officer), to be fined £1. Agreed unanimously.

VII.

Every member arriving too late to answer to his name when the Roll is called shall be subject to the following fines:—Officers 10s; Non-commissioned Officers 5s.; Privates 2s. 6d. Resolved unanimously. July 25, 1833.

VIII.

PARADE BUTSASH, Monday, March 7, 1831.

No Member shall leave the Troop until the expiration of three months after notice given in writing to the Captain of his intention so to do, and any Member leaving the corps at the expiration of the three months' notice agreed on, shall pay the first year the value of his dress; the second year two pounds; and the third year one pound.

IX.

Any Member who shall appear on Parade incomplete in any part of his Dress, Arms, or Equipments

RULES AND REGULATIONS

OF THE

NEW FOREST EAST TROOP

OF

YEOMANRY CAVALRY.

———

A N D R E W   R O B E R T   D R U M M O N D ,   E S Q . ,

Captain Commandant.

———

ESTABLISHED BY GENERAL CONSENT, JANUARY the 13th, 1831.

———

J. COUPLAND, PRINTER, SOUTHAMPTON.

RULEBOOK FOR CAVALRY MEMBERS

Stiff Rules for Yeoman Cavalry...

with which he shall have been furnished, shall forfeit for each irregularity, or for the omission of each article, one shilling.

X.

Any Member who shall appear on Parade without having his Dress, Arms, and Equipments, in neat, clean, and serviceable order, shall, on the commanding officer's decision, forfeit two shillings and sixpence.

XI.

Any Volunteer to become a Member shall be proposed at a General Meeting, and none shall be enrolled without being approved by a majority of two-thirds of the Troop, and who does not provide, as his charger, a horse with a short tail, to be

approved of by the commanding officer.

XII.

Any Member who may be actually away from the neighbourhood will escape being fined, if he shall have previously noticed to the commanding officer, either personally or in writing, his desire for leave of absence.

XIII.

Any Member refusing to pay the fines to which he has rendered himself liable under the Rules and Regulations of this Troop, exposes himself to be expelled, in addition to any other penalty to which he renders himself liable under the Yeomanry and Volunteer Acts.

XIV.

No Rule or Regulation can be

binding unless agreed to at a Meeting of two-thirds of the Troop; nor can any Rule be established unless proposed and sanctioned by the Commandant, who is responsible to his Majesty under the Yeomanry and Volunteer Acts for any Rule established in the corps.

The six last Rules were agreed to at a Meeting of the Troop for Drill, on April 11th.

XV.

PARADE, HILL TOP, July 22, 1833.

It was this day resolved unanimously,—

That every member of the Troop, having given notice to quit, shall return to the Quarter-Master previously to the expiration of his notice, in good order, the following articles:—arms, bridle, collar and chain, holsters, cloak and three straps, valisse, two baggage straps and pad, sword, belt, and knot, shacco and plume, pair of epaulettes, pair of spurs, forage cap, nose bag, cartouch box, and shall forfeit the prime cost of each article not so returned as a fine or penalty, and no Member of the Troop shall cease to be a Member until every article is so returned or the fine paid.

ANDREW ROBERT DRUMMOND.

Belgians in the New Forest

During 1914 and 1915 a number of Belgians—some military, some civilians—were received in Burley homes by public-spirited citizens.

In her *Chronicles of the Belgians* (or) *More Especially Those Relating to Blackmoor Convalescent Home*, Ruth Dent described the war-time hospitality accorded the visitors. The journal was dedicated to the girl's mother and her friend, Mrs. Arthur Clough, "as a souvenir of the Belgians who were the cause of much laughter during the sad years."

Continued on next page

FIREPLACE COMMEMORATES SITE OF PORTUGUESE ARMY CAMP

Well Known Landmark Honours War-time Portuguese Army Unit

There has seldom been a war in which the New Forest did not play some part. Foreign troops were often stationed within its boundaries, as well as home forces.

Usually these troops were in training for war, or convalescing from wounds sustained in fighting. There was, however, an instance during the first World War when Portuguese troops came to the New Forest to fill the gap in the labour force caused by the departure of many forest workers to the military services.

The camp of the Portuguese was about two miles west of Emery Down. Here they had a cookhouse where meals were prepared in the Portuguese tradition. Later, the fireplace from this kitchen was salvaged and re-erected as a memorial to Britain's allies who responded during this country's manpower shortage.

Beside the fireplace is a plaque which reads:

PORTUGUESE FIRE-PLACE

This is the site of a hutted camp occupied by a Portuguese Army unit during the first World War. This unit assisted the depleted local labour force in producing timber for the war effort.

The Forestry Commission have retained this fireplace from the cookhouse as a memorial to the men who lived and worked here, and acknowledge the financial assistance of the Portuguese government in its renovation.

Belgians...

Continued from previous page

The account gives the family background of each newly arrived Belgian. If they did not own photographs of themselves, Ruth made the snapshots herself.

In Belgium the entire population observed the King's "Name Day" each year, and the Burley hosts of the visitors duly arranged for King Albert's special day to be celebrated in the village. This thoughtfulness much pleased the Belgians.

After some of the Belgian ladies displayed talent for making lace, special exhibitions and sales of work became regular features. Those with a gift for working with wood were persuaded by young Ruth to take up toy-making. The pursuit of crafts amid the quiet village surroundings enabled some of the Belgians to recover their physical and mental health; a few, however, proved to have deep-seated problems.

On the whole, the crafts industry flourished, bringing happiness to the buyers and useful income to the invalids. "The chief toys we made," writes Ruth in her journal, "were parrots and cockatoos that balanced (1/6 each), crocodiles that waggled (1/3), polichinelles that turned somersaults (1/6), Kaisers on horseback (1/6), cocks and hens (8d), Red Indians, soldiers, goose girls, tits, poodles, black cats, see-saws, Red Cross nurses, officers, and jig-saw puzzles. The puzzles varied from 25 to 500 pieces for which we charged 2/- per 100 pieces packed in a box."

Towards the end of the experiment, Ruth wrote: "The toy accounts have all been settled up. I am still 1/- in debt to myself, but I have more than that worth of toys. Victor went away with £4.10 in his pouch, Leon about 10/-, Paul 6/-, Noulet 25/-, Henri 10/-, Pick 5/-, Soinet 12/6, and Delvin 25/-." She was sad when the end came. She wrote: "All my other debts are paid, and now I feel quite sentimental about the empty cash boxes in my room that used to contain the men's money."

INDIAN TROOPS IN BROCKENHURST IN 1914

J.W. Martin made the picture below of wounded Indian soldiers in front of his chemist's shop. His small son Ken stands in front of the first soldier. The men were quartered at Forest Park Hotel and Tile Barn (now demolished).

(Both photographs on this page are from the collection of the late K.J. Martin.)

KING GEORGE V INSPECTING TROOPS IN BROCKENHURST

In November, 1914, King George V came to the Forest to see Indian soldiers wounded in France. He is shown here inspecting the walking wounded. Queen Mary is visible in the background.

A 15-Year Old Girl Visits an Army Camp

What was the New Forest like when thousands of troops were camped within its borders? Thanks to a remarkable teen-age girl, Ruth Dent, we have a first-hand impression of the huge camp at Lyndhurst in 1914. Ruth also illustrated her account which appeared in the hand-written magazine, *The Pierrot*, which she edited for four years. She kept a journal (described elsewhere in this chapter) about Belgian convalescent soldiers in the New Forest. Dionis Macnair, daughter of Ruth Dent (later Mrs. Ian Macnair), is a member of the Verderers Court. In her preface below, she tells how her mother produced *The Pierrot*. (The original magazines are now at Edinburgh's Museum of Childhood.)

COVER OF *The Pierrot*
Like today's magazines, *The Pierrot* had a different cover for each issue. The cover above was used for the Christmas, 1912, issue.

Dionis Macnair writes: "My mother must have been lonely when she came to Burley from Edinburgh. She was an only child, educated at home. She decided to edit a magazine which would be read by her friends and relations. Contributions came to her by post: stories, pictures, verses, articles, do-it-yourself features, puzzles, etc. She produced a magazine every two months for four years, the last issue being Christmas, 1914. Most of the copies of these hand-written magazines were eventually returned to her. In later years, they were enjoyed by her children and her grand-daughter.

"That most copies were safely returned to my mother speaks volumes for the post of that time, since they went as far afield as East Anglia, Northumberland, Scotland and Northern Ireland. There were about 20 contributors ranging in age from ten to 16 and about as many addressees. Subscribers paid 3d to read each issue if they had not contributed to its contents, and readers had to pay a penalty of 1d if they kept an issue more than two days. Mother spent a great deal of her time badgering the contributors for material, and still was able to maintain a high standard. She received many appreciative letters, but she had to draw the line and refuse to accept any more first chapters of "serials" that were never completed."

Lyndhurst is a quiet little town in the New Forest and is the tourist centre of that district. On two sides it is surrounded by woods and on the other two by an open moor and golf links. It is about 11 miles from Southampton.

How it is completely changed; the whole of the moor and links are covered with hundreds of tents, soldiers are to be seen everywhere, and the road which runs through the camp is blocked by every kind of traffic.

Last week the 7th Division was temporarily encamped there previous to starting to the front via Southampton. Every day the men packed up and expected to receive their marching orders, but they were delayed owing to the presence of a German submarine in the Channel. The men were getting terribly impatient and longing to start, and the

uncertainty must have been very trying, but on Monday they really left and now more troops are expected at Lyndhurst.

The first time we went over to see them, we took about 100 apples which we threw to any soldier we saw along the road. They liked them very much, and sometimes a head would poke out of a tent and say, "Send us along one, please!" One apple was badly thrown and it knocked off one of the men's cap and hit him on the head. Another soldier who was walking with him said, "I hope the bullets won't do that."

Every man we asked if they were looking forward to going to the front answered with their faces lighting up, "I should think so," or "The sooner the better; our poor boys out there are wanting us," or something else to this effect. We saw the Grenadier

Guards coming in from route marching; it was five o'clock and they had been out since seven (a.m.) with all their kit on their backs and their rifles in their hands. They were very hot and dusty and tired, but as cheery as anything. It was only the officers who looked anxious. We also saw the "Queens," the "Warwicks," "Suffolks," the "Worcester Borderers," the "Scotch Fusiliers," etc., and the Royal Field and Royal Horse Artillery and the Royal Army Medical Corps. In the camp there are altogether 30,000 men and they all look splendid and in perfect condition.

The next time we went all the waggons were being inspected: Red Cross waggons, commandeered carts, pontoons, etc. The horses were very wild; an Army Service Corps man told us that a great many had never had on harness before, but had just been commandeered out of the fields. The big guns are all covered with spots of blue, red, yellow and green paint which makes them look as if someone had been amusing themselves throwing

30,000 MEN CAMPED ON LYNDHURST GOLF COURSE IN 1914
The tranquil surroundings of Lyndhurst were drastically altered during the 1914–18 war when many Army units pitched camp on the golf course near Bolton's Bench. The area served as a staging area for men awaiting embarkation to France, and was twice visited by 15-year old Ruth Dent and fellow reporters of *The Pierrot*.

The Camp at Lyndhurst ...

Continued from previous page

paint at them. It is really put to make them look less conspicuous in the distance.

Then we went over to the Gordon Highlanders' camp. They all wore khaki aprons over the front of their kilts. Some of them were packing up, others were practicing fixing bayonets. Suddenly an officer issued from a tent. "Pipe major," he called out, "have you got enough ammunition for your revolver?" (He answered:) "More than I can carry, sir." It made one realize how very near the war was. Some of the men, especially those on bicycles, wore white and blue ribbons round their arms; that meant that they were signallers. A red band round the cap meant the staff.—THE END.

NOTE: Since writing this, the 7th Division has left for the front and instead there are some mountain batteries of Indian troops. They are a very fine looking lot, tall and with mostly beards or moustaches and all with beautiful white teeth. They wear khaki and khaki turbans with a dash of red in them. Some, however, are still in white with orange or red turbans or waistcoats. They are mounted on mules, which they ride most beautifully bareback—each man leading a second mule. One man has two white mules which he always leads about. They nearly all have bare legs and heelless slippers and they look rather cold. The officers wear some sort of linen khaki, sun helmets and *very* thick overcoats!

FIRST WORLD WAR TRANSPORT AT LYNDHURST CAMP
A Red Cross waggon, a commandeered cart, and pontoons as drawn by the youthful editor and artist, Ruth Dent.

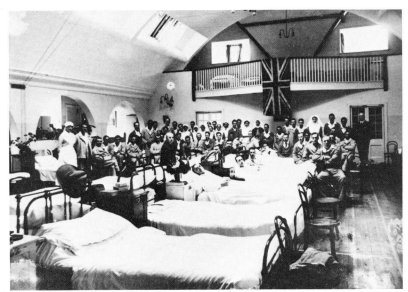

Courtesy late K.J. Martin

SERIOUSLY WOUNDED NEW ZEALAND SOLDIERS AT MORANT HALL

Brockenhurst's Morant Hall was converted into a hospital for seriously wounded New Zealand troops evacuated from France during the first World War. In the picture above some men lie in their beds while others are able to stand. At the rear of the hall is the hospital staff. Many of the New Zealand wounded did not recover, and over 100 are buried in Brockenhurst cemetery.

FURTHER SKETCHES FROM *The Pierrot*
Above: a soldier accidentally hit by an apple, and (below) a sentry on duty.
Both sketches were made by Ruth Dent.

NEW ZEALAND WAR MEMORIAL AND GRAVES

Simple headstones honour New Zealanders who gave their lives for "the home country" during the first world war. A small commemorative marker was erected by one young man's parents who travelled from New Zealand to see their son's last resting place.

Odette and the Beaulieu "School for Spies"

(The rigorous training of Odette Sansom at the Beaulieu S.O.E. school is detailed in Jerrard Tickell's *Odette: The Story of A British Agent* (Pan Books) from which these extracts are taken. After the war, Anna Neagle starred in the film, "Odette", and in 1986 when the actress lay on her death-bed, Odette was there to offer comfort. Odette today is the wife of Geoffrey Hallowes.)

In a letter to the editor of this volume, Odette (Hallowes) reveals how much the New Forest meant to her, both at the time of her training at the S.O.E. school in Beaulieu, and during the "dark days" she later experienced:

"Having lived in London since my arrival in England in 1933, I did not know the English countryside. The New Forest was my first revelation of the beauty and gentleness of this part of Southern England and I fell in love with it.

"It certainly made me very sad when I eventually had to leave the Training School in the New Forest."

"In the dark days that were to come, I used to think of its peace and beauty. It was a kind of solace."

In Baker Street a file was started and numbered 'S.23'. Between its blue covers went every document relating to Sansom (Mrs.), O.M.C., and this number - 'S.23' —was to be her permanent reference in the French Section. To a senior F.A.N.Y. officer she yielded up her identity card and received in exchange a small blue certificate of membership of the Regimental Association. This was numbered F.10. Having thus become two numbers as well as one person, Odette left for the New Forest.

The school was unobtrusively guarded by alert soldiery, and identification, both of visitors and of students, was meticulously carried out. Once past the cordon, Odette found a charming and modern country house. From the french windows, a lawn sloped down to an ornamental lake and, beyond the lake, there were deep woods. In this pleasant and tran-

quil place, she was to learn the arts of deception; the observant staff were to learn about Odette.

The weeks were strenuous. Most of all Odette liked the free outdoor work. Even the purpose of P.T. became clear to her, and if supple muscles were considered to be part of the equipment of a secret agent, well, she would do her best. On the lake, she learnt how to handle a canoe deftly and silently; in the dark forests, she could soon find here way unerringly with only the stars to guide her; she became an expert poacher. She could take a chicken out of a hen house at midnight without a sound or a squawk ... and trap, kill and cook a rabbit without the formality of removing the skin.

The war was gathering in fury and she was impatient to tread the soil and smell the smell of France and get at the throats of the King's enemies. She had burned her boats and because of this, because of the utter finality of her decision, the unavoidable make-believe of the school irritated her sometimes —with the result that she was apt to be terse and even offhand in her answers. The staff, well trained in the art of observing their fellow creatures, watched her with understanding.

She was shown into a small partitioned room and Major Buckmaster came to see her at once. He was tall and, on that occasion, in uniform. He greeted her with a sort of controlled nervous energy that had hidden in it somewhere a most engaging solicitousness for her comfort. For

The Philosophy of Odette...

"I am a very ordinary woman to whom a chance was given to see human beings at their best and at their worst. I knew kindness as well as cruelty, understanding as well as brutality. I completely believe in the potential nobility of the human spirit."

A young French mother living in England since the early 1930s, Odette Sanson had a profound sense of duty and a love for both England and France which led her to volunteer to be a British agent in World War II.

She was parachuted into German-occupied France and later captured, interrogated and tortured. Odette refused to inform on fellow agents and, instead, drew all responsibility to herself and saved the lives of two officers.

Subsequently sent to Ravensbrück, she survived and, in 1946, was awarded the George Cross and, later, the MBE.

The extract above, from her preface to Jerrard Tickell's *Odette*, exemplifies Odette's humility and humanity.

Odette and the Beaulieu "School for Spies"...

Continued from previous page

most of the time, she was conscious of his austere preoccupation with a cause. She decided after a few minutes that his features were cast in a curiously ecclesiastical mould. The painters of the very early Renaissance had portrayed faces such as his, thin, eager, remote. Then, being a Frenchwoman to her finger-tips, she modified the impression for there was a human liveliness in the heel of his eye, usually kept under strict control both in canvas and in pulpit.

He told her about the French Section and the general nature of the work she would very likely be asked to do. He spoke in French from first to last. At the moment, he imagined that she would be a courier but the specific role she would play would depend largely on her reports from school.

It was hidden away in a country house in the New Forest and there she would be taught a number of queer things. One of them, perhaps the most difficult of all, was the art of assuming a new identity, sometimes at a moment's notice, and assuming it so utterly and so completely that every vestige of one's own personality was lost.

She might think that was easy —even rather fun in a way, like dressing-up or playing charades. It was, in fact, extraordinarily difficult—as difficult as the spontaneous construction of the perfect cover-story.

The perfect cover-story—or fake life-story—must be full of imperfections. That sounded like a paradox but it wasn't. The cover-story started at one's birth—and nobody could be expected to remember every detail of his or her life since he or she had mewled and puked in his or her nurse's arms. Here came the art of imperfection. Those who answered questions too glibly were, *ipso facto*, under suspicion. The Gestapo were shrewd, trained interrogators and should never be underrated.

"In many ways it's a beastly life," said Major Buckmaster

THE S.O.E. PLAQUE IN THE CLOISTERS OF BEAULIEU ABBEY
More than one of every four agents trained at the Beaulieu S.O.E. school lost their lives during the second world war.

frankly. "It will be physically hard. More than that, it will be mentally exhausting, for you will be living a gigantic lie, or series of lies, for months on end. And if you slip up and get caught, we can do little to save you."

"To save me from what?"

He looked at her and shrugged.

"Oh, from the usual sickening sort of thing; prison, the firing squad, the rope, the crematorium; from whatever happens to amuse the Gestapo. Jepson told you." He said to her earnestly, "Mrs. Sansom, every single person in The Firm is a volunteer. Every job that we ask anyone to do is a

voluntary one. I know from your papers that you have three young children. Now that you know more of what it's all about and what it might involve, wouldn't you like to think it over?"

She shook her head.

"No. My mind is made up."...

(Another view of the rigorous training at the Beaulieu school is given by E.H. Cookridge in his book, *Inside S.O.E.*, quoted below by permission of the publishers, Arthur Barker.)

In the great hall, hundreds of

Odette and the Beaulieu "School for Spies"...

Continued from previous page
S.O.E. agents were given their final grooming. To mentally mould themselves into their new identities required many hours of assimilation. They met their Conducting Officers, many of whom had already been in the field and could impart advice from first-hand experience. The students became proficient in map-reading, coding, micro-photography and, particularly, in the hundred and one ways of guarding their own and their future comrades' security.

They learned how to find a 'safe house', how to establish contacts, use 'letter-boxes' at accommodation addresses, employ couriers, arrange 'dates', communicate with friends in the Resistance, prepare dropping grounds and receptions of other agents and material, use false documents and, above all, what not to do in order to avoid detection and capture. They were given micro-films and told to hide them on their bodies, in the rectum and elsewhere, or in personal articles. Then they were searched by experienced instructors, most of them Scotland Yard detectives. Some students achieved great skill and could have become peerless smugglers.

There were sessions of simulated *Gestapo Verhör* (interrogation). Short of being actually brutally manhandled, the 'prisoner' received somewhat rough treatment that had all the genuine flavour. '*Raus, Du Schweinehund!*' the pseudo-*Gestapo* men would shout, wield steel rods or use rifle buts, snarl commands and question the 'prisoner' under blazing lights, to frighten and bewilder him into telling something he should have kept secret. Afterwards, over a whisky-and-soda, he was told of mistakes he made; and how he should behave if he ever had to face the real thing.

Above all the would-be agents had to be impressed by the cardinal importance of communications. Everything the agent was expected to accomplish in the field depended on maintaining a regular contact with headquarters.

The main task of an SOE agent was to organize and instruct Resistance groups from which at a given time the secret armies would emerge to assist the Allied invasion forces by disturbing and destroying the enemy's lines of communications, by disrupting railway and road systems, telephone and telegraph communications by hampering his supplies, and finally by open attack at his rear and flanks. The lone agent in the field, even if helped by enthusiastic patriots, could do little of value if he was not told where, when and how to do it

The majority of the agents were, therefore, trained in the operation of a wireless transmitter. Those given a special task as organizers, liaison officers, or sabotage instructors were either sent into the field together with a 'pianist' (radio operator), or the operator was sent to join or to precede them.

When the "Hush-Hush Troops" Were All over the Place

The Beaulieu estate, with many of its outlying houses taken over by the Special Operations Executive for training agents, was a scene of great activity during the second world war. Happily the cover of the New Forest permitted just the cloak of secrecy the school required.

The Hon. Mrs. E. Pleydell-Bouverie, mother of Lord Montagu, knew in a general way what was going on and, in the interview below, tells something of the dramatic conditions that existed at the time.

We had eleven of the Beaulieu estate houses occupied by the S.O.E. troops. They were known locally as the "hush-hush" troops.

Why they liked the houses so much was because they could come and go as they liked through the woods, and no one was the wiser. From the moment they arrived they never came into the village of Beaulieu itself.

The training staff had to work very hard, having only a few days between classes to rest and plan before the next batch arrived. I understand that about 400 of some 1800 agents trained at Beaulieu never came back. Odette was one of those who trained here and, despite great suffering, she survived and there was a wonderful film made about her adventures. Many of the scenes in the film were made in and around Beaulieu.

It was probably because of the school that Palace House was not commandeered during the war. The school was just too "hush-hush" to have another military

THE HON. MRS. E. PLEYDELL-BOUVERIE

activity near by. The S.O.E. didn't want anything else going on within its training area. The school must have had dozens of specialists to train the agents. For example, Paul Dane, the actor,

Canada's Memorial Cross at Mogshade Hill

(Mogshade Hill, which knew the sounds of war preparations when the Duke of Connaught's men conducted manoeuvers there in 1895, again was host to servicemen in the second world war. This time it was men of the Canadian Third Infantry Division who were encamped nearby and who later were to take part in the invasion of Normandy. The press release below, jointly prepared by the Canadian forces and the Forestry Commission in 1984 to mark the fortieth anniversary of D Day, describes the service on that occasion, and the events that led to the erection of the memorial.)

The New Forest has witnessed many strange and momentous events in its thousand-year history but none perhaps more incongruous with its ancient splendour than the build-up of armoured might preparatory to Operation Overlord, the Western Allies' bellicose return to the European mainland in 1944.

For months previous there had been a massive concentration of troops and equipment across the southern counties of England known for the most part only to

SYLVAN MEMORIAL TO THE MEN OF THE CANADIAN THIRD DIVISION

The cross above was erected by the Forestry Commission to replace the temporary one where members of the Canadian division worshipped during their encampment in the New Forest in the months leading up to D Day, 1944.

the local inhabitants. The New Forest offered almost an ideal cantonment with its concealing trees and proximity to a major port of departure. It was here that the 3rd Canadian Infantry Division spent the winter of 1943–44 under canvas and their padre Canon Keith Perdue conducted services for them at Mogshade Hill, where in April 1944 he set up a makeshift pine cross. Today a sturdy oak cross stands in the same place as a memorial to all those (Canadians) who lost their lives in the Normandy landings.

To mark the fortieth anniversary of D-Day (in 1984), a thousand people gathered at Mogshade Hill for a service conducted by Canon Perdue with a march past of war veterans, the salute being taken by Brigadier General Christopher Snider, Chief of the Canadian Defence Liaison Staff.

The Forestry Commission, which now undertakes the maintenance of the cross and the area

When "Hush-Hush Troops" Were about...

Continued from previous page

was on the staff and taught the art of make-up and acting. Likewise, the head-keeper at Sandringham was brought down to teach wood lore. The agents were trained in many other fields, including languages, topography, and use of foreign currency. There were many nationalities.

There was one amusing incident that I remember. Laura Lady Troubridge lived alone in a small house in the middle of the woods where lively training exercises were going on day and night. At first the school's officers were concerned about her being there, but as she was stone blind, they came to accept her. She was there

the whole time the S.O.E. school was in operation, but there was never any question of security risk.

When peace was declared the Commander, Lt. Colonel Woolwich, sent a notice around to all of us on the estate who had been in the background. He asked if we would come to one of the houses for a kind of celebration. He and his staff made a wonderful bonfire and threw open their cellar and laid on wonderful food.

We have a rather lovely memorial plaque inside the cloisters at Beaulieu Abbey in honour of the gallant men and women who trained at the school.

When Eagles of War Soared over the Forest

Britain has been involved in many wars, but probably no others so threatened national survival as the Second World War.

The tranquility of the New Forest today belies the enormous military activity in the area during the last war. Soldiers, seamen and airmen gave thanks for the security the Forest provided, the easy access it afforded to enemy targets, and the comfort it offered in rare moments of reflection.

The most visible activity was aircraft movement. At times planes operated round the clock. The Forest had three major and several smaller air bases. They contributed greatly to the Allied war effort on the Continent. Some runways of the larger bases may still be seen, but little remains of the smaller ones and the visitor to the Forest may be unaware of their locations.

Happily for students of World War II history, a series of books has been published documenting virtually every air base that existed during the conflict. *Action Station 5*, by R.C.B. Ashworth, tells the story of airfields in the southwest of England. Published by Patrick Stephens, Ltd. (Dennington Estate, Wellingborough, Northants) in 1982, the volume lists all the air bases in the New Forest together with the names of units assigned to them and their missions. Extracts from *Action Station 5* are presented alphabetically.

Beaulieu, Hampshire

SU350005. 4 miles NE of Lymington on B3055

The first landing ground at Beaulieu was laid out close to the village of East Boldre in 1910 when the New Forest Flying School opened. The same site was used by the RFC/RAF from 1915 to 1919 and as a civilian field from 1933 to 1938 but the Second World War base was a completely new airfield built further to the west on Hatchet Moor, and originally intended as a satellite for Thorney Island.

It was modified at a late stage to accommodate two general reconnaissance squadrons and when opened on August 8 1942 the extensive building programme necessary had not been completed. The three runways were functional but required camouflaging, while the operations room and watch office were still temporary, and most personnel found themselves in tents.

To bolster 19 Group during the renewed U-boat offensive in the Bay of Biscay, 224 Squadron moved down from Tiree, their Liberator IIIAs arriving early in September. They were soon in action, the crew of 'H' attacking a submarine on October 20. The explosion of their depth charges damaged the aircraft but it managed to make a crash landing at Predannack. Three days later came the first attack on Beaulieu when a German bomber dived out of low cloud and dropped four bombs, but caused no casualties and little damage.

The desperate situation in the Bay, coinciding as it did with the *Torch* convoys, forced Bomber Command to lend aircraft to Coastal and one and a half squadrons were allocated to Beaulieu. 15 Halifaxes of 405 (RCAF) Squadron and five from 158 arrived on October 25. Both flew their first patrols two days later and were soon involved in anti-shipping strikes using St Eval as a forward base. The 158 Squadron detachment left for Rufforth on December 6 but 405 remained and steadily improved their reputation. A very determined attack on the surfaced *U-263* was made by the crew of *405/J* on November 27 and, despite intensive fire from the U-boat's escorts, two runs were made and the submarine damaged. On February 26 1943 Liberator *224/Z* sighted two U-boats and both were attacked, the second being badly damaged and probably sunk.

In March 405 Squadron returned to Bomber Command and 224 Squadron was joined at Beaulieu by a detachment of 1(C)OTU for Liberator conversion flying. When 311 (Czech) Squadron arrived for

Canadian Memorial Cross...

Continued from previous page

surrounding it, was represented by the Conservator Ian Skinner and Deputy Surveyor Nicolas Banister and other members of the staff. The memories recalled on this day had a particular poignancy for Nick Banister, who commanded a flotilla of landing craft which took many of the Canadian soldiers from the Forest camps across to France from Southampton.

The text of the plaque at the Canadian memorial:

ON THIS SITE A CROSS

WAS ERECTED TO THE GLORY OF GOD

ON 14TH APRIL 1944.

SERVICES WERE HELD HERE

UNTIL D DAY, 6TH JUNE 1944,

BY MEN OF THE

3RD CANADIAN DIVISION, R.C.A.S.C.

A SIKORSKY R-4 HELICOPTER

Museum of Army Flying Collection

After the war the Airborne Forces Experimental Establishment took over Beaulieu. The Sikorksy R-4 is shown hovering above the field's control tower. The AFEE experimented with several types of aircraft, among them helicopters, gliders and transport planes.

gets on the Cherbourg Peninsula. The airfield was also used by the Ibsley Wing for several *Rodeos* during the last days of the month. A typical effort was on the 29th when two Typhoons of 266, five of 193 and eight of 257 Squadron went on a sweep to the outskirts of Paris. A Do 217 and two German training aircraft were shot down for no loss, though three Typhoons were damaged by flak.

At the end of January 257 swopped places with 486 Squadron, and the Beaulieu Wing became heavily engaged in attacks on V-1 sites. On March 1 Beaulieu was transferred to 10 Group, ADGB, in readiness for the arrival of American units. The RAF moved out and in came 365 Fighter Group, 84 Fighter Wing, IX Air Force. P-47 Thunderbolt fighter-bombers were received later in the month and the three squadrons, 386, 387 and 388 used for bomber escort and dive bombing prior to D-Day. On D-Day + 1 the Group (together with 366 FG) put up a maximum effort over *Omaha* beachhead where American troops were taking a pounding from dug-in German defensive positions.

No 365 FG left for the Continent on June 28 and three weeks later 323 Bombardment Group, 98 Bomb Wing (453, 454, 455 and 456 Squadrons) arrived from Earls Colne during a general move south of B-26 Marauder units as the fighter bombers vacated the forward airfields. A little over a month later 323 BG also moved into France and on September 27 Beaulieu was returned to the RAF.

It remained empty until the Airborne Forces Experimental

training in May, 224 Squadron left for St Eval and with the dispersed accommodation sites now completed it was possible to dispense with the temporary billeting arrangements. Diversions sometimes overloaded the facilities and caused difficulties. During the night of August 13, for instance, five Wellingtons of 407 Squadron arrived, one of which collided with a Halifax from Holmsley South just after taking off for return to Chivenor. The overlapping circuits of the two airfields were a constant hazard.

No 311 Squadron remained at Beaulieu after conversion and recommenced operations in August, 'M' being attacked by a Ju 88 on the 30th. The gunners shot it down and the Liberator returned to base, but with a dead man in the rear turret. During September 53 Squadron arrived from Thorney Island and both units were heavily engaged in Bay operations, the marauding Ju 88s continuing to be very troublesome. Beaulieu was able to claim its first U-boat when the crew of *53/B* sighted one by Leigh Light during the early morning of December 13. The U-boat opened fire and hit the aircraft so the

searchlight was switched off and the Liberator positioned for an attack up moon. The six depth charges straddled the submarine just forward of the conning tower and after it disappeared bodies were seen in the water. The captain, Squadron Leader G. Crawford, AFC, was awarded an immediate DFC for this exploit.

No 53 Squadron left in January 1944 followed by 311 (Czech) the following month. Their replacement by Typhoon 1B squadrons had already begun, their servicing echelons arriving on January 13, followed a few days later by 257 and 263 Squadrons. Eight Typhoons of 257 took off on their first operation from Beaulieu on the 22nd—an attack on *Noball* tar-

---

Beaulieu Airfield History

Students of military history will find Robert Cole's *History of Beaulieu Airfield* an invaluable reference.

Published in 1982, the 64-page volume embraces all four period's of the airfield's history: those recording the two world wars, as well as the pre-war and post-war eras. With 131 illustrations—including the runway lay-out at various times, the history is one of the finest pictorial records produced about war-time airfields.

BEAULIEU IN AUGUST, 1945

Museum of Army Flying Collection

The thin soil of this part of the New Forest remained scarred for years after the airfield construction.

Establishment started arriving from Sherburn-in-Elmet during December. Beaulieu was ideal for AFEE operations and a very wide range of activities involving gliders, early helicopters, paratroop and freight transports was soon under way. Aircraft included the Stirling, Halifax, Lancaster, York and Dakota with Hadrian, Hotspur, Hamilcar and CG-13A

gliders plus a number of experimental types. The end of the war had no immediate impact on the AFEE for there were many new aircraft to test and the momentum built up during 1944–45 ensured that there was plenty of equipment trials to carry out.

During October 1946, C Flight of 657 Squadron arrived to be converted on to helicopters, leav-

ing in March 1947 for Andover as 1901 Flight with some of the temperamental Sikorsky Hoverflys previously on AFEE strength. By 1948 the major activity concerned Valetta and Hastings trials, including glider-towing, and it was these aircraft which provided most of the work right up to September 1950 when the AFEE was absorbed by A&AEE Boscombe Down. Beaulieu reverted to Care & Maintenance and was then allotted to the 3rd Air Force, USAF, on April 1 1953 as a standby base. It was not used for flying and the Americans returned it to the RAF two and a half years later. Beaulieu was finally disposed of in November 1959.

Most of the airfield was taken over by the Forestry Commission who broke up the runways and converted some of the building foundations into caravan parks. A piece of the old perimeter tract is used as a car park for a forest nature trail.

Bisterne, Hampshire

SU155030. 1½ miles S of Ringwood on B3347

During 1943 a number of temporary airfields were surveyed and

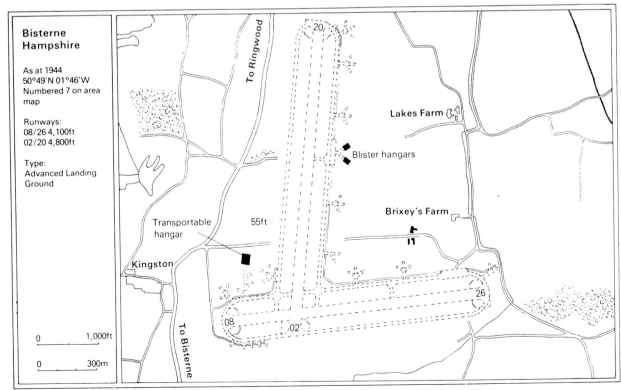

**Bisterne
Hampshire**

As at 1944
50°49'N 01°46'W
Numbered 7 on area map

Runways:
08/26 4,100ft
02/20 4,800ft

Type:
Advanced Landing Ground

built in the south of England to provide bases for the influx of aircraft into the area expected prior to the invasion of Europe. Known as Advanced Landing Grounds, they had the minimum facilities consistent with flying operational aircraft in support of ground forces—Bisterne was one of these ALGs.

Built on low-lying pasture land just to the east of the River Avon, a steel mesh runway paralleled the B3347 road and an east/west strip lay alongside the minor road to Lakes Farm. Arrowhead-shaped hardstandings were laid along a narrow taxi-track and PSP marshalling areas were constructed on either side of the runway thresholds.

Bisterne was completed in September 1943 but not used, apart from the odd visitor, until March 1944 when the 371st Fighter Group of IX Fighter Command, USAAF, moved in direct from the United States. The ALG was extremely primitive, the domestic accommodation being in tents, many of which became swamped when it rained. All technical work was in four Blisters or the open air until a large transportable hangar was erected in the south-west corner of the airfield. Operations commenced on April 12 when the P-47s made a sweep over France without loss. It was not long before the heavy pounding from the Thunderbolts took its toll of the wire mesh runways and at the end of a week they were badly rutted and extremely hazardous. The ALG was closed for hasty reconstruction during which the 371st operated from nearby Ibsley.

They returned to Bisterne on May 1 and were soon busy flying two missions daily attacking airfields and communications in France. A typical day was May 21 when the Group despatched 50 Thunderbolts on a sweep to the Loire river. They attacked three trains, but two aircraft were hit by the ever-dangerous German flak, and only just scraped into Warmwell. On D-Day the 371st were held until 09:00 hours when one squadron, the 404th, flew on a

dive bombing mission in support of forward troops. Operations continued on close support fighter-bomber work from Bisterne until the Americans moved to the Continent on June 23.

Its work done, Bisterne was soon abandoned, and was derelict by the end of July 1944. The wire track runways were taken up and early in 1945 the site reverted to agriculture after the Royal Engineers had bulldozed the hard core foundations. There are now few traces except culverted ditches and hedges replaced by wire fences where runways and taxiways crossed them. A few pieces of runway mesh are still scattered around the local farms.

Holmsley South, Hampshire

SZ215988. 5 miles NE of Christchurch on A35

Carved out of the New Forest, Holmsley South was built as a standard three-runway airfield during 1941–42. It was opened in a terrible rush on September 1 1942 to accommodate reinforcements for 19 Group, Coastal Command, during Operation *Torch*.

None of the domestic sites were complete when RAF personnel began to arrive and the first weeks were utter chaos. Fortunately last minute changes delayed the first flying unit until October 21, and then it was only the nucleus of 547 Squadron. Four days later, however, two USAAF officers arrived, and galvanised the station into action by stating that eight Liberators were flying in that afternoon to start operations. These B-24Ds were from the 330th Squadron, 93 Bomb Wing, VIIth AF, seconded for anti-submarine work with 19 Group. With only two hardstandings completed, the aircraft were parked on the secondary runways

> ## "one (Liberator was) attacked by five Ju 88's on November 21. The fighters' clumsy approach enabled the American gunners to shoot two down and claim a third damaged."

and missions started on October 28 with a Bay of Biscay search. More aircraft arrived and the 330th rapidly increased their sortie rate, though like most bomber units they found the anti-submarine role difficult, and while a number of sightings were made, no follow up attacks resulted.

Two aircraft were intercepted by Luftwaffe fighters, one being attacked by five Ju 88s on November 21. The fighters' clumsy approach enabled the American gunners to shoot two down and claim a third damaged before the Liberator reached the safety of cloud.

With *Torch* over the Americans returned to Alconbury and 58 Squadron, RAF, arrived from Stornoway to re-equip with Halifax GR 11s, replacing 547 which left for Chivenor after working up on Wellingtons. In March 1943 502 Squadron flew in from St Eval to complete conversion from Whitleys to Halifaxes, 58 moving out during the following month.

Holmsley South was being used as a conversion base for Halifax squadrons, amongst them a 38 Wing unit, 295 Squadron, which arrived from Netheravon in May. Previously flying Whitleys, they were to tow 36 Horsa gliders over Sicily. Intensive crew conversion and glider towing resulted in three crashes while at Holmsley, but both crews and Halifaxes were ready in time for the operation.

The airfield was now almost complete, a large number of pan-handle dispersals having been cut into the woods around the airfield and two Bellman hangars built. During July 1943 Nos 58 and 502 Squadrons returned for intensive anti-submarine operations. They were soon in action, a pack of three U-boats being caught on the surface by a Sunderland and two of 502's Halifaxes on July 30, while on August 2 Flying Officer Biggar took on a German des-

> ## "The crew sighted, attacked and sank U-221, but the Halifax was set on fire and the captain forced to ditch the aircraft."

troyer and claimed it damaged. This period coincided with increased activity by Ju 88s in the Bay and 58 Squadron lost three Halifaxes during August to these formidable aircraft. Two more were lost in accidents, a total of five in nine days. Things looked even blacker when Halifax *58/B* failed to return on September 27. It was carrying the Station Commander, Group Captain Mead, DFC, on his first operational sortie with the squadron. The crew sighted, attacked and sank *U-221*, but the Halifax was set on fire and the captain forced to ditch the aircraft. Six of the crew managed to scramble aboard their dinghy and after 11 days at sea they were found, by chance, by two destroyers. It was a thinner and wiser CO who subsequently returned to Holmsley. In December both Halifax squadrons left for St Davids, South Wales, and early in 1944 the station was transferred to 10 Group for fighter operations.

Three Canadian squadrons, 441, 442 and 443, moved in from Digby with their Spitfires and worked up as 144 Wing before exchanging places with 121 Wing (174, 175 and 245 Squadrons) which flew Typhoons and arrived from Westhampnett in April as 83 Group lodgers. This Wing had recently converted to rocket work and spent D-Day in direct support of troops on the beachhead. When the Army was established, they turned their attention to communications, harassing motor transport in the immediate rear of the front line.

Meanwhile, 418 (RCAF) Squadron, equipped with Mosquito FB VIs, started intruder operations from Holmsley South. On June 14 one of the crews reported the first V-1 sighted in flight and together with three other Mosquito squadrons they concentrated on night *Anti-Diver* patrols. During the first night

operations the squadron accounted for three V-Is and a probable in the five sorties flown.

No 121 Wing moved to the Continent in mid-June and was replaced by Nos 129, 306 and 315 Squadrons from Coolham. They went on armed recce, some of their Mustangs carrying bombs, but also became involved in several dogfights heavily outnumbered by German fighters. They also suffered from flak, losing several aircraft while at Holmsley South, but within days they were transferred to Ford and the airfield handed over to the IXth AF, USAAF, as Station 455.

It was used by the B-26 Marauders of the 394th Bomb Group (584-587 Squadrons) which moved forward from Boreham on July 24 and flew medium-level bombing raids behind the front line in France. Typical were operations on August 7 1944 when the 394th despatched 36 Marauders for a morning attack on the bridge at Nogent-sur-Seine and successfully severed this important communications link despite heavy flak. In the afternoon 34 B-26s were sent to an ammunition dump south of Nantes, leaving it in flames.

After a month at Holmsley the unit moved on to the Continent and the airfield was left empty until 116 Wing, Transport Command, took it over during October. Newly formed on the very troublesome Warwick transport, 167 Squadron began services to the liberated parts of the Continent in December. 246 Squadron arrived from Lyneham during the same month and flew to the Middle and Far East using Liberators and a few Yorks. The squadron absorbed the VVIO Flight of the Metropolitan Communications Squadron, Northolt, in February 1945 and received its first Skymaster in April, giving up its Halifaxes at the same time.

Meanwhile the unhappy 167 Squadron had moved to Blackbushe, and the long-range 246 settled down to operations to India on trooping until it merged with 511 Squadron at Lyneham in October 1946. A Battle of Britain display was held in September 1946 but it was virtually the end, for on October 16 Holmsley South was placed on Care & Maintenance as an inactive site.

Parts of the runways remain on the privately owned western end, but the rest of the airfield has been reclaimed by the Forestry Commission, except for a section used as a public road and a caravan site on one of the old dispersals.

Ibsley, Hampshire

SU155090. 2 miles N of Ringwood on A338

Built on low ground near the western edge of the New Forest, Ibsley was opened as a satellite of Middle Wallop on February 15 1941, though it was far from ready. 32 Squadron moved its Hurricanes in only two days later for convoy patrols, and the Luftwaffe soon took an interest, damaging one Hurricane during the night of March 13 when they dropped 30 small bombs.

The airfield was virtually completed around 32 Squadron, and things were just getting organised in April when they were replaced by the Spitfires of 118 Squadron. Engaged on defensive patrols over the south coast, they started badly by shooting down a Whitley on May 4, but were soon on the offensive, escorting Beauforts on dangerous anti-shipping strikes. They also flew some night patrols and during one of these the CO shot down an He 111. When 501 Squadron arrived in August the accommodation built on the north-east corner of the airfield was usable, but much requisitioned property had to be retained as the station's strength steadily increased. Equipped with Spitfire IIs the two squadrons launched into a round of *Rhubarbs*, *Ramrods* and *Roadsteads* as well as the inevitable convoy patrols.

Numerous squadrons used

Ibsley for operations over France, but the most significant event was the arrival of 234 Squadron in November 1941 and the commencement of operations as a Wing under the dynamic leadership of Wing Commander 'Widge' Gleed. The Wing was soon escorting bomb-carrying Hurricanes, 2 Group light bombers and the heavies of Bomber Command. Many of the *Circus* operations were very successful but a long-range sweep of 300 miles (492 km) made on March 16 nearly ended in disaster. Short of fuel in bad weather, 28 Spitfires landed at Exeter, four scraped into Bolt Head and four crash-landed with the loss of one pilot.

Meanwhile, ten month's hard work by a Works Flight had provided double fighter pens around the perimeter together with the only weather protection at Ibsley, nine oversize Blister hangars. On May 15, just after 66 Squadron replaced 234, the whole Wing was involved in a very sticky mission escorting eight Hurri-bombers of 175 Squadron against three minesweepers off Cherbourg. As they left the area one ship blew up, another burst into flames and the third was listing badly, but despite heavy flak only two Spitfires were damaged, and all the Hurricanes got back to base.

Operations continued at a slightly reduced rate throughout June, but then Gleed was posted and the Wing dispersed, Ibsley being handed over to the USAAF. A few days later the American advance party arrived and on August 27 the 1st FG (71 and 94 Squadrons) flew their P-38F Lightnings in from Goxhill. On the 29th came the Group's first operation, the 94th scrambling two aircraft to intercept a Luftwaffe bomber, but they did not make contact. By the time the 1st FG left for Tafaraoui, Algeria, on November 14 they had flown 273 sorties and claimed one victory.

Ibsley transferred to 10 Group on December 12 when 66 and 118 Squadrons returned from Zeals, to be joined later in the month by 504 Squadron. Only 504 stayed

very long and with 129 and 616 Squadrons it was soon heavily engaged in sweeps, *Circuses*, *Ramrods* and *Rhubarbs*, including top cover to the murderous B-17 daylight raids over France. The winter revealed one of Ibsley's main problems –flooding. Work was started on widening and straightening drainage culverts but proved of little value during severe gales in January when the southern half of the airfield was soon under water.

The Wing took part in the large-scale Army Co-operation exercise *Spartan* in March 1943, while 616 Squadron provided close escort to the Prime Minister's Liberator on his return from Casablanca, and later for HM the King homebound from North Africa. 310, 312 and 313 Squadrons were then gathered in from Scotland, Wales and south-east England and established at Ibsley in September as the Czech Wing. Still flying Spitfire Vs, the Wing concentrated on bomber escorts over France but saw little action apart from an early skirmish with Bf 110s on September 21. 263 Squadron arrived in December to convert to Typhoons but all RAF units left early in 1944 when the Americans returned.

The HQ of the 100th FW, IXth AF, moved in on January 13 and the aircraft dispersals and airfield defences were strengthened. The 48th FG (492, 493 and 494 Squadrons) arrived from the USA on March 29 and flew their first P-47 mission over France three weeks later. They were joined briefly by the 371st FG in April due to the condition of their base at Bisterne, but they left early in May. Intensive training using the bombing range just to the east of the airfield quickly brought the 48th up to operational standard and they carried out numerous sweeps before D-Day, attacking marshalling yards, airfields, bridges, coastal batteries and radar stations. D-Day itself was something of an anti-climax for they were confined to convoy and beach cover, but afterwards they reverted to their destructive sweeps. During June the 48th flew 68 missions

involving 1956 individual sorties.

As soon as ALGs on the Continent became available the squadrons moved in, the last leaving Ibsley on July 4. A liaison squadron was then based for about a week before being replaced early in July by the 367th FG from Stoney Cross. Flying P-38 Lightnings, their stay was also short and they left for Beuzeville, France on July 22.

With the end of the American occupation in October, Ibsley was used temporarily by Oxfords of 7 FIS, Upavon and on March 9 1945 the airfield was transferred from 11 to 46 Group, Transport Command. No operational units were based here, it being used as a satellite by Stoney Cross and Holmsley South, and for the Glider Pick-Up Training Flight, which arrived from Zeals with Dakotas and Hadrians. A variety of small ground units also appeared, including 160 Staging Post awaiting a move to Guernsey, and 200 and 201 Signals Unit which assembled at Ibsley in readiness for Tiger Force.

The Glider Pick-up Training Flight moved to Ramsbury in October and the station joined 47 Group, though the last flying unit had already gone and Ibsley had started to run down. Amazingly, work started on a new Station HQ in January 1946, but by March the grass between the runways was being ploughed up and Nissen huts were being sold off to local purchasers. Some of the Blister hangars were used by a detachment of 49 MU for storage but Ibsley became an inactive site in 1947 and was soon derequisitioned. The minor road between Ellingham and Rockford Common, which cuts across the old north/south runway, was reopened and in the early 1970s the airfield itself became an Amey Roadstone gravel pit and is now fast disappearing. A few air-raid shelters, a number of derelict huts and the large ATC tower remains as reminders of a short-lived but important airfield.

Lymington, Hampshire

SZ342960. 1 mile E of Lymington

Built specially for the invasion of Europe, the Advanced Landing Ground of Lymington had minimal facilities. Two temporary runways were produced by laying steel wire mesh reinforcements on low-lying ground on Snooks Farm near Lisle Court, and close to the Solent. A number of Blister hangars were erected but personnel were accommodated in tents.

The 50th FG (10, 81 & 313 Squadrons), IXth Tactical Air Command, USAAF, moved in during March 1944 and started intensive training on their P-47 Thunderbolts. Under the command of Colonel William D. Greenfield they flew their first operational mission on May 1 and soon all three squadrons were hard at work softening up communications on the Continent.

With landing strips available in France, the Group moved over the Channel on June 25 and Lymington was not used again, rapidly reverting to agriculture. A Blister hangar has been used as a farm building for many years and the position of another at SZ344960 can be deduced. Some bar and rod tracking is in use for fencing, but little other evidence of an airfield now exists.

Needs Oar Point, Hampshire

SZ402978. 1½ miles S of Bucklers Hard

One of the series of Advanced Landing Grounds built along the Sussex and Hampshire coasts, Needs Oar Point could have been scarcely further forward. It was on low-lying ground near the entrance to the Beaulieu River, south-west of Fawley. With clear approaches from the sea, it was screened by trees on the northern side, these providing some camouflage for aircraft.

The site was selected during the summer of 1942, work commencing in the spring of 1943. Steel wire mesh was laid as reinforcement on the grass but other facilities were minimal, the ALG being intended for occupation only during the build-up to the invasion of Europe. All accommodation would be tented and only first-line servicing would be undertaken. Additional work was done on the site by 4842 Works Flight from December 1943 onward in readiness for the HQ of 146 Airfield, 84 Group and 197 Squadron when they moved in from Tangmere on April 10 1944. They were joined by another Typhoon squadron the following day when 193 returned from an Armament Practice Camp, and the unit reached full strength when joined by 257 and 266 Squadrons. Like the other units of 83 and 84 Groups, it was fully mobile with some 200 lorries on strength. Each squadron had 30 aircraft, a total of 120 on this small landing strip, with 96 in use at any one time.

During the run up to D-Day the 'Tiffies' concentrated on attacking radar stations and communications. 193 and 257 Squadrons bombed a rail tunnel on May 19, succeeding in blocking it at both ends, while the latter squadron fired 9,615 rounds of 20 mm ammunition and dropped 62 500 lb bombs on just one day. A few days before the invasion the unit was renamed 146 Wing.

A maximum effort was made on D-Day itself when 146 Wing was on *cab rank* duty, on call to attack any strongpoint or target designated by the Army. Later they returned to harrassing enemy communications. East of Caen they found a train entering a tunnel, this time trapping the unfortunate occupants inside by repeating their earlier blocking tactic. Their major coup was on June 27 when the Wing Leader led an attack on a farmhouse used as the HQ of Generalleutnant Dohlmann, commander of the German infantry division facing the Americans at St Lô. While Mitchells carried out medium-level bombing the Wing went in low with rockets, bombs and cannon. The farmhouse was completely destroyed and Dohlmann killed.

This was virtually the end for Need Oar Point. 257 Squadron left for France on July 2 followed by 193 and 197 the next day. 266 Squadron had already gone to Eastchurch for a rocket-firing APC and suddenly the ALG was deserted. Within weeks it was abandoned.

The site was de-requisitioned in November 1944 and parts of it immediately reverted to farming, though it was used for storage by the Royal Navy as late as 1946. Very little evidence of the airfield now remains. A thorough search might produce scraps of wire mesh reinforcement, but there was never anything more permanent on the site.

Stoney Cross, Hampshire

SU246125. 7 miles NE of Ringwood

Set in a heavily wooded area of the New Forest just north of the A31 (T) road, Stoney Cross was originally planned as a secret airfield, a landing ground deliberately devoid of any of the usual facilities and with camouflaged hides for aircraft. Later it was decided to develop the emergency airfield into an advance base for both fighters and bombers and work started on the necessary buildings in 1942.

Stoney Cross was opened by 38 Wing, Army Co-operation Command, on November 9 1942 in an incomplete state, and with the contractors still occupying most of the airfield. It was not fit for the planned move of 170 Squadron but after Sommerfeld tracking had been laid over soft ground 239 arrived on January 13 1943—in gliders towed by 296 Squadron. A month later 123 Airfield HQ set up camp to the north of the airfield, joined two days later by Mustangs of 26 Squadron and at the beginning of March by 175 Squadron. With the runways cleared and Ashby Walk bombing range restricted in use, Stoney Cross was considered ready for action. 123 Airfield commenced operations during Exercise *Spartan*, a large scale Army Co-operation exercise.

Transport and Coastal Command representatives visited early in April but both turned Stoney Cross down. Wimpey, the contractors, were still finishing the runways, perimeter tracks and dispersals, and as if to emphasise its unsuitability a collision between a Mustang and a contractor's lorry occurred the following day, resulting in the death of three civilians. It was then offered to 38 Wing who agreed to use it for 295 Squadron but to delay the unit's arrival until the middle of May to enable Wimpey to complete their work. 123 Airfield units moved out early in April and with 295 going to Holmsley South instead the airfield was without flying units.

With the disbandment of Army Co-operation Command on June 1 1943, Stoney Cross was transferred to 10 Group, Fighter Command, while construction work continued. B-17 Fortresses of the VIIIth Air Force, USAAF, started to appear in increasing numbers from June onwards, bringing in American aircrew for rehabilitation at Broadlands, the Mountbatten family home at Romsey.

The airfield was at last fit for regular operations when 297 Squadron arrived from Thruxton in August 1943 with a mixed strength of Albemarles and Whitleys. More Americans appeared to herald fresh developments but they were only concerned with the erection and towing out of Waco Hadrian gliders. Meanwhile, 297 Squadron had dropped units of the 12th Commando at St Valerie (they were retrieved by the Navy) in September and had been threatened with re-equipment with Venturas. Then, on November 4 the squadron was split up, B Flight becoming the nucleus of 299 Squadron at Stoney Cross while C Flight moved to Tarrant Rushton to perform the same service for 298 Squadron.

No 299 Squadron received the Venturas and together with 297 was soon busy on intensive training with the Airborne Division on such oddly named exercises as *Try Again*. At the beginning of 1944,

299 Squadron re-armed with Stirling GT IVs while 297 carried on with the Albemarle on almost non-stop exercise paratroop drops by day and night. These exercises gradually got larger and more involved, 14 Albemarles of 297 Squadron taking part in the drop of 1,500 troops of the 3rd Parachute Brigade Group on February 6.

Supply drops over France were made by 297 Squadron during February, and by both squadrons in March. The whole station was beginning to work well when both squadrons were suddenly moved out of Stoney, 297 going to Brize Norton and 299 to Keevil. The USAAF took it over on March 13 1944 and P-38 Lightnings of the 367th FG, IXth AF, arrived on April 1. The three squadrons (392, 393 and 394) immediately commenced training, having arrived direct from the States. From their first combat mission on May 9 operations were almost exclusively aimed at airfields, rail junctions, road bridges and French coastal batteries in preparation for *Overlord*.

After D-Day the Lightnings roamed over France interdicting, operations which continued when the Group moved to Ibsley on July 7 and Stoney Cross returned to RAF control. Only very briefly, however, for on the 27th the Marauders of the 387th BG (556-559 Squadrons) arrived from Chipping Ongar. Operations were against communications in France but the BG was only waiting for landing grounds on the Continent to become available before they moved forward on September 5. The RAF element had warning

COLONEL YOUNG AND HIS P-38 AT STONEY CROSS

National Air and Space Museum/U.S. Air Force

U.S. Air Force pilots usually gave names to their aircraft. They may have been names of their wives, sweethearts, movie actresses or some allegorical concoction. Colonel Young's home state was Montana and he chose to portray its map with the name "Miss Helena" on the P-38's fusilage (Helena is the capital of Montana).

of a take-over by Brize Norton units—but this was cancelled and a detachment of No 1 Heavy Glider Servicing Unit, Netheravon, arrived instead. They took over two hangars and a workshop and repaired assorted glider parts retrieved in France and brought over to Southampton docks by landing craft.

On October 7 the airfield became a satellite of Ibsley. Nine RAF Regiment squadrons moved in to use the accommodation

Effect of Two World Wars on the Forest

(Although the New Forest contributed substantially to Britain's success in both world wars, it nonetheless suffered adversely from long and harsh occupation. Anthony Pasmore, in his history,— *Verderers of the New Forest* (1976), details these set-backs.

The New Forest of 1976 was still so littered with the debris of military occupation from 1939 to 1945, that the demands for land made upon the Open Wastes in the years following 1914 are easily forgotten. Indeed, the Forest's ability to heal the scars from that earlier conflict has been so effective that a learned archaeological society once embarked upon an excavation of unidentified earthworks at Matley Wood, until, to their disgust, the fin of a mortar bomb was revealed. ... Of course the Forest's contribution to both wars in terms of timber supplies was made much of in succeeding years, in order to further the interests of commercial forestry, but the story of military occupation as it affected the commoners in the First World War has never been fully told.

The Verderers' immediate and willing submission to military demands was an inevitable and no doubt laudable consequence of the national emergency, but it hastened the slow decline of the Court, and probably deprived it of a will to resist post-war development and plans for expansion by the Office of Woods and its successor.

The military authorities were quick to take advantage of the new concessions offered by the Verderers, and in September and early October 1914 the 7th Division was encamped on the Racecourse and Bolton's Bench at Lyndhurst with twenty thousand **Continued on next page**

When Eagles of War Soared over the New Forest...

Continued from previous page

whilst in transit, and a month later 116 Wing, Transport Command, took over the unit. A large influx of personnel in November heralded the formation of two Wellington transport squadrons, 232 and 242. Four of the established 25 Wellington C XVIs of 232 Squadron had arrived by the end of the month and training commenced, but a change of plan brought re-equipment with Dakotas in January 1945, and the Wellingtons were handed over to 242 Squadron.

No 46 Squadron re-formed on January 9 1945 with the first Stirling C Vs to reach an operational unit and the training role of Stoney was accentuated by 52 Squadron (Long Range Flight) which was attached for six weeks to convert part of 232 Squadron to C-87 Liberators. Two days after the LR Flight left, four aircraft of 232 were despatched to Karachi and more went later in the same month. At about the same time the Dakota element of the squadron moved to Merryfield and became 243 Squadron, the remnants of the unit remaining at Stoney Cross to convert to C-54 Skymasters later in the year.

This confusion and turmoil was only increased when 242 Squadron exchanged its Wellingtons for Stirling Vs and, using mainly ex-Bomber crews, started training flights to North Africa. 46 Squadron flew their first route service on March 3 and from early April were operating to India. They were just about to be joined by 242 Squadron when the latter was told it was to receive 15 Avro Yorks. By May 1 242 had three Yorks, 18 Stirlings, one Wellington and an Oxford, while 46 Squadron had 24 Stirling Vs on strength.

The MAP took over No 2 hangar (at the southern end of the airfield) during May and a party of Bristol Aeroplane Co personnel moved in to modify Stirling IVs to the trooping role. Much to 242 Squadron's disgust, these were delivered to them to replace their Mk Vs, the latter having already supplanted their Yorks which had suddenly been withdrawn in July. Despite these many changes the amount of flying increased during August with 46 Squadron shouldering extra tasks while other squadrons used Stoney as their route departure point.

A new passenger and freight building complete with a large hardstanding came into operation in September, just in time for the large trooping commitment at the end of the war with Japan. During December 242 Squadron moved to Merryfield but 46 continued services to India on a reduced scale, and in February 1946 they were told that they were to re-equip with Dakotas. They slowly completed the changeover in April and then flew services to the Middle East.

With the move of 46 Squadron to Manston in October 1946 Stoney Cross was rapidly run down and transferred to Care & Maintenance. Retained as an inactive site, it finally closed in January 1948.

The easterly perimeter track was taken over as a minor road to Lyndhurst and later the NE/SW runway was similarly used as the base of a road to Linwood. The three 'T2' hangars were still present in 1956 but after the Forestry Commission took over they were removed together with the remaining concrete runways, perimeter tracks and dispersals except on three camping sites. These use the foundations of the main barrack area on the edge of Kings' Garn Gutter Inclosure (SU250129), the Janes Moor Pond site (SU246136) and Ocknell Inclosure (SU250120) where aircraft dispersals were employed. The whole airfield has been successfully converted into a public recreation area by the Forestry Commission.

Effect of Wars ...

infantry, four thousand horses, artillery, and a great deal of other equipment. Then, as in the Second World War, the Forest served as an important staging post for troops destined for France. As might have been expected, the damage resulting from this use was considerable, with numerous trenches and pits left open throughout the Forest, and with the stock much disturbed.

After the initial excitement aroused by the massive troop movements of 1914, the presence of soldiers and equipment in the Forest became a matter of routine, with the Agisters being given general instructions to co-operate to the full. In June of 1915 for example, they marked military maps with the sites of dangerous bogs to be avoided during the manoeuvres, and indicated them on the ground with red flags supplied by the Army. Trouble with open trenches and litter continued, but was tolerated to an extent which would have been unimaginable before the war. As the years of conflict wore on, however, more serious consequences of troop movements became apparent, with gates left open or destroyed by motorised transport, and with a rising toll of ponies and cattle killed by military vehicles.

Manoeuvres certainly disrupted the use of the common grazings for their duration, but of much more significance were the demands for land which commenced within a few weeks of the outbreak of war. A hospital for wounded Indian troops had been established at Balmer Lawn, and in November 1914 the new Deputy Surveyor informed the Verderers that the officer in charge had selected a site on the Open Forest for a crematorium. Mr. Leese however had suggested an alternative in Perry Wood, and this had been accepted. Sightseers at the hospital had since proved such a menace that the troops had enclosed ten acres of open Forest around it with barbed wire, and

had posted sentries to keep people away. Under the circumstances the Verderers raised no objection.

After the establishment of the hospital, it was almost a year before further land was demanded from the Forest. There were then almost simultaneous applications for a grenade school at Bolton's Bench, and an airfield at Beaulieu. These two encroachments and their extensions were to cause the

Verderers more trouble than any other aspect of military activities, and in the meantime the Forest proceeded to contribute to the War effort in many lesser ways. For example, in the winter of 1914/15 quantities of heather were sent from Beaulieu for use in the saturated military camps around Winchester, while in the Spring of 1916, hand-picked heather tops

ALLUM GREEN SCENE, AS SKETCHED BY HEYWOOD SUMNER IN 1882

Sumner made the sketch for the Artists' Edition of Wise's *The New Forest*. Six decades later Allum Green was anything but peaceful. Allum Green House had been requisitioned by the military in 1940. Eventually the house suffered a direct hit from a German plane and there were casualties. In the spring of 1944 Vera Brittain, noted lecturer and author, was able to observe the massive buildup for D-Day from her cottage adjacent to the ruins of the Alum Green House.

Effects of Two World Wars on the New Forest. . .

Continued from previous page

were supplied for packing munitions and for bedding.

Tram lines were laid across the Forest from Hawk Hill to the Brockenhurst to Beaulieu Road to facilitate the extraction of pit wood and other timber, while at Millyford Green a Portuguese lumberjacks' camp was established with its numerous buildings and tram lines. Massive concrete footings still survive there, and the old cookhouse fireplace and flue has recently been restored and designated as a tourist attraction.

Charcoal was perhaps one of the most interesting natural products of the Open Forests specifically related to the war.[44]. The traditional method of pit burning had become virtually extinct in the New Forest by the beginning of the century, and the secrets of the craft survived with only one man —Frederick Cull of Cadnam. This was known to Briscoe Eyre, and with his encouragement the industry was re-established for the duration of the war by Cull and his two brothers. The products of their labours were sent to France, probably for use in water filtration, and possibly in the form of activated charcoal in gasmasks.

The construction of a bombing or grenade school was commenced in the vicinity of Whitemoor, east of Lyndhurst, at the end of 1915 and the site was in use by the following March. It eventually occupied an area of about 190 acres, and by the end of 1916 proposals were well advanced for the enclosure of an additional 230 acres, immediately adjoining and to the north west of Matley Wood for a trench mortar school. Concurrently with the establishment of the bombing school, the Army Council applied for Forest land to be used as an airfield at Beaulieu. The size chosen was one which had been developed as a private flying school in 1910 by a Mr. McArdle, and the Verderers had already experienced some problems with this gentleman's activities in levelling the Forest without permission. The War

Office now stated that the field would be required only for the duration of the war, and that it was not anticipated 'that any material damage to the surface will be done'. On this understanding permission was granted by the Court. There can be little doubt that the War Office application was intended as the most blatant piece of deception. Within a few weeks some buildings were already erected, and five aircraft installed. Throughout the remainder of the war the site was repeatedly extended and developed with innumerable concrete buildings, a sewage works, and ultimately a proposal for a railway link to the main line at Beaulieu Road. This last scheme arose in the summer of 1918 and never progressed beyond the drawing board, but the airfield itself may well have exceeded 300 acres in extent by this time.

In August of 1918, the Matley Trench Mortar School was closed, and its site occupied by a War Dog Training School. Some 200 dogs were accommodated on the site for training in message-carrying under battle conditions. Part of this training also involved taking the dogs to various parts of the Forest and releasing them with messages to be returned to Matley. The consequences might have been foreseen, and within a few months several commoners' animals (in particular pigs) had been killed and injured. The Verderers' patience was at last exhausted and, with the war now over, they wrote demanding that the school should be closed at once and the commoners compensated for their loss. The school was in fact closed in May of 1919, although the claims were not settled until the following November.

The Second World War left the New Forest in a physical and administrative mess. In addition to the three airfields, two bombing ranges, and cultivation areas, there were numerous lesser service installations and sawing sites. The whole area had been parcelled up

into different military training and firing zones, and damage by tanks was extensive. The military had destroyed many of the bridges and dug thousands of slit trenches and a number of anti-aircraft landing traps. Barbed wire littered the heath and live explosives made areas such as Acres Down perilous to animals and humans alike. A large prisoner of war camp disfigured Setley Plain, sprawling camps and depots had sprung up at several sites.

The 8,700 acres of military encroachments recorded by the Baker Committee as existing in 1946 gives a wholly inadequate picture of the real damage caused to the Forest and suffered by the commoners as a result of the war. Moreover, it quickly became clear that the Service Departments were not going to relinquish their newly acquired empire without a fight, and even had plans to extend it.

Gradually the pressure against continued military occupation began to make its mark, with condemnation coming from many sources and with continuing presentments in the (Verderers') Court calling for the reinstatement of the Forest. The War Department's application for 5,000 to 6,000 acres for training purposes, made in July of 1948, no doubt damaged the military case beyond repair, by uniting national and local amenity interests with those of the Verderers, the Agricultural Committee and the local authorities. The application was withdrawn late in 1949, and by that time the return of the major encroachments was well under way. Stoney Cross and Holmsley were opened to grazing (although not reinstated) in the summer of 1947 and the bombing ranges were cleared and returned by 1949, with the exception of the Millersford camp.

9
Gypsies and Their Lore
Juliette de Bairacli-Levy and the Wanderers

For centuries New Forest gypsies have been casually observed, but it remained for Juliette de Bairacli-Levy to live among them and write the definitive book about their everyday life. *Wanderers in the New Forest* has gone into several printings since it appeared in 1958. With gypsies barred from living in the open Forest today, her book has become a valuable record of the old pattern of life.

Juliette de Bairacli-Levy was born in Manchester, educated at Manchester and Liverpool universities, and since the age of twenty has been devoted to a "life of nature" with gypsies, foresters and shepherds as her friends. She also is an authority on veterinary herbal medicine and has written widely on the subject.

By courtesy of Juliette and her publishers, Faber and Faber, the following passages are reproduced.

Old Haunts Remembered

I do not forget a walk that I had once with Eiza Cooper, one of my longest-term friends amongst the New Forest Romanies. Her own people called her Black Liz, 'Black' being a Gypsy compliment, meaning a Gypsy of the purest type, the pure black blood, the *kawlo ratt*. Eiza's uncle, Nehemiah Cooper, who died at near ninety years of age, during my time in the forest, had been the recognized King of the Hampshire Gypsies, and Eiza has racial pride powerful upon her. On our walk she showed to me all the quiet, beautiful and well-chosen sites—by water and places in the sun—which had been the old camps of her pony-trading family when they had possessed the freedom of the New Forest.

Giving Birth in the Open Air

What impressed me about the change from Gypsy nomad life on the wild heaths to shack life in suburbia or slum-dwelling in the towns, was that the Romany women lost one of their truest characteristics, the ability to give birth to their babies with the ease of the fox vixen littering her cubs in the forest. The modern Romany woman goes into hospital for the birth of her baby and suffers a birth often as difficult and complicated as endured by the non-Gypsy woman from suburbia or town who does not take natural exercise or eat natural foods. There is a place on the moorland along Godshill ridge where grows a massive holly tree, around whose roots and beneath whose ample wind-defying shelter, it is known that in former times many Gypsy babies were born to their mothers who went to that place alone when their time came.

The Women Sing Beautifully

In contrast many of the English Gypsy women sing with the lilting sweetness of the woodlarks—of which the New Forest is a stronghold of those melodious birds who sing on the wing—and I loved to hear the women singing into the night over the hatches of their van doors or from the doorways of their shacks.

The Lamb sisters, especially Emma, possess amongst the finest voices of any of the forest Gypsies who I met at the inns. They attract a big audience including the foresters and get well applauded. They wear gaudy clothes and I have seem them with pieces of picture chains around their strong, full-throated necks, when short of other ornament.

Eiza Cooper told me how once she and her many brothers and sisters were commissioned by a Romany Rye (a Gypsy lover) to sing for him 'Danny Boy', throughout in Romany. Her mother dressed them all in white frocks, the boys and the girls, clothing borrowed for the occasion, and the *rye* presented each one of the large family with a silver five-shilling piece.

Augustus John and Jean Cooper

Augustus John remarked to me concerning Jean, how he had seen a young girl leaving Ringwood cinema, who must have been from a travelling Gypsy family passing through the town, there being such a shy, wild, air about her, as if a creature from the woods. That could only have been Jean Cooper, who belonged so much to the forest that she could only tolerate work in the fields as her father worked, and who had found a fox cub and tamed it herself, and ages after she had let it go back into freedom in the forest could have it instantly at her side, as loving as a dog, for the mere whistling to it. Those long-shaped, deep, true-Gypsy eyes, of the girl were perfection in the dusky, oval, face, shaded with the ungroomed hair, dark yet glinting-gold like a wood-copse into which sunlight filters. Those people would have made wonderful artist's models to give the true Gypsy type, but all were too shy to consider such work. As they each told me when I tried to persuade them to pose for artist friends—'Us might be asked to take our clothes off us!'

TWO PAINTINGS OF GYPSIES BY THE LATE ERYL VIZE
On the left is a painting of a family living in the Forest; the group on the right was painted in one of the compounds into which the gypsies were grouped when the open Forest was no longer available to them.

Two Names for the Same Children

Today, then, the New Forest Gypsies wear ordinary drab clothes now much prevailing in the English countryside, where drabness has become esteemed as respectability, and they further, with ashen powder, seek to conceal the natural swartness of their skin; they have almost ceased to speak their Romany language even amongst themselves, although it is one of their tribal laws that parents should instruct their children in their language. Only they still love their good ear-rings, and the old women also their fancy brooches, and they will all adorn themselves again in their former finery which they wear like artists, when they are alone in their family festivals, especially for their marriages and births.

The Gypsy men continue to cling pathetically to the neck-scarf, the *dicklow*, almost a badge of their race for the males, from the youths to the old men.

Also I learnt from Eiza Cooper that the New Forest Gypsy children mostly get two names, one *gawje* (non-Gypsy) plain, for school and work, and one Romany for the family. So that at school one gets Amy, Edie, Henry, Bill, Tommy, at home, Trinity, Liberty, Freedom, Levi, Reuben, Jasper, Whiskey, Trafalgar, Euphonius. They also frequently use two surnames as they travel, to confuse the police and other officials.

The Beauty of Easter and Christmas

The wild daffodils of the forest, gathered by the Gypsies, make one of their trades which I shall remember best. For many times I had met with the daffodil gatherers from Millersford compound, the Gypsy women and their children, passing to and fro along the forest roads, their old perambulators laden with the papery, glistening, golden flowers, often shining with rain, the heaped flowers, the brown babies and the lurcher puppies all in the prams together.

They walked fourteen miles in all, quite often and many times a week, to their special gathering places, where they picked the flowers with care so as not to spoil the harvest for the following years. Care for the daffodil flowers was worth while, for they sell well in the market-places of Ringwood and Salisbury, when neatly bunched and bound with green wool. The peculiar local Gypsy name for the wild daffodils is *dykes*, and if Easter festival comes early and spring itself begins late, held back by frosts, then the Gypsies have a special method of steaming open the closed buds into forced flowering, much care and work being entailed in that steaming process over kettles and pans of hot water.

In the forest the Gypsy flower and plant trade is continuous through each year, for when there are no wildings for the gathering there are always forest ferns and the bay bushes which grow around old ruined cabins, and the sweet gale which grows in the bogs, both providing scented foliage which is saleable.

How A Doctor Endeared Himself to Gypsies

In 1850 Philip Klitz published *Sketches of Life, Character, and Scenery in the New Forest*. He was a member of a prominent musical family that emigrated from Prussia to Britain in about 1790 and which, to this day, has members who are active in musical careers. Philip was born in Lymington, but moved to Southampton in 1829 when he was 24. He became a professor of music and composed many works, among them classical and ballroom pieces, and ballads.

He was always aware of the New Forest's charm and for many years collected stories, poems and legends that he heard from various sources. Some are based on fact, others are fictional. One of the most dramatic stories told in his book concerns a doctor, probably from Lymington, who was called out in the middle of the night to go into one of the wildest parts of the New Forest to assist a gypsy family.

SKETCHES
OF
LIFE, CHARACTER, AND SCENERY
IN
THE NEW FOREST:

A SERIES OF TALES,
RURAL, DOMESTIC, LEGENDARY, AND HUMOROUS.

BY PHILIP KLITZ.

LONDON: ORR & CO.   ROMSEY: LORDAN.
1850.

TITLE PAGE

The Doctor's Story

It was late on a stormy and boisterous night in the dreary month of November, that I had been reading, and feeling fatigued with the toils of the day had fallen asleep—an indulgence I rarely enjoyed out of bed. I must have slept some time, for on awakening I found myself quite alone, my sister and the servants having long since gone to their comfortable beds. A few last sparks were all that remained of what had been a cheering fire; the candles too showed me, by their long dark shadows, that it was high time to be off: I felt cold and uncomfortable, and hastened to seek the comfort of a night's rest. I had just reached my chamber-door, when a violent ringing of the night-bell interrupted my progress. Half asleep and cheerless as I felt, you may imagine I was not particularly pleased at the prospect of having to turn out at such a time and in such weather.

Sleep Interrupted

Before I could have found time to vent my dissatisfaction in the most summary form of words, the bell was again rung, and I bustled to ascertain by whom: throwing up the window, I shouted "What's the matter?—who are you?—what do you want?" The only reply I could get was—"Be quick—be quick—for the love of heaven, be quick!" and that too in a tone and with a peculiarity of accent not at all familiar to me.

By this time, my servant, aroused by the noise, had gone down to the surgery-door: I followed him, and having opened it, caught a glimpse of a low, shaggy, forest colt, with a man upon it, whose legs nearly reached the ground. Both were completely drenched by the rain which fell in torrents, and the wind, which was blowing a gale, extinguished the only light we had. Thus left in the dark, I had no further opportunity of ascertaining who or what the stranger was; for during the absence of my servant in quest of another light, my questionings were overwhelmed by the man's passionate entreaties that I would go along with him and be "quick—quick, for the love of heaven!"

"My Wife Is Ill"

This would of course have been a sufficient summons had I known the man or the whereabouts of the patient: his hurried answer to my inquiries on these two points was uniform—"I shouldn't know him by his name, if he told me:—he had no home; but Marian—his dear wife Marian—was ill: would I go to her?"

"Where to?" I again eagerly inquired.

"Into the forest," he this time replied.

"But," said I, "I know all the

Juiliette de Bairacli Levy...

Continued from previous page

There is also moss to be collected for sale to florists. Then the holly and mistletoe trade is important for the Gypsies, both to florists and private houses, and they know well to cut the best berried branches early before the birds spoil them, and how to keep them a good colour by frequent sprinklings with water, and further flinging old sacking over all. Licences to cut holly for Christmas are issued to the old Gypsy families.

The year through there is the making of household articles, ash clothes-props, willow or hazel clothes-pegs, ash dairy churns and casks for the forest people's home-made wines. The hand-made Gypsy articles are preferred by all who seek long wear.

The round bee skeps once found in nearly every New Forest cottage garden, woven of bramble and straw and reed, are made mostly by the Gypsies. There are still some in use and we possessed one ourselves, and I used to use one on which to balance my typewriter when working out of doors as it was springy and made typing more of a pleasure: no bees, naturally, kept in that one!

Doctor's Story . . .

Continued from previous page
people in this part of the forest: tell me your name."

"No, sir, I can't: I am a stranger, and know no one: my wife is ill—indeed, sir, she is ill and needs your aid; hasten, I beseech you."

My servant had now obtained a light, and the stranger, having stepped from off his forester, entered the surgery. If any addition circumstances had been required to strengthen my disinclination to accompany so mysterious a visitor into the wilds of the New Forest at such an hour and in such a night, it would most certainly have been supplied in the very appearance of the stranger: so dark, so gaunt, and so brigand-like. And yet there was an evident sincerity in the strong love of the man for his wife that counterbalanced in some degree the repulsiveness of his aspect: nevertheless, you would have as soon expected to hear a rough-hewn block of granite discourse sweet music, as that such an individual should betray emotions stirred by the tender passion.

My sister had by this time joined us—for you all know how the effect of a storm intensifies the interest of a night-alarm—and as she only saw the man, and heard him beg me to go with him into some unknown part of the forest, her affection imagined danger, and she conjured me not to leave her. On hearing this, the poor fellow betrayed the bitterness of his disappointment, and casting a supplicatory look at my sister he repeated a few sentences which, to us, were unintelligible. However, his anxiety increased with my objections; and as I hinted that his secrecy and his appearances might reasonably make me hesitate, he seemed to catch at the hope of succeeding: for he immediately threw off the slouched hat and uncouth covering in which he was enveloped, and placing himself erect, with a look of intense anxiety, he addressed me, accompanying all he said with the most animated gestures.

But now his appearance was altogether altered; I never saw a finer-looking fellow; his fiery dark eyes seemed to read my very thoughts—an olive, gipsy-like complexion, added to a fine set of features, full of energy; his head covered with a profusion of jet black curling hair, which hung down his neck, made up a picture which struck me by its boldness, vigor, and expression. Seeing that he was gaining on my opinion, he took advantage of the circumstance, and immediately proceeded to work on the feelings of my sister in his behalf. If I had been surprised at the manner in which he had addressed me, I was much more so at the style in which he pleaded to her;—to say the least of it, it was as much like that of a gentleman as anything I ever witnessed.

He commenced his attack by at once appealing to her kind feelings; and no drawing-room beau could have used more insinuating language, yet freer from nauseating flattery or coarseness. His affecting description of the situation in which he left his wife, was an eloquent appeal to our human feelings; my sister was won, and I could no longer withstand his plea. Fearing it possible I might object on the score of remuneration, he instantly produced a handful of gold, as if to assure me on that point; but it was his persuasive manner that won me; and I at once ordered my horse and chaise to be brought round. His satisfaction at this announcement was evinced most warmly. We were soon equipped for our mysterious journey, but before leaving he addressed my sister again—"Lady," said he, "may the great Ruler of the Stars, whose power governs all, protect you, until your brother's safe return, and as a tribute of gratitude accept this trifle from a wandering son of our tribe!

A Silver Ring

The star of my destiny has made me seek your aid, and never must it be said that the son of a chief of our race forgot his duty to those who befriended him in the hour of trial." Then placing a silver ring, marked with some outré character, on the middle joint of my sister's fore-finger, he continued—"Should aught of danger or trouble overtake you, seek one of our race; and if assistance or aid is within the power of all the tribes, that will demand it. Farewell!"

The chaise was now ready, and wrapping myself up for a dreary journey, I directed my servant to follow our guide, who had already mounted his forest pony. The wind still blew a hurricane, and the falling rain beat so violently into our faces as to render it necessary to keep our heads down;— fortunately we had lamps, or we should not have seen or kept up with our guide. Wind or rain made no difference to him—on he went, dashing forward most gallantly, while his steed seemed animated by the same spirit, and flew on with amazing speed.

We had, however, great difficulty in keeping up with him, and once or twice we lost him entirely:—calling was of no use. Hitherto we had kept on the high road, and our guide would sometimes halt and join us; then start again, and in the lull of the roaring wind, I could hear him shouting to his pony, or urging us to greater speed—a wish we found it impossible to gratify, for the hurricane often threatened to bring us to a stand-still: the moon, too—the "pale moon," wont to regard the traveller's benisons, seemed utterly unmindful of ours, and about this period in our drive withdrew her face entirely, thus increasing the obscurity of our route.

We had turned from the highroad, and were following the track of the forest timber-carriages— and that much to my annoyance, for it was a series of rolling into deep ruts and rapid risings out of them, suggesting at each descent the strong probability of our being tilted into the muddy ravine. We at length approached a dark mass, and as our guide suddenly shouted to us to halt, I congratulated myself on being at our journey's end; but this idea was soon dispel-

Doctor's Story . . .

Continued from previous page
led by his assurance, that I must now alight, as it was impossible for any carriage to proceed farther in the direction in which he wished to lead me. I had not the remotest knowledge of the locality—a very imperfect acquaintance with my conductor; however, his great anxiety for "Marian—his dear wife Marian" reassured me.

Crossing the Water

To expedite matters, he requested that I would mount his pony, which he then led, and in this manner we proceeded for awhile: then our course was checked by a broad expanse of water: at this obstacle my guide, pausing for a moment, gave a long and loud whistle, and immediately afterwards a commotion was heard from the water. Presently a boy emerged from the stream or lake, and to him the pony was resigned —my guide giving me to understand that I must cross on his shoulders, which, as all scruples were just then useless, I did—and thus laden he forded the tide and deposited me safely on the bank. We then moved forwards for about half a mile, and arrived at the tent which contained the object of all his anxiety—and here, while I perceived matter for astonishment, I saw none for fear.

A Son Is Born

My coming, delayed as it had been, was most opportune; and I am hopeful that it prolonged the patient's life. The result of her sufferings was the birth of a son, at the announcement of which the father's joy knew no bounds. The crisis over, I was led into another tent, where I found a table well laid out for me, with everything I could desire—a bottle of port and sherry, brandy, hot water, cold chicken and a ham, &c.; and to add to the surprise of the scene, two wax-lights in elegant and massive silver candlesticks, a profusion of plate, and on the table were five guineas as my fee. Having made as hearty a repast as I could desire, my guide informed me that, when it suited my con-

CUSTOMS REMEMBERED

(The year 1895 saw the publication of Rose C. de Crespigny's and Horace Hutchinson's *The New Forest: Its Traditions, Inhabitants and Customs*. The work quickly became a classic in its field and although much has changed in the Forest since the turn of the century, the book remains an authentic record of life as it existed in the area almost a century ago. The excerpts below, taken from the chapter on gypsies, are reproduced by permission of the original publishers, John Murray.)

Surely there is no man so practical or so worldly as not to have a soft place in his heart for the gypsy. The "immortal child," that survives somewhere in the nature of every one of us, puts out a hand instinctively to the picturesque nomad with his caravan, his Eastern aspect, and indifferent raiment. The New Forest and its immediate neighbourhood offer obvious attractions to the wandering tribes who love the sylvan glades and sheltering woods. ...
Fifty years ago the romance with which our fancy surrounds (the gypsies) was something of a reality. Among them there were excellent musicians, some of whom played the violin really well, while the rest would dance to its strains on the greensward according to all the best traditions. Now the violin is scarcely to be heard. ...
An anecdote that strikes us house-dwelling folk as curious is

venience, he was ready to accompany me back to my servant with the chaise.

I immediately availed myself of his services, crossed the water by the same process as before, mounted the pony again, and returned by the same route. I will not detain you by recounting all that passed on our homeward journey, in which nothing could surpass the eloquent gratitude of the gipsy. I reached home safely, and certainly none the worse for my singular and romantic adventure in the New Forest.

The Forest Gypsy in the Time of Wise

(In 1862 gypsies still lived in the open Forest without much hindrance. At that time John R. Wise had this to say about them in his classic work, *The New Forest: Its History and Scenery*:)

Here and there still linger a few (gypsies) in whose veins run Indian blood, against whom Henry VIII made bad laws, and Skelton worse rhymes. The principal tribes round Lyndhurst are the Stanleys, the Lees, and Burtons; and near Fordingbridge, the Snells.

They live chiefly in the various droves and rides of the Forest, driven from place to place by the policeman, for to this complexion have things come. One of their favourite halting-places is amongst the low woods near Wootton, where a dozen or more brown tents are always fluttering in the wind, and as the night comes on, the camp-fires redden the dark fir-stems.

The kingly title formerly held by the Stanleys is now in the possession of the Lees. They all still, to a certain extent, keep up their old dignity, and must by no means be confounded with the strolling outcasts and itinerant beggars who also dwell in the Forest. Their marriages, too, are still observed with strictness, and any man or woman who marries out of the caste, as recently in the case of one of the Lees, who wedded a blacksmith, is instantly disowned.

They are now content to live upon a stray fowl, or hedgehog, or squirrel, baked whole in a coat of clay, and to gain a livelihood by weaving the heather into mats, and brooms, and beehives.

More True Stories of Gypsies

At the turn of the century when gypsies lived contentedly throughout the New Forest, H.E.J. Gibbins took a special interest in their life and customs. He headed the "The New Forest Good Samaritan Charity" whose purpose was to assist those gypsy families most in need. In 1909 he compiled a book of recollections entitled, *Gipsies of the New Forest and Other Tales*, from which the extracts below are taken.

Fortune Telling

A year or two ago I told a lady where to find a Gipsy woman in the Forest who (upon introduction) would satisfy her curiosity in this (to some a most fascinating pastime). The lady and the Gipsy were absolutely strangers to each other; the former lived some twenty miles distant and had never been in the Forest before, and it was impossible that any knowledge of her or her affairs could by any means have reached this Witch of Endor, or rather of the New Forest, but after the usual formula of crossing the hand with a silver coin (nothing smaller in value suffices):

Gipsy: "My lady, you lives many miles away: I didn't think I've seen ye hereabouts afore."

Lady: "No; this is my first visit to this lovely Forest, and I hope often to come again. As you see, I have a good car, and distance and

CUSTOMS REMEMBERED . . .

Continued from previous page

related of a gypsy boy who recently came into a house, with some other children, to learn some badly-needed lessons. When the lesson was over he was told that he might go. The bare permission was not of the slightest use to him—he had never been in a room before, and had no idea how to open the door. ...

A favourite gypsy dish is snails toasted on the hot ashes with some salt sprinkled over them. No doubt they are very good. ... Those who are acquainted with the gypsy camps speak well, on the whole, of the code of morals that prevails in them. For honesty and sobriety they will bear comparison with most village communities.

time are small matters to me, especially when I have an object in view."

Gipsy: "There's no faith in faces, my lady, but I thinks I can trust ye."

Lady: "I hope so, or I would not have come; and, besides the name I have given you is sufficient to satisfy you of my integrity, I trust, in matters confidential."

Gipsy: "Quite so, my lady, but we has to be kortios (cautious). Well, trust not any man's words, if you please. You have had a deal of trouble, some bother over money and property, and it is causing you a lot of worry. You must perservere with it, and you will gain your end; but you have a cruel enemy, one whom you have looked upon as your best friend. She it is who is your worst foe; but it will all end in your favour, and before long you will be successful, and recover the property, and money will soon be paid to you which you may not have expected."

As it happened, this remarkable outburst of information, with a very graphic description of some of the parties engaged in the lawsuit that was pending between this lady and others, and several matters of small interest, with not so much as a question being asked to gain information, all turned out true in a marvellously short space of time, and in every detail, and a considerable sum of money was paid over to the lady's representatives in the following year, and she soon realised that the Gipsy's words, "Your best friend is your worst enemy," were not only true, but true as Gospel, though she was very loth to believe it at the time.

Some of the Gipsy children are by nature remarkably bright and sharp. Riding my bicycle through

Beaulieu on my way from Hill Top to Exbury, one morning, I met by the wayside a Gipsy woman whom I knew. She was in great distress at the loss of her little baby, only a few months old. She showed it to me in her tent close by. I asked her when she was going to bury it. She said at Beaulieu next day. I enquired what she had to pay, and finding that she wanted only a few shillings to complete the amount required, I gave it to her and passed on. It was then about eleven o'clock. Returning that way in the afternoon, and reaching Hill Top gate, I was surprised to see only one child at it, a dark-eyed, bright little girl of about eight years, and, recognising it was the woman's child I had spoken to in the morning, I got off my bicycle and spoke to her. I asked her what fortune she had had at the gate that day. Looking round to see that no other children were near, she stooped down, and, raking up a handful of dust from the foot of the gate-post, produced a lot of coppers.

A Dutiful Child

"How many pennies have you there?" said I.

Counting them over, she said, "Just twenty, sir."

So I gave her four more, remarking, "You have now two shillings. What are you going to do with all your money?"

"Going to give it to mother, sir, to help bury the little baby with."

About 1900 there was living in her tent in the Forest a very old Gipsy woman named Priscilla Sherred, feeble and very shaky with St. Vitus' dance, from which affliction she went by the name of "Trembling Polly." She was nearly ninety years of age, but hobbled about in a wonderful way for many miles daily, smoking her very short pipe (which disappeared entirely into her horny hand on the approach of Gentiles), and wearing a large coal-scuttle bonnet with a big curtain falling over her shoulders. In a high-pitched, shaky voice she would tell a pitiful yarn to any who would stop to hear it. Some years ago I

"A GYPSY ENCAMPMENT"
(From de Crespigny's and Hutchinson's *The New Forest*)

A New Forest Gypsy Tale

(For excerpts from a story about gypsy life in the New Forest, see the account about Ethel Stevens in the chapter, "Tales That Have Been Told.")

More True Stories of Gypsies

Continued from previous page
persuaded her to go into a cottage, and for the purpose took a small thatched house with a decent garden attached, a quiet, out-of-the-way spot at Bull Hill, near Lymington. I paid a month's rent in advance, and placed the old lady and her grandson therein. They seemed very comfortable, and the village grocer near by supplied them with a weekly allowance of tea and sugar. Going over one day, as I had done several times before, to see how they were getting on, I found the cottage deserted, and a man who was repairing the thatched roof told me he believed the woman had gone to Shirley Holmes, a well-known Gipsy camping-ground not far away in the Forest. Thither I at once betook myself, walking up to the first tent I came to, and looking in at the opening at the top, I saw the old lady quietly smoking her short pipe—"her pipe of peace." After a moment's contemplation of this poor old soul's "paradise", I spoke, but at that instant the pipe fell to the ground and the old woman fairly collapsed. I was sorry to have frightened her so much.

"Well, Mrs. Sherred, what brings you here?"

"Oh, pray, sir, how you did startle me. I couldn't abide that 'ere roof over my 'ed. I couldn't bide it no hows. If I'd a stopt there another day I should a died."

I have seen but few of them ill, and have never met one in a tent suffering from rheumatism. Colds they have at times, but not half so badly as house-dwellers; and bronchitis—or, as they persist in calling it, "The Brown Kitis"— is perhaps unknown, except amongst their baby children, and in these so-called cases I think it is more often only a cold, so magnified for the purpose of invoking charity.

Mrs. Lakey: The 'Queen"

(H.E.J. Gibbins, in his *Gipsies of the New Forest and Other Tales*. describes Mrs. Lakey, whom he regarded as the last of the New Forest gypsy queens.)

Mrs. Lakey, the so-called Queen of the New Forest Gipsies, who died at the ripe age of eighty-five, in October, 1903, spent the first four score years of her life in a tent, in robust health and apparent happiness, but during the year 1898 she was very ill, and after frequent visits to her in her camp, upon her subsequent recovery she was induced by me to go into a small cottage at Beaulieu Rails, a little hamlet of thatched cottages in the Forest, about a mile to the west of Beaulieu Village, where she lived in peace and quietness for the last five years of her life. Her funeral at East Boldre Churchyard attracted a large number of the different families of the tribe from all parts of the Forest to pay their last token of respect.

The old Queen was a remarkable woman in her way, and always spoke of the other "Travellers" (Gipsies) as her children. She had a hard, masculine face, which, from exposure to the air, and always sitting in the smoke of her wood fire (as they all do for choice), had become like the leather of an old saddle, seemingly as hard and brown, and as much wrinkled. She was the last of the "Gipsy Queens" in the Forest.

DIGNIFIED TO THE LAST
Mrs. Lakey pictured not long before her death in 1903 at the age of 85.

The Church Army and New Forest Gypsies

In the 1930s, when New Forest gypsies were confined to compounds, the Church Army undertook an evangelical mission among them. A Captain and a small team of Cadets visited the compounds, travelling in a "Van Evangelist." The extract below, from a booklet entitled *Gipsy Missioning in the New Forest*, describes the life of gypsies and the Church Army's work with them.

Tradition has it that the New Forest is the home of gipsies. In times gone by these people were free to move and settle where they pleased. Usually they pitched within reach of a spring or stream. Now, the gipsies have to live in compounds. These are small clearings of about an acre marked out by the authorities. Here the gipsies build their tents and "park" their caravans. The latter are perhaps in the minority, due to the difficulty of getting them into the forest, and partly because of the poverty of the gipsy. It takes him only half an hour to get a fair-sized tent erected. Hazel sticks form the framework; they are bent over to form a half loop and the ends stick in the ground. A number of them are placed in regular formation and then covered with sacks, canvas, oilskins, etc., according to the wealth and adaptability of the family concerned.

In a family tent there is a space in the centre of the top of the tent to allow the smoke from the fire underneath to curl out. Sometimes just one person will live alone. In this case the tent is built long and narrow, with the fire at one end. Often there is only just sufficient space for the occupant to lie down. Housedweller (Gorgios, as called by the gipsies) would be afraid of fires breaking out, but these people seldom seem to have any casualties, even though in the winter quite big log fires are kept.

In each compound there are anything from eight to fifteen families. There is very little privacy in the tents, as one often finds quite large families living together in a comparatively small place. However for all that, immorality is almost unknown. In most cases partners have not been married according to the Church or State laws, but they are nevertheless most faithful to each other. Their tents are very bare, containing only a box or two and the "beds". These are simply a mass of bracken or straw covered with old clothes and no proper pillows. Some, however, manage to obtain an old wooden bedstead with a mattress and some even rise to blankets. Those who have caravans are usually best off in that respect; but how two grown-ups and four or five children manage to sleep in such close quarters is often a source of wonder.

Many and varied are the means of livelihood open to the gipsy. Among those most followed are included the making and selling of clothes pegs from door to door, the making of holly wreaths, the buying and selling of tastefully arranged bunches of flowers, the picking and sale of wild watercress, and the sale of lace and other articles. In spite of reduced demands for horses, the gipsies still attend the horse fairs, endeavouring to do business. In the "old days" the gipsies worked hard and bought a large number of ponies with their savings, which they trained and then sold in many cases to the colliery owners of Yorkshire.

During the early summer months gipsies can be seen making their way towards the strawberry fields. The plants have to be bedded down with straw. As soon as the fruit ripens these people are working hard from early morning until last thing at night. Both men and women work, and also the children over fourteen years of age. This gives the Missioner an excellent opportunity to run schools among the younger children compelled to remain in the camp. It proves an interesting sight to see the gaily

A GYPSY DOUBLE WEDDING ARRANGED BY THE CHURCH ARMY

This wedding took place at Burley. Many gypsy couples were not married according to Church or civil law, but nonetheless were faithful in their relations.

"Sir Gustus:" Idol of the Forest Gypsies

Church Army . . .

Continued from previous page
painted caravans, resplendent
with their brass fittings, etc. Perhaps it is late in the evening, the
fire has been kindled, the boiling
pot is beginning to steam and
tempting odours arise from the
contents. The grown-ups are sitting or reclining around the fire,
smoking their pipes or cigarettes.
The children (who never seem
tired) are playing their games.
The Church Army Captain and
his Cadets draw near and are
greeted with enthusiasm by the
"travellers." Then some singing
of hymns and choruses follows.
The "Magic" Lantern plays a
great part in the work. The sheet
is rigged up between some trees or
on a caravan. Then later on, when
dark, the pictures are thrown on
the screen.

Sometimes when a service is in
progress the attention of all is
drawn away by the sight of some
men running a horse up and down
the road showing off its good
points in order to sell it. At other
times the noise of the children is
deafening. Those who can read
are given hymn books. Sometimes
a boiling pot left on the fire goes
dry, causing everyone to stir. Peals
of laughter ensue and the service is
practically broken up. In the fields
one meets lots of old friends from
the Forest and also many new ones
are made. Old friends are glad to
find the Church Army Captain
and talk over their joys and
difficulties with him.

Now the work in the Forest lasts
about nine months in the year.
The Evangelist is trying to treat it
as a parish and tries to visit the
various compounds periodically.
The area covered is something like
thirty miles square. The beaten
track is often left to get at these
people. During one season about
700 visits are made to 115 families
in about 10 compounds. Hundreds of miles are covered on a
cycle to do this.

All the families are visited, and
after a time the Captain mounts

Augustus John (1878–1961), renowned portrait painter of T.E.
Lawrence and many other subjects, was a devoted friend of the
New Forest gypsies. No one knows better the warm feeling John
had for the gypsies and the esteem with which they held him,
than Juliette de Bairacli-Levy—whose book, *Wanderers in the
New Forest*, remains the definitive work on gypsy life as it once
existed in the Forest.

The following extracts from her letter to the editor describe
the relationship between Augustus John and the wanderers
whose plight he championed.

John was the appointed King of
the New Forest Gypsies. They
loved and respected him, and he
returned their love. The Gypsies'
friendship name for John was 'Sir
Gustus.' Note the 'Sir.'

John allowed the Gypsies
camping places on his land, and
he helped them when they were
there. The Gypsies never took
advantage of their patron's kindness, and they in turn repaid with
many kind acts toward John and
his family.

It has always been very difficult
to get the Forest Gypsies to pose
for photos or paintings. I managed
both; so did the local Fordingbridge artist, Eryl Vize (whose

work was admired by John), and
John himself was able to have all
the Gypsy models he required.

(I remember once a crowd of
Hungarian Gypsies camping in
John's grounds. They were cop-
persmiths, and their presence
there was of great interest and
pleasure to the Forest gypsies.)

I also remember well, John
opening an exhibition of paintings
by the Berlins in a New Forest
hall. The Gypsies were there in a
crowd, to mingle with their King
and Queen (the Queen being
John's beautiful, graceful and
generous-hearted wife, Dorelia,
who herself wore gowns of the
traditional gypsy sort, with flowing, long skirts—usually patterned
with flowers more after the type of
Spanish and Hungarian Gypsies
than those of the New Forest).
The Gypsies came also to see pictures for which they had modelled.

Everyone 'wined' very well at
that Forest painting exhibition,
and there was Gypsy dancing of
the horn-pipe type, which is the
sort of dance performed by the
Forest Gypsies. In the 'olden days'
the Gypsies, mainly the women,
used to dance for the 'gentery' for
coins flung to them as they danced
(and they remembered often getting a golden sovereign coin if the

his "ready steed" and cycles
another six miles to the next compound. Then in the late afternoon
he cycles fifteen or sixteen miles
back to his caravan. In the evening a visit is made to a near-by
compound.

The children are particularly
anxious that the Captain should
come and take a service. As they
are not very keen to go into a
building for services the Captain
takes his cornet to the compound
and holds a service there. Imagine
a very dark night. The quietness
of the night is suddenly broken by
the sound of hymn tunes being
played on a cornet. Out from
among the bushes quickly appear
a number of children, who volunteer to lead the Captain into the
camp. "Follow me, sir," says one
little chap. "I know the way." And
we go through mud and water,
pursuing a way through bushes
and trees which would form a
veritable maze to the uninitiated.
Presently we find ourselves in the

centre of the camp. Around us
there are tents and a few caravans,
of all sizes and descriptions. We
start singing choruses. Practically
everything has to be learned by
heart as the majority cannot read.
But sing!! The singing is interspersed with simple talks and short
stories. A short Bible reading.
Then a hush as prayers are said.

"Sir Gustus" . . .

Continued from previous page

dancing was performed well). The dance was beautiful, which was quite often for the young girls, with their streaming black hair, dark as the Forest bog pools, and their eyes flashing as the spiralling sparks from Gypsy fires—windborne over the Forest.

John himself, in appearance, really was a Gypsy King. He was big built, and strong as one of the ancient Forest oaks. His grey hair was very bushy, and he wore his hair long, at a time when long hair for men was unusual. But I'm sure it was the eyes which gave him that title of 'Sir Gustus.' Big eyes, of unusual brilliance. Compelling eyes, and deep-seeing ones. Only their beauty somewhat marred by the red viening which fondness for alcohol often causes.

I remember a very historic meeting in the New Forest—in a public hall there. It was held to decide the future of the Forest Gypsies, especially in relation to their camping rights. I was one of the principal speakers at that meeting, and I had personal letters from Augustus John and Brian Vesey-Fitzgerald, and from the Gypsy Lore Society of Great Britain, all urging that the Gypsies should have restored to them their right to dwell and camp in the Forest wherever they chose, with the exception of private lands.

To the joy (and surprise) of those of us speaking on behalf of the Gypsies, the vote was quite heavily in our favour, and we left that meeting able to convey to the Gypsies the happy news (which all of them longed to hear) that the Gypsies now possessed their traditional living rights in England's New Forest.

The sad ending to this voting triumph and also to this piece of New Forest writing, is that higher authorities (above those of Hampshire), totally annulled those voted Gypsy dwelling rights in the New Forest, and to this day the Forest Gypsies suffer many dwelling restrictions, and possess only marshy and windswept areas of the Forest for lawful dwelling-

places and are largely directed into Council house permanent homes —thus cutting them off from their former true Gypsy life of forest and woodlands, which their King, 'Sir Gustus,' encouraged and helped them to follow.

Night Sounds

(The following extract is from C.J. Cornish's *The New Forest and the Isle of Wight*, published in 1903:)

Voices of children, calling or crying in the deep wood, are among the startling and unexpected sounds of night in the forest. More than once the writer has left the track and hastened into the grove, only to see the fire of a gypsy camp, with the children and parents lying at the mouth of their tent, lighted and warmed by the glow of their beech-wood fire. The smell of the woods on a still night, when dew is falling, is the essence of a thousand years distilling in the soil of this virgin forest.

It baffles description: suffice it to say, as Herodotus did of Arabia Felix, "from this country comes an odour, wondrous sweet."

"Granny" Cooper's Last Days

(Archie Cleveland, Verderer and a retired undertaker, has been a life-long friend of the gypsies. He recalls an elderly woman, known locally as "Granny Cooper," and her calls to his home on the edge of Brockenhurst.)

There was an old gypsy lady— Granny Cooper, we used to call her—who used to come here every week. She finally went to live in a house at Sway. This was her last call, my house here—my wife used to keep all sorts of things for her. She used to walk straight across the Forest—over there (pointing towards Sway)—back home. If we weren't here, my wife would leave whatever she had for

Gypsy Numbers Were Not Great

(The population of Forest gypsies never exceeded a few hundred. Their mobility made an accurate census impossible. Nonetheless, they comprised a considerable proportion of the New Forest's strictly rural population.)

Granny Cooper outside the door, but she'd *never* take it if we weren't here. She'd wait until we came. One day I came home and I saw her walking in the distance, staggering like a drunken person. I came indoors and said to my wife, 'There's old Granny Cooper going up over the hill. She looks bad. I'm going up with the van—I don' reckon she'll get very far.' And just over the brow there I couldn't see her when I go on top of the hill. So I watched and waited a bit. Then I had a look and she was crawling behind a bush. So I went up to her and said, 'Now, come on, Granny, you're not very well.' She looked at me and said, 'No, my boy, I'm not.' So I said, 'Well, now, I'm going to pick you up and put you in my van, and take you home.' She was overjoyed. 'Oh, God bless you, my dear,' she said. And that's what I did. I took the old girl home and I never saw her after that. She died, and they couldn't tell her age properly, but we knew she was well over 90.

When we did the gypsy funerals —the last one I think I did was for one old lady Sherwood—that used to be over at Norleywood. I don't know how many old cars and vehicles there were that followed us to church. Usually the gypsies would wait for you at the churchyard gate and say, 'Now, sir, how much do we owe you?' Then they would all pay their share, and pay in cash at the church gate. With this particular funeral, they came up the next day. 'How much do we owe you, Mr Cleveland,' they asked. Then they paid the money —as straight as a die, they were.

An Illustrated Account of A Gypsy Caravan

What must be one of the most attractive and detailed accounts of a gypsy caravan has been written by Jean Westlake whose family operates the Sandy Balls Holiday Centre near Fordingbridge.

Entitled *Gypsy Caravan, A 100-Year Old Story*, the 66-page volume is printed on fine paper and contains over seventy illustrations—most of them by Jean. She also executed the text by hand, giving the book an artistic appearance throughout.

Gypsy Caravan is a true story of the Westlake caravan going back almost a century. It contains illustrations of the original purchase documents, detailed sketches of the caravan's exterior and interior, and an account of happy holidays touring the New Forest. In addition, the volume gives a glimpse of Jean's remarkable father, Dr. Aubrey T. Westlake, a Cambridge-educated physician and a man devoted to Quaker ideals all his life.

The book is well researched, and is a valuable reference for anyone interested in the origins of gypsy caravans. (Copies may be obtained from the Sandy Balls Press, Sandy Balls Holiday Centre, Godshill, Fordingbridge, Hants.)

JEAN WESTLAKE STANDING BESIDE THE CENTURY-OLD CARAVAN

The caravan is permanently sited at the Sandy Balls Holiday Centre at Godshill, near Fordingbridge.

"HOW THE STORY BEGAN"
The first paragraph from Jean Westlake's *Gypsy Caravan*.

NCE upon a time a Gipsy boy fell in love with a Gorgio girl (a non-Gipsy, or house dweller). The family tradition that has been handed down from my Grandfather, to my Father, to myself is oral only, but I believe it to be true is this—before their marriage the girl told her husband-to-be, that if she was to spend her life travelling the roads of England, she wanted to live in a waggon as much like her original home as possible. Obviously well-to-do, the young man ordered the best "vardo" (caravan) that money could buy, stipulating that no expense be spared to make it superior to others built at that time. This accounts for the fact that it is longer (14ft 6in), wider (5ft 8in), higher (11ft 9in), and heavier (about 2 tons), than the usual Reading van, this being the type most favoured by Gipsies and the home most characteristic of a rich Romany family.

10

Happenings: Mischevious, Merry and Otherwise

Smugglers Made Great Use of the Forest

(Throughout its existence of over nine centuries, the New Forest has witnessed many dramatic events. Few, however, so stir the public imagination as the smuggling which occurred in the eighteenth and nineteenth centuries.

Looked at from the standpoint of geography, the New Forest could not have been better placed for smuggling. Its very borders coincided with the English south coast opposite the shores of France from which most of the contraband came. Within minutes the illicit cargo could be transported to the depths of the Forest and hidden or sorted, pending onward shipment to populous areas.

Although there were several points for landing cargo and multiple routes to the shelter of the Forest, much of the planning was done in a few, well-known inns. K. Merle Chackfield, an authority on smuggling in the south of England, in the copyrighted article below describes how the "Free Traders" operated.)

"LOVEY" WARNE. WHOSE SCARLET CLOAK WAS A SIGNAL
She and her brothers, Peter and John, worked as a family team in the running of contraband through the New Forest from beaches and ports on the English Channel. (From an old print)

We were sitting by the water on Mudeford Quay talking of the old Hampshire smugglers. "Ah," said the cheery old fisherman, glass in hand. "Nothing tastes as good as that stuff did," and he laughed heartily at the thought of the 'Preventer' being outwitted as the smugglers brought in their contraband brandy and disappeared with it into the hidden depths of the New Forest.

Smuggling, or 'Free Trading' as it was called, became big business in its heyday during the eighteenth and early nineteenth centuries, and it played an impor-

tant part in the economic life of the people at a time when a labourer's wage was seven shillings (35p) a week. Capital was invested, perhaps by the squire and local traders, doctors, farmers, and even the parson. One parson in 1778 who held strong views against smuggling told his parish clerk that it was a grievous sin. The clerk replied, "Then the Lord have mercy on the town of Christchurch, for who is there here who has not had a tub?"

This was a time when severe taxation, combined with the general poverty of the working people, led to smuggling on a very large scale. The operation consisted essentially of buying a shipload of dutiable goods across the Chan-

nel and shipping them to a lonely English beach, preferably by night, to be hidden away locally if necessary, and eventually distributed into the country. Tea, tobacco, brandy, silks, laces, pearls, spices and wines—even aristocrats escaping the French Revolution, and gold and spies during the Napoleonic wars—all passed through the smugglers' hands.

The New Forest offered excellent cover for smuggling, and its leafy ways and secret places were well known to the 'free traders.' In the Queen's Head, a seventeenth century inn at Burley, the smugglers would gather to make their plans for handling cargoes expected at Chewton Bunny, a miniature gorge where a stream

Smugglers ...

Continued from previous page

runs down from the forest to the sea at Highcliffe. This was a convenient landing place for goods destined for Burley, Ringwood, Fordingbridge and Salisbury. The contraband was brought up in waggons or on horseback along the track from the head of the Bunny over Chewton Common to the Cat and Fiddle Inn at Hinton, where the men would unload some of the tubs, and then moved on into the Forest.

Smuggling was an activity usually carried on by men, but there were some women who delighted in taking part in the excitement and profit of the illicit trade. One such was Lovey Warne who, said a Forester, "would hitch up her skirts, jump on her horses and join her brothers Peter and John in a contraband run." She would wrap silks and laces round her body under her voluminous dress and ride home to the family cottage at Knave's Ash, between Crow and Burley. Her chief task was to warn the free-traders during the daytime of the presence of the Riding Officer who was Abraham Pike in 1803. Dressed in

THE QUEEN'S HEAD, BURLEY: A FAVOURITE WITH SMUGGLERS

Tracks from Chewton Bunny and other landing points converged at the Queen's Head. With many local people secretly abetting the smugglers, the Queen's Head was a safe place for the runners to make decisions about concealing contraband or shifting it to populous areas.

a cloak of the brightest scarlet, she would stand, whenever danger threatened, at the top of Vereley Hill, close to Picket Post, from where she was clearly visible to the smugglers at almost every approach to Burley.

John King of Burley was a man who remembered the smuggling days. He was 'a big man like a gnarled oak, hard as iron,' and he had many times taken 'a couple of forest ponies with sacks on their backs and had gone down to the sea.' He said that the smugglers' route was 'across Crane's Moor, up the smugglers' path, through Vereley and Ridley up to Smugglers' Road there, and on to the Royal Oak at Fritham.' It is probable that there was a smugglers' walk over Poor Man's Common to Picket Post, and it is suggested that there is still a bricked-up cellar somewhere beneath the bracken where contraband was hidden. Cargoes landed at Lymington, Milford and Milton were often taken up the Boldre River into the Forest, and further east the Beaulieu River formed another route from the coast.

So when you see the ponies cropping the green sward of the Forest, or stumble upon a sunken track half hidden in the young bracken; or perhaps if you sail the tidal waters of the Beaulieu River along Fiddler's Reach to Buckler's Hard, you may remember the 'Gentlemen of the Night' who used these ways over two hundred years ago, and risked transporta-

FRITHAM'S ROYAL OAK, ONE OF THE FOREST'S FAMOUS INNS

Located adjacent to some of the most remote woodland areas, the Royal Oak was a convenient place for smugglers to meet and plan their movements.

A Famous Clergyman and the Smugglers

The Rev. Richard Warner's peripatetic life brought him both disappointments and happiness, but his residence in the New Forest area provides us with some amusing anecdotes in his *Literary Recollections*.

Warner's father, also named Richard, was a Londoner who late in life moved near Lymington. The young Richard attended school in Christchurch for four years, awaiting appointment to Winchester College (and eventually admission to New College, Oxford), but a friend failed to keep a promise to assist him on this path. Disappointed, he returned to his Christchurch for another seven years. Eventually he went to another Oxford college (St. Mary's Hall), but after eight terms failed to take a degree.

Through the assistance of Warren Hastings, Warner was ordained in 1790. This time, another friend—William Gilpin, kept a promise and named him curate at Boldre, where he stayed for four years despite meager pay. Eventually a curacy with improved conditions developed at nearby Fawley, and he remained two years.

It was Warner's boyhood days in Christchurch and his later curacies at Boldre and Fawley that inspired him to write so much about Hampshire (including the New Forest). At Boldre he was influenced by William Gilpin to take an interest in topography, and at one time he hoped to write a comprehensive history of Hampshire.

Warner's greatest success came from his pen. Over forty of his works became nationally respected, some of them going into several printings. His efforts covered a wide range: topography, history, science, theology, biography, economics—and even duelling. In archaeology he was the first to pinpoint the Roman settlement of Clausentum near Southampton. But even his writing produced pitfalls. In one work he reproduced the print of an artist without obtaining permission, was taken to court, and obliged to pay compensation and costs of £70—equivalent to several thousands of pounds today. In 1793 a two-volume topographical work was destroyed by fire at the printers; precious copperplates were also lost.

Smuggling flourished during Warner's school days at Christchurch and his later period at Boldre and Fawley. The accounts below, taken from his *Literary Recollections*, give the flavour of those times—including one occasion when he nearly lost his life to the moonrakers.

Smugglers: Heroes of the Schoolboy

It is scarcely credible, indeed, how many families were implicated, more or less, in this illicit and barbarising (smuggling) traffic; what large sums were accumulated by its practice; or, with what openness and insolence it was carried on; nor, can the reader well conceive, the deep interest which was excited in the minds of the school-boys; or how much our imaginations were inflamed, by the spirit of daring and adventure, which animated these defiers of the law; by the dangers they were seen to encounter; the hair-breadth 'scapes they were known to experience; and by the magnitude, and I may add, *pomp* of the scale, on which they conducted their operations.

No actual resistance (if perchance, there might be an occasional *show* of it) was opposed to the smugglers, though they were pursuing their calling under the meridian sun; for, what could the opposition of a handful of revenue-officers have availed, against bands of raw-boned ruffians, hardened, determined, desperate, and generally half-maddened with liquor, consisting of from one to three hundred in number?

20 to 30 Waggons

I have myself, more than once, seen a procession of twenty or thirty waggons, loaded with kegs of spirits; an armed man sitting at the front and tail of each; and surrounded by a troop of two or three hundred horsemen, every one carrying on his enormous saddle, from two to four tubs of spirits. The revenue troop, who had always intelligence of the *run*, were, it is true, present on the occasion; but with no other views and intentions, than those of perfect peace. A flood of homely jokes were poured upon them by the passing ruffians; but, these were always accompanied by a present of kegs, greater or less, according to the quantity of the smuggled goods; a voluntary toll received, as it was conferred, in perfect good humour, and with mutual satisfaction.

Murder—And A Narrow Escape

The unfortunate victim to the brutal revenge of the smugglers had been, for some years, one of the corps of the Christ-church custom-house officers; and resided at a small village, called Milton, about six miles from that town. It was in a dark winter night, after the worthy man had, for some hours, retired with his family to bed, that a loud rapping at the outer-door roused him from his slumbers. On looking through the chamber casement, he perceived

Smugglers...

Continued from previous page
tion or even hanging for two shillings and sixpence a keg, or five shillings for a night's smuggling.

Clergyman...

Continued from previous page

two men, though their countenances were not distinguishable, through the gloom of midnight. He enquired their business; when one of them informed him, that he had discovered a large quantity of smuggled goods, in a contiguous barn; to which he and his companion would lead Mr. Bursey, if he would reward them with a stipulated sum.

A bargain was immediately struck: and the unsuspicious officer hastily clothed himself; descended, unarmed, into the passage; opened the door; and, in one minute, his brains were dashed out upon his own threshold! The fact afterwards appeared to have been, that Mr. Bursey, a truly conscientious and zealous servant of government, had mortally offended the smugglers by his activity: and that they had deputed two of their gang, to rid them of so vigilant an enemy, by this barbarous murder.

Nor must I forget to mention, before I quit the subject, a danger that I escaped; or, at least, a dreadful fright which I experienced, *in propriâ pesonâ*, from this terrible banditti, a year or two after I had quitted school. I had been spending the day at Christchurch, and, mounted on my little *Forrester*, was returning at midnight, (a ride about ten miles) through the beautiful but lonely lanes, between that place and the house of my father, who then resided on the borders of the New-Forest. I could not boast of a very serene state of mind at the moment; as I well recollect, that the rustling of the fast-falling October leaves, effectually prevented that train of quiet thought, in which I certainly should have indulged, in so picturesque a scene, had the clock been but twelve hours *earlier*.

While thus pursuing my solitary way, under a cloudy sky; all ear, and with no very agreeable associations in my fancy; I suddenly, but distinctly, heard the trampling, of heaven only knows how many horses in my rear. I

How Lord Malmesbury Knew about Smugglers

James Howard Harris, third Earl of Malmesbury (1807 – 1889), spent a good part of his childhood at Heron Court, an old manor house near Christchurch, where he learned first-hand about smuggling. While bird-watching in a nearby copse, he was roughed up by a smuggler because he had seen the man and his companions hiding kegs of brandy amongst the trees. The man made the boy swear not to tell and insisted on giving him a drink.

The Earl went on to become Foreign Minister. In his *Memoirs of An Ex-Minister (1884)*, he relates the following anecdotes from those childhood days at Heron Court.

Surprise at Dinner

My childhood was passed chiefly at Heron Court, an old manor house near Christchurch, which, with a considerable property, was left to my grandfather in 1795 by Mr. Edward Hooper, the last of a very old Dorsetshire family. During the long war with France this wild country, which extended in an uncultivated state from Christchurch to Poole, was the resort of smugglers upon a large scale. The last Mr. Hooper was chairman of customs, and the late Lord Shaftesbury, father of the noble-philanthropist ..., told me this anecdote as characteristic of the times.

About 1780 Lord Shaftesbury was sitting at dinner in the low hall at Heron Court with this relation, the latter having his back to the window. The road, which has since been turned, passed by the front door of the house. Suddenly an immense clatter of waggons and horses disturbed their meal, and six or seven of these, heavily loaded with kegs, rushed past at full gallop. Lord Shaftesbury jumped up to look at the sight, but the old squire sat still, refusing to turn round, and eating his dinner complacently. Soon after a detachment of cavalry arrived with their horses blown, and asking which way the smugglers had gone. Nobody would tell them, and no doubt they got safely into the New

pushed my pony forwards; but the awful sound increased upon me. The *Forrester* now tried his swiftest gallop: the effort however was vain; for the pursuers were almost at my heels — when, happily, a notion of their real character flashed across my mind. I concluded they were smugglers; and as I fortunately chanced to be neither a custom-house officer nor an informer, I determined to pull up, and throw myself upon their mercy. In another moment two of the ruffians were at my pony's head. A brace of clubs were brandished over me; and, in a flood of blasphemy, it was enquired: 'Who I was? What my business? And whither going?' Though I felt my courage 'oozing out at every pore,' I notwithstanding mustered sufficient presence of mind, to respond without hesitation, 'A friend—Mr. Warner's son, of Sway—and getting home with all possible speed.'

A Close Call

My captors muttered a few words to each other; and discharging another volley of no very good wishes against my eyes, heart, blood, and limbs; released my nag; and bade me, at my peril, proceed incontinently, to the place of my destination. Assuredly I was not reluctant to obey the mandate; but started off like an arrow from a bow: and felt not a little grateful for my escape; more especially, when I heard, the next morning, that the same party had fallen in with the Lymington custom-house officers; attacked, defeated, and pursued the band; and beaten one of them almost to death!

Malmesbury ...

Continued from previous page
Forest. The smugglers had dashed through two deep fords in the Stour close by, which the soldiers had refused, and so lost their prey. These fords are the same through which Sir Walter Tyrrell rode red-handed for his life on his way to Poole after he had crossed the Avon at a place which bears his name, Tyrrell's Ford.

A Doctor Remembered

The following anecdote I learnt from Dr. Quartley, who had practised for nearly fifty years as a medical man at Christchurch. He had not long been in business there when he was awakened one night by a loud thumping at his door. Opening his window, he could distinguish two men muffled up in drab horseman's great-coats and with heavy whips in their hands, with which they were knocking at his door. On hearing the window open they exclaimed, 'Come, doctor, be quick! You are wanted!' Though he did not much like the look of the thing, he thought it better to slip on his clothes and go down to them. They told him they had a job for him, and that he must get his horse out of the stable and come along with them.

After a little hesitation he obeyed their call, and found himself, with a companion on each side, trotting towards the old bridge. When they reached it, they whistled and were joined by two other horsemen. All proceeded in silence some distance over the heath leading to the New Forest by Bransgore. At last they turned down a lane and came to a lone cottage, such as are to be seen in these districts. 'There, doctor,' cried one of his companions, breaking the long silence—'there is some work for you! Step in.'

On entering he found extended on the floor a fine young man in a sea-faring garb, who appeared to be suffering severely. On inquiring he found that he had been wounded in an affray with the custom-house officers. Dr. Quartley suc-

Three Instances When the Moonrakers Won

(H.E.J. Gibbins was a great friend of the New Forest gypsies, and he also collected tales and anecdotes about other aspects of the Forest. Many of these appear in his *Gypsies of the New Forest, and Other Tales*, published in 1909. In this collection are three accounts of smuggling, all—according to Gibbins— based on fact.)

The Smugglers' Captain

A very interesting tale is told of a visitor staying at a small village inn not far from the coast being awakened one night by the opening of a door. He looked out of his bedroom window just in time to see a man with a hunting crop in his hand mounting a horse by the moonlight and riding away. A short time after this he was again disturbed in his slumbers, and quickly slipping on his clothes, went down into the passage, and there met the same looking figure in top boots, spurs, and whip in hand, ready to be off.

'Come with me,' he said; 'I will show you some sport.'

Being a man of nerve, he accepted the invitation, and a moment later descended the steps. In the yard was the man already mounted, and a servant holding another horse in readiness for him. He sprang into the saddle, and away they went, silence being the order of the day. Getting out of the village by a path behind the houses, they were unobserved, and by the moonlight galloped

away across the open country and the downs till they came to a grassy descent from the cliffs to the seashore. At a slight distance in advance were a number of men waiting beside a rather large boat on the beach. His leader, now taking him by the arm, whispered,

ceeded in extracting a ball from his back, and when he had done this, one of his quondam companions came in and asked him (Dr. Quartley) what he thought of it. He answered that the wound was dangerous, and that the young man must be kept quiet. 'Well, Tom!' said the other, 'willst thee stay here and be hanged, or shall we tip thee into the cart?' The wounded man preferred the latter alternative to Dr. Quartley's injunction, and two of them took charge of him, and led him through a dark night and in dead silence back to the old bridge, and there bidding him farewell, cantered off.

At the conclusion of the same winter he was again awakened by a loud rap at his door, and in the morning his maid brought in a keg

of fine French brandy, which she had found on his steps, and on which was written, 'Left there for the doctor's fee.' Fifteen summers afterwards Dr. Quartley dined at Mr. Mills's at Bisterne, and in the evening they went on the Avon. In getting into the boat, Dr. Quartley observed that one of the men who rowed it was particularly attentive to him, so much so that he observed, 'My man, you look as if I ought to know you.'

'Know me! please your honour! I be he from whose back you cut out a slug fifteen years ago. Don't you mind on't? He had been carried into the forest, where by the aid of a good constitution he had recovered, and at the time of this second meeting was working in Mr. Mills's garden.

Three Instances

Continued from previous page

'Keep quiet, say nothing, but follow me.' Getting up to the men, they all saluted in their rough fashion. Few words passed, orders were given by the Captain on horseback, and very soon the last of the tubs of spirits had been carried up the cliff, the boat pushing out to sea, and the two riders following the last of the men with the kegs to the top of the cliff, where the tubs were loaded into some carts that had come in readiness to the spot. This being done, and the loads sent off by different routes, the men dispersed.

The two horsemen found their way back to the village inn, as they had come, without disturbing of meeting anyone. On arrival at the yard, the groom took the horses into the stable, and the riders betook themselves to the sitting room at the back of the house, where the windows, which were closed tightly with shutters, looked into a large garden. The room was dimly lighted, but a good fire was blazing, and some hot grog was soon provided. The host taking up the candle, and removing his hat, great was the astonishment of the

visitor to find it was none other than the young landlady of the inn, who had masqueraded as a man, and had given her orders to the smugglers as their captain.

A few weeks after another expedition was made, with similar results. Soon after this the couple were married, and carried on the inn and the smuggling business so successfully that in a few years they retired with comfortable means provided for the future. The young woman was the only child of the former landlord of the inn, who died the year previous.

Gluggity-Glug

Another interesting tale is given of a young commercial traveller, who made periodical visits to the old-fashioned inn in Hampshire, which adjoins the churchyard. On one of his visits, when returning to his evening meal, he complained of not feeling very well, and wanted some brandy. The landlady said she had not any in the house, but as he did not seem well, she would try and get him some, if he would not say a word to anyone about it. So, taking a dark lantern, she asked him to go with her across the churchyard, and reaching a door at the foot of an old ivy-covered tower, she unlocked it, and getting well inside, she turned on the light. Removing some old gravedigger's tools, a bag or two of cement, old sacks and rubbish, she revealed to sight a number of kegs of spirits. Selecting one, she produced from her pocket a gimblet such as brewers use, and boring a hole with it in the head of the cask, and another smaller hole with a small gimblet being made at the opposite side of the head to give vent, she poured out a jug full of white brandy. The man had meanwhile cut two pegs, or spiles, to put into the cask, but the woman stopped him, saying:

'That won't do, you silly fellow!'

'Why not?'

'Why, the first chap as takes up that 'ere keg will know it's been broached.'

'Why?'

'Why! Sure, it'll go gluggity-glug, just like some old sitting hen. No; I know a trick worth two o' that.'

So, producing from her capacious pocket a small bottle of sugar and water, she filled up the keg to its utmost capacity, and inserting a peg in each hole, cut them off level with the head of the cask. Then rubbing a little cement dust over, to hide all traces, they replaced the tools and bags of cement, etc., just as they had found them, masked the light, and once more gained the inside of the inn, where the traveller much enjoyed his meal, and still more the brandy.

Fooling the Coastguard

The Lymington Excise-man, with his pond in his garden, where it is said many a cask of good brandy was hidden, was long suspected of being a successful smuggler, and his doings were so carefully watched that it was thought impossible that he could land any more contraband. But Jack, his skipper, thought otherwise.

'You go ashore, Capt'n, and leave it to me,' was his remark.

Next day the Coastguard met Jack wheeling up a barrel from the beach, and stopped him for 'searching enquiries.'

'My master 'e's a fool, 'e is,' said Jack; ''is latest idee is 'e'll 'ave a bath o' salt water, an' I'm blow'd if I ain't got to wheel up this 'ere barrel full o' salt sea water for 'im every mornin' afore breakfast!'

'He be a fool!' roared the Coastguard, who went grinning away; but every day after that Jack wheeled his barrel of contraband, unquestioned, by the signal station, with a grin at the Coastguard's expense.

Kegs on the Move at Pitt's Deep

(This extract from Frank Perkins' booklet, *Boldre*, describes what happened to kegs of brandy after they arrived off Pitt's Deep.)

Kegs of spirits, roped together, were sunk and marked with a float, about one-quarter of a mile from the shore, in the Pitts Deep stream, at a spot known as Brandy Hole. The kegs were floated ashore by punts, as by this way it was easier to sink them if a coastguard arrived.

The kegs were carried from the shore by a gang of local men to carts which were waiting a short distance away; but if dangerous for the carts to load up, the kegs were carried into the forest and hidden; the kegs were easily carried slung across the shoulders, generally one in front and two behind. The pay was 2/6 per keg.

Mischief in the Making at the "Cat and Fiddle"

(No written record has yet been unearthed describing just what happened at the various New Forest inns when a smuggling operation was in progress. Fortunately, however, E.E. Cowper in his book, *The Moonrakers*, gives a fictional account of what may have occurred at Hinton's famous 'Cat and Fiddle' on such an occasion. The extract which follows is reproduced by permission of the publishers, the SPCK (Society for Propagation of Christian Knowledge).)

On the night that Mistress Hadlow came to her home, and Roden the Rider also came there to tell them of the outrageous attack upon the King's warehouse at Poole, the 'Cat and Fiddle' inn at Hinton Admiral, but a short distance off the main road to Christchurch, lay in unusual quiet.

It was a long, low, white building, with four irregular dormer windows in the thatch and as many below. Backed by thick wood—for here the Forest grew dense—it stood simply aside from the road, yet on it. There was no garden of division, nor courtyard. A few yards from the door—in the road—was planted the post that held the swinging sign, so well known to travellers. A stable or cart-shed adjoined and found accommodation for the few beasts that rested a night in this place.

The 'Cat and Fiddle' inn was kept by one Pateman Sherrard and his daughter Unity. It was commonly supposed that they were of gipsy extraction; both name and features pointed to it, but they did not claim kinship with the wandering folk of the Forest. Further, this forest inn bore no good name in the matter of trading in contraband, yet nothing had been brought home to its landlord; he went scot-free so far, and was likely to, it seemed, for the place was only patronized by the meaner sort; people who had their business in the Forest,

British Tourist Authority

OLD HAUNT OF SMUGGLERS: THE CAT AND FIDDLE
Many of the older inns of the New Forest served as informal meeting places for smugglers who almost always included local residents. The Cat and Fiddle at Hinton is a short distance from the sea and thus must have been frequently used as a rendezvous. Its famous sign has undergone many changes in design over the years.

seamen, farmers and their men; and these were always banded together to protect the free trader; nor dare they betray him. It was as much as Master Sherrard's neck was worth for him to consider the claims of Law and Justice; the best he could do was to shut his eyes.

A light had been burning since seven o'clock in the window of the 'Cat and Fiddle' inn. The open half-door of the tap-room showed a wood fire that threw a warm glow on the sanded floor and glimmered from the pewter pots on the table.

Two men sat by the table talking. The one was a packman, travelling from Christchurch to Lymington, selling small matters of ribbons, cottons, needles and

Mischief at the "Cat and Fiddle"...

Continued from previous page

pins by the way; the other a miller's man, sent to Poole on a matter of business from Master Hoby, who owned the big mill on the Danes-stream at Milford by the sea.

These sat and talked about the attack on Poole Custom House in low voices, because walls have ears, and night covers much; but the miller's man had seen the very place; indeed, he had seen so much and discussed it so long, that he was on his way back to Milford at half-past ten o'clock at night, instead of three in the afternoon. The wood ashes dropping on the hearth, the rough mutter of the men's voices, and the faint, far-away hum that proclaimed a sou'-westerly wind was waking the quiet sea to a quarrel with the shingly coast-line, were all the sounds.

Master Sherrard was not visible, and his daughter seemed to be moving about softly above stairs.

Suddenly the packman paused, his pot raised in act to drink; he listened; the miller's man slowly followed the direction of his eyes, and ceased to describe the appearance of the broken door of the Poole warehouse.

The packman's head was turned towards the road from the Forest that met the Christchurch road here in a sharp turn.

A horse was coming from the Forest at a smart trot; and if a horse, then, presumably a rider.

At this minute the half door was pushed open, and the traveller appeared. He crossed the kitchen, threw himself on the settle by the fire and stretched out his long boots to the warmth. His coat was open; and the men saw the glitter of pistol barrels; but he did not remove that nor did he lift his mask: the bright eyes observed them through the slits.

Both men fell silent. Nothing can be imagined more difficult than a friendly conversation to be carried on with a mask and two watchful eyes!

'Master Sherrard is abroad?'

remarked the newcomer to the girl.

'He has gone to Poole to-day, and something keeps him,' Unity answered indifferently, but her black eyes looked sideways at the questioner.

'Who doesn't go to Poole now! All the world wants to see the King's Custom House, eh? And no one will say who broke it. A man might do worse than try for the reward they'll offer. A hundred pounds or so wouldn't hurt a man with the winter coming on. What do *you* say, gentlemen?'

'I say nothing at all,' answered the packman, with hasty fervour. 'The less to do with such business the better.'

'In these days a man must live with his eyes shut and his ears plugged,' added the miller's man. 'If you don't want to be hanged by one, shot by another, and transported by the King, you'll live a blind, deaf mute.'

The eyes twinkled through the slits of the mask.

'You are a philosopher, my friend.'

'I don't know what you call a philosopher! If it's caring for your own skin, perhaps I am.' As he spoke the miller's man raised himself regretfully from his chair. He had fully intended to prolong his talk with the packman for another hour, but this company was beyond him! A smuggler he could stand—nay, feel sympathy with. A 'moonraker' he would have defended, as much for fellowship as for fear. But the 'Flyer'! The mysterious gentleman of the road whose face no man had ever seen. The highwayman to whose charge many wild doings were laid—whether with truth or no mattered little to the making of a reputation.

For the last two years the Forest had been his haunt. He appeared at irregular intervals, and sometimes patronized one of the meaner inns, as in this case. For the rest, no one knew anything certain of him, except that he had never molested the King's Mail, nor taken a man's life; that is, not since he had haunted the Forest.

When the 'Flyer' disappeared from the New Forest men gave him the credit of unlawful doings in other directions. Possibly true

FORCING OF THE CUSTOMS HOUSE DOOR AT POOLE
Smugglers usually operated within their own immediate areas. One exception was when Sussex smugglers came to Poole, broke open the King's Custom House, and made away with confiscated goods—inflicting casualties in the process. This old wood cut depicts that occasion (1749).

Mischief at the "Cat and Fiddle"...

Continued from previous page

enough. In any case the miller's man believed the worst, and the packman was one with him in extreme distaste for the cynical glitter of the eyes from the eyelet holes of the black mask. So these good men shortened their conversation.

'Stay and share my tardy supper, gentlemen,' said the 'Flyer,' as the two men stood up to go, and the packman began looking to his straps.

But they shook their heads, and presently departed with a regretful look backward at the warm hearth.

''Tis a thousand pities when a man allows his imagination to master him, eh, Mistress Unity?' said the remaining guest to the landlord's daughter as she brought in his supper.

The girl looked at him sideways through her thick black lashes and proceeded to set the food on the table. She was tall, slim and agile; her dark face betokened something untamed, and certainly little enough respect for authority, but there was nothing in its expression mean or false.

'These good fellows wished to remain here and discuss the lively doings of our friends of the Forest. They had promised themselves another hour by your hearth. Imagination has driven them forth into the rain.'

'They don't like you, I suppose,' said the girl, with a short laugh. It may be allowed that she was afraid of nobody and nothing herself.

'Or their own conclusions about me.'

''Tis the same thing,' said Unity.

'Not at all, my dear,' said the 'Flyer,' stretching his long legs with a yawn. 'I am as sleepy as a six months' infant, and shall want no entertainment but a bed.'

He sat down to his supper, which consisted of a venison pie. Venison was cheap enough in the Forest at all times; and, if truth be told, few Forest-dwellers paid any-

thing at all for it.

After that he spoke little except once to ask the girl where her father was.

'He should be back now,' said she, and that was all. Clearly she could keep her own counsel.

After supper this suspicious traveller retired to the little room in the roof, and later the 'Cat and Fiddle' shut and bolted its doors, leaving not so much as a glimmer behind the small window pane.

Whether Sherrard was out or in was uncertain. But the guest believed him to be in, and not only in, but busy.

In spite of his professions there was no appearance of weariness about the 'Flyer' when once the door was shut upon him. He glanced round at the place in which he found himself. A truckle bed, a chair, a poor cupboard; a box; and you had it all. He crossed to the window and found he could see nothing. The trees over the road made the darkness denser than the night; fine rain fell evenly, blowing towards the house; far away the moaning song of the sea came from the westward. To an unused ear it might have passed unnoticed, but to one who knew it was a clear portent of a rising westerly gale. After watching and listening for a few minutes the man threw himself on the bed; it creaked in all its crazy joints, and moving, he took care to make it creak more.

There he lay motionless, a long dark figure with the strange sinister face; the mask was never lifted, and the eyes stared watchfully through at the objects in the room growing out of the darkness. His ears the while strained at listening.

Nearly an hour passed; it would seem to be drawing towards one o'clock in the morning when the

listener felt rather than heard a stir near his door.

He breathed heavily as one who sleeps sound, and turning, creaked the bed again. Someone was listening outside the door. So thin was the poor panel, so rickety the structure of this upper floor, that he could hear the breathing, as they, no doubt, could hear his.

A minute, and the person passed down-stairs.

At the same moment the 'Flyer' sat up with a quick movement, and from his coat pocket took something which he tied over his feet. Then he stepped to the window and crouching hidden, looked down. Long watching in the dark had made sight easier, and so he saw clearly enough the figure of a young man step from the door and turn toward the stable.

That is to say, he deemed the man young from the lightness of his build and his manner of moving.

A faint sound came from the shed that served as a stable, and a small horse was led out. The man mounted and rode away, at first walking his beast gently on the grass at the side of the road.

The 'Flyer' crossed his room in a step, was out of the door and down-stairs in a very few more. He moved like a cat—as silent of foot from the pads on his boots. The door was latched, but of course unlocked: it presented no difficulty; a moment after he was in the stable. There he treated his horse's feet in much the same fashion he had his own, putting them into thick leather cases that left no print and made no sound. Then, mounting, he cantered off on the track of the other—to the eastward along the road to Chewton Glen.

When he came to the head of the glen he dismounted and tied his horse up securely among the

---

> ***The girl looked at (the "Flyer") sideways through her thick black lashes and proceeded to set the food on the table.***

The Key People in A New Forest Smuggling Run

(Landing, hiding and distributing an illicit cargo was a highly organized venture with lines of authority as carefully drawn as in a military operation. E. Russell Oakley in *The Smugglers of Christchurch* (Hutchinson, 1944) gives a brief account of the roles played by the principal characters in the smuggling drama.)

It is quite a mistake to imagine the smugglers were a band of individuals apart from the rest of the community, or a distinct tribe such as gipsies. The sea-going smugglers were generally in ordinary occupations, as fishermen, oyster dredgers, or working small cargo boats. The land smugglers were farm hands, tradesmen, workers in various trades, and smuggling for them was largely a spare-time occupation. But whether a large or small band, their methods and procedure were much the same.

The procedure and individuals concerned, were briefly as follows:

The Venturer

First there was an invisible man, the Venturer. He provided the capital for the business, and, like many financiers to-day, was in the background. His qualification was solely the ability to put up a sum of money in gold coin, with no security except the word of the captain of the smugglers' crew. It is obvious that he must have been a wealthy man, so it may be that he was known to his neighbours as an ordinary law-abiding citizen, such as a rich tradesman, or perhaps squire of the village.

Ship's Captain

Secondly, there was the captain of a well-equipped fast-moving boat. Often as in the case of old Gulliver of Poole, he was also owner, and therefore in a dual capacity of responsibility for the risk. The first step in negotiations was an agreement between the Venturer and the Captain, that in consideration of the Venturer handing to the Captain a bag of gold (guineas or, later, sovereigns) amounting to £300, £400, or £500, according to the cargo intended to be run, the Captain would agree to purchase the commodity in France or the Channel Islands, bring the same to some place on the mainland, run it ashore, and eventually dispose of it. He would then collect the proceeds, and when all was settled hand back to the Venturer the money loaned, plus an agreed share of the profits. In the event of disaster the Venturer lost the whole of his advance, but the next time could come in on the same terms.

Lest it be thought that such an arrangement weighed against the invisible man, it must be remembered that the actual net profit on contraband successfully run was enormous. If one of three runs was successful it was known they were all right even with the loss of the other cargo and perhaps confiscation of boats and gear in the two unlucky cases. Therefore the Venturer was on a pretty good thing, particularly if the Captain were owner as well.

The Landing Team

Thirdly there were the 'Lander' and his men. The Lander was responsible for the whole of the cargo immediately it was put ashore. His men were selected for strength, activity and secrecy. Many were, for instance, carpenters, bricklayers, woodmen, gamekeepers, or farm workers. Their pay was usually ten shillings a night. Think of the glorious opportunity for spare-time employment at this rate of pay when the agricultural labourer's wages were seven shillings and sixpence to ten shillings a week.

The Lander was responsible not

Mischief at the "Cat and Fiddle"…

Continued from previous page
trees. He followed the sheep track to the broken ground above the shore and there looked out upon the water.

The sea was quiet; yet there was about it the sense of sullen waiting that comes before turmoil. A fresh west wind blew landwards, carrying rain in the face of the watcher.

Close in shore lay anchored a fine smack. Her foresails down, the peak of the mainsail swinging. A boat lay alongside, and even as the man took in the situation, it left the side of the anchored vessel and was rowed ashore. A dozen men were busy, some in the boat, some on the beach, transferring small kegs from the one to the other, and piling the kegs into a light cart. Sitting on his horse overlooking the business was the young man from the inn. The eyes of the highwayman dwelt upon him.

When the work was near complete the 'Flyer' returned to his horse silent as he came, and was back at the 'Cat and Fiddle' with a speed which proved he'd earned the name he went by. Instead of returning to his room he rode into the wood at the back of the house and there tied up the horse again; then he came as close to the stable as he could with safety, and there waited in the shelter of it, and in view of a large heap of broken flint stones for road mending that lay piled at the side of the road to the eastward of the inn.

He had not long to wait.

Presently came a small party of men; with them a light cart, and one man on horseback.

They drew up by the pile of flint stones. Presently the kegs were laid on the ground in careful order, rising higher in the centre to the number of at least fifty. When all were safely set the flint stones were shovelled over the heap till all was covered in and every keg hidden.

The work being completed in the cleverest fashion possible, the men engaged returned the way they came, taking the cart with them.

The Chewton Bunny Route into the Forest

CHEWTON BUNNY—THE PERFECT PLACE FOR LANDING
This old print shows Chewton Bunny in its original wooded state, a condition which provided smugglers with perfect cover right into the depths of the New Forest.

(A remarkable journal was kept by one Abram Pike, an officer of the Customs and Excise based at Christchurch. In it he listed every inspection trip he made, the distance involved, and what transpired. For the years 1803 and 1804 his journal is intact; the record for other years has not been found. Pike's diary shows that Chewton Bunny, the outlet for Chewton Glen, was a favourite landing place for illicit cargoes. The glen ran right into the New Forest itself, making concealment easier than by some other routes. The excerpts below regarding Chewton Bunny and Hangersley, and the manner in which the smugglers operated, are taken from E. Russell Oakley's little volume, *The Smugglers of Christchurch*, and are reproduced here with the permission of the publishers, Century Hutchinson.)

Chewton Bunny

Chewton Bunny is a narrow, deep ravine, down which for centuries has gurgled a forest stream making for the outlet to the sea in the centre of Christchurch Bay. The Bunny extends well into the New Forest, and was much used by smugglers who wished to avoid town and village when making a run for the benefit of their many good customers at Burley and further north.

The landing on the beach here was perilous, and could never be undertaken at night except by those intimately acquainted with the coast owing to an extensive area of quicksands formed at the mouth of the glen by the fresh water meeting tidal water. It was a nature-made death trap for the unwary, and is now, as many fatalities there in recent years have been reported.

For this reason, and its desolate land approaches, Chewton Bunny proved an excellent Smugglers Way in the direction of Burley, where it is recorded in the Old

The Key People

Continued from previous page
only for moving the cargo from the shore or beach, but for arranging for temporary hiding places until it was marketed, arranging for horses and farm wagons, for signals and signallers and watchers for roads. He alone knew what the final destination for the cargo would be if all arrangements went according to plan.

Very often, if it were known beforehand what the contraband would be, whether brandy, tobacco or tea, the whole was sold at agreed prices to various purchasers for C.O.D. There were, of course, a few others connected with the smugglers, not paid helpers, but sympathizers anxious, perhaps, to do their one good deed, and delighting in the adventure and sport of the undertaking,

and there was also one other invisible man. Remember these were the days when few could read or write—and the smugglers were no exception.

As the success of all smuggling operations depended upon those who could neither read, nor write, it was obvious someone possessing these accomplishments must also be included, and so there was a 'quill driver' or 'writer man.' To-day he would be termed a secretary. The smugglers therefore made terms with a man who had these necessary qualifications. He was usually a clerk in a wine-merchant's employ, perhaps a bank clerk, brewer's clerk, vestry clerk or bookseller. The high acme of efficiency was once achieved by enlisting the services of a Town Clerk in one town on the south coast. The 'writer man' had no responsibility except to keep the

Chewton Bunny Route. . .

Hangersley

Continued from previous page

Journal so many cargoes of contraband disappeared. The occupiers of an old cottage near the Forest end of the glen assisted the smugglers by receiving parcels of silks and laces. On one occasion Riding Officers of Excise arrived here a few hours after it was known a consignment had been delivered, and although they made a careful search of the premises nothing was found as the four women there, in the interval, had undressed and swathed each other's bodies with lengths of silk and lace and had then re-covered themselves with the usual capacious gown and crinoline of those

days which were of a size capable of concealing much or little. The crinoline has gone with the red flannel petticoat. Both were useful and much appreciated.

The track from the head of the glen was almost direct to Burley and here on a hill not far from Picket Post, and visible for miles around, an old lady stood for many hours wearing a bright scarlet cloak to warn the villagers of the coming of Excise men if they were likely to approach. The result was often as stated in the Old Journal: 'Searched several suspected places, no success.' The name of this loyal helper was a delightful one: 'Lovey Warne.'

Here at an old thatched cottage near Merryweather Farm, at a time when the cottage was empty, birds made holes in the thatched roof, and in doing so disclosed under the eaves a number of letters addressed to various persons in the district. These on examination were found to be communications relating to consignments of smuggled goods in transit from the coast. No doubt the papers had been put there as a simple but safe hiding place when evidence was being searched for by Excise men working in this village. The discovery is interesting as showing the long distance from the coast contraband was then moved.

The Key People in A Smuggling Venture. . .

accounts for and on behalf of the smugglers.

Hide-and-Seek

Smuggling was a gigantic game of hide-and-seek through the country-side. The hiders were the smugglers, assisted by almost the entire resident population. The seekers were a handful of Riding

Continued from previous page

Officers of Excise with a few assistants in each district, and in and near the large ports, the establishments of collectors of Customs and Excise as at Portsmouth, Southampton, Plymouth, Poole, and so on.

It is apparent that the odds were in favour of the smugglers, yet from official records the pluck,

pertinacity and resource of the Preventive men under most difficult circumstances was such that they must be admired. It is marvellous that the Government of the day could have found such fine fellows for very poorly paid duties, under legislation which was thoroughly detested by all classes.

CHEWTON GLEN, HOTEL WITH DOUBLE CLAIM TO HISTORY
The route used by smugglers from Chewton Bunny to the New Forest passed within yards of the present hotel, rated as one of the country's finest. The original building was the home of the Marryat family. Frederick Marryat (author *Children of the New Forest*), commanded the *Rosario* during 1821–22 to prevent smuggling in the Channel. As late as 1852 the house was occupied by a Marryat (George).

AT a MEETING of the MAGISTRATES, acting in and for the Eaſt Part of the *New Foreſt* Diviſion, in the County of *South-ampton*, and alſo the MAYOR, CORPORATION, and principal Inhabitants of the Borough and Town of *Lymington*, and the Neighbourhood, aſſembled at the *ANGEL INN*, in Lymington aforeſaid, the 28th of October, 1795, for the purpoſe of taking into Conſideration the Practice of the BUTCHERS in ſelling out their Meat, and the Cauſe of the preſent high Price thereof.

PRESENT:

THOMAS ROBBINS, Eſq. in the Chair.

Sir JOHN D'OYLY, Bart.	J. H. WOLCOTT, Eſq.	Rev. Mr. LANCASTER
Sir HARRY NEALE, Bart.	ROBERT ALLEN, Eſq.	Mr. BRIDGER
JOHN WALTER, Eſq.	JAMES ALLEN, Eſq.	Mr. JAMES M'ILWAIN
PHILIP BROMFIELD, Eſq.	Mrs. MANN, by T. ROBBINS.	Mr. JAMES M'ILWAIN, Jun.
PERCIVAL LEWIS, Eſq.	THOMAS MAITLAND, Eſq.	Mr. GEORGE M'ILWAIN
WILLIAM ROOKE, Eſq.	CHARLES DODD, Eſq.	Mr. JOHN MITCHELL
CHARLES BOWLES, Eſq.	CHARLES BLOIS, Eſq.	Mr. ROBERT RICE
THOMAS BECKLEY, Eſq.	WILLIAM ROBBINS, Eſq.	Mr. JOHN NEWELL
THOS. BECKLEY, Jun. Eſq.	I. P. I. ROCHFORT, Eſq.	Mr. THOMAS COLBORNE
JAMES SAMBER, Eſq.	Rev. Mr. DIXON	Mr. JOSEPH COLBORNE
WILLIAM ROBERTS, Eſq.	Mr. RICHMAN	Mr. THOMAS SHEPPARD
WILLIAM TRATTLE, Eſq.	Mr. St. BARBE	Mr. JAMES BAUGHAN.

IT WAS RESOLVED UNANIMOUSLY,

I. That the Butchers of this Town demand a higher Price than thoſe of Ringwood, Chriſtchurch, Poole, or any of the Neighbouring Towns; and that the manner of obliging their Cuſtomers to take a conſiderable Quantity of what is called *Rough Meat*, to be weighed in with the *Prime*, is peculiar only to the Butchers of Lymington.

RESOLVED,

II. That every Perſon at this Meeting is determined not to deal with any Butcher who ſhall inſiſt on ſuch practices; — and in order to put a ſtop to all unfair Combinations, it was reſolved, that every due Encouragement be given to all Butchers round the Neighbourhood, who may be willing to attend this Market; and who will give the Poor an opportunity of being ſupplied with the Ordinary Pieces, which cannot be the caſe with the Butchers of Lymington, whilſt they continue to inſiſt on weighing in Rough Meat, at the ſame Price with the Prime.—And although many who buy the Prime Meat, are deſirous of taking a moderate quantity of inferior, yet they do not conſider themſelves as unreaſonable in being left to a choice, to take either of Prime or Rough Meat, as may ſuit the Purchaſer, when they are willing to pay a full and reaſonable Price for what is Prime. But ſuch has been the uniform arbitrary practice with the Lymington Butchers, that when any of their Cuſtomers have deſired to have Twenty pounds of Roaſting Beef, they have inſiſted on weighing in with it Two-thirds of Rough Meat; by which conduct it is fair to ſay, that Roaſting Beef at Lymington is more than Eight-pence per pound. This cuſtom, which gave riſe to this very neceſſary and proper Meeting, is found to obtain no where, but with the Lymington Butchers.

RESOLVED,

III. That temporary Stalls be erected every Saturday in the Town, for the accommodation of all Butchers, not reſident therein, who may be deſirous of attending the above Market.

RESOLVED,

IV. That One Hundred of the foregoing Reſolutions be immediately printed; and that it be alſo inſerted once in each of the following County Papers, viz. *The Saliſbury and Wincheſter Journal*, and *Portſmouth Gazette*; and that the Expence attending the ſame be paid by Mr. F. G. BRIDGER, Clerk to the Magiſtrates, acting in and for the Diviſion, Borough, and Town aforeſaid, out of the Subſcriptions, received from the Gentlemen preſent.

The Reſolutions being ſubſcribed to by all preſent, the Butchers of Lymington were deſired to attend—and on being aſked what Prices they were willing to ſell the different claſſes of Meat at, ſeparate, they all agreed not to ſell any of the Prime Meat ſeparate: the Meeting therefore was prevented from coming to any Terms with them. It was then determined to carry the foregoing Reſolutions into effect.

BUTCHERS BEWARE!

Consumer action is often regarded as a 20th century achievement, but the 1795 handbill shown here reveals how the inhabitants of Lymington, in concert with local magistrates and officials of the town, successfully brought about a change in pricing meat by Lymington butchers. The dramatic public meeting was held in the Angel Inn.

The Southampton and Dorchester Railway was the first line to operate through the New Forest. It was the brain-child of a Wimborne solicitor, Charles Castleman who, with his brother Edward, had law offices in Wimborne and Ringwood.

A meeting held at Southampton on 9 May 1844 showed great public enthusiasm for the proposed line. Castleman would have put the railway across the heart of the Forest, passing south of Ringwood, but Captain William Scarth Moorsom proposed a winding route through Brockenhurst, Ringwood, Wimborne, Poole and thence to Dorchester. Although the line became known as "Castleman's Corkscrew," the circuitous route was, in fact Moorsom's idea.

The story of the Southampton-Dorchester Railway is told in *Castleman's Corkscrew*, by J.G. Cox, published by the City (Record Office) of Southampton (1975). The extracts below give some idea of the problems encountered in getting the parliamentary bill approved, and later, in the construction. (The line was formally opened on Saturday, 29 May 1847).

11 Horses Lost in Building Railway Line across Forest

Bill Opposed

When the Southampton and Dorchester Bill reached the House of Commons the following April, the only opposition came from Mr. Compton, the member for South Hampshire, who had been on the provisional committee of the now defunct Salisbury and Dorsetshire company and, as a verderer, was against any railway which encroached upon the New Forest. He proposed that the Bill should be deferred for six months, in effect, thrown out for the current session. His move was strongly resisted by Mr. Mackinnon, the member for Lymington.

Compton found no support. Even George Bankes, a Dorset member who had supported the L & SWR proposals the previous year, refused to obstruct the passage of Southampton and Dorchester bill, saying that in his opinion an unsatisfactory line was better than no railway at all. After a few words of support for the project from Lord Palmerston—a Hampshire landowner as well as a distinguished politician—Compton withdrew his motion and the Bill received its second reading on 21st April 1845 without a division.

The route through the New Forest at last decided, an agreement was signed between the Commissioners and the company in July 1846. This provided for the payment of £12,000 by the company for the land they required, the money to be used for improvements such as drainage in the Forest as specified by the Act. For the contractor Peto the long delayed agreement meant that he could at last start work on this part of the railway. Further delay would have meant disbanding his labour force at a time when navvies were in short supply due to the large number of railway projects in progress throughout the country.

To encourage Peto now to complete the railway as quickly as possible, the company offered him a bonus of £5,000 if he could finish it by 1st May 1847. The challenge proved considerable. The ensuing winter brought severe frosts and heavy rains, which in turn held up the work. Between Brockenhurst and Ossemley Ford, Peto lost no less than eleven horses in a few weeks during the course of cutting through a treacherous layer of heavy clay. Nevertheless the Forest section was completed by the appointed day and Peto qualified for his bonus.

Deer Protection

A problem peculiar to the New Forest section of the line was the type of fencing to be used to prevent animals from straying on to the railway. (The engineer), concerned for the deer and fawns, proposed an elaborate barrier, consisting of a screen of bushes, a ditch and bank and a continuous line of wood palings beside the track. Moorsom said this was unnecessary and that the bushes would not grow on the sandy soils

TRAIN ON "CASTLEMAN'S CORKSCREW"
A south-bound train sweeps past the Ashurst camp-site, following the "corkscrew" route devised by Captain Moorsom, but named after Charles Castleman, principal promoter of the line.

Situated adjacent to the English Channel, the New Forest receives more than its due share of violent weather.

Sometimes this "share" is so great as to merit mention in historical works, leading publications of the day, and even in fiction. A leading reference work, *Our Own Country*, tells of the devastation of an early 18th century storm:

"The terrible gale of November 1703, which wrought as much damage in England as a tropical hurricane, uprooted some 4,000 fine trees in the (New) Forest."

Richard Blackmore, in *Craddock Nowell*, gives a vivid description of the hurricane of 1859. The force of the gale in this storm was so great that a man was unable to stand and was obliged to crawl if he wished to get about. The storm of 16 October 1987 was undoubtedly the most devastating the New Forest has known from the standpoint of number of trees lost. Excerpts from *Craddock Nowell* and a Forestry Commission assessment give some idea of the havoc created by these last two gales.

Stormy Weather in the Forest

The 1859 Tornado

(In October, 1859, the New Forest was devastated by a tornado. William Beach's account of the storm appears in Sarah Robinson's autobiography, *My Book*.)

Old William Beach, telling me of that storm, said he was then a young married man at work in the Forest, and could only crawl home on hands and knees, lying flat at intervals; he saw more than one dead man, a haystack carried bodily up and torn to pieces in mid air, sheds crushed like eggshells, tops of great trees sliced off and carried right away. When he reached home, his wife was in the doorway with the "cheeld" in her arms; chimney fallen, cottage rocking; they could only crouch together in a ditch until the worst was over; when seven hundred of the largest old trees lay uprooted in the Forest, besides the damage done to numberless others.

11 Horses Lost Building Railway...

Continued from previous page

which covered most of the area. They eventually agreed on a post and wire fence, with a ditch on either side of the line to deter the animals. As this could not be completed by the time the railway was opened, Peto was compelled by the company to employ watchmen along the open portions to warn the train drivers if animals strayed on to the line.

The postponed dinner to celebrate the opening was held on 8th June 1847, at the Crown Inn, Ringwood, with John Mills in the chair. After pointing out that the occasion marked the termination of all their labours and praising Castleman, saying that without him the line would not have been carried or constructed, he defen-ded the railway from those critics who had already nicknamed it "The Corkscrew". He said that, had it been straight enough to have silenced their objections, it would have accommodated no person or place; though it would not have been so much like a corkscrew, had it not been for the demands of those who had driven them through the New Forest, first one way and then another.

The advertised passenger services between Southampton and Dorchester consisted of five trains in each direction on weekdays, four of which had London connections. The fastest down service left the L & SWR's London Station at Nine Elms at 12.30 p.m. reaching Dorchester at 5.45 p.m.

From *Craddock Nowell* (the 1859 Storm)

The first sough of the wind thrilled throughout the Forest—a prolonged deep-drawn, dry sob; a hollow and mysterious sound, that shivered through the shadowy leaves, and moaned among the tree-boles. Away went every beast and bird that knew the fearful signal; the deer lanced away to the holm-frith; the cattle in huffs came belloking to the lew of the boughy trees; the hogs ran together, and tossed their snouts, and skittered home from the ovest; the squirrel hied to his hollow dray, the weasel slunk to his tuffet lair, and every rabbit skipped home from grass. The crows and the magpies were all in a churm; the heavy-winged heron flapped off from the brook side, the jar-bird flicked out from the ivy drum, the yaffingale darted across the ride with his strange discordant laugh; even the creepers that ply the trees crept into lichened fastnesses, lay flat to the bark and listened.

First came fitful scuds of rain, 'flisky rain' they call it, loose out-riders of the storm, lashing the woodman's windows—then a short dark pause ensued, in which the sky swirled up with clouds, and the earth lay mute with terror; only now and then a murmur went along the uplands. Suddenly, ere a man might say '*Good God!*' or, '*Where are my children?*' every tree was taken aback, every peat-stack reeled and staggered; every cot was stripped of its thatch on the opposite side to that on which the blow was expected. The first squall of that great tempest broke from the dark south-east, it burst through the sleet and dashed it upwards like an army of archers shooting: ere a man could stay himself one way, it had caught him up from another—the leaves from the ground flew up again through the branches which had dropped them, and then a cloud of all manner of foliage, whirling, flustering, capering, flitting, soared high over the highest tree-tops, and drove through the sky like dead shooting-stars.

Stormy Weather in the New Forest...

Continued from previous page

Faster and faster flew the mad squalls after one another, screaming onward and bellowing back; dashing in and swooping out, lashing themselves and everything. Then there came a lull! so sudden that the silence was more stunning than the turmoil. A pause for sunset; that evening the sun-down gun from CALSHOT was heard over all the Forest.

Forest Commission Report (16 October 1987 Storm)

During the early hours of October 16 the wind from the south west increased rapidly to 45 mph in the wake of the storm centre, with gusts of twice that velocity. The gusting and turbulence of the air flow at ground level, funnelled by natural features, was responsible for most of the damage. Although this was widespread, the greatest effects were felt in a swathe which passed across Holmsley, Wilverley, Rhinefield, Pound Hill, Hurst Hill and Highland Water Inclosures. Even there, the effect was of a very heavy thinning; only relatively small areas were flattened but many single trees were lost, almost all by uprooting.

The fact that most of the oaks and beeches were in leaf added to their vulnerability to wind pressure, and the waterlogged soil was holding their roots less securely than usual. Beeches tended to blow over whilst oaks with their long tap roots were more likely to lose boughs, although many of course did fall.

Shallow rooting of conifers on poor soil was another significant factor. The root plates of the Douglas fir toppled at Bolderwood are like a thin crust torn off pure gravel. At least 15,000 trees, and possibly as many as 20,000 were blown down in the Forest.

Forestry Commission

A BOLDERWOOD SCENE AFTER THE 1987 STORM
Some parts of the New Forest suffered severely from the October 1987 storm. A particularly wide swath swept through Bolderwood, felling dozens of ancient trees.

An Epoch-Making Natural History Event

Creating An Artificial Badger Sett

Filming history was made in the summer of 1975 when badgers first occupied an artificial sett. Constructed by the New Forest wildlife photographer, Eric Ashby, the sett has been more or less continuously occupied since that time.

When badgers were filmed in the sett and shown to millions by the BBC, public response was overwhelming. In the account that follows Eric Ashby tells how he first became interested in wildlife photography and how he tackled the "impossible" challenge of erecting an artificial sett that would serve as home for badgers.

(In June, 1987, Eric Ashby was granted an injunction against the intrusion of New Forest Foxhounds on his land—a 2.5 acre wildlife sanctuary at Linwood, on the grounds that trespasses there had disturbed wildlife and had been a constant worry to him on hunting days. During the case, heard at Winchester County Court, he related how badgers in the artificial sett had failed to produce cubs after two incursions by foxhounds.)

As far back as I can remember I have been keenly interested in wildlife and my sympathy was always for those animals that are persecuted. Probably this is the reason my favourite subject is the badger.

My keenness for wildlife led me to wish to record in some way the wonders of nature and so the next step in 1931 was to try my hand at photography. Then by dint of selling some of my photographs to various publications, by 1935 I bought my first 16 mm cine camera, even though a national newspaper paid as little a five shillings for the reproduction of one of my efforts.

By the Spring of 1938 I had taken my first still photograph of a badger in the New Forest but was later shocked to find the sett which is the badgers' home, dug by the foxhunt after a hunted fox had gone to ground. The resulting devastation made me furious and was the cause of my first letter of complaint to the Forestry Commission, followed by many others when setts are attacked, to the present day. The most interesting and harmless of mammals is regretfully still persecuted in the new Forest.

Overwhelming Response

In 1938 a friend mentioned to the Natural History Unit of the BBC about my amateur badger filming and as these animals had not been filmed before in daylight, the Producer, Christopher Parsons, suggested making a programme about Forest Wildlife featuring badgers in particular. After over two years hard work this was duly transmitted in 1960 entitled "The Unknown Forest." The response from the public was so overwhelming that I was asked for more material which was made into one of Sir Peter Scott's "Look" programmes entitled "The Silent Watcher"—transmitted under a year later. At that time Chris went around gift shops but nowhere could he find anything depicting badgers. Nowadays shops have plenty to offer.

During the years that followed many of the programmes I filmed for the BBC included some badger material. The type of films I was making took so much time that I had to consider it a hobby—one could not live on the payments. I felt I had to carry on for the sake of wildlife, particularly in the New Forest.

Then one year, in 1974, I had been up to Bristol to help with the editing of "The Private Life of the Fox", when I was told that the BBC could not consider any more badger material unless I could go underground to film their private lives. I explained that that would be impossible.

I knew that any interference with their underground home would cause them to desert. I am one of the very few wildlife filmmakers who would not consider

ERIC HAS A 500-MM LENS ON HIS CAMERA

Artificial Badger Sett...

Continued from previous page

using tame or confined animals and pass them off as wild.

The Badger: A Shy Animal

Even walking over a badger sett will cause the occupants to emerge late that evening and to act unusually shy. And so I had a problem. But most wildlife filming creates problems. I knew that badgers are not so shy away from their home, in fact if they are eating one's strawberries for example, it is very difficult to deter them. Also badgers have been known to have setts under houses, in sheds, even in heaps of hay in thick hedges. Another point was that the local badgers came to eat my poultry food leavings.

I came to the conclusion therefore that if I made an artificial sett in a shed, with a copy of a typical badger sleeping chamber for filming and another compartment where they would feed, it might be possible to film truly wild badgers at their natural underground activity. In the wild, badgers have outlying setts away from the breeding sett near their feeding grounds where they might take short naps or even stay for a few days. This was what I hoped to create—an outlying sett next to a never failing tree of plenty.

Concrete Pipes Arrive

The BBC agreed to give it a try, then a contract after I had shot my first successful roll of film. And so it was in January, 1975, that a load of concrete pipes arrived, kindly donated by an interested director of a well known company. These pipes varied from ten inch to twelve-inch internal diameter, in fact nine-inch is large enough for the biggest boar badger to pass through.

The sett was built when our heavy soil was wet and sticky making the work slow and hard. I made two entrances into a bank from the orchard, joining a curving pipeline into one sleeping chamber under a holly bush and the other end into the shed leading into the filming sleeping chamber which I called the "film sett" adjacent to the feeding room. I intended leaving the concrete chamber under the holly bush completely private and untouched for the badgers to retire to which I called the "private sett", hoping that perhaps cubs may one day be born there. In the twelve years since then I have only opened it up three times.

By March 8th trenches had been dug and pipes were in place and the two sleeping chambers completed. On the 14th all the outside pipes were covered with soil and the bank turfed over around the entrances, making the site neat and tidy.

The First Badger Enters

Although the arrangements inside were very far from complete I threw some food up the entrances on 22nd March and this was taken two nights later. A few days later the feeding room was opened for the badgers to enter and one was disturbed feeding at 7.40 p.m. on the 9th of April.

There was still a lot to be done and it wasn't until the 29th of April that electricity was laid on from the cottage to the shed. Meanwhile on the 16th I was excited to find oak leaves and grass had been dragged into the "film sett" by the badgers for their bedding which proved the animals felt quite at home in the structure even though I was working outside during the day and they did not object to my scent on everything I handled. Things were working out even better than I had expected.

At long last on 7th May a 15 watt lamp was switched on in the feeding room while a badger was feeding, it took no notice and so the next night a 60-watt lamp was used but the light disturbed the animal and I went back to the 15-watt. It was obvious that I had to slowly increase the light over a long period.

Crowded Feeding Chamber

Wonderful news on 14th May! Two adults arrived and fed at 8.15 p.m. Going out to look at 10.45 there were four adults accompanied by three cubs! There was still only a 15-watt lamp in the feeding room but still none in the film sett. Later cubs could be heard playing there. On May 31st the lighting arrangements were complete and a 15-watt bulb was placed in the film sett. This was found to be too bright in the confined space, the badgers peeping in and retreating, so I fitted a 5-watt lamp but after a few days this was increased to 15-watt. The light in the feeding room had meanwhile been increased to 180-watt.

Soon it was getting near to the time I could try the flood lights in the sleeping chamber. Here the lamp had been increased to 40-watt and on June 19th I had tried a 500-watt flood light at half power but the badger only peeped in. However on the 28th one adult and three cubs were asleep and I took an experimental shot on 16 mm colour film, the badgers not noticing the increased power.

A serious fault was found in the resulting print which was found to be slightly out of focus. This was believed to be caused by the quarter-inch plate glass which covered the chamber through which the camera lens viewed the action at an angle. The chamber therefore had to be redesigned, removing the plate glass and fitting a double paned window through which the camera viewed the scene fairly squarely. The camera test then was found to be perfect, and the BBC in their careful way sent me the first part of a three part contract to guard against any failure.

A Filming "First"

Never before, so I was told, had any truly wild animal been filmed underground in their homes, all previous filming having been carried out with tame subjects or those completely under control. I was making no attempt to tame these badgers and they could come and go just as they wished and my plan was to record behaviour just as it occurred in their own natural setts, never before seen by man.

At about this time a ginger tom

> *"Almost immediately a badger entered to feed; therefore, badger and cat must have passed each other in a lay-by underground."*

Artificial Badger Sett...

Continued from previous page

cat was seen in the feeding room eating the food. This was very interesting and I wondered what would happen if a badger appeared. Then one evening as I was watching Ginger feeding he suddenly turned around and went through the pipe. Almost immediately a badger entered to feed, therefore badger and cat must have passed each other in a lay-by underground.

For some time I had noticed many cat footprints on the sandy mounds at the natural sett two hundred yards away and seen the cat several times on the sett when it would dive down the nearest hole. One day when this happened I waited for five minutes and Ginger emerged from a far hole. Evidently he lived in the sett and knew the underground workings and the occupants. Later I saw him on the bank above the home-made sett entrances watching the badgers a few feet away. In due course I was able to tame this lost pussy and he became an affectionate pet still interested in watching badgers, foxes and deer.

Constant Activity

The behaviour of the badgers was becoming more interesting as they became more at home. If I put dry Molinia grass outside the pipes on the field the badgers would bring it into the film sett or private sett. During the night the bedding would disappear from the film sett only to be brought back again later. This constant movement would keep it in good dry condition. I am quite sure that this activity is carried on day and night in natural setts. It is surprising the amount of air movement through the tunnels. No wonder the animals don't emerge when watchers foolishly place themselves where any slight breeze is blowing

human scent towards any one hole of a sett.

Most of the badgers visiting the artificial sett were coming from a natural sett situated in New Forest woodland almost against the

SOW BADGER SUCKLING HER CUBS UNDERGROUND

boundary of our field about two hundred yards away from the shed. Being on public land anyone could visit the natural sett and during the summer visitors would disturb the animals; one persistant photographer was even found sitting in the middle of the group of holes with a camera fitted with flash. This continual disturbance made the animals wary during the summer, coming to a climax in the Autumn when the foxhunt blocked the holes on frequent occasions.

The Blockage Problem

I therefore dug a pit on my side of the fence and spaded the start of a

hole facing away from the Forest. A few days later badgers were enlarging the hole and within a few weeks several holes were on our side of the boundary. I planted brambles to provide cover and fenced the section off. A letter to the Forestry Commission pointed out the absurdity of the Hunt blocking the Forest side of the sett when holes were open on my side resulted in an agreement not to block. The outcome was that the badgers could be more prosperous not having to put up with eight months of earth stopping and in

the summer the animals could find refuge from visitors amongst the thick brambles and holes in our sanctuary.

Not much filming was done this first year. The badgers were getting fat in preparation for winter. During December and January badgers tend to live off their fat and eat very little. Visits to our sett became unpredictable. Territorial fights occurred now and again, but the smaller quantity of food placed in the feeding room was partly or mostly consumed by morning, the full grown cubs being the hungry ones.

As is usual, the badgers became more wary during the winter and spring, up to the time the cubs are

Artificial Badger Sett...

Continued from previous page

weaned. One had to be extremely quiet entering the shed.

The Cubs Arrive

Adult badgers were arriving regularly during the first months of 1976 and we were keenly waiting for the first sight of cubs. On the first day of June we had our suspicions that "someone" was in the private sett because our dog Suzie was very interested. At 4.10 p.m. in the afternoon of the 5th of June an adult was feeding and we were delighted to see two cubs with two adults at 11.45 p.m.

At 4.05 p.m. the next day some food had already been taken and we were getting confident that badgers were staying in the private sett a few feet down the pipes. At 10.10 p.m. two cubs and two adults were feeding and at 10.40 p.m. three cubs with a different adult.

In the afternoon of the 7th of June I looked in at 2.55 p.m. and found an adult and one cub with a third of the food eaten and at 3.45 there were three cubs and most of the food gone. But the greatest surprise came the next morning at 8.30 a.m. when I found six adults sleeping in the film sett but they were unfortunately disturbed later at 10.35 a.m. when the coal lorry came just when we were preparing to go to London. Such is life.

We were now quite certain the badgers had temporarily taken up residence in my home-made "outlying" sett near to their feeding grounds as is their nature, even though the feeding grounds were not natural. This was fine, but I knew I had to be very careful not to disturb them by starting filming too soon and so spoil the wonderful good luck.

I had to make quite sure that the sound of the cine camera and the bright lights for colour filming would not unduly disturb the animals. The first really long length shot came at 2.30 p.m. on the 18th of June when I was able to take a three minute film of two cubs playing in the film sett without any sign that the cubs were in the least worried. It was clear the best way was to turn up the lights and start the cameras during action.

When the bedding in the film sett was getting low through wear and tear or dragged away down the pipes out of sight, all I had to do was to place some Molinia grass near the entrance outside and the badgers would bring it in later and this I filmed, also the bundle dragged away again later! Sometimes a badger would go to sleep on the bundle of bedding outside before being brought in later by another animal.

Upside Down Posture

During the hot summer evenings one of the occupants would sometimes be seen upside down in the pipe enjoying the cool air coming in from the field. Outside I had placed a drinking trough and one clever cub had the bright idea on several warm nights of sitting in the cool water, leaning back and with his front paws splashing water up his front.

Sometimes a fox looked into the film sett, listened to the badgers feeding in the next compartment and then withdrew. I managed to film this, notwithstanding the bright light must have been quite painful to the poor fox's eyes. I also took some still photographs, one a big close up which brought forth the remark from a friend,

"Hasn't he got kind eyes; you wouldn't think he would take poultry" to which I rejoined, "You have kind eyes and yet you also eat poultry." Which I think sums up the many quite unfair misunderstandings made about our predators.

The year sped on, with the film camera set up and long waits or continual look-ins to see if anything interesting could be filmed. Gradually the film footage increased. One has to shoot about ten times as much film as is likely to be used in a television programe to provide plenty of material so that the edited programme runs smoothly.

The Badger's Diet

The badgers staple food in the wild is worms plus almost anything animal, vegetable or fruit in season. I am often asked what food do I give them. I try not to provide too much unbalanced material such as bread but include pies, sausages, meat and other left-overs which can be obtained free or practically so, to which can be added balanced poultry laying pellets or one of the all-in-one dry dog foods. Water of course must be supplied. The badgers take a little time to get used to any strange food that might be offered.

In due course the programme "At Home with Badgers" was completed and the BBC contracts department in London offered me the normal rate for a project. I thought all the extra work and costs involved and the risk of failure ought to mean a better offer. The reply came back that considering the risk the BBC had taken the offer was quite fair!

It is now 13 years since I built the artificial sett and badgers are still using it. Though it is unlikely that any of the first visitors are still alive the present ones are several generations younger. The natural sett across the field has grown year by year. Sow badgers produce one, two or three cubs a year, often only every other year in the poor feeding conditions in remote parts of the Forest. Wild animals control their numbers according to food supply.

> *"During the hot summer evenings one of the occupants would sometimes be seen upside down in the pipe enjoying the cool air."*

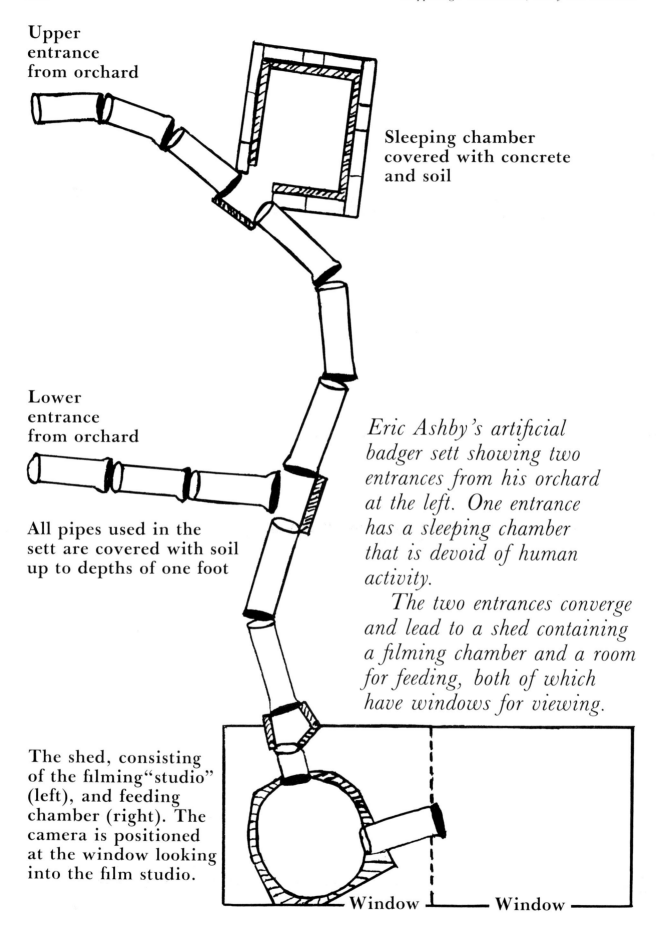

Upper entrance from orchard

Sleeping chamber covered with concrete and soil

Lower entrance from orchard

Eric Ashby's artificial badger sett showing two entrances from his orchard at the left. One entrance has a sleeping chamber that is devoid of human activity.

The two entrances converge and lead to a shed containing a filming chamber and a room for feeding, both of which have windows for viewing.

All pipes used in the sett are covered with soil up to depths of one foot

The shed, consisting of the filming "studio" (left), and feeding chamber (right). The camera is positioned at the window looking into the film studio.

Window   **Window**

11
Some Who Came and Went

Fanny Burney, George III's "Court Reporter"

(British and European royalty, as well as other leading figures from many lands, have visited the New Forest. Few of them boasted a chronicler so gifted as Fanny Burney. She was attached to George III's household and from this vantage point was able to report both the monarch's, and her own impression of the New Forest and the reception accorded the royal visitors by the local population. The account of the progress is taken from the *Diary and Letters of Madame D'Arblay*; the period covered is 25–30 June, 1789.)

FANNY BURNEY
A lively description of George III's visit to the New Forest,

Thursday, June 25—This morning I was called before five o'clock, though various packages and business had kept me up till near three.

The day was rainy, but the road was beautiful; Windsor great park, in particular, is charming. The crowds increased as we advanced, and at Winchester the town was one head. I saw Dr. Warton, but could not stop the carriage. The king was everywhere received with acclamation. His popularity is greater than ever. Compassion for his late sufferings seems to have endeared him now to all conditions of men.

At Romsey, on the steps of the town-hall, an orchestra was formed, and a band of musicians, in common brown coarse cloth and red neckcloths, and even in carters' loose gowns, made a chorus of "God save the king," in which the countless multitude joined, in such loud acclamation, that their loyalty and heartiness, and natural joy, almost surprised me into a sob before I knew myself at all affected by them.

The New Forest is all beauty, and when we approached Lyndhurst the crowds wore as picturesque an appearance as the landscapes; they were all in decent attire, and, the great space giving them full room, the cool beauty of the verdure between the groups took away all idea of inconvenience, and made their live gaiety a scene to joy beholders.

Carriages of all sorts line the road-side:—chariots, chaises, landaus, carts, waggons, whiskies, gigs, phaëtons—mixed and intermixed, filled• within and surrounded without by faces all glee and delight.

Such was the scenery for miles before we reached Lyndhurst. The old law of the forest, that his majesty must be presented with two milk-white greyhounds, peculiarly decorated, upon his entrance into the New Forest, gathered together multitudes to see the show. A party, also, of foresters, habited in green, and each with a bugle-horn, met his majesty at the same time.

Arrived at Lyndhurst, we drove to the Duke of Gloucester's. The royal family were just before us, but the two colonels came and handed us through the crowd. The house, intended for a mere hunting-seat, was built by Charles II., and seems quite unimproved and unrepaired from its first foundation. It is the king's, but lent to the Duke of Gloucester. It is a straggling, inconvenient, old house, but delightfully situated, in a village,—looking, indeed, at present, like a populous town, from the amazing concourse of people that have crowded into it.

The bowmen and archers and bugle-horns are to attend the king while he stays here, in all his rides.

The Duke of Gloucester ·was ready to receive the royal family, who are all in the highest spirits and delight.

I have a small old bedchamber, but a large and commodious parlour, in which the gentlemen join Miss Planta and me to breakfast and to drink tea. They dine at the royal table. We are to remain here some days.

During the king's dinner, which was in a parlour looking into the garden, he permitted the people to come to the window; and their delight and rapture in seeing their monarch at table, with the evident hungry feeling it occasioned, made a contrast of admiration and deprivation, truly comic. They crowded, however, so excessively, that this can be permitted them no more. They broke down all the paling, and much of the hedges, and some of the windows, and all by eagerness and multitude, for they were perfectly civil and well-behaved.

In the afternoon the royal party came into my parlour; and the moment the people saw the star, they set up such a shout as made a ring all around the village; for my parlour has the same view with the royal rooms into the garden, where this crowd was assembled,

Fanny Burney...

Continued from previous page
and the new rapture was simply at seeing the king in a new apartment!

They all walked out, about and around the village, in the evening, and the delighted mob accompanied them. The moment they stepped out of the house, the people, with one voice, struck up "God save the king!" I assure you I cried like a child twenty times in the day, at the honest and rapturous effusions of such artless and disinterested loyalty. The king's illness and recovery make me tender, as Count Manuccia said, upon every recollection.

These good villagers continued singing this loyal song during the whole walk, without any intermission, except to shout "huzza!" at the end of every stanza. They returned so hoarse, that I longed to give them all some lemonade. Probably they longed for something they would have called better! 'Twas well the king could walk no longer; I think, if he had, they would have died singing around him.

June 30—We continued at Lyndhurst five days: and the tranquility of the life, and the beauty of the country, would have made it very regaling to me indeed, but for the fatigue of having no maid, yet being always in readiness to play the part of an attendant myself.

I went twice to see the house of Sir Phillip Jennings Clerke, my old acquaintance at Streatham. I regretted he was no more; he would so much have prided and rejoiced in showing his place. His opposition principles would not have interfered with that private act of duty from a subject to a sovereign. How did I call to mind Mrs. Thrale, upon this spot! not that I had seen it with her, or ever before; but that its late owner was one of her sincerest admirers.

Miss Planta and myself drove also to Southampton, by the queen's direction. It is a pretty clean town, and the views from the Southampton water are highly picturesque: but all this I had seen so far to greater advantage, with Mr. and Mrs. and Miss Thrale. Ah, Mrs. Thrale!—In thinking her over, as I saw again the same spot, how much did I wish to see with it the same—once so dear—companion!

On the Sunday we all went to the parish church; and after the service, instead of a psalm, imagine our surprise to hear the

GEORGE III
His state dinner was rudely interrupted.

whole congregation join in "God save the king!" Misplaced as this was in a church, its intent was so kind, loyal, and affectionate, that I believe there was not a dry eye amongst either singers or hearers. The king's late dreadful illness has rendered this song quite melting to me.

This day we quitted Lyndhurst; not without regret, for so private is its situation, I could stroll about in its beautiful neighbourhood quite alone.

The Huntington Library

LYNDHURST CHURCH AT THE TIME OF THE KING'S VISIT
This sketch is from Thomas Rowlandson's "A Tour in A Post Chaise," probably made in 1784, five years before George III's visit described by Fanny Burney.

ROWLANDSON'S VISIT TO THE NEW FOREST

The autumn of 1784 is the time usually assigned by art historians to Thomas Rowlandson's post-chaise tour through the south of England.

His route took him to Southampton, thence to Lyndhurst and the New Forest, and on to Lymington (where he may have remained for as long as five nights), and to the Isle of Wight.

One sketch, the locale of which probably is the New Forest, is of a rustic barber shop; it may have been in the Brockenhurst area.

(In 1964 The Huntington Library, San Marino, California, published a 150-page book, *Rowlandson's Drawings for A Tour in A Post Chaise.*)

Royal Dislike of "Wild Beauties of Nature"

George Rose (1744–1818) was one of the most influential men ever to reside in the New Forest. Born of Scottish stock, he was educated at Westminster School, and after a short period with the navy in the West Indies, became a civil servant in the office of the Chancellor of the Exchequer. He proved an able administrator and rose rapidly in government service. He became secretary of the treasury where his financial ability and judgment were highly regarded.

In the 1780s he bought Cuffnells (sometimes spelled Cuffnalls) from the heirs of Sir Thomas Tancred and this was to be his principal residence for the rest of his life. In March, 1778 he was elected a verderer of the New Forest. In 1808 he was appointed Deputy Warden of the New Forest by the Duke of York. At one time or another he was a member of parliament for Launceston, Lymington, and Christchurch.

As George III's spells of illness became more and more frequent, he found some relief by quitting London and residing in Weymouth. On his trips to and from Weymouth he called on his friend, George Rose, at Cuffnells. The passage below from C. J. Phillips' *New Forest Handbook* (1876) describes some of the king's visits to Cuffnells.

Towards the close of the last century and the beginning of the present many distinguished men visited the place as guests of the Right Hon. George Rose, one of the most celebrated statesmen of that time, who lived at Cuffnalls, close to the village, and here twice or three times received George III, with the Queen and several of their children. At one of these visits Sir Charles Mills, the bow-bearer of the Forest, discharged an ancient tenure under which his family held Bury manor within its borders, by presenting to His Majesty two milk-white greyhounds; and it was on a similar occasion that the King, walking in the grounds then occupied by Lord Londesborough at Northerwood—a house bearing traces of Nash's handiwork—and viewing the prospect here presented, gave it the name of "Mount Royal," by which it is known among the older inhabitants to this day. In 1804 the Duke of Cumberland's regiment of Light Dragoons and Sir George's eldest son's regiment of South Hants Yeomanry Cavalry met His Majesty near Stoney Cross on his way from Weymouth, and in the park at Cuffnalls he was received by some eighteen hundred of the Volunteers of the neighbourhood. The Queen, the Princesses, and the Duke of Cambridge, with the ladies in waiting, accompanied His Majesty, who, we find, with

Mr. Rose, the following day, in a heavy rain, rode through the Forest to Cadland, a seat between Hythe and Fawley which previous to the Reformation belonged to Titchfield Abbey. Here they dined with Mr. Drummond, the king's banker:—

"The ground, continues the diary, after long and incessant rain for some days, was wet and spongy, which made the ride extremely uncomfortable to the King, who therefore chose to come the roadway back by Eling, though five or six miles further. The next day, after breakfast, we rode to Lymington, by the high road, on our way to Walhampton, to dine with Sir Harry Neale, and on our return in the evening the King began the conversation again about being the naked and dreary waste we rode over yesterday, abusing it as worse than any part of Bagshot Heath, and said on the whole he thought Windsor Forest incomparably a more

CUFFNELLS, WHICH GEORGE III VISITED SEVERAL TIMES

This beautiful home with its spacious grounds near Lyndhurst was occupied by George Rose for the last thirty years of his life. Here Rose entertained King George III on several occasions and many other great men of the day, including Prime Minister William Pitt. On one occasion nearly two thousand members of the South Hants Yeomanry assembled to see the king. Rose died here in 1818. Cuffnells has long since been demolished. The engraving is taken from Bayley's and Britton's *Beauties of England and Wales* (1803).

William Cobbett's Unhappy Forest Ride

William Cobbett (1762–1835), the noted critic, economist and reformer, visited the New Forest in 1826 during one of his famous expeditions on horseback.

He had little to say about the Forest, and was highly critical of its management. En route to Beaulieu he was diverted to the site of an ancient chapel and barn (a mile south of Buckler's Hard at the present-day St. Leonard's farm) which he said deserved the name of Beaulieu ("fine place") more than the abbey and village of that name.

Cobbett's *Rural Rides*, from which these extracts are taken, was first published in 1830 and has been reprinted many times. It is available today in J. M Dent's "Everyman's Library" series.

Having made all preparations for a day's ride, we set off, as our first point, for a station in the Forest called New Park, there to see something about *plantations* and other matters connected with the affairs of our prime cocks, the surveyors of woods and forests and crown lands and estates.

We had to go about three miles to New Park, which is a *farm* in the New Forest, and nearly in the centre of it. We got to this place about nine o'clock. There is a good and large mansion-house here, in which the "commissioners" of woods and forests reside when they come into the forest. There is a garden, a farm-yard, a farm, and a nursery. The place looks like a considerable gentleman's seat; the house stands in a sort of *park*, and you can see that a great deal of expense has been incurred in levelling the ground and making it pleasing to the eye of my lords "the commissioners."

My business here was to see whether anything had been done

Royal Dislike. . .

Continued from previous page
beautiful one than this. To which I replied, It was fortunate in this as well as other matters of taste, that all did not think alike—but His Majesty replied that he had no taste for what was called the fine *wild* beauties of nature; he did not like mountains and other romantic scenes of which he sometimes heard much."

towards the making of *locust plantations*. I went first to Lyndhurst to make inquiries; but I was there told that New Park was the place, and the only place, at which to get information on the subject; and I

WILLIAM COBBETT
(From an old engraving.)

was told, further, that the commissioners were now at New Park; that is to say those experienced tree-planters, Messrs. Arbuthnot, Dawkins, and Company. When I heard this, I was at breakfast, and of course dressed for the day. I could not, out of my extremely limited wardrobe, afford a clean shirt for the occasion; and so off we set, just as we were, hoping that their worships, the nation's tree-planters, would, if they met with us, excuse our dress, when they considered the nature of our circumstances. When we came to the house, we were stopped by a little fence and fastened gate. I got off

my horse, gave him to George to hold, went up to the door, and rang the bell.

Having told my business to a person, who appeared to be a foreman or bailiff, he, with great civility, took me into a nursery which is at the back of the house; and I soon drew from him the disappointing fact that my lords, the tree-planters, had departed the day before! I found, as to *locusts*, that a patch were sowed last spring, which I saw, which are from one foot to four feet high, and very fine and strong, and are, in number, about four feet apart each way. I found that last fall some few locusts had been put out into plantations of other trees already made; but that they had *not thriven*, and had been *barked* by the hares!

And what are the *hares* kept *for* here? *Who* eats them? What *right* have these commissioners to keep hares here to eat up the trees? Lord Folkstone killed his hares before he made his plantation of locusts; and why not kill the hares in the people's forest; for the *people's* it is, and that these commissioners ought always to remember. And then again, why this farm? What is it *for*?

Why, the pretence for it is this: that it is necessary to give the deer *hay*, in winter, because the lopping down of limbs of trees for them to *browse* (as used to be the practice) is injurious to the growth of timber. That will be a very good reason for having a *hay-farm* when my lords shall have proved two things; first, that hay, in quantity equal to what is raised here, could not be bought for a twentieth part of the money that this farm and all its trappings cost; and, second, that there ought to be any deer kept! What are these deer *for*? Who are to *eat* them? Are they for the royal family?

For what, and *for whom*, then, are deer kept in the New Forest; and why an expense of hay-farm, of sheds, of racks, of keepers; of lodges, and other things attending the deer and the game; an expense

> "... *any man may be transported if he go out by night to catch any part of this game!*"

Continued from previous page amounting to more money annually than would have given relief to all the starving manufacturers in the north!

This New Forest is a piece of property as much belonging *to the public* as the Custom House at London is. There is no man, however poor, who has not a right in it. Every man is owner of a part of the deer, the game, and of the money that goes to the keepers; and yet any man may be *transported* if he go out by night to catch any part of this game! We are compelled to pay keepers for preserving game to eat up the trees that we are compelled to pay people to plant!

From New Park, I was bound to Beaulieu Abbey, and I ought to have gone in a south-easterly direction, instead of going back to Lyndhurst, which lay in precisely the opposite direction. My guide through the plantations was not apprised of my intended route, and, therefore, did not instruct me. Just before we parted, he asked me *my name*: I thought it lucky that he had not asked it before! When we got nearly back to Lyndhurst, we found that we had come three miles out of our way; indeed, it made six miles further from Beaulieu Abbey than we were when we were at New Park. We wanted, very much, to go to the site of this ancient and famous abbey, of which the people of the New Forest seemed to know very little. They call the place *Bewley*, and even in the maps it is called *Bauley*.

We ... turned away from Lyndhurst, as soon as we got back to it, and went about six miles over a heath, as barren as it is possible for land to be. A little before we came to the village of Beaulieu (which, observe, the people call *Beuley*), we went through a wood, chiefly of beech, and that beech seemingly destined to grow food for pigs, of which we saw, during this day, many, many thousands. I should think that we saw at least a hundred hogs to one deer. I stopped, at one time, and counted the hogs and pigs just round about me, and they amounted to 140, all within 50 or 60 yards of my horse.

After a very pleasant ride on land without a stone in it, we came down to the Beaulieu river, the highest branch of which rises at the foot of a hill about a mile and a half to the north-east of Lyndhurst. For a great part of the way down to Beaulieu it is a very insignificant stream. At last, however, augmented by springs from the different sand-hills, it becomes a little river, and has, on the sides of it, lands which were, formerly, very beautiful meadows. When it comes to the village of Beaulieu, it forms a large pond of a great many acres; and on the east side of this pond is the spot where this famous abbey formerly stood, and where the external walls of which, or a large part of them, are now actually standing. We went down on the western side of the river. The abbey stood, and the ruins stand, on the eastern side.

Happening to meet a man before I got into the village I, pointing with my whip across towards the abbey, said to the man, "I suppose there is a bridge down here to get across to the abbey." "That's not the abbey, sir," says he: "the abbey is about four miles further on." I was astonished to hear this; but he was very positive; said that some people called it the abbey; but that the abbey was further on; and was at a farm occupied by farmer John Biel. Having chapter and verse for it, as the saying is, I believed the man; and pushed on towards farmer John Biel's, which I found, as he had told me, at the end of about four miles.

When I got there (not having, observe, gone over the water to ascertain that the other was the spot where the abbey stood), I really thought, at first, that this must have been the site of the Abbey of Beaulieu; because, the name meaning *fine place*, this was a thousand times finer place than that where the abbey, as I afterwards found, really stood. After looking about it for some time, I was satisfied that it had not been an abbey; but the place is one of the finest that ever was seen in this world. It stands at about half a mile's distance from the water's edge at high-water mark, and at about middle of the space along

Beaulieu River.

BEAULIEU RIVER, FROM SUMNER'S NEW FOREST GUIDE
Cobbett wrote: "After a very pleasant ride on land without a stone in it, we came down to the Beaulieu river."

William Cobbett and the Forest ...

Continued from previous page

the coast from Calshot Castle to Lymington haven.

It stands, of course, upon a rising ground; it has a gentle slope down to the water. To the right, you see Hurst Castle, and that narrow passage called the Needles, I believe; and, to the left you see Spithead, and all the ships that are sailing or lie anywhere opposite Portsmouth. The Isle of Wight is right before you, and you have in view, at one and the same time, the towns of Yarmouth, Newtown, Cowes, and Newport, with all the beautiful fields of the island, lying upon the side of a great bank before, and going up the ridge of hills in the middle of the island. Here are two little streams, nearly close to the ruin, which filled ponds for fresh-water fish; while there was the Beaulieu river at about half a mile or three quarters of a mile to the left, to bring up the salt-water fish.

The ruins consist of part of the walls of a building about 200 feet long and about 40 feet wide. It has been turned into a barn, in part, and the rest into cattle-sheds, cow-pens, and inclosures and walls to inclose a small yard. But there is another ruin which was a church or chapel, and which stands now very near to the farm-house of Mr. John Biel, who rents the farm of the Duchess of Buccleugh, who is now the owner of the abbey-lands and of the lands belonging to this place. The little church or chapel, of which I have just been speaking, appears to have been a very beautiful building.

A part only of its walls are standing; but you see, by what remains of the arches, that it was finished in a manner the most elegant and expensive of the day in which it was built. Part of the outside of the building is now surrounded by the farmer's garden; the interior is partly pig-stye and partly a goose-pen. Under that arch which had once seen so many rich men bow their heads, we entered into the goose-pen, which is by no means one of the *nicest* concerns in the world. Beyond the

goose-pen was the pig-stye, and in it a hog which, when fat, will weigh about 30 score, actually rubbing his shoulders against a little sort of column which had supported the font and its holy water. The farmer told us that there was a hole, which, indeed, we saw, going down into the wall, or rather into the column where the font had stood. And he told us that many attempts had been made to bring water to fill that hole, but that it never had been done.

Mr. Biel was very civil to us. As far as related to us, he performed the office of hospitality, which was the main business of those who formerly inhabited the spot. He asked us to dine with him, which we declined, for want of time; but being exceedingly hungry, we had some bread and cheese and some very good beer. The farmer told me that a great number of gentlemen had come there to look at that place; but that he never could find out what the place at Beuley had been. I told him that I would, when I got to London, give him an account of it; that I would write the account down, and send it down to him.

He seemed surprised that I should make such a promise, and expressed his wish not to give me so much trouble. I told him not to say a word about the matter, for that his bread and cheese and beer were so good that they deserved a full history to be written of the place where they had been eaten and drunk. "God bless me, sir, no, no!" I said I will, upon my soul, farmer. I now left him, very grateful on our part for his hospitable reception, and he, I dare say, hardly being able to believe his own ears at the generous promise that I had made him, which promise, however, I am now about to fulfil. I told the farmer a little, upon the spot, to begin with. I told him that the name was all wrong: that it was not *Beuley* but *Beaulieu*; and that Beaulieu meant *fine place*; and I proved this to him in this manner.

You know, said I, farmer, that when a girl has a sweetheart, people call him her *beau*? Yes, said he, so they do. Very well. You know also that we say, sometimes, you shall have this in *lieu* of that; and that when we say *lieu*, we mean in *place* of that. Now the *beau* means *fine*, as applied to the young man, and the *lieu* means *place*; and thus it is, that the name of this place is *Beaulieu*, as it is so fine as you see it is. He seemed to be wonderfully pleased with the discovery; and we parted, I believe with hearty good wishes on his part, and I am sure with very sincere thanks on my part.

As for the ruins on the farm of Mr. John Biel: they were the dwelling-place of Knights' Templars, or Knights of St. John of Jerusalem. The building they inhabited was called an hospital, and their business was to relieve travellers, strangers, and persons in distress; and, if called upon, to accompany the king in his his wars to uphold Christianity. Their estate was also confiscated by Henry VIII. It was worth at the time of being confiscated upwards of *two thousand pounds a year*, money of the present day.

This establishment was founded a little before the Abbey of Beaulieu was founded; and it was this foundation and not the other that gave the name of Beaulieu to both establishments. The abbey is not situated in a very fine place. the situation is low; the lands above it rather a swamp than otherwise; pretty enough, altogether; but by no means a fine place. The Templars had all the reason in the world to give the name of Beaulieu to their place. And it is by no means surprising that the monks were willing to apply it to their abbey.

From the former station of the Templars, from real Beaulieu of the New Forest, we came back to the village of Beaulieu, and there crossed the water to come on towards Southampton. Here we passed close along under the old abbey walls, a great part of which are still standing. There is a mill here which appears to be turned by the fresh water, but the fresh

William Allingham, Friend of Tennyson

William Allingham (1824–1889), the Irish poet, was born in Ballyshannon. After[a] brief formal education, he entered the customs service and remained in it for most of his working life.

He was determined to earn a name for himself in the literary world and took every occasion to visit London and meet the leading figures of his time. These included Leigh Hunt, Carlyle, Coventry Patmore, and Rossetti. Through Rossetti he gained an introduction to Tennyson. His first volume of poems appeared in 1850.

When he was transferred to the customs house in Lymington in 1863 he seized the opportunity to cultivate the friendship of Tennyson, then living on the Isle of Wight. At times he may have perceived himself as a kind of "Boswell" to Tennyson, but his lack of confidence and the need to earn his living at the customs house were barriers to reaching the kind of relationship Boswell had with Johnson. In his diary he referred to Tennyson as "T," Mrs. Tennyson as "Mrs. T," and the boys as "H and L."

During his seven years in Lymington, Allingham visited the New Forest many times, sometimes alone, sometimes with Tennyson or other friends. The extracts from his diary that follow reveal how Allingham made his way to most of the well-known Forest scenes and villages. Allingham did not marry until he was fifty and fifteen years later he died without achieving the literary fame to which he had aspired. Unwittingly, he contributed much useful background about his contemporaries through his diary, notes and correspondence.

Early in 1863 fortune not choice fixed my abode at **Lymington** in Hampshire.

"You will be near Tennyson," said Carlyle, when I was taking leave of him. "I doubt if I shall see him," I replied, disheartened by a second failure to settle in London, and disinclined for even the best company. "Yes, yes," said C., "you are sure to come together."

I went to **Lymington** on Friday the 8th of May, pleasant little old Town on its green hill, looking across the Isle of Wight some five miles away, to which a steam-boat plied three or four times daily. I was **Lymington's** Custom-House Officer, the only one, my office being a small first-floor room over the Coastguard Station, looking upon the little Harbour (muddy at low water, occupied chiefly by pleasure yachts) and the woods of **Walhampton** behind.

A little higher up a Ferry-Boat rowed by a big man in a Jersey, a Blue Giant, kept crossing to and fro, and higher still was a Toll-Bridge, to which the **Boldre Water** or **Lymington River** ran down in its green valley, a quiet rural stream, from the oaks, beeches and brackens of the **New Forest**.

WILLIAM ALLINGHAM
On a walk through the Forest, Rossetti told Allingham he should become an artist, so highly developed were his powers of observation.

Depressed tho' I was, I felt a great deliciousness in the quiet green lanes and hedges, thickets, woods and distances; and the evening after my arrival, standing at the field gate close to the Town, I heard four nightingales.

Tuesday, Wednesday, July 7–8.—Wandered in the **New Forest**—view of the wide woodland from **Emery Down**. Slept at the **Crown, Lyndhurst—Church**, window designed by Jones; Fresco, half-done, of the "Foolish Virgins" by Leighton.

Sunday, October 11.—Walk, **Boldre, Hayward Mill, Common**. Gypsies—old woman asks me to look at her son who is very ill in waggon. I see him, lying pale with heavy black eyes and tangled hair, speechless, has

William Cobbett and the Forest ...

Continued from previous page
water falls, here, into the salt water, as at the village of Botley. We did not stop to go about the ruins of the abbey; for you seldom make much out by minute inquiry. It is the political history of these places, or, at least, their connection with political events, that is interesting.

Just about the banks of this little river there are some woods and coppices and some corn-land; but at the distance of half a mile from the water-side we came out again upon the intolerable heath, and went on for seven or eight miles over that heath, from the village of Beaulieu to that of Marchwood, having a list of trees and enclosed lands away to our right all the way along, which list of trees from the south-west side of that arm of the sea which goes from Calshot Castle to Redbridge, passing by Southampton, which lies on the north-east side. Never was a more barren tract of land than these seven or eight miles. We had come seven miles across the forest in another direction in the morning; so that a poorer spot than this New Forest there is not in all England; nor I believe, in the whole world.

William Allingham's Diary ...

Continued from previous page

"lumps in his throat" she says—quinsy? I promise to send someone to him if I can. Call on Marshall, the relieving officer,—"at church," leave him a letter about the sick gypsy.

Saturday, October 17.—Fine evening. **New Forest**. **Holmsley**, **Wilverly Post**, heath and woods in front, russet gold; rest by a rivulet, thick beech woods, cottage—the woman says it is unheathly and very lonesome—'Under the shade of melancholy boughs.' Two woodpeckers, green as parroquets. The setting sun, the fiery ferns, the gold beechen-leaves. **Lyndhurst**, bed at **Crown**.

Sunday, October 18.—To **Rufus's Stone**, moorlands under heavy sky, thick embossment of russet golden beechwoods filling the vales, blue-distance—showers.

Monday, October 19.—News of the gypsy. "Getting better. Lump broke."

Friday, October 23.—Very fine; in the **New Forest**. Holmsley—path to **Burley**, field-lane fern-banked, delightful. Hamlet on its gorsey common, a big oak among the hollies. Sat down and read Woolner's *Beautiful Lady* which the post brought me today from the author. Tender and sweet. Well tastes poetry thus on a solitary ramble. ... Passing a Keeper's Lodge, came to the "**Twelve Apostles**," old oaks, most of them rugged hollow pillars with a few living branches. Sunset light, lonely road running through great beech-woods; doubled-dyed with sunset gold: I picture myself attacked by ruffians, with various dénouments. Such things never do happen in the Forest. The gypsies only beg and perhaps filch. Pass **Alum Green**, the moon rising over the hamlet, and strike a dampish forest path to **Brockenhurst road**, where I enter a wayside inn, and sit comfortably by a great peat-fire, two antlers above the chimney, drinking beer and reading in Woolner's book. Home by rail about 8.

Wednesday, December 30.—

Walked to **Pitt's Deep** and visited the Coastguard Station; returned at dusk, dirty roads, starry sky. Be content: what folly in a poor man to wish for an easy life and at the same time for much that he could only get by hard work.

1864

Monday, June 6.—Very fine. Tennyson and the Boys come across the Solent to me and we

"OF WHAT USE IS JOHN MORANT?"

"Walk—the old pathway to Brockenhurst Church, through Mr. Morant's park, obstructed by an old oak lying across it. ... The Old Domesday Book Church with its yew and hollow oak, always a delight to me."

make an excursion to **Beaulieu Abbey**. I take them through **Walhampton** by the **Fir Walk**.

Monday, August 29.—To **Aubrey House**, where Mr. and Mrs. Weld are now settled. It is near **Keyhaven**, on the way to **Hurst Castle**, and has the cliffs of the Island in full view. Walk back through the marsh under bright stars.

Monday, October 31.—Fine, chilly. ... Walk with George St. Barbe to **Boldre Church**. He knows Grantley Berkeley, and has gone otter-hunting with him.

1865

Wednesday, March 8.—Woolner comes across from the Island in the 1:30 steamer. I meet him and go on to **Brockenhurst Church** and show him the Old Yew and Oak, with which he is

well pleased and promises to come down and visit me. I walk into the **Forest** by **Ladycross**, get into swamp and have to try back. Shower of sleet. Ruined cottage with two yews beside it; meet Under-Gamekeeper, who tells me he lived in that old place for twenty-one years; has seven children; is now in a new cottage. (I ask:) "Which do you like best?" "I'd sooner be hanged at the Old Cottage than die a natural death at the other!"—an odd way of expressing his feeling. **Healthy Dilton**, farmyard, wood and ferns, **Royden Bridge**, **Boldre** and **Lymington**.

Sunday, August 6.—Lonely. Walk, field-path, **Pennington Farm**, standing corn. Ditch crowded with wild-flowers. Would I had a companion!

Monday, November 27.—... Walk, **Pennington Common**, moonlight. **Solentisms**.—The folk who live by the **Solent** say *mash* for marsh, *'ood* for wood, *waps* for wasp, *year* for here, *postes* for posts, *haps* for hasp, *porching* for poaching! *acker* is to stammer; *butt* a beehive; *I'll twist 'en*! means I'll do it—i.e., some troublesome feat. They say *sha'n't us* for *sha'n't we*, *to he* for to him, and make many or most neuter objects masculine; it being a jocular saying among

William Allingham's Diary ...

Continued from previous page
themselves, "In 'Am-sheer everything's 'e but a tom-cat—see one, and *There she goes!*"

1866

Friday, June 22.—Very fine. Train to **Lyndhurst Road** and walk into **Forest**—beeches cut down—warm—pretty country towards **Dibden** and **Southampton**. Tents, with folk like gypsies (but they so *no*), peeling rushes for rushlights: you leave a strip of green on the pith for backbone. **Beaulieu**, the Duke's park, old church and ruins. Village, tide in. Cottage hung with roses, man in front garden tells me he has lived there fifty-three years. I praise the beauty and quiet, but he often thinks he "ought to a-pushed out into the world—gone to London or some large place." Boys fishing for bass. The miller's, a piano going inside ("it's the miller's daughter," no doubt). Rasher and ale at the inn. The young lady at the bar with short

curls and towny air finds it "very dull here." I walk away at 20 to 9, sunset light over heath and forest, long road. The night-jar whirring.

Saturday, July 14.—Returning to lodging from office find that a telegram has come and the servant has gone out with it to find me, taking wrong way. Frightened— my Father (ill)? Turns out to be very pleasant: "**Crown Hotel, Lyndhurst**. A. Tennyson to W. Allingham. Will you come to us here?" Dine hastily and rush to train.

Sunday, July 15.—Breakfast at **Crown** at 9:30. A. T., Mrs. T., (and the boys) Hallam and Lionel. A. T. and I out at 12. **Swan Green**, forest path, **Halliday's (Holiday's) Hill**, we *swim* through tall bracken. T. pauses mid-way, turns to me, and says solemnly, "I believe *this* place is quite full of vipers!" After going a little further, he stopped again and said, "I am told that a viper-bite may make a woman silly for life,

or deprive a man of his virility." We enter *Mark Ash*, a wood of huge, solemn Beech trees, the floor thick-matted with dead leaves; a few trees were broken or fallen; some towered to a great height before branching. We sat on the roots of a mighty Beech. T. Smoked. We shared in sandwiches and brandy. Then he produced a little pocket *As you Like It*, and read some parts aloud. Returned by **Holm Hill**—View to the Isle of Wight, with six or seven distances one behind another. ... We strike again into the woods and reach the hill over **Swan Green** at 4. The donkey-chair with Mrs. T. and the boys appears, and a stupid little donkey-driver. It jolts down the rough wood-path. Huge flies draw blood. H(allam), L(ionel), and I go in search of the great **Knightswood Oak** and find it, looking fresh and healthy, but one limb lost. "**Kelt and Saxon**." Dine 7:30. ... I out, and take a dark walk to corner of **Fox Leas** and back. Owls shouting. Corncrakes.

Monday, July 16.—"**The Crown**." Breakfast—rough wait-

THE OUTER GATEWAY, BEAULIEU ABBEY
"I praise the beauty and quiet," wrote Allingham after his visit to Beaulieu. (Illustration from Heywood Sumner's *A Guide to the New Forest*.)

William Allingham's Diary ...

Continued from previous page
ress, poorly managed Inn. I pack up and go down the **Brockenhurst Road**, A. T. having started before me. At **Fox Leas** corner find him sitting under tree. ... Good-bye, walk to station, train to **Lymington**.

Wednesday, July 18.—... **Brockenhurst**. Walk to **Lyndhurst** by **Holland's Wood** and **Pondhead**. Inquire at two places for lodgings,—"taken." **Crown**, all out, engage a room. Dinner, A. T., Mrs. T., H. and L. The sherry here, T. says, a compound of spirits and wine—a bottle of it "stunned me." ... T. and I out in starlight, down street, lower road. He is surprised to find I have a habit of taking a walk after dinner.

Thursday, July 19.— **Lyndhurst**, fine. Walk with T., **Fox Leas**, **Whitley Wood**, **Queen's Bower**, brook dry; a heron rises. Another brook, brisk and clear, which pleases T. "I should like to lie in that pool for an hour. Nothing so delightful to the mind as a brook." I say good-bye, cross **Ober Green** and hurry to train, thunder-shower in the evening.

Sunday, July 22.—T. and I walk to **Swan Green**, turn off to **Emory Down** and into **Compton Manor** by path which leads us into a Park and then flower-gardens. We are posed, till a gardener shows us the way, with a remark that, "It is not liked that people should come through the Manor." We explain that we lost our way. See a jay. Cross a brook. Take a wrong turn to the left, and inquire at a cottage where the folk are at dinner and civily offer us beer. The wood-paths puzzle us again. T. says, "I want some forest," and leans over a gate while I go scouting to the top of the hill and scratch my new umbrella amid the brambles (important at the time!). Reach **Stony Cross Inn** and make inquiries, then back to T., who is lying under a hedge reading. ... To the **Stony Cross Inn**; bread and cheese and shan-

dygaff (i.e., beer and ginger-beer), good; civil girl. We look at rooms upstairs and T. opens a door disclosing folk eating, and shuts it. View of woods below the ridge. We descend; felled trees, bare spaces. ... We look about for the big yews, and can't find them. Ask Rural Postman, who says, "The **Sloden Yews** are *all cut down*. They were offered me, the whole of 'em, for £50. It was the head place for Yews." I think he said they were bought for £30 by an upholsterer at **Southampton**. We much vexed; T said he would have paid £30 himself to have preserved this famous Yew Wood, old beyond memory, and fit to live beyond reckoning. The cutting probably done by order of some London official down for the day. But surely the Deputy Ranger (Surveyor) here might have interposed? The wood is valuable, but very hard to cut and work. We now had wide prospects Eastwards, over forest and field, dale and down, towards **Southampton** and **Winchester**.

Saturday, August 18.—Very fine, South wind. Ned, Georgie and I to **Brockenhurst**. Field-path, stiles, **Ober Green**, heather: **Queen's Bower**. Sit by the little

bridge. **Oakenshaw**, big oak, brook, insects, big beech. Ned sketches. ... Skirt **New Park** to the other wood, they tired. Ned does paint down here (it's his holiday), and only makes a few sketches.

Sunday, August 26.—Fine. Rail 4.5 to **Brockenhurst**. The old **Church**. Service over, we peep in and encounter the Vicar, Rev. "Paddy" Falls. I apologise, introduce my friends. "Come in. Why not?" he says, with a strong brogue and funny twinkle of eye. "I was just saying a few words to a poor woman—pouring out the 'leperous distilment' into her ear." I remarked that we *ought* to have come in service-time. "Not at all, sir, not at all!" says Paddy politely, and showed us round the church. N. and G. were delighted with this Vicar ("hot from the service," as Georgie remarked), and thought the quotation "leperous distilment" very happy. Through **Brockenhurst Park**, where N. likes the woods. **Roydon**. They tired—**Boldre** —**Lymington** about 7, very tired.

November 9.—Walk—the old pathway to **Brockenhurst Church**, through Mr. Morant's park, obstructed by an oak lying across it, so that the rain has formed a small morass. The Squire evidently allows it to lie there for the annoyance of people

Sloden Wood

AN ILLUSTRATION FROM SUMNER'S *Book Of Gorley*

William Allingham's Diary ...

Continued from previous page
using the path, which he would fain shut up. What an ugly trick. Hear guns, and see M. in shooting-dress, dark-haired, florid, rather dandified man between thirty and forty, something like an opera Baritone. Dare- say he would like to shoot me for being on this path, which has certainly been public since before the Norman Conquest, while his family have only been here two or three generations. The Old Domesday Book Church with its yew and hollow oak, always a delight to me. There is talk of building, mainly by the Squire's wish, a new one in another place—cutting one more of the threads that join Past and Present. Of what use is John M. in the world? Towards the village he has closed up lately a beautiful bit of byroad.

Monday, November 12.—Meet G. St. Barbe. He applied *viva voce*, to oblige me, to the Parson of **Ellingham**, whom he knows, for leave for me to look over the Parish Register. I want to see if I can discover any traces of my ancestors (Allingham and Ellingham are, I believe, identical), who came to the northwest of Ireland in, Petrie thought, Elizabeth's reign. The old Vicar answered gruffly, "Shilling a year, shilling a year!" that is, I must pay a fee of a shilling for each year that I look at. This might come to a good deal of money, so I give the thing up.

1867

March 30.—Ride to **Hurst**. Returning, I rode by the edge of the sea till in one place the horse suddenly sank to his belly in the muddy sand. I had a real fright for half a minute, and then we scrambled out, I don't know how. At **Keyhaven** I got the horse well wisped.

Saturday, May 4.—**Lymington**. By train to **Brockenhurst**, and walk to **Queen's Bower**. The brook be-starred with white flowers (water crowfoot), little fishes gliding. Sit under the Big Oak reading *As You Like It*,—and

this might be Jaques very brook in Arden. Then through forest glades appears a carriage with Aidé, George du Maurier and his wife, and Miss Middlecoat.

Monday, June 10.—Fine, warm. To **Brockenhurst** by invitation to the Bowden Smiths, croquet, roses, hot sun. Field-path to station, red campions and king-cups. Down train comes in with Mrs. Cameron, queenly in a carriage by herself surrounded by photographs. We go to **Lymington** together, she talking all the time. "I want to do a large photograph of Tennyson, and he objects! Says I make bags under his eyes—and Carlyle refuses to give me a sitting, he says it a kind of *Inferno*! The *greatest* men of the age (with strong emphasis), Sir John Herschel, Henry Taylor, Watts, say I have *immortalised* them—and these other men object!! What is one to do—Hm?" This is the kind of interrogative interjection she often uses, but seldom waits for a reply. I saw her off in the Steamer, talking to the last.

June 18.—Very fine. Picnic in **Forest**, Schoolgirls and grown folk, youth and maidens. A Club Day also—children in waggons— noise and laughter—wood walks. We dine on the grass at 2:15.

Monday, August 19.—... Tremendous thunder and light for a long time. ... A thunder-bolt apparently falls on the mainland eastwards.

Tuesday, August 20.—Hearing that lightning did mischief out eastwards, I cross Ferry, walk to **Baddersley**, and find a two-storey cottage burned, only the blackened walls left; the ivy and flowers scorched, and the apples on some trees close by *roasted on one side*. Among a heap of half-burnt things, mixed with charred wood and ashes, lay some fused photographs of the old daguerreotype sort in metal frames, such as hang on cottage walls. The father stood grave and reserved, a girl, his daughter, near him, both seeming stunned. The man told me he

went to the upper room during the thunderstorm and sat down on a chair near the fireplace. His wife was in bed, and two sons in another bed. Suddenly the lightning darted through the thatched roof and down through the floor of the room, and the whole place was in a blaze in a moment. Up started wife and sons, the feather beds were thrown out of the window, all rushed out into the rain, and nothing else was saved from the fire. I offered to lend them a little money, but they declined. This was perhaps the work of the thunderbolt I saw last night; the time fits. I could not find that the lightning did anything as lightning save set the house on fire; this it did very effectually.

September 12.—Very fine. My landlady grumpy—"didn't tell me of the gentleman," etc. I explain (about D. G. Rossetti's sudden arrival). We walk by the river-side to **Roydon Farm**, path to **Brockenhurst Church**. **Crown Inn**. Rail to **Lymington**. Dine 7; Bed about 1. He had thought **Lymington** to be on the very edge of the **New Forest**.

Friday, September 13.—D.G.R. and I walk out to **Rope Hill** and Captain Barton shows us beautiful roses and offers us some for the picture—a very kind man. R. and I. to **Shirley Holmes** and lie in the grassy circle surrounded with oaks, hollies, etc., pierced with little green alleys and tunnels, a fit place to act the *Midsummer Night's Dream* in. We talk of the Forest Gypsies; this is one of their camping places.

Sunday, September 15.—... Out about 1:30; R. and I call at **Pennington Cottage**, and young Skinner joins us. **Milford church**—congregation in it, but D.G.R. and S. go in all the same, take a look and come out again —path, millpond, cliff, sea; delightful view.

Monday, September 16.—... (D.G.R. and I) walk through **Sowley Copse** and lie under an oak by the pond-side, reed-beds. ... Then to **Norley** and the cottage burnt by lightning-stroke. The scorched walls and trees remain much as when I saw them. An old

BOLDRE FORD BRIDGE NEAR THE QUEEN'S BOWER

This illustration was one of a dozen etchings by Heywood Sumner for the Artists Edition of John R. Wise's *The New Forest: Its History and Scenery.* **Walter Crane also contributed 63 illustrations for this limited edition of 350 copies.**

William Allingham's Diary ...

Continued from previous page

woman, who had been in the house when it took fire, told us she was "all skivered with sparks." R's comment on the whole was this—"What a dammed world where such things can happen!" In the garden was a little clump of box clipt in the form of an armchair; R. wanted to buy this, have it dug up and transplanted to his garden at Chelsea, but the bargain did not take effect. The *live* chair tickled his imagination.

September 17.—... We go by 1:45 train to **Brockenhurst** and walk by **Whitley Wood** to **Lyndhurst**—see Leighton's fresco in the church. Returning, we go over a roomy cottage-villa on the roadside, "To Let," with a garden behind, and Rossetti says in his emphatic tone, "I think I had better take it at once!"

Wednesday, September 18.— Fine—D. G. R. and I walk to **Boldre Church** Gilpin's tomb and its inscription. ... Back by **Pilley** and **Walhampton House**.

Friday, September 20.— D.G.R. and I take a short walk to **Pennington**, then early dinner, and he departs by the 5:45 train, I going with him to **Brockenhurst**.

Monday, January 20.—Fine; walk to **Pitt's Deep**—vernal and pleasant; Coastguard station. Beautiful **Sowley Copse**—men destroying it by order of Lord Henry Scott, since he finds he cannot close up the footpath —what a noble action!

Tuesday, January 21.—Fine. I go with (Mr. Cameron and Mrs. Prinsep) as far as **Brockenhurst**, pleasant. Walk to **Lyndhurst**, vernal, call at Miss Dickson's, poorly. ... Hurry to **Brockenhurst**, hot, catch train.

April 22.—Walk to **Sowley Pond**. Lord Henry Scott, after trying illegally to close the Path (charming shady short-cut from the dusty road) and failing, has now cut down the trees and grubbed up all the hazels and hollies, and left it a path through a

bare field. Oaks lying on the ground, piles of oak bark. The Magistrates decided against his claim to shut the Path, the Judges at Winchester decided against it, and now, instead of humbly apologising, his Lordship does this!

Saturday, October 10.—... With a party to the **New Forest**— **Swan Green**, **Queen's Bower**, rich red sunset through the trees; old oak and brook like old friends now, yet how little they care for us! This longing for Nature to return us some friendship, some affection, created Naiads, Dryads, and Oreads. Yet how could a Poet turn back to these? ... Cross **Ober** or **Over-Green** and pick some Butcher's-Broom.

October 11.—Very fine. Walk, **Norley Wood**; lakes of mist on **Beaulieu Heath**.

October 12.—Walk to **Keyhaven** by marsh.

Thursday, October 22.—Walk to **Setley**, and find gypsies encamped. Coming back I overtake a little girl carrying with difficulty two bags of sand, and just as I am

The Kaiser's Visit to the New Forest

An awkward situation occurred in 1907 when Gerald Lascelles, Deputy Surveyor of the New Forest, had to be absent from the Queen's House in Lyndhurst.

He knew that the Kaiser was on a visit from Germany, but hoped he would not come to the Queen's House until he returned there. Unfortunately, the Kaiser came on to Lyndhurst, apparently without being told by his aide that Lascelles was away. In his memoirs Lascelles describes the mix-up and how the Kaiser left behind his signature on a piece of notepaper.

In 1907 (the Emperor, Kaiser William II) came to reside for a brief period at Highcliffe, near Christchurch, and spent his time in motoring all over the country. I knew that he would be sure to want to see the King's House, but at that time it was a house of mourning, and a black shadow lay across it.

I took pains, however, to convey to the Kaiser, through Metternich, my hope that he would give me one week's grace before he came, after which time I would be willing and anxious to show him the house, and tell him all that was of interest about it.

His Imperial Majesty, however, selected to come at a time when I was perforce away. He looked over the house, being shown, of course nothing of interest, and, calling for a sheet of letter paper, wrote for me, as a visiting-card, a large "William I.R.," and a second sheet was covered with the signatures of his distinguished staff.

But I am bound to say that he

Allingham's Diary ...

Continued from previous page asking how far she is going, up drives Rev. P. F. ("Paddy" Falls) in his gig, who offers me a lift. I say, "Help this little girl with her two heavy bags," upon which his Reverence reddens and drives off. I carry one of the bags.

October 28.—... Walk alone into **Forest**, among coloured trees; **Whitley Wood, Gretnam, Tollgate**, back by brookside, among beautiful beeches; spindle tree seeds; maple yellow like a ripe quince.

November 2.—... Out and walk in the dusk on **Boldrewood Road**, sunset fading, dark trees, owls do cry. Already a drift of withered leaves.

Tuesday, November 3.— **Lyndhurst**. To Meet of the Foxhounds at **Bolton's Bench**, carriages, horses, hounds.

Tuesday, August 3.—... I walk off over moor, **Matley Wood**.

August 6.—Walk to **Whitley Ridge**; cowboy says the bull "Blared" (i.e., bellowed).

Sunday, August 22.—Out to **Sway** and **Mead End**, dine under old tree, near sunset time.

Gertrude Jekyll (1843–1932) became a cult figure in the 1970s and 1980s when her gardens and Sir Edwin Lutyens' homes became the subjects of numerous books, articles, television and radio programmes, and exhibitions.

Sometimes overlooked is the fame which Miss Jekyll achieved in her own lifetime when homeowners throughout Britain queued up to enlist her services in designing their gardens. From 1868, when she was 25, until she died, Miss Jekyll worked tirelessly in planning gardens of all sizes and shapes. She broke with the formal "straight-line" tradition of the past, letting nature dictate the pattern of her designs. Her gardens tended to blend with the houses in the background, as if they were of the same tapestry.

For many years she planned an average of nine to ten gardens, but never took on more work than she could conscientiously complete. On some occasions when new houses were being built she and Sir Edwin Lutyens combined their gardening-architectural designs as an harmonious "package." Her influence abroad was considerable: home owners in France, Switzerland, Ireland and the United States eagerly sought her services. She was highly regarded in the United States where a collection of her garden plans is now held (University of California).

The New Forest was fortunate in having four gardens designed by Miss Jekyll, all of them in the village of Burley. The extract below, taken from *Gertrude Jekyll, A Memoir*, by Francis Jekyll (1934), gives the date, house name, and owner at the time the gardens were laid out. Unfortunately none of the gardens has survived intact, or is open to the general public.

GERTRUDE JEKYLL GARDENS IN THE NEW FOREST		
Year designed	Name of house	Owner
1906	HIGHCROFT, Burley	Miss Sarrin
1907	LITTLE HAY, Burley	Lady Isobel Ryder
1907	DURMAST, Burley	Miss Baring
1925	BURNT AXON, Burley	Col. H. B. Strang (Architects: Read and Macdonald)

Roosevelt's "Crowning Joy:" Forest Trek

Theodore Roosevelt was a remarkable man. Born a sickling, he adopted a rigorous physical training regime to boost his health, and for the rest of his life was a lover of the "great outdoors." He was a keen conservationist and ornithologist, and during the building of the Panama Canal, operated a giant steam shovel.

He was the youngest person ever to become president of the United States when he succeeded William McKinley on September 14, 1901. McKinley had been shot by an assassin, leaving the 41-year old Roosevelt—then vice-president—to be sworn in. As president, he fought the corruption of "big business" in American politics, rigorously enforced the anti-trust (anti-cartel) laws, fought for employee liability rights, and mediated the peace between Japan and Russia. He won the Nobel Peace Prize and was the first American president to use the International Court at the The Hague. He was named president in his own right in the election of 1904.

In early 1910 he came to Britain and Europe to meet national leaders and to give a series of addresses to universities and scientific and cultural groups. In May that year he represented the United States at the funeral of King Edward VII and the following month visited both Cambridge and Oxford universities where he enjoyed meeting and talking with undergraduates.

He booked his return passage to the United States aboard the Holland-American liner *Kaiserin Auguste Victoria* on June 10, but informed his British hosts that he would like to be escorted to some rural part of England by a lover of birds sometime shortly before his embarkation from Southampton. Sir Edward Grey, the British Foreign Secretary, volunteered himself for the assignment. The requested "rural adventure" took place in the New Forest on Thursday, June 9. That event, and the former president's departure from Southampton the next day were reported in *The Times* of June 11th, as given below.

THEODORE ROOSEVELT
A keen naturalist all his life, the former president considered his walk through the New Forest one of the highlights of his 1910 visit to Britain and Europe.

Arriving at Basingstoke by train in the middle of the day, Mr. Roosevelt and Sir Edward Grey went from that place by motor car to a village in the New Forest (Stoney Cross-Fritham), and they (then) walked for several hours.

Each time a bird was heard, Mr. Roosevelt asked to be told about it, and produced paper and pencil so that Sir Edward Grey might write down its name. Thus a considerable list was made in the course of the day, and Mr. Roosevelt was not a little concerned to be (immediately able) to find this list in his pockets yesterday when he wished to refresh his memory.

Birds Seen or Heard

But he recalled as among birds which he had seen or heard the lark, the blackbird, the thrush, the wren, the nightjar, the robin, the chiffchaff, the hedge sparrow, the willow-wren, the creeper, the golden-crested wren, the rook, the starling, the jackdaw, the black-cap, the garden warbler, the coot, the moorhen, the tufted duck, the swallow, the martin, and the swift.

The two ornithologists were unaccompanied and they had a charming country walk, which was all the more (appreciated by) Mr. Roosevelt, inasmuch as he had been feeling thoroughly worn out in consequence of his more serious engagements earlier in the week.

Severe Thunderstorm

They were caught in a severe thunderstorm, and arrived at the Forest Park Hotel, Brockenhurst, their clothes wet through and soiled with mud, but themselves in high spirits. Their luggage had been sent to the hotel by car.

This (New Forest) experience (Mr. Roosevelt) described in conversation with the Mayor of Southampton and others as "the crowning joy" of his visit to Europe, and (returning) to it later, he declared emphatically: "I have just finished about the most pleasant 24 hours I have had in all my trip. I have had a delightful time among your English birds."

The Kaiser's Visit . . .

Continued from previous page
afterwards sent me a very kindly worded letter through Count Metternich to the effect that, if he had ascertained that we were away from home, he would not, at such a time, have come to the house at all, though he wished to visit it. It is now naturally with somewhat mixed feelings that I regard these papers and these reminiscences, after all that has happened since. But there they are, and they cannot but come into my records.

Walter Wilkinson, the Peep-Show Man

Half a century ago Walter Wilkinson was probably the best known puppeteer in the English-speaking world. He toured widely in Britain, the United States, Canada and Australia, performing at some of the world's finest art museums. Universities vied for his visits and on one occasion he performed at the White House before Mrs Eleanor Roosevelt and her friends. He wrote eight delightful books detailing his adventures. They bore such appealing titles as *The Peep Show*, *Vagabonds and Puppets*, *Puppets in Yorkshire*, and *A Sussex Peepshow*. Other works dealt with his wanderings in Lancashire, Wales, Scotland, and America.

Born in 1889, Wilkinson lived to the age of 81 when he died suddenly before completing his autobiography. After his death Wilkinson was almost forgotten. Then, in 1985 and 1986 two British television channels filmed episodes from his puppet adventures in the south of England and overnight, he again became the beloved figure so widely admired in the 1920s and 1930s.

Walter Wilkinson was a true scholar and artist. At the age of 25 he walked across Italy and France and here cemented his earlier interest in marionettes. But puppets attracted him more, for the puppet show demanded more of the artist than the marionette. His love of outdoor life convinced him he should construct a light-weight barrow containing his peep-show theatre, and tour the countryside with a Punch and Judy repertoire. This goal he achieved with astounding success. Happily for his thousands of admirers, he kept illustrated diaries and turned them into some of the most popular reading of his day. His wife accompanied him on many of his visits to the English-speaking world where, he frequently would be shown his books about Yorkshire, Lancashire, Sussex, Wales and Scotland—shipped over from Britain by relatives or friends.

The Times, in a critical assessment, said "Wilkinson gets into the landscape and rubs against the inhabitants with an intimacy that even Cobbett did not achieve." The extracts that follow are taken from the manuscript of the diary entitled *The Peep Show* and are reproduced through the courtesy of Wilkinson's niece, Miss Joan Wilkinson. The passages describe Wilkinson's adventures in and around the New Forest in 1924 when he was thirty-five.

evening. Keep to tent and get on with jobs.

Friday, May 23—Get to work on Punch's hands and get them well under way by dinner time. ... Take a stretch after lunch towards *Godshill* and get into the fringes of the New Forest. The village very quaint—the real thatched cottage and thatched-barn sort of place. Back to (*Breamore*) for tea, heavy rain, and then to school. Good audience and do them a good show. Much applauded and appreciated. ... Rains all evening and I make Punch a cap. Am

WALTER WILKINSON

feeling cheered up by *Breamore*. As soon as I came round the corner and into the village and saw the pretty cottages spaciously set apart and the poplars and the large school open to the fields, I felt here was something for me. Such an open, pretty place with its streams and willows and green fields. Indeed, it has been kind to me, getting my shoes mended so quickly, giving me a convenient pitch from a kindly man, and rewarding the show with a good collection.

Saturday, May 24—Heavens, how it rains! ... To *Fordingbridge* in afternoon. Walk the streets and shop and (have) tea, and admire the river scene from the bridge and the fair ground. Back to jobs

Wednesday, May 21—My boys are round again by seven and very interested in watching me get breakfast. They edge into the tent by degrees and the heat nearly suffocates me. So I clear them out but they soon edge in again. Get turned down by the *Downton* school. They've had unfortunate experience with entertainers and the managers have put a stop to the practice. ... Cold feels rotten tonight.

Thursday, May 22—Very wet-looking morning but I proceed with toilet and packing. Am away

by nine. ... The long wet grass was getting on my nerves and my shoes have been wet through since Tuesday evening. ... Get to *Downton* and shop, and try to hook on to someone for a show, but don't catch anything. Then to *Breamore* and persuade the master to let me. ... Mr. Hall is very nice and kindly lets me into his paddock with a pony 30 years old. Leave shoes to be mended. This is a great relief as I have been nervous of every step today expecting them to fall to pieces. Eat some tough cakes and make a soup. Dismal

WALTER WILKINSON CAMPING IN THE NEW FOREST

Walter Wilkinson . . .

Continued from previous page

in very threatening evening.

Sunday, May 25—Still threatening, but I tidy up and set off for *Godshill*. Fine walk through *Woodgreen* after which one passes into the precincts of the Forest and under large trees. But this is only a narrow belt of forest land for presently one comes out on rough moorland of heather and gorse now in glorious bloom—and away for miles and miles all Hampshire lies below. Such an illuminated picture this morning with glimpses of sun wandering about amongst the deep blue shadow of storm clouds. The air is so fresh and fine up here as scented by the gorse. Am directed by a nice cowman to the Charman's house which stands on the hilltop over the valley. ... Met Tom and the little Russian girl just coming out, going to visit a schoolmaster in *Woodgreen* and so I returned with them. Back to nice lunch and

chatter and talk about shows and manage to pull my caboose up here and camp. Fine evening; promises well for the morrow.

Monday, May 26—Up early and away in lovely, lovely morning. The many streams, the flowery fields and the willows are fairyland this morning. The schoolchildren give me great greetings as they pass. The Forest is wonderful this morning with the abundance of yellow gorse and the wide panorama and the fine sky. Delightful pull up to *Godshill* and not too hard. Get pitched here and then the Misses Nicholls arrive to enquire about show and they seem pleased with the idea and take on, and are going to arrange it.

Friday, May 30—To *Fordingbridge*, then lunched early, packed up and away to *Hatchet Green*. Good rest and tea in the forest on the way. Mistress had forgotten to announce me to the children, but

she kept them all and paid for them. Was very pleased with show and had enjoyed it herself. Home late but cheerful. More chats with the Charmans.

Thursday, June 5—Up early in another gloomy morning, but no rain. ... Pull through *Gorley* but the thundery weather heavy. Make tea under a birch. ... Good going to *Ringwood* which is early closed and deserted. At *Kingston* pull down side road to a common; there seems to be no one to give permission. Stout man advises me to take bull by the horns and camp, and if anyone objects, say you thought it was a common, etc., etc., and that you are only staying the night and won't do it again. Take his advice and camp. Gives me water the colour of beer. Says it is very good, has had it analysed—it's full of iron.

Friday June 6—Up at six in fine, bright morning. Great treat this. Paddled about in the dew and shaved—quite like old times. Breakfasted and packed and had

Walter Wilkinson. . .

Continued from previous page

grand tramp as far as *Sopley*. Here found the children at play and got permission to show from a lovely dark girl in a primrose dress and not at all like a school marm. She cried with delight, "O, a puppet show!" Rested in a pine wood and watched a mouse running up and down bracken stems and a squirrel in the tree tops. Rhododendrum in full bloom. ... I got back at three and did show in the playground with the washing hanging out—a dress and some stockings looking very like the pretty property of the pretty schooltea-

married, and it breaks my heart once again to pull out of *Sopley*.

Monday, June 16—To *Burley* this morning ... but find the kids have had a recent entertainment and a holiday and next week go to Wembley, so am squashed out.

Thursday, July 2—Up early this morning and away to *Hinton* school where old dame must interview the managers and send (me) word. Wandered round to *New Milton* and went to post and fixed up the school there. Very aimiable master but the schools are Army huts. Long morning tramp, but

packed and away to *Burton*—bit of a rush but got there in good time. Two or three adults and the vicar's children in the audience. Show a roaring success—teacher says they want me in the winter. ... To Burton Common for camp. Lovely camp, this among the heather and gorse.

Sunday, July 27—Walk along to *Barton* which looks very difficult for the Peep Show. Good day on the shore and the cliffs and am glad to get on with the book. Some louts came to bathe and brought a gramophone with them to play ... while they undressed. It is surprising how quiet a gramophone sounds on the seashore and that it sounds more gruesome and

cher. After the show I am asked if I would like a cup of tea. Wouldn't I just! Accordingly I find myself sitting on a sofa drinking tea and eating bread and butter and strawberry jam. An unconventional (teacher), this. Has read of puppet shows in *The Teacher's World* and is going to Africa to help in a school. Doesn't trouble her children about lessons —tries to make them happy. No use educating them: the girls will go out to service and the boys to farms. "They all know much more than I do about real things," (she said.) ... She lives on the heathrug all the winter, never sits in a chair. I like my dark and handsome schoolmistress who lived in (my) dreams until (I found) she was

have a good lunch and repose writing in afternoon which is wet and stormy.

Saturday, July 5—Up early and bathe in the stream. Packed and on the road by ten. Shop in *New Milton* and then pull on to *Milford*. Approach Brownie Girl Guides who are running about the cliff. They accept (a show) at a penny each. So there and then I put the show over the heather and thyme on that lovely windy cliff above the sea, with the white breakers below, and over the blue Solent the white cliffs of the Isle of Wight and the Needles. That is my part fee, to have the privilege of performing under such healthy and lovely conditions.

Thursday, July 24—Lunched and

unmusical than ever.

Thursday, July 31—Out to *Pennington* this morning on the bicycle. Find the school has gone to Bournemouth and half the adults in the village as well. ... Get to *Sway* but can't fix up with master though he is willing. Chase away to *Thorney Hill* after the "Good Templars Treat" but they can't have me because they have promised the caterers that nobody else shall collect pennies from the children.

Lymington Town Crier

Saturday, August 2—... Early tea and away to *Lymington*. Interview the town crier and toll man and get permission to pitch. ... I set up the Show in a gutter and crowd began to gather curiously at once. ... Do the Show three times to

Walter Wilkinson...

Continued from previous page

interested audiences. Boys exclaim "This is a grand show." Pack up and away at nine o'clock. Cheerful old couple say they have had a good entertainment and thank me.

Thursday, August 7—Feeling fitter this morning. ... Fixed up outside *Chewton Glen* and two or three sudden gusts nearly blew the Show over—had to hold it down with my leg on the side rails—very awkward position. Then moved along to refreshment booth and did another show. ... A wild child threw his mother's hat in and then his own and then seized a leg of the theatre and nearly shook it over. Little things like this help me along. Somewhat irritated by children throwing stones at the theatre—have to go out and stop them doing this. Good collecting: have some sixpences and a whole shilling.

Wednesday, September 24—Up at 6:30, packing and clearing up. Lovely morning, though damp. Shady lanes and then—Heavens! What exhilaration out on the high open heath beyond *Sway*. Green grass and heather and the pretty Forest ponies, and a great blue and white sky rolling grandly onwards before the wind. A great open view, shadows wandering over heath and forest. Through *Brockenhurst* and into the forest. Pull into a glade with silver birches and a grand old oak or two, and lunch. Peep Show, (I will) forget. Such shady little jungles of bracken and briar, and such vistas beyond into sunny swards. ... It is all made to look at. The trees pose in picturesque screens and the glades are all a mist of greenery and sunniness. I am going to enjoy this, (for) this is a day of freedom and carelessness. I will not bother my head about wagging dolls, but dismiss them, lock them away. Nor worry myself with permissions and persuasions to be allowed to show. Here is an entertainment, an exhilaration for *me*. A present from the gods—not to be refused. A fine, bright September day, all green and blue

and white, mellowed with golden sunlight. A keen air that cleans me through and through to the tips of my nose, my cheeks my ears. Even my hair is sensitive to its influence. If I take in no pennies, I am taking in all this brightness and glorious sunlight—all this forest loveliness into my soul. It all speaks to me in wordless poems. It exhibits itself in endless pictures. This is a day in Paradise.

The General Who Saw the Forest Only from His Car

Dwight Eisenhower, like Theodore Roosevelt, may have longed to see the innermost beauty of the New Forest, but he had no chance to do so.

As Supreme Allied Commander in the European theatre of operations during the second world war, Eisenhower worked day and night to oversee the planning and preparation for the Normandy invasion on 6 June 1944. His headquarters were at Southwick near Fareham, but he also met with Prime Minister Winston Churchill many times—including one crucial occasions in a railway coach on a siding in the Meon valley.

Eisenhower also visited Allied troops scattered over the whole of southern England. These morale-boosting trips to units scheduled to take part in the D Day invasion of France often took the general through the New Forest. One

Library of Congress

DWIGHT D. EISENHOWER
As Allied Supreme Commander in World War II, he passed through the New Forest frequently in the months leading up to D Day.

American unit he visited was quartered at Brockenhurst's Balmer Lawn Hotel. On most of his forays by automobile Eisenhower was driven by his English chauffeur, Kay Summersby, who later wrote two books about her war-time experiences with the general.

Unlike Theodore Roosevelt, Eisenhower was unable to visit the Forest in retirement. He was twice elected American president, but during his second term suffered a heart attack which much restricted his life thereafter.

None of the four presidents who followed President Eisenhower is believed to have visited the New Forest.

The 1969 Visit of Princess Elizabeth

The 1979 celebration to mark the 900th anniversary of the New Forest was not the first time the Queen visited the Forest.

Almost exactly 30 years earlier she (then HRH the Princess Elizabeth) came to open the national youth centre at Avon Tyrrell. En route to Avon Tyrrell the royal party stopped briefly in Burley where the Princess received a bouquet of New Forest wild flowers collected by village Girl Guides.

Afterwards the Princess wrote a letter of appreciation which remains a treasured possession of the Burley Guides.

The Queen's 1979 Visit to the New Forest

In 1079, historians generally agree, the New Forest was officially designated. To mark the 900th anniversary of the Forest's founding, extensive celebrations took place in 1979—culminating in the visit of Queen Elizabeth II.

Hundreds of Forest residents made their way to points on the official route to get a glimpse of the Queen and the Royal entourage. Sally Taylor, feature writer of the *Salisbury Journal*, was there to record the atmosphere of the occasion.

The extracts below are taken from the *Journal's* issue of 19 April.

The Queen and the Duke of Edinburgh met the people who administer its laws, those who earn their living within its boundaries, and the residents who live in its historic setting, during their first official visit to the New Forest.

The Royal couple, here to mark the 900-year celebrations of the New Forest … could not have toured the Forest on a more spectacular afternoon. As the rain clouds which had dogged the morning activities in Winchester swept away, the crowds in the New Forest swelled to 10 deep in places.

It was whispered, at the end of the day, that the Queen herself was delighted at the response. The Queen and the Duke started their tour at Bolderwood … (Here) the Queen set out on her first New Forest walk. She followed a nature trail under a canopy of magnificent Douglas firs familiar to residents and visitors. …

As the Royal visit continued, the crowds snowballed. Children, who throughout the tour were placed at the front, had a magnificent view of (the) Queen and the youngsters were speechless with excitement as the Queen accepted their gifts of flowers and Easter eggs.

Knightswood Oak Scene

Throughout the progress along the Ornamental Drive knots of people, some in large groups waving flags and others in twos and threes, stood among the trees to see the Royal couple pass. Cheers went up as the escorting Agisters trotted into view at the Knightswood Oak where many disabled people and more schoolchildren … waited.

H. Wills

THE ARRIVAL OF THE ROYAL PARTY AT BOLDERWOOD
The Queen is escorted by G.D. Holmes, Director General of the Foresty Commission.
Immediately behind the Duke of Edinburgh waves to onlookers.

The Queen's 1979 Visit to the New Forest...

Continued from previous page

The Duke put on a mackintosh as he rode in the open carriage—one of two sent down by the Royal Household for the New Forest visit. Both landaus were pulled by a pair of grey horses.... The first stage of the journey brought the Queen to Knightswood Oak where she met Forestry (Commission) staff, and commemorated her visit by planting an oak tree.

The Queen met the Verderers at Whitefield Moor and said farewell to her mounted escort of four Agisters—Raymond Stickland (Head Agister), Brian Ingram, Raymond Bennett and John Booth, who had ridden Arab horses bred from a mare given to Sir Dudley Forward, official Verderer, by Queen Elizabeth the Queen Mother.

The Queen's second and longest walkabout ended at Appletree Court where her visit ended with tea in a marquee and the presentation of district councillors and former MPs for the New Forest and Christchurch.

In the final moment before her departure for Windsor, the Queen was shown a tapestry commemorating the (New Forest) anniversary. (It was) made by Belinda Lady Montagu and a group of helpers who took two years completing the work.

The signing of the visitors' book and two colour photographs brought to an end the Royal visit to the Forest.

H. Wills

THE QUEEN ENJOYING HER VISIT TO THE FOREST
Here the Queen admires one of the fine horses assembled on the official route. A young boy, hoisted on the shoulders of his parent, gets an inobstructed view of Her Majesty.

12
Places, Diverse and Wonderful

The "Hidden Beauties" of Heywood Sumner

The "true lover of the New Forest" is not content to gaze from afar—by car, bus or train—on the vast expanses of forest and heathland, but will seek out what Heywood Sumner calls the "hidden beauties."

Sumner, in his *New Forest Guide* (1923), divides the Forest into northern, middle and southern areas. With the help of the Forestry Commission's guide (*Explore the New Forest*), the Ordnance Survey's 2½-inch to 1-mile map of the Forest, and one of the excellent books on walking in the New Forest (see bibliography), the enthusiastic adventurer will find that Sumner's beauties need not be hidden.

In the extracts below from Sumner's guide, towns and villages have been omitted, as they occur in other parts of this work. Also omitted are out-of-date passages.

The illustrations accompanying the text are taken from Sumner's guide and his *Book of Gorley* (1910)

The Northern Area

The main feature of the Northern area is open moorland—level, upland plains, capped with gravel, covered with heather, furze and bracken, worn into five parallel ridges and bottoms by streams that trickle in dry and rush in wet weather down to the Avon.

Here and there the hills are overgrown with thickets, with old woods, with planted Inclosures, or with self-sown Scots pine, but the open Forest is never far distant. From all the roads and tracks the wayfarer sees far views over wild foregrounds to distant cultivation, over a tract of primaeval wastes set in the midst of a more fertile formation, over heathlands surrounded by the chalk hills of Dorset, Wiltshire, Hampshire and the Isle of Wight. The lie of the land and the vegetation show that the sandy gravelly, clayey soil of the Forest rests on a chalk basin that extends from Cranborne Chase to "the Island," and from Purbeck to Hampshire South Downs.

The streams in this area run down parallel bottoms, as before said, separated by gravel-topped ridges terminating in bluffs which line the Forest side of the Avon valley. Each of these bottoms has its own special character—Follow a stream—or—Follow a ridge—are the best directions for those who seek to find wild beauty for themselves. In following these streams and ridges the outflow of hill-side springs should be noticed. The sheets of plateau gravel that cap these hill-tops are only of a few feet in thickness, and they rest on sand, below which is clay. The surface water, percolating through the super-imposed gravel and sand, is held up by the clay, and peezes out of the hill-sides through the exit of least resistance: then behold, a spring! "Jack and Jill went up a hill, to fetch a pail of water." So do we, here, and the water does

not fail. But, in times of summer drought, the overflow of such hill-side springs is absorbed by the thirsty soil long before it reaches the brook below. Thus the dry brook is not evidence of the waterless state of this district.

Throughout the Forest there are special places where ponies and cattle congregate in summer—places where breezes always blow though hot air quivers above the heath, and where flies merely tease, but do not torment—as they do in the still woods. Such places are called "shades" in local speech—shade meaning a cool place. Generally shades are on high ground where ponds lie on the plains—for example, in this part of the Forest, Ocknell Pond, Janesmoor Pond, Longcross Pond, Stony Cross, Handy Cross Pond, Broomy Plain Pond, and Latchmore (the last being on open, but not high ground). On sunny, summer mornings, quite early, ponies, foals and cattle make dewy tracks from their feeding grounds to the shade that serves their haunt; there they will bide throughout the hot hours of a long summer's day, when flies are bold, shifting, whisking, stamping, nibbing unceasingly, making the best of a bad time, until the cool of the evening descends—and then they disperse to feed, unmolested by flies, amid lawns and thickets where nightjars churr in the gloaming.

Observant explorers on these heaths may notice small, embanked, rectangular areas which occur at Hive Garn Gutter, near Ashley Rails; on Ibsley Common; in Newlands above Moyles Court; on Rockford Common; and at Pinnick above Greenford Bottom; and they may question their purpose. Such relics tell of a custom that was followed by local bee-keepers until about 100 years ago. They used to send their hives to the Forest heathlands when the

FROM HEYWOOD SUMNER'S *Book of Gorley*

heather was in bloom, in order that their honey might profit thereby. Some neighbouring forester looked after them, and kept them in such embanked "bee-gardens" secure from disturbance by ponies or cattle. This custom is remembered as hearsay by old men now living, but has quite died out.

Places of Interest

Amberwood. Planted in 1815. Oak with thorn and holly undergrowth, and an outer belt of Scots pine, cut in 1918. In the same year a clearing for a nursery was made within the wood South of Amberwood cottage. There is a good track from here to Hyde, and rough tracks to Bramshaw Telegraph and to Fritham.

Anses. Old beech, oak and holly. The regeneration of an old wood by self-sown seedlings may be well seen here, for the young trees are protected from the nibbling ponies and cattle by dense thickets of holly out of which they rise. This wood is remarkable for its great beeches—the largest of which is 17 feet 6 inches in girth at 4 feet from the ground—and for its numerous examples of ingrowth—of branches growing into each other, or into their parent stem. The lower part of Anses is bounded by the twisting upper course of Dockenswater which perfects the charm of this, the most beautifully wooded bottom in the Northern area.

Ashley Lodge is a Crown keeper's cottage, built in 1773 near the site of an older lodge. Pitt's wood adjoins the grounds of Ashley Lodge, and its name commemorates John Pitt, surveyor general of the Forest when this wood was planted in 1775. It stands below the hills of Ticketsbury on the South and of Cockley Plain on the North, in a little valley down which meanders the Ashley brook to join Ditch-end brook near Green House Farm. In 1903 it was re-inclosed, partly planted with Scots pine, larch and oak, and a nursery made at the Western end.

There are good tracks from here to Hyde and to Godshill.

Bentley, North and South. Planted in 1700. Both are pure oak woods of fine growth.

Bramble Hill. A beautiful, old wood, mostly beech. On the Southern slope of the hill is a large residence built on the site of a Forest Lodge. Pipers Weight (cf. Denny Wait, in the Southern area; *wait* old English for water)—North of Bramble Hill—is the highest ground in the District, 422 feet above the sea.

Bramshaw Church had the curious distinction of standing in Hampshire and Wiltshire, but in 1895 the Wiltshire portion of the parish was transferred to Hampshire. Bramshaw wood is said to have provided the timber used in building Salisbury Cathedral (1220–1258).

Bramshaw Telegraph is marked by a belt of Scots pine that crowns the ridge—419 feet above the sea—whereon the highroads from Fordingbridge and Downton join on their way to Southampton. This was one of a chain of stations on high ground that was used during the first half of the 19th century for conveying messages by semaphore signals (Greek *sema*, a sign, and *ferein*, to bear), from Plymouth to London and vice versa. The Telegraph station was occupied by an officer and two men, one of whom was always on the look-out.

Brook is a typical hamlet on the edge of the Forest. It belongs to Bramshaw parish, and is situated in a spacious semi-circular valley-head below Stony Cross and Fritham. The ill-omened name of Gibbet Wood—below Salisbury trench—is said to record a Gibbet which stood there in the days when such dreadful display was supposed to proclaim the reign of Law and Justice. (cf, the tale of castaways on an unknown land, seeing a gibbet, and saying: "Thank God, we are in a civilized country.")

Broomy. Planted in 1809, mostly oak with bracken undergrowth. Broomy Lodge is a private residence. Holly Hatch, a woodman's cottage beside Dockenswater. The view Westward from Broomy Plain is very extensive. There are by-roads from here to Linwood, and to the Ringwood and Romsey highroad. Stags-horn moss and lilies-of-the-valley may be found near here by those who know where to look for them.

Cadnam is a hamlet lying partly in the parish of Eling, and partly in that of Minstead. It was famous for an oak which, like the Glastonbury thorn, was reputed to come into leaf on old Christmas day (Jan. 6). Gilpin in his "Remarks on Forest Scenery," (described) the premature vegetation of this tree. ... Two points may be noted in (his) account. (1) It mentions that the tree had been injured. (2) Twigs, with leaves on them, are assumed to represent similar vegetation all over the tree. A "super-annivated" Cadnam woodman tells me that the only evidence of such traditional growth is to be found in premature shoots around tree injuries—where young sap meets with old spine wood—and such premature budding is local, around the injury, not all over the tree. I give (and retain) this saying for future observation.

Canterton is in the parish of Minstead. At the

junction of King's Garn Gutter and Coalmere brook, there are curious earthworks adjoining, that appear to mark the site of a mediaeval mill of which there is record.

Crock Hill has recently been replanted with silver fir beneath a canopy of oak planted in 1850.

Eyeworth is an old beech wood with holly undergrowth. A specially fine tree that stands on the verge of Eyeworth and Studley is known as the "Queen beech"; its trunk rises about 20 feet from the ground without a fork, and measures 16 feet 10 inches in girth, 4 feet from the ground.

There was a powder factory on the Southampton side of the wood.

"Ivare," is the Domesday version of his place-name. It is interesting to note that locally—Eyeworth, of the Ordnance Survey—is still locally pronounced *Iver*—and used to be 150 years ago—cf. "Ivory Lodge," a site here recorded in "Warner's Collections for a History of Hampshire." *Ivers* as a place-suffix occurs along the Ebble and Nadder valleys; and marks what is called in Petersfield district—"a hanger," i.e., a wood on a steep hill. Perhaps connected with "oves"—eaves—the edges of a declivity.

Godshill Wood. Planted in 1810. Oak and Scots pine with holly undergrowth—much of which has been cut during the war, leaving spacious fern-grown vistas that now add to the beauty of the wood. At the Western end of the wood there is an out-lying bluff, overlooking the Avon, called "Castle Hill," which is fortified by earthworks that appear to belong to the Norman period. A mile distant from Godshill wood, to the South, on the edge of a wooded scarp that falls abruptly down to the Avon, stands Frankenbury—the largest British camp of defence in the Forest district.

The Northern end of Godshill wood is bounded by a grassy, deep-rutted track, running West to East, that separates it from Densome, or Densham Wood. There is local tradition that this was the old way along which Cranborne Chase wheat was carried to Southampton; and the Court Rolls of the Hundred of Ford, (1834), support such tradition of an ancient way in the following presentment—"We present that every person going through Densham Wood except by ancient path shall forfeit for every offence five shillings."

Hasley. Planted in 1846. Scots pine, larch, oak and sweet chestnut. On the Northern side of the Inclosure the sandy soil is stained orange by iron, and limonite iron-stone occurs—which may account for the old diggings on the North-Eastern side.

Holly Hatch. Planted in 1808. Oak and Scots pine. The word "Hatch" indicates that a hatch gate stood here.

Islands Thorns. Planted in 1850. Oak, larch and Scots pine.

King's Garn. Planted in 1860.

Latchmore is the most spacious bottom in this area. It is covered with heather, furze-brakes, and thickets of holly and thorn, through which a brook flows at will down Latchmore bottom—now rippling over flats of flood-washed gravel—now oozing through marshes of sedge, sweet-gale and bog-bean—now cutting its channel in fantastic loops through grassy lawns. Scattered ponies and cattle feed over this expanse, or congregate in times of summer heat around the shallow pool known as Latchmore "shade". Time's changes have

Latchmore shade.

FROM SUMNER'S *A Guide to the New Forest*

left Latchmore untouched, and it is typical of the prospect that the open Forest must have presented for centuries past.

A rough track leads up the bottom from Ogdens to Fritham.

The place-name *Latchmore* also occurs at the Northern extremity of Setley plain. (*Laece, Lache, Latch,* Old English, a stream through a bog.)

Linwood is a hamlet belonging to Ellingham parish.

Milkham. Planted in 1861. Scots pine—most of which were cut during the war. After the lapse of six years a few Scots pine and oak self-sown seedlings are growing up, but no birch.

Moyles Court

FROM HEYWOOD SUMNER'S *Book of Gorley*

Moyles Court stands beside Dockenswater on the verge of Rockford common and outside the Forest Boundary—but so near, that we may be allowed to overstep our limits in order to include this historic site. Moyles Court was first so called in 1392. *Moyles*, from the family of Meoles, or Meoles, who held this manor in the 14th century. *Court* probably from the Court Baron, incident to the manor, being held there. It is built of red brick, with hipped gables to its tiled roof, projecting eaves, and great chimney stacks. It may have been built in the reign of Charles II. The South wing and the stables retain the character of this period. There is a wood-cut of Moyles Court in the "Gentleman's Magazine" 1828, which shows a large wing, now pulled down, on the West of the existing building.

The execution of Dame Alicia Lisle is the historical tragedy connected with Moyles Court.

Near Moyles Court, on the South side of Dockenswater, stands the finest oak in the District. Wise, writing in 1860, states that its girth measured 18 feet

8½ inches—but he does not state at what height his measurement was taken. I measured this oak in 1902 at 4 feet from the ground, and recorded its girth as being 19 feet 8 inches and again in 1921 at the same height as being 20 feet 4 inches. Measurements of gnarled trees, standing on uneven ground, are liable to vary, but it seems that this oak has increased its girth since 1860. The longest lateral spread of branch is on the North-Western side, namely 55 feet from the trunk to the outermost twigs. Now, 1923, this old tree seems to be failing, judging from its extremities.

Ocknell. Planted in 1775. A beautiful wood of oak and beech with holly undergrowth, channelled by the head springs of Highland water. On the Northern side of the wood stands a clump of Scots pines which was probably then planted as an experiment to see if this "foreign" tree would thrive in New Forest soil. It seems to have completely died out in this part of England, but the remains of submerged forests found in making Southampton docks show that it was indigenous in prehistoric times.

Ocknell Pond is on the summit of the plain, 360 feet above the sea on the North-West side of the wood. It is a natural "mist" pond, solely dependent for its supply on rainfall and mist. In times of drought it rarely gives out, but in 1911, it was quite dry—for the first time in fifty years—and yet again in 1921. Its circuit is 317 paces, its greatest depth about 2 feet, and it is encircled by grassy lawns where ponies and cattle come to "shade" in summer when the woods and valleys are unbearably hot. A clay and "callous" (gravel-stone indurated with iron) floor retains the surface water, and when the wind blows across the exposed plain the lapping waves crumble the surrounding banks of sandy clay; their erosion suggests the gradual making of Ocknell Pond as we now see it. Janesmoor Pond, Longcross Pond near by, and Hatchet Pond on Beaulieu heath appear to have been made by similar action.

Picked Post is about 2 miles from Ringwood on the highroad to Cadnam, and marks the summit of one of the gravel bluffs that flank the Forest side of the Avon valley. The view from here is very extensive. This place is now usually spelt "Picket," but "Picked" was the spelling in the Ordnance Map of 1817, and in all maps previous to that date. The name probably referred to the pointed angle of the roads that join here. *Picked* is a Wessex word in present use, meaning *pointed*. "*Picked piece*", and "*Picked rough*," constantly occur as names for triangular fields.

Pinnick and Redshoot are fine old woods of oaks, thorn and holly, with scattered crab-apple trees, growing on the stiff clay hill-sides that flank Greenford Bottom. Linford brook flows through this bottom, and access to Pinnick is generally more or less waterlogged. Pinnick is crowded with self-sown seedling trees which form continuous thickets overshadowed here and there by old oaks of contorted growth. Redshoot is less crowded, the old trees are of finer growth, and they stand amid glades of bracken that slope down to Greenford Bottom.

A Forest track leads along the Redshoot ridge from Broomy to Highwood and Linford. *Red*, here, perhaps marks the colour of the clay soil. *Shoot*, from French *shute*, a steep, inclined plane, is a common Forest place-name suffix for a hill-side track—e.g. *Whiteshoot*, which occurs frequently, the prefix marks the colour of the top-spit gravel stones, bleached by the acids from the heath roots.

Roe Wood. Planted in 1811. Oak with occasional sweet chestnut and Scots pine, and thorn undergrowth. The chestnuts have grown much better than the oaks. Castlepiece, Roe, is a circular pre-Roman camp of defence, much concealed by trees. A Forest track leads through the wood from Linwood to the Ringwood and Cadnam highroad.

Rufus' Stone stands in the Canterton Valley below Stony Cross, surrounded by beautiful old beech woods; it marks the place where, according to tradition, William Rufus was killed, 1100 A.D. Chroniclers are either silent, or give different versions as to how it happened, but agree in regarding his violent end as a just punishment for evil-doing.

Sloden Hill

FROM HEYWOOD SUMNER'S *Book of Gorley*

Sloden is an old wood of great variety, oak, ash, yew, whitebeam, crab-apple, holly and thorn; with "ivy drums" clasping old trunks, and branching aloft to find a place in the sun for their glossy foliage. Anses has been claimed as the most beautiful valley-wood of this area, now Sloden shall be claimed as the most beautifully wooded hill-side, both in respect of the lie of the land, and of the growth and contrast in foliage of the trees that crown the hill. Nowhere in the Forest do yews and whitebeams grow in such profusion.

Sloden Inclosure. Planted in 1864. Oak, ash and Scots pine, with a few well-grown Douglas and Silver firs. A Forest track leads along the ridge from Fritham to Ogdens.

Slufters. Planted in 1862. Scots pine—much of which has been cut during the war—with some well-grown Douglas firs near the high-road.

Stony Cross is a hamlet belonging to the parish of Minstead, consisting of "the Compton Arms" hotel, and a few detached houses near by. It stands on a plateau gravel ridge 369 feet above the sea, commanding spacious prospects on all sides. Stony Cross and Picked Post may claim to have the finest air, and the

finest views, of any inhabited sites in the Forest. The Cross, marks the intersection of the road from Ringwood to Romsey with the road from Lyndhurst to Downton. Stony, or Stoney? Both spellings have the sanction of local print, cf. Pony, or Poney? The latter, old-fashioned. There is no meaning at issue in such variant spellings, as there is in *Picket* and *Picked*.

Wood Green is a beautifully situated village at the extreme North-Western corner of the Forest. Here, for about a mile, the Avon flows as the Forest boundary, below the wooded bluff of Castle Hill before mentioned. It lies on gravel, sloping West, and faces a fine view across the Avon valley to the chalk of Cranborne Chase. Merry trees (black cherries), and orchards abound here—and the cottage gardens vie with those at Breamore as the gayest in the District.

The Middle Area

The main feature of this area is woodland. Old woods in all stages of maturity and decay. Inclosures of young trees. Thickets of undergrowth. Woods that seem to be interminable. Excepting heathland that stretches from Brockenhurst to Thorny Hill, to Burley, and thence on to Bratley plain, and excepting cultivated land around Lyndhurst, Minstead and Burley, the roads that traverse the Middle area, East, West, North and South, pass through continuous woods. Planted woods.

The pedestrian will explore here to the best advantage, either by seeking the old woods wherever lofty trees may be seen rising above young trees; or by following up the courses of Highland water, Bratley water, or Ober water, which will lead him by devious, lonely ways, through great woods to upland moors whence their sources issue. Every time of year has its own especial beauty. Winter reveals lichens that grow like grey fur on bare branches, mosses that clothe boles and limbs with vivid green, buds that show subtle difference of colour such as can only be seen in a smokeless district, and moorlands clad in sober vesture of dun brown. In spring the tender green of young leaves contrasts with the ruddy buds of backward beeches, the golden furze-brakes with the silver bloom of thorns and crab-apples, the rust-coloured catkins of sweet-gale with the withered bog-sedge. In summer the old woods are in heavy foliage, the thickets are wreathed with honeysuckle and crowded with bracken and foxgloves breast-high; the heather is in bloom, and the bogs are starred with cotton-grass and gilded with asphodel. So the year waxes, and then wanes; until woods, heaths, and bogs assume their final splendour of autumn colouring; but whatever the season the Forest vegetation bestows its fullest beauty of colour when it is wet. Of these seasons, summer is my last choice, because the Forest streams are then reduced to trickling shallows and stagnant pools and because a plague of flies then torments both man and beast. But at all times of year, the first thing needful for progress through the Forest is that the pilgrim should be well shod, for here he must always reckon with bogs and water-logged bottoms.

Ridley wood supplies evidence of the protective

method of Inclosure employed by the mediaeval tree-planter. This old wood is still surrounded by a wasted bank and ditch, on which, and outside which, fine self-sown trees now grow. We know that in 1571 a fence stood on this bank, because the regarders also then indicted the said tenant for "divers and many young oaks felled for stakes for the hedge." Protection by bank, ditch and "hedge," (fence); varied tree-planting; natural regeneration by the up-growth of self-sown seedling trees; and the chances of Time; have all helped to produce the old woods that we now seek and admire—but we cannot look forward to such ultimate beauty arising from Inclosures that protect pure woods of Scots pine.

The care and cultivation of woodlands appear to have been practised for centuries before Ridley "coppice" was planted – even before the date of Domesday (1085–6), for it records the measurements of woods, their capacity for yielding profit, their different kind of growth, and the number of swine which their pannage (fallen mast of oak and beech trees), would support. The prevalence of old beeches in the Forest represents survival of pannage purpose in tree-planting, while the comparative rarity of old oaks is due to constant demand for navy timber during past centuries.

In times past the Forest high-roads, running straight across heathlands and through woodlands, added beauty to the scene. The yellow road belonged to the soil—as the road-side gravel-pits testified, and when the sun was low these golden roads were barred with blue-purple shadows that gave mystery to the passage of the high-way. Now, such old fashioned roads are being superseded by granite, tarred tracks of dull slate colour, whereon black shadows lie, and gravel—as high-road metal—will soon be only a memory.

Deer may often be seen in the great woods of the Middle area.

Places of Interest

Aldridge Hill. Planted in 1775 and 1809. A re-inclosed wood of well-grown oaks which have been thinned, and are now surrounded by young plants of oak and occasional beech, sweet chestnut, and birch. Aldridge Hill and Rhinefield Sandy near by (also planted in 1775), are good examples of the cultivation of trees by natural regeneration.

Backley Inclosure. Planted in 1829, mostly sweet chestnut, the mast of which is sought after and gathered in the autumn. The sweet chestnut is supposed to have been introduced into Britain by the Romans. There is little planting of chestnuts done nowadays. Its timber after about sixty years growth is apt to become "shaky," but if cut young, it is as durable as oak for posts and piles, and its wood is almost all spine.

Berry Beeches; not pollarded; crown the ridge that leads from Burley moor to Backley Plain, and are specially fine on the Eastern slopes of the ridge; they are remarkable both for their beauty and for the curious examples of ingrowth shown in their stems and branches. Vipers are said to abound on this ridge. Referring to snakes—those that frequent the Western

side of the Forest, are grass snakes, vipers, and the smooth snake (Coronella Austriaca). In order of frequency. The last named is rare and harmless, only found on the Western heaths of the New Forest, and on the heaths between Avon and Stour valleys. There is great variety in the colour of vipers in the Forest—from silvery grey with black zigzag markings, to buff, to reddish, with brown markings.

Brockenhurst (area). Balmer Lawn, Setley Plain, Hincheslea, Rhinefield and Queen's Bower are place-names that may recall the varied scenery to be found near Brockenhurst. The old oaks along the course of the stream in Queen's Bower are specially characteristic of the growth of these trees in the Forest.

Burley Lodge stands in the midst of the great woods, near the road from Burley to Lyndhurst. It was occupied by the Dukes of Bolton from about 1700 to 1809. The Old Lodge has been pulled down. There used to be a group of old oaks standing in the grounds adjoining that were known as the Twelve Apostles, of which few now remain.

Burley Rock is the name given to stone which has been dug on Rock Hill (near Markway Hill), and on the ridge near Bisterne Close Farm. It is a conglomerate of gravel-stones and sand indurated with iron, a durable, impervious, intractable material of dull rust colour, used nowadays for foundations, rough walling, and rockeries.

Bushy Bratley is a famous old wood standing above Bratley water, to the East of the Ringwood and Cadnam highroad. These venerable beeches are now in a stage of gradual decay. Gaps and clearances occur in the wood. Here, the ruin of an up-rooted tree, there, piles of cord-wood and crowds of foxgloves, telling of latter-day windfalls, and of "sign (assigned) wood" awaiting clearance. And we cannot console ourselves with good hope for the future. There is not much chance for natural regeneration in Bushy Bratley, because there are few thickets here to protect young seedling trees from the destructive nibbling of Forest cattle and ponies.

The distant view of Bushy Bratley from Mogshade Hill, on the way from Lyndhurst to Ringwood, is a vision that haunts one's mind's eye. The old trees rising eminent in massed verdure —the irregular verge of self-sown beeches, making shadowy bays and sunlit promontories of foliage —the surrounding stretches of fern brake and heather—and Bratley water below, meandering through thickets.

Emery Down is a residential district, half a mile distant from Lyndhurst to the North West. The sudden rise and fall of the land here, and the medley of buildings, gardens, orchards and forest give special charm to the village. "St. James' Hill" (place-name in 6 inch ordnance survey map) was named "Gravel Hill" in 1789 according to Richardson King and Driver's map. Old gravel-diggings on the top surface of the hill testify to the name. This abrupt mount, 300 feet above the sea, is a curious example of an outlying, isolated hill of which the gravel-capping has resisted sub-aerial denudation.

Highland Water Inclosure. Planted 1869. Scots

pine, cut down during the war, thereby improving the wide prospect from Mogshade Hill. The folds of the hill-side descending to Highland water, make a fine, broken foreground to woods below, with the grove of old trees at Puckpits marking the summit of the hill opposite, while Southward the view extends across Southampton Water, and its adjacent lowlands to the distant South downs and Spithead. Mogshade Hill used to be covered with beautiful thickets of old holly trees, now alas, badly burnt by a recent (1918) fire, which is remembered as a war-time careless mishap, to the discredit of over-seas woodmen.

Holmsley Inclosure. Planted in 1811. Oak and Scots pine. Holmsley bog and the Avon water valley are natural preserves for the botanist. Thorny Hill Holms near-by, are dense groves of hollies that fringe the Forest Boundary at Thorny Hill. "Devil's Den" (*Devill's Den*). Perambulation of 1681. *Develdon*. Perambulation of 1301) is now unknown as a place-name, but a track through the Holms is known as "Devils Walk."

Knightwood Oak stands near the Lyndhurst and Bournemouth high-road, beside Knightwood Inclosure (planted 1867 cut down during the war). It is a fine pollard in vigorous old age, and is protected by an encircling spiked-pale fence. J.R. Wise, in 1862, records its girth as being 17 feet 4 inches. W.F. Rawnsely, in 1906, "nearly 19 feet at 4 feet from the ground." The Rev. C. Darling, in 1921, 21 feet 6 inches, at the same height.

Malwood Castle is the site of a small pre-Roman camp of defence. There is no evidence in support of the tradition that a Norman Castle once stood here. Castle place-names connected with ancient earthworks occur on this side of the Forest. For example—Castle Hill Burley, and Castle Piece Roe Wood (pre-Roman camps of defence). Lucas' Castle (a hill above Highland water near Ocknell). Studley Castle (a small pastoral earth-work near Bramshaw Telegraph). Thompson's Castle (a barrow on Latchmore). Castle Hill Godshill wood is the only Castle place-name that probably marks a Norman site.

There is, however, evidence, dating from 1358, that a Forest Lodge stood here, and that it was called *Hardebourgh, Herbarwe*, or *Harebergh*. Hardus Green appears to be a survival of this forgotten place-name.

Mark Ash is an old wood, mostly consisting of ancient pollard and free-grown beeches in every stage of prime growth, past prime, and gradual decay (the last predominating) with an undergrowth of holly and thorn. Some of these old beeches have remarkable girth. The 'Queen Beech'—a pollard of beautiful growth—is 18 feet 1 inch at 4 feet from the ground, and near by stands a beech that divided into six vertical stems at 10 feet from the ground, which shoot up 30 feet before they branch. This tree measures 20 feet 11 inches. Marked boundary-tree place-names frequently denote the limits of primitive West-Saxon settlements—e.g., Cut-thorn—Marke oak—Bound oak, etc. Possibly the name Mark Ash is older than the afforestation of William I. in 1079 A.D. Anyhow, here and now, the marked boundary ash tree will be looked

FROM SUMNER'S *A Guide to the New Forest*

for in vain.

New Park, on the left of the highroad from Brockenhurst to Lyndhurst, is Crown property; its name is in distinction to the Old Park of Lyndhurst—now disparked. Old Park dates from 1291. New Park is first mentioned in 1484. It was added to by Charles II. in 1670 "for the preservation of our red deer, newly come out of France." (It is now the venue for the New Forest show).

Oakley. Planted in 1853. Oak and Scots pine. There is an avenue of fine Douglas firs in this Inclosure which shows how much their growth exceeds that of the other trees, all having been planted at the same time.

Ridley Wood stands on the South-Eastern side of the highroad from Ringwood to Cadnam— below Picked Post. This fine old wood of pollard beeches has already been referred to, and we know its approximate age from written records. The Western side of this wood is approached by a hollow way, and there is authentic hearsay tradition that this concealed hollow was used as a meeting-place by smugglers and their local customers. "Smugglers' Lane", crossing the heath from Crow, marks this line of access from the Avon valley.

Setley Plain is a gravelling expanse of heather and furze-brakes by the side of the highroad from Brockenhurst to Lymington. Three well-preserved disc barrows stand on the plain (the only examples of this type within the Forest Boundary, but there is a small disc barrow on Ibsley common just outside the Boundary). The outer earthen circles of two of these barrows intersect each other.

Vinney Ridge is crossed by the highroad from Lyndhurst to Christchurch, and is crowned with old beeches whose tree-tops used to sway beneath nesting herons, but now this heronry is deserted. In 1861 Wise says there were fifty nests here, and also a few at Bolderwood.

The Southern Area

This area is bounded on the Southern side by a low-lying stretch of cultivated sea-board beside the Solent. The landward slant of "bustle-headed" trees tells of prevailing sea winds, the stream estuaries tell of neighbouring tides, and the disused salterns, in marshy flats of a sea-water industry. Here the wayfarer arrives at a natural boundary of the Forest— the Solent.

Inland, from Sway Common to Butts Ash, gravel-capped plains rise about 100 feet above the sea, through which streams have cut their courses towards the Solent. The valleys made by these streams are clayey and well-wooded, while the gravel plains are mostly bare heath-land, overgrown in places with self-sown Scots pine. Farther inland lies boggy ground extending from Hincheslea—Brockenhurst—Beaulieu Road—to Ashurst, much of which is below the 50 foot line. This low-lying area gradually rises towards the

North, across the woods of Ramnor, Park Hill, Denny, and Matley Ridge, towards Lyndhurst which stands behind them, on higher ground, 170 feet above the sea.

Places of Interest

Balmer Lawn is a spacious grazing ground near Brockenurst, surrounded by an amphitheatre of woodland that rises gradually towards the North and North-East.

Beaulieu Abbey was founded by King John in 1205 A.D., and here he placed thirty Cistercian monks. He endowed the Abbey with lands, exempted it from the numerous tolls and taxes of feudal times, gave it privileges and immunities, and surrounded it with a disafforested tract of land. Forty years elapsed from the date of its foundation to that of its completion and dedication. The ceremony took place about 1246, Henry III. and his Queen being present with a great retinue. The Abbey church was larger than any belonging to the Cistercian order in England, being 336 feet in length and 186 feet across the transepts. "About this period (1327 A.D.) Pope Innocent received the convent of Beaulieu under the protection of the apostolical see; and by his bull, conferred on its members several great ecclesiastical privileges. Such as that of Sanctuary; an exemption from the payment of tithes; from the attendance on episcopal synods, or courts, together with a power of electing their abbot, and regulating the affairs of their convent, without the interference of the dioscesan." (Warner, "Topographical Remarks"). Thus the Beaulieu Cistercians obtained a hazardous immunity from both secular and

Sloden Hill — from Splash bridge.

FROM SUMNER'S *A Guide to the New Forest*

diocesan local authority—for which they ultimately paid the full penalty.

Such hazardous immunity lasted for about 200 years. Then the price was paid. Beaulieu Abbey was dissolved in 1538 A.D. Most of its buildings were pulled down, but the outer and inner gate-houses still remain, with portions of the cloisters, and of the chapter house. The Refectory also stands, and is now used as the parish church. The Abbey precincts were surrounded by a wall, parts of which still remain, and wasted earthworks indicate the site of fish stews and of ducts for water supply. The field-name of *Vineyards* confirms documentary evidence as to the monks having made their own wine here; the Cistercians were farmers as well as monks, of which we are further reminded by the remains of a noble stone barn at St. Leonards Grange (216 feet long by 61 feet wide, standing near a 13th century chapel), by the place-name *Bergerie*, sheep farm, and *Beufre*, ox farm, and by the evidence of their constant encroachments on the Forest.

Beaulieu Heath, and **Beaulieu Hill-Top Heath**. The wayfarer's estimate of these heaths will probably vary according to the weather that he meets with. If he chances to cross them on a wet day, when low clouds blot out the distance, and rain drifts across the plains, he will remember them as tracts of desolation. But if he chances on a fine day, when warm air quivers above the heath, and when distant views are clear, he will remember them as spacious, sunny moorlands fringed with woods, within sight of the gleaming Solent, of its shipping, and of the bare downs that dominate "the Island." Nowhere in the Forest are so many barrows, or (in local parlance) "butts" to be seen as here. Fifty-four stand on the plains of these two heaths. They suggest considerable Bronze Age occupation at a period when the land stood higher than it does now, and when the Solent may have been a fertile valley.

Beaulieu Rails. This place-name marks a row of squatters' cottages on the Southern side of Beaulieu heath. All round the Forest Boundaries, and those of the commons adjoining, such small holdings represent the original choice and occupation of bygone squatters.

Bishop's Ditch is the name given to a curiously shaped area of boggy ground, containing about 500 acres surrounded by a rambling bank between two ditches. It is situated near Denny and Woodfidley, and is crossed by the Southern Railway, from which there is a good view of the site. Forest pasturage and sport appear to have been sought by John de Pontoise, or Pontisarra, Bishop of Winchester, when he obtained the grant of Bishop's Ditch from Edward I. 1284 A.D. The area thus enclosed is now an open, low-lying, boggy waste, a favourite feeding ground of Forest ponies, intersected by runnels and shallow pools which gradually unite their flow at Pig Bush Passage and become a little brook which joins the Beaulieu river. It seems probable that the present boggy condition of this area has increased since it was first enclosed. The damming of the flow of Beaulieu river in later times may have caused such change. Bishop's Ditch and Matley

bog—a mile distant—are examples of bogs formed under different conditions, the former lying in wide, open, converging bottoms amid expanses of heather; the latter in a narrow bottom overgrown with alders.

There is a tradition relating to this neglected inclosure, namely, that in ancient times one of the Prelates of Winchester was given as much of the Forest as he could crawl round, and that Bishop's Ditch was the result. The legend —which occurs elsewhere—seems to express country humour, attributing a fantastic origin to an unusual earthwork of which nothing was known.

Buttsash is a place-name that marks a site on Beaulieu Hill-top Heath beside a barrow, and also beside an old road from Applemore, near Dibden, which has claims for consideration as a Roman road to Lepe. cf. the "streets" at Buttsash and Langley in New Forest Perambulations.

Denny is one of the few old beech woods that can be seen from the Southern Railway in its twisting course through the Forest, and it is the finest in this area. Like Matley its beauty is enhanced by a fringe of self-sown birch trees that surround the irregular verge of this wood, and that make lovely contrast at all times of year with the background of stately, spreading beech-groves on Denny Hill. Denny Lodge is occupied by the head keeper of the Forest.

Exbury is a little village situated on the Eastern side of the mouth of the Beaulieu River. There was a chapel of St. Catherine here (pulled down in 1827), which was served by the Cistercians of Beaulieu Abbey.

Hatchet Pond is a large, irregular, crescent-shaped sheet of water at the Eastern extremity of Beaulieu Heath. In Richardson King and Driver's map above mentioned, scattered circles are figures on this site, and marked "Old Marl pits." The site is very exposed and the soil crumbling. Probably this pond, as we now see it, was made by wind-driven water lapping and wasting away the edges of these separate marl pits, till, gradually, they were joined up and became one pond. The name is derived from the hatch gate near by, separating the heath from the cultivated land. The same name in a similar situation occurs at Hatchet Green, Hale, on the Northern side of Forest. (cf. also Holly Hatch, beneath Sloden; *Hatch*, gate, is a common suffix in the neighbourhood of ancient forests).

Matley is a beautiful old wood of oak, thorn, and holly, with a fringe of self-sown birch trees growing around its outskirts, and leading down to the dense thickets of alders that mark the line of Matley bog. The fine, matted rootlets of alders, create and increase boggy ground. Walk warily in forest bottoms where alders grow.

Park Hill is on the site of the "Old Park of Lyndhurst," of which the earliest record dates back to 1291 A.D. In 1300 its acreage and value were thus estimated: "The park of Lyndhurst contains in covert 200 acres, the pannage thereof is worth yearly when the acorn comes 34s. 3d. Item, the honey in the same park is worth yearly 2s. Item, the herbage can sustain 40 beasts and 20 foals and that pasture is worth 23s.

Place Names Are Important Clues to History

Arthur T. Lloyd read history at Reading University just before the second world war. His mentor was the renowned medievalist, Professor Sir Frank Stanton. After taking his degree, Lloyd served six years in the Army before becoming senior history master at Ashley county secondary school (converted to Arnewood Comprehensive in 1970). He held this post for almost 30 years, using his summer holidays and other spare time to produce numerous articles and publications and to undertake research in a variety of historical fields. In the 1950s he discovered and later translated 300 medieval deeds at Winchester College related to Milton.

One never to keep his acquired knowledge to himself, Arthur Lloyd's community service is legendary. He founded the Milton local history group; is a past president of the Bournemouth, Christchurch and Poole branch of the Historical Association; is chairman of the Lymington and District Historical Society; a past chairman of the Wessex Numismatic Society, and has lectured for more than three decades to WEA (Workers' Education Association) and adult education classes.

The study of place names has long been a particular interest of Arthur Lloyd. He has searched through over 900 charters, many held by the British Library, for the earliest references to place names in and around the southern part of the New Forest. His "Place Names and Personalities," reproduced below, is taken from *Explore the New Forest*, published by the Forestry Commission.

Place Names and Personalities

To an historian the names on a map summon up the past and supply vital clues to events which might otherwise be lost. They are living signposts, but caution is needed, as frequently the obvious meaning is not the correct one.

The oldest place names in this area are those of the waterways that bound the Forest, namely the Avon (Celtic word for "river") and Solent (origin uncertain). Flowing through the Forest is the Lymington river; the prefix means "elm".

Iron Age hill forts were usually called in Saxon times "bury". South west Hampshire has several such as Burley, Tatchbury and Exbury. The name "Rings" at Buckland also indicates such a fort. But in the case of Holbury the suffix may refer to a Roman building, and the prefix show its ruined state (in holes). "Drakenhorde" in Rockbourne probably points to the discovery of a Roman treasure; it is close to the fine villa found in 1942. Similarly, Hordle, south of the Forest, means "treasure hill".

One reference in Domesday shows that as late as William I's reign people remembered the celtic name "Andret" for this stretch of woodland along the south east coast. On the death in

---

The Hidden Beauties of Heywood Sumner...

Continued from previous page

4d.'' The boundary of this old park is still traceable by a wasted bank and ditch. It appears to have been disparked in the 16th century.

An old salt-way from Lymington to Southampton crossed this site. The salterns along the shores of the Solent were worked with profit until the beginning of the 19th century.

Sowley Pond in mediaeval times was variously called *Colgrimesmore, Frieswater*, or *South legh*. Fish from South legh pond replenished the monastic fish stews at Beaulieu.

In later times iron works were established at Sowley Pond, the blast furnaces were supplied with fuel from the Forest, and with iron-stone from Hengisbury Head and the Hordle cliffs—''on the Southern shores of the county, particularly the coast of Beauley manor, iron-stone was formerly gathered in some quantity: this, it seems, was generally rolled up by the surf; and such was the eagerness at those times for collecting this mineral, that even in wheat harvest the fields became abandoned, and the shores were thronged with people, who gathered and conveyed it to the iron works at Sowley.'' (Vancouver's ''General view of Agriculture

in Hampshire,'' 1810 —at which date the smelting works were still being carried on here). ''There will be rain when Sowley hammer is heard,'' was a local proverbial saying that preserved the memory of these iron works.

Owing to its low-lying situation, and to its wooded surroundings, this large sheet of water is hidden, and is nowhere seen as a feature of the local prospect. Tall reeds invade its shallows, fringed landward by birch trees in beautiful contrast with the surrounding Scots pine woods that cast dark reflections in the still water broken here and there by scuttling wild-fowl.

Woodfidley is an old wood of free-grown beeches standing on a knoll to the West of Bishop's Ditch. They rise as landmarks above the tops of the surrounding Scots pine and oaks which were planted 1860–66. The girth of the finest beech, in full prime, on the top of the hill, measures 15 feet 4 inches at 4 feet from the ground; of another, past prime, on the Northern slope of the hill, 15 feet 8 inches. There is a rough track leading from here to Beaulieu Road station.

''Woodfidley rain'' is the local name on the Northern side of the Forest for persistent rain from the South-East.

Place Names and Personalities...

Continued from previous page

1100 of William Rufus a chronicler wrote that the old name for the New Forest was "Ytene". Philologists have known for eighty years that this means "(land) of the Jutes", proving Bede's assertion about 730 that the Jutes had settled in southern Hampshire as well as the Isle of Wight and Kent.

The Forest has interesting links with the Saxon Royal House, for the Chronicler stated that Cerdic landed in 495 at "Cerdicesora", which might be Ower, Calshot. Cerdic's battle in 508 against the Britons led by Natanleod may have taken place at Nateley; if so, the name is derived from that of the chief. These are surmises, but with Charford we have a name that is definitely derived from Cerdic's battle in 519 at "Cerdicesford".

Eling is the next oldest name of Saxon origin in this area, meaning "Edla's followers". Ellingham, far to the west, means "homestead of Eling men". Keeping, in the Beaulieu area, may be a Jutish type of -ing name. Canterton near Brook, "farm of men from Kent," shows a link with the earlier Jutish settlements there.

South-west Hampshire may have been the last English area to retain its Germanic heathenism. Here two heathen Jutish princes fled in 680 from the Island. Nearby, in the bounds of Millbrook, Thunor was worshipped—the god who gave his name to Thursday. On the Forest's western bounds are Godshill and Devilsden the latter being named in 1300.

Place names prove the area was well-wooded in early times. Six incorporate the word "wood", besides another five on the Forest edge like Arne- ("Eagle"), Ring- ("edge") and Wootton ("farm in the wood"). Lyndhurst ("lime tree wooded hill"), Brockenhurst ("broken woodland"), and Bramshaw ("bramble copse") tell

the same story. So do the 36 examples in the Forest and 25 nearby of the ending -ley, meaning "wood" or "clearing". Oakley, Bartley ("birch") and Ashley specify the tree species; others give each owner's name, as Sopley and Woodfidley: the latter's owner was probably a lady, Wulfgyth. Apple and Alder also appear as prefixes, as does Maple in the lost Domesday name "Mapleham".

The Danes, of course, made little impact. Only "Colgrimesmore" on the Beaulieu bounds in John's reign is definitely Danish, whereas the name Dane Stream arising near Wootton is derived from the Saxon "denu" (valley). A few Norman names survive, especially in the area of Beaulieu, itself of course French, from the Latin "Bellus locus regis", where kings had owned a hunting lodge before the Abbey was founded. On Abbey lands are Beufre and Bergerie (beef and sheep farms). The word "Purlieu" is used, associated with Dibden and Ogden, and close to the Forest edge are Hinton Admiral, reminding us of the Albamarlia family, and Tiptoe, the name a family brought with them from their Norman village.

Of course, the name New Forest derives from William I's afforestation. Domesday named 45 manors reduced to little value once the King's hunting took precedence. Of these identified only recently, the most important historically is "Thorougham", wrongly linked with Fritham (homestead in woodland) since the eighteenth century. It is definitely the area now Park Farm, on the Beaulieu Estate. its significance comes from it being the site identified earlier than any other with the death of Rufus.

When William I created the Forest his officials and local people had to know its bounds. Named tumuli, for example, Lugden's

Barrow and Knave's Ash on West boundary, were used; more interesting is "Rodedic" on the bounds, for this was a meeting place for the local Hundred. Within the Forest is Bishop's Dyke, which is said to demarcate an area round which the Bishop of Winchester crawled in one day to secure land for his church. Queen's Bower must be the medieval hunting lodge called "Queenboure" (named after Eleanor, wife of Edward I).

At the end of the Middle Ages, both the widow of Warwick the Kingmaker and Perkin Warbeck claimed sanctuary at Beaulieu, but soon all such monastic property fell into lay hands. The Forest saw many armed horsemen again in the Civil War, but it must be remembered that Marryat's children's story is all fiction.

It was Charles II who enclosed New Park near Brockenhurst, and it was his brother's judge (Jeffreys) who dealt so harshly with Dame Alice Lisle of Moyles Court, after Monmouth failed to reach Lymington and escape by boat.

Bolton's bench commemorates a member of that Ducal family which held the office of Master Keeper of Burley Bailiwick throughout the eighteenth century.

In Boldre churchyard lies asleep the Reverend William Gilpin, lover of the Forest Scene; the historian John Wise is buried in the new cemetary at Lyndhurst, the grave of Sir Arthur Conan Doyle is at Minstead, Brusher Mills the snake catcher is buried in Brockenhurst churchyard, and in the family vault at Lyndhurst parish church lies Alice Hargreaves, who as a little girl was given immortality as Lewis Carroll's Alice.

Where the Forest begins to slope towards the sea, Peterson's Sway Tower built in 1884 stands as a curious memorial to one man's faith in reinforced concrete as a material for building.

13
Fun in the Forest

WHEN FOREST VILLAGES HAD MAYPOLE DANCES
Virtually every child in the village of Burley attended the colourful fete depicted above on "May Day" in 1852.

A Sylvan Setting for A 1852 Maypole Dance

That most English of customs, the Maypole dance, caused the editors of the *Illustrated London News* in 1852 to seek a site where the event could be portrayed in a picturesque rural setting. They settled upon the New Forest and, in particular, the village of Burley. Here, on Shappen Bottom, the artist captured the flavour of the traditional dance as the villagers followed the movements of their offspring. Below is the text of the article that accompanied the sketch, as it appeared in the *ILS* of May 8th.

The little village of Burley, in the New Forest, Hampshire, was the scene of a very interesting festivity on Saturday last, the 1st of May; and whilst we reflected on the pretty scene which there surrounded us, we rejoiced that our pages might still further extend this pleasure by Illustration, and be perhaps the means of stimula-ting some of the richer inhabitants of such localities, in future years, to adopt a somewhat similar celeb-ration of May-day; and show how trifling expense, trouble, and good management may insure much happiness to a class who enjoy but little of the sweets of this life.

Burley is delightfully situated in one of the loveliest parts of the New Forest, the prettiest spot in which was selected for the day's pleasure and amusement to the children belonging to the church and chapel schools. And here we would express our gratification at finding the promoters of the *fête* permitted no sectarian views of their own to induce their favour-ing one class of children above another.

This lovely spot is known to the foresters as Shappen-bottom. It is a long-extended lawn, the smooth grass of which appeared more luxuriant in contrast with the heath and furze, the bright and golden blossom of which added not a little to the enchantment of the scene; bounded by gently rising eminences, and shaded here

Maypole Dance...

Continued from previous page
and there by beeches varied by the darker hue of holly, which were growing in pretty knolls about the hills. A Maypole was erected in the centre of the lawn, tastefully decorated with green and garlands; and at a little distance was a tent, wherein cake, buns, oranges, gingerbread, &c. were most liberally distributed.

At three o'clock, the children, numbering 140, came upon the lawn, preceded by an excellent brass band, and accompanied by W. Clement D. Esdaile, Esq., of Burley Park; and Mrs. Laurence Hill, of Burley Lawn; the originators of the *fête*.

The May Queen, chosen by lot from the three best girls of each school, walked under a muslin canopy tastefully decorated, and surmounted by a floral crown, supported by her four maids of honour.

Many visitors from Ringwood, the neighbouring town, and Burley, with the parents of the children, conduced to make a large assemblage. A dance round the Maypole was commenced, whilst its outspreading ornaments of natural form and growth, in the shape of boughs and branches of evergreen, interspersed with the stag-horn, characteristic of the Forest, were hung around with sundry little presents to be afterwards distributed, that no child might go empty-handed from the gay scene.

The amusement was diversified by the approach of a 'Jack-in-the-Green,' who danced to the lively strain of two cornopeans.

After a plentiful supply of cake and tea, the children were addressed by the Rev. C. H. Maturin, vicar of Ringwood, and the Rev. Benjamin Maturin, the curate. They took the opportunity of imparting very excellent advice—in terms so simple, that the youngest child might understand; and in matter so important, that the oldest present might with

The greatest Prodigies this Kingdom ever produced!!!

TWO CELEBRATED

DWARFS,

Natives of Devonshire,

Of the Parish of Southleigh, between Honiton and Sidmouth.

JUST ARRIVED IN THIS TOWN,

MR. & MISS BATSTONE,

BROTHER AND SISTER,

THE SHORTEST

MAN & WOMAN,

Of English Production, (well proportioned,) that was ever exhibited in this Kingdom

Mr. BATSTONE is now 25 Years of Age, only 40 Inches high, of a Manly appearance, and weighs only 40 Pounds.

Miss BATSTONE is 19 Years of age, 36 Inches high and weighs only 35 Pounds.

Extraordinary as it may appear, Mr. and Miss BATSTONE have a Brother Six Feet in height! and three Sisters of the Stature of Women in general.

To all who have beheld those astonishing Prodigies of Human Nature, they have given the utmost Satisfaction; and are two of the most complete and surprising Little People ever exhibited in this Kingdom.

☞ *Open from Ten in the Morning until Half-past Nine at Night.*

Families waited on at their own Houses, in the Evening, at an Hour's Notice.

WHEATON, Printer, Binder, Stationer, &c. RINGWOOD.

FORESTERS' AMUSEMENT IN THE MIDDLE OF LAST CENTURY
Wheaton's, a well-known Ringwood printer, prepared this handbill for circulation in the New Forest and its adjacent area. Such attractions always caused great interest in market towns.

profit take it to himself.

Thanks were proposed to Mr. Esdaile, who though a resident at Burley Park of but six months, has already, by his active benevolence, endeared to himself all the inhabitants in the village. Rustic games followed, and not only kept the children, but their older participators, till the lengthened shades of evening warned them to depart. Before separating, however, the various presents were distributed, and we saw nicely-dressed dolls, bookmarks, housewifes' bags, with other gifts, car-

ried away by happy girls; from which we suspected what we have afterwards learned, that the fair hands of many ladies of the place had not been inactive in this labour of love. Ninepins, balls, bags of marbles, tops, etc., were distributed amongst the boys.

To the Queen of the May a nicely-bound Bible was presented by Mrs. Esdaile; in handling which the husband of that lady made a very suitable address, reminding one and all of the children assembled, that, however happy the day may have been to

Cricket in the Forest: Then and Now

In the August, 1880 issue of the *New Forest Magazine*, a proud reporter from Bramshaw relates how the local cricket team bested players representing the rest of the Forest. Clergymen headed the list of players for both teams, although neither led in runs. The reporter generously attributes part of Bramshaw's success to the bad weather which befell the New Forest team at crucial moments.

NEW FOREST

Rev. W.E. Coghlan, b Olliver	5
Mr. C. Duplessis c A. Jeffreys	14
Mr. Nunn, c Judd, b Davis	24
Mr. Sims, run out	1
Mr. Kail, lbw, b Judd	2
Mr. G. Ashby, b Judd	10
Mr. Purkiss, c A. Jeffreys, b Judd	0
Mr. E. Hammick, c A. Jeffreys	2
Mr. Strange, b Davis	0
Mr. Forman, b Judd	1
Mr. Nicholls, not out	0
Bye 1; Wide 1	2
	61

BRAMSHAW

Rev. W. Truell, c Forman, b Nicholls	6
Mr. Judd, b Nicholls	5
Mr. A.F. Jeffreys, c Forman, b Nunn	65
Mr. P. de Crespigny, run out	74
Mr. Olliver, c Kail, b Duplessis	9
Mr. F. Jeffreys, b Forman	5
Mr. Davis, b Strange	2
Mr. Hiscock, b Strange	0
Mr. F. Strange, c Duplessis, b Strange	0
Mr. Henbest, not out	17
Mr. Crutcher, b Coghlan	3
Byes 5; Leg Bye 1; Wides 5	11
	197

Maypole Dance...

Continued from previous page

them, such happiness, at the most, was but for a season; that true joy was to be found in the path of righteousness, and the book he then presented would direct the way to treasures that faded not, to the peace which the world cannot give, and to happiness which will endure forever.

The band, which had played with great spirit during the games, concluded the entertainment with the National Anthem. The weather was most propitious, the sun shining brightly. The children's holiday was made a general one, and the clean, neat, tidy appearance of the dwellers of the New Forest, contrasted strongly with the pale and care-worn countenances, etc., of the inn-dwellers of the crowded town to which we were about to return.

"Squogging:" An Old Sport

("Squogging" was a rustic sport practiced by many a New Forest youth (and their fathers, too) around the turn of the century. On occasion there was organized competition and New Year's Day was regarded as the ideal time for the sport.

Rose de Crespigny and Horace Hutchinson, in their study of the Forest and its customs (*The New Forest*, John Murray, 1895), describe how foresters went about "squogging.")

One thing the New Forester can do, against any man—he can throw a stone or a cricket ball. A great amusement of the foresters is to turn out in bands and go

We are glad to be able to record a signal success in cricket. In a match played at Lyndhurst, July 8th, against the New Forest, one of the best clubs in the county, we were victorious. The weather was unfortunately against our opponents, who had to field and bowl in the wet; this, of course, gave us an additional advantage and contributed considerably towards our victory. The full score follows:

TODAY'S CRICKET IN FOREST SETTINGS
Cricket is played throughout the New Forest, and rivalry between clubs is often fierce (see account below). Two especially delightful settings are those at Swan Green, near Lyndhurst (above) and Burley (below).

An Exciting Sports Day at Lyndhurst

Lord Londesborough

On Saturday last a series of athletic sports, promoted by Lord Londesborough and other residents of Lyndhurst, took place on the old race course adjacent to the village, and were in every respect most successfully carried out. With brilliant weather throughout the day—the sunshine at times with almost summer power, the concourse of some three or four thousand spectators assembled on the occasion, and the keenest interest was manifested in the sports. A reserved inclosure was provided, a number of carriages lined the course, and the following comprised the fashionable gathering of the neighbourhood patronising the day's pleasures: Lord Londesborough and party; Major Candy; the Hon. Gerald Lascelles; the Hon. Lascelles and Mrs. Lascelles; Mr. and Mrs. and the Misses Meyrick; Mr. and Mrs. Macfar and party; Mr. Bryan and party; Mr. Cumberbatch and party; etc.

Besides the inhabitants and tradesmen of Lyndhurst, who made a holiday for the day, there was a large attendance from the surrounding places, and many from Southampton were attracted by the fine weather, the amusements, and the privilege of spending several hours in a part of the Forest commanding in its higher parts healthful breezes and charming glimpes of distant scenery. The sports were admirably conducted by a committee ... all of whom, with Lord Londesborough for the countenance and assistance he gave to the undertaking, deserved congratulations upon the happy result of their combined efforts.

Volunteer Band

There was no lack of competition in the various events which were spiritedly contested. A feature of remark in connection with them was the success of Cubitt who, hailing from Kimberley in Norfolk, appears to be an all-round athlete of promising qualities for,

Probably the largest crowd ever to see an athletics meeting in the New Forest gathered on the old Lyndhurst race track on 18 April 1885 to see exploits of running, jumping and hurdling. There were also other spectacular events, including pony races, bicycle and tricycle handicap sprints, a donkey race, climbing a greased pole, and a zoological race pitting snakes, pigs, guinea fowls and other creatures against each other. (Roy Jackman of Lyndhurst discovered this account in the *Hampshire Independent* of 22 April 1885.)

successful in several of the races, etc., he displayed powers which are likely to bring him well to the front in feats of running and jumping in more pretentious gatherings than this, which was of course of a merely rural character. Mr. Bryan and Mr. Wilson acted as starters and the rest of the committee as judges. The proceedings were enlivened by the playing of the Lyndhurst Volunteer Band and supplementing the sports were plenty of amusements for the villagers to engage in: shooting galleries, roundabouts, peep shows, knock-'em-downs, etc. In the enforced absence of Mr. Superintendent White, Sgt. Russell was in charge of several of the County Police Force who assisted in keeping the course clear.

The following were the various events:

100 yards men's race: 1, Fletcher; 2, Cubitt; 3, Moore.

This was a splendid race, there being eight competitors, all being in a cluster of a few yards throughout, and Fletcher won by only a yard. Time: 11 sec.

Quarter-mile hurdling handicap: 1, Cubitt; 2, Kennett. Cubitt, a capital runner residing at Castle Malwood and who is the captain of the Lyndhurst Football Club, won with ease, coming in some 15 yards ahead of Kennett who had been leading until three quarters of the race had been accomplished.

Close Hurdle Race

Hurdle race: 1, Fletcher. The event was run in heats, the winners of the first being Fletcher and Barnes; the second, Palmer and Loader. Kennett and Holley and Miller also competed. There were 10 flights of hurdles, and the first contest was a rare good one, the difference between the three runners at the close being but a matter of inches.

Squogging: An Old Forest Sport...

Continued from previous page

"squogging" with a "squoyle". A "squog" is a squirrel and a "squoyle" is a handy little club of wood, like a policeman's truncheon, weighted with wood or lead. It us used as a missile, and is, therefore, rather a knobkerry than a truncheon. New Year's Day is the great date for these squirrel-slaying enterprises. They hunt the poor little beasts from tree to tree. Wherever one shows round a trunk or branch, whang goes a "squoyle" at him.

The foresters become great adepts at the throwing, and

numbers of 'squogs' are brought to bag. They are eaten in pies, or are baked, as the gypsies bake the hedgehogs, in moulds of clay, and their flesh is excellent eating. This "squogging" develops a wonderful power and accuracy of throwing in the forester, and when you impress him into service as substitute on the cricket field you will be surprised to find this creature who runs after the manner of the plantigrade, and uses his bat as if it were his fern-sickle, returning the ball from long-off like Briggs from coverpoint.

A Forest Pageant Two Generations Ago

(One of the most ambitious public spectacles ever arranged in the New Forest was staged in Brockenhurst Park on 1 and 2 June, 1921. Organized by the Brockenhurst Women's Institute, it was called "A New Forest Pageant" and through a succession of "episodes" the history of the Forest was paraded before the audiences. The pageant had roles for Brusher Mills, the snake catcher; the gypsies; returning soldiers; the Gullivers of smuggling fame; and the Purkess family. The programme of the pageant is held in the University of Southampton's Cope Collection. Reproduced from it is the scene below, re-living a "visit" of Queen Elizabeth I to the New Forest in 1589).

SCENE.—*Brockenhurst, 1589*
Enter Mr. Alban Knapton (Lord of the Manor) and a Crowd of Villagers, a Wicker Giantess (Madam Magog), a woman dressed as Britannia (Mistress Neptune), Mistress New Forest, Plantations, Tobacco (a little girl), Potato (a fat little boy), Justice (bearing scales), Freedom (bearing a glove), and Commerce (the latter leading a little black boy by the hand).
   Mr. Alban Knapton. Now then, good people! Haste and make way for our good old giantess! Do you not see that to celebrate the advent of our gracious Queen, our Gloriana, we have collected all the

A New Forest Pageant

Arranged by the Brockenhurst Women's Institute

Held in Brockenhurst Park

by kind permission of Lady Kathleen Hare

On June 1st & 2nd, 1921

Price One Shilling.

All the Scenes are laid in the New Forest, in the Neighbourhood of Brockenhurst.

PROGRAMME FOR NEW FOREST PAGEANT

Exciting Day...

Continued from previous page
Zoological race:—which was an interesting event. A snake, fowls, guinea fowls, rabbits, a pig and a fox-hound being placed in the handicap positions, somewhat after (an) order according to their estimated natural race progress —each with a driver. Eventually Mr. J. H. Palmer of the Crown Hotel was successful with his pig. Mr. G. Meyrick was second with his hound.
   Greasy pole: The leg of mutton was won by Mr. J. H. Palmer.

(Other events included pony races, 13 hands and under and 13.3 hands and under; 100 yards for boys under 13; 200 yards for boys under 13; bicycle and tricycle handicap; combined long and high jump—won by Cubitt; quarter-mile race, 1, Cubitt and 2, Fletcher; donkey race, mile race; 300 yard race for strangers, and another for local people; obstacle race for men, 1, G. Broomfield and 2, Fletcher; and

an obstacle race for boys.)
   The conclusion of the day's sports was about 6 o'clock when the prizes, consisting of cups and clocks, etc., were presented to the successful competitors by Mrs. Lascelles. Afterwards Mr. Bryan called for three cheers for this lady which were heartily given, and were likewise given to Lord and Lady Londesborough, Rev. W. E. Coghlan and others ere the proceedings terminated.

A Memorable Forest Pageant

Continued from previous page

female divinities of the classics? I am not so young as I was, and my learning is somewhat rusty; but I trust I can still present an allegory which shall be to her Majesty's taste—though she hath an excellent discrimination in these matters.

They all range themselves in order

Enter Queen Elizabeth and her page, and four ladies and four gentlemen of her Court. (Much cheering).

Mr. Alban Knapton (bowing). Madam, your very humble servant! Your poor subjects of Brockenhurst have prepared an Allegory in your honour, and beg that you will see fit to rest here, on your progress through the Forest, and will receive our humble and loyal devotion.

Queen Elizabeth. Good Mr. Knapton, we thank you and our good subjects of Brockenhurst. We have ever felt that our New Forest did give us hearty pleasure. Not that we, like our great forerunner, Diana, the chaste huntress, do enjoy the chase above all pleasures. For our tender heart forbids us to take delight in the death of beasts. But we love well to recreate ourselves in this pure air, to gaze upon these glorious scenes, and, more than all, to contemplate this noble timber, which doth give promise of such store of tall ships for our Navy, and for the settling of our plantations beyond the seas. Wherefore proceed, good people of Brockenhurst, with your Allegory.

Mistress Neptune. Since Master Francis Drake and his Argonauts have of late years "opened to your Highness the gates of the sea, and given you the keys of the world," we beg you to accept the sovereignty of our watery realm. *(Presents the Queen with a trident), The page receives all gifts.*

Madam Magog. And I do tender to your Majesty the loyal heart of Hampshire. *(Presents casket on cushion).*

Mistress New Forest. And I will crown you Queen of the Forest

(Places wreath of oak leaves on the Queen's head).

Plantations. My name is Princess Pocahontas, and I am come from far Virginia, to offer to your Majesty the very loyal devotion of your new subjects, the Red Skins. *(Hands the Queen a head of maize with its leaves).*

Tobacco, a little girl, and Potato, a little boy, come forward hand in hand.

Tobacco and Potato (together). And we, the newest comers to your court, bring with us gifts to soothe your people's erstwhile too lively imaginations, and to assuage the pangs of hunger. *(They hand her a gigantic model of a cigar, and a large potato in its skin).*

Justice. Mine be the nobler part! For I bear witness to your Grace's equal affection for all your subjects, high and low alike. *(Hands her the scales).*

Freedom. I do nevertheless, Madam, most shrewdly give you leave to keep your preference for this fair New Forest, and herewith offer you a mailéd glove to protect the hand of justice. *(Offers glove).*

Commerce. And I am full of promise of good gifts to come, what time your Majesty's old sea-dogs of the West shall have enabled me to exploit your late glorious victory over the Spaniard.

Mr. Alban Knapton. Come, children, dance, that her Majesty

may see how our Forest air doth inform our very limbs, and give them strength and grace. *(The children dance.)*

Queen Elizabeth. Thanks, thanks, good folk! We do assure ye that we shall not soon forget this Allegory—which you, according to your means, have made for our delight. Fain would we hear yet more. And yet our Royal business of state calls us hence. How say you, though, good Mr. Knapton, would not our subjects here deem it a favour, if we did present for them some slight description of those dances which are now performed at our Court? We would very willingly reward our loyal Brockenhurst folk for their good will. So now, my ladies, and you gentlemen, *(to the ladies and gentlemen of the Court)* a measure!! Music, strike up!

(The Ladies and Gentlemen dance).

Queen Elizabeth. Now, Mistress Barbara, let us hear one of your joyous songs.

SONG.

"Orpheus with his Lute."

Queen Elizabeth. We thank you. And now, alas! We must heartily bid you all farewell.

All. God keep your Majesty. *(Cheers).*

Exeunt the Queen and her ladies and gentlemen and page, followed by the Crowd, hurra-ing and tossing their caps in the air.

The New Forest Show: Past, Present and Future...

(From humble beginnings the "New Forest Show" has grown to become a two-day event attracting 77,000 people, with the prospect of one day developing into a three-day attraction drawing over 100,000 visitors.

Phillip Shanks, executive secretary of the show (now called the "New Forest and Hampshire County Show"), relates below some of the landmarks in the show's progress since its modest start near Cadnam in 1920.)

The New Forest agricultural and

Horticultural Association was formed during the latter part of 1919 and the first "Live Stock Show" took place at Bartley Cross, near Cadnam in the summer of 1920. The event showed a surplus of £14.9s.2d.

Soon renamed The New Forest Agricultural Society, it prospered throughout the twenties and thirties at a number of venues in the New Forest area: Bartley Cross until 1924, then Tile Barn Hill, Brockenhurst, Hinton Admiral, Totton and Northerwood Park, Lyndhurst until 1939. Throughout this period the Show retained its traditional date of the

Foxlease: Girl Guide Centre with A History

(Tens of thousands of Girl Guides and their leaders have known the joy of staying at Foxlease, the national training and conference centre located in the edge of Lyndhurst. Twice, in 1924 and 1930, Foxlease was the site of international conferences.

The story of Foxlease's evolution from a Tudor house in the 1600s to its present status is one filled with drama, luck and most of all—hard work by two generations of dedicated supporters of Guides. This remarkable story is told in a booklet, *Foxlease*, published by the Girl Guides Association, extracts of which are reproduced below.)

PRINCESS MARY HOUSE, FOXLEASE, LYNDHURST
The house, which dates back to Tudor times, was donated to the Girl Guides Association in 1922 by Mrs. Archbold Saunderson, an American.

Early History

The first house to be built on this site was a sixteenth century Tudor timber-framed house called Cox Leyes or Coxlease. Ley, lea or lease was a clearing, meadow or pasture; 'Cox' may have been a family name, or a short form of 'cocks', but there is no record of the origin or meaning of the name. This was a Forest-Keeper's Lodge with wide rooms, low ceilings and oak beams. Parts of the Tudor house can still be seen in the square hall, with a wide fireplace and chimney, stone floor and low ceiling; the oak-panelled study

Continued on next page

had a dramatic effect on the Show, attracting in 1987, a crowd approaching 70,000 and achieving a turnover exceeding £290,000 thus confirming the claim that the event is one of the most important in the Mid-Southern Counties.

Quality Events
As one might expect in the New Forest area, a major feature of the Show is the exceptionally high quality of the Equestrian classes. There is particular emphasis on the wheeled classes which in 1986 featured 68 turnouts in the Private Driving classes, nine in the Coaching class and 33 in the Light Trade class. The high prize money in the Show Jumping competitions attracts all the "names" and it has become necessary to restrict entries to invited riders only. Other features of particular quality are the Horticultural exhibits, the Rural Crafts marquees (now for invited exhibitors only), and the varied and spectacular Ring Programmes.

The considerable success of the Society's recent shows has prompted discussions about extending the length of the Show and almost certainly a three-day New Forest & Hampshire County Show is a very real probability within the near future.

The New Forest Show...

Continued from previous page
last Wednesday in July; the choice of Wednesday, the local "early closing day" was to encourage local participation.

Various Sites
The first Show after the war took place at Cuffnells Park, Lyndhurst in 1946 and remained at this venue until 1954. The title of The New Forest Agricultural Show Society was adopted in 1949. In 1955 the Show moved to its present home at New Park, Brockenhurst, and continued to prosper through the next two decades, building up to an attendance of 38,000 people in 1977. During this period the "New Forest Show" became the Society's annual Show title in 1962, the year the Society was honoured by its first Royal Patron, H.R.H. The Duke of Gloucester, K.G.

The highly successful 1977 Show prompted the Society's Council to extend the Show to two days in 1978, following which the Society's fortunes went from strength to strength. The first major permanent facilities were installed in 1979 and to-date in excess of £110,000 has been spent on services, roads and other equipment.

In 1985 the Society adopted the title of the "New Forest & Hampshire County Show." This

C.J. May Collection

GUIDERS AT FOXLEASE IN THE 1920s
Camping has always been a feature of Guide training at Foxlease.
Today there are 10 campsites scattered over the 65-acre site.

Foxlease Guide Centre...

Continued from previous page

next to the hall; and two little rooms under the eaves, with solid roof-beams, sloping ceilings and uneven floors.

The first written record of the house was in the reign of James I. In 1604 Coxlease was 'part of the demesne lands of the manor of Lyndhurst . . . in the tenure of William Brown, by grant of Charles, Earl of Devonshire.' After the Restoration of Charles II, in 1667, 'Mabel, wife of John Cole of Odiham, petitioned the King for a lease in reversion for her husband for the house and grounds called Coxlease as a reward for her attendance on the late King in his imprisonment in the Isle of Wight.' There is no evidence to the success, or otherwise, of the lady's request, but there is a tradition that King Charles II planted a tree on a little hill in the garden behind the house. This tree was a Scots Pine which grew to be a landmark known as the Sentinel Pine until 1944 when it had to be felled.

By 1770 the house was owned by Sir Phillip Jennings-Clarke, Bart., and now known as 'Foxlease'. There is no record of how or why the name was changed, but there is a theory that it was an error in the writing or copying of manuscripts. Sir Phil-

lips built Foxlease as we see it today, and the North front has remained unchanged, the well-proportioned white stucco frontage is a permanent memorial to Georgian good taste.

A Generous Gift

The Girl Guide Movement was first registered in 1910 and spread through Britain and abroad, so that by 1920 when the first International Conference was held, 15 countries were represented. Guiding in Britain needed a permanent centre, a Guide house where Camps, Conferences and Trainings could be held. Among the suitable houses on the market at this time was Foxlease; Mrs. Archbold Saunderson was still the owner, but was now living in the U.S.A. During 1921 an experimental Training week-end was held in the empty house, Guiders spread their sleeping bags or camp beds on the bare boards of the bedrooms and met in the downstairs rooms and in the old thatched barn. Some camps were held in the grounds that summer; with their tents and fires they were the pioneers for thousands of Guides and Rangers to come.

Early in January of the next year, Sir Robert and Lady Baden-

Powell visited Foxlease to judge for themselves whether the house would suit the Guides. They enjoyed the garden and grounds, noticed the ten bathrooms and the many bedrooms, the light, airy rooms downstairs—and there was even a dark blue wallpaper in the hall, covered with fleurs-de-lys, the Scout emblem. There was the roomy barn, the old stables, the cowsheds and other out-buildings, trees and a shrubbery, and the whole forest just outside the gates. The whole estate was not only very suitable, but beautiful. Following the Chiefs' enthusiastic report, the owner offered to give her house to the Guides.

If this generous gift was to be accepted, the Executive Committee would have to be sure of enough funds to equip and maintain the house and grounds. By 22nd February, 1922, all was settled: this was the wedding day of the Guide President, Princess Mary. Mrs. Archbold Saunderson sent a cable to Girl Guide Headquarters that she gave Foxlease to the Guides 'in honour of the occasion of the marriage of our beloved President'. The Princess herself was most generous in giving £6,000 to Foxlease out of the wedding gift subscribed by all the Marys of the Empire. There was an additional £4,000 from the exhibition of her wedding presents.

Alterations and repairs were begun at once, to be followed by many volunteer cleaners. Then the Guides themselves sent money and other gifts to furnish the house and make it a home.

The rooms at Foxlease are still known by their original Guide names: Scotland is the white and gold Adam drawing room with its bay windows opening onto the side lawn; London is the garden room and is full of gifts from all over the world; Hampshire is the old Adam dining room with Iphigenia still white above the fireplace; Wiltshire upstairs, at the end of a corridor, is the panelled library with wonderful views over the grounds to the forest. The open-sided nursery play area was enclosed and glazed to form a

Foxlease: Girl Guide Centre with a History...

Continued from previous page
large dining room in the name of India, but is now looked after by India and Pakistan.

The house, now 'Princess Mary House', was ready to open its doors to Guiders at Whitsun in May 1922, when the first Training Week took place. Many thousands have stayed in the house since, Commissioners, Guiders, Rangers and Guides, even husbands and children for holidays—and all have enjoyed the atmosphere of gracious living which Foxlease offers. H.R.H. the Princess Royal was a frequent visitor to her house in the early days and she often brought another treasure with her, but she always brought sympathy, understanding and inspiration to all who worked or stayed here.

In 1924 the third International Conference of Girl Guides and Girl Scouts was held at Foxlease, linked to the First World Camp in the grounds. The sixth Conference was sited in Foxlease in 1930: by this time the World Bureau had been formed and the World Association of Girl Guides and Girl Scouts as we know it today was newly constituted.

From 1922 Foxlease—that is, Princess Mary House, the outbuildings, cottages, gardens, and grounds, were all held by a Trust on behalf of Mrs. Archbold. Saunderson and the Girl Guides' Association. This was to safeguard the estate in case the Movement could not make full use of Foxlease as a viable concern. During the first twenty-one years at Foxlease, Guides and Guiders proved that this was a well-loved and much-needed amenity, and the Trust was dissolved in 1942 and Foxlease became fully the property of the Girl Guides' Association.

Wartime Adventures

Life at Foxlease is never without event but the years of war saw the house responding to needs of a kind it had not met since it had become the home of Guides.

First came the necessity of blacking out the house. Many people remember the trial and problem that was, but not many people had 116 windows—not to mention a few skylights—to deal with. However, it has always been a matter of pride for Foxlease to be able to produce anything that is asked for, so as its campers hastily packed up and went home, their ground-sheets returned with the other camp equipment and went up as improvised curtains, and a new duty was added to each

inmates and the very first postcard home drew the picture 'We are in a palace kept by Guides, we have a bed and a dressing table each, so don't worry, Mum.'

During those years Foxlease met the British Army as she had never done before. Commandos were billeted for a night in the barn and gave a demonstration to the Guiders.

Camping was not allowed. Foxlease was just the wrong side of the road and came within the 10 mile from the coast ban.

A PRESENT DAY CAMP NEAR PRINCESS MARY HOUSE
Training takes place at Foxlease the year round, except for a short period in December.

patrol's list.

The first patrols to undertake it were unfamiliar to the house. Fifty-six schoolboys from Portsmouth were in the house for a fortnight. That was a wartime adventure on which the house and all concerned in it look back with happiness. True, the visitors were unexpected, the Guider-in-charge had asked especially for girls and girls had been promised, but owing to the vagaries of the evacuee trains it was boys, large and small, with a few baby sisters hanging on, who tumbled out of the cars at six o'clock in the evening. The house charmed its new

This account cannot be concluded without some mention being made of the Christmas parties. They were a wartime institution that will not be forgotten. Each year a group of Guiders who would have been alone, or who wanted to get their Mother, their Father, or their Aunt away for a peaceful Christmas, met and had a party in the short time the house is normally closed. Once again the house showed itself peculiarly fitted for such activity. During the time a party was always given to all the evacuee children in the area. Invitations were sent to the boys and girls who spent the first

> **"We are in a palace kept by Guides; we have a bed and a dressing table each, so don't worry, Mum."**

Foxlease…

Continued from previous page
fortnight of war at Foxlease, and it is these contacts, that otherwise would not have been made, that will stand out in the memory of those who spent 1939–45 in the heart of the New Forest.

Post-War Years

After the war a full programme of training started again though over the years courses have become shorter and nowadays the majority last for only forty-eight hours.

One of the most popular events of recent years had undoubtedly been the annual 'Patrol Day' when through the medium of *Today's Guide* an invitation has been issued to any Patrol Leader to bring her patrol to Foxlease for the day and join in a programme of activities, tours of the house, the Forest, and Campfire singing. There have been working weekends when parties have tackled such jobs as tree felling, logging up and stacking, clearing of the camp sites, even laying paving stones round camp buildings and helping with the maintenance of these buildings.

Since the first World Camp was held at Foxlease in 1924 many international gatherings have taken place. In 1950 delegates on their way to Oxford for the 13th World Conference spent four days

AT BURLEY, GOLF AND GRAZING GO SIDE BY SIDE
Golf has been played in the New Forest for over 100 years. Bramshaw (founded 1880) has two courses, one of 18 holes; Lyndhurst (1890), makes use of the old Lyndhurst race course and also has 18 holes; Burley (1905), has nine holes and at times boasts as many ponies as players; Brokenhurst (original spelling) Manor Golf Club was founded in 1919 and has 18 holes.

PASSAGEWAY
The stone floor is indicative of the house's great age.

learning about British Guiding, the World Committee met in 1968 and every three years there is a conference of Chief Commissioners of the Commonwealth, a gathering which has grown steadily larger as more and more independent countries send representatives.

Hungarian Refugees

A memorable event of the post-war years was the occupation of Foxlease by a number of families who fled from Hungary after uprisings in the autumn of 1956. From November 1956 to February 1957 fifty-eight people, including twenty-two children, received shelter and hospitality at Foxlease. A wonderful amount of help was received in service, money and gifts, from a vast number of friends, mainly in the Guide Movement.

The Forest Forever

In these days the beauty of the New Forest is enjoyed by many thousands in the course of the year, most of whom traverse it in cars. Those who venture further on foot may glimpse deer grazing under the dense branches in the stillness as the sun sinks over the open ground. They may see the ponies drinking from shallow pools amidst the amazing variety of plant and animal life.

Even Guides and Scouts are no anachronism, for the spirit of chivalry, the love of adventure and devotion to high causes have found expression in many a New Forest breast since Canute himself first appointed officers to watch over the fairest part of the Kingdom, teach woodcraft, and instil loyalties. The Guiders are but a fresh manifestation of an old tradition, and their home in the woodland gives them just the background that a great inspiration deserves. Long may they have their dwelling in the heart of the Forest, responding to the wonderful appeal of its beauty, learning its secrets, identifying themselves with its spirit, which is the spirit of universal fellowship in natural things.

A Visitor Enjoys Some of the Forest's Many Attractions

Nearly one million people visit the New Forest each year, and the number is growing.

Most come in their cars and remain several days either in local hotels or guest houses, or in camp-sites. Each day the visitors set forth to see the varied attractions of the Forest. Guide-books, maps, and leaflets enable them to follow trails and see first-hand the animal and plant life that give the Forest its particular beauty.

When one such holiday visitor, Mrs. Lesley M. Eldred, who lives at Earl's Colne near Colchester, wrote about her holiday, the account was published in the 1985 annual report of the New Forest Association. That account follows.

A Stroll in the Forest

A nature lover's paradise; heather, shrubs and gorse, interrupted at intervals by the grazing forms of the occasional cattle, donkeys, or numerous wild ponies. Clearings amassed with the abundant variety of trees housed within the 92,000 acres of the New Forest.

The walks we enjoyed, known collectively as The Ornamental Drives, enabled us to absorb in detail, the dense beauty, realising that in the past on day trips we had scarcely scratched the surface.

One morning after having deposited the car in one of the many car parks supplied by The New Forest Forestry Commission, we proceeded along the walks of Boldrewood and Rhinefield. An avenue of the most breathtaking trees, the height of many creating dizziness. Each tree of interest was clearly marked and recorded with historical evidence and detailed information of type, provided by narrator posts dotted at intervals along the route. The ancient and ornamental woodlands abound with oak, ash, beech, redwood and conifer to name but a few.

The information supplied had us constantly reaching for pen and paper, how many of us realise that 417,000 tons of wood contributed by the New Forest went towards the war effort? The Sitka Spruce, over 140ft. high, would supply enough boards to floor a 3ft. cor-

ridor, 1/4 mile long. The two immense Wellingtonia introduced in 1853, belonging to the same family as the Californian Sequoia coniferous tree which live to over 3,000 years, dwarf the foliage of their smaller counterparts. One of these trees, the second tallest in Britain, is 60ft. high and was planted in the year 1859. We also passed at 132ft., the tallest Redwood in Britain. The amount of seeds required to amount to just one pound would be an incredible 190,000 of one variety of tree.

On our travels we passed the deer viewing platform; if fortunate you may catch a glimpse of the Red, Fallow, Sika, or Roe deer, some evidently hand reared by their keepers in the past, that roam in this enclosure. This time we were disappointed, but vowed a revisit.

As we followed the marked pathway, we encountered waterholes of the wildlife, created courtesy of the numerous bombs that were deposited in the New Forest area during the last war.

The grey squirrels tapping their presence high amongst the dense foliage provided us with the solitary break of silence apart from the snapping of twigs and pine needles underfoot. One grey squirrel scurrying down an immense fir and across our path nudged our thoughts towards Winter and the sight that a blanket of snow would provide, with the variety of birdlife causing us to momentarily pause for risk of intrusion, a living Christmas card

would be created.

Upon returning to the car park which, due to an unusually warm day in September, was considerably full, we noticed a mid-air collision. The hive of activity was due to a variety of wrens, approximately 50 of them, the tiny exquisitely marked birds, verging from different shades of blue to yellow and green on wingtips, being thrown titbits by a delighted and consistently willing picknicker. They swooped in unison, grabbing remorselessly and the occasion was soon transforming into a "free for all". The slightest movement or noise had them disappearing into the sanctity of treetops returning only when any movement or disruption had dispersed.

The following day, the disused railway line was to be the objective of our travels. The length of disused railway, lines having been removed, provides a walk of immense beauty; we passed beneath the bridges and debris of former activity. We imagined a stream train trip, the engine chugging through the vast carpeted acres of the New Forest. On passing a small clearing, we discovered that a caring station master had planted a variety of fruit trees, now bearing the fruits of his labours.

We crossed over a small bridge where on one side sleepers lay forever at rest, water filled the other side, a further oasis for wildlife we suspected. Unused, created by the course and progress of time, lay the still immaculate station, still seeming as if activity was pending.

We experienced sorrow that this railway was no more. Progress normally resulted in a loss of this nature, which is a tragedy, as once gone so often forgotten.

After walking the entire length as far as we were able, we returned to our holiday retreat, vowing to return and complete the other various walks that time prevented on this vacation.

After rising early next morning, our final day, I enjoyed a short pre-breakfast stroll and apart from meeting a paper-boy and scurry-

Forest Ponies

"To be woken by ... the occasional whinnying of a pony is a rare tonic" (Sketch is from Heywood Sumner's *Book of Gorley*)

A Visitor Enjoys the Forest...

Continued from previous page

ing grey squirrel which ran across my path, I was in solitude. To be woken by a dawn chorus and the occasional whinnying of a pony is a rare tonic and a person would have to be totally void of the appreciation of nature and imagination not to respond to the natural beauty that New Forest acres provide; not for the first time did this nature lovers' paradise create the vow of a revisit.

Staying in a Forest Hostel

(Kim Higgins of Yorkshire first visited the New Forest nearly a decade ago when she stayed at the Burley youth hostel. She recalls her arrival and stay at the hostel in the brief memoir below.)

I remembered the road to follow out of the village, and bearing in mind the old hostellers' proverb that 'the steepest track is always the right direction', I walked through the overhanging trees past the mellow brick school buildings to the open sward of the golf course. On through the trees the narrow track forked off towards some half-glimsed property, shaded by beech and oak and lime. At my feet a reassuring sign, emblazoned with the letters 'YHA'.

There was no sound save the birds and squirrels in the branches above me and twigs cracking underfoot. Early evening light filtered through the thick foliage. I began to think I'd missed a turning, when suddenly through a break in the hedge, I beheld Cottesmore House in all it's Victorian splendour, red brick and cream paint, the door wide open, a welcome at the journey's end, in the shelter of a massive copper beech tree.

An encouraging smell of hot food wafting through the quarry tiled hall-way and the menu chalked up on a blackboard at the foot of the stairs, confirmed what my nose had already decided—I would not be cooking for myself tonight!

Burley YHA is a building of great charm and as I wandered around its tranquil grounds, studying the building from all angles and discovering brambles, bay trees and bamboo in overgrown corners of the garden, it was easy to feel I was staying among friends.

There was time after dinner to stroll down to the pub. Luckily someone remembered to bring a torch and so the return journey was not as fraught as it might have been; avoiding the muddier puddles on the track and tangled undergrowth.

I was awakened in the morning by a most peculiar sound. I was sure I could hear animals snorting

THE NEW FOREST'S ONLY YOUTH HOSTEL: BURLEY Cottesmore House has been "home" to thousands of hikers and cyclists.

A Favourite Walk of Anne-Marie Edwards

Staying in A Forest Hostel...

Continued from previous page and chomping on grass. Bleary eyed I looked out of the window and there was a herd of cows wandering around the cycle shed, contentedly cropping the vegetation, and swishing their tails—no wonder the lawn was so neat!

TWO FORMER HOSTELS

Once the New Forest boasted two other youth hostels to accommodate visitors to the north and east of the area. These World War II snapshots depict Norleywood (above), between Lymington and Beaulieu, and Godshill (below), near Fordingbridge. The Norleywood building no longer exists; the Godshill building is today part of the Sandy Balls holiday centre.

> Anne-Marie Edwards, a former teacher, lives in the New Forest and has written a series of guides to walking in the Forest. She is a free-lance writer and broadcaster, and some of her walks have been presented on Radio Solent. She is also the author of *Discovering Hardy's Wessex* and *In the Steps of Jane Austen*.
>
> By permission of Anne-Marie and Arcady Books, Walk 4 from her guide, *New Forest Walks* (1975, with several reprintings), is reproduced here.

Walk 4
High Corner and
Dockens Water

In some parts of the New Forest you sense a feeling of mystery. Perhaps this is because so much has happened there in the past that, in spite of so few traces remaining, the Forest still holds these secrets. This is particularly true of the more remote parts of the Forest to the north-west. Here small rivers wind through woods and over moorlands to the Avon valley. There are some glorious walks along their banks and under the trees on the hillsides. I would like to describe one of my favourite walks through countryside which at various times in history has been bustling with activity and is now the most serene and peaceful part of the Forest.

There is nothing at all mysterious about our starting point! This is High Corner Inn; one of those quaint old inns that thrived in coaching days but now lie off the beaten track in the New Forest.

Coming from the west, take the A31 which runs across the north of the Forest from Ringwood to the Cadnam roundabout. About six miles east of Ringwood turn left along a minor road signposted 'Linwood'. In a little over a mile, the road bears left to cross Broomy Plain. Several tracks branch off over the heath, but continue for about half a mile when you turn right down a track signposted 'High Corner Inn'. Travelling west, take the A35 through Lyndhurst. Just through the village at Swan Green, turn right for Emery Down. Drive through Emery Down and just past the New Forest Inn turn left along the road signposted 'Bolderwood' and 'Linwood'. Keep to this road as it bears north under the A31 when it becomes the 'Linwood' road I mentioned above. As the track dips down the hillside to High Corner the going is rather rough but I think you will agree that the Inn and the beautiful valley it overlooks are well worth a few bumps on the way!

High Corner Inn is low and rambling and picturesque. The house was built in the 1700s originally as a farmhouse. When I was last there it was the sort of day when you cannot decide whether to take a mackintosh or not—that maddening mixture of sunshine and cloud that is known locally as 'clouberry weather'. I took my 'pint and ploughmans' out into the garden. It seems almost unbelievable now, but until I came south I had no idea what a ploughman's lunch was. However, it did not take long to discover this nice combination of crusty bread,

THE FOLK HOUSE

A Favourite Walk of Anne-Marie Edwards...

Continued from previous page
cheese and pickles. As I ate, chaffinches hopped about pecking up the crumbs and cloud shadows chased each other across the wooded slopes in front of me.

This walk begins along the gravel track that leads left from the Inn, downhill at first through trees then over lawns of close-cropped turf. Follow the main track as it bears right to go through the gate into Broomy Inclosure. Walk past the Forestry Commission's car free area barrier and through the woods which is a pleasant mixture of many kinds of trees, pines and the traditional oaks, beeches and holly. Go straight over all cross-tracks, keeping to the main track. Another gate brings you into a quite different wood.

You are surrounded by green glades of young oak trees, the ground beneath them rich with ferns. Just past the gate, the way divides: keep to the main track which bears a little right. (Ignore a gravel track on your right). Now you will really feel you are in the heart of the Forest. The air is very still and quiet and if you see foot-prints they are likely to be those of deer or badgers! You come to a wide gravel crosstrack just before a gate. Turn left down into the river valley with Dockens Water ahead of you. As you come out of the trees there is a choice of routes. If you would prefer a shorter walk along the streamside turn left and follow the path past the nicely-named Splash Bridge until you come to the edge of Broomy Inclosure again. Turn left here and walk uphill to High Corner Inn. The whole walk is about four miles.

For our longer walk, turn right along the valley, past the keeper's cottage at Holly Hatch. Turn left just past the cottage to cross Dock-ens Water by the small wooden footbridge. By the way, this is a perfect place for a picnic! The stream ripples over clean stones between smooth green lawns and beyond the bridge we can see our path winding gradually up the

opposite hillside to enter the woods of Sloden. It is hard to imagine a more peaceful scene but Dockens Water has seen its share of stirring events. Not far away, at the point where the stream flows across the New Forest boundary, stands Moyles Court. This was the home of Alice Lisle, who, like Nurse Cavell, died because she also believed 'patriotism is not

ANNE-MARIE EDWARDS MAKING NOTES ON ONE OF HER FOREST WALKS

enough'. Although she was a staunch royalist she sheltered two wounded fugitives, supporters of the Duke of Monmouth, who were seeking refuge in the Forest after his defeat at Sedgemoor.

The notorious Judge Jeffries deemed her humane act to be trea-son and the gallant old lady was beheaded. She has her memorial in the House of Commons but her grave in Ellingham churchyard is a very simple one. Legends have grown up about her, but none so strange as this from *It Happened in Hampshire* told by an old inhabit-ant of Furze Hill. 'One dark night when Mother and I was coming up Ellingham narrer Leane, we heard waggon wheels a rattlin behind us. "Run child," says

Mother, "run to the side long by Ellingham cross, lane's too narrer for night pass." So us ran, all over trimble, to the side-long, and Mother said "I allow t'will be Dame Lisle a coming to Moyles from Ellingham churchyard." So t'was—waggon passed us all a-rattling, drawed by four horses with never no heads and no driver, but inside waggon Dame

Lisle was a setting. Horses knowed there way and rattled 'cross high road and up backways to Moyles. She must have got there, for they do say she were heard along the passages o' the house and her high heels went tap-tap-tap and her silk dress went swish-swish-swish agen the bare floorboards. But she don't hear en no-a-days. I allow it's got sorter tired, wore out by time along.'

The walk continues over the footbridge and along the path leading into the opposite woods. Now you can walk uphill and under the dark yew tress of Sloden. This is one of the stran-gest places in the New Forest. The yews stand heavy and forbidding

Anne-Marie Edwards...

Continued from previous page

and among them are ancient oak trees, crumbling with age and twisted into all sorts of fantastic shapes. Gardens of fern flourish in the hollows of their gnarled branches. These yews were planted when our ancestors needed their wood for their long-bows and arrows. I suppose some of the yews' sombre look is associated with the fact that we often see them in churchyards and the reason for that must date back to pre-Christian times when they had an important religious significance. Their wood was one of the three sacred symbols of the Druids who also venerated the form of a circle and water. If we were able to see ghosts of former inhabitants it would be here at Sloden, but they would be busy men hard at work making pottery! For in these woods are the remains of a large pot-making industry that flourished for several hundred years while the Romans ruled England.

You can see banks and mounds and entrenchments marking the site of quite a large community and the outline of two kilns. A typical kiln was about twelve feet in diameter and was constructed of puddled clay. Inside was a combustion chamber where wood or charcoal was burnt with the aid of suitably arranged flues and an upper dome where the pottery was arranged to be fired. You can still find fragments of their pottery which covered a wide range of bowls, platters and flagons, usually decorated with a linked design and often with a distinctive purple glaze. From coins found near the kilns it is believed that these potteries ceased production about AD380.

After entering Sloden wood the way forks. Leave the gravel track which bears a little right uphill, and follow the green track to the left. This takes you uphill, then to the left of a cleared area to a gate. Go through the gate and follow the wide green ride ahead straight over all crosstracks down into the

valley of the Latchmore Brook. Go through a gate in the valley and now turn left along one of the most beautiful green paths in the Forest, fringed with groves of silver birches, young oaks and graceful larches. Hidden among the trees on your right in Alderhill Inclosure runs the Latchmore Brook which will try to tempt you from your way with glimpses of little wooden footbridges. Keep to the path when it leaves the woods behind and follow the streamside through open heathland.

You are now crossing Latchmore Bottom. 'Bottom' is a word to beware of on any New Forest

A Forest stream.

FROM HEYWOOD SUMNER'S *Book of Gorley*

map! It means wet, boggy ground so be prepared to pick your way carefully in wet weather. When the path divides, bear left, a little away from the brook, to meet a gravel track running in front of a group of cottages called Ogdens. Ogdens car park is on your right. Turn left along the gravel track, and keep to the main track as it bears left, then uphill to Hasley Inclosure. This is a small hill crowned with woods with a path running all round it. There are splendid views across the Forest towards the Avon Valley from here and a lake edged with Scots pines. You will see a path into Hasley leading from our track on the left. Just past the track into Hasley, bear right round the pine trees to pick up a good track which runs downhill towards Dockens Water. You will see parts of this hill have been dug away to reveal

the clay which is stained bright orange and red by iron. Possibly the Sloden potters delved here for the fire-resisting ironstone to use in their kilns.

Just before you cross Dockens Water, you will pass a fascinating farmhouse built three sides of a square called Ogdens Purlieu. With its small windows, single-storey wings and low thatch over its huge arched doorway it looks like a Saxon farmstead. You will find purlieus in various parts of the New Forest. Purlieu is, of course, a French word, dating back like the Forest itself to William the Conqueror and derived

from 'pour allez,' to walk round an area. This land was once subject to Forest laws but by special dispensation it became part of a farm and was allowed to be enclosed and cultivated. Naturally these fertile areas were specially tempting for the deer and other wild animals who invaded them if they could. So a special Forest officer or Ranger was created to chase them back into the Forest again!

Cross the bridge and follow the road ahead. It leads uphill and back to High Corner Inn again. This whole walk is about eight and a half miles, but if you would prefer a shorter distance, a glance at the Ordnance Survey map will show you several short cuts. If you would like to walk further you can plan this easily too, beautiful remote Forest land surrounds you but remember to take a map as

Traditional New Forest Cooking Recipes

(Irene Soper was born in Wiltshire and came with her husband to live at Abbots Well about 20 years ago.

"When we occupied our house", she said "the old cob cottage standing in the garden was in a state of disrepair. It is reputed to be three hundred years old and one of the few remaining original New Forest cabins. We spent some time restoring the old cottage, revealing an open fireplace complete with bread oven and chains hanging in the large open chimney. The atmosphere of this old dwelling led me to wonder how the old foresters existed in such humble surroundings, particularly having to cook in an open hearth." This was when the idea was born for her book, *New Forest Cookery*.

"Because we cannot use the cottage as a dwelling place," she said, "we now use it as a studio as we both paint in oils."

The wells of Abbots Well, recorded in ancient chronicles of **1217**, still produce their pure water which the Sopers use for wine making. Living as they do surrounded by open forest, they have a great fondness of the natural wild life and spend a lot of time walking and cycling in the Forest. They have regular visits to the house by foxes and badgers as well as the smaller mammals.

Excerpts from *New Forest Cookery* are reproduced through the courtesy of Irene Soper and Arcady Books.)

The Forest farms were quite small, and stock consisted mainly of pigs, cattle, chickens and ban-

IRENE SOPER PREPARES A MEAL IN HER COB COTTAGE

tams. The farm-houses were often old thatched cottages with the pigsties and cattle byres attached.

The peasant usually kept a small herd of cattle that would graze on the Forest for the best part of the year and eventually provide him with a supply of beef, most of which he salted down and stored for use during the long hard months of winter.

This salted beef was utilized in many ways. For supper it was eaten cold with pickle. Any slices left over were fried with cooked vegetables and eaten for breakfast the next morning.

Bubble and squeak

Cut up some slices of cold boiled salt beef, and fry together with any left-over vegetables and potatoes until lightly brown. Form ingredients into cakes when frying, season with pepper and salt.

Outside the farmhouse there were always a few bantams and chickens running around, providing eggs for the family and the occasional bird for the table.

Breakfast eggs

Butter thickly half a dozen small

moulds, mix *two tablespoons of minced parsley, and two tablespoons of cooked ham*, and shake into each mould, so that the sides may be covered by the mixture, and reject the surplus. Break *one egg* into each mould, sprinkle with *salt and pepper*, stand in a pan containing water, allowing the water to come within half an inch of the top; simmer slowly till the eggs are just set, then take out the moulds from the pan. Toast some bread and cut into rounds a little larger than the moulds, butter them, and turn out the eggs, one on each piece of toast, and serve.

The small Forest mushrooms are the button type, their caps being scaly and brownish, quite delicious to eat in their raw state when freshly picked.

Mushroom soup

Take *one pound of freshly picked mushrooms* and skin them, *slice one small onion, heat a little butter* and fry in it the mushrooms and the onion for three or four minutes, lift out about one dozen of the smallest mushrooms and set aside. Add *three pints of water* to the mushrooms and the onion in the pan, season, boil for half an hour or

Anne-Marie Edwards...
Continued from previous page
there are fewer roads in this area, and a confusing number of footpaths in some of the inclosures. You might like to take binoculars too as these quiet woods are the home of deer and other interesting wildlife.

Traditional Forest Recipes...

Continued from previous page

until the mushrooms are quite soft; pour the soup through a fine sieve and rub through the pulp; put back into the pan, add the dozen small mushrooms, *one ounce of flour mixed with one ounce of butter* into a ball, boil gently for five minutes and pour into a tureen in which *quarter of a pint of cream* has been placed, and serve.

The rabbit was perhaps the most popular food from the Forest for both peasant and gypsy alike. The gypsies used to catch rabbits by means of a net after dark; the nets were placed near the rabbit burrows, dogs were sent out and the rabbits, cut off from their holes, were easily caught. These nets were made by the gypsy women with string, some were several yards long. The Romany just cooked his rabbit together with wild onions in his stew pot. The peasant preferred his made into a pie.

Rabbit pie

One rabbit, half a pound of bacon, two hard boiled eggs, one small onion, half a teaspoonful of mixed herbs, seasoning, one tablespoonful of flour, half a pint of stock, and pastry crust.

Cut the rabbit into joints, dip in seasoned flour, and fry until golden brown in a little hot fat. Place in a pie-dish with slices of eggs and strips of bacon. Sprinkle in more seasoning and herbs. Pour in stock. Cover with pastry and bake for about two hours in a moderate oven. Do not forget to leave a hole in the pastry to allow the steam to escape.

Apple tart

A pound and a quarter of apples weighed after they are pared, sliced and cored, will be sufficient for a small tart, and four ounces more for one of moderate size. Lay *a border of pastry* round the dish, just dip the apples into water, arrange them compactly in it, higher in the centre than at the sides, and strew amongst them

from *three to four ounces of pounded sugar*, or more should they be very acid: the *grated rind and strained juice of half a lemon* will much improve the flavour. Lay on the cover rolled thin. Place the tart in a moderate oven for half an hour. This may be converted into an *old-fashioned creamed apple tart* by cutting out the cover whilst it is still hot, leaving only about an inch-wide border of pastry round the edge, and pouring over the apples when they have become cold *some well drained cream* piled high and lightly over the fruit.

Rhubarb pie

Peel the *rhubarb*, and if it is very large divide it into two or three strips, and then into short lengths. Fill the dish as full as it will hold, *sprinkle some sugar* over it, and if liked mix with the fruit a flavouring of *grated lemon-peel and ground ginger, or a little nutmeg grated*. Line the edges of the dish with pastry,

moisten these with water, and lay a cover of pastry over all. Press the edges close together and ornament them, then *sprinkle a spoonful or two of cold water* over the pie and dredge *a little white sugar* upon it; bake the pie in a moderate oven until the pastry loosens from the dish, about twenty minutes to half an hour. Serve hot or cold.

In winter, with a log fire in the cabin, we sometimes have girdle scones for tea. A girdle (sometimes called a griddle) is a round piece of thick iron hanging on a chain and heated over an open fire. It can also be used on a range or stove. You can use a grill burner for these recipes or a griddle if you have one. The griddle should be well heated whilst preparing the dough. Before cooking, it can be either greased or sprinkled with flour. Afterwards, the girdle should never be washed. Clean it by rubbing with coarse salt and a piece of paper, then give it a final dust.

Our girdle was given to us by the Forest Naturalist, Eric Ashby. It came from 'Badger Cottage' where it was regularly used by his

The Apple Mill

FROM HEYWOOD SUMNER'S *Book of Gorley*

Traditional Recipes...

Continued from previous page
mother to make these delicious scones.

Badger cottage girdle scones

One pound of flour, half a teaspoonful cream of tartar, one teaspoonful carbonate of soda, a little salt and sour milk.

Sieve all the dry ingredients into a basin and make a well in the centre. Add enough milk to make a light dough, turn out on a floured board, and divide into four. Then take one piece at a time and flatten it into a round scone, about half an inch thick. Cut in four again and place the scones on a hot greased girdle. Cook about five minutes on either side. The scones should be nicely browned on both sides, and they are ready when the edges are dry. Serve with butter.

A few currants may be added if liked.

Most cottage gardens are invaded in some form by wild vegetation of the Forest. The hedges surrounding our own garden are entwined with brambles but this is to our advantage in the late summer when we are able to pick the clusters of juicy sweet berries. My mother loved to make jams and jellies, and this is one of her favourite recipes.

Evelyn's Bramble jelly

Two pounds of blackberries and a quarter of a pint of water.

Pick the berries over and remove all stalks. Put them into a preserving pan with the water and bring to the boil; then simmer until the fruit is soft. Strain through a piece of muslin. Put liquid back into saucepan, add sugar allowing one pound of sugar to one pint of liquid, stir until dissolved, then boil briskly until set.

My mother never removed her jam from the jars to serve as she

PONY SALES: POPULAR ATTRACTIONS FOR VISITORS

Beaulieu Road Pony Sales

Some people attend the Beaulieu Road pony sales to acquire animals for their children or their own pleasure. Others go for the atmosphere: the display of the ponies and horses, the excitement of the auction, the chance to meet old acquaintances.

Four times a year, in April, August, September and October, animal lovers make their way to the sale site where the Lyndhurst-Beaulieu road intersects the Waterloo-Bournemouth railway line.

At the sale all eyes are turned to the pens full of ponies and the auctioneer's stand where the action occurs. Valerie Russell, in her book *New Forest Ponies* (1976), tells what it is like to attend a Beaulieu Road pony sale.

Going to Beaulieu Road is rather more than just going to another pony sale—it is an opportunity to observe a slice of traditional Forest life. The sales start at 10.30am, but from early morning the scene is one of great activity, with lorries, horse-boxes and trailers discharging their loads of ponies. As the lorry doors open, the ponies come out, uncertainly at first and then with a rush, and are herded into the pens by the sale ring. With the final indignity of a catalogue number stuck on their quarters, they stand more or less patiently and wait their turn for auction. The commoners and their families also wait, looking forward not only to seeing their animals knocked down for good prices but to one of the important 'days out' of the year.

Most of the crowd collect round the pens, leaning over or sitting on the rails, and the talk is naturally

centred on the ponies—the quality of animals for sale, and whether prices will be up or down on last time. For the prospective buyer a little discreet eavesdropping could pay dividends. The commoners' ability to recognise individual animals, even foals, is well known, and an overheard remark—'I see that old chestnut colt of Jackie's is here. That's by old so-and-so's horse. It could be a good one'—may be worth acting on. The sale ring itself is surprisingly small, and seems smaller still when the crowds of buyers and spectators pack into the tiered stand as soon as bidding begins.

At 10.30 the door to the chute opens and the first foal comes in, perhaps erupting into the ring and rushing about in the confined space, threatening the safety of the stewards, who try and direct their wild charges with flags. At least one has been known to leap the

Traditional Recipes...

Continued from previous page said the flavour was lost when exposed to the air for too long. Instead she stood the jar on an attractive saucer, patterned with moss roses or bold nasturtiums, reminiscent of cottage gardens. I treasure her favourite, decorated with a spray of blackberries.

Honey cake

Eight ounces of self-raising flour, one teaspoonful mixed spice, four tablespoonfuls of honey, four ounces of margarine, two eggs, split almonds and milk.

Mix flour, sugar, and spice together. Put the margarine, honey and a little milk together and warm, add the beaten eggs, and pour into the dry ingredients.

Mix to a soft dough. Put into a shallow square tin lined with grease-proof paper. Brush with milk and scatter the top with the split almonds.

Bake in a moderate oven for about one hour. Cut into small squares.

Roast loin of pork

Take one pint of cider, one small onion peeled and chopped, three bay leaves, three cloves, half a teaspoonful of salt, black pepper, two ounces of butter and a few peppercorns.

Put the ingredients together in a saucepan and bring to the boil. Leave to cool, then strain and pour over the joint. Leave for twenty four hours. Turn the joint occasionally and baste thoroughly. Cook the joint in *butter* over a gentle fire (burner) until browned, using some of the marinade to keep it basted. Cover and simmer slowly for two hours.

Prepare a sauce by cutting *the rind from two oranges*. Slice the rind. Rub *three lumps of sugar* on the oranges. Put the sugar into a basin with *six tablespoons of red currant jelly, a little white pepper, one chopped shallot, one spoonful of mixed mustard* and enough *port wine* to make the sauce as thick as a good cream; add the

Farmers' Weekly

STUDENTS AND STAFF ON A WINTER'S DAY

Aims of the Fortune Centre, a registered charity, are to train and rehabilitate the lesser handicapped school leaver through extended residential courses, to train specialist instructors and riding therapists, to provide riding instructions for handicapped young people, and to contribute to research in the therapeutic sports field.

Riding for the Handicapped

(In February, 1986, *Farmers' Weekly* magazine sent Ann Rogers to the Fortune Centre, on the edge of the New Forest, to report on the centre's work for disturbed and handicapped young people. Her account follows.)

Whatever that strange power is that horses have over certain people, the Fortune Centre puts it to good effect.

Here, on the edge of the New Forest, horses bring happiness and hope into the lives of disturbed and handicapped young people.

Beaulieu Road Pony Sales...

Continued from previous page fence, scatter the startled crowd, jump out of the yard and disappear into the depths of the Forest. Others enter hesitantly, and stand, forlorn and frightened, in the centre of the ring. But no matter what happens in the arena below him, the auctioneer launches into his patter: '*What a lovely foal this is, and a filly too! Isn't that a well grown foal! What am I bid? Thirty guineas, thirty-five—and a half. Thank you, sir. It's against you, madam. Come along, he's only a man, don't let him beat you!* And so it goes on, hour after hour, until the last pen is empty, the last animal sold.

Then comes the business of new owners loading their purchases into boxes, lorries or trailers—some going easily, some resisting violently. Many a lorry has left the sale yard with its sides reverberating from the sound of hooves (fortunately unshod) battering at the boards, or a trailer departed with a pony's head sticking out through the small gap between ramp and roof.

The majority of animals sold at Beaulieu Road go as children's riding ponies. A buyer with a real 'eye for a horse' might pick up a genuine bargain. Black Ribot, for example, was bought at a sale in 1959 for fifteen guineas. He was broken and schooled by the owner's daughter, Marilyn Jewell, who then took him show-jumping. He was upgraded to J A in one season, and by 1967 was valued at £1,500.

orange rind which should be cut very thin, heat gently in a saucepan, then pour over the carved slices of the joint. Serve with *wild apple jelly*.

Riding for the Handicaped...

Continued from previous page

This stable at Avon Tyrrell, Bransgore, takes horse therapy a stage further than the usual Riding for the Disabled schemes. Its residential training courses help disturbed young people to come to terms with themselves and educate the less handicapped ones so that they may lead full lives and hold down jobs.

Many will have had little to do with horses before, but all are motivated by the love of that animal and the desire to care for it.

"That's one of the most effective way of learning maths," said Jennifer Nelson, as she showed me round the well-ordered stables and pointed to the charts on which students had calculated feed quantities for Maxwell, Mary Poppins and the other horses and ponies.

Reading and writing are mastered through concern for the horse too—keeping its records, writing its signs and writing about it in letters home.

As we walked round, one group was having a riding lesson in the indoor school. Up in the gallery another party was playing a version of Kim's game with horse accessories, while one student was in the kitchen helping prepare lunch.

Domestic chores form part of the curriculum, as well as stable and estate ones, as do crafts, music and sport—including tennis, swimming and cycling.

Up in the library two students were doing some private study. They were student therapists. A small group of these, most of them university graduates, come to the Fortune Centre from all parts of the world to train for riding therapy jobs with schools and hospitals.

Jennifer Nelson, the centre's nurse, is, like all its staff, doubly qualified. As well as being a state registered nurse she hold a British Horse Society qualification.

Her mother, Yvonne Nelson,

Courtesy Olive Forshaw

HANDICAPPED YOUNG PEOPLE AT AVON TYRRELL
Up to 80 young people can use the residential facilities at Avon Tyrrell's centre at one time. Besides the physically and mentally handicapped, other groups using the centre include schools, youth clubs, community and church groups, and government-sponsored training organizations. The centre offers its residents a swimming pool, canoeing, fishing, badminton, tennis, volleyball, football and an assault course. Avon Tyrrell does not itself offer courses, but allows visiting groups to organize their own programmes while using the centre's facilities.

SIX THOUSAND PASS THROUGH ITS PORTALS ANNUALLY
Avon Tyrell is the National Association of Youth Club's residential centre, and its location on the edge of the New Forest allows young visitors to go away with a deeper appreciation of nature. It was officially opened by H.R.H. Princess Elizabeth (now the Queen) on 1 July 1949. In September, 1985, the then Princess Anne visited the centre and saw severely disabled young people tackling Outward Bound-type courses. (Avon Tyrell will soon be 100 years old, having been constructed for Lord Manners in 1891.)

Driving in the New Forest

(As Marylian Watney points out in the account below, the New Forest is ideally suited to driving.

It is sometimes forgotten that Commoners once drove from their small-holdings to the nearest village or town to sell their produce and buy life's necessities. The New Forest remains today one of the few areas in Britain where country lanes, heathland, and woodland combine to permit driving amidst tranquility and beauty.

Marylian has lived in the Forest area for more than 20 years and has written for *Country Life* and other national journals. Her books include *The Elegant Carriage* (1961), *Show Driving Explained* (1978) and *Royal Cavalcade* (1987). She was co-author with her late husband, Sanders Watney, of *Horse-Power* (1975). While her husband was president of the British Driving Society, she was editor of the society's annual journal.

Marylian derives great pleasure from helping to organize driving for disabled people.)

DRIVING ALONG A WINDING FOREST LANE

Over the centuries, the New Forest has been a veritable haven for horsemen for, in addition to the very obvious pleasure of being able to explore dense thickets and open moorland, many aspects of wildlife can be better viewed when in equine company. Deer, for instance, frequently stand and stare before darting away into the undergrowth.

For this pursuit, New Forest ponies with their inherent sure-footedness and "feel" for the land are an obvious choice, and with the breeding of strong-boned stallions, many ponies are capable of carrying comparatively heavy weights. Riding, however, is not the only means of enjoyment in the Forest, but driving—the method by means of which many commoners formerly made their livings, has, and perhaps surprisingly, also remained a popular activity—and for both young and old.

As is the case with the majority of sports, enthusiasts prefer to participate in company, and the formation of Driving Clubs has, since Georgian times, been recorded in various parts of England. In the New Forest, one such club, called "The Cavaliers", came into existence shortly before the outbreak of World War II, but due to hostilities did not last very long. More recently, the British Driving Society, formed in 1957, had its Hampshire Area-Commissioner living in Burley. So the new Forest, with its many routes through woodland, became a mecca for members of the driving

Learning for Life...

Continued from previous page began the centre almost 10 years ago, with the Hon Mrs Peter Baillee, as an extension to their work with Riding for the Disabled.

Now it is a registered charity. Running costs are met by fees paid by students—who are usually grant-aided—but development of the centre is financed by fund raising activities.

There is a large staff, with a staff-student ratio of 1 to 1 ensuring personal attention and individual timetables.

Not every Fortune Centre student will end up working with horses. Some may find jobs in old people's homes, for example, or become kennel assistants. But all will have benefited from learning through love of the horse, its dependence on them and the routine and discipline that its care imposes.

What to See and Do In the New Forest Area

Apart from its natural woodlands, heathlands and wildlife, the New Forest boasts dozens of attractions spanning a wide variety of interests.

A selection of these is reproduced below from "In and around the New Forest," a leaflet issued by the New Forest District Council. Intending visitors to the Forest can obtain tourist information (including leaflets on where to stay, sport and recreation) by writing the NFDC, Appletree Lyndhurst, Hants SO43 7PA. A New Forest miniguide is also available at nominal cost. Times of opening and admission charges may be obtained from the Centre in Lyndhurst.

RUFUS'S STONE

FROM SUMNER'S
A Guide to the New Forest

Archaeological and historical sites

Rufus Stone, Brook. Marks the spot where it is said William Rufus met his death in 1100. Situated north of A31 between Brook and Stoney Cross.

Naked Man, Holmsley. Relic of gibbet tree where legend has it a highwayman hung until his bones were laid bare. Situated close to A35 Lyndhurst–Bournemouth road at Wilverley Post.

Bolton's Bench, Lyndhurst. Named after Lord Basing when as Lord Warden of the Forest in 1688, he was appointed Lord Bolton.

Knightwood Oak, Bolderwood, near Lyndhurst. One of the oldest pollarded trees in the Forest and nearly 400 years old. Located close to Bolderwood Ornamental Drive, off the A35 Lyndhurst–Bournemouth road.

Ocknell Clump, Stoney Cross. Where Scots Pine were reintroduced into the Forest in 1775.

Bramshaw Telegraph. Situated in the north of the District, off the B3078, this was the site of a signalling station in the Napoleonic wars. Fine views over the Forest.

Hatchet Pond, Beaulieu. An artificial pond once used for local hammer mill, west entrance gate

to Beaulieu estate. Pleasant lakeside car park and picnic area. Coarse fishing by permit.

Canadian Memorial, near Emery Down. A simple wooden cross commemorating the presence of the Third Canadian Division in the Forest. Erected in April 1946, at Mogshade between Emery Down and Bolderwood.

Portuguese Fireplace, near Emery Down. A restored remnant of the occupation of Portuguese Forest Corps in the 1914/18 war. Situated between Emery Down and Bolderwood.

Walhampton Obelisk, Lymington. 18th Century Egyptian style pillar commemorating Sir Harry Burrard Neale.

Petersons Tower, Sway. Built in 1879–84 to prove the qualities of concrete. Not open to the public.

Churches of interest

Among the many interesting village churches are:

Boldre—Secluded 13th Century parish church, north of village.

Breamore—Fine example of a Saxon Church built in the 10th Century.

Brockenhurst—Church of varying styles from Norman to Victorian. Burial place of "Brusher" Mills, a famous Forest snake-

Driving in the New Forest...

Continued from previous page

world from all parts of England.

Driving on gravel paths, however, constituted a threat to the delicate paintwork on the wheels of traditional horse-drawn vehicles, and so the building of more stoutly-made varnished exercise carts was begun—again in Burley—and these proved so popular that they were bought for use in many other parts of the country. Similarly, leather harness with either silver or brass fittings became too valuable for everyday use, and so the same firm in Burley began producing a more serviceable type of harness made from rawhide and Fire Brigade hose with sheepskin breast-collars, and this again is now widely used.

These exercise carts and harness are ideal for attending the

many picnic drives organised during the summer months —when the ponies can be easily removed from their vehicles and tied up under trees to munch hay while humans eat sandwiches, but it is when put to elegant and traditionally-built vehicles and with shining harness that the New Forest pony comes into its own. Many New Forest ponies have won championships and became famous in driving events at horse shows throughout the country.

Whatever the event, New Forest ponies are fun to own, but most people would probably agree that there is nothing to beat the charm of driving a New Forest pony in its natural habitat— among the trees, the gorse, and the heather.

BREAMORE CHURCH: EXAMPLE OF SAXON ARCHITECTURE

ELLINGHAM CHURCH

catcher.

Ellingham—12th Century church with unusual and ornate interior features. Dame Alicia Lisle, a victim of the infamous Judge Jeffreys, is buried in the churchyard.

Fordingbridge—Dating from the 13th Century with five 15th Century carvings and a magnificent roof.

Lyndhurst—Victorian church with fine stained glass. Burial place of Alice Liddell—the original "Alice in Wonderland".

Minstead—Containing the grave of Sir Arthur Conan Doyle, three decker pulpit, 12th Century font and 18th Century galleries.

Sopley—A 13th/14th Century church containing a number of items of interest including a medieval font.

Touring, Parking and Walking

For the visitor, the Forestry Commission has provided over 140 car parks, accessible from both major and minor country roads. These vary from viewpoints to sites in woodland, forest, open heathland or beside streams. From many of these the visitor is welcome to explore on foot.

Picnic facilities at most car parks, but picnic fires are not allowed. Special barbecue hearths are available to booked parties at Beaulieu Heath and Millyford and can be reserved by application to the Forestry Commission, Queens House, Lyndhurst, telephone Lyndhurst 3141.

Some forest walks have been provided with wayside information and are accessible from Bolderwood, Brock Hill, Blackwater, Puttles Bridge, Whitefield Moor, Knightwood Oak and Wilverley car parks. Leaflets describing the walks may be purchased from the leaflet dispenser in most of these car parts. A special short walk, of about a quarter of a mile designed for the disabled is to be found at Wilverley.

Some guided walks are arranged during the summer. Check the New Forest Centre for more details.

Bolderwood Walk (Forestry Commission) Five miles west of Lyndhurst through Emery Down. Yellow and green waymarked walk amid majestic Douglas fir trees leads to a sculptured memorial stone to the 7th Earl of Radnor. There is a deer observation platform overlooking the deer sanctuary.

Bramshaw Common. A series of commons owned by the National Trust extending to some 90 acres. Nearby is the highest point in the Forest, Pipers Wait, 421 feet above sea level.

Hale Purlieu. An area of heath and woodland about 512 acres in extent. Undulating country including the wooded Millers Ford plantation.

Ober Water Walk (Forestry Commission), Brockenhurst. A peaceful walk alongside a Forest stream accessible from car parks at Whitefield Moor or Puttles Bridge.

Tall Trees Walk (Forestry Commission), Rhinefield. A waymarked walk between an avenue of magnificent trees planted in 1860. Accessible from two car parks, Blackwater or Brock Hill on the Rhinefield Ornamental Drive.

For those who might prefer it, horse-drawn wagon rides through the inclosures are available from Balmer Lawn near Brockenhurst and at Burley.

Parks and Gardens

Exbury Gardens, Exbury. Woodland garden extending to over 200 acres on the East bank of the Beaulieu River, containing the world famous Rothschild collection of rhododendrons and azaleas with group and individual plantings of magnolias, camellias, specimen trees and flowering shrubs; also, fully stocked plant centre, pools, 2 acre rock garden, rose garden and picnic areas.

Furzey Gardens, Minstead. 8 acres of delightful landscaped gardens, beautiful banks of azaleas, rhododendrons and heathers, flaming Chilean Fire trees and many other interesting and rare shrubs. Also 16th Century cottage and craft gallery displaying the

400-YEAR OLD COTTAGE AT FURZEY GARDENS

work of local craftsmen.

Lepe Country Park, Lepe. On the Solent foreshore, this area of outstanding natural beauty has commanding views over the Isle of Wight. Restaurant, picnic and beach area. Ideal for boardsailing.

MacPenneys, Bransgore. Nursery covering approximately 14 acres including a woodland garden. At its best in the Spring, the garden is free for visitors to wander at will. The woodlands form part of the "living catalogue."

Spinners, Boldre. Mainly a woodland garden. Rhododendrons, azaleas, magnolias, pieris, hydrangeas—interplanted with primulas, blue poppies, iris, trilliums, erythroniums, rodgersia, geraniums, hostas and other choice shade loving and ground over plants.

Vineyards Open to the Public:
Beaulieu Vineyard, John Montague Building, Beaulieu. Open May – October. Necessary to telephone in advance to book visit.
Lymington Vineyard, Wainsford Road, Pennington, near Lymington. Guided tours.

Walking
Lyndhurst
Arranged by the Foresty Commission, these tours operate from the New Forest Centre in Lyndhurst. Numbers on these walks, which cover various Forest and historical themes, are strictly limited. Tickets and further information should be obtained from the Centre in Lyndhurst.

Ringwood/Fordingbridge
Arranged by the local Footpath Society, guided walks take place in each month throughout the year. Evening tours are also organised. Further information on starting times and places available from Ringwood Tourist Information Centre and the Ringwood and Fordingbridge Community Centres.

For details in general on cycling/cycle hire consult the New Forest Centre.

Entertainment
Dances and live entertainment are often provided in local hotels, pubs and inns. Some towns and villages in the New Forest District have their own local theatre and opera groups. A full range of entertainment is to be found throughout the year in the nearby towns of Bournemouth and Southampton, including cinemas, theatres, and concert halls.

Ferries
Lymington to Yarmouth (Isle of Wight). Passenger and vehicle ferry operating throughout the year.
Hythe Pier to Southampton. Short trip across Southampton Water. Access to embarkation point along hundred year old pier with railway.
Keyhaven to Hurst Castle. Regular ferry service to and from the Castle during the summer months, with limited sailings in the winter. Also cruises to the Needles and the Isle of Wight.
Beaulieu River Cruises. Half hour cruises in the boat 'Swiftsure' from Bucklers Hard to Beaulieu from Easter to September.

Museums and historic houses
National Motor Museum, Beaulieu. Beaulieu offers much more than just England's most visited stately home. It is the home of the National Motor Museum with its superb exhibits which tell the story of motoring from 1894 to the present day. Also comprehensive exhibition of monastic life in the atmospheric Abbey ruins. "Wheels" is a major new feature which transports visitors in space age 'pods' through 100 years of motoring.

Breamore House and Countryside/Carriage Museums, Breamore, near Fordingbridge. Fine Elizabethan Manor house owned by the Hulse family since 1748 and containing a fine collection of art and furniture. Countryside Museum displays some of the history of agriculture and rural life, whilst the Carriage Museum is housed in the old stables.

Buckler's Hard Maritime Museum and Cottage Displays. 18th Century village where ships of Nelson's fleet were once built. Maritime Museum traces its his-

THE NEW FOREST MUSEUM AND VISITOR CENTRE, LYNDHURST
A visit to the Museum begins with "The Changing Forest," a film that traces the rich and exciting story of the Forest from the days of the Norman kings to the present. Open daily from 10 a.m., the Museum and Centre is an introductory "must" to a visit of the New Forest. Contained in the same premises are also a tourist information centre and gift shop.

tory with models, pictures, ship-builder's drawings and relics. 18th Century homes of a master ship-builder, a shipwright and a labourer—together with an Inn scene—have been recreated in the original cottages with costumed figures. Cruises on the Beaulieu River, riverside walk.
Calshot Castle, Calshot. Built in the middle of the 16th Century by Henry VIII to defend the Solent,

like Hurst Castle it is situated at the end of a spit protruding into the Solent. It was built with stone from Beaulieu and Netley Abbey.
Eling Tide Mill, near Totton. Restored in 1980 as a working Tide Mill Museum. The only surviving mill in the world harnessing the power of the tide for the regular production of wholemeal flour. Solent Protection Society Award 1980, National Heritage

Museum of the Year 1981, Institution of Mechanical Engineers Award 1986.
Hurst Castle, Keyhaven. Built in the middle of the 16th Century by Henry VIII to defend the Solent. During the Civil War, Charles I was imprisoned there. The Castle was modernised in the 19th Century against possible invasion and was used in the last war. Ferry from Keyhaven to Hurst Castle.

British Tourist Authority

A FAMILY PICNIC IN THE EARLY DAYS OF THE MOTOR CAR
The scene above is only one of several in "Wheel," a "ride-through" display at Beaulieu's National Motor Museum. The Museum is one of the top tourist attractions of the nation.

14

In and around the Forest
During Queen Victoria's Reign

Was there a time, beyond living memory but still relatively recent, when both a written and an artistic record of places in and around the New Forest was made?

Extensive research reveals that *Hunt's Directory of Hampshire* (1852) and Robert Mudie's illustrated *History of Hampshire* (1838), taken together, go a long way toward depicting life in the hamlets, villages and towns of the Forest and its adjacent area during the first quarter of Queen Victoria's reign. *Hunt's* is valuable for showing families who then lived in the area (and some of whose descendants reside there today), and for listing the trades they followed. Mudie's work portrays the local churches and other prominent landmarks of the time.

The period encompassed by the two books (1838–1852) was an exciting one. Stage coaches were still running, but trains had been introduced. Agriculture was still the dominant industry, as is evidenced by the number of people who were farmers, and by the many traders and craftsmen who relied on farming for their livelihoods. Yet the "supporting towns" — Christchurch, Lymington and Ringwood — possessed a surprising array of specialist shops such as would be found in much larger places.

The annual fairs for bullocks and horses have long since been discontinued at Christchurch, and Lymington's cheese, broom and cattle fairs are likewise events of the past. Only Ringwood has kept its status as a market town where sales of farm animals and produce still attract buyers not only from the whole of the New Forest, but other parts of southern England as well.

In addition to listing the occupations of the principal residents of the New Forest area, the directory entries give descriptions of the various places in 1852, information about carriers, coaches and railways, and postal arrangements.

HUNT & CO.'S DIRECTORY
OF
HAMPSHIRE,
COMPRISING COMPREHENSIVE

LISTS OF THE COMMERCIAL, PROFESSIONAL,
AND
PRIVATE RESIDENTS,

IN EVERY TOWN, VILLAGE AND HAMLET
THROUGHOUT THE ENTIRE
COUNTY OF HANTS,
INCLUDING THE
ISLE OF WIGHT,
ALSO IN THE
CITY OF SALISBURY,
TOGETHER WITH

A Descriptive Account of each Town,
AN EPITOME OF EACH VILLAGE,

Particulars of Carriers, Coaches, Railroads, and Water Conveyances,
Postal Arrangements and other Useful Information.

1852.

PRINTED FOR E. HUNT & Co.
PRACTICAL PUBLISHERS OF PROVINCIAL DIRECTORIES;

By BENSON and BARLING, Royal Library, Weymouth;

And may be had of B. W. GARDINER, Royal Blue Book Office,
Princes Street, Cavendish Square, London.

Subscribers Copy.—Price Eight Shillings & Sixpence.

TITLE PAGE, HUNT'S DIRECTORY
This comprehensive directory lists not only the gentry for each village, but also the tradesmen and farmers of the period.

BEAULIEU, a village & parish located on a river of its name, and 6¼ miles N.E. from Lymington. This village is noted for its once famous abbey, founded by King John. Here it was that Margaret of Anjou took refuge after the battle of Barnet. The parish is rich in antiquarian remains. Fairs chiefly for horses and cattle are held on the 15th of April and 4th of September. Population 1177. Acres 8880. County court town, Southampton. *Post Office*, at William Payne's; letters delivered at 7 a.m., and despatched to Southampton at 6.30 p.m.

Baker Rev. Frederick Walker,
Burt Rev. John Bartlett (Baptist minister), Beaulieu rails
Davies Rev. Geo. Jennings (curate)
Pocock Henry esq.

Adams John, Farmer, Bucklershard
Aldridge George, '*Horse & Jockey*', Beaulieu manor
Ball Eliza, butcher
Bennett Ann, baker

Bennett Charles, boot & shoemaker
Biddlecombe Benjamin, farmer
Biles William, farmer, St Leonards
Burden James, veterinary surgeon, Hazle copse
Burt John Bartlett, miller, Beaulieu rails
Carpenter Saml. farmer, Dock farm
Carpenter Samuel Jun. farmer
Carpenter Stephen, farmer, Godfrey's farm
Carpenter William jun. farmer
Cooper Stephen, farmer

BEAULIEU CHURCH

Cullen George, tailor
Dawkins Thomas, farmer
Dodds Isaac, farmer, Sowley
Eames James, farmer, Beck farm
Farlow James, '*Chequers*'
Figgins Thomas, farmer
Fletcher James, '*Montague Arms*'
Fry George, blacksmith
Gregory Thos., beer retailer, Beaulieu rails
Huggins Charlotte, farmer
Kemp Henry T.C. grocer & Baker
Judd Thos., farmer, Bargery farm
National school, Stevens James, & Vincent Elizabeth
Payne William, wheelwright; *Post Office*, and parish clerk
Pike Michael, farmer
Pinnock Thomas, farmer
Pinnock William, farmer
Randall Joseph, cooper
Rawlings Edward, blacksmith
Rowe John, grocery dealer, East end Beaulieu rails
Seager James, farmer
Scanes Wm., '*Ship Inn*' Bucklershard
Snook James, '*Forge and Hammer*', Sowley
Stote John, boot & shoemaker
Suffield Thomas, grocery dealer, Beaulieu rails
Tarver George, farmer
Wallis William, beer retailer, Beaulieu rails
Ward Benjamin, '*Royal Oak*' and tailor, Hill top
Ward John, saddler and harness maker
West William, grocery &c. dealer
Westbrook James & Francis, twine &c. spinners

White William, tailor
Willshire James, farmer, Swinleaze farm
Withers Henry, farmer

BISTERNE, a village 3 miles S. from Ringwood, and 6 N. from Christchurch. Population is included with the parish. County court town, Fordingbridge. Letters *via* Ringwood.

Dent Villiers, esq.
Mackie Rev. Charles, M.A. (curate)
Mills John, esq.

Foot John, parish clerk
Fowler Benjamin & William, farmers
Free School, Snelling William, and Neave Elizabeth

Hurdle Saml. '*George and Dragon*'

BOLDRE with its tythings of **Pilley, Rails, South Baddesley, Sway, Walhampton, & Warborne.**—Boldre is an extensive parish divided from Lymington, the County court town, by the river Boldre, and distant from it 2½ miles N. by E. Acres 10,394. Population 2874. *Post Offices* at Jesse Jenvey's, Boldre; and at Elizabeth Kemm's, Sway. Letters delivered about 7 a.m., and despatched to Lymington from Sway, at 6 p.m., and from Boldre at 7.

Beetham Albert William, esq. F.R.S. (barrister at law) Rope hill
Brine Rev. August. Jas., Boldre hill
Christian John, esq. Flexford
Cunningham Mrs. Battramsley
Gilbert Lt. Gen. Wm. Tweed villa
Gunning Rev. Joseph W. B.A., East Boldre
Heathcote Misses, St. Austins
Lewin Robert H. esq., the Elms
O'Brien Rev. Wm., East end cottage
Pardoe Mrs. Warborne
Peacock George, esq., Pylewell
Sivewright Capt. Edw. Vicar's hill
Shrubb Rev. Charles, M.A., (vicar,) Vicar's hill
Weld Jospeh, esq., East end

Bartlett William, beer retailer, Kettle Thorns
Buckle John, smith, Bowling green
Burt John B., miller, Hatchett mills
Burton Richard, farrier
Butt William, farmer and miller
Crouch Mrs., farmer, Sheepwash
Cull Charles, blacksmith
Dore Ann, '*Swan*,' Bridge
Egg William, farmer, East end
Hobbs Thomas, farmer Bull hill
Hopkins Thos., farmer, Mead ends
Jenvey Jesse, carpenter
Jones Thomas, carpenter, Portman common
Lancaster Charles, farmer
Lancaster William, smith East end
Macey Robert, relieving officer
Marshall William, farmer
Orchard William, farmer, Bull hill
Parker John, wheelwright
Penny John, farmer, Bowling green
Phillips James, farmer
Rowe John, baker, grocer, & draper, East end
Salter William, grocery dealer

BOLDRE CHURCH

Savage Thomas, farmer, Bull hill

Shephard Joseph, blacksmith and beer retailer, Portmore common

Smith William, '*Red Lion Inn*'

Spencer Robert, farmer, Baddesley

Sque Samuel, farmer, Norley

Suffield Thomas, miller and grocery dealer, Pilewell

Ward James, farmer, Norley

Wheeler Benjamin, farmer, East end

White Jas., '*New Inn*', Battramsley

White Mrs., farmer

Wooldridge William, beer retailer, Baddesley

Pilley

Breaker Alfred, blacksmith

Free School, Wyatt George and Answorth Jane

Kedgell John, shoemaker

Pinnick James, painter, &c.

Silk Jeremiah, '*Fleur de Lis*'

Waterman John, '*Carpenters' and Wheelwrights' Arms*' & carpenter

Withern William, farmer

Sway.

Jeffrey Rev. George F., M.A. (curate)

Jones, Rev. William

Mills Thomas, esq.

Clark William, farmer

Dible Sarah, '*Rose Inn*'

Hopkins Thomas, sen., farmer

Kitcher William, '*Hare and Hounds*'

Reed James, grocery, &c., dealer

Rickman James, woodman

Wicher John, farmer

Walhampton.

Burrard George, esq., Blake cottage

Burrard Rev. Sir George, bart.

Cooper Rowland, E., esq.

Geary Capt. John, R.N.

Lewin Robert H. esq., the Elms

Rooke Capt. Leonard Charles, R.N.

Curtis Henry, '*Waggon and Horses*'

Dore Amelia, '*Swan*,' & brick maker

Downer James, farmer

Downer Thomas, farmer

Gilbert Joseph M., marine painter

Shephard Edmund, carpenter

BRAMSHAW, a scattered village on the borders of Wilts, 5½ miles N. from Lyndhurst, (the County court town,) 8 W.S.W. from Romsey, and 13 S.E. from Salisbury. The parish contains about 280 acres of land, and about 1,000 inhabitants. Post Office, at Flora Henbest's; letters delivered about 9.30 a.m.

and despatched to Lyndhurst at quarter before 6 p.m.

Blake Mrs. Sarah

Cooper Rev. Mark, A.M.

Eyre George esq. Warrens

Shute Thomas D. esq.

Wilson Mrs. Elizabeth

Andrews Jno., farmer & parish clerk

Bredman Daniel, farmer

Cooper James, farmer

Fowkes Edward, dairyman

Free School, Woolridge Elizabeth

Gay Henry, farmer

Gill Henry, farmer

Henbest Charles, farmer

Henbest Flora, post office

King James, farmer

Knowlton James, blacksmith

Knowlton Robert, blacksmith

Lawrence John, beer retailer

Marshall Sarah, grocery dealer

Miller Henry, farmer

Page Hannah, '*Dragon*'

Snellgar William, grocery dealer

Stares John, farmer

Waldran James, grocery dealer

Wicks James, blacksmith

Wolfe Fanny, '*Bell*'

Young Charles, carpenter

Young John, carpenter

BRANSGORE, a chapelry in the parish of Christchurch, 5 miles N. of that town. Population about 700. County court

town, Christchurch; letters via Ringwood.

Bingham Lady

Castleman Henry, esq.

Jesson Thomas, esq.

Jesson, William Percy, esq.

Macdonogh Rev. Terence Michael, (curate)

Pocock Sir George, bart.

Abbott Priscilla, grocery dealer

Bebin Geo & Bros. brickmakers

Bolton James, farmer

Brown John, parish clerk and brick maker

Collins James, brickmaker & farmer

Head William, boot and shoemaker

Hopkins John, farmer

Jarrad John, brickmaker

National School, Sprod Samuel

Pardy Ann, grocery &c. dealer

Penny Henry, grocery &c. dealer

Petty Thomas, brickmaker & farmer

Pounds Stephen, beer retailer

Saunders Edward, beer retailer

Selfe John, '*Crown*'

Tuck John, grocery &c. dealer

White William, farmer

Whittle James, '*Three Tuns*'

BREAMORE, a village & parish 3 miles N. from Fordingbridge, the County court town, and 9 S. from Salisbury.

Population about 700. Acres 3440. Letters *via* Salisbury.

Hulse Sir Charles, bart.

Palmer Rev. James N. M.A. (rector)

Rooke Mrs. Sarah

Whitchurch Samuel, esq. Charlford

Absalom William, farmer

Barns William, farmer

Cook Charles, farmer

Curtis Henry, miller

Edsall Henry, blacksmith

Edsall James, blacksmith

Free School, Edsall John, and Absolom Letitia

Hall John, grocery dealer

Hall William, farmer

Hobbs Samuel, carpenter

Holloway John, farmer

Hood Daniel, farmer

Robertson Charles, '*Bat & Ball*'

Rooke Michael, farmer

Witt William, farmer

BROCKENHURST, a chapelry to the parish of Boldre, on the road leading from Lymington to Lyndhurst 4¼ miles N. by W. of the ormer place, and 3½ S. of the latter, is skirted on the north and east by the river Boldre, and in the vale below towards the north is a station on the Dorchester and Southampton railway. Acres

BROCKENHURST CHURCH

3,500. Population 1000. County court town Lymington. Post Office, at William Scorey's; letters delivered at 8 a.m. and despatched to Lymington at quarter before 10 a.m. *All letters delivered beyond a quarter of a mile from the village are subject to a small fee.*

Cumberbatch Lawrence H. esq., New park
Devey William, esq.
Lovell Francis F. esq.
Morant John, esq.
Mudge Mr. Richard R.
Smith Nathaniel Bowden, esq.

Aldridge John, bricklayer
Aldridge Sarah, glover
Ballard Henry, farmer
Barnes James, parish clerk
Brown James, farmer, butcher and maltster
Collis Elizabeth, '*Rose & Crown*'
Fuller Frederick, farmer
Godden Thomas, farmer
Hall Sarah, maltster
House Aaron, farmer
Jolliffe James, school
Humby Thos. baker and shop-keeper
Humby William, farmer
Kiddle Samuel, supervisor
Kidgell Thomas, shoemaker
Linney Thomas, shoemaker
Masters James, blacksmith
Mould Charlotte, grocery dealer

National School, Ash Mary Ann
Reed William, officer of Royal forest
Reed William, jun. ditto
Rogers William, blacksmith
Rooke William, tailor
Scorey John, baker and maltster
Scorey William, '*Railway Inn*'
Short John, shoemaker
Taylor Edmund, '*Bat & Ball*'
Wallis William, farmer
Wareham, R. carpenter & shopkpr.
Waterman, James, tailor
Waterman, Luke, blacksmith

BURLEYVILLE is a tithing in the parish of Ringwood, 5 miles east from that town. Population 533. County court town, Fordingbridge. Letters via Ringwood.

Craigg Rev. John Kershaw
Edwards Sampson, esq.
Esdaile Clement, esq.
Hill Lawrence, esq. Burly lawn
Jenkins Bev. Henry
Phelps Mrs. Picket post house
Robberts Mrs. Burly lawn
Robin Mr. Lewis, Shalden hill

Barron Charles, carpenter
Barrow William, bricklayer
Bond – , farmer, Stocks
Bradford Wm., carpenter & wheeler
Bromfield John, farmer, Highcroft

Bromfield Wm. farmer, Varley
Browning George, blacksmith
Cooper George, New forest keeper, Holmslay lodge
Davis James, farmer
Dowden Thomas, tailor
Garrett Thomas, blacksmith
Head Joseph, grocer and baker
Holloway, John, New forest keeper
Holman William, grocer & baker
Ingram Thos. farmer & shoemaker

Marchant George, wheelwright
Parmiter Thos. farmer, Pound farm
Scammell James, boot & shoemaker
Shelly George, grocery &c. dealer
Taylor Henry, '*Picket Post Inn*'
Taylor William, beer retailer
Taylor William, farmer, Burley st.
Vincent Robert, '*Queen's Head*'
Young Jane, grocery &c. dealer

CHRISTCHURCH, a market and county-court town, sea-port and corporate and parliamentary borough 12 miles W. from Lymington, 10 E. from Poole, 9 S. from Ringwood, 27 S. from Salisbury, 100 W.S.W. from London, and 7 S.W. from Osmondsley, where there is a station upon the Southampton and Dorchester railway.

In ancient times this place was denominated Twyneham-Bourne, but it now takes its name from the parish church, it is situated in the vale of Avon, between the rivers Avon and Stour, these streams forming a junction near the town and falling into Christchurch bay. The houses are mostly structures of the olden time and but few have been modernized, the town is nicely paved, lighted with gas and well supplied with pure water.

The principle source of employment and profit in Christchurch arises from the manufacture of watch and clock fusee chains which furnishes constant employment to about 400 young women and children, assisted by foremen. These articles are supplied to the watch, clock and chronometer makers of London, Liverpool, Coventry, and many other parts of England, and to different firms on the Continent. Fishing also furnishes employment for about 50 men, during the summer months, at the harbour's mouth, and many fine salmon and other fish are annually caught in the Avon and Stour. The prawn and lobster fisheries on the ledge off Hengistbury Head,

CHRISTCHURCH

CHRISTCHURCH (Continued)

likewise provide profitable employ for 20 boats, having two men, the produce of which are forwarded to the London markets, with the exception of enough being reserved for the consumption of the residents and visitors of Mudeford and neighbourhood. A small coasting trade is carried on, but access to the harbour is only attainable at high water, in consequence of the bar at its entrance; here, as at Poole, are two high waters in one tide, a phenomenon occasioned by the situation of this coast with respect to the Isle of Wight, and from the contraction of the channel, by the jutting out of the peninsula upon which Hurst Castle stands.

Christchurch being a prescriptive corporation was not interfered with by the Municipal Reform Act, it has a mayor and an indefinite number of burgesses, but the jurisdiction of the town is invested in the county magistrates, who sit in petty sessions every other monday. Previous to the Reform Act it returned two members to parliament, the franchise being vested solely in the corporation, about 35 in number, 20 being the greatest number who had voted for 30 years, it now sends one member to the British senate; the boundaries of the borough have been considerably extended, and the present constituency numbers about 320.

The Church was anciently the collegiate church of a priory, but of so remote a date, that all records of it are entirely lost. In the time of Edward the Confessor, it had a dean and 24 canons. It appears that the entire re-construction of this edifice was effected by Ralph Lambard, bishop of Durham, in the time of William Rufus, this prelate re-built it on a more extensive and superb design and dedicated it with deep solemnity to Christ. The church, although greatly altered since its re-construction, is a noble and interesting building, especially the nave, south aisle and the northern transept. In the interior is a magnificent sculptured altar-piece, representing the root and branch of Jesse, the figures, foliage, and architecture are combined with exquisite effect. The Wesleyans have an excellent chapel, and there is also a commodious one for Independents; there is likewise an extensive National School, besides another provided by the Independents upon the British system. Some few charities exist, in connection with the church, one being for apprenticing poor boys, others are bequests left for the needy and aged. A weekly market is kept on monday, and two annual fairs for horses and bullocks one on Trinity thursday and the other on October 17th. Christchurch parish contains 24,640 acres of land, with a population in 1851 of 6248, of which number 3002 are in the town.

POST OFFICE AND MONEY ORDER OFFICE, Bridge street. *Postmaster*, Mr. Abraham Pike. Letters are delivered daily at 7 a.m. and 4 p.m. and despatched to London at 11 a.m. and 9 15 p.m.; box closes at 9, p.m.

Adams Mrs. Sarah, High street
Aldridge Mrs. Ann, Castle street
Belford Mrs. Clara, the Priory
Bayley Saml. esq. Hengistbury place
Best Mr. Robert, Bargate
Brander Fredk. esq. the Priory
Burrows Rev. William F., (vicarage)
Collins Charles, esq. Jumper's park
Corbin Miss Ann, Bridge street
Elliott Capt. John, Burton
Elms Mrs. Ann, Purewell
Ferry Mrs. Charlotte, Castle street
Fletcher Rev. Joseph, High street
Gale Mr. Robert, Purewell
Gillum Mrs. Ann, High street
Goddard Mr. and Mrs. Bridge street
Green Mr. James, Purewell
Hannaford Mrs. Jane, Barrack road
Jeans Mr. William, Bargate
Lloyd Rev. Richd., (curate) High street

Lyte Miss Harriet, Purewell
Macauly George, esq. Purewell
Palmer Charles esq. Bridge street
Preston Mrs. Hester H. Church st.
Raaks Miss Elizabeth, Bargate
Steel Mr. Richard, Millhams street
Spickernell Mrs. Harriet, Bargate
Taylor Misses, Meeting house lane
Tice Misses, High street
White Mrs. & Miss, Millhams street
Wright Miss Susan, Church street

Miscellany of Traders, &c.

Aldridge Edward, farmer, Purewell
Austin Thos. coach builder, Purewell
Baker Benjamin, maltster & farmer, Bargate
Belbin Charles, collector of property and income taxes, Purewell

Bemister Samuel, relieving officer, Barrack road
Butler Richard, marine store dealer, Bargate
Cheatle Edward, serjeant of county police, Bargate
Crabb Edward, Thomas, inland revenue officer, Castle street
Davey Augustine, clothes dealer, Church street
Hiscock Hiram, stone mason, High st
Holloway Geo., boat builder, Bridge street
Holloway John Edward, architect, Barrack road
Lemmon Chas. accountant, High st.
Lockyer John, tinman, Pound lane
Lockyer William, crier, High street
M'Diarmid James, barrack master
Mintern Edward, currier, Purewell
Mott Sarah, upholstress, Castle st.
Orchard William, gardener, Bargate
Pain Henry, vestry clerk, Bridge st.
Pitt John, cooper, High street
Preston Henry, organ &c., builder, Purewell
Rose James, turner, Purewell
Sharp Richard, Millhams street
Sharp Risdon D., advocate in the County court, Millhams street
Union Workhouse, Church lane, *clerk*, Pain Henry; *master*, Gould John
Young Elizabeth, staymaker, High street

Agents—House & Estate.

Abbott John, Bridge street
Pain Henry, Bridge street

Auctioneers and Valuers.

Abbott John, Bridge street
Cranston George, Castle street
Farmer, Henry, Castle street
Reeks Charles, Castle street

Bakers.

Brixey Eliza, High street
Cluett William, Purewell
Cox Joseph, High street
Dowling Edward, Bargate
Feltham Edmund, Bargate
Goodbody Horatio N., Church street
Lockyer Henry, Bargate
Miller George, Church lane
Shirvell John, Purewell
Tizard William, Bargate
Troke John, Bargate
Walden George, High street

Bankers.

Wilts and Dorset Banking Co., Castle street, (draw on London and Westminster Bank,) *manager*, Stokes Henry

Beer Retailers

Button Henry, Purewell
Davis George, Gravel pits
Durndall Daniel, Bargate
Feltham Edmund, Bargate
French William, Bargate
Newman Samuel, Purewell
Pratt Charles, Purewell
Saunders Betsy, Bargate
Shirvell Edwd. Canteen, Barracks
Tarrant James, Millhams street

Blacksmiths.

Bemister James, Gravel pit
Caines James, Whitehall
Hext Giles, (whitesmith) Barrack road
Keffen Edward, Purewell cross
Lemmon Wm. (and farrier), Millhams street
Witcher Henry, Purewell cross

Booksellers & Printers.

Tucker William, High street
White Joseph, High street

Boot and Shoemakers.

Argyle Matthew & John, Purewell
Bound John, Whitehall
Brownen John, Church lane,
Clark Edmund, Church street
Cram John, Purewell
Dowden John, Purewell
Gritten William, Purewell
Hart Henry, High street
Hart Marmaduke, Purewell st.
Lockyer Henry, Bargate
Keeping George, High street
Payne Anthony, Bridge street
Preston John, Bargate
Vick John, Purewell
Whiffen George, Purewell

Brewers and Maltsters.

Aldridge George Olive, High street
King Joseph & James, High street
Pratt Charles, Purewell

Bricklayers & Plasterers.

Belbin George, Purewell
Davis Charles, Purewell
Eveleigh John, Bridge street
Preston Charles, Purewell

Brickmakers & Limeburners.

Belbin Brothers, Purewell
Holloway John, Hengistbury works

Builders.

Belbin Brothers, Purewell
Cornish Thomas, Purewell
Holloway John, Bridge street

Butchers.

Best Robert, High street
Domone Edmund, (and dealer in game), Castle street
Gubbins George & Wm. High street

CHRISTCHURCH (Continued)

Reeks John, Bridge street
Scott William, Castle street

Cabinet Makers.
Hooper John, Bridge street
Preston Henry, Purewell

Carpenters and Joiners
Bower Charles, Purewell
Hinton James, Pound lane
James Samuel, Purewell
Stone James, High street
Walden William, Bargate

Chemists and Druggists.
Jenkins Henry Maine, High
   street
Sharp Henry, High street
White Joseph, High street

Chimney Sweepers
Clark William, Bargate
Evans Thomas, Bargate

China, Glass, &c. Dealers.
Abbott John, Bridge street
Cranston George, Castle street
Hooper John, Bridge street

Coal Merchants
Bemister James, Barrack road
Elliott Edward Sleat, Castle
   street
Holloway John E. Barrack road
Tucker Benjamin, Purewell

Corn and Seed Merchants.
Fuller Gilbert, Purewell street
Hatchard William, High street
Hicks Charles, High street
Reeks Charles, Castle street

Fire & Life Insurance Agents.
Marked thus * denotes Fires,
   thus + Life.
* + *Atlas*, Abbott John, Bridge
   street
+ *Clerical & Medical*, Stokes
   Henry, High street
* *County &* + *Provident*, Lane
   Wm. Church street
* + *General*, Aldride G.O., High
   street
* + *Globe*, Farmer H. Castle
   street
* *Hants, Sussex & Dorset*, Sharp
   Risdon D. Millhams street
* + *Legal & Commercial*, Bennett
   Henry, High street
+ *London Mutual, and Guarantee
   Society*, Woodcock C., Pur-
   ewell
* *London Union*, Jenkins H.
   Bridge street
+ *Mentor*, Williams F.E., High
   street
* + *Norwich Union*, Pain Henry,
   Bridge street
+ *Palladinm*, Druitt J. High
   street
+ *Pelican*, Sharp R. Millhams
   street
* *Phoenix*, Tucker Wm. High

   street
* + *Royal Exchange*, Cranston
   Geo. Castle street
* + *Royal Farmers*, (and hail
   storm,) Reeks Charles, Castle
   street
+ *Solicitors and General*, Druitt
   Jas. High street
* *Sun*, Druitt James, High street
* *Sun*, Tucker William, High
   street
+ *Western*, Jenkins H. High
   street
* + *Yorkshire*, Lane E. Purewell

Fishmongers.
Butler John, Bargate
Clark Thomas, Purewell
Cutler Joseph, Church street
Pardey James, Church street

Furniture Brokers
Abbott John, Bridge street
Cranston George, Castle street
Oxford Jane, Purewell

Grocers & Tea Dealers.
Lane Elias, Purewell
Lane William, Church street
Pike Abraham, Bridge street
Tucker William, High street
Williams Frans. Edw., High
   street

Grocery & Sundries Dealers.
Burry Richard, Church street
Dale Elizabeth, Church street
Dowden John, Purewell
Dowling Edward, Bargate
Durndall Daniel, Barrack road
Feltham Edward, Bargate
French William, Bargate
Fripp Sarah, Purewell
Goodbody Horatio, Church
   street
Gregory Jane, Gravel pit lane
Grocatt Matthias, Purewell
Holloway John, Bridge street
Keffen Edward, Purewell cross
Jenkins Henry, Purewell
Lockyer Henry, Bargate
Newman Stephen, Bargate
Saunders Betsy, Bargate
Stone James, High street
Tarrant James, Millhams street
Tizard William, Bargate
Troke John, Bargate
Witcher Henry, Purewell cross

Hair Cutters and Perfumers.
Attewell William, High street
Bore Richard, Bridge street
Lockyer Edward, High street
Lockyer John Richard, Pur-
   ewell

Horse and Gig Proprietors.
Ball Frederick Edw. Purewell
Keeping George, High street

Inns and Public Houses.
Crispin, Purewell, Rose George
Cross Keys, Barrack rd. Hext, G.

Crown, Barrack rd. Summers,
   Dav.
Dolphin, Church st. Tongue,
   Ann
Eight Bells, Church street,
   Pardey, James
George Inn, (commercial), Castle
   st. Chiswick, William
Horse and Groom, Bargate,
   Sparks, William
King's Arms Hotel, (family,
   commr. and posting) Castle
   st. Humby, W.
Rising Sun, Purewell, Preston,
   C.
Ship, (commerical & market
   house), High street, Axford,
   George
Wellington, Barrack Road,
   Pardey, Sarah

Ironmongers, Braziers, &c.
Abbott Henry, Bridge street
Farmer Henry, Castle street
White George, High street

Linen and Woollen Drapers.
Bennett Henry, High street
Broadway, John, High street
Ferry Geo. and Wm. High
   street
Hicks Samuel, Purewell
Small George, Castle street
Woodcock Thomas, Purewell

Millers
Aldridge George O. High street
Miller George, Place mill

Milliners & Dress Makers
Dixon Jane & Harriet, High
   street
Barnes Mary A. Purewell street
Beames, M. & S. Purewell
   street
Footner, W. Purewell
Ginn Elizabeth, High street
Jennings Jane, Millhams street
Mitchell Sarah, High street
Tucker Elizabeth, High street

Painters, Plumbers & Glaziers
Belbin George, Purewell
Berry George, Purewell
Burry Richard, Church street
Holloway George, Bridge street
Jenkins Henry, Purewell
Long Robert, High street

Poulterers.
Betteridge George, High street
Corbin Henry, Purewell

Registrars of Births, &c.
Bemister Samuel, Barrack road
Pain Henry (superntndnt.)
   Bridge street

Saddlers & Harness Makers.
Burry David, High street
Burry Joseph, Purewell
Lemmon John, Bridge street

Schools
Marked thus * take Boarders
* Burrows Rev. Francis W.

   Vicarage
Bargate, Dunn Sophia
Bragge Jane, Purewell
Cornish Elizabeth, Church
   street
Grammar, Church st., Young
   Edwd.
Infants', High st. Lemmon
   Mary
Lemmon Eliza, Bridge street
Miller Mary Ann, High street
National, High st. Wheeler
   Henry and Maynard Susanna
Protestant Dissenters, Meeting
   house lane, Steel Rod., and
   Young Mary; *Infants*, White
   Edan
* Rickard Sarah, High street
* Sopp Jane & Sarah M. High
   street
* Sopp John, Amsterdam house
Stroud Mary, Church lane
Young Jane, Barrack road

Solicitors
Druitt Jas. H. (and clerk to
   county court, and to magistrates and town clerk), High
   street
Sharp R. and J. Millhams street

Straw Bonnet Makers.
Dixon H & J. High street
Ginn Elizabeth, High street
Tilley Keziah, High street

Surgeons.
Goddard John Bryer, Purewell
Palmer Arthur, Bridge street
Pocock James, High street
Welch James Kemp, High
   street

Wheelwrights
Butler James, Gravel pits
Guy George, Purewell
Head George, Purewell

Tailors.
Marked thus * are Drapers also
* Bennett Henry, High street
Billett John, Bridge street
* Broadway John, High street
Cutler George, Church lane
Davis John, Gravel pit
Durndell William, Pound lane
Freemantle James, High street
* Ferry Geo. & William, High
   street
Innes James, Purewell
Phillips George, Purewell
Wagg George, Whitehall

Watch & Clock Makers.
Butler George, Bridge street
Hardy Albert, Purewell
Hext Giles, Barrack road
Watt Edward, High street

**Watch & Clock, Fuzee Chain
   and Hook Makers.**
Cox Charles & Co., High street
Hart William & Co., Bargate
Jenkins Henry T. Bridge street

CHRISTCHURCH (Contd.)

Wine & Spirit Merchants.

Aldridge George G. High street

King Joseph & James, High street

Omnibus.—To Christchurch road station from the 'King's Arms Hotel,' daily at 11.10 a.m. and 3.30 p.m.; and to Bournemouth daily at 9.15 a.m.

Carriers.—To Christchurch road station, *Newman*, from his house Purewell, daily at 8 a.m.—To Bournemouth, *Butler*, from the 'Horse & Groom,' daily 8.30 a.m.—To Lymington, *Soden*, from his house, Bargate, mon. wed. and sat. at 8.45 a.m.—To Poole and Bournemouth, *Curle*, from his house, Bridge st. mon. tues. thurs. & sat. at 8.30 a.m.; and *Sparks*, from the 'Horse and Groom,' mon. tues. thurs. & sat. at 8.30 a.m.—To Ringwood and Wimborne, *Tilley*, from the 'Cross Keys,' tues. thurs. and sat. at 9.30 a.m.—To Salisbury, *Bowers*, from the 'George,' mon. and fri. at 8 a.m.; and *Roberts*, from his house, Purewell, mon. & fri. at 9 a.m.—To Southampton and Lyndhurst, *Tilley*, from his house, Bargate, mon. and thurs. at 9 a.m.

Bure.

Hunt Mr. James

White William, esq. Bure Homage

Baker William, farmer

Clapcott Henry, gardener

Stanpit.

Burden Miss Mary

Dobson Rev. John (rector of High cliff)

Hooper Mrs. Caroline

North Mr. John

Barnes Thomas, coal carrier

Bemister John, carpenter

Cox Francis, carpenter

Derham George, master mariner

Derham, Sarah, farmer

Gannaway Walter, grocer

Groves Lemuel, farmer

Head George, wheelwright

Head George, '*Ship in Distress*'

Holloway Sarah, laundress

Hopkins William, wood carrier

Jones John, corn and coal dealer

Keffen Edwd. grocer and smith

Leary Susannah, lodging house

Meadus John, shoemaker

Preston William, bricklayer

Scott William, painter

Smith John, carpenter

Vick John, pilot and fisherman

Vick Joseph, pilot and fisherman

Vick Joseph, jn. ditto

ELING is a very extensive parish, and includes the hamlets of Bartley, Cadnam, Calmore, Hounsdown, Marchwood, Ower, Rumbridge, Totton, Winsor & Woodlands. Eling is about 5 miles N.W. from Southampton, either by rail or road. At Marchwood are the Government powder magazines. Totton is a pretty hamlet, bordering upon the river Test; the whole neighbourhood is picturesque and beautiful, abounding as it does with river and inland scenery, besides being studded with agreeable residences. The parish contains three churches. Population 5,817. Acres 24,500. County-court town Southampton. *Post Office*, at Thomas Read's, Totton; letters delivered at 7.30 a.m., and despatched to Southampton at 9 p.m. Box closes at 8.30, but letters may be posted up to the despatch, by affixing to each an extra penny stamp.

Bourne Miss, Testwood house

Duckworth Wm. esq., Beechwood house

Haddon Mr. James, Salisbury road

Horton Mrs. Salisbury road

Kneller Mrs., Ashurst bridge

Lynn Walter, esq., Rushington ho.

Oke Rev. Wm., (curate) Mountfield

Paulet Sir Henry, bart., Little Testwood

Paulet Rt. Hon. Lady Henry, ditto

Phillips Rev. Wm., Joseph George, Vicarage

Phillips Rev. George, M.A., ditto

Saunders, Andrew, esq., Downs ho.

Stanley Wm. Sloane esq., & Wm. H.S. junr. esq., Paulton's house

Thomas Jas. C. esq., Colbury house

Timson Rev. Edward, Tatchbury mount

Wake Geo. Anthony esq., Manor house, Tatchbury

Westmacott Mrs. Sarah, Lampits

Wilson Mrs., Langley cottage

Adams James, cattle dealer, Rushington

Adams William, '*Anchor*'

Anthony Edward S., corn merchant

Bessant Wm., farmer, Ashurst lodge

Blake John, farmer

Capon William, yeoman

Crook Samuel and John, & Walter, builders, Jacobs' gutter lane

Crook Samuel, parish clerk

Dumper George, maltster,

Water lane

Eeles Benjamin, yeoman, little Testwood

Facey William, boot & shoemaker

Giles John, yeoman, Rushington

Glen David, yeoman, Fletchwood

Godden James, grocery dealer

Graveley Edward, Hy. soap maker

Haddon Jas. jun. miller, Fleetwood

Hunt George, miller & mealman

Hurst Henry, yeoman, Wade farm

Kimber Wm. farmer, Newbridge

Kitchen John, pilot

Lainson Wm. corn & coal merchant

Lane James, Chevess' farm

Lane William, yeoman, Calmor

Longland Geo. highway surveyor

Lowman Thomas, carpenter

Lowman William, coal merchant

Maber John, farmer, Willswood

Martin John, boot and shoemaker

Mintram William, yeoman

Moody Henry, farmer, Woodlands

Parker Geo. pilot, Crackmorehard

Penford George, yeoman, Little Testwood

Philpot Henry, yeoman, Durley

Rooke Sarah, ladies school

Soffe & Adams, millers, Eling mill

Spooner Wm. Charles, bone and guano merchant, manufacturer of super-phosphate & other chemical manures—and bone mills

Stote George, blacksmith

Taylor Ann, beer retailer

Union Workhouse, New forest, master, Miall George Horatio

Trowbridge Chs. yeoman, Tatchbury

Whitmarsh, Robt. farmer, Waterman's farm

Bartley

Coffin Capt. Henry Edward, R.N.

Eyre Robert, esq.

Jones Ashur, esq. Bartley mount

Broomfield Aaron, baker

Dunnings Mark & Henry, farmers

Emery Henry, boot & shoemaker

Gear William, yeoman

Light John, timber merchant

Osman John, yeoman

Rebbeck Henry, yeoman

Roe James, post office

White Edward, yeoman

Cadnam

Forbes Mrs. Laura cottage

Boham Henry, yeoman

Goddard Thomas, farmer

Hussey George '*White Hart*'

Lovell George, blacksmith

Luker Joseph, '*New Inn*'

Pope George, '*Coach and Horses*'

Stevenson, William, nail maker

Young Wm. grocery &c. dealer

Hounsdown

Tomlinson, Lieut. Nicholas, R.N.

Bunday George, brickmaker

Cheetham Samuel, brick, draining tile and pipe works—res. Totton

Dawkins Thomas, blacksmith

Ford John, grocery &c. dealer

Green James, '*Hunters Inn*'

Green Robert, beer retailer

Hale James, bricklayer

Hewer Francis, farmer

Hillier Thomas, baker

Hobbs Thomas, grocery dealer

Lowe Thomas, tailor

Marchwood

Martelli Rev. Thomas, M.A.

Phipps Col. Paul, Byam's house

Saunders Mrs. Margaret, Byam's h.

Aldridge James, blacksmith

Edsoll George, blacksmith

Grimstead James, baker & grocer

Jones George, market gardener

Loney John F. surveyor of taxes

Paice Robert, farmer & maltster

Payne Thomas, farmer, Ipley

Philpot Nathaniel, farmer

Reeves Samuel, farmer

Register George, '*White Horse*'

Richman Charles, wheelwright

Topp Edward, farmer

White Arnold, farmer

Netley

Bull Christopher, farmer

Cave Elias, farmer

Cave Elias, yeoman

Coffin John, '*White Horse*'

Gilbert William, baker

Osman William, blacksmith

Smith, William, painter &c.

Ower

Soffe John, farmer

Underwood Richard '*Vine Inn*'

Winsor

Budd Richard, farmer

Fuller John, farmer

Gear Abraham, boot & shoemaker

National School, Jerram Thomas

Light John, farmer

Prior John, farmer

Scammel Thomas, yeoman

Taylor William, beer retailer

Whitmarsh Robert, farmer

ELING (Contd.)

Woodlands

Brownjohn Henry, esq.
Westmacott Miss Sarah

Moody Henry, yeoman
Shide Joseph, yeoman
OMNIBUSES,—from Eling, Totton and Rumbridge, to Southampton four times daily (except sundays)

ELLINGHAM, a village and parish 2 miles N. from Ringwood, the County-court and post town. Acres 1680. Population 346.

Gabbatas John, esq.
Green Rev. Frederick (vicar)
Paget Arthur, esq.

Ayles Daniel, farmer
Bailey Wm. '*New Inn*' & smith
Brown Alexander, farmer
Harvey George, farmer
Hatchard Isaac, farmer
Ingram Charles, shoemaker
Jeffries John, parish clerk
Lucas George, farmer
Lucas Roberts, farmer
Neale James, farmer
Toms Robert, farmer
Young Ann, grocery dealer

FAWLEY CHURCH

FAWLEY with the chapelry of Exbury, and the hamlets of Hardley, Lepe, and Langley. This very extensive parish is about 5 miles S.E. from Hythe. Population 1830. Acres 6590. County-court town Southampton. Exbury, standing on the east bank of the river Beaulieu, is about 10 miles N.E. from Lymington, and 9 from Southampton by water. Lepe, a tything, lies nearly opposite COWES, being about 2 miles S. from Exbury, and 7 from Hythe. Langley and Hardly are both hamlets, the former is 5 miles from Hythe, and Hardly is about 2½ miles S. from Hythe. *Post Office*, Fawley, at John Johnston's. Letters are delivered at 7 a.m. and despatched to Southampton at 7.15 p.m. *Post Office*, Exbury, at Ann Stephen's. Letters are delivered at 8 a.m. and despatched to Southampton at 5.30 p.m.

Cleggett Mr. Ashlett
Drummond Andrew Robert, esq., Cadland park
Drummond Major Gen. Eagle-hurst
Foster James, esq. Copthorne house
Gibon Rev. Wm M.A. (rector)
Harrisson Mrs. A.M. Rime hall
Harrisson Rev. Robt. E., M.A. ditto
Lambert Hon. O.G. Stonehall

cott.
Langford Mrs. Rime hall
Mitchell Lieut. William Charles, Calshot castle
Munday John, esq. Cadland
Robins Capt. George, Forest lodge
Soffe Mrs. Thomas, Spring cottage
Studds Mr. William, Rimehall
Trattle Miss Mary Ann, Laura cott.

Arnold James, farmer, Stonehills
Barnard Thomas, builder, Copthorne
Barns George, '*Falcon Inn*'
Blow Thomas, blacksmith
Bound Thomas, beer retailer, Lazy town
Budd Robert, surgeon
Caton Jas. saddle & harness maker
Caton Richard, boot & shoemaker
Cheyney John, farmer, Stone farm
Cheyney Thomas, farmer, Stanswood farm
Churchill Samuel, surgeon and M.D.
Cullen Robert, boot and shoemaker
Elliott Edwin B. maltster
How Frank, painter &c. Ashlet
Johnston John, baker, grocer & c.
Lane William, Farmer, Stanswood
Martin Richd. '*Jolly Sailor*'

Ashlet
Munday Jsph. farmer, Church farm
National School, Marsh John and Amelia
Pinnick James, carpenter
Pitt William, brewer and maltster
Sharp Bichard, farmer
Soffe Thomas William, builder
Thicks John, stone mason
Waterman Wm. grocer and baker
Westbrook Peter, tailor
Westbrook Robert, farmer
Westbrook William, butcher
Wheeler Dinah, dressmaker
Wheeler Henry, parish clerk
Wyatt Charles, bailiff, Rhime hall
Wyatt William, farmer, Field's farm
White Richard, boot and shoemaker
Willis Richard, carrier to Southampton, tues. thurs. and sat.
Wyatt Wm. farmer, Field's farm

Exbury

Hoskins Rev. E.H. (curate) Parsonage
Royde John, esq. Exbury House

Carpenter James, farmer
Cull Robert, blacksmith
Cresswell Sophia, farmer
Haywood John, beer retailer, Iper's bridge

Henwood Mary, farmer
National School, Smith Matilda
Norris William, boot and shoemaker
Plascott Henry, carpenter &c.
Stephens Ann, baker &c.
Tillyer Sarah, '*Mitford Arms Inn*'
Tullidge George, game keeper
Waterman William, farmer

Lepe.

Callender Thos. esq. Inchmerry h.
Robinson Lieut. James Chas. R.N.
Drudge William, farmer
Wheller John, '*Ship*' and baker

Langley

Bundy Francis, blacksmith
Bundy James, farmer, &c.
Lampard John, grocery dealer
Lewis John, farmer
Nicholas John, brick maker
Tiller John, carpenter &c.
White Betty, farmer
White Henry, yeoman
White Joseph, farm bailiff

Hardly.

Ayles William, grocery &c. dealer
Cooper Thomas, yeoman
Hearn George, yeoman
Pewsey John, grocery &c. dealer
Rann Thomas, farmer

FORDINGBRIDGE, a market and county-court town and parish, delightfully situated near the borders of and in the division of the New Forest, chiefly on the north west bank of the upper Avon, here bestrided by a substantial, well-built stone bridge of seven arches. The town is partly located on the main road between Salisbury and Ringwood, distant 12 miles S. from the ormer place, and 6½ N. from the latter, 20 W. from Southampton and 92 S.W. from the metropolis. Flax spinning and the manufactures of bed ticking and sail cloth, form the main stay of the town, furnishing employment to a large number of industrious operatives, whose wages being chiefly expended in the place add most materially to its general prosperity. Another source of considerable emolument to the town is derivable from an extensive corn mill, which calls into daily requisition the assistance of very many persons to carry out its various ramifcations. This town rendered itself conspicuous for its manufactures as early as the formation of Domesday book, in which it is written Forde, and stated to have contained one church and two mills, an indisputable proof of its original consequence. Fordingbridge has repeatedly suffered from fires, the ravages of which have tended in a great measure to decrease its ancient importance. Friday is the market day, and a fair is annually held on the 9th of September. The parish church of *St. Mary* is an interesting structure of considerable antiquity, having a square embattled tower, containing a clock and five bells; the living is a vicarage in the presentation of the provost and fellows of King's College, Cambridge, and now possessed by the Rev. Charles Hatch. The other places of worship here belong to the Independents, the Wesleyans and the Society of Friends, and there are public schools on the British and National systems, and some charities, connected with the church. Bicton, Burgate, Gorley, and Stuckton, are all hamlets within the parish of Fordingbridge, and altogether comprise 5818 acres of land, and by the census of 1851, contained 3357 inhabitants.

POST OFFICE AND MONEY ORDER OFFICE. *Postmaster* Mr. James Chubb; letters delivered at 8 a.m. and despatched to Salisbury at 7.30 p.m.; box closes at quarter past 7, but letters will be received till 7.25 p.m., if an extra 1d. stamp is affixed.

Blakeman Mr. John
Brice Major George Tito
Chubb Mr. Samuel
Coote Eyre, esq.
Fricker Mrs. Betsy
Harrisson Thomas, esq.
Hatch Rev. Chas. M.A. (vicar)
Heath Miss
Hodding Matthias Thomas, esq.
Joyce Archibald Duncan, esq.
Joyce Misses Gertrude & Martha
Joyce Mr. Edward
Key Mr. Jonathan M.
Lukin James William, esq.
Oates Mr. Robert
Veal Mr. Joseph
Williams Rev. Morgan
Wormington Edward, esq.

Miscellany of Traders, &c.
Alexander Js. plumber, painter, &c.
Andrews Jno. Wm. vetnry. surgeon
Applin Thos. baker and confectioner
Atkins John, registrar of births, deaths, and relieving officer
Bailey Arthur, blacksmith
Bailey Robert, blacksmith
Ball Thomas, basket maker
Bartlett Eliza, milliner
Bartlett Francis, shoemaker
Blachford Richd. boot & shoemaker

Brazier Edmund, builder
British School, Rawkins Thos. Geo. and Elizabeth
Brothers Chas. boot & shoemaker
Brothers John, tailor
Brothers Wm. painter
Brown Joseph, cooper
Browning Philip, maltster
Budd Benj. John, solicitor
Chalk Arthur, bricklayer

Chubb James, surveyor and post master
Chubb Jas. jun. draper &c.
Coles John, miller
Cottman John, builder
Croft Saml. & Jas. R. tailors
Curtis Ann, grocery dealer
Curtis James, miller
Dale George, hair dresser
Davy Robert, solicitor
Day Jno. basket & chair maker
Dorrington John, glover, &c.
Eastman Saml. turner & chair mkr
Edsall Henry, smith
Fulford Ann, bookseller and grocer
Gray William, grocer and draper
Griffin Sarah, grocery dealer
Hall William, butcher
Hannen Charles, '*King's Arms*'
Hannen John, insurance agent
Hannen John jun. auctioneer
Haydon Fredk. K. chemist & agent to Medical invalid & gen. life office
Hayter Henry, butcher
Hayter James, saddler, &c.
Henbest Francis F. carpenter
Hennen Solomon, boot maker
Hicks Emma, seminary
Hicks Thomas, boot and shoemaker
Hilary Charles, ironmonger
Hooper John, '*George Inn*'
Horsey William, wheelwright
Huxtable George, grocery dealer
Inland Revenue Office, at the '*Greyhound*,' *officer*, Dunn James
Jeffries John, parish clerk
Jeffries, Thomas, shoe maker
Jeffries, Wm. brewer and maltster
Jenkins Thomas, tailor
Keay John, grocery dealer
Kerly John, boot and shoemaker

Langford Thomas, tailor
Lawes George, tailor
Legg Benjamin, general dealer
Maidment Joel, saddler &c.
Manning Jane, dress maker
Marsh George, grocery dealer
Mercer Elizabeth, grocery dealer
Merrie George, cooper
Mitchell Titus, grocer
National School, Maton Elizabeth
Neave Josiah, miller
Pain William, boot and shoemaker
Pinhorn Francis, draper
Pinhorn Humphrey, surgeon; agent to the Wilts and Dorset Banking Co. and to Sun fire & life office
Pope George, clothier
Precey Edmund, watchmaker
Rawlence G.C. supernt. registrar
Rawlence George Curtis & Brothers, maltsters
Read Nathaniel, blacksmith
Reeves J. grocer, and agent to the county fire & provident life offices
Roach Edmund, farmer
Rose John, '*Rose and Crown*'
Rouse Charles, carrier
Russell, John, baker
Senior George, surgeon (and coroner for Fordingbridge hundred)
Sims Daniel, blacksmith
Spratt John, '*New Inn*'
Stewart Jas. '*Star Inn*' (commercial and posting)
Stickland Selina, day school
Sworn George, '*Greyhound Inn*' (commercial)
Thompson, Penny, and Westlake, flax spinners & canvas manufacts.
Tiller Stephen, carpenter
Verge Anna, dyer

FORDINGBRIDGE CHURCH

FORDINGBRIDGE
(Continued)

Wakeley William, tailor
Waters George, 'Crown'
Watts Charles, carrier
Watts George, butcher
Welch Benjamin, boot & shoemaker
Withers Richard, spirit merchant
Witt William, farmer

COACH.—To Ringwood from 'Grey-hound,' daily (except sun.) at half past 10 morng. and returns for Salisbury at ¼ past 1, afternoon.

CARRIERS—To Christchurch through Ringwood, *Bower*, from the 'George', and *Roberts*, from the 'Greyhound,' both tues. & sat. at 4 aft.—To Poole, *Rouse*, on thurs. and sun. at 10 night. To Ringwood, *Rouse*, daily at 10 morn.) (*also per Christchurch carriers*)—To Salisbury, *Bower*, from the 'George', mon. and fri. at 2 aft.; also *Roberts*, from 'Greyhound' on mon. and fri. at 2 aft.; and *Rouse*, on tues. thurs. and sat. at 8 morn.—To Southampton, *Watts*, on mon. at 12 night, and fri. at 9 morn.

Bicton.
Early Joseph, beer retailer
Pinhorn Vincent, farmer

Burgate.
Bartlett James, farmer, Midgham
Bryant James, farmer
Hayter Stephen, farmer
Parrett James, farmer
Phillpott James, farmer
Sweatman Adam, farmer
Sweatman William, farmer
Union Workhouse; master & matron, Dewson William and Frances
Wing Vincent, farmer

Gorley.
Bartlett Rev. John, Pemberton

Cheater James, farmer
Cheater James, jun. farmer
Collins Elizabeth, beer retailer
Cutler James Pottle, farmer
Hayter William, farmer
Ingram Charles, farmer
Jones Benjamin, farmer
Read Peter, beer retailer
Thomas William, farmer
White Eleanor, farmer

Stuckton
Coles, Charles, shop keeper
Collins Francis, farmer
Rose John, farmer
Viney Richard, farmer
Witt Richael, miller and farmer

GODSHILL is an extra parochial hamlet to Fordingbridge, and 2 miles east from it. Population included with that town. Acres about 860. Letters via Fordingbridge.

Chubb Thomas, farmer
Kent George, farmer
Mowland Matthew, farmer
Newman Mary, farmer
Nutbeem Jane, farmer
Witt George, '*Fighting Cocks*' and blacksmith

HALE is a village and parish 4 miles N.E. of Fordingbridge, the county-court town. Population about 1000. Acres 1210. Letters via Salisbury.
Goff Joseph, esq.

Cooper Stephen, farmer & parish clrk.
Harrison John, farmer
Long William, farmer
Philpot Nathaniel, blacksmith

HORDLE, a chapelry united to Milford, 4 miles W.S.W. from Lymington, the county-court and post town, and 8 E. from Christchurch, containing rather more than 3,879 acres; & about 850 inhabitants.

Chambers Wm. F. M.D. Hordlecliff
Falconer Alexander Pytts, esq.
Heathcote Rev. Samuel, (curate)
Howkins Theophilus, esq.
Milner John, esq. Arnewood park
Symonds Rear Adml. Thos. Edw.

Thomas Edward, esq. Downton
Wright Major, Arnwood

Beck Thomas, farmer
Bell William, shoemaker
Buddon John, grocery dealer
Calway John, farmer
Corbin James, farmer
Hawkins John, farmer
Jerrard Josiah, farmer
Linney John, farmer
Meaton James, farmer
Peckham George, baker & grocer
Rogers Joseph, blacksmith
Saunders Charles, carpenter
Swift James, beer retailer
Tyler John, '*Royal Oak*'
Wearn George, blacksmith
Wilson John, farmer

HYTHE is a chapelry in the parish of Fawley, 12 miles by land from Southampton, but by water only 3, and across which boats from the latter town are constantly plying. Population 680. County-court town Southampton. *Post Office*, at Thomas Tovey's; letters are delivered at 8 a.m. and despatched to Southampton at 8 p.m.

Barnes, Miss Mary Ann
Bower Rev. William Henry, (Independent minister)
Bray Mr. George
Browne Capt. Richard, R.N. Frost lane
Covey Mrs.
Dancaster Mrs. Sarah
Deschamps Mrs. Mary
Dodd Rev. Henry Luke
Dodds Mrs.
Dowden Miss Mary, Frost lane

Dudman Capt. Robert
Greeves Mr. Henry
Hobart Hon. Mrs.
Hughes Mrs. Jenny, Frost lane
Irby the Honbl. & Rv. Adolphus Frederick A.M. (perpetual curate)
Jones Mr. James
Kelsall Charles, esq.
Lejeune Mrs. Mary
Pare Rev. Frederick
Simon Mr. John
Soffe Mrs. Ann
Smith Mr. Thomas
Spencer Mr. Arthur
Westcott Mr. George

Baker John, boot and shoemaker
Baker William, grocery &c. dealer
Bound Thomas, boot & shoemaker
Bound William, farmer, Frost lane
Bower Rev. Wm. Henry, academy
Bowie Sarah, ladies school
Bunday Geo. carpenter, Frost lane
Cosens Mary, draper and grocer
Cotten Richard, bricklayer
Cotten Richard jun. grocery dealer
Dixon William, grocery &c. dealer
Ediss Thomas, carpenter
Elcock James, baker and grocer
Elcock William, tailor
French Mary, grocery dealer
Fry Frederick, relieving officer, and registrar of births and deaths for Fawley district, Buttash

IBSLEY CHURCH

HYTHE (Contd.)

Froud Wm. boot and shoemaker
German George, bricklayer
Gird Benjamin, tailor
Holloway Thomas, brewer & retailer of beer
Jarman Thomas, grocer & tea-dealer
Langar Joseph, ironmonger
Marks Joseph, saddler and harness maker
Martell William, builder
Martell William, jun. builder
National School, Collins Richard and Wyatt Mary
Phillips Henry, carpenter
Pinnick Robert, butcher
Ralfs Samuel, '*Anchor and Hope*'
Rann James, farmer, Frost lane
Smith Frederick, Robt. beer retailer
Stephens Henry, beer retailer
Stephens John, '*Lord Nelson Inn*'
Stephens Thomas, pier toll keeper
Tyson Thomas William, tailor
White George, builder
White Josiah, blacksmith
Wiukworth Wm. '*Drummond Arms*'
Withers William, baker
Witt Ann, grocery &c. dealer
Wyatt Thos. clerk of Hythe chapel

IBBESLEY, a village and parish midway between Ringwood and Fordingbridge. Acres 870. Population 316. County-court town Fordingbridge. Letters *via* Ringwood.

Coles Jeremiah, wheelwright
Curtis Charles, beer retailer
Curtis Stephen, farmer
Free School, Brown Elizabeth
Hayter Wm. farmer & parish clerk
Head Stephen, farmer

LYMINGTON.—This is a market town and parliamentary borough, governed by a corporation; it is 18 miles S.W. from Southampton, 27 S.S.E. from Salisbury, 29 S.S.W. from Winchester, 94 S.W. from London, and about 4½ S. from Brockenhurst, where there is a station upon the Southampton and Dorchester railway. In Domesday book we find the town styled *Lentune*, subsequently it was called *Limentun*, thence modernized to the more euphonius appellation of Lymington.

The town stands on a gentle acclivity upon the western bank of the Boldre, a stream falling into that part of the English channel called the Solent, across which to Yarmouth, Isle of Wight, it is about 5 miles. It consists principally of one long street which is spacious and open, and the houses therein are in general good erections, more especially those of recent date,—those located near the coast side commanding fine marine prospects. Many improvements have been latterly effected by pulling down several old and unsightly houses and buildings, modern ones occupying their sites; also a general improvement in the shop fronts, &c., giving the town a much more respectable appearance. Concerts, balls, and other amusements occasionally take place in the Assembly Rooms at the Angel Hotel, and there is a Literary and Scientific Institute, the members holding their meetings at a building formerly used as a theatre, but which is now discontinued for dramatic representations, and converted into lecture and reading rooms, and provided with a well-selected library. In the summer season Lymington is much frequented for sea-bathing, and the Baths, which are arranged in a superior manner, render this an agreeable spot for visitors and others; independent of this, the scenery around the neighbourhood is picturesque and beautiful. The town is well lighted with gas and abundantly supplied with water. Medicinal salts and the common salt for domestic uses, are manufactured here, and universally acknowledged to be of superior quality; ship and yacht building is carried on with spirit, especially the latter, and many of those swift sailing vessels, as well as H.M.R. cruizers, are constructed here; brick-making also forms an important branch of commerce. Cargoes of coals and slates are brought hither—the former in large quantities. The foreign imports are timber and deals from Canada, and timber, tar, hemp, &c. from the Baltic; but as the harbour is safe and of late years great attention having been paid to encourage and encrease the foreign trade, there is every probability that its various ramifications will eventually be fully developed. The exports are timber, bricks, cattle, and forest colts; and a considerable traffic is carried on with the Isle of Wight by means of a steam vessel.

James I. originally incorporated this town, which charter was acted upon until the passing of the Municipal Reform act; by this latter measure the governing power is entrusted to a mayor, 4 aldermen, and 12 councillors with their subordinate officers, who are styled "the mayor and burgesses of the borough of Lymington." Petit sessions take place every alternate Saturday, for the division of Lymington and New Forest, and a court is held monthly at the Town Hall, under the recent County Court's Act, for hearing and determining plaints, not exceeding £50. Queen Elizabeth, in the 27th year of her reign, empowered Lymington to return two representatives to parliament, a privilege it still enjoys. At county elections this town is a polling place for South Hants. The church, (St. Thomas-a-Becket,) though devoid of uniformity and architectural grace, nevertheless convenient in its internal arrangement and is capable of holding 2000 persons—it is constructed of bricks and stone, having a castellated quadrangular tower, which is surmounted by a cupola. The Baptists and Independents have each a chapel here, the latter one was erected in 1847, and is a handsome building in the Gothic style; attached are spacious school rooms where about 300 scholars are daily instructed; there are likewise boys' and girls' schools (with residences for master and mistress,) forming a neat building of modern erection, where from 300 to 400 poor children are taught upon the National system; and a small endowed Grammar School. Lymington gives name to a parochial union under the Poor Law Amendment Act; it comprises six parishes. Fairs for cheese, brooms, and cattle, are held on May 12th and October 2nd, and a weekly market on saturday. The parish of Lymington contained in 1851, 4164 inhabitants.

POST OFFICE & MONEY ORDER OFFICE, High street. *Post master*, Mr. Wm. Le Jeune Galpine. Letters for London, Southampton, &c. must be posted before 12.30 noon and 10 p.m. for Weymouth, Dorchester, Poole, Wimborne, Ringwood, Wareham, &c., before 1.15 p.m. and 10 p.m.;—for Lyndhurst and Brockenhurst before 10 p.m.;—for Boldre, Milford, Pennington, Sway, Wootton, Woodside, &c., must be posted before 5.30 a.m.

Letters delivered at 7 a.m. in summer, and 8 in winter, and at 5 and 9 p.m.

Ahmuty Mrs. Letitia M. High st.
Andres Miss C. Stewart cottage
Badcock Mr. John L. 11 Nelson pl
Bailey Miss, 20 Southampton bgs.
Bannerman Mrs. Bellmore lane
Barfot Mrs. & Misses, Church lane
Bartlett William, esq. St. Thomas st
Beckley Rev. Thomas, High street
Beckwith Miss Cath. R. High st
Beeston Miss Frances R. High st.
Bennion Mrs. Ann, Woodend cott.
Brown Mrs. & Miss, 12 Nelson pl.
Bull Rev. Edward, High street
Burer Lieut. Col. Gabriel, Gosport street
Bursey Mr. John, Mrs. and Miss, High street
Carnac Sir John Rivett, bart. Warborne
Castle Capt. W.L. R.N. New lodge
Clark Mrs. Elizabeth, High street
Creighton Mrs. C. Woodside
Dalton George, esq. Woodside
Dannell Mrs. & Misses, Fairfield
D'Arcy Mrs. Catharine L.E. High st
Dennett Miss Ann, Old town house
Drawbridge, Mr. Wm. High street

Elgar Mr. Benj. St. Thomas street
Emmott Philip Keele, esq. St. Thomas street
Ferris Mrs Mary, 8 Nelson place
Fluder Mrs. Elizabeth, High street
Furner Mr. Jas. 36 Southampton buildings
Gipps George. esq. Wainsford
Glover Mrs. & Misses, 6 Highfield
Goodchild Misses, 9 Captain's row
Harnett Mrs. Mary A.40 Southampton buildings
Harrison Capt. John G. R.N. Withy bed cottage
Heathcote Rev. Samuel J. Downton lodge
Hicks Edward esq. High street
Hicks Mrs. Mary, High street
Hobbs Mrs. Mary, Southampton buildings
Hockings Misses, Woodside
Home Miss Amelia, 2 Highfield
Hunt James, esq. Ramley
Hunter Miss M. 39 Southampton buildings
Inman Mr. Thomas, 23 Southampton buildings
Jones Miss Ellen, St. Thomas st.
King Mrs. Jane & Misses, High st.
King Mrs. Lucy, St. Thomas street
Lempriere Miss Mary, 2 Highfield

LYMINGTON FROM MOUNT PLEASANT

LYMINGTON
(Contd.)

Lewin Robert H. esq. the Elms
Lloyd Rev. David, High street
Martin Rev. James, High street
Merryfield Mrs. Mary S. 3 Victoria terrace
Michell Miss Maria E. High street
Michell Henry C. esq. 1 Highfield
Millard Rev. James, Church lane
Neuville Misses, High street
Newell Mrs. Ann, 39 Southampton buildings
Oake Mrs. and Miss, 39 ditto
Parham George, esq. Church lane
Parker Joseph esq. the Grove
Patey Mrs. Eliza, New lane house
Phillips Mr. Edward, High street
Rennalls Mrs. Jane F. New ln. ho.
Rice Edmund, esq. 4 Highfield
Rice Robert, esq. 3 Highfield
Riddett Mrs. Sarah, 4 Nelson place
Rogers Miss Hannah, High street
Rooke Capt. Leonard, R.N. Formosa house
Rooke Wm. W. esq. Viletta, Woodside
Salter Mr. Robert Geo. 29 Southampton buildings
Smith Mr. Richard, Gosport Street
Smith Mrs Martha, Highfield
Southey Mrs. Caroline, Buckland
St. Barbe Fras. W. esq. St. Thomas st
St. Barbe, Geo. Foster, esq.

High st
St. Barbe Samuel, esq. High street
Templer Miss Jane, St Thomas st.
Tinling Capt. Geo. V. Bellmore ldg.
Towsey Wm. esq. M.D. Gosport st
Walton Miss Ann, St. Thomas st
Ware Mrs. Charlotte, Northover cot.
Watson Mrs. Ann, New lane house
Wynch Mrs. & Misses, 5 Highfield
Young Mrs. & Misses, Wellington pl

Miscellany of Traders, &c.

Ackland William, fly proprietor, St. Thomas st
Baths, Quay, manager, Coles Jno.
Bellows J. Bath chairman, New ln.
Clayton John, hatter, High street
Curtis W. bird preserver, Church ln.
County Court Office, St. Thomas st. *clerk*, Brown James; *high baliff*, Rogers William
Custom house, Quay, principal coast officer, Grunsell George
Dalton Wm. tobacconist, High street
Gas Works, High street, *lessee*, Mitchell John
Gerrard George, turner, Gosport st.
Grunsell Wm. harbour master, Quay
Hayward John, relieving officer, St. Thomas street

Hopkins Wm. cowkeeper, Church ln
King Charles, poulterer, High street
Literary Institution, New lane, *treasurer*, Chubb William; *hon. sec.* Sharp Richard; *librarian*, Banks George
Morris George, currier and leather cutter, Ashley's lane
Murray Wm. D. pilot, Quay
Nelson Rodolph, marine store dealer, Captain's row
Pearce Hy. high constable, High st.
Pinnick John F. dyer, 13 Southampton buildings
Salway John, inland revenue officer, Priestland
Thorn Thomas, fishmonger, High st.
Union Workhouse, New ln. *clerk*, Robins Jph.; *master and matron*, Thompson Alexander and Mary
Woolfrey G. umbrella mkr. High st.

Accountants

Robbins Joseph, 6 Captain's row
Thring Wm. (& vestry clerk) High st

Auctioneers and Valuers

Banks William, High street
Colborne Thomas, High street
Figg Henry & Son, High street

Bakers.

Marked thus * are also Confectioners
*Behr John, High street
Coote John, High street
Hampton George, Stanford row
Haslett James, Gosport street
*Hatchard Charles, High street

*Hookey Henry, High street
Hookey Joseph, High street
Jenvey Louisa, 22 Southampton bg.
Lawes Stephen, St. Thomas street
*Malser James, High street
Milledge Benjamin, Quay hill
Rogers Josiah, St. Thomas street
*Smith Samuel F. & Co. High st
Thomas Stephen, Old town

Bankers.

St. Barbe Chas. Samuel, & Geo. F. High St. draw on Lubbock & Co. London
Wilts & Dorset Banking Co. High st. draw on London & Westminster Bank, manager, Chubb William
Savings', High street, open on sat. from 1 to 2; actuary, *Wilkinson* Chiels Cripps

Beer Retailers.

Best Mary, New lane
Bran William, Bellmore lane
Chandler John, Gosport street
Cull John, New lane
Etheridge John, Buckland
Gatrell James, Ashley's lane
Hall William, Bridge lane
Harbour Jane, Quay
Jeffery John, High street
Preston William, Old town
Scorey William, Gosport street
Tarver James, St. Thomas street
Thring William, High street

Berlin Wool Warehouses.

Gatrell John, St. Thomas' street
Rogers Sarah, High street

LYMINGTON
(Contd.)

Blacksmiths
Bennet John, Gosport street
Bower John, New lane
Grunsell Wm. (& ship smith) Quay
Light Samuel, New lane
Macey Henry, (& ship) Quay hill
Stickland Thomas, St. Thomas' st.
Tarlton John, Old town

Booksellers, Stationers, and Printers.
Doman Henry, High street
Galpine Wm. Le Jeune (and circulating library & news room) High st.
King Richard, High street
Watterson Charles (and circulating library & billiard room) High st.

Boot and Shoemakers
Allen James, Quay hill
Ballard John, Gosport street
Burton Jas. (& leather cut.) High st.
Collins William G. High street
Earley Isaac, High street
Gauntlett Francis, High street
Goodfellow James, St. Thomas st.
Gosling Daniel, High street
Holmes George, Rosetta place
Lewis Leonard, High street
Lewis Thomas, Captain's row
Lobb W. Andw. 8 Southampton bg.
Meadows Charles, New lane
Pavey George, Quay hill
Stroud Robert, High street
Weeks William, High street
Welch Edward, Priestland place
Whitchell James, High street

Brewers
Bran William, Bellmore lane
Cooper William, High street
Mew Thomas Parker, Quay
Preston William, Old town
Stephens Humphrey, Quay hill
Tarver James, old town

Brick and Tile Makers
Colborne Thomas, Church lane
Read Joseph, Croyden

Bricklayers and Plasterers.
Colborne Thomas, Church lane
Flora John, Church lane
Gardiner Samuel W. St. Thomas st
May Wm. & Edward, Bellmore lane
Preston John, Church lane
Reeks William, Gosport street

Builders
Banks Geo. (& architect) High st.
Banks William, High street

Butchers
Gatrell Wm. Verling, High street
Goulding James, Quay hill
Lobb Andrew, Quay
Pedler George, High street
Preston William, Old town
Prince Henry, High street
Spencer William, High street

Cabinet Makers & Upholsterers.
Banks William, High street
Baskett John & James, Old town
Bright George, St. Thomas street
Gatrell John, St. Thomas street
May Richard, Old town
Shephard William, St. Thomas st.

Carpenters and Joiners
Allison James, 8 Gosport street
Bench John, Sea side cottage
Colborne Thomas, High street
Jenvey Geo. 22 Southampton bldgs.
Jenvey Jas. 24 Southampton bldgs.
King Charles, High street
Payne Richard, Bridge street
Richman John, Quay
Richman William, High street
St. John Charles, Bridge street
St. John Henry, Captain's row

Chemists and Druggists.
Corbin James, (and stamp office) High street
Peat Edward, High street
Wheaton Frederick, High street

Chimney Sweepers.
Batts John, Gosport street
Brown William, Waterloo
Rogers Thomas, St. Thomas street

China, Glass, &c. Dealers.
James Richard, High street
Morris George, High street
Scarle Willam, High street

Coach and Gig Builders.
Austin John, High street
Lewis Samuel, St. Thomas street

Coal Merchants and Dealers.
Bath William, Quay
Blake Philip, (and timber and slate) Captain's row
Cheesemen George, Quay
Dennett Edward, High street
Hookey Joseph, jun. High street
Howard John, High street
Mitchell John, High street
St. Barbe C.S. & G.F. High street

Coopers
Cooper William, High street
Stevens George, Quay hill

Corn Merchants and Dealers
Bath William, Quay hill
Clark George & Sons, High street
Dennett Edward, High street
Fryer Robert, High street
Hookey Joseph jun. High street
Howard John, High street

Farmers
Edmonds James G. and Burges, Woodside
Emmott Philip, Little Buckland
Gatrell Wm. V. High street
Hendey Chas. 17 Southampton blgs.
Hobbs Andrew, High street
Perry Samuel, Ampress farm
Pulteney Mrs. Bucklands
Worthy James, Woodside

Fire & Life Insurance Agents.
Marked thus * denotes Fires, thus Life.
Clerical & Medical, Robins Joseph, Captain's row
*County and Provident, Clayton John, High street
* Guardian Sharp R. Captain's row
*Hants, Sussex & Dorset, Hayward John, High street
* Imperial and Palladium, Guy Anthony, High street
Legal and General, Figg William, High street
* London, Galpine William, Le J. High street
Medical, Invalid, and General, Wheaton Fred. High street
Mentor, King Richard, High street
Minerva, Chubb William, High street
National Mercantile, Gibbs Richd. High street
* Norwich Union, Brown James, St. Thomas street
*Phoenix, Badcock Elzbth. High st.
* Royal Exchange, St. Barbe Chas. S. and Geo. F. High street
* Royal Farmers (and hail storm) Chubb William, High street
* Sun, Mitchell John, High street

Furniture Brokers.
Bowler William, St. Thomas street
Hampton Elizabeth, High street
Welch Edward, Priestland place

Gardeners & Seedsmen.
Barter William, Quay Hill
Beach Richard, High street
Howard John, High street

Greengrocers & Fruiterers
Ash Frederick, High street
Hapgood Ann, High street
Hatchard Charles, St. Thomas street
Hobby Joseph, Old town
Jerome Charles, High street
Pardy Ann, Quay

Grocers and Teadealers
Barnes Robert, St. Thomas street
Clark Geo. and Sons, (wholesale & tallow chandlers) High street

BATH HOUSE, LYMINGTON

LYMINGTON (Contd.)

Craft Daniel, Gosport street
Gibbs Richard, High street
Hayward John (and ale and porter merchant) High street
Purchase Isaac Bentey, High street
Smith Thomas, High street

Groceries & Sundries Dealers.
Burgess William Henry, High street
Head John, Quay Hill
Hicks John, Gosport street
Ivamy Sarah, Quay Hill
Kitcher Henry Robert, Quay
Lawes Stephen, St. Thomas street
Pavey Thomas, North street
Pearce Harry, High street
Rogers Josiah, St. Thomas street
Scott Robert, St. Thomas street
Slater Elizabeth, Quay
Smith Elizabeth, 2, Southampton buildings
Smith Samuel Fluder, & Co. High street
Tarver James, St. Thomas street

Gun and Pistol Makers.
Clayton Alfred, High street
Jeffery John, High street

Hair Dressers
Frampton Luke, Quay hill
Joulin Anthony, St. Thomas street
Searle William, High street
Wright John, High street
Woolfrey George, High street

Inns and Public Houses.
Anchor and Hope Inn, (com. & post.) High street, Acland Elzbth. & Hen.
Angel Inn, (family & posting) High street, Norris William Benjamin
Blacksmith's Arms, Old Town, Rogers John
Bugle, High street, Eves Henry
Chequers, Woodside, Marshall Mary
Fighting Cocks, St. Thomas street, Bench John
King's Arms, St. Thomas street, Bollen Charles
King's Head, Quay hill, Avery Rebecca
Nag's Head Inn, (family, coml. & post.) High st. Perry Samuel
Red Lion, High st. Gosling, Elzbth.
Ship, Quay, Crowfoot Charles
Six Bells, St Thomas street, Bran George
Solent, Quay Hill, Stephens, Humphrey
Swan, Bridge, Dore Amelia
Waterloo Arms, Priestland place, Wilton James

Wheatsheaf, Gosport street, Reeks William
William IV, Quay, Graham Wm.

Ironmongers, Braziers, &c.
Hapgood George, High street
Mursell Wm. & Blake Robt. (and iron & brass founders) High st
Tanner Benj. and Sharp Thos. C. (and implement makers) High st.

Linen and Woollen Drapers.
Badcock Elizabeth, High street
Bennett George, High street
Furner James, Oliver, High street
Good William, High street
Hatchard Thomas, High street
Lacey Wm. (& clothier) High st.
Shrimpton Henry, High street
Staples Walter, High street

Maltsters.
Hatchard Thomas, High street
Hookey Joseph jun. High street
King John, Old town
Nike Charles, St. Thomas street

Master Mariners.
Alston Henry, 9 Nelson place
Cribb John, Bath road
Hayward Henry, 7, Nelson place
Hughes John, 31, Southampton bgs
Hinks William, Captain's row
Jacobs William, 3, Nelson place
Lowe Eli, 6, Nelson place
Slater William, 5, Nelson place
Spracklin James, Bath road
Watt James, Gosport street
Way William, Bath road
Webster Edward, Quay
Webster Robt. C. 16, Captain's row

Millers.
Butt Zachariah, Haywood mill
Dexter Joseph, Lymington mill
Hatchard Thomas, Efford mill

Milliners & Dress Makers.
Baskett Olivia, Priestland place
Bevan Fanny, 21, Southampton bldg
Curtis Martha, Church lane
Court & Read, High street
Gould Agnes & Emma, High st.
Green Mary Ann, St. Thomas st.
Hendey Elzth. 17, Southampton blg
Ingram Elizabeth, High street
May Sarah & Frances, Belmore lane
Savage Elzth. Jane, Gosport street
St. John Sarah, High street
Read Eliza, Church lane
Rogers Elizabeth, St. Thomas st.

Painters Plumbers & Glaziers
Banks John Charles, New lane
Drake Andrew, Old town
Figg Henry & Son, High street
Keay Wm. & Elgar Saml. High st.
Wearn Mary, Gosport street
Winsey Benjamin, St. Thomas st.

Professors of Music.
Klitz Charles, High street
Klitz Rbt. Jno. (& musicial instrument seller & tuner) High street

Registrars
Burford Geo., (of marriages) Captains row
Guy Anthony, (suprt.) High street
Hapgood Henry, (births & deaths) High street

Saddlers and Harness Makers.
Blake Charles, High street
Hayter William, Old town
Russell William, St. Thomas street
Shrimpton Samuel, High street

Salt Manufacturers.
Mitchell John, High street
St. Barbe Chas. Samuel & George Foster, High street

Schools.
Marked thus * take boarders.
British, High street, Gibbs Edwd.
Darling Joseph B. Old town
*Domine Chas. Bowling-green-ln.
*Galpine Mary, (boarders only) High street
Infant, High street, Taylor Elizabeth
National, New lane, Cole Thomas & Newman Sarah
*Perress Mary & Sarah, High st.
*Pittis Jane, High street
*Noake Francis L. & Harriett S. Gosport street
Rogers Henry, St. Thomas street
Suffield Lydia, Captain's row
Smith Susanna, 2, Southampton buildings
Wells John, Anglesea place

Ship and Boat Builders.
Dagwell Philip, (boat only) Bath rd.
Inman George & James (& yacht & rope makers) Quay

Solicitors
Brown Jas. (& town clerk & clerk to county court), St. Thomas st
Guy Anthony, High street
Moore Edw. H. & St. Barbe Francis W. (and clerks to county magistrates) Captain's row

Royle William, High street
Sharpe Richard, Captain's row
Wilkinson Chiels Cripps, Nelson pl.

Stay Makers.
Day Elizabeth, Church lane
Hogan & Moss, High street
Knight Patience, High street
Rogers Sarah, High street

Stone Masons.
Colborne Thomas, Church lane
May Wm. & Edw. Bellmore lane
Newman Jno. Rd. West-end cott.

Straw Hat Makers.
Atwell Martha, New lane
Pedler Martha, High street
Salter Ellen, 10, Southampton bldg.
Springer Kezia, New lane

Surgeons
Adams & Chatfield, High street
Fluder & Chinery, St. Thomas st.

Surveyors and Agents–Land.
Darling Joseph Benj. Old town
Dennett Edward, High street

Tailors.
Ayes Henry, High street
Bowden Edward Rawlins, Quay
Burford George, Captains row
Dixon Catherine, High street
Dore Samuel, St. Thomas street
Good William, jun. High street
Hapgood Charles, Church lane
Ings John, High street
Jenvey George, Bridge street
Lewis Thomas, High street
Loder Charles, St. Thomas street
Mason John, Church lane
Pitt James, Captains row
Saunders William, High street
Tarlton Henry, D. St. Thomas street

Watch & Clock Makers.
Ellsworth George L. Captain's row
Henning Robert, Church lane
Marriott John, High street
Padbury Chas. (& jeweller) High st.

Wheelwrights.
Cole John, 26 Southampton buildgs.
Haskell Bartholomew, Bridge street
King Charles, High street
Payne Richard, Bridge street

Wine and Spirit Merchants.
Corbin Jas. (& ale & porter) High st
Mew Thos. P. (spirit only) Quay

LYMINGTON (Contd.)

Omnibusses.—To Brockenhurst, daily from the 'Angel, & Nag's Head' Inns, to meet all the trains

Carriers.—To Lond, *Hapgood*; also *Herridge & Co.* from the 'Anchor and Hope,' High st. daily, via rail, from the Brockenhurst station.—To Christchurch and Poole, *Soden*, from the 'Anchor and Hope,' mon. wed. and sat. 4 after.—To Ringwood, Roberts from the 'Bugle,' sat. at 1 noon.—To Romsey, Moody, from the 'Bugle' sat. at 1 noon,—To Salisbury, *Edwards*, from 'Anchor and Hope,' mon. and fri. at 10 morn.

Steam Vessels.—To Cowes, Portsmouth, Ryde, and Southampton, tues. & fri., and to Yarmouth daily

---

LYNDHURST, a large and respectable village, occupying a very pleasant situation nearly in the centre of the New Forest 8 miles N. from Lymington, 10 S.W. from Southampton, 10 S.S.W. from Romsey, and 18 S.E. from Salisbury. Petty sessions are held here on the first wednesday in every month, the verderer's court about the 26th of August, the Swainmote court on the 14th of September, and the courts Leet and Baron in October. The parish comprises an area of 3560 acres, and in 1851 contained 1571 inhabitants. *Post Office*, at John Smith's. Letters are delivered at 8 a.m. & despatched to London & all parts at 12.30 noon. and at ½ past 9 p.m. Box closes at 9, but letter will be received till 12 noon, and 9.30 p.m. by affixing an extra 1d. stamp to each.

Bailey Captain, T.J.
Breton Capt. Frederick John
Bully John Blagrave, esq. Holles Mount
Burrard Capt. Sir Charles, bart. R.N.
Compton Rev. John (rector)
Dashwood Admiral William
Davies Thomas, esq. Shrubbs hill
Duckworth Wm. esq. Beechwood
Erroll Dowager Countess of
Eyre Robert, esq. Bartley
Gilbert Edward, esq. Lamburne
Heathcote, T. Jenkins esq.
Hoare Rev. George (curate)
Hodges Henry, esq. Linwood
Hogg Colonel John
Low Isaac, esq. Cottage
Powell Mrs. Cuffnells
Powell Capt. Buckworth
Pulteney Mrs. Evelyn E. Northerwood Lodge
Robins Genl. Thos. Castlemallwood
Rowley Capt. R.N. Emery down cot.
Shedden Lindesay, esq.
Williams Walter, esq.
Young Robert, esq.

Adams Henry, file cutter
Arnold Elizabeth, baker and grocer
Bennett Betsy, grocery dealer
Brixey William, brewer, cooper, and *Stag Inn*
Bugden Wm. B. grocer and draper
Butt William, baker and grocer
Collins Humphrey, beer retailer
Coxwell Edward, supt. registrar
Crook John, bricklayer
Fielder Isaac, registrar of births and deaths
Figg Henry and Son, painters and plumbers
Fripp Robert, tailor

Gerrard James, furniture broker
Goffe George, tailor
Golding James, carpenter
Hillyer David, shoemaker
Hinter William, '*White Swan*'
Hinves Catherine, maltster
Hoskins George, shoemaker
Ives John, '*Fox & Hounds*'
Keddle William, supervisor
Lemmon Dorcas, blacksmith
Lowman Lucy A. '*Crown Hotel*'
Macey Charles, carpenter
Maskew John S. surgeon
Masters Geo. & Jno., basket & chair makers
Mathews Samuel L. grocer &c.
Millard David & Son, saddlers
National School, Hillman Thomas and Alexander Anne
Neale Mary Frances, school
Nightingale Richard, surveyor &c.

Nike Charles, brewer & maltster
Norton Charlotte, grocery dealer
Nunn George, surgeon
Payne Fanny and Sarah, dressmakers
Payne Joseph, builder
Ruffett Elizabeth, milliner & dress maker
Shelly Isaac, baker and grocer
Short Frederick, baker
Short Henry, coach builder
Short Joseph, jun. grocer and ironmonger, and agent to the Sun (F.&L.) insurance office
Short Wm. chemist and draper, and agent to the Norwich Union fire, life, and hailstorm insur. office.
Sidford Matilda, school
Smith Chs. Edwd. tailor & stationer
Smith John, postmaster
Stote Alfred, blacksmith
Stote Philip, blacksmith
Strange Robert, butcher
Taplin Charles, carpenter

Taplin Wm. & Jno. painters & glaziers
Tate Thomas, timber merchant
Union Workhouse, New Forest, *master and matron.* Miall George Horatio and Jane
Walton Elizabeth, dressmaker
Watridge James, carpenter
Whitcher Joseph, butcher
Whitehorn Chas. glass & china dlr.
Wolfe George, blacksmith

RAILWAY CONVEYANCE—*Omnibus* from the 'Crown Hotel' to Lyndhurst-road station (3 miles distant) three times a day to meet the trains.
CARRIERS—To Christchurch, *Tilly*, from the 'White Swan', tues. and fri. at 3 aft.—To Southampton, *Tilly*, from the same place, at 3 aft.; *Bradley*, also *Waterhouse*, tues. thurs. and sat., and *Shelley*, mon. and fri.—the latter start from their own houses.

MILFORD with its tythings of **Key Haven, Efford** and **Pennington**.—Milford is delightfully situated about 4 miles S.W. from Lymington, the county court town, having on its south and west Christchurch bay, and on its southeast the Solent channel, which divides Hants from the Isle of Wight; a small stream of water, frequented by trout and some other members of the finney tribe, runs through the village which is surrounded by exquisite scenery. The cliffs hard by abound with fossils and antediluvian remains, and the country hereabouts is studded with splendid seats and noble family mansions; their occupants attracted hither, no doubt, by the extreme salubrity of the circumambient atmosphere. The parish contains rather more than 4518 acres of land and in 1851—1,782 inhabitants. Hurst Castle, 2½ miles from Key Haven, situated on a narrow neck of land jutting into the Solent will be viewed with satisfaction by the admirers of the romantic and picturesque. Pennington, lies near Lymington, about 3 miles N. by E. from Milford, and contains about 700 inhabitants. *Post Office* at William Ireland's, Milford. Letters delivered at 8 a.m. and despatched at ½ past 6 p.m.

OLD KING'S HOUSE, LYNDHURST

MILFORD (Contd.)

Barrow Mrs.
Brown Robt. M.D. Kivernells house
Carnac Dowager, Lady Rivett, Rook Cliff
Chambers Miss, Everton
De La Tour Augustus, esq.
Edwards Lieut.—Everton
Halliday Miss Maria
Hare Hon. William Henry
Hastings the Marchioness of and Baroness Grey de Ruthyn, Efford house
Jennins Richard, esq. Carringtons
King Mrs. Sarah, Rose Cottage
Palmer Capt. J.B. Milford house
Peers Capt. Henry D. Everton
Robinson Rev. Thomas, M.A.
Symonds Mrs. Julianna
West Fred. Rd. esq. M.P. Newlands
Yelverton Capt. Hastings Reginald, R.N. Efford house

Adams John, butcher
Batts William, parish clerk
Berry William, plumber, painter &c.
Chase William, shoemaker
Cole Louisa, straw hat maker
Cole George, smith and farmer
Cole Richard, baker and grocer
Dowden Thomas, tailor
Elgar William, tailor
Etheridge Alfred, grocer & draper
Hatchard Thos. miller, Efford
Hayall Rob. agricultural machine maker
Hobby Henry, carrier to Lymington daily at 11 morn.
Ireland William, carpenter
King Charles, tailor
King John, builder and maltster
King Martha, dress maker
Lightfoot Isaac, shoemaker
Newham Abr. brewer, miller, baker, and farmer, Westover
Peckham Edw. grocer and baker
Phillips John, '*Crown Inn*'
Pope Charles, turner
Russell William, saddler
Scammell Mark, '*Red Lion Inn*'
Strange Walter, butcher
Tyrrell John, shoemaker
Udal & Son, painter & plumbers
Vile Emma, grocery dealer
Williams George, surgeon

Hurst Castle.
Hanson William, master gunner
Page John, light keeper
Pepper John, chief boatman
Reed James, beer retailer

Key Haven
Carnac Sir John Rivett, bart. Aubry house

MILFORD CHURCH

Hawker Col. Peter
Skynner Major, Belaire
Wilson Capt. E. R.N. Harewoods

Cocks William, '*Gun Inn*'
Guy James, land surveyor
Jennins Henry & Arthur, farmers
Thomas William, farmer
Wheeler John, farmer

Pennington.
Dickson Sir William
Ducket Captain
Gaven Mrs. Jane, Ridgway
Hockings Miss Ann, Woodend cot.
Lambert Rev. William
Norbury Earl of Priestland house
Taylor Lieut. Col. Pringle, K.H.
Vincent Rev. O.P.
Welch Capt. Robt. Gregory, R.N.

Baverstock Grace, farmer
Collins William, butcher
Conway Aeneas, baker
Hayter Jeremiah, farmer
Hampton Joseph, pig jobber
Hookey George, beer retailer
Hookey William, grocery dealer
Ingram George, carpenter
Ingram Henry '*White Hart*'
Ingram William, market gardener
Marshall Mary, '*Chequers*'
Martin Matthew, farmer
Miles John, farmer
Newman William, beer retailer
Norris John, '*Duke's Head*'
Pardy Charles, pig jobber

Pardy John, farmer
Read Charles, shoemaker
Read James, shoeing smith
Read Thomas, shoemaker
Stote George, baker and grocer
Taylor Thomas, grocery dealer

MILTON, with its hamlets of **Ashley, Barton, Bashley, Chewton, Gore & Wootton**, a parish 4¾ miles E. by N. of Christchurch, the county-court town, and 7 W. of Lymington, comprising 5000 acres of land, and a population of 1386. *Post Office*, at Jas. Olding's Milton. Letters delivered at 8 a.m. and despatched to Lymington at 5 p.m.

Tyrell Rev. Francis M.A.
Martin Chs. W. esq. Belvidere ho.

Aldridge Matthew, farmer
Best Stephen, farmer
Brake George, tailor
Bramble John, farmer
Brownen Charles, blacksmith
Brownen John, '*Wheat Sheaf Inn*'
Cooper Wm. farmer
Cox Joseph, carpenter
Dawkins Wm. farmer & grocer
Hayward Edward, registrar *National school*, Brownen Edmd.
Olding James, parish clerk
Peck Thomas, blacksmith
Peckham George, baker & grocer
Randell James, shoemaker
Randell John, '*George Inn*'
Rogers John, carpenter
Self Henry, carpenter

Sheave George, blacksmith
Udall Joseph, painter &c.

Ashley.
Clinton Lieut. Col. Frederick
Roebuck John Arthur, esq. M.P.

Adams George, farmer
Hood William, wheeler & grocer
King Richard, farmer
Macdonald William, surgeon
Ward George, farmer

Barton.
Bevan Lieut.—R.N.
Dent Mrs. Ann Jane

Corbin Robert, farmer
Preston George, shoemaker

Bashley.
Beames John esq. Bashley lodge

Burton Stephen, beer retailer
Church John, farmer
Brown John, '*Bee hive*'
James Charles, grocery dealer
Lightfoot Abraham, beer retailer
Sheave Joseph, farmer
Vale James, bricklayer

Chewton
Cameron Col. William, Nea house
Hopkins Capt. Hn. Hubborn lodge
Jesson Thos. esq. Hord cottage
Marryatt Geo., esq. Chewton glen
Shipworth-, East close

MILTON (Contd.)

Burton Robert, farmer
Clapott Jane, grocer &c. New town
Frampton James, wheeler, Newton
Hailey James, miller and farmer
Pack John, '*Globe*' & grocery dealer
Plowman Herbert, farmer

Gore.
Bramble Hooper, farmer
Cox Joseph, farmer

Wootton.
Dickinson John, esq.
Falconer Thomas, esq. the Farm

Bashford Richard, farmer
Beal George, farmer
Day George, farmer
Fish William, farmer
Gulliver George, woodman
Hayward Charles, shoemaker
King Mary, farmer and shopkeeper
Pack Isaac, '*Rising Sun*'
Spicer Henry, blacksmith
Wallace William, post office

MINSTEAD, or **Minesteed**, memorable as being the place where William Rufus, the Red King, was accidentally shot dead by a wandering arrow from the bow of Sir Walter Tyrell. The body was soon after picked up by a charcoal burner named Purkiss, who placed it in his cart and carried it to Winchester. Near Stony Cross, in this parish, a suitably-inscribed stone was erected to mark the spot where the monarch fell, but time and the elements have long since obliterated the ancient inscription, yet through the liberality of a late ranger, Sturges Bourne, esq., the stone is still preserved, that gentlemen having had it enclosed in a strong frame work of iron. Minstead is in the New Forest, 3 miles N. from Lyndhurst, and 16 S.S.E. from Salisbury; the parish contains 3200 acres of land, and about 1200 inhabitants. County court town, Southampton. *Post Office*, at John Frampton's and Arthur Scorey's. Letters delivered at 8 a.m. and despatched to Lyndhurst at about a quarter before 7 p.m.

Compton Henry Combe, esq. M.P. Manor house
Compton Rev. John, M.A. Parsonage
Hilyer Mrs.
Parker Rear Admiral Hyde, Lodge

MILTON CHURCH

Preston Wm. Robert, esq. Lodge
Robbins Major Gen. Castlemalwood
Broomfield Charles, baker
Broomfield David, miller
Compton John, parish clerk
Compton Wm, '*Trusty Servant*'
Dymott John, wheelwright
Farmer Samuel, cattle dealer
Frampton John, shopkeeper and Post Office
Gain James, carpenter
Golding & Brothers, timber fellers, Canterton
National School, Rose Thomas
Payne Joesph, bricklayer, Emery down
Phillips Henry, blacksmith
Pope John, '*Compton Arms*'
Pudney John, charcoal dealer, Emery down
Purkiss George, '*Robin Hood*'
Reeves William, farmer
Scorey Arthur, grocery dealer and Post office
Smith William, grocery dealer

MUDEFORD, a much admired, and, during the summer season, well frequented watering place, situated in the bay of Christchurch, and 2 miles E.S.E. from the town of that name. An hotel, two inns and some lodging houses afford accommodation for visitors; and, in the neighbourhood, are several mansions inhabited by wealthy residents. At Highcliff is a neat new church. *Post Office*, at the 'Sandford hotel'; letters are delivered at 8 a.m. and despatched to Christchurch at 7 p.m.

Arnott Henry, esq. Mulberry cott
Berkeley Hon. Grantley, Beacon lodge, High cliff
Brown Mr. Jno. Brook cottage
Buffett Mrs. Sarah G.
Butler Mr. Wm. Victoria cottage
Cook Rev. John
De La Tour Madame, Mudeford ho
Eyre Rev. Fredk. Willow lodge
Kennett Lieut. John, R.N.
Martin Charles William, esq.
Reade William, esq.
Rose Sir George Henry, bart. G.C.H. Sand hills
Stewart de Rothsay Lady, High cliff castle
Tanner Mr. William

Tanner Mrs. Mary

Bradshaw Geo. lodging ho. keeper
Brown Henry W. '*Sandford Hotel*' (family, com. & posting)
Butler Wm. lodging house keeper
Clark John, '*Haven house*'
Derham John, pilot & fisherman
Derham Peter & Edmund, farmers
Edgehill Felix, gardener
Foster Anthony, music master
Tucker John, pilot & fisherman
Vickers Christopher, '*Isle of Wight Hoy*', High Cliff
West Jane, bath proprietor & lodging house keeper.

RINGWOOD, a parish and market town, in Fordingbridge County-court district, intersected by the Southampton and Dorchester railway, is situated on the high road from Salisbury to Christchurch and on the eastern bank of the Avon, which river is here divided into two channels, each spanned by a bridge on the road leading to Wimborne and other parts of Dorsetshire; distant 9 miles N. from Christchurch, about the same distance N.E. from Wimborne, 18 S. from Salisbury, 20 W. from Southampton, 93 W. from London.

The commerce of Ringwood is rather circumscribed through having no other manufacture but that of a particular kind of knitted woollen gloves and stockings peculiar to the place, still this with its well attended weekly corn market, and the advantage derivable from its thoroughfare situation both by road and rail, together with the farming operations carried on in the immediate neighbourhood, cause a considerable amount of money to be spent in the town, and which probably places it on a par with other towns whose manufactures are more numerous or extensive. The river Avon, at this part, is famed for its eels, which, in favourable seasons, prove a source of profit to the renter of a pound here, wherein they are sometimes caught by hundreds; many fine trouts also and some other fish are found in the rapid running waters of this rippling and translucent

RINGWOOD (Continued)

stream, which occasionally overflows the adjacent meadows, and materially tends to increase the fertility of the land.

The church is an ancient cruciform structure, and the living, which is annexed to the rectory of Warbridge, is a vicarage in the gift of King's College, Cambridge. The Wesleyans, Independents, and Unitarians, have each their respective chapels here; and there are six almshouses liberally endowed by the late William Clark, Esq., a noted resident brewer. In pursuance of the will of this benevolent donor the almshouses were, in 1843, erected, and, with the new National school (into which the anciently endowed Grammar school is now merged) form the chief modern architectural attractions of the town. The market is held on Wednesday, and fairs principally for forest colts, and pedlery, take place on the 10th of July and 11th of December. Petty sessions are held (at the town hall) on the second Wednesday in each month; and manorial courts, at which a high constable and other officials are chosen at Lady-day and Michaelmas. CROW, HIGH TOWN, KINGSTON, and POULNER, are hamlets belonging to Ringwood parish, and altogether comprise 10,550 acres of land, and by the census of 1851, contain a population of 3953.

POST OFFICE, and MONEY ORDER OFFICE. *Post Mistress* Sarah Benson; letters delivered at 8 a.m. and 4 p.m. Box closes for Southampton and London, and Exeter and the West at 11 30 a.m. and 10 p.m., but letters will be received up to 11 35 a.m. if an extra stamp is affixed to each.

Baldwin Mrs. Mary
Baylis Rev. J., Wesleyan minister
Brown Mr. Thomas
Castleman Charles, esq.
Critchell Mr. John
Edwards Capt. Richard, R.N.
Etheridge Mrs.
Gilbert James, esq.
Hamper Misses Lydia Ann Dawson and Mary Jane
Harris Rev. George, (Independent minister)
Jones William, esq.
Maffey Mr. Stephen
Maturin Rev. Benjamin
Maturin Rev. Chas. Henry, M.A.
Metcalf Miss Ann
Ness Miss Caroline Elizabeth
Ness Rev. Edward, Hawke
Newman, Mrs. Mary
Oake Mr. Henry
Shoey Mr. George
Slater Mrs. Mary

Miscellany of Traders & c.
Adams James, watchmaker
Appleford James, miller
Arnold James, grocery dealer
Ayles George, farmer
Ayles Harry, farmer & land survr.
Ayles Stephen, relieving officer and registrar of births and deaths
Baker Joseph, wheelwright
Baker Thomas, grocer and tallow-chandler, corn and provision dealer
Barnard Henry, '*Globe*'
Barnes James, draper
Bartlett John, saw mills
Beavan Jas., maltster and corn dr.
Benson Geo. Hen., ironmonger and agent to the Sun fire office
Benson Sarah, straw bonnet and dress maker, and post mistress
Biles Peter, farmer
Bioletti James hair dresser
Birt & Head, milliners & dressmks.
Blake Henry, '*Crown Coml. Inn*'
Blake William, saddler, &c.
Brown Anne, seminary
Brown and Riggs, coal merchants
Brown John, cooper
Brown Rich., wine merchant
Buckland James, '*Royal Oak*'
Burford John, tailor & coal dealer
Burgess Jane, baker and grocer
Carter Alexander & Co., brewers & spirit dealers
Cave William, glover
Chapple Wm., manager of Bank
Cheater George, shoemaker
Cheater George, blacksmith
Chilcott Robert, '*Red Lion*'
Coates Wm. Thomas, draper
Colborne Alfred, tailor
Colborne John, boot & shoemaker
Colborne John, tailor
Coles William, farmer
Coasby Henry, carpenter & '*Star*'
Cosby James, tailor
Conway Brothers, tanners & curriers
Cottman Robert, builder
Cottman William, '*New Inn*'
Cox Charles, grocer & draper
Cox James, beer retailer
Cranston Geo., auctioneer and spirit dealer, and agent to the Royal Exchange fire and life offices
Cranston John L., upholsterer
Critchell William, corn merchant & maltster
Cross Henry, currier, leather seller and shoe mercer
Darley Henry, chair maker
Davy Robt., solicitor and clerk to the magistrates
Day James, boot and shoemaker
Domone William, butcher
Drodge William, tailor
Dunkerton James, shopkeeper
Dyer Thomas & Son, surgeons
Dyett Richard, tax gatherer
Early John, painter and glazier
Early Samuel, grocery dealer
Early Sarah, painter and glazier
Eldridge George, '*Lamb*'
Etheridge Geo., china, glass, &c., dealer
Etheridge Jas., painter & glazier
Etheridge John, carver and gilder
Feltham Anne, toy dealer
Fowles William, grocery dealer
Frampton Robert grocery dealer
Free Grammar School, head master, Maturin Rev. C.H.
Gardner Chas., bricklayer & mason
Gilbert Hen., grocer & corn dealer
Gay Aaron, seedsman
Haskell Stephen, bootmaker
Hayter Thomas, Saddler, &c.
Hayward John, grocer
Hiscock James, wheeler
Hoare Wm., leather cutter
Hopkins Henry, '*King's Head*' and baker and grocery dealer
Hounslow William, nurseryman
Hunt William, commercial school
Hutton John, linen & woollen drpr.
Independent School, Holmes Sarah
Infant School, Soar Julia
Ings Philip, marine store dealer
Jameson Wm. R. builder and registrar of marriages
Johns Henry Tremenheere, solicitor and clerk to the county court at Fordingbridge and Christchurch
Kent Moses, grocery dealer
Kingsbury John Biles and Sons, grocers and tallow chandlers
Lane Henry, hair dresser
Langer William, tailor
Lawrence Henry, grocer & mealman
Lee Thomas, grocery dealer
Low Geo. grocer, and agent to the County fire & Provident life offices
Maffey John, chemist & herbalist
Masterman William, tailor
Mitchell Mary & Jane, boot & shoemakers
Morris Edwd. grocer and tea dealer
Mouland Charles, '*Nag's Head*'
Mouland Wm. '*Smiths Arms*'
National School, Clark Mr. & Miss
Neale Henry St. John, solicitor, superintendent registrar and conservator of the local rivers
Neale John, farmer
Newton Albert, ironmonger & agent to Anchor fire and life office
Paice George, '*Kings Arms*'
Pearce Edward, day school
Pearce Joseph, tin plate worker
Philemore Sarah, milliner
Phillips Joseph, shopkeeper
Polden Robert, butcher
Powell Susan, seminary
Ridout John Early, woolstapler
Ridout William, draper
Ringwood and Poole Bank, (draw on Roers, Olding & Co. London,) *proprietors*, Ledgard and Sons; *agent*, Chapple Wm.
Riggs Joseph, '*George*'
Roo John, shoemaker
Rose William, shoemaker
Russell Charles, auctioneer

Saunders Edward, land surveyor & auctioneer
Savage Edward, shoemaker
Savage John, boot and shoemaker
Sharp Charles, surveyor and timber merchant, and agent to the Royal Farmers Fire and Life offices
Small Thomas, coal dealer
Smith Chas. superintendent of police
Spicknell Wm. '*Railway Arms*'
Stark Anne, '*Railway Inn*'
Stainer David, butcher
Stevens George, tailor
Stevens William, baker
Street Charles, beer retailer
Street Fabian, coal dealer
Summerhays Thomas, railway station master
Tanner Hannah, straw hat maker
Travers Mary, '*White Hart Inn*' (commercial and posting)
Union Poor House, master & matron, M'Daniel James and Jane

Veale Isaac and Son, brewers
Vincent John, '*Antelope*'
Ward George, '*Fish*'
Ward Horatio, tailor
War John, jun. tailor
Ward Sarah, milliner
Ward Wm. grocery dealer & baker
Ward William, jun. baker
Watton Harry, grocery dealer
Westcott Charles, surgeon
Wheaton Wm. bookseller, printer, and chemist (& stamp office)
White Frederick, sheriffs' officer
Whitchell James, boot & shoemaker
White John, pastrycook
Wiltshire Edward, '*White Lion*'
Witt George, builder
Woodroffe Chas. H. inland revenue officer
Woodford Spencer, bookseller

RINGWOOD

RINGWOOD
(Continued)

and printer, & agent to Clerical and medical life & Hants, Sussex, and Dorset fire offices
Wyatt Matilda, grocery dealer
Wyatt Robert, seedsman

COACH.—To Salisbury through Fordingbridge, from 'Crown Inn' daily (except sun.) at ¼ past 12 noon. A Bus from 'Crown Inn' to the railway station to meet every train.
CARRIERS.—To Christchurch, *Bower*, from the 'Star'; and *Roberts*, from the 'George', both on tues. and sat.; also *Tilley*, from the 'Star,' on mon. wed. & sat., all leave about 4 aft.—To Fordingbridge, *Rouse*, from the 'Antelope,' daily at 4 aft.—To London, South-

ampton, Exeter, and all parts West, *Ford and Co.* (agent, Chillcott Robt.) and *Lipscombe & Co.* (agent, Lawrence Thos.) both via rail daily—To Poole, *Simmonds*, from the 'Antelope' on tues. and sat.—To Salisbury, through Fordingbridge, *Bower*, from the 'Star, on mon. and fri., and *Ford and Co.* from the 'Red Lion,' on tues. and sat., also *Roberts*, from the 'George,' on mon. and fri. and *Rouse*, from the 'Antelope,' on tues. thurs. and sat.—To Southampton, *Simmons*, from the 'Antelope,' on mon. and fri.

Crow.
Holloway Harry, land surveyor
Targett Thomas, farmer
Trill John, wheelwright

High Town.
Ayles James, farmer
Middleton James, farmer

Kingston.
Ayles William, farmer
Downton Joseph, farmer
Independent School, Moyle Jane
Keeping John, grocery dealer
Tuck Charles, blacksmith
Wiseman, Joseph, farmer
Wright Isaac, wheeler
Wright Thomas, carpenter

Poulner.
Bennett James, farmer
Etheridge Thomas, farmer
Hayter James, farmer
Jones Elizabeth, shopkeeper
Roberts John, farmer
Smith Joseph, blacksmith
Street Stephen, farmer
Tanner John, farmer
Warn Joseph, '*White Hart*'
White Charles, farmer

SOPLEY, a village and parish three miles N. from Christchurch, the County Court own.

Acres 3730. Letters *via* Ringwood.

Clapcott Mr. John
Hammond Rev. John P. (vicar)
Honeywell Mr. Frederick
Paris Robert, esq.
Tice William, esq.

Barrow George, parish clerk
Barrow Mary, farmer
Blacklock Robert, farmer
Clapcott Henry, farmer
Corbin Richard, wheelwright
Crouch Mary, grocery dealer
Dowden William, grocery dealer
Moyle James, grocery &c. dealer
Shave William, '*Woolpack*'
Wareham Thos. boot & shoemaker
Whicher Henry, farmer

RINGWOOD CATTLE MARKET CLOSED IN JUNE, 1988
The town of Ringwood was given a charter to sell agricultural animals and produce in 1266, and it is believed cattle and other animals have been sold continuously since then, and probably some years previously. The last cattle market in the town's Market Place was held on 29 June, 1988. The general market in the town's Market Place will, however, continue.

15
A Forest Pot-Pourri

Telegraph Hill's Remarkable Signal Station

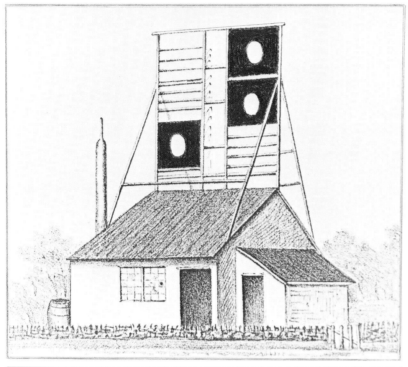

← THE STATION

Simplicity and speed were two essentials in the operation of the semphamore system linking Britain's ports with London. Of each station's complement of three men, one was on the look-out constantly. Poor visibility was a problem for which there was no solution.

In the first quarter of the nineteenth century the telegraph station near Bramshaw was an indispensable link in the Admiralty message system between Plymouth and London.

The Bramshaw station and others in the chain were built to the same specifications and therefore were similar in appearance. Likewise, they employed the same number of specialists—an officer and two men. Shown here are the signal station and code in use from about 1816 to 1825, the hey-day of the Plymouth-London line.

Stations were ideally positioned about 10 to 15 miles apart on the highest available ground. At Bramshaw the altitude reaches 419 feet. From here the line ran toward Plymouth through stations near Verwood, Chalbury Hill, Blandford, Bell Hill, Nettlecomb Tout, High Stoy, Toller Down, Lambert's Castle, and on to the coast. Going toward London, the line from Bramshaw went to Chilworth, Farley, the hill near Winchester prison, Chessford Head, Four Marks, and Monkton Binstead. Here the line joined the London-Portsmouth system.

Just how the semaphore system operated was described by T. B. Groves in a paper given before the Dorset Natural History and Archaeological Field Club. His paper, and additional information, are contained in the Society's *Proceedings* of 1890 (Vol. XI), from which the accompanying extract is taken.

The first attempt in this country to improve Telegraphy seems to have been made by the Rev. J. Gamble. His apparatus was constructed of five boards, arranged as shutters. This, however, was soon after superseded by a somewhat different plan, submitted to the Admiralty in 1795 by Lord George Murray, and adopted between London and Dover in the following year. This consisted of six shutters, arranged in two vertical rows with an interval space, in which worked the ropes and pulleys which controlled the shutters. This plan was modified in 1805 by Davis, who adapted to the frame signal lights for use by night. His idea was, however, not generally carried out.

The ball once set going, numerous were the inventions for increasing the efficiency of the instrument; but as they mostly added to the complexity of the arrangement they were not often adopted. In fact, all the shutter machines were in 1816 superseded by the Semaphore of Sir Home Popham, which consisted of a simple mast with two moveable arms. The use of this was continued until December 31st, 1847, when it gave place to that necessity of modern society—the Electric Telegraph. The Semaphore is still found useful on board ship, especially when fleets are lying in a roadstead and there is not wind enough to extend a flag.

Of the original Murray Telegraph … I fortunately found a contemporaneous drawing. The shutters are painted black with a white spot (or possibly open space) in the centre, and for rapidity of working are divided into three. Ropes attached to the cranks which actuate the shutters pass through the roof of the building to the operating room underneath.

At the back of the drawing will be found a diagram showing the number of changes that might be made by displaying all the shutters

Telegraph Hill's Remarkable Signal Station...

Continued from previous page

simultaneously, some being vertical, and therefore visible, the others horizontal, and presenting only a thin edge to the sight, practically invisible. The number of changes obtainable is 63, which would suffice for the letters of the alphabet, the numerals, and certain commonly recurring words and phrases. Considering how much the work was influenced by atmospheric conditions we should not be far wrong, I imagine, in including 'Repeat last signal' among the said phrases.

The Telegraph Station was occupied by an officer and two men, one of whom was always on duty marching backwards and forwards in the instrument room, applying his eye alternately to the fixed telescopes directed to the

stations right and left of him. At night there was nothing to do beyond watching for the beacon fire, provision for which was made by having ready adjacent a large stack of firewood for immediate kindling.

The rapidity of the shutter Telegraph attained very respectable proportions. As many as six signals could be transmitted per minute, and with the Semaphore it is said that the dropping of the time ball at Greenwich could be signalled to Portsmouth and back again in 45 sec. This was, of course, simply indicated by the dropping of an arm.

The shutter Telegraph was equally well adapted for cypher correspondence, and it is presumable that for ordinary use spelling

was distinguished rather by brevity than correctness. Its range was limited to 10 or 12 miles either way. There was a difficulty often experienced in inducing the shutters to remain in the position required. The wind, when high, would very much impede operations and induce mistakes. This was observed by Henry Ward, of Blandford, when watching the working of the Telegraph on the Race-down. Being a man of singular inventive faculty (he obtained several valuable medals, as well as money prizes, from the Society of Arts) he speedily devised a method of overcoming the difficulty. It consisted of a spring clutch, which firmly held the shutter in either of its two positions, vertical or horizontal.

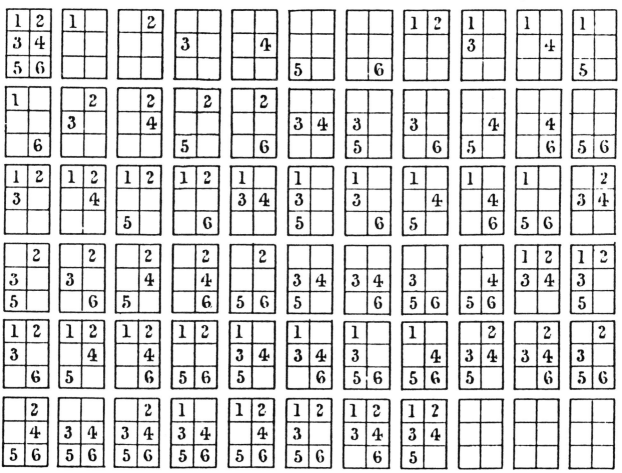

SIGNAL CODE IN USE AT BRAMSHAW STATION

An examination of the arrangements shows that 63 variations are possible, more than enough for the 26 letters of the alphabet and the numerals. The arrangements left over were used to signal the most commonly used messages, thereby assuring rapidity of delivery.

How the Commoners Earned A Living

**G.E. Briscoe Eyre worked for
nearly half a century to save the
New Forest from massive cutting, and the Forest "parliament"—the Verderers Court,
from being stripped of its
powers. He was a Verderer from
1877 to 1922 and took the lead
whenever the independence of
the New Forest and its institutions was threatened.**

**The extract below, from a study
he prepared in 1883, reveals
how the conscientious commoner could more than make
ends meet. (From *The New Forest
and Its Common Rights*.)**

It is estimated by our cottagers
and small farmers that, if there
were no wastes, a minimum of 3
acres of our forest meadows would
be required to keep a single cow,
i.e. an acre for hay and 2 acres for
the usual little crops of mangel,
&c., and to be used for pasture
alternately. The rent of such a
3-acre lot would not be less than
4l., and might be considerably
more. But with the use of the
wastes, the usual house-plot of 2
or 3 roods, if a good cow common
adjoin, will support a single cow,
except possibly in a winter of
exceptional severity.

The cow lives by the common
from May to November, while
two crops of hay are secured from
the heavily manured orchard, and
a good after-grass is growing
which is sometimes mown twice;
but everyone who can afford to do
so will give the cow a little something nightly. An expenditure of
2s. to 2s. 6d. per week in winter
on hay, swede-turnips, and pollard, and on the materials for a
mash (to the amount of about 50s.
3l.) will increase the average
weekly produce of butter
throughout the year by one-half,
say, from 3 lbs. to 5 lbs. per week.
This butter is sold at the gate for
1s. 2d. a lb. on the average.

Cases occur where a small

capital of about 10l. will enable a
second cow to be kept on the
house-plot and common by the
purchase of additional food. The
calf will be sold at six weeks old for
about 10s. profit, and all the skim
milk will then go to fatten the pig.
Each pig bought, fatted, and sold
at about four-score weight may
produce in six or eight weeks a
profit of 1s. per week up to 10s.,
and with high feeding will produce
a little more; but the value of the
pig has lain, until lately, rather in
the fact that it helps to turn everything to use and provides a valuable manure. Of course the
number bought and sold annually
will depend on circumstances,
capital, and on the mast-time.

Widows and such-like owners of
a single cow often kill and salt a
pig, the cost of which may be
cheapened by about a third if
there is a good mast. The profits of
a house-plot and single cow, with
its complement of pigs, may be
estimated at from 4s. to 10s. per
week, according to the means and
opportunities of the cottager, and,
speaking roughly, it is probable
that our labourers not unfrequently earn the double of their
weekly wages by such stock-
keeping as the foregoing.

If an acre of 1½ acre of meadow
can be added, there will probably
be two cows and a sow, and two or
three fatting pigs on the premises.

With the third cow, expenses
out of pocket begin. Few wives can
now manage without a boy to
help, and the husband, obliged to
be more and more at home, must
substitute task work for day work.
Or he will set up a pony and cart
and begin dealing first, as a hig-
gler, or dealer in butter, eggs,
poultry, and garden produce,
which he buys of the cottager and
sells in the market town—and
later, as a general dealer on a
larger scale. He employs his spare
time in carting turf, fuel, wood,
chalk, &c., for his neighbours at
5s. a ton. But the middleman's
business is not without its
drawbacks, and the careful house-
wife regards with some anxiety the

social habits and long absences
which it involves.

The next and most important
stage is reached when the cottager
can rent about five acres of
meadow and stock it with three or
four cows, a couple of sows, and
can rear a heifer and sell two
calves, and fat 10 to 12 pigs yearly.

It is possible to give the actual
profits of a twelvemonth's stock-
keeping on a "little place" of six
acres, with cottage, cowpen, and
pigstye. The stock kept was three
cows, one heifer, and one wean-
ling calf; twenty-four pigs also
were bought and sold in the year.
The labour-bill included haymaking, emptying the pens and
styes, and all rough work, the
cottager being a middle-aged
bachelor, with considerable
savings. The profits on the cow-
kind—made by sale of butter,
new milk at 4d. per quart, skim-
milk (to oblige) at 1d. a quart
—amounted to 39l. 18s. 6d. The
profits on the pigs—fatted largely
on bought food and sold at about
five score weights—amounted to
21l. 14s. 9d.

The year's net profits therefore
amounted to 61l. 13s. 3d. The
maximum profit made by this
cottager in any year was 77l. 5s.
11d. and the minimum 59l., say
10l. an acre.

The general results may be
summed up briefly. The cottager
lives the life of a labourer, but the
profits of his little holding will
compare with those of a farm in an
enclosed country of about three
the size, and of about twice the
rent. The cow provides a weekly,
the pig a quarterly, and the heifer
or pony an annual income, which
can be reinvested in a business
which the cottager thoroughly
understands, at a good or even
very high interest.

The effect on character in forming habits of industry and thrift is
obvious, and experience shows
that it is generally permanent.
Financially, also, the result seems
to be permanent notwithstanding
a stroke of ill luck or a bad season
or two. Bankruptcy in this class is,
as far as I can learn, unknown.
Neither does the cottager fall a
prey to the money-lender.

Charcoal Burning, An Old Forest Industry

Charcoal burning was for several centuries an important New Forest industry. Writers and artists depicted the burners and their picturesque pits. Historians, however, neglected to record where the pits were or the technique employed in making charcoal.

Anthony Pasmore, aware that the last vestiges of this ancient industry were fast disappearing, interviewed the one remaining charcoal burner in the Forest. After extensive additional research, he wrote his conclusions, "Surviving Evidence of the New Forest Charcoal Burning Industry" for the journal, *Industrial Archaeology*, in 1964.

HISTORICAL BACKGROUND

In view of the fact that charcoal burning was one of the oldest of the Forest's industries, it is surprising that it was never recorded in detail by the 19th century local historians. It is described in a casual manner in some of the earlier guide books to the Forest, but the picturesque appearance of the charcoal burner's hut seems to have been the chief object of interest, and no attempt was made to describe the kiln itself or the methods of production. It seems probable that the kilns were then so numerous and commonplace, that a detailed description was considered quite unnecessary from the historical point of view. John Wise writing about the middle of the century for example, could scarcely have foreseen that within 40 years the entire industry would be little more than a memory.

In order to obtain contemporary impressions of the industry, therefore, it is necessary to look for other sources. It appears that for at least the last two centuries of the industry's history, there was considerable friction between the colliers and the forest authorities. Throughout this period, increasing importance was being attached to the production of 'Navy Timber', and the alleged destruction of this timber by the colliers appears to have given rise to great official concern. In 1698, an Act was passed 'for the Increase and Preservation of Timber in the New Forest in the County of Southampton'. This Act, which is generally considered to have marked a turning point in the history of the Forest, contains the following provisions relating to charcoal burning:

'... nor shall any Collier presume to make or any Keeper or Under Keepers suffer any Coal-Hearths or Coal-Fires for making Charcoal within the said Forest to be made

CHARCOAL BURNERS AT WORK NEAR THEIR HUT IN BOLDERWOOD
This artist's impression depicts the pit recorded by Anthony Pasmore at Bolderwood Grounds. The sketch, by Lancelot Speed, is from C.J. Cornish's *The New Forest and the Isle of Wight* (1903).

Charcoal Burning...

Continued from previous page

(as hath of late been practiced contrary to Law) except in the waste Ground of the said Forest to be then appointed by one or more of the Verderers and two or more of the Regarders and the Surveyor or Woodward and not within One thousand Paces of any Inclosure to be made by this Act nor shall any of the said Coal-Hearths or Coal-Fires be fenced with Bushes but with Heath or Furse only but every Collier making such Coal-Hearths or Coal-Fires and every Forester and Under Keeper or other Officer permitting the same to be made within the said Forest shall forfeit and lose for every offence the Sum of one hundred pounds ...'

The penalties mentioned above appear to be unexpectedly severe, and this, perhaps, gives some indication of the extent of the collier's depredations. The Act, however, like so much of the subsequent legislation affecting the Forest, appears to have failed in its object. In 1789, the Fifth Report of the Land Revenue Commissioners revealed that the activities of the charcoal burners were in keeping with the general atmosphere of corruption and lawlessness which prevailed in the Forest at that time. It was stated as part of a list of offences which were being committed in the Forest that:

'7thly. That the salutory Provisions of the Act of 9th and 10th William III (1698) are almost wholly disregarded in many other respects ...

The Charcoal Hearths are all allowed within the woods, because that is more convenient to the Makers, though attended with the Danger of burning the Woods, and affording Opportunities of stealing young trees or Branches with less Probability of Detection.'

The examination of the Groom Keepers of the various Walks also provides some interesting facts concerning the extent of the industry, although it should be remembered that many pits were probably situated on private land adjacent to the Forest. It appears that more than 20 pits were operating in the Forest at that time, and that as a result, considerable damage was being done to the timber. Perhaps this is hardly surprising, however, when even the administration of the Forest contained few officials who were above suspicion of committing one crime or another.

In 1848, a Select Committee of the House of Commons revealed that conditions in the New Forest were, if anything, rather worse than they had been in 1789. The examination of W.L. Freeman, who appears to have been an inspector from the central body of the Office of Woods, contains the following references to charcoal burning:

'Do you burn much charcoal in that part? Not any now.

Did you formerly. Yes; I found a good many charcoal-burners, and I turned them all out, because I found that charcoal-burning encouraged the stealing of cordwood, and encouraged people to sell it, for charcoal-burners are not generally the most reputable people.

Are you aware that by the Act of William III, every collier making charcoal, and every forest-keeper or other officer permitting the same charcoal to be made is liable to forfeit £100? Yes, I am.

Are all the charcoal-pits stopped now? Yes; there are some in the manors, which, of course, we cannot interfere with.

Were there charcoal pits burning close to the road, near Mr. Sign's, when you first went down? Yes, he himself had one there.'

(James Sign was prosecuted for irregular dealings in timber, but was never tried, as it was claimed that he was insane; he was taken from the court to an asylum.)

From this it appears that the authorities were at last making a stand against the abuses which were rife in the Forest. Three years later, however, the Deer Removal Act was passed, and this was followed by over 30 years of intense conflict between the Office of Woods and the Commoners, during which time the charcoal burners seem to have quietly re-established themselves. Then, apparently within a period of about 20 years hinged on the turn of the century, came the death of the industry. In his *History of Hampshire* 1892, Shore makes the following reference to the decaying industry, but fails to provide any reason for its death:

'The art of charcoal burning has survived in Hampshire from the time of the Romans, or earlier, until the present day, there being a few charcoal burners, who will probably be the last of their kind, still following their craft in the New Forest.'

Pit burning was to continue in other parts of the country for many years to come, until superseded by the modern cylindrical iron kilns.

The commencement of the 20th century, might, but for an unusual set of circumstances have seen the last charcoal pit vanish beneath the Forest's undergrowth, and with it all knowledge of the local methods of production. These circumstances were related to me by Mr. Robert Cull of Copythorne, and to him I am also indebted for the following account of the construction and firing of a charcoal pit as it was done in the New Forest. In reading the account given below it should be borne in mind that it depends upon the memory of one man stretching over half a century and on my own attempts to visualize a charcoal pit from a purely verbal description. Despite this, however, I hope that any errors or misdescriptions which may have been included will be outweighed by the very fact that such an account has been produced while it is still possible to do so.

Towards the end of the last century, the Culls were living at London Minstead, where Maurice Cull, my informant's father, was engaged in charcoal burning at

Charcoal Burning: An Old Forest Industry...

Clay Hill. The cottage which they occupied was Crown property and their subsequent eviction might suggest that the Office of Woods was still exerting pressure on the industry. On leaving Minstead, the Culls moved to Copythorne, where Maurice and his four sons continued to practise their trade. By this time the industry was collapsing, and Maurice Cull and Mark Veal of Lyndhurst were probably the last colliers supplying the traditional markets. In the course of his business, Maurice Cull obtained supplies of wood from the Eyres' estate at Bramshaw. It seems that it was the custom for a number of oaks to be felled each year on that estate and the bark sent to the tan yards at Romsey. As a result of his purchase of 'rinded' cord wood from the estate, Maurice Cull came to the notice of Mr. Eyre, and so it was that on the outbreak of war in 1914, Mr. Eyre knew one of the remaining charcoal burners in the New Forest.

With the war came the first extensive use of toxic gas as an offensive weapon, and the consequent development of the box respirator brought about an unexpected revival of the industry. The principles upon which this respirator worked are rather complicated, but very broadly they depend upon the ability of activated charcoal to absorb and hold molecules of gas, roughly in the same way that a magnet attracts and holds iron filings on its surface. It follows from this, that in the early stages of the war there was a great increase in the demand for charcoal for which the industry was unprepared and not in a position to meet.

It appears that Mr. Eyre, through his work in London, had become aware of this demand and accordingly he attempted to locate the charcoal burners who had formerly purchased wood from his estate. In this he was at first unsuccessful since Maurice Cull was by this time dead. Further research, however, revealed that

Continued from previous page

Frederick, his eldest son, had learned the trade from his father; but Frederick was at first unwilling to co-operate. His political views were strongly radical and he had no wish to serve a government which he considered had been largely responsible for his family's eviction from their former home. After a great deal of persuasion, however, based on the argument that the charcoal was for the 'boys at the front' and not for the authorities, Frederick and his brothers started work in the Nomansland area, enjoying an almost complete monopoly of the trade in the New Forest.

TECHNIQUE OF PRODUCTION, c.1914

The methods employed at this time were briefly as follows. Assuming that the kiln is to be erected on the site of an existing pit, a circle with a radius of 7 ft. is laid out. Around the edge of this circle, a bank of 'dirt', i.e., charred bed fuzzing, charcoal dust and soil(?), is erected. This bank has a width of about 3 ft. and an inner height of between 18 and 24 in. which tapers down to ground level at the outside of the ring. In constructing this bank, a gap is left sufficient for the passage of a

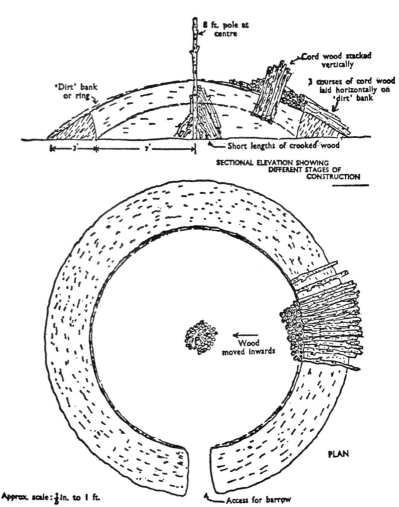

SECTIONAL ELEVATION SHOWING DIFFERENT STAGES OF CONSTRUCTION

PLAN

Approx. scale: ⅛ in. to 1 ft.

The cord wood is then stacked in roughly the form of an inverted pudding basin centred on the pole. As this stacking process is continued, the working space develops into a ring which moves outward towards the edge of the kiln as the

Charcoal Burning...

Continued from previous page

wheelbarrow from the outside.

Three courses of split cord wood are then laid horizontally on top of the bank forming radii to the circle. The object of this is to provide support for the split cord-wood which is brought into the kiln at the next stage. An average pit contained about eight cords or approximately 1,000 cubic feet of wood, the remainder of which is brought into the kiln and stacked vertically against the three courses described above, in diminishing concentric rings. Throughout this process, the passage through the outer bank is extended, until, on its completion, there remains a small working space at the centre of the kiln connected to the outside. An 8ft. pole is then erected at the centre of the kiln, and around

are incorporated in the stack. At this stage, a 'V' shaped notch is visible between the edge of the stack and the dirt, and into this notch is packed 'bed-fuzzing'.

Bed-fuzzing consists of gorse tops which are cut on the open Forest, and commencing at the foot of the stack it is packed tightly into the gaps between the cord wood until the whole kiln is covered to a depth of 6 in. The dirt is then shovelled up and spread over the bed-fuzzing to form a further covering 6 in. deep which is thoroughly soaked with water. All is now ready for firing, and accordingly the pole is removed and two shovels of red-hot embers are placed in a 3 ft. deep hole which has been preserved at the top of the kiln during construc-

Cull, a number of amateur attempts to produce charcoal during the first war, failed because of a lack of knowledge of the correct methods of firing.

After firing, the kiln has to be watched day and night to ensure that the outer covering does not burn through. It is also necessary to refuel with 'feeding-wood', that is, short lengths of dry wood which are put into the kiln by removing the turf covering from the top. Feeding wood is added four times daily, on each occasion about one barrow load being used. After three days no more feeding wood is added, while on the fourth day the kiln has subsided to a height of about 5 ft. There follows the 'flare', i.e. the turf covering is burned through and a sheet of flame appears at the top of the kiln. When the flare has died down the wood is completely converted and an inspection of the hole at the top (approached by ladder) reveals a glowing red mass. At this stage the fire is extinguished by adding two tubs of water and completely sealing the kiln with the remaining dirt in order to exclude the air. When the kiln has cooled, the outer covering is cleared away and the charcoal removed, the whole process having been completed in about one week.

Because of its light weight, charcoal was sold by volume before the war, the standard market price being about eight shillings per bushel. During the war, however, probably because the purchase was arranged by some unimaginative official in London, the charcoal was bought by weight. Under these circumstances, it is hardly surprising that rather more water was used in extinguishing the kiln than had formerly been the case.

Post-war Period

After the war, this brief revival of pit-burning came to an abrupt end, although Frederick Cull continued to practise his traditional craft until his death. Living in a caravan, he set up a pit just inside Furzey Lawn Inclosure opposite the New Forest Foxhound kennels, and here the industry finally came to an end.

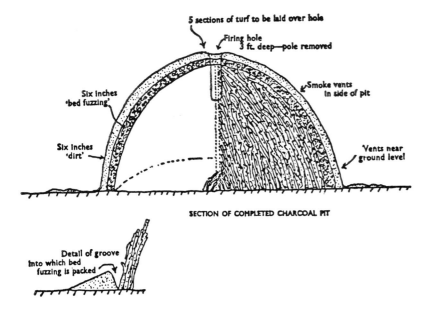

SECTION OF COMPLETED CHARCOAL PIT

its base is placed a quantity of short crooked wood. The cord wood is then stacked in roughly the form of an inverted pudding basin centred on the pole. As this stacking process is continued, the working space develops into a ring which moves outward towards the edge of the kiln as the charcoal burner reaches behind him and brings forward each length of wood. Finally, there remains only the three courses laid horizontally on the dirt bank, and these also

tion. The hole is then covered with about five sections of turf and a number of small vents are made near ground level in order to admit draught to the kiln; further holes are made in the sides to allow smoke to escape. The method of firing was a jealously guarded trade secret, a fact which is confirmed by a number of old people living in the Forest who relate that a charcoal burner would never fire his kiln while being watched. According to Mr.

Glossary of Forest Words

(In his *New Forest Commoners*, 1969, Anthony Pasmore lists examples of Forest terms used by the Commoners in their everyday life. Some of the terms are passing out of use.)

The language of the commoners is full of words which, although not necessarily confined to the New Forest, may be unfamiliar to the visitor. This glossary is by no means exhaustive, but may be of interest as so many of the old Forest words are falling into disuse. Of the "Glossary of Provincialisms" thoughtfully provided by J. Wise in his "*New Forest*", 1863, less than half a dozen words remain in use today, and many of those listed below are becoming less common.

Agister: A servant of the Verderers employed in the care of commonable animals. Formerly an officer of the Forest.

Clip out: To cut away the hair covering a brand.

Colts: May mean ponies in general, or foals, or male foals.

Colt hunting: The art of rounding up individual ponies required for a particular purpose.

Cord Wood: A stack of firewood 4 ft. x 4 ft. x 8 ft. used in the supply of wood for fuel rights.

Dier: A sick animal likely to die.

Drift: A round up of animals organized by the Agister for official purposes.

Driftway: A track running between two pieces of enclosed land.

Forest Eye: A disease of the eye in cattle which originated, and remains prevalent, in the Forest.

Furze: Gorse. Pronounced "Fuzz".

Haunt or Run: The portion of the Forest within which a particular pony lives.

Lane Creeper: A pony which leaves the Forest and habitually grazes the road verges outside the peramublation. (Obsolete.)

Holms: Holly trees.

Mare colt: A filly foal.

Marking fee: Money paid annually to the Verderers in respect of an animal depastured in the Forest.

Open Forest or Open Waste or Crown Waste: The commonable lands of the Forest in Crown ownership.

Ovesting: To mark and depasture pigs. As "agisting" with commonable animals. (Rare.)

Passage: A path across a bog as "Matley Passage" or "Admiral Murray's Passage".

Perambulation: Current meaning is the boundary of the Forest.

Portable Pound: A portable heavy sectional enclosure used for drifts.

Presentment: A request, complaint or announcement made in public before the Court of Verderers.

Purlieu: Land once within a forest and subject to Forest Law, but subsequently disafforested.

Ring Rope: A rope with a steel ring at the end. Used in catching ponies.

Shade: A place where animals congregate in Summer, usually an open ground, to escape the attacks of flies.
Also used as a verb: "She shades at Ocknell Pond".

Shoot: A small pig (under one year) for which a small payment is due to the Crown for pannage.
Also a steep path in the Forest (obsolete except in place names; e.g. Whiteshoot).

Small Commoner: A working commoner deriving all or part of his living from the Forest.

Sucker: A foal.

Sucked Yearling: A yearling which still feeds from its mother.

Tailing: A method employed in colt hunting where the colt is caught by the mane or tail.

Turn out: To turn out is to depasture animals. Sometimes used as a noun meaning the right to turn out.

Walkers: Commoners assisting at a drift on foot.

HUNTING HISTORY

Sporting historians agree that the New Forest Hounds had their origin in 1781 with Vincent Hawkins Gilbert whose home was at Bartley Lodge (then called "Lamb's Corner") near Cadnam.

Gilbert was born in 1753, went to Oxford and later spent much time hunting with two close friends, Andrew Berkeley Drummond and John Compton, both of whom came from prominent New Forest families. For the last seven years of his life Gilbert was Master of the New Forest Hounds. He died in 1798.

The history of the New Forest Hounds is a tabulation of many famous names, some Forest residents and others from without who came to the area for sport. For students of hunting history in the New Forest, three useful references are *A History of Hunting in Hampshire* by Brigadier-General J.F.R. Hope (1950); *A Hunting Pageant* by Mary S. Lovell (1981); and *Sport and Sportsmen* in the New Forest by C.R. Acton (1936).

Charcoal Burning...

Continued from previous page

SURVIVING EVIDENCE

The physical traces left by the industry on the ground are very slight, but with patient searching of the Forest's deciduous woodlands, they can be discovered with little difficulty. The sites of two abandoned pits are shown on the 1909 edition of Six Inch Ordnance Survey maps, namely those at Clay Hill (Minstead) and Wooson's Hill. With these exceptions, the recording of charcoal pits provides an almost virgin field for those who derive satisfaction from collecting scraps of unwritten history. It also seems possible that complete distribution maps and analysis of the different types of charcoal might provide information about former areas of woodland in the Forest. In considering this, it should be remembered that the charcoal pits were set up wherever a suitable supply of timber was available, as is still the case today; the fuel was not generally moved to the pit.

CHARLIE POULTON MAKING EEL TRAPS HALF A CENTURY AGO

Made of seasoned hazel rods, the traps were carefully woven to allow eels to enter one end with no chance of escape. The completed trap was three feet long. Charlie, who lived at Woodgreen, once made five traps in a day: two before going to work, one at lunch, and two more in the evening. He made traps when in his 90s and they were always in demand. Up to three pounds of small eels could be caught in a single trap during the spring and summer seasons when they were most plentiful. Charlie put his long life down to outdoor activity. "We caan't bide een doors," he was quoted as saying, "the rhe'matics do get at ee somethin' tara'ble. 'Ee must be oot a potterin' aboot; there's al-ays summat to do."

A Pictorial Pot-Pourri...

FIRST WOMAN TO BE ELECTED A VERDERER
Dionis Macnair, secretary of the New Forest Pony Breeding and Cattle Society, astride her Forest pony. She was the first woman to be elected a Verderer.

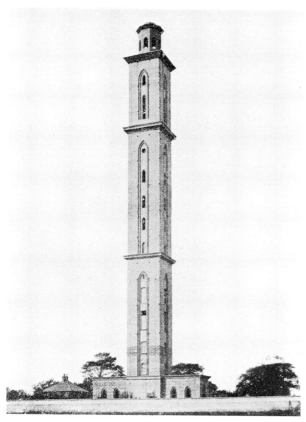

PETERSON'S FOLLY AT SWAY

TWO POPULAR BEAUTY SPOTS
Looking down "Ragged Boys Hill" from Sloden
Woods toward Holly Hatch. (Below): Wootton
Bridge, a favourite wading spot for children.

A Trusty Servants portrait would you see
This Emblamatic Figure well survey
The Porkers Snout not nice in diet shows
The Padlock shut no secrets he'll disclose
Patient the Ass his Masters wrath will bear
Swiftness in errand the Staggs feet declare
Loaded his Left hand apt to labour saith
The Vest his neatness Open hand his faith
Girt with his Sword his Shield upon his arm
himself and master he'll protect from harm

"TRUSTY SERVANT" SIGN AT MINSTEAD

A HUNTING CENTRE—The New Forest
This reproduction of an old print appears in Mary S. Lovell's history of the New Forest Hunt Club, *A Hunting Pageant*. It depicts some of the well known landmarks associated with hunting in the Forest a century ago; left to right from the top they are The Compton Arms, Stoney Cross; Minstead Manor; Beaulieu Abbey; the kennels at Lyndhurst; stables, and Bolton's Bench, Lyndhurst.

The 1869 Duel of Words between Freeman and Trollope

The "pros and cons" of hunting wild animals is a lively issue in the New Forest, as elsewhere in Britain, but seldom has the case for and against this sport been put so well as when two prominent figures battled in print over a century ago.

In 1869 the attention of the nation was focussed on the columns of the respected journal, *Fortnightly Review*, as a leading historian, E.A. Freeman, and the novelist Anthony Trollope, took opposing sides. Freeman was well known for his forthright views on many subjects and his abrasive manner no doubt contributed to a series of failures to gain a seat in Parliament. He wrote extensively for leading publications and eventually was named regius professor of modern history at Oxford. Trollope at the time was at the peak of his popularity and could command a price of a thousand pounds or more for his novels, usually serialized.

Freeman saw no place for hunting in the life of "an educated man," and his article, "The Morality of Field Sports" was resented by the sporting fraternity when it appeared in the October, 1869 issue of *Fortnightly Review*. Trollope, a keen supporter of fox-hunting, felt obliged to reply to Freeman's thesis and received permission from the magazine's editor to respond in a subsequent issue. The *Dictionary of National Biography* says the nation was much amused by this duel of "two very rough diamonds."

After the two original points of view had been published, Freeman followed up with a rebuttal, but when Trollope asked for space to make a rejoinder of his own, the editor would only reluctantly agree. Trollope therefore abandoned the attempt, perhaps realizing the argument could go on indefinitely. Freeman then offered to print the opposing views in a pamphlet. Trollope agreed, but only on condition that he have the last word inasmuch as Freeman had had the first. Freeman refused, and the pamphlet never appeared. The "classic" presentation of opposing views, as set forth by Professor Freeman and Anthony Trollope, are reproduced here in key extracts from the original arguments.

FREEMAN ...

The true question lies in a nut-shell. Is it right to inflict, and to seek pleasure in inflicting, needless suffering on any creature whatever?

The subject is one on which one is commonly met with simple amazement, with mere bluster or ridicule, or with answers so absurd that they cannot be meant seriously. I need not stop to discuss an answer which I have heard more than once, namely, that "the fox likes it." Fox-hunting is said to have some social advantages, I mean real social advantages in linking together class and class. In this I believe there is some truth as regards some particular classes; but supposing it to be more true than it is, it does not touch the question.

We are told too that, if there were no field-sports, country gentlemen would find nothing to do. This again does not touch the question, and the saying is a libel on very many country gentlemen, both among those who hunt and among those who do not. I could point to a good many country gentlemen, to men who are the salt of their class, who—whether for my reasons or for any other I cannot always say—never join in field-sports, and what is more, whose public and private duties would not allow them the time to join in them.

We are told that many men, if they were not hunting, would be doing something worse. This I can well believe; but it only proves that hunting is not the worst of all occupations, and I never said that it was. Then we are told that the amount of animal suffering inflicted in other ways, by drovers, by cabmen, by butchers, is much greater than what is inflicted in hunting. This is doubtless true, but it does not touch the point. It is no excuse for one form of cruelty to show that other, perhaps worse, forms of cruelty may be found.

TROLLOPE ...

The effect of Mr. Freeman's essay on an uninitiated reader would be the creation of a belief that the ordinary English fox-hunter is always riding about the country up to his elbows in fox's blood. This, however, is not the case. The recreation experienced in the hunting field is very various in its nature; but a promiscuous intercourse with the mangled limbs of the quarry is not a part of it. Men are thrown together who would not otherwise meet, and converse on all subjects common to men. Politics are discussed, and agriculture, social habits, the affairs of the country, the preservation of foxes, the enmity of this enemy to the sport, and the devoted friendship of that friend.

Perhaps of all the delights of the hunting field conversation is the most general. Fresh air and exercise are gained by men who greatly need it;—for the hunting field is not made up of men who, because they hunt, are therefore idle; out of the crowd of those assembled nine out of ten are men who work hard and earn their bread. There is enterprise in riding to hounds, and skill. Ambition, courage, and persistency are all brought into play. A community is formed in which equality prevails, and the man with small means and no rank holds his own against the lord or the millionaire as he can do nowhere else amidst the scenes of our life. City-men learn country lore, and country-men are told the ways of cities.

Hunting is, of all amusements, the most fit for a hard-worked educated man, who desires to foster the outer vigours of his manliness in those hours which he has been able to take from his work and devote to the preservation of his health and the recreation of his senses.

As Mr. Freeman has implied that the man who shoots is no better than an "amateur butcher" and that

FREEMAN ...

Continued from previous page

And there is this all important difference. Whatever cruelties are committed by drovers or cabmen, however great may be their aggregate amount, are still incidental. A cabman or a drover perhaps seldom is, but he always may be, a perfectly humane man, who takes all heed never to occasion any needless suffering to the animals under his care. A butcher too may be a thoroughly humane man, who takes all heed that no animal which passes under his hands undergoes anything beyond simple and speedy death. In all these cases, though cruelty is frightfully common, yet it is always an abuse, it is no essential part of the occupation. But a humane fox-hunter is a contradiction in terms, because in his occupation cruelty is not an occasional incident but the essence of the whole thing.

Creatures, we are told, are made to prey on one another; the dog has the instinct of prey, so has the man himself. He is therefore in no way sinning by following his own natural instinct and by witnessing and encouraging the instinct of the dog. The manifest answer to this is that, if this argument proves anything at all, it justifies every sort of cruelty, or rather every sort of wickedness to which a man may profess to feel a natural impulse. And if there be a natural impulse towards pursuit and destruction, which may be lawfully gratified because it is a natural impulse, any inhumanity, whether towards man or towards beast, may be justified on the same ground.

We have in us an impulse of self-defence, an impulse of wrath at wrong done to ourselves or to others, which, especially when heightened by the natural desire of success, may give a zest to warfare or conflict of any kind. And such an impulse as this may easily degenerate into mere love of fighting, and from mere love of fighting it may degenerate into something like a mere love of destruction. The combative instinct is one given us for good purposes; but, like some other instincts given us for equally good purposes, it needs to be specially controlled and kept in order.

The whole existence of death and pain, of evil of any kind, is the deepest and saddest of mysteries. But it is plain that, for whatever ends pain and evil may be allowed in the world, it is at least our business to lessen their amount, not to increase it or to seek our pleasure in them. The line of argument of which I speak, if consistently carried out, would give full scope to all the fiercer, and would stifle all the gentler, emotions of our nature. If we may take pleasure in the infliction of pain and death, because pain is a part of the order of nature, there is no knowing where we are to stop.

I have also been told that my argument proves too much, that, if I condemn fox-hunting, I should in consistency be a vegetarian and condemn all slaying of animals. But surely the distinction on which my whole argument rests, between the infliction of simple death for an adequate purpose and the infliction of needless suffering in sheer wantonness, is a perfectly tenable one. Even if we did not kill animals for food, it would be necessary to kill them for other purposes. If animal

TROLLOPE ...

the man who hunts is worse than the man who shoots, I have thought it well to endeavour to clear the ground in regard to hunting. I say that no man goes out fox-hunting in order that he may receive pleasure from pain inflicted; that no fox-hunter seeks or ever receives such pleasure; ... At a fox-hunt no man or woman goes to see blood, agony and death, and not one in twenty does see the animal at its death.

I can understand that any complainant against fox-hunting other than Mr. Freeman should say that in this argument I am hiding myself behind a subterfuge, in that the cruelty to the animal is there, though the sportsman does not witness it. Mr. Freeman cannot object this to me, because he distinctly and prominently brings this charge against fox-hunters—that pleasure taken in the infliction of pain and in beholding that pain is the essence of ... fox-hunting. There is no such pleasure derived from fox-hunting either as its essence, or even as a possible outside result. Mr. Freeman may assert that fox-hunting cannot take place without agony to the fox, and that assertion may be unanswerable, or may be answerable. ... In fox-hunting the visible agony of the fox is never longer present to the eye than is that of the wasp that is crushed without remorse by a lady's fan, and is rarely visible at all.

And now I will go on to that graver charge of cruelty to the animal. We do not become callous to life and death by knowing that men die, but we do so by seeing them when dying. But the injury, though less in degree, may still be injury. But before we allow our minds to settle down on the vehement denunciation of this or that special cruelty, we should know what cruelty is. Is it cruel to kill a wasp? It is not held to be so, because it is done in self-defence. To kill a fly may be exceeding cruelty. To kill a hundred merely because they are a slight nuisance, is considered an action by no means cruel. The hundred flies have been killed for what Mr. Freeman calls "need."

Mr. Freeman say that "neither death nor torture should be turned into matter of amusement." But we daily subject both men and animals to pain for our amusement. Does the clown at the theatre not suffer —ay, and the singer! It is a world, it may be said, necessarily burdened with pain for men; but the animals need not be made to suffer. Do we not know that horses suffer in their work, and must suffer?

It is a world in which delights and pains are mingled, and in the midst of it all the fox, who is lord of the copse and possessed in fee of the covert, has by no means the worst time of it among animals.

Mr. Freeman has admitted that if there were no hunting there would be no foxes. The fox owes his existence, therefore, to the sport. Then, though he is not absolutely nurtured as a house lamb, he receives all the care that is essential to his well-being and education. Mr. Freeman, laughing with good cause for laughter as a non-sporting man, says truly enough that the fox becomes so precious that the word vulpicide has

FREEMAN ...

Continued from previous page

life were absolutely sacred, human life would become intolerable. But I cannot see that the right to torment is at all involved in the right to kill.

It sometimes strikes me that sportsmen, those at least among them who have any capacity or any inclination for thought, often show a lurking feeling of doubt as to the rightfulness of their own pursuit. The big words of bluster and ridicule which are so often used are not only void of argument, but they betray a certain, perhaps an almost unconscious, uneasiness which seeks relief in this kind of talk. Sportsmen are sometimes rather too loud in the praises of their pursuit; they are sometimes too eager to defend it even when it is not attacked.

I ask nothing of any reader of this essay except boldly to look the question in the face and honestly to weigh what I say. Cast away all prejudices, all conventionalities, all subterfuges, look the thing boldly in the face, and will any one tell me either that it is really right to seek amusement in the suffering of any living creature, or that hunting is anything but amusement sought in the sufferings of a living creature? Will any one who engages in such sports tell me that he does not, for the time at least, stifle the divine voice of mercy within him, that he does not, for the time at least, give the reins to the passions of the wild beast or the savage?

Now, as a man's views and arguments are commonly more or less affected by his personal position, I think it right to say that my views on these matters are wholly the result of reflection. I was brought up in a way which gave me no incentives or opportunities for field-sports, but, on the other hand, I was not taught to look on them as wrong.

Whatever may be thought of my views, they have not been hastily taken up, nor are they the result of any prejudices of family, class, or sect. Circumstances have enabled me to look at the matter without any prepossessions either way. My opinions have been at least thought out by myself, honestly, independently, and, I may add, fearlessly.

The advocates of humanity have a hard battle to fight, but I am not without hope. As in everything else, there are fluctuations and reactions, and perhaps of late years there may have been a certain reaction in favour of cruelty. So it has been with the growth of political freedom; still political freedom has advanced, and so I feel that it must in the end be with the cause of humanity.

TROLLOPE ...

been created to denounce a most hated crime. The fox is almost worshipped, and becomes, as I have said, lord of the coppice and great freeholder of the covert.

To be hunted,—or to think that he is hunted,—and to take safety in flight, is the nature of a fox. We cannot doubt but that his scent was imposed upon him in order that he should fulfil his destiny of falling a prey to his pursuers. Till fatigue induces the fear that escape may not be achieved, the animal probably does not suffer. Then he has a sharp ten minutes, and a final half-minute of agony in his death-struggle. In all this, is his life as bad as that of a cab-horse, or of a half-starved dog, or of a caged bird, or an imprisoned fish?

In accordance with Mr. Freeman's theory, that fox should not be made to suffer the slightest pain, even though its single death would give balmy recreation to all mankind in all ages. He lays it down as a law that neither pain nor death should be made matter of amusement. No such law can stand, or be of any guidance whatever to mankind.

The hunted fox suffers that death to which it seems that he was devoted by nature, without any added circumstances of torture, in which his death-struggle is not prolonged as is that of the mouse beneath the cat, in order that a large number of men may enjoy a sport which is by them thought to be salutary, noble, and beneficial. Mr. Freeman doubtless objects to the sport on other grounds, thinking it to be neither, salutary, noble, or beneficial;—but that is not now the question. The objection now urged is solely that of cruelty, and is so urged as to be intended to prevail even were the advantage of hunting confessedly very great. In answer to that objection, I plead that the end justifies the means, that a minimum of suffering produces a maximum of recreation, and that the fox's life serves as good a purpose as that of any animal which falls that men may live.

(Animals) hunt each other from day to day, and suffer the double agony of hunger and of bloody destruction. Seeing that this is so,—that the soft-hearted, rose-leafed, velvet life which Mr. Freeman would desire for animals is not in accordance with Nature, I cannot bring myself to feel that the fox suffers unworthily when he is done to death by a pack of hounds for the gratification of a hundred sportsmen. As far as he is concerned he owes his existence to the prospect of his death. As regards those who ride after him, I maintain that no part of their pleasure comes from his suffering.

The Best Ways to See the Forest

(Gerald Lascelles in his autobiography, *Thirty-Five Years in the New Forest* 1915 maintains there are only two proper ways of viewing the forest.)

There are only two ways really to see the New Forest and realise what it is like. One is to go on foot with a pair of extra stout boots and a walking-stick, but this takes a long time, and is a fatiguing process. The other—the only way fit for a gentleman—is from the back of a pleasant, well-mannered horse, with good shoulders and a trained eye for ruts and rabbit holes.

With such a conveyance, the most delightful summer's day imaginable can be spent in rambling about the beautiful heaths and woodland scenes of all kinds that make up this beautiful Forest.

1. NEW FOREST M.F.H.

2. THE MORNING KISS

5. THE MEET: THE RIDING-MAS

3. 4.30 A.M.: "HERE BE HIS SLOT"

4. NATIVE SPORTSMEN

11. THE SURVIVAL

12 THE RETURN OF THE HIRED MOUNT

13 CHANGING HORSES

HUNTING WITH THE

DEER-HUNTING IN THE NEW FOREST AS DEPICTED BY *The Graphic* **A CENTURY AGO**
Sporting events in the New Forest frequently attracted national attention a century ago, as is shown by the sketches on these pages. They were the centre spread in one of Britain's most widely read illustrated journals, *The Graphic*. In its issue of 14 February, 1885 *The Graphic* sent its artist to the

6. GONE AWAY

7. ACROSS THE PLAIN

9. A CAREFUL HUNTER.

10. WELL JUMPED

8 THE HIRED MOUNT

ACK TO HIM"

15 GOING HOME

10 "MR. MUDGE, HAVE YE CATCHED THE DEER TO-DAY, SIR?"

OREST DEERHOUNDS

New Forest to record the atmosphere of deer-hunting, but the artist did not miss the humour of the occasion. He depicted the dangers awaiting an inexperienced rider, a lady changing horses without alighting, and (in the last cartoon) Forest children querying a hunter about the deer not caught.

West Saxon Speech Lasted Longer in Forest

PUBLICATIONS OF THE PHILOLOGICAL SOCIETY

IV

THE DIALECT OF THE NEW FOREST

IN HAMPSHIRE

(AS SPOKEN IN THE VILLAGE OF BURLEY)

BY

SIR JAMES WILSON, K.C.S.I.

OXFORD UNIVERSITY PRESS

LONDON Amen Corner EC · EDINBURGH · NEW YORK

TORONTO · MELBOURNE · BOMBAY

TITLE PAGE OF SIR JAMES WILSON'S LANGUAGE STUDY
Wilson concentrated on the oldest Forest residents in compiling his study, recognizing that the younger generation already had become more mobile and would have lost much of the old West Saxon dialect spoken by their elders.

Just before the first world war Sir James Wilson, the noted philologian, set out to find if there was any place in southern Britain where remnants of the old West Saxon language were still spoken. Rural villages offered the best possibility, but even then some were being settled by people from nearby towns and young people were moving away for lack of employment.

Wilson's search narrowed to the New Forest, a "pocket" then largely immune from outside influences. Within the Forest he sought, and found, a village not yet affected by main arterial roads and an influx of people from without. This village was Burley and it was to become Sir James' "laboratory" on two occasions before he compiled his study, *The Dialect of the New Forest in Hampshire (As Spoken in the Village of Burley)*.

Born in 1853, Wilson was educated at Perth Academy and the universities of Edinburgh and Oxford. He became secretary to the Government of India in the Department of Revenue and Agriculture, and spent most of his free time documenting the customs and language of the areas where he worked. His Indian studies include *Code of Tribal Custom in Shahpur* and another for Sirsa, as well as *Grammar of Western Panjabi*. On retirement, he returned to his native Scotland and produced *The Lowland Scotch*, *Farm Workers in Scotland*, *The Dialect of Robert Burns* and *Dialects of Central Scotland*.

His New Forest dialect study appeared in 1913 when he was 60. He died at 73. A few of the rare language forms documented by him are still used by some of the older Forest families. The extracts below are taken from Sir James' introduction to his study, and from representative sections of the 48-page treatise. (Unfortunately, it is not possible to reproduce Wilson's 700-word New Forest vocabulary here.)

INTRODUCTION

During two short visits to Burley, a quiet country village in the New Forest in Hampshire, I made some notes of the dialect, as spoken by the older residents, who had spent all their lives in the village. I have now put them together, in order to give some idea of the differences between that dialect and standard spoken English, in pronunciation, grammar, vocabulary, and idiom. They are by no means exhaustive, but, so far as they go, I have tried to make them accurately represent the actual language still used by the present generation, the words and phrases having been noted down from the memory of the people, not taken from books. In giving illustrative sentences (printed in bold type) I have written every word of the sentence as I understand an old resident of Burley would pronounce it, if he were speaking unthinkingly in his own mother-tongue.

I presume that the dialect of Burley may be taken as fairly typical of the speech of the New Forest, and as representing what remains of the language of the West Saxons.

J. WILSON.

59 CADOGAN SQUARE, LONDON,
20 November, 1913.

West Saxon Speech ...

Continued from previous page

GRAMMAR

NOUNS

The following plurals are peculiar:

E.		N.F.
	Singular	*Plural*
house	**hous**	**houzin or houzinz**
furze	**vuz**	**vuzin**
deer	**deer**	**deerz**
child	**cheild**	**childern or chillern**
foot	**veet**	**veet or veets**

After a numeral nouns of time do not take the **s** or **z** of the plural. Examples:

E.	N.F.
six months	**zix munth**
twenty years	**twenty yeer**

PRONOUNS

PERSONAL PRONOUNS.

Us, slurred into **'s** or **'z**, is often used in short phrases for **mee**. Examples:

Gi'ss wun	Give me one.
Let's av mei speks.	Let me have my spectacles.
Laiv us aloan.	Leave me alone.
Bist gwein wee uz?	Are you going with me?

In the second person singular **dhee** is used in all cases (**dhou** and **dhy** are not used), and is often slurred into **ee**. Examples:

Bist dhee cooud?	Are you cold?
How'z dhee mudhur?	How's your mother?
Caas'n dhee goo?	Can't you go?
Dhee woald zow	Your old sow.
Ei tell dhee	I tell you.

The second personal pronoun dhee is often omitted when the termination of the verb shows that the second person singular is meant. Examples:

N.F.	E.
How bist?	How are you (art thous)?
Dust meind?	Do you (dost thou) remember?
'Snoa?	Do you (dost thou) know?
Dist eer oi?	Did you (dist thou) hear me?

See other examples under the verbs.
Sometimes other pronouns are omitted. Examples:

Doan dhink much oa dhay, nun oa um.	I don't think much of any of them.
Baint much good, not wair hee iz.	He isn't much good, where he is

In the third person singular the slurred forms, **un**, **en**, **in** or **'n** for **him**, **ur** for **hur**, and **em** or **um** for **dhem** are very common.

Ei aess un hiz naaeem.	I asked him his name.
Ei zin in yesterday.	I saw him yesterday.
Ei het'n on dhe laig.	I hit him on the leg.
Get hoald on un.	Get hold of him.
Hee laivz dhum yeer.	He leaves them here.
Nun oa um (or on em).	None of them.
Wee em.	With them.

The neuter third personal pronound **it** is often slurred into **'t** before a vowel or **w**. Examples:

'Tiz—'twoz—'tiddin.	It is—it was—it isn't.
Ei dhaut 'twoz.	I thought it was.
'Tiddin fair.	It isn't fair.

It is much more common that in ordinary English to personify an inanimate object and, when speaking of such an object, to use the masculine or feminine personal pronoun instead of the neuter. I have noticed the masculine **hee**, **hiz**, **un** used of the sun, the moon, a tree, house, waggon, spade, knife, cigar, book, and poem; and the feminine **shee**, **hur**, **ur** of a ship, train, motor-car, bicycle, kite, and ditch. Examples:

Hee nivvur feilz.	He (the moon) never fails.
Haast zin un yet?	Have you seen him (the moon) yet.
Hee'll wair yoo out, spaid wull.	He'll wear you out, the spade will.

RELATIVE PRONOUN.

The relative pronoun, both singular and plural, masculine and feminine, is **wot**, which stands for *who*, *which* or *that*. Examples:

A man wot wuirks in vaarist.	A man who works in the forest.
Voag wot caamps in vaarist.	People who camp in the forest.
A buird wot bildz in dhe treez.	A bird that builds in the trees.
Dhe haas wot yoost too wuirk.	The horse that used to work.

OTHER FORMS.

Perhaps in the following sentences **ar** stands for **er a** and **nar** for **ner a**.

N.F.	E.
Haast got ar looud oa dung too sell mee?	Do you happen to have a load of dung to sell me?
Haas'n dhee got nar littul woald mair?	Haven't you got any little old mare?

NOTE. A double negative is common. Examples:

N.F.	E.
Ei nivvur aits noa braid.	I never eat bread.
Tidd'n herdly fair.	It's hardly fair.
Ei nivvur killd noa voxiz.	I never killed any foxes.

INTERJECTIONS

N.F.	E.	N.F.	E.
Oi, yaas, ees.	Yes	**Dus noa?**	Dost thou
Noo.	No (noa).	**'snoa?**	know?
Loo see.	Look ye.	**Beid still**	Stand still
Cum on yeer.	Come on here.		—be quiet.
Ei sez.	Said I.	**Haih?**	Eh?—what?
Mee deer.	My dear.	**Good eevnin.**	Good evening.
Waal.	Well.	**I 'low.**	I allow—I dare say.
Dee noa?	Do you know?	**Oa maaee!**	O my!
		Ei dunnoa.	I don't know.

West Saxon Speech ...

Continued from previous page

CONSONANTS

As compared with standard English, one of the most marked characteristics of the New Forest dialect is its tendency to substitute voiced consonants for voiceless ones, especially at the beginning of a word, as z for s, zh for sh, v for f, dh for th, b for p, g for k, d for t.

PRONUNCIATION

Examples—z for s:

English		New Forest	English		New Forest
Written	*Spoken*		*Written*	*Spoken*	
see	*see*	**zee**	sell	*sell*	**zell**
sun	*sun*	**zun**	same	*saim*	**zaaeem**
set	*set*	**zet**	scythe	*siith*	**zoiv**
sow, *n.*	*sow*	**zow**	seek	*seek*	**zaik**
seven	*sevn*	**zevn**	sold	*soald*	**zooud**
south	*south*	**zouth**	certain	*sertin*	**zertin**
said	*sed*	**zed**	saucer	*sauser*	**zaasur**
such	*such*	**zich**	cider	*siider*	**zoidur**

v for f:

	E.	N.F.		E.	N.F.
Written	*Spoken*		*Written*	*Spoken*	
fire	*fiir*	**veier**	fat	*fat*	**vat**
four	*foar*	**vouer**	fly	*flii*	**vloi**
furze	*furz*	**vuz**	fall	*faul*	**vaul**
fern	*fern*	**vuirn**	fell	*fell*	**vell**
field	*feeld*	**veeld**	find	*fiind*	**veind**
foal	*foal*	**voal**	frog	*frog*	**vrog**
feet	*feet*	**veet**	full	*fool*	**vool**
from	*from*	**vrom**	fox	*fox*	**vox**
first	*furst*	**vust**	fifty	*fifti*	**viftay**
fish	*fish*	**veesh**	faggot	*faggot*	**vaagit**

When followed by r, th becomes d:

	E.	N.F.		E.	N.F.
Written	*Spoken*		*Written*	*Spoken*	
three	*three*	**dree**	throw	*throa*	**droa**
throat	*throat*	**droat**	thresh	*thrash*	**draash**
through	*throo*	**droo**	thrush	*thrush*	**drush**

Other instances of a voiced consonant taking the place of a voiceless one. Examples:

	E.	N.F.	Change of Consonant
Written	*Spoken*		
kettle	*kettul*	**kiddil**	d for t
spider	*spiider*	**zbeidur**	b for p
buskin	*buskin*	**buzgin (gaiter)**	g for k
scythe	*siith*	**zoiv**	v for th
cuckoo	*cookoo*	**gookoo**	g for k

Examples of non-participles:

	E.		N.F.
Written		*Spoken*	
gelding		*gelding*	**geldin**
morning		*morning*	**maarnin**
starling		*staarling*	**staarlin**
pudding		*pooding*	**poodin**
nothing		*nuthing*	**nudhin**

Other changes of consonantal sounds:

	E.	N.F.	Change of Consonant
Written	*Spoken*		
chimney	*chimnay*	**chimlay**	l for n
		chimblay	l for n
tremendous	*tremendus*	**tremenjus**	j for d

DROPPING OF CONSONANTAL SOUNDS

The New Forest does not, like the Cockney dialect, put an h before a word which begins with a vowel-sound in English, and does not drop the h of English nearly so often as in the Cockney dialect, though there is some tendency in that direction.

	E.	N.F.		E.	N.F.
Written	*Spoken*		*Written*	*Spoken*	
home	*hoam*	**oam**	head	*hed*	**id**
half	*haaf*	**aaf**	horse	*hors*	**oss**
house	*hous*	**ous**	hardly	*haardli*	**aardlay**
hear	*heer*	**eer**	hound	*hound*	**oun**
holly	*holli*	**ollay**	perhaps	*perhaps*	**praps**

T.

There is a tendency to drop t where it comes after another consonant at the end of a word. Examples:

	E.	N.F.
Written	*Spoken*	
kept	*kept*	**kep**
must	*must*	**muss**
art (thou)	*aart*	**s (for ist)**
insect	*insekt*	**insek**

and all auxiliary verbs in the second person singular followed by *not*:

	E.	N.F.
Written	*Spoken*	
wast not	wost not	**woz'n**
canst not	canst not	**cass'n**
wouldst not	woodst not	**woos'n**
couldst not	coodst not	**coos'n**
art not	aart not	**bis'n (for bist not)**
shalt not	shaalt not	**shaa'n**

R.

r is often dropped, especially before s or z. Examples:

	E.	N.F.		E.	N.F.
Written	*Spoken*		*Written*	*Spoken*	
burst	*burst*	**bust**	worth	*wurth*	**wuth**
first	*furst*	**vust**	girl	*girl*	**gel**
purse	*purs*	**puss**	February	*Febroouri*	**Feboouray**
worse	*wurs*	**wuss**			
horse	*hors*	**haas**			

TRANSPOSITION OF CONSONANTS.

In a few words the consonants are transposed. Examples:

	E.		N.F.
Written		*Spoken*	
great		*grait*	**girt**
wasp		*wosp*	**wops**
children		*children*	**childern**
			chillern
hundred		*hundred*	**hunderd**

A Gunpowder Factory in the New Forest

At the turn of the century the New Forest boasted "the premier Nitro-Compound Gunpowder Factory in the World." This claim was made by the directors of the Schultze Gunpowder Company in a booklet issued on 1 March 1895 for the general public; the factory so described was located at Eyeworth near Fritham.

Schultze started slowly with "crude and imperfect" samples being offered to the shooting public in 1865. By 1868 a small company was formed, and thereafter the Schultze reputation among the hunting fraternity grew rapidly—as did also the firm's factory at Eyeworth. In 1878, at international field trials, Schultze gunpowder outperformed its rivals and thereafter the company went on to achieve honour after honour. At the London International Exhibition of 1885, Schultze won the highest award for smokeless powder. This was followed by similar honours at the Chicago International Exhibition of 1893, the California International Exhibition of 1894, the Antwerp International Exhibition of 1894 and the Milan International Exhibition of 1894. Concurrently the world's best shooters used, and praised the Schultze product.

The key person behind the Eyeworth factory was young R.W.S. Griffith, company chemist, who lived in Eyeworth Lodge. Rebuilt and enlarged by the company, it was originally a royal hunting lodge.

At the height of its prosperity, the Schultze company employed over 100 people in 70 buildings. It had its own electricity generation plant and a large pond (known as Eyeworth Pond today and maintained by the Forestry Commission) for water supply. Despite occasional explosions and casualties, morale was good and the firm's marching band proudly performed at many public functions in the area.

In the account below, F.E. Stevens, in his *The New Forest Beautiful*, describes the operations of the Schultze company.

that the raw material of the trade was available in abundance, may have been the determining consideration in establishing the factory at Eyeworth, as was done in the late sixties of the last century.

Ideal Location

At that time black powder was the basis of nearly all propellent explosives; and charcoal was the leading constituent of black gunpowder. But the remoteness of the whole district of which Eyeworth Lodge is the centre made it an ideal place for the carrying on of a dangerous trade. As smokeless powder came into more general use so the demand for the black variety declined, and it was with this change that the factory at Eyeworth began to assume significance.

It started in a very small way. In the early weeks the total output did not exceed ten pounds in weight, and the transport problem, when the manufacture of the weekly batch was complete, was a simple matter of a man and a wheelbarrow. Then the whole process of manufacture was carried on in three wooden huts.

Big Business

But it was a business which eventually became a very big thing, employing a large number of men at Eyeworth and Redbridge,

One of the biggest industries of the Forest area in modern times was that of powder manufacture, which was carried on at Eyeworth on the northern plain. Charcoal-burning was at one time the basis of the processes which went to the manufacture of gunpowder, and the fact that this was still being carried on within the Forest and

---

West Saxon Speech...

SOME IDIOMS

N.F.	E.
A neis girt maaeed.	A fine big girl.
Eer'z taakin.	Here's talking.
Ei'v aird taak.	I've heard say.
Dhay'd keep sukkin doun.	They'd go on being sucked down.
Oi, Ei gottun wun, 'z wantin?	Yes, I've got one, art wanting it?
In dhe vurdher paart oa Burlay	At the other side of Burley.
Dhe weif.	My wife.
Dhis twintay yeer.	These twenty years.
Ei doan noa dhat ivvur Ei heerd on un.	I don't know that I ever heard of him.
Bist gwein on too baid?	Are you going to bed?

CALLS TO ANIMALS

Pigs are summoned by the call, **choog, choog**; cows, **woaee, woaee**; ponies by **kip, kip**.

Commands to a horse:

Cry.	Meaning.
Kum idhur.	Go to the left.
Woag, woag ee, woag aaf.	Go to the right.
Steddee now.	Steady.
Git baak sti.	Go back.
Jee, jee-up.	Go faster.
Way, way dher.	Stop.

CHILDREN'S RHYME

Henray oaray itturay aan,
Stoar dhe vinegar in dhe paan;
Oarum stoarum poapshee loarum,
O-u-t spellz 'out'.

Gunpowder Factory...

Continued from previous page
which is on the Forest-Southampton main road. The three wooden huts became seventy on the Eyeworth site alone; the man and the wheelbarrow was displaced first by a horse transport system which employed forty animals, and then a fleet of cars. The ten pounds per week became fifteen thousand pounds per week.

Charcoal did not go to the making of smokeless powder; the basis of it was wood pulp, and for this purpose alder was chiefly used, and this was imported in prepared sheets from overseas. The pulp was first dried, and then treated with acids which changed the pulp into an explosive nitro-compound. The surplus acid was removed by washing, and the material was afterwards dried again and ground, the drying being carried out by hot air. By this time the compound was an explosive, and needed careful treatment in danger houses, with the most carefully devised safeguards, and it was there that the sifting, grading and packing took place.

Nobel Took over
The Company which carried out the process was the Schultze Gunpowder Company, the active head of which, during the whole of his working life, as a highly skilful chemist, was Mr. R.W.S. Griffith, who was appointed to the managership in 1874 at the age of 22.

During the war explosive material for time fuses and the like was manufactured at Eyeworth, but since then the Schultze undertaking has become a part of the Nobel Combine and its operations have been transferred to Scotland, and the buildings at Eyeworth have been demolished.

EYEWORTH POND
The Eyeworth Pond car park is adjacent to the well known chalybeate (iron) well, source of water for the pond.

EXTERIOR VIEW OF GUNPOWDER WORKS

THE RESEARCH LABORATORY WHERE THE CHIEF CHEMIST WORKED

R.W.S. Griffiths, a brilliant man, became manager of the Schultze factory in 1874 at the age of 22. He was deeply interested in the welfare of small-holders and was a driving force behind the Commoner's League.

IN THE HARDENING HOUSE OF THE FACTORY

A QUIZ ABOUT THE NEW FOREST

(In 1979 the Division of the Hampshire County Library serving the New Forest prepared a quiz for young people to test their knowledge of the Forest. Questions from this quiz, and the answers, are given below.)

1. What was Brusher Mills' profession?
   (a) cricketer, (b) snake catcher, (c) road sweeper, (d) woodman.
2. In which graveyard is Brusher's grave?
   (a) Lymington, (b) Minstead, (c) Brockenhurst, (d) Sway
3. Who is believed to have shot the arrow that killed William Rufus?
   (a) Sir Francis Cooke, (b) Earl Godwin, (c) Sir Walter Tyrrell, (d) Captain Burleigh
4. What is the maximum height of a New Forest pony?
   (a) 13.2 hands, (b) 14.0 hands, (c) 14.2 hands, (d) 15.0 hands.
5. From where did Henry Adams launch the Agamemnon in 1774?
   (a) Lymington, (b) Hythe, (c) Buckler's Hard, (d) Keyhaven.
6. A place on the open ground where cattle gather to escape flies is called:
   (a) a shoot, (b) a slade, (c) a shade, (d) a purlieu.
7. About which real person was the book, *Alice in Wonderland*, written?
   (a) Alice Lisle, (b) Alice Liddell, (c) Anne Neville, (d) Caroline Bowles.
8. Which Order of Monks occupied Beaulieu Abbey?
   (a) Cistercians, (b) Benedictines, (c) Dominicans, (d) Franciscans.
9. Who wrote the New Forest classic, *Remarks on Forest Scenery*?
   (a) Gilbert White, (b) William Cobbett, (c) William Gilpin, (d) W. H. Hudson.
10. Where was King Charles I imprisoned in 1642?
    (a) King's House, (b) Calshot Castle, (c) Hurst Castle, (d) Rhinefield House.
11. Which Beaulieu Abbey farm owes its name to the cattle kept there?
    (a) Gins, (b) Beaufre, (c) Bergerie, (d) Swinesley.
12. Which "Common Right" deals with fuel wood?
    (a) Mast, (b) Marl, (c) Estovers, (d) Wicinage.
13. Where did the Bisterne Dragon have its lair?
    (a) Castle Malwood, (b) Woodfidley Knoll, (c) Buckland Rings, (d) Burley Beacon.
14. "Sowley Hammer" was used in which industry?
    (a) a shipyard, (b) a sawmill, (c) a gravel pit, (d) an iron works.
15. Which species of Forest deer has palmate antlers?
    (a) red, (b) roe, (c) sika, (d) fallow.
16. Who stood on Vereley Hill wearing a scarlet cloak to warn smugglers of the excise men?
    (a) Mary Dore, (b) Alice Lisle, (c) Lovey Warne, (d) Lavinia Cooper.
17. Who collects marking fees?
    (a) Agister, (b) Verderer, (c) Forest Keeper, (d) Regarder.
18. How often does the Court of Verderers meet?
    (a) monthly, (b) six times a year, (c) twice a year, (d) annually.
19. On whom did King Charles II bestow King's Coppice at Fawley and Irons Hill Coppice at Brockenhurst in 1664?
    (a) Frances Wells, (b) Winifred Wells, (c) Alice Hargreaves, (d) Bessie Catchpole.

ANSWERS TO THE QUESTIONS ABOVE:

1 (b); 2 (c); 3 (c); 4 (c); 5 (c); 6 (c); 7 (b); 8 (a); 9 (c); 10 (c); 11 (b); 12 (c); 13 (d); 14 (d); 15 (d); 16 (c); 17 (a); 18 (b); 19 (b).

(The quiz has been reproduced with permission of Ronald Hansford of the Hythe Library, who prepared it, and the Lymington Divisional Headquarters of the Hampshire County Library.)

Boys' Games

(In his history of the village of Nomansland, H.M. Livens describes several of the games played by boys around the turn of the century. Poverty was no problem for these ingenious lads who made improvised sticks and used stones for balls.)

The games and sports of the boys of the Forest side eighty years ago are worthy of a note. First there was a kind of rough hockey, known as "*Bandish*," played with a crooked stick, and with a stone for a ball.

"*Christened Beast*" was a game played in parties from trees as bases; the players dividing into two parties and trying to run one another down, as in chevy. The name is a mystery. For this, as for most other games, the green was the natural playground.

In "*Dreaden Grammer's Needle*" (Threading Grandmother's Needle), a party of, it might be, twenty holding on to one another, would pass under a bridge of hands which would descend at intervals during the recitation of certain mystic sentences and cut off one or another of the players. In this we recognise "the Bells of St. Clement's."

Tip-cat was known as "*Juggle Cat*." It was played with a short stick and a wooden cat, the object being to knock the latter, with as few strokes as possible, into a hole about the size of a hat.

Forest Publications

The following booklets are available at a nominal price at the New Forest Museum in Lyndhurst, or by post from Mrs. D. Seaton, Springer's cottage, Brockenhurst, Hants or Mrs. L. Errington, Rockford End, Ringwood, Hants:

Snake Catchers of the New Forest, Agisters of the New Forest, Commoners of the New Forest, Woodmen of the New Forest, Verderers of the New Forest, New Forest Commoners (in the year) *AD 1792*, and *The New Forest Embroidery*.

16
The New Forest:
Are It's Days Numbered?

A Grandiose Plan for A Forest Model Town

At least twice in the last 300 years "planners" have come up with schemes to build a town—usually referred to as a "model city"—within the New Forest.

The first was Daniel Defoe (1661–1731). His plans were set forth at length in his work, *London to Land's End*. His aim was to re-people the Forest by offering 20 families £4,000 each and 200 acres. In the centre of this 4,000-acre settlement would be a town in which the farm families lived, together with 600 supporting tradesmen, craftsmen, and their families.

Defoe's dream was never seriously considered, but in 1849 another model city was proposed by James S. Buckingham. The frontispiece of his book (*National Evils and Practical Remedies*), reproduced below, shows the proposed town of Victoria, located on the River Exe (now called the Beaulieu River) with the Isle of Wight in the background.

Buckingham's town would have cost £3 million to build and would have had five churches, 2,000 houses, a university and a library. He estimated the population would reach 10,000. His plan was widely publicized and as late as 1908 it was brought up again in the *New Forest Chronicle*, a weekly newspaper read by many Forest inhabitants.

His scheme, like Defoe's came to nothing, but the New Forest has seen intense urban development southwest of Southampton, on the "Waterside", along the south coast, and east of the River Avon.

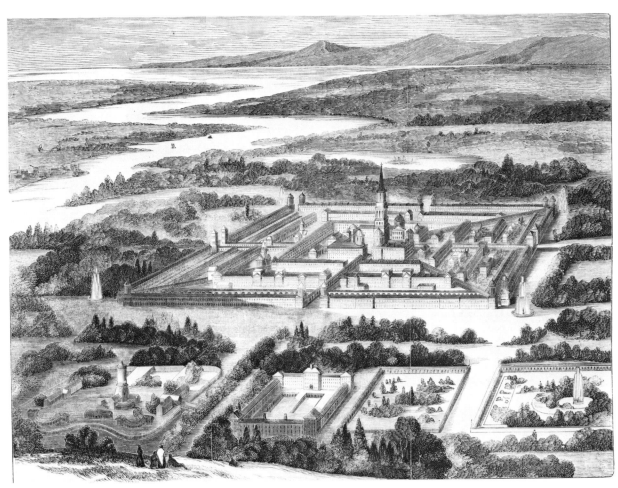

THE MODEL TOWN OF VICTORIA   *By permission of the British Library*

Auberon Herbert: Multi-Talented Eccentric

Although Auberon Herbert was not Forest-born, he spent the last two decades of his life in the area, and at his request, was buried near his home, "Old House," near Burley.

Born at Highclere near Newbury, Auberon Edward William Molyneux Herbert (1838–1906) was educated at Eton and St. John's Oxford. During his Oxford years he became fascinated with warfare and took time out to witness some of the battles in the Prussian-Danish War, the American Civil War and the Franco-German War. Perhaps because of these experiences, he was later to give up riding, the taking of life (hunting), and eating of meat.

In 1870 he was elected M.P. for Nottingham. Although he was to have a parliamentary career of only four years, there was hardly a cause that was debated that did not see him taking a vigorous, radical position. In 1872 he took a leading role in the passage of the Wildlife Protection Act.

On leaving Parliament he went first to Ashley Arnewood Farm (near Lymington), but after his wife's death in 1886 moved to "Old House" near Burley where he was to remain until his death. He frequently wintered abroad and in 1902–3 revisited the United States. He was a prolific writer; besides books on a variety of subjects and a book of verse, he enjoyed sending letters to the editor of *The Times* and other leading publications. His fondness for the New Forest was best expressed in an article, "The Last Bit of Natural Woodland," which appeared in *Nineteenth Century* in September, 1891.

Herbert's annual teas at "Old House" received national attention. They are described in a passage below from Felicite Hardcastle's *Records of Burley*. Also reproduced is a poem from Herbert's collection of verse. Entitled "A Forest Scene," it could represent a real or imaginary girl seen by Herbert near "Old House."

"A Forest Secret"

Oh! there is a nook, if ye
   will not tell—
Deep down in the Forest
   glade;
And nowhere in the
   land doth dwell,
A sunnier-hearted maid.

For, oh! She's blithe as a
   bird on the bush,
That carols all day long;
Mid-morning light till
   dewy night;
Her heart goes out in song.

Selected Passages from "The Last Bit of Natural Woodland"

(Auberon Herbert opposed the cutting down of the ancient woods of the New Forest, and attacked the Deputy Surveyor, Gerald Lascelles, for felling as many as 2,000 old trees in a single year. Herbert believed these old woods should be left alone and that only decayed trees should be removed. He made a number of suggestions for preserving these ancient and ornamental woods of which the first two are extracted here. Ironically, some of Herbert's concerns about the New Forest are as timely today as they were in 1891 when the article containing these excerpts was published.)

I ask the English people to try to understand what has taken place, and is now taking place. Towards the end of last century, and through all the earlier part of this century, the New Forest still remained the most beautiful and interesting spot in England. You might have passed through mile upon mile of natural woodland without drawing rein. It was a bit of country that had escaped modern changes. It was a bit of the older England—the England of the outlaw, of the singer of ballads, of the lover of the greenwood life—which, belonging to the past, had by some fortunate accident survived into the present.

To a country, like ours—crowded with this modern busy life —such a fragment should have been priceless. But to a public department, as to a French sapper, there is nothing sacred, whether in the earth below or in the heavens above. Bit by bit the old woods were destroyed, and the new plantations were put in their place. Hundreds and hundreds of acres of woodland, rich in beauty and historic interest, were sacrificed—and for what? The authorities knew—or might have known—that what they were doing could not pay. They knew that their expensive processes would eat up all profit, that salaries were piled upon salaries, and that the poor blindfolded nation could not watch over its concerns. Why, then, did they pursue this destructive course?

I think the answer must be, first, that they did not in the least understand or care about the thing with which they were dealing; and, secondly, that they were possessed with a feverish wish to appear to be doing something, and to have something to show— whether the something was good or bad in itself, whether it would yield less or more than the expense incurred upon it—in return for the official salaries. And to-day there is the same feverishness, and therefore just the same danger. Rather than do nothing, rather than discharge carefully and conscientiously the ordinary useful duties of their office, our officials

The Renowned Teas at Old House

The "Old House Teas" to which (Herbert) invited all "while the Tea Pot lasts" made him known, literally to thousands. His guests found a most unconventional host, clad in baggy, homespun trousers, loose woollen shirt, and shapeless coat, who preferred to sleep in an eyrie on the roof of his house, and shunned rooms where a fire burned, or the window was not wide open.

Auberon Herbert...

Continued from previous page long to distinguish themselves by doing something big—to cut, to enclose, to plant, quite careless of what is destroyed in the process, quite careless whether they will be able hereafter to justify their last work any better than, if called upon, they could justify the earlier work of their predecessors.

The object is not to grow as much timber as can be grown per acre, but to continue the natural woodland, which has come down to us from the past, with its many varying and beautiful incidents. From dense woods of beeches, so dense that nothing grows under their shade, you pass to groups of trees growing in their own fashion, from them to single trees, to open spaces of heath and fern, to glades of closs-cropped lawn, to tangles of holly and thorn—each succeeding the other in charming variety—until you reach the boundary of the wood, where the eternal war of trees and plain goes on, each striving to encroach on the territory of the other.

Nothing is more interesting than this warfare. The wood, constantly throwing out fresh out-

posts, wherever circumstances in the least favour an advance, gains in several directions, whilst it is apt to lose in the one special direction from which the strong south-west gales make their attack. Amongst the results of this warfare is that broken line of boundary which is so pleasant to the eye.

Now it has to be remembered that really natural woodland exists hardly anywhere in England. Plantations, mixed timber and coppice, parks, arboretums, pleasure grounds, you have in any quantity scattered over the country; but natural woodland —in the sense of forest, that through a long course of time has grown up untended, where art and artifice have had no part, where the cattle have roamed at will, where there is no need to cut the finest trees for purposes of market, where the young growth has to avail itself of those wiles and defences against its enemies, which those, who know how to look, find in all parts of nature— is so rare as to be hardly seen anywhere in England away from the New Forest.

Granted that the object is not to

grow timber but to preserve a bit of nature, no man is fit to meddle with these old woods and to improve their wild and varying beauty. There are, of course, plenty of persons who think themselves specially designed by their artistic perceptions to go into these old woods, cut here, clear there, and plant somewhere else.

There are two great dangers that always threaten a beautiful bit of nature—meddlesomeness and conceit. There are, unfortunately, very few men who care much about what is beautiful in itself; but there are plenty of men who care about their own little ideas, and delight in peddling and pottering over fancy creations of their own.

I plead for the old woods, being left entirely alone, not only for the sake of the artist, but of the forester as well. I claim it in the first instance for the artist and the lover of nature. I ask the artist if it would not be a priceless boon for him that somewhere in England there should be a sanctuary of nature, where ash and beech, holly and thorn, fern and gorse, all struggled for possession of the soil, where trees were left to ripen and slowly decay to their fall, where the cattle wandered at will, forcing their own path through the undergrowth, where the 'self-comers' struggled up, eluding danger by nestling in the tangle, and bit by bit replacing the older wood, as the storms opened up for them spaces of light and air, where the hand of man played no interfering part, but from generation to generation the struggle of nature went on, and the battle of the trees was lost here to-day and won there to-morrow.

But I appeal also to the forester. I have no opposition of any kind to offer to a school of forestry, except to a Government school—on the grounds that it is much best for Government, with its cumbrous machinery and third-rate motives, not to play with any kind of science, not to undertake researches which those principally interested should be undertaking for themselves, not to dabble in providing posts for those who learn to serve

The Unspoiled Forest of the Edwardian Era

Within the space of only two generations the threat to the future of the New Forest has accelerated to such an extent that no one can say with assurance that the next generation will know the Forest as it exists today.

The article below, preserved in the archives of the Hampshire Library Service, is taken from an unidentified national periodical in the decade immediately preceding the first world war. It is a fitting "landmark" for this chapter, as it depicts the New Forest before large-scale development of tourism and emasculation of its ancient wooded areas.

Brusher Mills was by now dead, but far from forgotten. There were then four railway stops within the Forest. There was no danger from motor traffic, although cars were by then common sights. Many of the area's hostelries received high marks for their care of visitors.

King Alfonso XIII of Spain, then in his twenties, much enjoyed his motoring trip through the Forest. Yet the writer of the article felt comparatively few people appreciated the charm of the New Forest—in reality "a holiday paradise."

The writer pointedly remarks that the 1877 act of parliament required balance between the "ornamental as well as the profitable use of ground," and added: "All the famous beech and oak are watched by the keepers."

> *"The greatest charm of the Forest is preserved in the magnificent masses of beech wood"*

Nothing is more surprising in these days, says a writer in the "Tribune" when everyone seeks a holiday at least once a year, that such a comparatively small number of people seem to be familiar with the peculiar charms of the New Forest. And yet here, within two hours' railway journey from the Metropolis, is to be found as fine a combination of beautiful landscape as exists in any area of like proportions. It is true that the varied amusements afforded at seaside resorts are not provided; but for a complete contrast to the form of recreation with which so many persons are familiar, nothing could be more enjoyable than a few days spent amid the countless attractions which Nature offers in the New Forest, with its broad lawns, its wide ranges of moorland, the sylvan splendour of its woods and vales, the magnificent views its heights unfold over land and water, and the simple life led in all its centres of population.

A Holiday Paradise

The greatest charm of the Forest is preserved in magnificent masses of beechwood, whose long branches are now seen covering the roads like massive Gothic arches. In spite of the great clearances effected in earlier days, in order to meet the requirements of the British Navy, many exceptionally fine oaks are still standing, and in two woods known to ramblers as the North and South Bentleys there remains a lot of fine timber which was originally intended for shipbuilding. When one becomes acquainted with the infinite variety of the scenery, it is difficult to understand why so few artists are led to penetrate the bewitching nooks of the Forest. Exceptional

Auberon Herbert...

Continued from previous page them in some fashion or another, not always the worthiest fashion, nor to take money compulsorily from those who don't wish to apply it to such purposes.

The science of forestry is like every other science in the world; it is rich in its own interests, rich in its own rewards, and worthy of hearty encouragement at our hands. All that I specially claim in this matter is that the 4,600 acres of old wood should not be used for *experimental* forestry. Preserved by some blessed chance in their wild condition, they are too sacred to be allowed to undergo experiments from the hands of any of us, simple or learned.

These special old woods, whose like we shall never see again, should be only for the forestry of observation. In them let us be content to watch natural experiments without lifting a finger of our own.

I will conclude by stating what I practically advise. So long as the nation owns the New Forest—an owning which I do not justify, or attempt to justify—so long it should carefully guard these old woods.

1. It should stop in the most summary way the cuttings which are now carried on against the intention of Parliament. Except to remove a fallen tree—that has fallen, ripe with old age, or overpowered by the storm—the ring of axe should never be heard in the old woods.

2. The expenses of the Forest should be mercilessly cut down. It is monstrous that in order to pay officials who are not required, trees should be cut and sold from the old woods. ...

> *"Nothing could be more enjoyable than a few days spent amid the countless attractions which Nature offers in the New Forest"*

The Unspoiled Forest...

Continued from previous page
interest, therefore, always attaches to the exhibition at Lyndhurst of Mr F Golden Short's pictures of scenery of the Forest.

In the early spring the golden bog myrtle is seen amid the sedges and the mosses, which together form a remarkable mass of colour. The blackthorn and the crabtree blossom immediately follow, and there is, indeed a constant succession of bloom right through spring. Then, as soon as May has passed, the dog-roses come out, the foxglove rears itself on a tall stem, and the moorlands give delightful shade and aroma from vast banks of purple heather. Next appears the bracken, which, as it turns from green to gold, supplies a picture of exquisite loveliness in many parts of the Forest. The closing scene is presented in the first week of November, when the rare visitor beholds the last tints of

autumn. Then the woods are almost bare, the foliage has died away, and the first cold snap is experienced. Throughout this long period the Forest is veritably a holiday paradise.

Preservation of the Forest

In the summer months, especially on hot and oppressive days, these leafy shades are truly delightful to the motorist, the cyclist, and the pedestrian, for each of whom abundant opportunities of recreation are provided. Nearly the whole of the enormous areas under the jurisdiction of the Court of Verderers is thrown open to the

public, and the rambler penetrates the enclosures at will. Danger from any kind of wheeled traffic is thus escaped, and the molestation of ladies or children in the woods, is happily, unknown. The Crown lands at the present day cover nearly 65,000 acres, but the dis-

> *"... the bracken ... as it turns from green to gold, supplies a picture of exquisite loveliness in many parts of the Forest"*

trict afforested by William the Conqueror between 1079 and 1085 included the entire south-western corner of Hampshire, extending from the Avon to Southampton water.

Much good has obviously been done by the Act passed in 1877, under which Commissioners were empowered to keep the woods, "having regard to the ornamental

A LYNDHURST SCENE CONTEMPORARY WITH THE ABOVE ACCOUNT
Sketched by Alexander Ansted and entitled "Cottage at Lyndhurst," this view appeared in C.J. Cornish's *The New Forest and the Isle of Wight*, published in the same decade as the accompanying description of the Forest.

> *"Much good has obviously been done by the Act passed in 1877 (requiring) 'that the ancient ornamental trees shall be carefully preserved and the character of the scenery shall be maintained'."*

The Unspoiled Forest...

Continued from previous page

as well as the profitable use of the ground," and even strangers are able to realise the benefits which have followed from the further requirement of the statue, "that the ancient ornamental trees shall be carefully preserved and the character of the scenery shall be maintained." Ruthless decimation by villagers and nomads has come to an end, and the national property is now jealously guarded alike against absorption and damage. It is true that trees are still cut, but these are the short firs, sold for use in the colliery districts as pit-props. All the famous beech and oak are watched by the keepers, and, as a rule, visitors refrain from acts of vandalism, which, if detected, are followed by severe punishment.

A Grand "Hunting Ground"

Rich almost beyond comparison, in many species of wild flowers, the New Forest has, unfortunately, been robbed of specimens of fern that once grew in abundance, but the Osmunda Regalis, the Sweet-scented Mountain Fern, the Lady Fern, the Hart's Tongue, the Common Polypody, and other good varieties may still be seen in different places, especially near Lyndhurst and Brockenhurst. Butterflies, moths, and insects are equally numerous, and the Forest is, therefore, a grand hunting-ground for the entomologist, who comes from Southampton, Bournemouth, London, and places much farther afield. The presence of a "snake charmer" in the quaint personality of the late "Brusher Mills" has before now created an erroneous impression concerning the denizens of the New Forest. For many years Mr Mills found a profitable occupation in catching the small and perfectly harmless grass snakes, which he forwarded once a week to the authorities of the Zoological Gardens as food for the reptiles: but since that gentleman's death this industry has, up to the present, at least, become a "lost art". Foxes, otters, rabbits and squirrels abound; badgers are occasionally detected in unfrequented corners, and hares are killed only by gentlemen who hold shooting and fishing licenses, which cost £20 a year.

Accommodation for Visitors

There are four stations in the Forest belonging to the London and South-Western Railway, and eight more on the borders. To any of these points passengers may travel direct from Waterloo by a service of fast trains. Lyndhurst Road is the first station reached, and the bracing drive from the railway line to Lyndhurst, the capital, prepares the visitor for the unalloyed pleasure that he may confidently anticipate during his sojourn. At the Crown Hotel he will find excellent accommodation, and the Lyndhurst golf links, close at hand, occupy one of the finest natural sites in the Forest. There is always a breeze on the open moorland, with its short turf and its patches of heather, and, with far-reaching views on every side, it would be difficult to discover a finer inland course.

The best class of visitors are attracted to the little town, of which the late Lord Leighton was so fond, and in the church opposite they may at any time inspect the grand fresco that the artist painted and presented to the parish in token of his love. Strangers are always impressed with the peculiarly peaceful character of Lyndhurst and its associations. At this season of the year the hotel garden is a veritable home of roses. Flowers are, indeed, seen growing in profusion in the grounds of the smallest cottage, and the peculiarly health-giving characteristics of the spot has in recent years induced many well-known physicians to strongly recommend it to those who require pleasant rest from brain fag.

Sports of the Forest

In the course of the year the New Forest attracts many distinguished and prominent persons. Princess Henry of Battenberg drives through occasionally, and the Duchess of Argyll sometimes stays there with friends. Motorists appear in considerable numbers, the drive from London through Kingston, Esher, Ripley, Guildford, over the Hog's Back to Farnham, and thence to Winchester, Southampton, and Lyndhurst, being a favourite run. The King of Spain motored in the Forest on the occasion of his recent visit to England, and was particularly struck by its grand appearance. But the majority of people prefer less expeditious means of travel amid such surroundings, and consequently carriages are as much in use as ever.

Otterhounds hunt the Forest streams, and deer hunting begins in August. Fox hunting follows, and until the end of April next

> *"(The New Forest is) rich almost beyond comparison in many species of wild flowers"*

The New Forest Association

(The New Forest Association is the primary organization concerned with the welfare of the Forest. Founded in 1867, its aims have been broadened over the years as threats to the Forest have increased. Reproduced below from the leaflet, "How the New Forest Association Works," are its aims. Further information can be obtained from the Association Secretary, Mrs. L.K. Errington, Rockford End, Ringwood, Hants BH24 3NB.)

The elected council of the New Forest Association draws its members from virtually all the specialist fields with interests in and influence on the Forest. The Association's sources of information, experience, and specialised knowledge are thus exceptional. Additionally, this widely representative council provides a forum for establishing a common viewpoint, and occasionally for bringing out into the open a conflict of interest, influencing directly the parties concerned, and ensuring a knowledgeable and comprehensive debate.

Unspoiled Forest...

Continued from previous page

good sport will be provided. Capital mounts can be obtained from Mr Bradford, at Brockenhurst, and sportsmen are now able to secure accommodation in or near that village, at the Rose and Crown Hotel, one of the oldest hostelries in the Forest; at the Balmer Lawn Hotel, which has a golf course and a polo field at its own doors, and at the Forest Park Hotel, looking out upon the "Queen's Bower". It is at Brockenhurst that the day tours arranged by Messrs Thomas Cook and Son begin, and a drive through some of the prettiest parts of the Forest invariably induces those who take advantage of these excursions to resolve upon a longer stay in its midst at the earliest opportunity.

The Association was founded in 1867, when the Government was grimly determined to enclose and plant more and more of the Forest for timber production. Working with the Commoners, the Association triumphed over Whitehall, and the all-important Act of Parliament of 1877 was the result.

Today the Association's rules define its objectives and powers as follows:

1. (a) To promote the preservation for the benefit of the Commoners and the public generally of the New Forest including the areas added by the New Forest Act 1964 and generally to protect and preserve the areas of scientific and ecological importance and the flora and fauna therein.

   (b) To do all such lawful acts or things as are incidental to the attainment of the primary objects of the Association and so far as may be necessary or desirable to do such acts or things in collaboration with any

person body institution authority or otherwise.

2. For the purpose of carrying out the foregoing objects but not otherwise the association shall have the following powers:

   (a) Power to raise money from the public generally.

   (b) Power to attend and be represented at Planning Enquiries Public Meetings and Planning Appeals.

   (c) Power to promote or oppose or assist in the promotion of or opposition to legislation affecting the New Forest.

   (d) Power to provide funds to the Court of Verderers for the furtherance of the objects of the Association.

   (e) Power to organise concerted action and promote co-operation between Local Authorities, Local Societies and other persons.

   (f) Power to arouse, form and educate public opinion in order to ensure the promotion of the aforesaid objects.

THE NEW FOREST UNDER WATER
Conservation of the Forest embraces not only the woods and heathlands, but the Pylewell foreshore on the West Solent which is also within the perambulation.

Engraver Crusades to Save the New Forest

(In the long history of the New Forest many residents have fought for its preservation when threats arose. Since the second world war, Jean Cobb has been in the forefront of efforts to keep the Forest safe from self-destruction and outside incursions.

Born in Scotland of a naval family she worked for the Admiralty during the war. Her duties were top secret; among them were charting the movements of Allied ships for the Normandy landings. When the war was over, she met her husband-to-be, David, who had served six years in the Navy—some of this time on MTBs (Motor Torpedo Boats). They merged their naval interests by living the first seven years of their married life on "White Heather," a small boat.

After their daughter was born and the need arose for a land base, they chose the New Forest. Here they would also be near Lymington harbour and its sailing opportunities. Having decided on the Setley area, south of Brockenhurst, they erected—with the help of a friend—the A-frame house that still serves as their combined residence and studio-a-deux.

Glass Engraver

Both Jean and David are artists. Jean, using her maiden name of Main, is an Associate Fellow of the Guild of Glass Engravers, and her work is to be found in various buildings—commercial, public and ecclesiastic—as well as in many private collections. Her artistic talent is by no means confined to glass engraving; she also has done portraiture, stone carving, book illustrations and cartography. David is a marine artist of international renown. He has documented the Falklands conflict in paintings and during 1978–1983 served as president of the Royal Society of Marine Artists.

Jean has taken a deep interest in the conservation of the New Forest since the day she and her husband settled near Brockenhurst. She is not content merely to join New Forest and other conservation societies, but can always be counted on to cut through bureaucracy and obstructionism when threats to the Forest surface. At hearings and enquiries her presentations are concise, logical and to the point. "Her technique can sometimes be spectacular," a fond admirer admits, "but she gets results, and that's what counts."

Hardwoods Felled

When the Forestry Commission cut down hundreds of acres of hardwood trees in the late 1960s, Jean spearheaded a protest that led to the banning of such felling by the then Minister of Agriculture, James Prior. The eyes of the nation were focussed on the New Forest during that critical period and when the strong words were over and the felling had ceased, *The Spectator* carried an article by Jean in its 16 October, 1971 issue entitled "How We Saved the New Forest." Although Jean did not give the article this title, no other could have better told the dramatic fight she led to save what was left of the Forest's magnificent hardwoods. The account follows.)

There is only one New Forest in the world. Over the last few years it very nearly ceased to exist as we know it, because of the combined pressure of bureaucratic logic and commercial demand. This article is the story of how the New Forest was threatened, and how it was saved. At least for the moment. And the events which I describe call into question the whole process by which we act to preserve our national environmental heritage: by these acts shall the professions of governments, politicians, planners and civil servants be judged. And by them we will see how much say we, the people, have in the preservation of our surroundings.

The process of destruction, which for long went unnoticed, is simply described. The traditional New Forest consists of both Forestry Commission 'Inclosures' and the 'Open Forest' of heath, bog, lawn, and the natural woodlands of gnarled oak and beech, interspersed with younger trees, chestnut, silver beech, holly and scrub. The latter are called, in the act of 1877, 'Ancient and Ornamental Woodlands,' and Section 8 of that Act decreed that they 'shall be preserved'. That trust, since 1824, has been shared between the Forestry Commission and the Court of Verderers of the Forest, on which sit a nominee of the Queen, nominees of the Ministry of Agriculture, the Forestry Commission, the Planning Authority and the Countryside Commission, as well as five Verderers elected by Commoners.

In 1964 the New Forest Act allowed the Forestry Commission "after consultation with the Verderers" to carry out "all such silvicultural maintenance work as may from time to time be necessary." In 1969 the then New Forest management stretched this provision to allow the felling of over 1,400 mature oak and beech trees from the Ancient and Ornamental Rushpole Wood, a process which also destroyed, by mechanical timber extraction, many of the random grassy rides and paths. Though the Verderers' approval is by statute required for all works of silvicultural maintenance, this scheme was never submitted to nor approved by them. It subsequently emerged that the Verderers had agreed to dispense with consultation during the administration of the Forest by Mr. W.A. Cadman, a keen naturalist, who enjoyed the confidence of all concerned with the preservation of the Forest. But in 1968 (three years before retirement) Mr.

Engraver Crusades to Save the New Forest...

Continued from previous page

Cadman resigned his post following the joining of the New Forest to the Forestry Commission's South East Conservancy Area—including the rest of Hampshire, and all Surrey, Sussex, Kent and Berkshire. Bound by the Official Secrets Act, Mr. Cadman said only that he had "lost the confidence of his superiors." The 'Working Plan for the New Forest' and the 'Rushpole Scheme' were the creations of his successor, Mr Dallas Mithen. The occasion of Mr Cadman's resignation was also the occasion of a protest, bearing more than 7,600 signatures, against the absorption of the New Forest in the South East Conservancy Area. It was contemporaneous with protests about changes in the 'Inclosures.' And the Rushpole Scheme led to further protest against what appeared to be, against the provisions of the 1877 Act and the instincts of most, the destruction of the Ancient and Ornamental Woods. It now appears that, since 1963, some 1,090 acres have been felled in the hardwood areas alone.

All earlier protests having failed, a public meeting was held on February 14, 1970, in Lyndhurst, 'capital' of the Forest and seat of the Verderers' Court. The object of the meeting was to protest, not only against the creeping illegal destruction of the Forest, but against the fact that this destruction was being carried out evidently for the purpose of commercial exploitation. Four people were chosen to publicize the Commission's policy. On March 5, 1970 they produced a brochure, 'Destruction of the Environment in the New Forest.' signed by naturalists, broadcasters, writers, scientists, artists, and officers of the Hampshire Field Club. This brochure was

> **"a brochure, 'Destruction of the Environment in the New Forest,' (was) signed by naturalists, broadcasters, writers, scientists, artists and officers of the Hampshire Field Club. ... The reaction of the scientific world was immediate"**

widely distributed and accompanied by separate reports on the 'Ancient and Ornamental' Woods by Dr Francis Rose of London University and Mr Fred W. Haynes, Senior Lecturer in Botany at Portsmouth Polytechnic. The reaction of the scientific world was immediate. Professor

THE "RUSHPOLE GOBLET" Jean Cobb's goblet commemorating the "Rushpole Incident" when twelve people prevented the wholesale felling of hardwoods throughout the New Forest and their replanting with conifers.

G.W. Dimbelby wrote to the Minister of Agriculture, to whom the Forestry Commission are responsible, and visited the Forest to make his own report; Dr Bruce Cambell telephoned from Oxford and contributed articles in the national press; and Dr Frank Fraser-Darling spoke of the Forest in his Reith Lectures, and offered his assistance.

The official reaction was not so forthcoming. On March 13 the Secretary to the Ministry of Agriculture merely acknowledged receipt of the brochure, and said it had been forwarded to the Commission. The Duke of Edinburgh, likewise re-routed his copy to the Commission. The Nature Conservancy, who have one representative in the New Forest, appeared unwilling to become involved; communication with their representative is, in any event, difficult, as, like every Forestry Commission worker, he is bound by the Official Secrets Act. The Commission's own reply to the brochure lacked nothing in sentiment on the issue: the Commission, its Secretary wrote, 'recognizes that the New Forest is a priceless heritage and that its conservation, not only for today, but for posterity, is of immense importance, and we are sorry that you do not accept our good intentions or that what we are doing will achieve the objectives we all share." The utter meaninglessness of these professions was shortly to be revealed.

To return again to the Commission's reaction to the brochure of March 5. In an effort to allay rising public indignation, the Commission on September 10, 1970, announced their intention of setting up a 'New Forest Consul-

> **"It now (1970) appears that, since 1963, some 1,090 acres have been felled in the hardwoods alone"**

Engraver Crusades...

Continued from previous page
tative Panel.' Leading conservationists immediately welcomed the decision, imagining that it implied the appointment of about fifteen experts to advise the Commission. When announced, however, the panel turned out to be "a sounding board for public opinion," with a membership of over sixty representatives from societies, invited by the Forestry Commission itself to take part. The matter was debated in the House of Lords on November 3, 1970. Lord Malmesbury, the Official Verderer, appointed by the Queen, expressed himself as "rather hurt because the Verderers had not been consulted"; and Lord Montague of Beaulieu said "it was widely felt that the panel had reached such a size as perhaps to render it completely ineffective."

Within days of the formation of the Panel the action group (as those who had met on February 14 had come to be called by the press)

> ### "The intention ... was extracting a commercial crop of 123,000 cubic feet of hardwoods annually from 350 acre blocks of the Ancient and Ornamental woods"

annually from 350 acre blocks of the Ancient and Ornamental woods, which had always been inviolate from commercial timber production. This programme was to be repeated on a twenty year rotation and "in addition, in these 350 acre blocks a thinning will take place."

In the Inclosures, legal, amenity and landscape requirements were dismissed as follows: "Section 6 of the 1877 Act states *inter alia* that the woods must be replenished having regard to the ornamental as well as the profitable use of the ground. This has at times been interpreted as a sword of Damocles hanging over forestry. It has not proved so in practice." Then there was the quite erroneous statement, "It is only in the

strips of hardwood around some of the conifer plantations, and along some of the roads. This would cause the greatest loss of traditional trees in the history of the New Forest, and change its character beyond recognition.

When they realized the full import of the Working Plan, the MP for the New Forest Mr Patrick McNair Wilson, and the acting Official Verderer, Sir Oliver Crosthwaite-Eyre, visited the new Minister of Agriculture, Mr James Prior, on September 22. Within forty-five minutes the Minister had slapped a total ban on all hardwood felling in the New Forest.

On November 23 Mr Prior visited the New Forest and confirmed his ban. He also stated that he would return in the Spring to discuss recommendations about a new role for the Commission in New Forest affairs. On April 1, 1971, Mr Dallas Mithen was appointed Conservator for West Scotland, and a Deputy Surveyor, Mr Donn Small, was again in sole charge of the Forest. The Minister returned and spelled out his charter for future management. He said it was his belief that, with the passage of time, the balance between commercial timber production and conservation and amenity would have to be considered afresh.

We could claim a victory for the action group who have saved the Forest from a rising tide of regimented conifers, but at the same time we acknowledge the difficul-

> ### "In the Inclosures the areas of oak, beech and other hardwoods were to be reduced to only four per cent ... . This would cause the greatest loss of traditional trees in the history of the New Forest and change its character beyond recognition."

obtained a copy of the parts of the New Forest Working Plan relevant to the timber cropping programme. The shattering exposure of true Forestry Commission policy which this paper revealed endorsed every fear of the destruction of the New Forest. In the Open Forest, from the 7,500 acres of the Ancient and Ornamental woods, where no timber crops may be taken, and where any felling had always been severely restricted, according to the document, "the selection type of felling had been fairly extensively done during the last ten years and this had been recorded as a thinning." The intention was stated of extracting a commercial crop of 123,000 cubic feet of hardwoods

broadleaved high forest (A and O woodlands) that amenity obligations apply." This Working Plan also assessed the expected yield from Scots Pine crops on the Open Forest—where the Commission has a statutory duty to keep the grazing free from encroaching conifers. In the Inclosures, the areas of oak, beech and other hardwoods were to be reduced to only 4 per cent, in the form of

> ### "We could claim a victory for the action group who have saved the Forest from a rising tide of regimented conifers, but at the same time we acknowledge the difficulties of the Forestry Commission"

> **"... we realize that the Forest is a living entity and acknowledge its changing role for the future. Our aim is to keep it alive. Pressures come from many sources besides commercial forestry"**

Engraver Crusades to Save Forest...

Continued from previous page

ties of the Forestry Commission, who strove to hold an untenable position where their statutory duties "of promoting the interests of forestry, the development of afforestation, the production and supply of timber, and the maintenance of reserves of growing trees in Great Britain, including the Crown Woods, transferred to it in 1924," and their "primary duty to the Commission" were in direct conflict with the conservation of the New Forest and the laws for its preservation. Could it be that because of these very duties the Forestry Commission are the wrong people to manage the Forest? Possibly the alternatives could be to relieve the Commission of their statutory duties of commercial timber production in the New Forest, or to hand over the management to some other government department on the same basis as management of the Royal Parks.

This is the third time since the Commission took over management of the New Forest that their commercial exploitation has had to be stopped by the public. Restitution has never been made for the depredations the Forest has suffered. This time, this small action group of twelve people, whose only official backing came from the Hampshire Field Club, have, with the invaluable support of leading scientists and conservationists, overcome the combined bureaucratic indifference and even publicly-expressed disbelief of the Ministry of Agriculture, the Forestry Commission, the Nature Conservancy, the Verderers, and the New Forest Association. Through their intervention, all hardwood felling was stopped in the New Forest between Novem-

ber 1970 and May 1971; and for 1971 has been reduced from the Commission's proposed felling rate of 120 acres per annum to 30 acres. They achieved this result by insisting on the truth and exposing all attempts to conceal it. They sacrificed their own interests to the future of the Forest, knew their subject, and judged the Commission not by its propaganda but by its actions.

For our part we realize that the Forest is a living entity and acknowledge its changing role for the future. Our aim is to keep it alive. Pressures come from many sources besides commercial forestry. We have co-operated with the county planning department and the Forestry Commission in their report 'Conservation of the New Forest,' which underlines our belief that the added pressure of commercial forestry is unnecessary in these overcrowded acres. This, moreover, is a pressure that has been created by the Forestry Commission itself and one which only they can remove. We look to the new management to work to this end. They have inherited a legacy of mistrust. We await their moves; and watch.

Mrs Jean Cobb was one of the original four action group members selected at the meeting of February 14, 1970, together with Eric Ashby, Anthony Pasmore and Desmond Polack. They were late joined by David Cobb, Richard Eurich, R.A., Raymond Galbraith, Fred Haynes, June Irwin, Ruth and John Lavender, Geoffrey Squires and David Stagg who was co-opted for the Hardwood Survey.

Postscript...

(The following passage by Mrs. Cobb up-dates the conservation position of the New Forest.)

Since the above article was written, great changes have taken place in the New Forest management. Under the Deputy-Surveyorships of Nicolas Banister and David Perry, management has become much more open.

Members of the New Forest Consultative Panel are invited to inspect the areas of proposed felling and silvicultural treatment, and to submit their comments to the Forestry Commission, while discussions (open to the public) on all matters affecting the Forest are held every two months. Members of the public may not speak but their comments and questions can be raised by their parish representative or other members of the Panel.

The New Forest Review Group, consisting of representatives of the Forestry Commission, Hampshire County Council, Countryside Commission, New Forest District Council, Verderers, and Nature Conservancy Council, keep an eye on all Forest matters and appoint working parties to consider the character and specific demands of the Forest.

Comments on its draft reports from interested individuals and societies are invited and considered before publication of the final report. (The latest draft report appeared in 1987; as an auxiliary to this document, Hampshire County Council has produced "Highway Strategy for the New Forest" which considers the problems of transport.)

The greatest problems these days for the New Forest arise not from the Forestry Commission, but from those pressures just beyond the perambulation verging on its borders; pipelines and oil-drilling in the south and east, and the building of Fawley-B power station. Most recently and possibly most destructive of all, is the Central Electricity Generation Board's proposal to establish a giant coal-importing terminal at Fawley to distribute coal to power stations throughout the southern half of the country. This is a proposal which must be fought to the death.

A Verderer's View of the Forest's Future

> Archibald ("Archie") Cleveland was born not half a mile from where he now resides at South Weirs near Brockenhurst. He has lived in the area all his life except for six years in the Navy during the Second World War.
>
> Apprenticed to a carpenter and joiner when he left school, he eventually started his own business—incorporating funeral directing in common with many other country builders. He has been retired for several years, but his interest in the New Forest has been lifelong. He has been an elected Verderer of the New Forest for over ten years and is passionately devoted to its preservation.
>
> In the interview below Archie tells of his concern for the Forest's future and what, in his view, should be done about it.

When I was a boy, working families in the New Forest, of which our family was one, always reckoned to be as near self-supporting as possible.

That meant keeping ponies for transport, pigs and poultry for food, a cow for milk and butter, and so on. My father also kept bees. I never liked bees—perhaps its more true to say that bees didn't like me. But I've always liked their honey.

I was in my mid-twenties when the Second World War ended. So many things had happened that it was as if my whole life had to be started over again. My father had died and my brother, too—he was out in the Middle East. I got married in 1945, and to start with we bought a cow and a goat. Did you know goat's milk is disease-free? There's no problem of tuberculosis with goats. We also bought pigs and poultry, so we were pretty well self-supporting when it came to food.

Freedom of the Forest

There's nothing about the Forest I don't like. I have loved it since I was a boy. I suppose the best thing is its freedom. There's nowhere in Europe where you have the same measure of freedom you get in the Forest.

I enjoy riding horses, colt hunting—rounding up the Forest ponies and cattle, and I enjoy collecting and cutting wood, which we use for our fuel.

I first became an elected Verderer of the New Forest in November, 1976. To be an elected Verderer you have to occupy at least one acre of land to which common rights are attached. You don't have to own the land, just occupy it. I'm lucky in that I do own my land. Verderers are elected every three years for six-year terms.

Conservationists

There are so many bodies—agencies and the like, in the Forest today, each with its own particular interest, that they can be a danger to the very survival they claim to support. They are very strong and have voices in high places; yet they are really destroying what they intend to preserve.

I'll give you an example. At Shappen Bottom there have always been passages across the bogs, just above the water level. The conservationists have now gone across the bog at Shappen and raised the passages by something like two to three feet. That is proof enough that the bogs are spreading and destroying grazing land for the animals. That's a classic example of why New Forest bogs are spreading—they have to, because the main streams that used to run through them are now silting up.

Coarse Herbage Problem

Another case, not far from here. The Forestry Commission, by agreement with the conservation lobby, cleared a river between North and South Weirs, cutting down all the coarse herbage either side of the stream. But the land, on both sides, where these lateral ditches run into the stream, is now silted up and big clumps of bushes are grown over them. So the water can't get into the main water courses anymore. This kind of situation is one of the biggest problems we are faced with in the New Forest today.

The conservationists won't allow these over-grown areas to be cleared. There used to be Forest by-laws that gave the Forestry Commission the task of keeping the Forest clear of coarse herbage while at the same time keeping its main drainage routes clear. Unfortunately, since the last war "odd words" have crept into the by-laws which have left the situation wide open. For example, in many of the by-laws today they set out what should be done but add the words "with regard to other interests." There you allow the arguments to creep in.

These conservation bodies are made up of paid civil servants—nearly all scientists, and they've got the Ministry of Environment right in the government as their friends and spokesmen. They've been building up this last 20 years before we in the Forest realized what was happening.

Oil and Gas

Another peril is oil and gas development. They've done some exploration but they've been stopped for the time being. The companies keep on making applications for development either in or near the Forest. I'm afraid, in the future, there won't be enough people, or enough financial resources, to stop them.

Still another threat is the Hampshire County Council. There are several Acts of Parliament covering the New Forest, but the law says the Verderers have power of veto where the welfare of the Forest is concerned. If anyone thinks the Verderers are unfairly opposing permission for some project, the law states the matter must be referred to arbitration.

A Verderer's View...

Continued from previous page

Hampshire County Council

Take the Lyndhurst by-pass issue. The County Council refused to go to arbitration and instead promoted a new act of parliament that would enable them to override the Verderers. The danger there is that this would represent a precedent. Since precedents are important in law, this means the whole concept of Forest management would be at risk.

You see, the Hampshire County Council once tried to take over the Court of Verderers and their authority. A central point was the Verderers' shortage of funds; they never have much because their only income is from marking fees of animals grazing on Forest land. Now some years ago the County Council put forward proposals to take over the Verderers and to take care of their financial problems. Of course that would have given them control. We had a terrific fight to keep them out, but we did—and they've never gotten over it. They always seek to get back to us. They—not the people of the Forest itself—would like to hold the power. The Verderers Court is the only means of keeping the forest independent and free of intrusion, so its authority must be maintained.

Speeding Cars

Another Forest problem is speeding cars. I would like to see the Ministry of Transport put a speed limit on all Forest roads. This could be advertised prominently on entry into the Forest from any direction. If there was a speed limit—even as high as 40 miles an hour—we could cut down the number of animal deaths dramatically. But they will not do it.

We've been trying to get a speed limit for a long time, but the Ministry won't budge. Speed on the dual carriage from Cadnam to Ringwood doesn't matter, because that's fenced all the way. I'm speaking of the roads that are open to the Forest. The Ministry say a

speed limit can't be enforced, but that's nonsense. If you visit special areas in other parts of the country, as we all do, you'll see that speed limits there *are* enforced, and they could be here.

Few Commoners Left

Perhaps the greatest danger to the Forest is the demise of the Commoner. The Forest now has many urban people living in it, as opposed to the country stock who once resided here. These newcomers are buying up properties that in olden days would have been bought by Forest people.

The prices are so inflated that local people—sons and daughters of the Commoners—can't afford to buy.

I admit you can't prevent Forest people from selling their properties in the first place. This is something that has happened largely since the last war. These people who sell think they will come back one day, but they can't, for the prices of Forest properties will be even higher.

Many of those from urban areas who come to settle here want to preserve the Forest and do contribute toward its preservation. But most are not Commoners with animals to keep the Forest clear and they usually don't have sons and daughters interested in earning a living from the Forest.

THE CLEVELANDS AT THEIR SOUTH WEIRS HOME
One of the highlights in Archie Cleveland's tenure of office was the presentation of the New Forest Verderers to the Queen in 1979 on the occasion of the Forest's 900th anniversary celebration.

PRIMARY AIM: New Forest Review Group (1987)
As a well-loved part of our national heritage, the character of the (New) Forest must also reflect how it is perceived in the national consciousness—how people want it to be—and in this regard, surely its essence is that of that of a unique throwback to medieval times when man had only begun to exploit his surroundings, in harmony with nature, and had not yet succeeded in bending them entirely to his will.

"The Forest Should Survive—Forever!"

The New Forest has survived for over 900 years because there have always been dedicated people who have fought for its future, by protecting it from those who tried to use it for present gain and personal profit.

The New Forest Acts were drawn up for its protection but few people seem to know them, and even those who do, and ought to know better, tend to ignore them and hope they won't be found out. For instance, there was once a plan to build a new main road across the Forest along the length of the disused Southampton to Dorchester railway line through Longslade Bottom at Brocken-hurst and on to Ringwood. This erosion of Forest land was only stopped when the relevant section of the Southampton to Dorchester Railway Act of 1845 was read out in the Verderers Court in the full glare of publicity, and the proposed road was proved to be illegal because, according to that Act, any land taken from the Forest for the railway, if disused for two consecutive years, had to be restored and rights of grazing reinstated.

> For over a generation Jean Cobb has fought to save the New Forest from one threat or another. The campaign she led to save the hardwoods of the Forest has for the moment reduced risks from this quarter, but other perils are constantly surfacing. The Editor asked Mrs. Cobb to set forth the outstanding threats of the future, based on her knowledge of past events and perceptions of things to come.
>
> Her concerns, presented below, read like a catalogue of vested interests, and one may well wonder how the New Forest can survive with so many powerful bodies enviously eying it. Indeed, the Forest is inanimate—able only to bask in its beauty and majesty so long as mortals enable it to do so.
>
> Are there enough dedicated people to speak up and fight for the Forest? Are they prepared to inform themselves about the threats to whittle away at the Forest's independence?
>
> Jean Cobb hopes so. "The New Forest", she says, "*should* survive. Forever."

death.

In the days before universal transport, the over-use of the Forest was non-existent. Now one of the main threats to its future is the increased mobility of the masses. The propinquity of big cities like Bournemouth and Southampton, and the motorway bringing traffic from London, all increase the numbers of people travelling to, or through, the New Forest. Perhaps there can be no

Can one blame them for wanting to use the New Forest for their own profit? For treating this threatened part of an international heritage as one great recreation ground? So many think only of what they can get out of the Forest without putting anything back—except, dare one say it?—their litter.

As well as increasing the traffic problem, the urbanisation of land around the Forest perimeter, the growth of building development creeping out from Ringwood, Totton and areas which were once villages, is consuming paddock land needed for animals in winter when they may have to be taken off the Forest as food shortages arise, or the animals need extra care. Without this "back-up land" there could be so few animals left to graze and browse on the Forest that the land could deteriorate into an impenetrable scrub of bramble, sloe, gorse and (illegal) self-sown conifers spread from Forestry Commission inclosures.

This effect can be seen at Setley in the south of the Forest where much of the land was "gridded-

Continued on page 352

> *"Drivers do not realize that animals in the Forest have every right to be on the roads, and motorists are held responsible for their injury or death"*

Animals and Roads

Further encroachment of grazing land takes place whenever roads are repaired and the edges built up and widened. Traffic in the New Forest should be restricted by the narrow roads, not the roads widened to accommodate more and heavier vehicles. Each time a road is thus repaired more land is lost. The widening of roads, too, leads to an increase in the speed at which traffic travels, and because of this more and more animals are killed each year, often left to die agonising deaths. Speed limits will have to be introduced. Drivers do not realize that animals in the Forest have every right to be on the roads, and motorists are held responsible for their injury or

way of halting this flood. So often the crowds destroy the very peace and quiet which they come to find. Is education the answer? To teach people the value of silence; and to watch, without destroying their surroundings?

Opposed to keeping the crowds at bay, of course, would be the local shop-keepers, the tourist trade of hotel and guest-house keepers, and, of course, of those whose employment depends on tourism.

> *"Is education the answer? To teach people the value of silence and to watch, without destroying their surroundings?"*

The Forest under Threa

The New Forest Acts... our SAFEGUARD

Fordingbridge

Ringwood

Burley

Bransgore

Sway

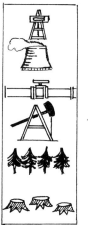 Oil, gas prospecting		 Gravel extraction	
Coal-fired power station		Housing development	
Pipelines		By-passes, motorways	
Nodding donkeys (oil wells)		Planning encroachment (Grazing lands)	
Conifer plantations			
Tree-felling		Military manoeuvres	

— A Perspective View

> *"It has often and truly been said that the Commoners' animals are the architects of the New Forest."*

The Forest Should Survive...

Continued from page 349

out" by the changed "perambulation" of 1964 when many roads and private lands were cut off by cattle grids to prevent animals straying onto main roads or into towns. Here, when grazing ceased because Commoners' animals were fenced out, the vegetation changed into patches of self-sown pine-wood with a few forlorn silver-birches, from what had been an area of wild heath and bog, the home of rare plants, deer, badgers, foxes and otters, where the buzzards nested and harriers hunted.

Animals are Architects

It has often and truly been said that the Commoners' animals are the architects of the New Forest. Many of the duties of the Verderers (the protectors of the New Forest) are bound up with the well-being of these animals and their use of the Open Forest. The Court of Verderers has the great task of preserving their grazing rights, which keep the New Forest open for the enjoyment of so many people.

The Verderers have no jurisdiction over the inclosures which are worked by the Forestry Commission—and here too, actions contrary to the Law have occurred. The New Forest Acts protect the woodlands but the Commission, as a Government department, has to be watched. The 1877 New Forest Act dictates that no clear-felling to leave the land without trees or vegetation shall be allowed in inclosures (in order to protect the look of the Forest) and that "care shall be taken to maintain the picturesque aspect of the ground." How then, without contravening this law, has the Forestry Commission been able to grow over 12,600 acres of regimented even-aged conifers (i.e.

planted at the same time) in their plantations? The answer is, no doubt, that it hoped no one would read the Act, or if they did, they would not dare to challenge so large a Government department. This continuing disregard of the Act must be stopped, or the felling of oaks, beeches, chestnuts and deciduous trees and replacement with conifers will change the

Jean Cobb (Jean Main, Associate Fellow of the Guild of Glass Engravers) working on the chalice presented to Her Majesty the Queen and Prince Philip on their visit to the New Forest to celebrate its 900th anniversary. Mrs. Cobb feels the Forest can be saved only through the efforts of dedicated people.

Forest into a land of stark green darkness in the name of commercial achievement.

"No" to National Park

It has often been suggested that the New Forest ought to be designated as a National Park under the aegis of the Countryside Commission, another Government department.

But, watch out! Remember all Government departments are bound by the Official Secrets Act which can conceal their plans, and one Government department does not interfere with another. Then consider the conifers spreading across the Brecon Beacons, Lake District and other National Parks, and take fright! Then what of the Okehampton Bypass for instance, built to run through one of the most attractive parts of the Dartmoor National Park; where, as well, vast areas are turned over to military use as they are in the Northumberland National Park or along the Pembrokeshire coast?

Nuclear power stations have been built in the Snowdonia National Park and the North Yorkshire Moors, while Fylingdales early warning radar station is being redesigned and enlarged. Quarrying is being carried out in the Peak District National Park and in that of the Yorkshire Dales. Surely these examples are numerous enough to show that to become a National Park would offer no protection for the New Forest, but would be a Trojan Horse introducing further destruction.

A Limit to Tourism

One suspect duty of the Countryside Commission is to "secure access for open air recreation."

> *"This continuing disregard of the (1877) Act must be stopped, or the felling of oaks, beeches, chestnuts and deciduous trees and replacement with conifers will change the Forest into a land of stark green darkness in the name of commercial development"*

> *"Even the national government works, perhaps unwittingly, to destroy the New Forest. They have issued licenses covering the whole area to give oil companies permission to explore for oil or gas"*

The Forest Should Survive...

Continued from previous page

Their efforts in the New Forest should be curtailed; as, also should be those of the New Forest District Council's Leisure Department. Both increase the tourist influx to what ought to be a place of peace and quiet. The number of licensed riding establishments should be restricted; relentless riding churns up tracks over grazing land. Cycling should be allowed only along gravel tracks, and even the number of these should be minimised and built only in consultation with the Verderers. The Forestry Commission should allow camping only from mid-April to mid-September, and mass events, rallies, and parties should be strictly controlled under New Forest by-laws.

Local Government Threats

As well as encouraging tourism, an unexpected threat comes from local government by their efforts to undermine the protective clauses of the New Forest Acts. In 1972 the Hampshire County Council tried to introduce a Bill into Parliament which would have reduced the majority of the elected Verderers, who represent New Forest interests on the Court, by increasing Council representation; thereby gaining control of the Verderers' decisions. All Forest societies and many individuals worked to outlaw this, and the Bill died at birth.

Even the national government works, perhaps unwittingly, to destroy the New Forest. They have issued licences covering the whole area to give oil companies permission to explore for oil or gas. These companies hide their mechanical erections with pet names; "Nodding Donkeys" and "Christmas Trees", and explain

there will be only one small drilling rig in each area, but how many people realise that if they don't strike it rich first time they can go on drilling again and again in their area allocated for exploration? Also the public has been led to believe that once oil or gas is discovered it need not be extracted, but the companies fail to disclose that they have a statutory duty to extract it. They wouldn't spend thousands of pounds on exploratory drilling if they knew there would be no profit to be made!

Then, what of the hard-core roads to carry heavy machinery to and from the site, or an ever greater number of pipelines across the Forest, and the "collecting area" of tanks for oil storage, and the effect all this would have on the peace and quiet of the Forest itself? The noise, the danger of fire (always played down, of course, but "Red" Adair had to be called in from the United States for one blow-out in the north of England) and what would be the impact of extra heavy traffic on New Forest villages? No. Oil-drilling must never be allowed to begin in the New Forest. Once started it could take over the whole area. Go and look at Wych Farm in Dorset!

Oil-Drilling Illegal

The Shell Company in 1982–83 was prevented from drilling by New Forest Acts. The 1877 Act states that inclosures shall be used

only for the production of trees and timber, and the oil-drilling site was in one such inclosure. Subsequent Acts could have provided for this inclosure to be "thrown open" to become unfenced Forest but then Commoners' animals would have been allowed to graze there, and how could there be drilling rigs and all their accompanying paraphernalia without destroying any of the grazing, or with ponies and cattle wandering around?

According to another New Forest Act, extra land might have been provided in exchange from a "bank" of "Crown Freehold" land held by the Forestry Commission, but the difficulties became too apparent, and Shell, bless their hearts, withdrew their application. Again the New Forest was rescued by its Acts. But those areas licensed for oil exploration still remain, and the whole place must be watched with suspicious eagle eyes.

New Forest Acts have protected the Forest for over 900 years. Keep them intact, strengthen them if necessary, but never let them go. They are more of a safeguard than any other legislation.

Dedicated People Needed

The very conflict of interests between the Commoners who want the land for grazing, the Forestry Commission for growing commercial timber, the Nature Conservancy for the protection of flora and fauna, and the tourist trade for recreation, has helped to keep the Forest as it is today. To save it, though, there must always be dedicated people who work to keep the New Forest free from those who want to grab something from it, or it will be doomed. Only those with determination that the Forest shall not be overwhelmed

> *"New Forest Acts have protected the Forest for over 900 years. Keep them intact, strengthen them if necessary, but never let them go. They are more of a safeguard than any other legislation"*

Who Will Save The New Forest?

(Increasingly, national attention is being focussed on the preservation of the New Forest. In former times this concern was aimed mainly at saving the ancient trees; nowadays the very existence of the New Forest as a separate entity is under attack on many fronts. In its leader of 14 April 1988, *Country Life* magazine analyzed the perils that face the Forest.)

Because the New Forest has successfully preserved both its name and its nature for nine centuries, it is tempting to suppose that it will be able to do so in the future. But unless Parliament takes effective measures to protect the forest, it will slowly be crushed between the expanding forces of Southampton and the Poole-Bournemouth-Christchurch conurbation.

To counter this threat, the New Forest Review Group was set up by the Forestry Commission in 1986. The Group, consisting of representatives of the Commission, Hampshire County Council, New Forest District Council, the Countryside Commission, the Nature Conservancy Council and the New Forest Verderers, published a draft report in 1987. Comments have now been received, and the Group will publish its final report this year.

The forest's problems are not due only to external pressures. Economic change is destroying from within the system of com-

moning on which, for centuries, the forest depended. Rising land values make it next to impossible for would-be young commoners to get started. Young men or women with a rural forest background can no longer buy a cottage with a few acres of land, which would give them the right to run livestock in the forest. Such a cottage would cost £100,000 or more. Agricultural land in the forest, even without a cottage, is fetching up to £10,000 an acre.

Commoning is itself no longer a profitable activity. Many of the commoners' ponies are sold for meat at poor prices. Cattle of various and mixed breeds are still run in the forest by commoners, but they do not fetch good prices at market compared with cattle from local farms. Pigs can still be run profitably, in a good autumn pannage season, but that season is short. Finally, commoners' animals are killed on the roads; some 200 in the past 12 months.

When the Review Group reports, it will have to balance many conflicting interests. It must try to preserve the forest ecology against the pressures of commoning, forestry, tourism and motor traffic. It must try to maintain the traditional landscape. Above all, it must stop the spread of urban and industrial development.

It has been suggested, by the Countryside Commission among others, that the forest needs a status akin to that of a National Park. It needs more than that. In the forest, county councils are seen as threatening forces. Hampshire County Council's disgraceful

conduct in brushing aside the views of the Verderers, and forcing through its own plan for a Lyndhurst bypass by a special Act of Parliament, is not a recommendation for it as a forest custodian. Dorset County Council has plans for a new housing development west of Ringwood.

Who can save the forest? What Parliament should do is to reconstitute the New Forest Verderers, who effectively guarded the forest for nine centuries, broaden their membership to include conservation and tourist interests, and give them draconian powers that the local authorities would not be able to override.

The Forest Should Survive...

Continued from previous page can save it for all time.

They must prevent the growth of tourism, the building of roads, pipelines and other constructions on Forest land, the start of oil-drilling, proliferation of gravel extraction, the loss of near-by paddock land, the creeping urbanisation of adjacent country, any increase in conifer growing by the Forestry Commission (even at the Government's instigation) and the military use of the Forest. Most of all they must ensure that the New Forest Acts are kept intact and not undermined.

No small Task! However difficult it is, though, it is worthwhile. The important thing is that the New Forest *should* survive. Forever.

Decision by House of Commons Select Committee

After months of deliberation by select committees in both the House of Lords and the House of Commons, the Lyndhurst by-pass bill (a Hampshire County Council-sponsored private bill) was thrown out of Parliament in July, 1988.

Noting that "none of the parties before the committee argued that a by-pass was unnecessary," the report went on to say:

"The committee wishes to make it clear that even if it had been convinced that the Bill route represented a reasonable balance between the wider interests of conservation and the proper interests of the inhabitants of Lyndhurst and that alternative solutions to the problem had been fully investigated and found wanting, we could not have agreed that the promoters had proven the need for the Bill when, in fact, general powers are already available to them. We thus find that the primary purpose of the Bill, namely the building of a by-pass on the route specified, could have been effected without the authority of Parliament, although the less controversial matter of fencing the road would have required that authorisation. The committee thus finds that the Preamble is not proven."

BIBLIOGRAPHY

About New Forest Bibliographies

Over the years the number of New Forest bibliographies has grown, their lengths increasing as more and more titles have appeared.

Some authors have included short bibliographies at the end of their books about the Forest. One of the earliest efforts dealing with the New Forest as a separate publication, however, was Heywood Sumner's 14-page booklet, *A New Forest Bibliography and List of Maps*, 1925.

The first extensive (30 pages) bibliography devoted solely to the New Forest probably was that of the newspaper publisher, W. Frank Perkins (*A New Forest Bibliography*, 1935). Apart from its considerable length, this list included many local histories—some of which were already rare in 1935.

In 1969 the Botany Department of the University of Southampton published *A Select Bibliography of New Forest Literature*. This list (12 pages) was heavily weighted with natural history titles.

In 1979 Rita M. Popham compiled a brief, but well annotated basic bibliography (mainly for teachers). It is available from the Bournemouth Local Studies unit, The Teachers' Centre, 40 Lowther Road, Bournemouth, Dorset.

The most extensive New Forest bibliography published to date was compiled by Dr. Nicholas Flower for the Nature Conservancy Council in 1979 (with an addendum in 1981). Predictably, it is unsurpassed in natural science references with more than 300 works listed in the fields of archaeology and palynology; botany, ecology and forestry; bryology, lichenology, and mycology; geology, geomorphology, hydrology and soil science; invertebrate and vertebrate zoology, and animal behaviour; agriculture, animal husbandry, and local industry; and conservation, planning and the social sciences. This 40-page bibliography is sold by the Nature Conservancy Council, Calthorpe House, Calthorpe Street, Banbury, Oxon OX16 8EX.

No attempt is made here to repeat specialized references dealing with the Forest. The general reader will find many of the references that follow in the larger libraries of the Hampshire and Dorset systems (Winchester, Southampton and Bournemouth). For local histories, the Cope Collection at the University of Southampton is unrivalled. Exceedingly rare works may be found at the British Library or the libraries of Oxford and Cambridge universities.

GENERAL AND HISTORICAL

ACTON, C.R. *Sport and Sportsman of the New Forest*, 1936. Heath Cranton.

AFLALO, F.G. *Half A Century of Sport in Hampshire* (excerpts from Lord Malmesbury's Journals). 1905. Country Life.

AITCHESON, S. *The Ancient Manors of Minstead and Bisterne*, 1906. Privately printed.

ALLINGHAM, William. *William Allingham's Diary*, 1967. Centaur Press. Introduction by Geoffrey Grigson. Many references to the New Forest. Index. (Also see P. WALKER).

ALLISON, Phillip. The New Forest: *A Photographic Record of 100 Years of Forest Life*, 1979. Pioneer Pubs.

ANGEL, H. *The Jarrold Book of the Countryside of the New Forest*, 1977. Jarrold.

ANON. *The Hampshire Wonder or the Groaning Tree*, 1742. W. Smith. Describes the mysterious groaning tree at South Baddesley. Pamphlet.

ARNOLD, ROBERT and SIMON KEYNE. *Painters of the New Forest, 1800–1920*, catalogue of exhibition at the Hampshire Gallery, Bournemouth, 1973. Ills.

ASHWORTH, R.C.B. *Actions Stations 5*, 1982. Published by Patrick Stephens Ltd., Dennington Estates, Wellingborough, Northants. Many maps, ills. Lists missions and activities at all air bases in New Forest and south western England during second world war.

BAIRACLI-LEVY, Juliette de. *Wanderers in the New Forest*, 1958. Several reprintings. Faber and Faber. Ills.

BEAUTIES OF ENGLAND AND WALES, THE (Series on the counties). *Hampshire and Herefordshire* (including the New Forest), 1814. J. Harris; Longman.

BEGBIE, Joan. *Walking in the New Forest*, 1934. Alexander Maclehose & Co. Endpaper maps, ills.

BERKELEY, G.C.G.F. *Reminiscences of A Huntsman*, 1854. Longman.

BOEL, Geoffrey. *Picturesque Pubs of the New Forest*, 1981. G.F. Wilson and Co.

BRAYLEY, E.W. and J. Britton. *A Topographical and Historical Description of the County of Hants*, 1805. Sherwood, Neely and Jones.

BURLEY & NEW FOREST PONY & CATTLE SOCIETY. Annual reports (1906–80). (See also NEW FOREST PONY STUD BOOK.)

BURY, May. *In the New Forest with the Fairies*, 1922. telford E. Stone.

CADMAN, W.A. *Dawn, Dusk and Deer*, 1966. Country Life.

CAINE, William. *The New Foresters*, 1913. James Nisbet and Co. Travels with a donkey in the Forest. Ill., map.

CHACKSFIELD, K. Merle. *Smuggling Days*, 1966. *Christchurch Times*. Map, sketches, glossary. Describes stuggling in and around the New Forest, the Isle of Wight, Dorset and Devon.

CHURCH ARMY. *Gipsy Missioning in the New Forest*, c. 1930. Booklet describing Church Army work among the New Forest gypsies.

COATTS, MARGOT and ELIZABETH LEWIS. *Heywood Sumner: Artist and Archaeologist, 1853–1940*, catalogue of exhibition at Winchester, Cheltenham, and Portsmouth. Published by Winchester City Museum. 54 ills. (14 in colour).

COBBETT, William. *Rural Rides*, 1830, with numerous reprintings to the present day. In J.M. Dent's *Everyman's Library* (no. 639).

COLEMAN, Monica. *Monica Coleman's New Forest*, 1987. Paul Cave Publications. Reproduces 14 paintings (in full colour) of the Forest with maps of sites. Additional text and photographs by Anne Ruffell.

COPE, William Henry. *Glossary of Hampshire: Words and Phrases*, 1883. English Dialect Soc.

CORNISH, C.J. *The New Forest and the Isle of Wight*, 1895. Seeley & Co. Sketches by Alexander Ansted and Lancelot Speed.

—— The New Forest, 1899. Horace G. Commin.

COX, John Charles. *The Royal Forests of England*, 1905. Methuen. Several mentions of the New Forest, especially in Ch. 26. Ills.

COX, J.G. *Castlkeman's Corkscrew, The Southampton and Dorchester Railway, 1844–1848*, 1975. The City of Southampton. Maps, Ills.

CROLY, Elizabeth. *The Lure of the New Forest*, 1925. Mills & Boon. Map, ills.

CROSS, A.L. (ed.) *Eighteenth Century Documents relating to the Royal Forests, the Sheriffs, and Smuggling, Selected from the Shelburne Manuscript, 1928.* Macmillan.

DALLAS, C.C. *New Forest Shooting: Past and Present*, 1927. C.T. King.

DANIEL, William Barker. *Rural Sports*, 1801, 1812. 2 vols. Supplementary volume, 1813. Contains passage on "Slut," the sporting pig.

DARBY, H.C. and E.M.J. CAMPBELL. *The Domesday Geography of Southeast England*, 1962. Cambridge University Press.

DE CRESPIGNY, R.C. and H.G. HUTCHINSON. *The New Forest: Its Traditions Inhabitants and Customs*, 1895. John Murray.

DE CRESPIGNY, Mrs. Philip CAMERON and Captain E.C. TROLLOPE. "The Legend of the New Forest," an original operetta in three acts. 1889. Contained in the Bodelian Library, University of Oxford.

DEFOE, Daniel. *A Tour through England and Wales, 1724–1726*. Vol. 1. includes the New Forest. Dent's Everyman Edn.

DE PELCHIN, P. *Promenades Historiques Chez les Anglais*, 1881. Includes the New Forest.

DOMAN, Henry. *Songs in the Shade*, 1881. Marshall and Co.

EDLIN, H.L. *The Queen's House, Lyndhurst, and Its Links with the Crown*, 1962.

EVERSLEY, Lord. *Commons, Forests and Footpaths*, 1910. Cassell.

EYRE, G.E.B. *Cottagers and Open Wastes in the Districts of the New Forest*, 1882. British Assn. Report, 645–53.

—— The New Forest: *Its Common Rights and Cottage Stockkeepers*, 1883. John G. Short.

FOWLER, Sir J.K. *A History of Beaulieu Abbey*, 1911. *The Car Illustrated*.

FOXLEASE. Booklet published by the Girl Guides Assn. (1st edn., 1980) giving the history and description of the Girl Guides centre at Foxlease, Lyndhurst. Sketches.

FREEHOLDER WITHIN THE FOREST, A. 1843. Pamphlet, author anonymous. C. Boor.

GIBBINS, H.E.J. *Gipsies of the New Forest and Other Tales*, 1909. W. Mate. Ills.

GILPIN, William. *Remarks on Forest Scenery and Other Woodland Views*, etc., 1791. 2 vols. Ills, map. R. Blamire. Several edns (4th edn. edited by Sir T.D. Lauder, 1834).

GODFREY, Elizabeth. *The New Forest*, 1912. Blackie and Son. In "Beautiful England" series.

GRAPHIC, THE. "Hunting with the New Forest Deerhounds," 1885. Two pages of drawings, 14 February issue.

—— "The Shaker Settlement in the New Forest," 1875. Front page of the 9 January issue; devoted to drawings of the Hordle Shakers with accompanying captions describing their plight.

GRINNELL-MILNE, Duncan. *The Killing of William Rufus*, 1968. David & Charles. Maps, ills.

GROVES, T.B. "The Telegraph in Dorset before the Days of Electricity," 1890. *Proceedings, Dorset Natural History and Field Club*; Vol. XI.

HALL, P.L *A Few Topographical Remarks Relative to the Parishes of Ringwood, Ellingham, Ibbesley, Harbridge and Fordingbridge; and to the New Forest*, 1869. W. Wheaton.

HAMPSHIRE TREASURES, New Forest Rural District, 1973. Hampshire Council of Social Service.

—— New Forest District West, 1978. Hants Council of Social Service.

HANSFORD, Ronald Joseph. *New Forest Glimpses*, 1975 (2nd edn.) Poems.

HASSELL, J. *Tour of the Isle of Wight* (with the New Forest and southern Hampshire), 1790. 2 vols. T. Hookham.

HAWKER, Peter. *The Diary of Col. Peter Hawker, 1802–53*, 1893. 2 vols. Longman Green.

HAWKINS, Desmond. *Wild Life in the New Forest*, n.d. C.J. Newsome & Associates, Bournemouth, Photographs by Eric Ashby. Ills.

HEATH, F.G. *Autumnal Leaves*, 1881. Sampson Low, Marston, Searle and Rivington. With drawings by F. Golden Short. 1885.

—— New edn. Kegan Paul, Trench and Co. Ills.

HOCKEY, S.F. (ed.) *The Account-Book of Beaulieu Abbey*, 1975. Royal Historical Society.

—— *Beaulieu, King John's Abbey: A History of Beaulieu Abbey, Hampshire, 1204–1538*, 1976. Pioneer Pubs.

HOLLAND, A.J. *Ship Building, Mainly for the Crown, in the Southampton Area, 1650 to 1820*, 1961. Southampton University (master's thesis).

—— *Ships of British Oak: the Rise and Decline of Wooden Shipbuilding in Hampshire*, 1971. David and Charles.

HUDSON, W.H. *Hampshire Days*, 1903. Longman. 1923 edn., J.M. Dent.

HUTCHINSON, Horace, G. *The New Forest*. 1904. Methuen. Ills. (includes 31 colour plates by Walter Tyndale and one by Lucy Kemp Welch).

JACKSON, John. *Deer in the New Forest*, 1977. Moonraker Press. Map, many sketches, ills.

JAMES, Jude. *Comyn's New Forest*, 1982. Based on manuscripts of the Rev. Henry Comyn who had charge of the combined parishes of Boldre and Brockenhurst in the early 1800s. Documents many families and their lifestyles. C.J. Newsome and Associates in conjunction with Lymington Historical Records Society.

—— Hurst Castle, *An Illustrated History*, 1967. Dovecote Press.

JEANS, G.E. (ed.). *Memorials of Old Hampshire*, 1906. Bemrose.

JENKINSON, H.T.J. *The New Forest*, 1871. W. Ridgeway.

JOWITT, D.M. and R.L.P. *History, People and Places in Hampshire*, 1975. Spurbooks.

KENCHINGTON, F.E. *The Commoners' New Forest*, 1944. Hutchinson. Endpaper maps, ills., bib.

KENDALL, S.C. (ed.) *The Hants County Book*, 1939. Contains section on the New Forest. Lindsay Drummond. Map, ills.

KING, C.T. *Round Lymington and the New Forest*, c. 1890. Charles T. King.

KING, R. *A Handbook for the Town of Lymington, the New Forest and the Surrounding Neighbourhood*, 1853. R. King.

KLITZ, Robert. *Sketches of Life, Character and Scenery in the New Forest*, 1850. Described as "a series of tales, rural, domestic, legendary and humorous, Orr & Co.

LASCELLES, Gerald. *Thirty-Five Years in the New Forest*, 1915. Edward Arnold. Lascelles was the best known of the New Forest's Deputy Surveyors; his period of service was 1880 to 1914. Ills.

LEFEVRE, G.S. *English Commons and Forests*, etc., 1894. Cassell.

LEWIS, Percival. *Historical Enquiries Concerning Forests* (with remarks concerning the New Forest). 1811. T. Payne.

LOVELL, Mary S., *A Hunting Pageant*, n.d. Saiga Publishing Co., Ltd., Hindhead, Surrey. Ills.

MAKING OF THE NEW FOREST, historical account of, 1751. M. Cooper. (Paired with an account of the making of Richmond New Park.)

MALMESBURY, Earl of (James Howard Harris). *Memoirs of An Ex-Minister*, 1884.

MANNING, S. and S.G. GREEN. *English Pictures Drawn with Pen and Pencil*, 1808. Religious Tract Society.

MEE, Arthur. *Hampshire and the Isle of Wight*, 1939 with later edns. Hodder and Stoughton. In King's England series. Ills., map.

MILLS, Ethel M. *Tree Poems*, 1917. Fifield.

MONKHOUSE, F.V. (ed.) *A Survey of Southampton and its Region*, 1964. British Assn. for the Advancement of Science.

MONTAGU, Lord. *The New Forest and Its Old Woods*, 1926. Privately printed.
—— *Lady Troubridge and Archibald Marshall*, 1930. Macmillan.

MOORE, John C. *The New Forest*, 1936. Chapman and Hall. The author's adventures on horseback.

MUDIE, Robert. *Hampshire: Its Past, and Present Conditions and Future Prospects*, 1838. 3 vols., ills, map. James Robbins. Vol. 2 (pp. 217–332) deals with the New Forest. A facsimile edn was published by Laurence Oxley in 1975.

NEW FOREST ART EXHIBITION, 1892. Catalogue of exhibition held in the New Forest Hall, Lyndhurst in 1892 (5th year). Prepared by William Gerrard, manager and honorary secretary. H. King. 390 works listed. In British Library.

NEW FOREST ASSOCIATION. Annual reports from 1933 to present. Ills. for most years.,

NEW FOREST BUCKHOUNDS. 1921. Hunt Club Associates.

NEW FOREST GOOD SAMARITAN CHARITY, 1908. Report on the work of this charity by H.E.J. Gibbins (see reference in this bib.) in 23 June issue of *Ringwood Chronicle*. The charity was devoted to work among the gypsies.

NEW FOREST HOUNDS. c. 1932. Official handbook edited by "Sonech." Chase and Hunting Assn.

NEW FOREST PAGEANT. A. Programme of a pageant staged in Brockenhurst on 1–2 June, 1921, by the Women's Institute. Copy available in Cope Collection, University of Southampton Library.

NEW FOREST PONY STUD BOOK, THE. Yearbook of The New Forest Pony Breeding and Cattle Society. Contains registrations, transfers, miscellaneous information, including tail markings for Agisters' districts, and list of brands. Ills. (See also BURLEY AND NEW FOREST PONY AND CATTLE SOCIETY.)

NEW FOREST, THE, 1960. A symposium by several authorities with an introduction by Lord Radnor. Galley Press. Revised edn., 1966, J.M. Dent. Map. ills.

NEW FOREST (THE) AND HAMPSHIRE IN PICTURES, 1952. Introduced by Sir William Beach Thomas. Oldhams Press. Ills., map.

NISBET, J. *Our Forests and Woodlands*, 1900. J.M. Dent.

NORTHCROFT, Dorothea Mary. *A.B.C. of the New Forest*, 1966. Wilding and Son. Ills., map, bib. Brief notes on Forest subjects.

OAKLEY, E. Russell. *The Smugglers of Christchurch, Bourne Heath and the New Forest*, 1944, Hutchinson & Co., London. Ills.

OWEN, J.A. *Forest, Field and Fell*, 1893. Lawrence & Bullen. Contains a section on the New Forest.

PASMORE, ANTHONY, *New Forest Commoners*, etc., 1969. Privately printed. Ills., map, bib.
—— *Verderers of the New Forest: A History of the New Forest, 1877–1977*, 1977. Pioneer Pubs. Ills., maps, tables, bib.

PASMORE, Anthony and Jude JAMES. *The New Forest and Heywood Sumner*, 1985. New Forest Section, Hampshire Field Club and Archaeological Society. Ills.

PATTERSON, A.T. *Hampshire and the Isle of Wight*, 1976. Batsford.

PENROSE, M.A.M. "Some Aspects of Life in the New Forest." 1957–8. Bournemouth Nat. His. Soc. *Proceedings*: 48, 34–5.

RAWNSLEY, Mrs. Willingham. *The New Forest*, 1904. A. & C. Black. Observations on the Forest, month by month. 20 colour ills.
—— *The New Forest* (Beautiful Britain Series), 1915. A. & C. Black. 12 colour ills.

ROBINSON, Sarah. *The Soldier's Friend*, 1913. T. Fisher Unwin.
—— *My Book*, 1914. Autobiography. S.W. Patridge.

SEABY, A.W. *British Ponies: Running Wild and Ridden*, 1936. A. and C. Black. Contains 32 pages on ponies of the New Forest; includes 26 pen-and-ink drawings.

SIBLEY, Patricia and Robin FLETCHER. *Discovering the New Forest*, 1986. Robert Hale. Maps. ills.

SMITH, Gilbert. *Gilbert Smith: Man of the New Forest*, 1986. Biography of a Forest Keeper. Paul Cave Pubs. Ills.

SOFTCOTT, B.L. *Hants and Dorset's New Forest*, 1975. James Pike. In the "Viewing Hants and Dorset" series.

STAGG, David J. *New Forest Commoners*, 1983.
—— *Agisters of the New Forest*, 1983.
—— *Snake Catchers of the New Forest*, 1983.
—— *Verderers of the New Forest*, 1984.
A series of pamphlets published by the New Forest Association and available from the NFA Secretary, Rockford End, Ringwood, Hants BH24 3NB

STAGG, David J. *New Forest Documents, 1244–1334*, 1979.

——*New Forest Documents, the 15th to the 17th Centuries*, 1983. Hampshire Record Office, Winchester.

STEVENS, F.E. *The New Forest Beautiful*, 1925. Methuen. ills., map.

STUART, BRIAN. *William Shayer, Snr., 1787–1879*, catalogue of exhibition at Southampton Art Gallery, 1987. 19 ills. (seven in colour).

SUMNER, Heywood. *Cuckoo Hill: The Book of Gorley*, 1987. J.M. Dent & Sons, Ltd. Based on the original manuscript and containing many colour plates. Ills.

SUMNER, Heywood. *The Book of Gorley*, 1910. Contains black and white illustrations redrawn from original (coloured) manuscript. Chiswick Press. Ills.

SUMNER, Heywood. "The New Forest," (pp. 158–174 in *The Book of Bournemouth, 1934*, published for the 1934 annual meeting of the British Medical Association.) Ills., bib.

TATE, Peter. *The New Forest 900 Years After*, 1979. Macdonald and Jane's. Endpaper maps, ills.

TAVENER, L.E. *The Common Lands of Hampshire*, 1957. Hampshire County Council.

TSCHIFFELY, A.F. *Bridle Paths*, 1936. Heinemann. The author travels over England by horse, visiting the new Forest briefly.

TUBBS, Colin R. *The New Forest: An Ecological History*, 1968. David and Charles. Ills., tables, charts, bib.

——*The New Forest: A Natural History*, 1986. Maps, charts, ills., bib.

TWEEDIE, George R. *Hampshire Glorious Wilderness*, 1925. Homeland Assn., Ltd. Ills., map, bib.

VESEY-FITZGERALD, Brian. *Hampshire and the Isle of Wight*, 1949. Robert Hale. In "County Books" series.

——*Portrait of the New Forest*, 1966. Robert Hale. Reprinted 1969, 1974, 1977. Ills., map.

VICTORIA HISTORY OF THE COUNTIES OF ENGLAND. Hampshire and the Isle of Wight. 5 vols. and index. 1900–1914.
Vol. 2. pp. 409–470. Forestry and the New Forest.
Vol. 4. pp. 615–638. The Hundred of the New Forest.
Vol. 5. pp. 565–574. Sport in the new Forest.

WALDREN, William George James. *My New Forest*, 1982. Privately printed. Once owned the village shop in Norleywood.

WALFORD, Mike, *Pollards, People & Ponies*, 1979. Short Publications. Endpaper maps, many ills.

WALKER, Patrius (pseudonym of William Allingham). *Rambles in England and Ireland* (includes the New Forest), 1873. Longman Green. (See also William ALLINGHAM).

WARNER, Richard. *Topographical Remarks Relating to the Southwestern Parts of Hampshire* (includes New Forest), 1793. R. Blamire. 2 vols.

——*Literary Recollections*, 1830. 2 vols.

WESTLAKE, Jean. *Gipsy Caravan*, 1982. Sandy Balls Press. The 100-year story of a gipsy caravan. Many ills. (maps, designs, sketches).

WILKINSON, Walter. Unpublished manuscript, *The Peep Show*, 1924. Handwritten diary of the renowned puppeteer, illustrated with his sketches. Privately held.

WILSON, Sir James. *The Dialect of the New Forest in Hampshire, as Spoken in the Village of Burley*, 1914. Oxford University Press. No. 4 in Philological Society series.

WISE, John R. *The New Forest: Its History and Its Scenery*, 1863. Smith Elder & Co. Several edns: 3rd edn., Henry Sotheran & Co., 1880; Artists' edn., 1883 (with 12 original etchings by Heywood Sumner and 62 India proof wood-engravings by Walter Crane; edn. limited to 350 copies); Facsimile edn., 1971, S.R. Publishers. Map, ills.

WOODWARD, Bernard B. *et. al.* *A General History of Hampshire or the County of Southampton*, 1861–9. 3 vols. James S. Virtue. Vol. 3 includes the New Forest.

PERIODICAL LITERATURE

ADAMS, R.B. "The Story of Buckler's Hard," 1929. *Notes and Queries*, 156, 420–424.

ANON. "A Glimpse at the new Forest," 1889. *Tinsley's Magazine*.

——"Around the New Forest," 1891. *All the Year Round*, Vol. LVI.

——"The New Forest," 1977. *Holiday Which*, February, 1977. pp. 39–40.

——"The New Forest," 1882. *Leisure Hour*.

——"The New Forest," 1910. *Blackwood's* Vol. CLXXXVIII.

——Review of John Wise's History of the new Forest, 1863. *British Quarterly Review*, Vol. XXXVIII.

——"The New Forest," 1868. A Poem.

BAKER, Richard St. Barbe. "Among the Trees of Wessex," *The Wessex Magazine*, 1935. May (Vol. 1, No. 2), 84–9. Includes passage on the New Forest.

BARING, F.H. "The Making of the New Forest," 1901. *English Historical Review*; 16, 427–438.

CADMAN, W.A. "The New Forest," 1962. *Forestry*, 35: 27–34.

COBB, Jean. "How We Saved the New Forest," 1971. *Spectator*, 16 Oct., 563–64.

COCHRANE, C. "Early Roads of the New Forest," 1970. *Hampshire*, May.

COLLINS, Mabel. "In the New Forest," 1885. *English Illustrated Magazine*.

CRYPT, THE, or Recepticle for Things Past. A journal published by W. Wheaton, Ringwood, with articles on the new Forest. Vols. I–III (1827–29).

DARBY, H.C. "The Preservation of the New Forest, 1948. *Geographical Journal*; 112, 87–91.

DIMBLEBY, G.W. "*The Ancient and Ornamental Woods of the New Forest,*" 1971. *Ecologist*, 1: 16–18.

DONKIN, R.A. "The Cistercian Settlement and the English Royal Forests," 1960. *Citeaux*; 11.

DRAYSON, Major General A.W. "Among the Snakes and Vipers,"

1889. *Boys' Own Paper*, July and August.

DUGDALE, Sir. W. *Monastican Anglicanum*, etc., 1817–30. 6 vol. series on history of ancient abbies, monasteries, etc. (Beaulieu Abbey is included in Vol. 5)

EDWARDS, Elizabeth. "The New Forest Snake Catcher," *Country*, 1982. Magazine of the Country Gentlemen's Assn. *September*, 476–7.

ESCOTT, T.H.S. "The New Forest," 1875. *Belgravia*, Vol. VII.

EVANS, C.I. "The New Forest," 1915. *The Friend*, (Dec.)

EYRE, G.E.B. "The New Forest: A Sketch," *Fortnightly Review*, 1871. 1 April, 433–51.

FAWCETT, Millicent Garrett. *The new Forest Magazine of Art*, 1885. Vol. VIII.

GOODLAND, Norman. "The New Forest: Animals and Men," 1961. *Contemporary Review*, February.

GRAHAM, J.A. Maxstone. "England's New Forest," *American Forests*. Sept., 1971 (Vol. 77, No. 9), pp. 22–6, 60–63.

GRIGSBY, Joan. "A Forest GP in the Twenties," 1974. *Hampshire Magazine*, February, 49–50.

HAMPSHIRE. The county magazine. Established 1960. Contains many articles not listed here on New Forest subjects. The Bournemouth Reference Library maintains an index. The University of Southampton Library (Special Collections) has a partial index that includes articles and advertisements.

HERBERDT, Auberon, "The New Forest," 1891. *Fortnightly*, Vol. XLIX.

HOLLISTER, C.W. *The Strange Death of William Rufus*, 1973. *Speculum*; 48, 637-53.

ILLUSTRATED LONDON NEWS, 1852. Accounts of the Maypole dance at Burley. 8 May issue. (See also NEW FOREST; Ils. 1848).

JEFFERIES, Richard, "In the New Forest," 1893. *Cornhill Magazine*, Vol. XX.

LAVENDER, Ruth. "Rescuing Wild Flowers in the Forest," 1967. *Hampshire Magazine*, October, 23–4.

LEFROY, W. Chambers. "The New Forest," 1883. *The Portfolio*.

LLOYD, A.L. "Slums under the Trees," 1949. *Picture Post*, January 29. 5 pp., ill.

LLOYD, Arthur T. "Where Did Rufus Die?" 1962. *Hampshire Magazine*; 2 (11), 17–18.

——"A New Look at the New Forest," 1965. *Hampshire Magazine*; 5 (5), 26–8.

NEW FOREST, THE. *Illustrated London News*, 1848. Vol. 13, 247–8, 268.

NEW FOREST CHRONICLE and Lymington, Ringwood and Fordingbridge Times. Weekly newspaper in existence from 1 June 1905 to 30 May 1907. Succeeded by *Ringwood and New Forest Chronicle and Lymington, Christchurch and Fordingbridge Times*, 6 June 1907 to 26 March 1925.

NEW FOREST MAGAZINE. Monthly magazine issued in the last quarter of the 19th century for villages in northwest of the Forest. Predominantly religious news, but with some coverage of sport and other subjects.

ROSE, F. "New Mandate for the New Forest," 1973. *Arboricultural Assn. Jour.*; 2, 139–145.

RYLE, George. "The Future of the New Forest," *The Countryman*, 1971 (pp. 58–63).

PARKER, F.H.M. "The Forest Law and the Death of William Rufus," 1912. *Historical Review*; 27, 26–38.

SEYMOUR, William. "The New Forest from Norman Times," 1968. *History Today*, Vol. XVIII (No. 9, September, 614–20).

SISLEY, Timothy, "One Hundred Years of the New Forest Court," 1977. *The Field*, 12 May.

TAZEWELL, Kathleen, M. "An Eel Trap Maker of the New Forest," 1938. *Wessex Magazine*, (organ of the University College, Southampton), Vol. IV, No. 2; pp. 163–4.

TUBBS, Colin R. "The Development of the Smallholding and Cottage Stock-Keeping Economy of the New Forest," 1956. *Agricultural History Review*; Vol. 13, 23–9.

J.G.W. "The Children of the New Forest," 1862. *London Society*, Vol. 1.

WALKER, Patricius (William Allingham). "Rambles in the New Forest," 1868. *Fraser's Magazine*, Vol. LXXVII.

WARREN, W.L. 'William Rufus' Death," 1959. *History Today*; 9, 22–9.

WOOD, C.W. "In the New Forest," 1881. *Argosy*; Vol. 31.

YOUNG, D.W. "The New Forest," 1935. *Forestry*, 9, 1–16.

FICTION

BENSON, Edward Frederick. *The Angel of Pain*, 1906. Heinemann. Associations with Brockenhurst.

BLACKMORE, Richard. *Craddock Nowell, A Tale of the New Forest*, 1866. Chapman and Hall.

BRADDON, Miss M.E. *Vixen*, 1879. 3 vols. Several edns. (Nelson's Library, 1911).

COWPER, E.E. *The Moonrakers*, 1910. A fictional account of smuggling in and around the New Forest. S.P.C.K.

DOYLE, Sir Arthur Conan. *The White Company*, 1891. 3 vols. Smith Elder and Co. Many edns. (Nelson's Library, 1907). Set around Beaulieu and Lyndhurst in the reign of Edward II.

FINNEMORE, John. *The Lover Fugitives*, 1902. C. Arthur Pearson.

GASKILL, Mrs. *North and South*, 1855. Chapman and Hall. Many edns., including those by Walter Scott, J.M. Dent, etc.

GRANT, Peggy. *The Gate of Dreams*, 1915. Andrew Melrose. Set in Burley.

HILL, Headon, *Her Grace at Bay*, 1906. Cassell. (Nelson, 1925.)

HORN, Kate. *Susan and the Dukes*, 1912. Stanley Paul and Co.

HUNTER, Vespen, *A Head on My Shoulders*, 1985. Malvern Publishing. Biographical novel about Dame Alice Lisle.

KELLY, R.J. *Jim Unclassified*, 1916. Mills and Boon.

LEEK, Sybil. *Mr. Hotfoot Jackson*, 1965. Story of a jackdaw. Frederick Mueller.

——*A Foal and A Tree*, 1964. Lambarde Press.

LEIGH, Victoria, *Rustle of Spring*, 1967. Written by a teenage girl living in the Forest. Frederick Warne.

LUKENS, John. *Adders Abounding*, 1954. Hodder and Stoughton. The author uses fictitious name places.

MACNAMARA, R.S. *Golden Dishes*, 1923. Hurst and Blackett.

MARRYAT, Frederick. *Children of the New Forest*, 1847. Many edns. and several publishers. Current publisher: J.M. Dent & Sons; ills.

MARSHALL, Archibald, *Richard Baldock*, Set in Burley and Christchurch.

——*Exton Manor*. Set in Beaulieu.

MOGRIDGE, Stephen. *New Forest Exploits*, 1956. Thomas Nelson.

MYRTLE, Harriet. *A Visit to the New Forest: A Tale*, 1859.

PUGH, Edwin William. *The Stumbling Block*, 1903. Heinnemann.

REYNOLDS, Mrs. (Amy D.) Fred. *Trefoil*, 1923. John Lane.

——*It Might Have Been Otherwise*, 1925. John Lane.

SEABY, Allen W. *Skewbald the New Forest Pony*, 1923 (many reprints). A. & C. Black. Map, many sketches.

——*Sons of Skewbald*, 1937. A. & C. Black.

——*Purkiss the Charcoal Burner*, 1946. Harrap.

——*The White Buck*, 1939. T. Nelson and Sons.

SMITH, Horace. *The New Forest: A Novel*, 1829. 3 vols. Henry Colburn.

STEVENS, Ethel S. *Allward*, 1915. Mills and Boon. Gypsy life in the Forest.

—— *The Long Encampment*, 1912. Mills and Boon. Gypsy life in the Forest.

VACHELL, Horace Annesley. *Fishpingle*, 1917. John Murray. Describes hunting in the Forest and golf at Bramshaw.

—— *John Verney*, 1911. John Murray. Set at Beaulieu and in the Forest.

—— *The Yard*, 1923. Hutchinson and Co. Set in Lyndhurst (Puddenhurst).

—— *Blinkers*, 1921. Cassell and Co.

—— *The Soul of Susan Yellam*, 1918. Cassell and Co.

—— *Waters of Jordan*, 1908. John Murray. Set at Brook.

VALLINGS, J.F. *The Severing Sword*, n.d. Gall and Inglis. A Civil War story laid partly in the New Forest.

WARNER, Miss. *Herbert Lodge: A New Forest Story*, 1808. 3 vols. Longman.

WESTRUP, Margaret. *The Devil's Problem*, 1919. Hurst and Blackett. First world war setting.

WEYMAN, Stanley. *Queen's Folly*, 1925. John Murray.

GUIDES AND MAPS

AMYES, S. *The New Forest*, 1969. Jarrold. Coloured pictures.

BULLAR, John. *A Companion in A Tour Round Southampton*, 1799. Other edns., 1801, 1819. T. Baker, Southampton.

CARNE, P.H. *The Echo Ramblers' Guide to the New Forest*, 1960. Southern Newspapers.

DELDERFIELD, E.R. *Isle of Wight and the New Forest*, 1962. Raleigh Press.

DICKENSON, David. *Short Walks in the New Forest*, 1987. Inklon Publications. Map, ills., sketches.

EDWARDS, Anne-Marie. *New Forest Walks*, 1975. BBC. Maps, sketches. New edition, 1982. Arcady Books, Ashurst, Southampton. 64 pp., maps, sketches.

EVENING, Peter. *Walks in the New Forest*, 1975–76. illus., maps, 3 vols. (Bournemouth Local Studies Publications).

Part 1. The Northern area. Booklet no. 620.

Part 2. The Central area. Booklet no. 621.

Part 3. The Southern area. Booklet no. 622.

FANSTONE, R.M. *The New Forest*, 1934. British Publishing Co. Ills., map.

FORESTRY COMMISSION. *New Forest* (guide), 1950. 86 pp. map, many ills. 4th edn., 1969. End-paper maps, many ills.

FORESTRY COMMISSION. *Explore the New Forest*, 1975. 2nd impression, 1981. Many maps, illsd. (mostly in colour).

GIBBONS, G. *Dorset and the New Forest*, 1969. Geographia.

GILBERT, M. *The New Forest*, 1947. St. Catherine Press. In Footpath Guide series.

HATTS, Leigh. *Country Walks around the New Forest*, 1976. Circle Pubs. Ills., maps.

HENDERSON, A.E. *Beaulieu Abbey and Hayles Abbey, Then and Now.*, 1952. S.P.C.K.

JOWITT, R.L.P. and Dorothy M. *Discovering Hampshire and the New Forest*, 1969. Reprinted 1975. Shire Publications. Maps, ills.

KNIGHT, Charles. *Journey Book of Hampshire*, 1841. Charles Knight Pubs.

KNOWLTON, D. *Discovering Walks in the New Forest*, 1976. Shire Pubs.

LYON, W. *The New Forest: A Comprehensive Guide*, etc., 1976. *Hampshire* magazine.

MAPS, NEW FOREST. For early (1609–1875) maps of the New Forest, see the Nature Conservancy Council's bibliography of the New Forest (No. 3 in the NCC bibliography series) compiled by Dr. Nicholas Flower. Where applicable, call-marks of the Public Record Office are supplied.

MAP, ORDANCE SURVEY (General series). Sheets 179 (Bournemouth) and 180 (The Solent) embracing the New Forest, 1971. 1 : 63,360 (One inch to 1 mile).

—— First metric edn., 1974. Sheets 195 (Bournemouth and Purbeck) and 196 (The Solent). 1 : 50,000. Replacement for 1 inch–1-mile edn. above.

—— (Routemaster series). Sheet 9, Southeast England.

—— (Landranger series). No. 195 (Bournemouth and Purbeck), No. 196. (Solent and Isle of Wight). Scale: 1 : 50,000 (1¼ in. to 1 mile).

MAP, ORDNANCE SURVEY, (Tourist series). *Tourist Map of the*

New Forest, 1966. 1 inch to 1 mile.

—— *New Forest* (Outdoor Leisure No. 22), 1986. 2½ inches to 1 mile (4 cm to 1 km).

MATE, C.H. *The New Forest*, 1908. W. Mate.

MOENS, W.J.C. *Map of the Ancient and Modern Areas of the New Forest*, 1903. Scale: 2 miles to 1 inch.

NEW FOREST, THE, 1964. J. Salmon. (In Salmon's Cameracolour series.)

NEW FOREST, A Pictorial and Descriptive Guide to, n.d. Ward, Lock & Co. Many edns (5th edn., 1961). Ills., maps.

NEW FOREST LEISURE GUIDE, 1983. Automobile Association and The Ordnance Survey. Walks, historical notes, maps, many ills. (mostly in colour).

NORTHCROFT, Dorothea Mary. *An A.B.C. of the New Forest*, n.d. Wilding and Son. Map, ills.

OFFICIAL GUIDE TO THE NEW FOREST, 1956. New Forest District Council. Burrow. Another edn., c. 1975. British Publishing Co. Maps, ills.

PHILLIPS, C.J. *The New Forest Handbook*, 1873. J.G. Short. (3d edn., 1880). Ills.

PRATT'S PLAN OF THE NEW FOREST, 1930. Illuminated map of the Forest drawn by A.E. Taylor for Pratt's "High Test" fuel (later taken over by Esso).

ROGERS, William Henry. *Guide to the New Forest*, 1878, with many reprints. Rogers was Headmaster of All Saints School in Southampton.

RUSSELL'S GRAPHIC GUIDE TO THE NEW FOREST (many editions). British Publishing co. (44th edn., 1975). Ills., maps.

SUMNER, Heywood, *A Guide to the New Forest*, 1924. Brown & Son. Map, 10 black and white drawings by the author/artist.

—— *A Map of Ancient Sites in the New Forest, Cranborne Chase and Bournemouth District*, 1923. Mounted and folded in case. Scale: 2 miles to 1 inch, coloured; 2 ft. by 1 ft. 7 in.

—— "Old Maps of Hampshire, Dorset and Wiltshire," 1918–19. *Bournemouth Natural Science Society Proceedings*; 11, 52–5.

WARD, A.W. and G.E. STARTUP. *Bournemouth and the New Forest*, 1894. Darlington. (In Darlington's handbook series.)

ARCHAEOLOGY

AKERMAN, J.Y. *"An Account of Excavations on the Site of Some Ancient Potteries in the Western District of the New Forest*, Conducted by the Rev. J.P. Bartlett," 1853. *Archaeologia*; 35, 91-9.

ANON. "Various Notes on Potters' Kilns, etc.," 1858. *Gentleman's Magazine*.

CRAWFORD, O.G.S. "Cerdic and the Cloven Way," 1931. *Antiquity*; 5, 441–458.

FULFORD, Michael G. *New Forest Roman Pottery: Manufacture and Distribution, with a Corpus of the Pottery Types*, 1975. British Archaeological Report No. 17. Maps, tables, charts, bib.

GRINSELL, L.V. *The Archaeology of Wessex*, 1958. Methuen.

HAMPSHIRE FIELD CLUB AND ARCHAEOLOGICAL SOCIETY. Papers and proceedings, 1885, to the present. Contains many articles and references on the New Forest. New Forest Section, inaugurated in 1959, has its own reports.

HOPE, W.H. St. J. and H. BRAKSPEAR. *The Cistercian Abbey of Beaulieu in the County of Southampton*, 1906. *Archaeological Journal*; 63, 129–186.

MOENS, W.J.C. "The New Forest," 1903. *Archaeology Journal*; 60, 30–501.

PASMORE, Anthony. *New Forest Pottery Kilns and Earthworks*," 1967. A record of field work in Sloden, Pitts Wood, Alder Hill, Amberwood and Islands Thorn inclosures. Privately printed. Ills., map.

—— "Surviving Evidence of the New Forest Charcoal Burning Industry," 1964., *Jour. of Industrial Archaeology*; 1, 27–35.

PIGGOTT, C.M. "Excavations of Fifteen Barrows in the New Forest, 1941–2," 1943. *Prehistoric Society Proceedings*; 9, 1–27.

—— "An Iron Age Barrow in the New Forest," 1953. *Antiquaries Jour.*; 33, 14–21.

PRESTON, J.P. and C. HAWKES. "Three Late Iron Age Barrows on the Cloven Way," 1933. *Antiquaries Jour.*; 13, 414–454.

SUMNER, Heywood. *The Ancient Earthworks of the New Forest*, 1917. Chiswick Press. Maps, plans, ills.

—— *A Descriptive Account of the Roman Pottery Made at Ashley Rails, New Forest*, 1919. Chiswick Press.

—— *A Descriptive Account of Roman Pot-* *tery Sites at Sloden and Black Heath Meadow, Linwood, New Forest*, 1921. Chiswick Press. Ills, map, plan.

—— *Excavations in the New Forest Pottery Sites*, 1927. Chiswick Press. Ills., plans.

—— *Geography and Prehistoric Earthworks in the New Forest District*, 1925. Paper given at the British Assn.; later published (March, 1926, pp. 244–8) in *The Geographical Journal.*.

—— *Local Papers*, 1931. Chiswick Press. Various papers on New Forest and adjacent area. Maps, plans, black and white drawings.

—— *A Map of Ancient Sites in the New Forest, Cranbourne Chase and Bournemouth District*, 1923. Reprinted 1973. Scale: 2 miles to 1 inch. Dolphin Press.

SWANN, V.G. "The Structure of Romano-British New Forest Pottery Kilns," 1971. *Antiquity*; 45, 45–8.

TUBBS, Colin, R. "Earth Encoppicements in the New Forest," 1964. *Forestry*; 37, 95–105.

TUBBS, Colin, R. and G.W. DIMBLEBY, "Early Agriculture in the New Forest," 1965. *Advancement of Science*; Vol. 22 (no. 96), 88–97. Bib.

FOREST MANAGEMENT

BISHOP, A.C. "The New Forest," 1881. *Journal of Forestry and Estate Management*. 5; 225–242.

BUCHANAN, C. and partner. *South Hampshire Study: Report on the Feasibility* of Major Urban growth, 1966. 3 vols.

COUNTRYSIDE COMMISSION. *The New Forest Commoners*, 1984.

—— *The new Forest Landscape*, 1986.

EVANS, N.V. *Dibden Inclosure and Environs: A Study of Six Contrasting Habitats with Suggestions Regarding Future Management*, 1977. Dissertation: University of Southampton, Adult Ed. Dept.

FLOWER, Nicholas. *An Historical and Ecological Study of Inclosed and Uninclosed Woods in the New Forest, Hampshire*, 1977. London University (doctoral thesis).

FORESTRY COMMISSION. *Protection of the New Forest: Report of the Committee of Planning Officers, 1938–39*, 1939.

—— *New Forest Management Plan, 1982–1991*.

—— *New Forest Review: Consultation Draft Report*, 1987.

GRAHAM, C. *A Study of Three-day Visitor Sites in the New Forest*, 1977. M.Sc. thesis, London University.

GREEN, M.J. *Camping in Great Britain. Part 2: A Study of Camping*. Portsmouth Polytechnic, School of Architecture.

HAINES, H.H. "Some Aspects of the New Forest with Special Reference to the Changes Wrought by Direct or Indirect Human Agency," 1929. *Proc. Linn. Soc.*, 141:57.

—— *Preservation of the New Forest*. 1928. Privately printed.

HAMPSHIRE COUNTY COUNCIL. *Southwest Hampshire Structure Plan*, 1983.

JENKINSON, Henry T.J. *The New Forest: The Preservation of the Old Timber, the Open Commons and the Common Rights*, 1971. William Ridgway.

KEELING, A.E. *A Study of Recreation and Its Impact on the Environment in Part of the New Forest, Hants*, 1967. London University, conservation course.

LAND USE CONSULTANTS. *A Brief Assessment of the Enclosed Landscapes* of the New Forest Heritage Area, 1987.

LEWIS, Percival. *Historical Inquiries Concerning Forests and Forest Laws, etc.*, 1811. T. Payne. Map.

MILLAR, L. *A Study of the Long Term problems of Traffic and Accessibility in Rural Areas of High Amenity Value with Specific Reference to the New Forest*. 1967. M.Sc. thesis, University of Southampton.

NATURE CONSERVANCY COUNCIL. *The Food and Feeding Behaviour of Cattle and Ponies in the New Forest*, 1982.

NEWBOLD, P.J. "Conservation in the New Forest," 1961. *New Scien-*

tist, 9, 805–7.

NEW FOREST and ADVISORY PLANNING COMMITTEE. *Protection of the New Forest: Planning Officers Report, Technical Committee's Revision,* 1945.

NEW FOREST DISTRICT COUNCIL. *Forest and Downland Villages Local Plan,* 1983.

NEW FOREST JOINT STEERING COMMITTEE. *Conservation of the New Forest* (final recommendations), 1971.

NEW FOREST TECHNICAL REVIEW GROUP. *Progress Report on the Implementation of Conservation Measures, 1972–76, and Proposals for Future Strategy,* 1976.

——*Statement of Future Strategy,* 1978.

NEW FOREST WORKING PARTY. *Conservation of the New Forest,* 1970.

OPEN FOREST ADVISORY COMMITTEE ON GRAZING AND DRAINAGE. *A Strategy for the Maintenance and Continuation of the Commoning System,* 1986.

PARLIAMENTARY COMMISSIONER FOR ADMINISTRATION. *Management of the New Forest Woodlands by the Forestry Commission,* 1982.

PUGH, S.C. *New Forest Information Centres,* 1972. Portsmouth Polytechnic, School of Architecture.

REES, M.J. *Urbanization and the Influence of Demand on the New Forest,* 1976. Portsmouth Polytechnic, Surveying Dept. (Project 284).

RSPCA (Royal Society for Prevention of Cruelty to Animals). *Behavioural Ecology and Body Condition Changes in the New Forest Ponies,* 1980.

SKELTON, I.A.N. *Recreational Usage of the New Forest: A Sample Study of Two Sites over the Winter Period, 1973–4,* 1974. University of Southampton, Adult Ed. Dept.

SPEIGHT, M.C.D. *A Study of Recreational Use of the New Forest,* 1966. London University College, conservation course.

STAMP, Sir Dudley (ed.) "*Planning Problems in the New Forest,*" 1965. *Advancement of Science,* 22 July, pp. 134–46.

LOCAL HISTORY

(Beaulieu) COLES, Robert. *Beaulieu Airfield, History of,* 1982. Profusely illustrated. Privately printed.

(Beaulieu) ELSWORTH, Walter. *Beaulieu in World War II,* 1982. A villager's recollection of the war. Map, ills. Published by Philpott Publications.

(Beaulieu) WIDNELL, H.E.R. *The Beaulieu Record,* 1973. Pioneer Pubs.

(Boldre) PERKINS, W.F. *Boldre: the Parish, the Church, and the Inhabitants,* 1927. King's Library.

(Bramshaw) MERSON, Elizabeth. *Once There Was ... the Village School,* 1979. Reprinted, 1980. Paul Cave Pubs. Ills., sketches, map.

(Brockenhurst) STEVENS, J.R. *Brockenhurst and its Antiquity and Interest,* 1921. Several edns.

(Buckler's Hard) MONTAGU, John, Second Lord (Montagu of Beaulieu). *Buckler's Hard and its Ships,* 1909. Privately printed. Map, ills.

(Burley) HARDCASTLE, Félicité. *Records of Burley,* 1951. Raleigh Press. Maps, many ills.

(Burley) HARDCASTLE, Félicité, *Aspects of a New Forest Village: Records of Burley,* 1987. Chameleon International. Greatly expended edition of the 1951 imprint. First 500 copies printed as limited edition. Maps, many ills.

(Exbury) HOLLAND, A.J. and Edmund DE ROTHSCHILD. *Our Exbury,* 1982. Paul Cave Publications. Many ills.

(Fawley) GOULD, Mary. *Three Hundred Years in A New Forest Parish,* being a short history of Fawley, 1920. Warren & Son, Winchester.

(Fordingbridge) HANNEN, R. *A History of Fordingbridge,* 1883. Later edns. 3rd edn., 1909.

(Fordingbridge) HANNEN, R. and J. *Tales of the Hundred of Ford,* 1928 (3d edn.)

(Fordingbridge) MORELY-HEWITT, A.T. *The Story of Fordingbridge in Fact and Fancy,* 1966. Map, ills. privately printed.

(Gorley) SUMNER, Heywood. See *Book of Gorley* under General works.

(Hordle) SMITH, E.P. Boys. *Hordle,* 1913.

(Nomansland) LIVENS, H.M. *Nomansland—A Village History,* 1910. Compiled from articles that originally appeared in the *Salisbury Times and Wiltshire Gazette.*

(EDITOR'S NOTE: Virtually all of the parish churches of the New Forest have excellent guides. These tell not only the story of the respective churches, but much about their villages as well.)

"THE VILLAGE GREEN"
(From H.M. Livens' *Nomansland*)

REFERENCE WORKS

CLAIMS ON THE NEW FOREST, *An Abstract of, 1670*, 1776. Entries made at the Eyre's Court, Lyndhurst. 1853 edn. by Commissioners of Her Majesty's Woods, Forests and Land Revenue; includes incroachments. 1858, register of decisions on claims to Forest rights.

ECCLESIASTICAL CASES RELATING TO DOCTRINE AND DISCIPLINE, with a preface by the Bishop of London, 1865. John Murray. Pages 50–63 describe the appeal, *Craig vs. Farnall*; the Rev. J.K. Craig was the first Vicar of Burley.

FLOWER, Dr. Nicholas. *The New Forest* (bibliography), 1979. No. 3 in the Nature Conservancy Council's "Bibliography Series." Addendum, 1981. Over 500 references; predominantly in natural history fields.

GILBERT, Henry March and G.N. GODWIN. *Bibliotheca Hantoniensis*, 1891. An early bibliography of books about Hampshire (including the New Forest). Lists some magazine articles. Ye Olde Boke Shoppe, Southampton.

GREEN, Margaret. *Hampshire Churches*, 1967. Chapter 2 deals with New Forest churches. Winton Pubs. Ills., maps, bib.

HAMPSHIRE DIRECTORY, Hunt and Company's 1852. With an epitome of each village in the county (including the New Forest).

MANWOOD, J. *A Treatise on the Laws of the Forest*. London, 1615.

PARLIAMENT. Acts relating to the New Forest: 1698, 1808, 1851 (Deer Removal Act), 1877, 1949, 1964, 1970.

——Select Committees dealing with aspects of the New Forest: 1789 (24 July), 1792 (6 February), 1848 (25 July), 1849 (17 July), 1854 (17 July), 1868 (Deer Removal Act, 27 July), 1875 (5 May), 1889 (26 July), 1890 (30 July), 1938–9 (protection of the New Forest), 1947, 1964 (House of Lords, 11 March and 15 July).

PERKINS, W. FRANK. *A New Forest Bibliography*, 1935. C.T. King and H.M. Gilbert.

PEVSNER, Nikolaus and David LLOYD, 1967. *Hampshire and the Isle of Wight* (includes the New Forest). In "Buildings of England" series. Ills., maps, plans. Penguin books.

POPHAM, Rita M. *A New Forest Bibliography*, 1979. A Bournemouth Local Studies publication (No. 645).

PUBLIC RECORD OFFICE. Case of *Craig vs. Farnall*, an appeal before the Judicial Committee of the Privy Council based on a Court of Arches decision rendered on 11 November 1847. The PRO document PCAP 3/14 gives the complete background of the original Court of Arches case, but little on the appeal. For background on the appeal see *Ecclesiastical Cases*, etc., in this section of the bibliography.

SELECT BIBLIOGRAPHY OF NEW FOREST LITERATURE, 1969. Compiled by the Botany dept. of the University of Southampton. Emphasis on natural history.

SUMNER, Heywood, *A New Forest Bibliography and List of Maps*, 1925. H.M. Gilbert.

VICTORIA COUNTY HISTORY OF HAMPSHIRE, 1900–1911. 4 vols. Extensive references to the New Forest. Constable.

VIGNETTE FROM SUMNER'S BIBLIOGRAPHY

INDEX

(N.F. stands for New Forest)

"GOOD NIGHT!"

TAIL-PIECE FROM CHARLES W. WOOD'S "In the New Forest" (*The Argosy,* February, 1891)